UNDER THE EDITORSHIP OF

*Herold C. Hunt*

CHARLES WILLIAM ELIOT PROFESSOR OF EDUCATION

HARVARD UNIVERSITY

*Teaching the*

# Elementary School Child

LILLIAN M. LOGAN  VIRGIL G. LOGAN

EVANSVILLE COLLEGE

HOUGHTON MIFFLIN COMPANY · BOSTON

# Editor's Introduction

The elementary school provides a basic foundation for the entire educational program and is all-encompassing in its involvement of the youth it serves. The importance of the elementary school cannot be overemphasized; nation-wide census figures revealing an eleventh-grade level of adult accomplishment serve to focus attention on the vital responsibility of elementary education, and any concern for the improvement of secondary and higher education must take into account this first stage of the total educational design.

A general awareness of the significance of elementary education is resulting in fresh appraisals of its philosophy, objectives, curriculum offerings, and, above all, the teaching methods employed to maximize effective learning. New organizational and administrative patterns, new concepts in teaching, and new techniques and devices characterize the considerable modification of the elementary school program that has taken place during the present century. The content of instruction has expanded, a wholesome variety of teaching procedures has come into being, instructional materials have increased greatly, educational services have been extended, and school buildings are now better designed to serve children and the community more adequately. Increasingly, teachers and administrators are recognizing that elementary education must respond to individual and societal requirements, both permanent and changing.

The American people are taking a greater interest in their schools because of an increasing awareness that the welfare of the nation depends on the development of individual talents. Public concern for education on all levels is leading to new appraisals of the educational process and a new appreciation of its contribution.

It is in such a climate of interest and immediacy that two highly competent, experienced, and skilled teachers, Lillian M. Logan and Virgil G. Logan, have directed their talents to a consideration of teaching methods and curriculum design in the elementary school. This book, *Teaching the Elementary School Child*, has grown out of long and intimate knowledge of the field with which the Logans have been identified. Comprehensive in its treatment, this book provides a superbly creative approach to the tasks that face the teacher in today's elementary school. It will serve the prospective teacher seeking information and assistance, the in-service teacher looking for new ways to vitalize the teaching-learning process, the college instructor eager to stimulate the improvement of teacher education, the administrator looking for ways of motivating the teaching staff to a higher quality of excellence, and the parent who would understand his role in cooperating in the education of the child.

Well written, based on authoritative research, and replete with helpful illustrations, sample units of instruction, and anecdotal materials, *Teaching the Elementary School Child* offers what is probably the most complete coverage of elementary school teaching methods available between the covers of a single book. Designed to help the teacher bring children, knowledge, skills, and understanding together in a meaningful, integrated, and creative manner, this text meets a long recognized need and constitutes an important contribution to the literature of the field.

HEROLD C. HUNT

# Preface

*Teaching the Elementary School Child* was written to help meet the challenge of teaching childern to live successfully in a changing, dynamic society. Such teaching requires a rare breadth and depth of knowledge, understanding, insight, and ability on the part of the teacher as he works with children in individual and group situations.

Central to the plan of this book is its integrative approach. Content is the warp and creativity the woof that runs through the design the teacher weaves with a group of children. Through a union of content and method, material and process, the teaching-learning experience comes alive; today's teacher must be uniquely equipped to provide learning experiences that are challenging in their own right and at the same time correlative with other aspects of the curriculum. The function of this book is to help the prospective teacher understand the interrelatedness of the teaching tasks he faces and to suggest ways of solving the problems he will meet in carrying out the functions of teaching. The principles and teaching methods set forth herein are based upon actual experiences in the classroom under the guidance of teachers convinced that the child's greatest need is a teacher who will challenge him to achieve his highest potential.

This book deals specifically with important tasks and problems facing today's teacher: the problem of understanding the world in which the child lives, appreciating the demands of the culture upon the child, and taking into account the factors that shape each stage of his development; the task of developing skills in the key curriculum areas — selecting, organizing, planning, developing, and evaluating learning experiences that will equip the child to solve problems and meet the demands of living in the modern world; the problem of providing for the child with special needs; the task of formulating a philosophy of teaching based on a broad liberal education, sound professional training, and a creative approach to the teaching experience; and the challenge to become a teacher who exemplifies the characteristics of a professional person in the classroom, as a member of the staff, and as a citizen in the community.

New developments in teaching and new approaches to problems of class and school organization are taken into account. This book explores such innovations as the nongraded primary school, the multigraded class, and team teaching. Other recent developments such as teaching machines and educational television are incorporated here to extend the teacher's background and help him to improve educational experiences.

Throughout the book we have emphasized the teacher's responsibility for challenging the child to think, to learn, to create, to extend his horizons, and to develop an insatiable appetite for knowledge.

We wish to acknowledge the invaluable assistance of the editorial, art, and production staffs at Houghton Mifflin Company.

We are especially grateful to Professors Herold C. Hunt and Robert H. Anderson of Harvard University for their careful reading of the manuscript and thoughtful commentary on it.

Finally, we express our gratitude to the many fine teachers whose practices are reflected in the pages of this book.

LILLIAN M. LOGAN
VIRGIL G. LOGAN

# Table of Contents

PART FOUR The Opportunities We Face

part one

The Growing Child

1 And the world was filled with things which you will enjoy, unless you are too proud to be pleased with them.

JOHN RUSKIN

# The world of the elementary school child

Atomic energy, supersonic aircraft, space ships, rocket races, nuclear discoveries, and transoceanic television — this is the exciting world of today's child. It is a dynamic world in which the one constant is change and in which modern transportation and communication erase the boundaries that once separated cultures. As the child is thrust upon the scene he begins the lifelong process of adapting to a constant acceleration. He must get along with the people around him, discover answers to questions and solutions to problems, master the various phases of his culture, and develop inner resources.

The preschool child takes for granted concepts that many of his elders may never have fully comprehended. Teachers who had little contact with radio until they were adults must cope with children who have never known a world without television. Teachers who have traveled only within the borders of their home state often teach children who have been around the world. Through radio, films, recordings, television, and travel the child early senses his citizenship in a world that is "only ninety minutes in circumference."

In this world the child finds that people are friendly, supporting, and helpful, or they are just the opposite. They minister to his needs and wants or they fail to respond to his demands. They make him the center of attention or they neglect and ignore him. What others do for him, and how, and why, affects his responses, influences his personality, governs his aspirations, and determines his ways of reacting. It is through people that a child is oriented to life.

In his earliest years the child needs to develop trust in the love, affection, dependability, support, and understanding of the adults who make up his world. He needs also to gain a growing sense of his own powers, acceptance of his own feelings, recognition, and an awareness of himself as an individual. As he matures he needs, moreover, to develop confidence in his own abilities, a belief that he can do things for himself, enjoy his own company, and protect himself in the crises that arise in daily living.

As he matures he becomes acquainted with a wider world. He discovers other people from whom he can learn and with whom he can share ideas. Each child has a different cultural environment; each child's manner of responding to it varies. For the process of adjusting individual responses to the society's pattern of culture Titiev employs Herskovits's definition of enculturation: "Enculturation may be regarded as the manner in which each society molds the biological organization of its neonates to a set of pre-existing cultural norms."[1] As children progress from infancy through early childhood, middle childhood, and adolescence, physical maturation proceeds by degrees. At each stage of development certain specific patterns of behavior and expectations are set up by the society (see chart opposite).

[1] Mischa Titiev, *Introduction to Cultural Anthropology* (New York: Henry Holt and Company, 1959), p. 310.

### THE PROCESS OF ENCULTURATION

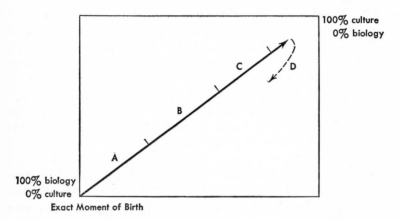

*In every society each neonate must go through the process of enculturation. This is divided into four stages: A stands for infancy, B for adolescence, C for adulthood, and D for old age. It should be noted that in each society A has the highest percentage of biological behavior and that D reverts somewhat to A.*

Source: Mischa Titiev, *Introduction to Cultural Anthropology* (New York: Henry Holt and Company, 1959), p. 310.

Each child must progress through stage *A*. Cultural groups differ in the minute details transmitted, the manner in which they are applied to the child, the type and severity of punishment meted out for failure to conform, the definition of a transgression, and the length of time allowed before the child is expected to move on to stage *B*. Stage *B* is characterized by the problems of adolescence. Stage *C* represents maturity. Stage *D* is entered in old age as defined by each society.

Each child reacts differently to the demands of the culture, the needs of his growing organism, and the inner world of feelings, perceptions, and ideas. Learning the ways of society is a difficult process even when the cultural values are stable and clearly defined. It is even more difficult in a period of rapid change. As the child interacts with others in his environment he develops an awareness of self. His growing personality is a reflection of the attitudes and behaviors of those with whom he comes in contact.

The significance of the influence of cultural patterns upon personality and social development is pointed out by Mead,[2] who observed the development of personality and character in a number of primitive tribes. She reported that such characteristics as sex traits of aggression on the part of the male and submission on the part of the female were largely a product of the culture rather than of innate sex roles. Among the Arapesh males there was a spirit of cooperation, gentleness, and solicitousness equal to that of the female. On the other hand, among the Mundugumur tribes the women assumed the aggressive, violent, competitive, and hostile behavior characteristic of the men of their tribes. Among the Tchambuli the women were the powerful leaders and dominated the scene while the men engaged in artistic, sensitive, and nonutilitarian pursuits. The men were timid and dependent; the women were efficient and dominant — the practical members of the tribe. Deviation from the established role was looked upon with disfavor. Mead concluded that such standardized personality differences between the sexes are the result of cultural patterns and expectations. The implication of such information is not that we need to remember the exact pattern set by a cultural group but that we should understand the relationship between the cultural patterns and the possibility of the individual's achieving them.

## The Child in a Democratic Society

Cultural modes may vary, designs for development may differ, educational patterns may change, but the way of life that is handed down as the social heritage of a people is determined by the values the society holds and the significant concepts of appropriate relationships between the individuals and the group. It does more than supply a set of skills for making a living and a set of blueprints for human relationships. It makes assumptions about the purposes of

[2] Margaret Mead, *Cooperation and Competition Among Primitive Tribes* (New York: McGraw-Hill Book Company, 1937); *Growing Up in New Guinea* (New York: Blue Ribbon Books, 1930); *Sex and Temperament in Three Primitive Societies* (New York: William Morrow and Company, 1935).

human existence, what individuals have a right to expect from one another, and what constitutes fulfillment or frustration in meeting the demands of society.

As the child begins the long and arduous task of adjusting to the culture he must learn the ways not only of his family but of his neighborhood and expanding community. These patterns are not clear cut, nor are they always easily understood. In order to teach the child, it is important to re-examine the basic tenets of a democratic society. Among these are the following:

1. A deep and lasting respect for the supreme worth and dignity of the individual. The institutions, processes, laws, and governmental operations of society make possible individual achievement and self-realization.

2. A belief in and protection of the right of the individual to freedom. Laws, civil rights, and other social controls operate to insure freedom. However, children must be taught that freedoms are not gained easily or maintained without vigilance and cooperative effort.

3. A faith in the intelligence of man. Man can make intelligent decisions, can and will judge fairly, and can solve problems through cooperative action. In order to assume such responsibilities the members of a democratic society must be assured of educational opportunities that develop maximal potentialities.

The family is responsible for providing the child with the first lessons in democratic living. In almost every society the family is the most important institution affecting the life and growth of the child: it guides his socializing experiences, begins the process of transmitting the culture, and inculcates a set of cultural and social values.

It is in the family that patterns of living, of behavior, of emotional response and attitudes, and of ideals are established. Hartshorne and May[3] reveal some of the influences of the home in the development of character. Brown,[4] and Havighurst and Neugarten[5] illustrate

[3] H. Hartshorne and M. A. May *et al.*, *Studies in the Nature of Character* (New York: The Macmillan Company, Vol. I, 1928); *Studies in the Organization of Character* (New York: The Macmillan Company, Vol. III, 1930).

[4] F. J. Brown, *Educational Sociology* (Englewood Cliffs, N.J.: Prentice-Hall, Inc., 2nd ed., 1954), Chaps. IX and X.

[5] R. J. Havighurst and B. L. Neugarten, *Society and Education* (Boston: Allyn and Bacon, Inc., 1957), Chaps. I, IV, and V.

some of the types of home training that contribute to misunderstanding between parents and children. It is imperative for the teacher to know the type of home training a child has, the kind of atmosphere he lives in, the kind of punishment and rewards he receives at home, and what the personal relationships are between members of the family and especially between parent and child. Often the lack of affection in the home accounts for the child's negative attitudes toward all adults — including his teachers.

Shirley concludes that "a child that is oversheltered and underloved goes forth from home with misgivings and doubts, and gives an impression of inadequacy and immaturity in his encounter with new experiences that make him unwelcome whether in the society of adults or children."[6]

Sears, Macoby, and Levin questioned 379 American mothers about their methods of bringing up children from birth to kindergarten age. They concluded: "[It is] our opinion that child-rearing practices are important determiners [of personality]. . . . Every moment of the child's life that he spends in contact with his parents has some effect on both his present behavior and his potentialities for future action."[7] Symonds[8] points out that the basic patterns of personality are formed in the first five years of life.

American society has made a fetish of immaturity, with the result that children generally are unprepared for the adjustment to school. They often find the transition from home to school difficult. Not only on the first day of school but for days and even months thereafter children who have not learned to trust adults, to act on their own initiative, and to make decisions have an utterly miserable time. "It is human," says Erikson, "to have a long childhood; it is civilized to have an even longer childhood. Long childhood makes a technical and mental virtuoso out of man, but it leaves a long residue of emotional immaturity in him."[9]

[6] M. M. Shirley, "Children's Adjustment to a Strange Situation," *Child Development*, 37:217 (1942).

[7] R. R. Sears, E. E. Macoby, and Harry Levin, *Patterns of Child Rearing* (Evanston, Ill.: Row, Peterson and Company, 1957), p. 466.

[8] P. M. Symonds, "What Education Has to Learn from Psychology," *Teachers College Record*, 61:317, March 1960.

[9] Erik H. Erikson, *Childhood and Society* (New York: W. W. Norton and Company, 1950), p. 2.

## The Child's View of Himself

It takes years of growing before the child acquires a full realization of self. He strives to become a member of the group and to build ties with other persons. At the same time he struggles to become more of an individual, to develop independence, and to have a voice in the affairs of men. It is necessary to understand the inner thoughts and feelings that make up a child's awareness of himself as a unique individual — his concept of what he is, what he has, and his feelings about his abilities, characteristics, aspirations, and properties. And our understanding must be in terms not only of his outer world but of his inner world and the manner in which he relates the two. It is his inner world that determines what he hears when he listens, what he sees when he looks, and what he concludes when he thinks. He selects and rejects experiences, ideas, and people on the basis of his feelings, perceptions, and thoughts.

Characteristic ways of reacting, responding, behaving, thinking, and feeling are acquired through interaction with others, as is one's image of the person he would like to be. The young child's feelings are close to the surface; his motives are easily read. As children develop, however, they tend to become secretive about their feelings. Millard and Rothney point out that "It is during the latter elementary school years that the child feels a real conflict between . . . his own inner concepts and the outside demands of the world in which he finds himself."[10]

A certain amount of frustration is inevitable. The child soon discovers that if he does what he is told to do he is rewarded; if he doesn't, he is punished, or at least punishment is threatened. He is faced with the dilemma of doing what he wants to do and being punished, or doing what he is told to do and being frustrated. If he is constantly prevented from doing what he desires he will not be contented. The answer to the dilemma may lie in the solution that many a youngster discovers: if he can develop the feeling of *wanting* to do what the adult in his life thinks he *should* do the frustration is minimized. This is the essence of self-discipline. It is defined as

[10] Cecil V. Millard and John M. Rothney, *The Elementary School Child: A Book of Cases* (New York: The Dryden Press, 1957), p. 8.

"the affinity for wanting to do what you have to do in harmony with social, natural, and physical laws."[11]

How the child accepts himself, how he adjusts to his social and physical environment, will be determined in large measure by his concept of who and what he is at any given point in life. Whether or not he is able to respect himself determines his ability to respect others. "Self respect and respect for others," says Oliver, "are not two opposites that may on occasion happily occur. . . . They are inextricably intertwined, like the warp and woof of a piece of cloth. Neither can truly exist without the other."[12]

Each child's concept of self is affected by the manner in which he reacts to and interacts with the internal and external forces in his world. His unique potentialities may be fostered or hindered by the purposes and goals that arise from inside and outside himself. Family relationships, cultural patterns of home and community, early patterns of adjusting to deprivations, and susceptibility to frustration affect his image of self.

The child comes to school already educated. He has been learning from his parents, his playmates, and the numerous social contacts and influences that surround him from the moment of birth. When he enters kindergarten or first grade he already possesses patterns of behavior, social skills, points of view, mechanical skills, communication skills, hopes, attitudes, and a wealth of information. "The child does not leave the world behind him when he enters the doors of the school, no matter how isolated from ordinary social activities the educational program may be."[13]

## What the School Expects of the Elementary School Child

The function of the school has always been to induct the young into membership in group, society, and nation. Although other agencies share in this process it is the school's specific charge. The

[11] Lillian M. Logan, *Teaching the Young Child: Methods of Preschool and Primary Education* (Boston: Houghton Mifflin Company, 1960), p. 427.

[12] Robert T. Oliver, *Psychology of Persuasive Speech* (New York: Longmans, Green and Company, 1957), p. 101.

[13] B. Othaniel Smith, William O. Stanley, and J. Harlan Shores, *Fundamentals of Curriculum Development* (Yonkers-on-Hudson, N.Y.: World Book Company, rev. ed., 1957), p. 93.

school was established to insure the transmission of the core values, ideals, understandings, and behavior deemed essential for successful living when society was unable to do it through informal experience alone. As the culture became more and more complex, the school took over the residual functions of society as other agencies tended to shed the responsibilities they once embraced.

In a democracy the school emphasizes the creation of a literate society, the improvement of the physical, mental, and spiritual well-being of the individual, development of his latent talents and skills, and the inculcation of good citizenship at every level. The goal has always been to develop the individual as far as his capacities and interests allow.

Traditionally the elementary school has been considered the school of the three R's. Here the child is supposed to receive the fundamentals of education. Here he is expected to master the techniques needed for further education. The school is responsible for achieving balance between the development of the individual and the improvement of society. It has the task of helping children achieve desirable attitudes, values, and socializing experiences — a task it has accepted in the belief that education is more than an accumulation of facts. "It cannot be compared to filling up an empty pot, but rather to . . . lighting a fire. The proper test of an education is whether it teaches the pupil to think and whether it awakens his interest in applying his brain to the various problems and opportunities life presents."[14]

*Objectives of Education.* In all cultures the functions of education remain essentially the same, although they differ in the manner and extent to which the school is used for transmitting the cultural heritage, for creating new social patterns, or for cultural renewal.

In our society the broad over-all objectives have been based on one of the tenets of democracy — the belief that the ultimate goal is the development of an individual who will be a contributing member of society. As Gwynn states, ". . . we have to synthesize in American society four different philosophies of education, namely, (1) preparation for life in a fast-moving scientific world, (2) intellectual development of a high order, (3) education for life in a democracy,

[14] Sir Geoffrey Browther, "English and American Education," *Atlantic,* 205:42, April 1960.

and (4) continual development of high moral and ethical values."[15]

Krug points out that "Educational objectives consistent with democracy . . . should include the development of those skills and understandings needed by individuals in carrying out democratic processes. Prominent among these are the skills of cooperative planning, reflective thinking and discussion."[16] In the light of our democratic heritage such statements of objectives are valid. Translating them into action in the classroom, however, is dependent upon having teachers who can create an environment in which group action and the democratic process are integral parts.

Butts emphasizes the importance of a broad base for determining elementary school objectives as he warns, "Schooling without rigorous knowledge is no education at all; but if the acquisition of organized knowledge is the *only* goal, then education may become rigid and lifeless. Schooling without self-development may become undisciplined and soft-headed. Schooling without social responsibility makes of education the impractical plaything of the dilettantes, but if social responsibility is the *only* goal, education may impose a cheerless and drab conformity."[17]

*Democracy in the School.* The school that makes democratic processes an integral part of daily living is characterized by the following practices and principles:

1. Each child is accepted as a worth-while individual. His opinions are respected by the teacher and the group. The teacher is sensitive to his concerns, values, problems, and needs, and understands the world in which he lives.

2. The teacher is concerned with the development of each individual — the gifted as well as the average and slow learner. Children are encouraged to proceed at their own rates through differentiated assignments, individualized instruction, flexible groupings, varied materials, and the use of effective evaluation techniques.

3. Children have opportunity to plan, organize, develop, and evaluate progress as they assume responsibility for certain phases

[15] J. Minor Gwynn, *Curriculum Principles and Social Trends* (New York: The Macmillan Company, 3rd ed., 1960), pp. 135, 136.

[16] Edward Krug *et al., Administering Curriculum Planning* (New York: Harper & Brothers, 1956), pp. 304, 305.

[17] R. Freeman Butts, "Scholarship and Education in a Free Society," *Teachers College Record*, 61:289, March 1960.

of the curriculum. The mature judgment of the teacher is respected as plans move forward and evaluation progresses.

4. Children are taught to use the scientific method: to define problems, seek solutions, gather data, weigh evidence, and form conclusions on the basis of evidence.

One has only to visit a classroom in which children are working together in a democratic atmosphere to understand its values. The contribution of each child is accepted and valued. Because each child knows that the teacher accepts him as an individual he assumes responsibility by becoming a contributing member of the group. His concerns, problems, and needs are considered in planning, developing, and evaluating learning experiences. To the extent that the curriculum design permits, the teacher involves children in the planning and development of the activities.

The formulation of objectives should consider various facets: the relation of the individual to society; the needs of youth; the nature of the learning process. Examination of educational objectives reveal that they are concerned with (1) physical development, (2) individual, social, and emotional development, (3) ethical behavior, (4) social relations, (5) the social world, (6) the physical world, (7) aesthetic development, (8) communication skills, and (9) quantitative relationships. Such objectives assume that changes will take place in understandings, knowledge, competence, skills, interests, and attitudes, and that patterns of behavior will be reflected in critical thinking, the creative use of intelligence, and improved work habits.

The following graphic presentation of elementary school objectives, from a report prepared for the Mid-Century Committee on Objectives in Elementary Education, Russell Sage Foundation, illustrates the idea that growth, development, maturation, and learning are interrelated and continuous as the child progresses toward the defined objectives of the school.

THE BEHAVIOR CONTINUUM

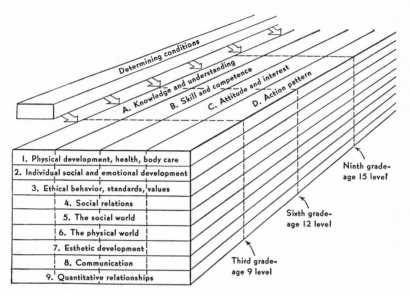

*Broad curriculum areas intersect major behavior categories.*
Source: Nolan C. Kearney, *Elementary School Objectives* (New York: Russell Sage Foundation, 1953), p. 38.

## Priorities in Education

The wide range of objectives encompassed by the elementary school makes clear the need for straightforward and realistic thinking about the limits of the school's energy, resources, and responsibilities. Anderson points to the failure of the school "to distinguish between the essentials for which society (or at least non-school agencies) should be held responsible and the essentials in which the school has a legitimate interest and for the realization of which the school is uniquely qualified. *Concern* for the whole child is by no means the same as *responsibility* for the whole child."[18] He further emphasizes what is obvious — that some schools try to do the job of all the other agencies whose concern happens at some point to coincide

[18] Robert H. Anderson, "Time Allotment: A View on Priorities," *Educational Horizons*, 37:35, Winter 1958.

with that of the school. Unless the school establishes some system of priority and limits itself to those tasks for which it is qualified and responsible it will fail in its purpose.

Today's teacher too often finds he cannot carry out the objectives of education when he must assume the roles of clerk, baby-sitter, secretary, and professional worker. He spends his time on chores that could be performed by other agencies or by persons of less training and experience in teaching.

Efforts have been made to define and analyze the teacher's job. As a result, many schools are using aides to relieve the professional teacher of such nonprofessional tasks as preparing instructional materials, maintaining and making available teaching equipment, recording data for permanent records, supervising playgrounds, monitoring lunchrooms, getting books from the library, putting written work on the board, putting up exhibits, helping children with wraps, collecting funds for numerous causes, watering plants, mixing paints, and numerous jobs that take up valuable time.[19]

The problem of priorities might be examined in the light of two questions: What should our schools accomplish? For whom should they accomplish it? In countries in which schools are admittedly the organs for shaping youth to the needs and purposes of the state these questions are readily answered. In our country they must be examined in terms of a dual purpose — the development of the individual and the improvement of society. One has but to look at the objectives of the school through educational history to see the pendulum swing at times in one direction and at other times in the opposite direction. During the nineteenth century public schools served as the chief instrument to preserve the cultural heritage and to develop state and national communities. With the advent of the twentieth century the goal of individual development came to the fore and the improvement of society received minor emphasis as an educational goal. Both goals are important. When they are harmoniously balanced education will be strengthened.

[19] Accounts of experiments with teacher aides in the classroom giving the purposes of the experiment and samples of opinion both pro and con may be found in the following writings: *Report of the First Two Years of Study* (Bay City, Mich.: The Superintendent, n.d.); Dorothy McCuskey, "The Bay City Project," *NEA Journal*, 45:284–285, May 1956; Alexander J. Stoddard, *Schools for Tomorrow: An Educator's Blueprint* (New York: Fund for the Advancement of Education, 1957), pp. 19–24; *The Yale-Fairfield Study of Elementary Teaching*, abridged edition of the report of 1954–1955 (New Haven: Department of Education, Yale University, 1956).

## Quality in Diversity

In spite of the common objectives there are vast differences in quality and quantity in educational opportunities in different sections of the country. Unless priorities are established many of the school's efforts will become increasingly nondirectional, nonfunctional, and nonproductive.

Because of the complexity of the problems facing our society educators are giving serious consideration to the proposal of a National Commission on Curriculum. Two major assumptions undergird the proposal: (1) that the commission will have no authority to implement its recommendations other than the weight of logic they carry, thus relieving individuals of the fear of losing local initiative and prerogatives, and (2) that there will be no strings attached. New developments come rapidly, require much research, and are often too costly for the local resources. Many curriculum changes are broad in scope. Pooling resources of competent, qualified individuals to get the research done in a manner that meets both local and national needs is the purpose for such a commission. It is not a question of trading local for federal control; it is simply a question of getting the job done.

There is a growing belief that "the schools of our nation need some curriculum experiences in common. . . . Some common understandings, and some common qualities must bind our people together in these times when factions from within and enemies from without would tear our nation asunder."[20]

Hanna proposes a permanent National Commission on Curriculum, nongovernmental, widely representative, and continuously at work on educational goals and a balanced curriculum design. It is his belief that:

> Because we live in a dynamic era of profound change which we believe we can, with widening limits, shape to our desire and will;
> Because the local and the state educational authorities are now and should remain in final control of curriculum choices and programs;
> Because modern science and technology have united local and state

[20] Paul Hanna, "A National Commission for Curriculum Research and Development" (Palo Alto: Stanford University, mimeographed, n.d.), p. 2.

communities in a great national community, the preservation and improvement of which makes certain demands on school curriculum;

Because few if any local or state systems of education can attract or can afford the rare talent required continuously to study and to propose priority of objectives and alternative curriculum designs that will specifically serve the national interest; and

Because the national community has no recognized and comprehensive body responsible for continuous study of educational objectives and for making the curriculum recommendations necessary to our continuing national progress:

Therefore, it follows that we should engage in nationwide discussion of how best to accomplish curriculum improvements desired.[21]

In spite of differences of opinion on the manner in which education meets the demands of the times there is general agreement that our educational objectives and our educational program must be strengthened in order to achieve balance in individual development and social improvement. The times demand that we develop well-educated individuals equipped to meet and solve problems. The curriculum, then, must emphasize accumulations of human experience and knowledge and interpret them in the light of scientific, technological, and economic advances. It must help the growing child not only to develop a keener appreciation for and understanding of the society and subculture in which he lives but to re-examine, evaluate, and bring critical and creative thinking to the problems therein.

This curriculum requires a teacher who combines respect and love for tradition with a willingness to open new doors. "Such a teacher, if she had the additional opportunity to keep herself eternally abreast of a changing world, with the latest song on her lips and the most amazing scientific discovery to wonder about,"[22] would challenge children to become their best creative selves.

Also required is a school that takes responsibility for developing basic communication skills and scientific understandings; for discovering and nurturing creativity in children; for engendering positive thinking; for promoting understanding of peoples of other lands

[21] *Ibid.*, p. 23.
[22] Margaret Mead, *The School in American Culture* (Cambridge: Harvard University Press, 1951), pp. 36, 37.

and good relationships at home; for teaching the fundamentals of learning; for providing practice in the democratic process in school and community; and for helping the child develop aesthetic and spiritual powers. For every child the school must provide the opportunity to attain the highest, most excellent goal.

## Conclusion

The world of the elementary school child is exciting, changing, and accelerating. To become a part of this world the child must master the ways of the culture, get along with the people around him, develop inner resources, and discover answers to the problems that confront him.

The home is the first socializing agency the child meets. Here he acquires his first image of self. Here he interacts with others and develops a concept of who he is, deduced from the attitudes and behavior of the people around him. How he accepts himself and others is largely determined by his relationships with people, places, and situations in his environment.

The school, too, is an important agency for the transmission of the cultural heritage and providing experiences that will lead him to become a contributing member of society. In the school he experiences group living under the guidance of skilled teachers who understand him and who help him reach his maximum potential. The school must make clear what it expects of him and how he is to achieve the expectations. Thus he will learn to meet each situation in such a way that it will have meaning for him. In addition, new concepts will make living in this world more rewarding and more comprehensible.

Only as the home, the school, and society clearly understand their functions in the enculturation, socialization, and education of the child in a democracy can they help him fully to contribute to the various groups to which he will belong. Only as he learns to achieve the purposes set up by these agencies in harmony with his own growing needs, abilities, and interests will he achieve his maximum potential and thus discharge his responsibility to society and himself. Every aspect of his environment, within and without himself, influences the choices he makes, the tasks he masters, and the results he achieves.

## ACTIVITIES AND QUESTIONS

1. How does the process of socialization and enculturation take place?
2. What basic values must the child in a democratic society assimilate? How can the school help him?
3. Why is it essential that the teacher know the inner world of the child as well as the discernible exterior world? Is it enough for the teacher to see a problem from the point of view of the child? Cite authorities for your answer.
4. Organize a panel to discuss: Should the school continue to assume many of the tasks once performed by other agencies? In establishing the panel, define the terms, determine the extent of the problem, limit the scope of the topic to the time available, suggest possible solutions, choose the best solutions.
5. Examine objectives in at least two curriculum guides and compare them with those suggested by Kearney.
6. Plan a role-playing situation in which the school staff explains its objectives at a meeting of parents and teachers.
7. Visit in a first grade and find out how many nonteaching tasks the teacher is performing — routines that call for no special skill. Which of these might be performed by nonprofessional personnel?

## BIBLIOGRAPHY

Ambrose, Edna, and Miel, Alice. *Children's Social Learning: Implications of Research.* Washington, D.C.: Association for Supervision and Curriculum Development, NEA, 1958.

Association for Supervision and Curriculum Development, 1952 Yearbook. *Growing Up in an Anxious Age.* Washington, D.C.: The Association, NEA, 1952.

East, W. Gordon, and Moodie, A. E. (eds.). *The Changing World.* Yonkers-on-Hudson, N.Y.: World Book Company, 1956.

Erikson, Erik H. *Childhood and Society.* New York: W. W. Norton and Company, 1950.

Estvan, Frank J., and Estvan, Elizabeth. *The Child's World, His Social Perception.* New York: G. P. Putnam's Sons, 1959.

Foshay, Arthur W., *et al. Children's Social Values.* New York: Bureau of Publications, Teachers College, Columbia University, 1954.

Frank, Lawrence K. *The School as Agent for Cultural Renewal.* Cambridge: Harvard University Press, 1959.

Freud, Sigmund. *The Basic Writings of Sigmund Freud.* Translated and edited by Dr. A. A. Brill. New York: Random House, 1938.

Gordon, Ira. *Children's View of Themselves.* Washington, D.C.: Association for Childhood Education International, 1959.

Gwynn, J. Minor. *Curriculum Principles and Social Trends.* New York: The Macmillan Company, 3rd ed., 1960.

Havighurst, Robert. *Developmental Tasks and Education.* New York: Longmans, Green and Company, 2nd ed., 1952.

Herskovits, Melville. *Cultural Anthropology.* New York: Alfred A. Knopf, Inc., 1958.

Hopkins, L. Thomas. *The Emerging Self in Home and School.* New York: Harper & Brothers, 1954.

Jersild, Arthur T. *In Search of Self.* New York: Bureau of Publications, Teachers College, Columbia University, 1952.

Kearney, Nolan C. *Elementary School Objectives.* New York: Russell Sage Foundation, 1953.

Landreth, Catherine. *The Psychology of Early Childhood.* New York: Alfred A. Knopf, Inc., 1958.

Lieberman, Myron. *The Future of Public Education.* Chicago: University of Chicago Press, 1960.

Martin, William E., and Stendler, Celia B. *Child Development: The Process of Growing Up.* New York: Harcourt, Brace and Company, 1953.

Mead, Margaret. *The School in American Culture.* Cambridge: Harvard University Press, 1951.

Mercer, Blaine E. *The Study of Society.* New York: Harcourt, Brace and Company, 1958.

Mercer, Blaine E., and Carr, Edwin. *Education and the Social Order.* New York: Rinehart and Company, 1957.

Midcentury White House Conference on Children and Youth. *A Healthy Personality for Every Child.* Raleigh, N.C.: Health Publishing Institute, Inc., 1951.

Muller, Theresa Grace. *The Foundations of Human Behavior.* New York: G. P. Putnam's Sons, 1956.

Oliver, Robert T. *The Psychology of Persuasive Speech.* New York: Longmans, Green and Company, 1957.

Otto, Henry J. *Social Education in Elementary Schools.* New York: Rinehart and Company, 1956.

*The Purposes of Education in American Democracy.* Washington, D.C.: National Education Association, 1938.

Shane, Harold, and McSwain, E. T. *Evaluation and the Elementary Curriculum.* New York: Henry Holt and Company, 1959.

Smith, B. Othaniel, Stanley, William O., and Shores, J. Harlan. *Social Diagnosis for Education.* Yonkers-on-Hudson, N.Y.: World Book Company, 1950.

Taba, Hilda. *School Culture.* Washington, D.C.: American Council on Education, 1955.

Titiev, Mischa. *Introduction to Cultural Anthropology.* New York: Henry Holt and Company, 1959.

Tyler, Ralph. "The Curriculum, Then and Now," *Elementary School Journal,* 56:364–374, April 1957.

**2** The decisive moment in human development is a continuous one.

FRANZ KAFKA

# Understanding the child

As the child travels the road toward maturity, certain significant moments in the developmental cycle serve as guideposts along the way. To know the elementary school child it is essential to understand not only the cultural factors in his external world but also the developmental factors within the organism. This knowledge helps orient the teacher to the children he will teach and helps parents in guiding children from immaturity to maturity.

## The Teacher and the Child

What does it mean to know a child? It means understanding his physical, social, emotional, and intellectual growth. It also means knowing his characteristics and needs, his motivations and frustra-

22

tions, his successes and failures. It means praising him when he achieves and helping him set more realistic goals when he fails. It means knowing his family, his peers, and the social and physical factors that influence his unique personality. It means recognizing the problems he faces as he grows from childhood to maturity. It means not being satisfied to evaluate him until all that can be learned about him is known. It means using this knowledge to teach him more effectively in group situations and individually.

In short, a teacher should be scientifically prepared to make use of the principles of development, behavior, and learning. Through study of children one can see how inherited behavior capacities, learning processes, and environmental experiences affect each child's design for development. By applying such knowledge the teacher can avoid many pitfalls. The science as well as the art of teaching "lies in understanding the dynamics that are operating in unique configurations in each individual and in dealing effectively with these dynamics in group situations and by group as well as by individual ized procedures."[1] Knowing and understanding children involves more than ability to verbalize age norms and grade expectancies in relation to behavior profiles; it can change a chaotic classroom environment into a laboratory for learning.

The teacher who understands the characteristics of children at a given age, recognizes the dominant feature of each stage, and appreciates the previous and succeeding development of the individual has a clearer picture of the continuity and interrelatedness of growth. By taking a panoramic view of child development from the preschool years through the middle years of childhood and approaching adolescence he gains insight into how a child progresses from age to age, stage to stage, and grade to grade and can use it for interpreting the behavior of any individual child, whatever his maturity level.

*Normative Studies.* Many studies of children have been normative in character — that is, they have indicated the average ages at which certain growth characteristics are evidenced. The normative studies conducted by Gesell and his associates[2] are among the best

[1] Daniel Prescott, "The Child, A Statement of Ideas About the Child for the Consideration of the Educational Policies Commission," quoted from Virgil E. Herrick, *Issues in Elementary Education* (Minneapolis: Burgess Publishing Company, 1952), p. 74.

[2] Arnold Gesell and Frances L. Ilg, *Infant and Child in the Culture of Today* (New York: Harper & Brothers, 1943), and *The Child from Five to Ten* (New

known of their type. The team studied the behavior of infants, children, and youth at regular intervals from birth on and established norms of behavior in four fields: motor, adaptive, language, and personal-social interrelationships. Certain children were able to accomplish specific acts or display a specific growth characteristic at an earlier age than others, but the average age at which the group as a whole performed the action or displayed the specific growth characteristic was used.

These norms can be useful; used unwisely they may do harm by pressuring children who are not ready to accomplish or evidence certain behavior. They are not, according to Gesell, infallible guides; "norms of behavior, as measures of maturity, must be applied with even greater caution [than norms of height and weight]. . . . They give a time flow-map of the way in which the child matures. It is not intended that a single profile should be used to determine whether a given child is bright or dull, good or bad. Individual deviations are almost as normal as they are numerous. The norms enable us to detect the deviations."[3]

Each child has his own design of growth which the teacher must consider in planning educational experiences. The over-all tempo may be slow or fast, the progress steady or spasmodic with spurts and plateaus intermingling. The urge to grow is innate and each child will, with the effective guidance of interested adults, accept and reject the offerings of his social and physical environment in harmony with his inner design of development.

The child does not know what his inherited capacities are. He must discover them, and the discovery depends upon the environment: the more stimulus and opportunity the environment offers, the more it will implement the native endowment. The more the teacher understands the child, the better he can provide the favorable environment for "self-discovery" on the part of each child.

The studies of growth that have been carried on during recent decades have made available a great deal of information about the nature of growth. Studies in child development have given us ad-

York: Harper & Brothers, 1946); Arnold Gesell, Francis L. Ilg, and Louise B. Ames, *Youth: The Years from Ten to Sixteen* (New York: Harper & Brothers, 1956).

3 Arnold Gesell and Frances Ilg, *Child Development: An Introduction to the Study of Human Growth* (New York: Harper & Brothers, 1949), p. 70.

ditional information about the early years of life. Two methods have been used to trace the course of human development. The first consists of measuring *different* large groups of children at different age levels to get norms, or standards of development, for these specific ages. The second consists of re-examining the *same* children at intervals throughout the years of childhood and adolescence. Although the second method undoubtedly gives a more accurate picture of the typical child's individual development, it is not always feasible. It is from studies by both of these methods that we have acquired norms of the typical design of development from the moment of conception until maturity is reached. Such studies form the basis of principles that will prove invaluable to the adult engaged in guiding children.

There are advantages in knowing what normal development is: we have an idea of what to expect from a child at every age and, in a general way, at what age different forms of behavior are likely to change to more mature forms. Thus the teacher can sense whether a particular child's behavior is typical or atypical at any age and can perhaps direct his development into the desired channels.

Prime requisites for understanding the child are to regard him as a growing, changing human dynamo; to recognize him as a unique personality, with a stubborn inclination toward developing according to his own design and to realize that his growth and development are in harmony with certain basic principles.

Prime requisites for guiding the child are a knowledge of (1) the basic principles of child growth and development, (2) the developmental characteristics and known sequences of behavior and development, (3) the principles of child behavior, and (4) the responsibility of the teacher in guiding growth and behavior.


## Basic Principles of Growth and Development

Growth is not haphazard. Neither does it follow a simple formula that enables the teacher or parent to predict with certainty its exact design and nature. However, certain basic principles do obtain and enable the teacher and parent to guide the child with a degree of equanimity and assurance.

*Continuity of Development.* Development is orderly and proceeds gradually; each stage is a direct outgrowth of an earlier stage. To understand the child at any age, it is essential to know the entire growth cycle from infancy to adulthood with special attention to the years from preschool through elementary school. The concept of growth as an unbroken sequence is important to the teacher as he recognizes the value of understanding what has happened in the previous stages of development, what is happening now, and what problems will arise in the next stage. "Every child has a unique pattern of growth but that pattern is a variant of a basic ground plan. The species sequences are a part of the established order of nature."[4]

*Variation Among Individuals and Within the Individual.* No two children are exactly alike. No two grow quite alike, not even twins. Wide differences exist among children of the same age, the same family, and the same community — differences in readiness for learning, in rate of growth, and in maximum potential. Although children follow an orderly pattern, each child has his own unique design that is consistent for him. The rapid developer continues in general to develop rapidly and the retarded child continues his slow, methodical pace. Over the years the chasm between the rapid developer and the retarded child widens. Each has his own limits beyond which he is unlikely to progress. However, late starters may develop in a manner that surprises parents and teachers alike. Teachers should apply the principles of growth judiciously. They should avoid putting undue pressure on the slow learner. They should also avoid aiding and abetting the child who achieves without effort and consequently is not challenged simply because he matures early.

Not all parts of the body grow at the same rate, nor do all aspects of mental growth proceed at the same tempo. To expect a child to be equally advanced in all phases of development is foolhardy. Teacher and parent must be aware that an "at-age-level" achievement goal for each child in every phase of development is unrealistic.

*Qualitative and Quantitative Aspects.* Development is *change.* In this sense it has a quantitative meaning. When you greet the child in the fall whom you have not seen for several vacation months you

---

[4] Arnold Gesell, "Growth Potentials of the Human Infant," *Scientific Monthly*, 68:252–256 (1949), quoted in Elizabeth Hurlock, *Child Development* (New York: McGraw-Hill Book Company, 1956), p. 11.

are likely to exclaim, "Susan, how you've grown!" This can mean that Susan is taller or heavier than she was at a previous period. But growth is qualitative as well as quantitative. Even during the period of leveling off, the period in which added maturity is gained, quality is still developing. Growth is always dynamic even when the change is less perceptible. This qualitative growth is not limited to physiological processes; it is in evidence in mental and social processes as well. The wise teacher looks for both quantitative and qualitative signs of growth. He knows that he can expect no more growth than is in harmony with the child's unique growth pattern and represents a reasonable progress on the road to learning and maturity.

*Development and Needs.* Needs, motives, and other personal-social drives are the result of living and interacting in a particular environment. They are not, that is, entirely determined by "growth" but are also affected by experiences. The impulse to grow is innate and is a singularly powerful force. However, new needs are created by growth. Growth may be accelerated under favorable conditions, but the gains are retained only through a continuous program of improving the total cultural environment.

The concepts of growth as creating new needs and growth as modifiable present a challenge to teachers and other adults engaged in guiding children. They underline the significance of providing a favorable educational environment and they emphasize the school's task of influencing child development in such a way that desirable needs are created and satisfied.

*Interrelatedness of Growth.* Every aspect of the child's life affects every other aspect. It is not enough for the teacher to show interest or concern with the child's emotional experience. He must realize that factors in the physical and social environment as well as factors of personality and physical development affect academic achievement. For example, in the complex task of learning to read, the child's emotional self, social self, physical self, and other selves are all involved along with his intellectual self.

In order to understand each child the teacher must be acquainted with the cultural factors that are shaping his personality; what he thinks, says, draws, sings, writes, reads, or experiences; how he feels about his family, his peers, his physical appearance; how he expresses his concerns about his physical appearance, size, prowess on the playground, achievements and failures in school. The teacher takes each phase of development into consideration — excluding none and overemphasizing none.

*From the General to the Specific.* In all phases of development the child's initial responses are of a generalized nature. Infants respond to stimuli with the whole body; later they gain control over parts of the body. Random movements precede specific. Watch a child as he learns to walk. He begins with random kicking before he can gain the necessary control for coordination of leg muscles in crawling, creeping, and walking.

Every new phase makes its appearance in a gross form, from which later emerge more skilled and specialized responses. This is true in the development of language as well as motor skills. The infant babbles before he becomes selective in the use of words. He uses general terms before he learns precise words. He does not identify the beagle or cocker spaniel at the outset — all dogs are "bow-wow" or "doggie." Later he learns to distinguish types. The significance of this principle cannot be overemphasized for the teacher. He must provide children with experiences and opportunities for reacting to situations with the entire body. He must in his teaching proceed from the simple to the complex, from the concrete to the abstract. He must see to it that young children use their large muscles before expecting them to develop the fine muscular coordination needed in writing or reading fine print. Finally, he must build upon what children already know in encouraging concept formation.

*Characteristic Traits of Each Stage.* A dominant characteristic, a leading feature, an outstanding need characterizes each stage of development and gives it uniqueness, coherence, or unity. Every individual normally passes through all stages. The rate and time required to complete each stage and to reach maturity varies. However, most people have gone through the major stages by the time they are twenty-one years of age. Unfavorable environmental factors, lack of motivation, poor health, or low intelligence may retard the normal rate of development, but their influence is not generally permanent.

*"Problems" as Normal Behavior.* Teachers and parents who understand the developmental patterns of boys and girls, and who are patient enough to allow each sequence to take its course, find

their problems simplified. Children may exhibit undesirable behavior characteristic of a certain age but they will outgrow it if they are helped to develop more mature ways of adjusting to their environment. They may be guided so that they modify or adandon it as they reach the next level of maturity. Children grow into frustrated and neurotic adults because adults lack understanding of normal childhood behavior, of problems children face as they grow up, and of the sequence of behavior at various ages and stages.

Understanding is necessary, but so is guidance. Adults must accept the children even though they cannot always accept the behavior. They must give assistance through difficult periods — not add to the children's problems. Knowing about children in general never relieves them of understanding children in particular. Knowing the principles is not enough: they must be applied in the classroom as the teacher organizes, develops and evaluates learning experiences and growth.

Since sequences of development follow a consistent pattern at specific ages for the majority of children, it is possible to set up norms of what the adult can expect at each age. Although age norms are not infallible guides or inflexible standards they can be used with profit for orientation and interpretative purposes.

Havighurst has made available a comprehensive standard for different age levels in his study of the problems children face in society. He has termed these problems developmental tasks. A developmental task is "a task which arises at or about a certain period in the life of the individual, successful achievement of which leads to his happiness and to success with later tasks, while failure leads to unhappiness in the individual, disapproval by society, and difficulty with later tasks."[5]

The origins of these tasks are threefold: physical maturation, cultural pressures, and personal values and aspirations of the individual or "self." The major developmental tasks for children are as follows:

INFANCY AND EARLY CHILDHOOD

*Birth to 6 Years*

Learning to walk.
Learning to take solid foods.

[5] Robert J. Havighurst, *Developmental Tasks and Education* (New York: Longmans, Green and Company, 2nd ed., 1952), p. 2.

ing to talk.
iing to control the elimination of body wastes.
hing sex differences and sexual modesty.
ieving physiological stability.
Forming simple concepts of social and physical reality.
Learning to relate oneself emotionally to parents, siblings and other people.
Learning to distinguish right and wrong and developing a conscience.

## MIDDLE CHILDHOOD

### *6 to 12 Years*

Learning physical skills necessary for ordinary games.
Building wholesome attitudes toward oneself as a growing organism.
Learning to get along with age-mates.
Learning an appropriate masculine or feminine sex role.
Developing concepts necessary for everyday living.
Developing conscience, morality and a scale of values.
Achieving personal independence.
Developing attitudes toward social groups and institutions.[6]

*Development of Fundamental Skills.* Most children learn to read, write, and calculate before they leave the elementary school. There is still much uncertainty on the part of parents and some teachers with respect to the developmental sequence of the basic skills. The following excerpt from Gesell and Ilg describes how one of these skills is acquired by "normal" children.

### READING

5 Years — Likes to identify repetitious phrases or words in familiar books such as exclamations or sounds that animals make. Also identifies word signs such as *stop* and *go*, or *hot* and *cold* on faucets, or words on cereal boxes. . . .
Recognizes own first name.
May read letters in sequence such as, "What does d-o-g spell, Mommy?"
May enjoy using wooden letters to represent names of people and may use these in combination with block building. . . .

[6] *Ibid.*, pp. 6–28.

6 Years — Interest in small as well as capital letters.
Recognizes words and phrases, and perhaps sentences. Finds words related to picture or story. Matches words. . . .
Beginning to develop a reading vocabulary. Beginning to recognize words out of context.
Gets clues from length of word, beginning sound or letter. . . .
Some like to pick out letters on a typewriter and have mother spell words for them. . . .
. . . apt to read and re-read it [a book] many times.

7 Years — Can now read sentences. Recognizes familiar words easily and rapidly out of context.
Individual differences in reading rate are marked. . . .
Enjoys finding familiar words in a child's dictionary.

8 Years — Masters new words through context, division into syllables, initial consonants, prefixes and suffixes.
Mechanics and reading for meaning now in better balance. . . .
Uses tables of contents and index. . . .
Reads more rapidly in silent reading, and usually prefers silent reading.
Also enjoys taking turns in reading a story orally. . . .

9 Years — Reading now more related to various subjects.
Individual differences in abilities and interests. Now some who have been slow have a real spurt.
Utilize dictionary.
May do better in silent reading but need to be checked by oral reading. . . .[7]

Children from ten to twelve years of age show rapid growth in reading skills, not only in recognition of words and their meanings, but also in reading aloud effectively, using the dictionary, enriching the vocabulary, developing versatility in word attack, evaluating material read, locating and remembering significant details, locating information in reference and source books for use in reports or problem solution, making outlines of material read and using them as a basis for a report. They are gaining new abilities in reading rate and technique according to purpose and type of material read. They interpret simple maps, charts, and graphs, selecting books for recreational reading with discrimination.

[7] Gesell and Ilg, *Child Development*, pp. 395–397.

An understanding of childhood tasks is important; an understanding of the child is even more important. The teacher who knows each child in the group is able to help him, by waiting for the proper moment, the "teachable moment," rather than standing with the "poised hand ready to fire the gun which will send the child hurtling into the next developmental lap."[8] Today's lap of the journey toward maturity is important not merely as a preparation for tomorrow, but because of its own significance.

A knowledge of the sequence of the educational levels will give the teacher and parent a clearer picture of what is expected of the child by the school. It will also show the interrelationships between the child's growth characteristics and needs, developmental tasks, and stages of growth during each period from infancy through middle childhood. Each period involves both progress and retrogression, gains and losses. Wise adults motivate, challenge, but do not force the child beyond his readiness for the new experience. They sense the continuing need for affection, acceptance, achievement, and emotional warmth and support throughout the years of infancy, childhood, adolescence, and adulthood.

## Ages and Stages

"Each stage represents a degree or level of maturity in the cycle of development. To ask how many stages there are in this cycle would be like asking how many minutes there are in a day. A stage is simply a passing moment, while development, like time, keeps marching on."[9] Gesell suggests that for the sake of clarity the stages be organized as follows: (1) the preschool years; (2) the elementary school years; (3) the high school years; (4) the pre-adult years.[10]

Erikson lists the eight stages of man in terms of the major problem to be solved, temporarily at least, at each stage. Personality development is always related to biological functions. The accompanying

---

[8] Walter Douglas Smith, "Those Transition Periods," *Childhood Education*, 32:170, December 1955.
[9] Gesell and Ilg, *Child Development*, p. 60.
[10] *Ibid.*, p. 12.

## Erikson's Eight Stages of Man

| | | | | | | | |
|---|---|---|---|---|---|---|---|
| **Oral Sensory 0-1 years** — Trust vs. Mistrust | | | | | | | |
| | **Muscular Anal 1-3 years** — Autonomy vs. Doubt, Shame | | | | | | |
| | | **Loco-Motor Genital 3-6 years** — Initiative vs. Guilt | | | | | |
| | | | **Latency 6-12 years** — Industry vs. Inferiority | | | | |
| | | | | **Puberty Adolescence** — Identity vs. Role Diffusion | | | |
| | | | | | **Young Adulthood** — Intimacy vs. Isolation | | |
| | | | | | | **Adulthood** — Generativity vs. Stagnation | |
| | | | | | | | **Maturity** — Integrity vs. Disgust, Despair |

Source: Erik H. Erikson, *Childhood and Society* (New York: W. W. Norton and Company, 1950), p. 234.

chart suggests the central problem of each stage of development and its biological orientation. ". . . The diagonal represents the sequence of enduring solutions, each of which is based on the integration of the earlier ones. At any given stage of the life cycle the solution of one or more nuclear conflicts adds a new ego quality, a new criterion of increasing strength."[11]

Witmer and Kotinsky interpret Erikson to mean that every problem

> . . . has to be solved, temporarily at least, if the child is to proceed with vigor and confidence to the next stage. These problems, these conflicts of feeling and desire are never solved in entirety. Each shift in experience and environment presents them in a new form.

[11] Erik H. Erikson, *Childhood and Society* (New York: W. W. Norton and Company, 1950), p. 233.

It is held, however, that each type of conflict appears in its purest, most unequivocal form at a particular stage in the child's development, and that if the problem is well solved at that time the basis for progress to the next stage is laid and a degree of "sturdiness" in personality secured for the future.[12]

According to this concept the infant is moving toward the mature, healthy personality, which combines a sense of trust, a warm confidence in others with feelings of autonomy, initiative, industry, identity, intimacy, generativity, and integrity.

Each stage of development brings with it not only new problems but new dangers, new anxieties, and new challenges. How the child relates himself and his needs and drives to the world of people, processes, and things determines the health of his emerging personality. As Jersild expresses it, "Every hurdle in development involves a hazard and every gain is made at a price."[13]

Growing up in society is not a simple matter. Neither is developing a healthy personality. The demands of the organism together with the expectations of the culture or society change as the child grows older. Likewise the child's thoughts, perceptions, actions, and behavior differ from those of the mature individual. As the child develops, he must learn to maintain a fine balance between the organismic demands, the emerging self, and the demands of society. As he does so, and resolves the conflicts that arise, he develops personality by building new strengths and adding new components. Erikson's design for personality development sets forth the nature of the personality components and the approximate periods in which they emerge.

Erikson bases his plan on the idea that the development of personality is subject to certain inner laws, just as the biological organism develops according to a plan, the various parts arising at a proper and specific time until all are functioning as an entirety. In the chart on page 33 read the growth stages, from infancy to maturity, downward at the left. The designations are derived from psychoanalytic concepts of personality. The first four stages correspond roughly to (1) the first year of life; (2) the years from one to

[12] Helen L. Witmer and Ruth Kotinsky (eds.), *Personality in the Making: The Fact-Finding Report of the Midcentury White House Conference on Children and Youth* (New York: Harper & Brothers, 1952), p. 4.

[13] Arthur T. Jersild, *Child Psychology* (New York: Prentice-Hall, Inc., 4th ed., 1954), p. 25.

three; (3) the years from three to six; (4) the years from six to twelve. The last four stages represent the years after the age of twelve. Because children vary so much during the period of puberty, and since we are concerned primarily with the child in the elementary school years, we shall not attempt to relate the remaining stages to specific years.

*The Sense of Trust.* In the first stage the child needs to develop his sense of trust. Most infants in our culture acquire the sense of trust before they are fifteen months old.

*The Sense of Autonomy.* The next step in the struggle for a healthy personality is attained by the age of three. By this time the child should have gone a long way toward developing what Erikson calls autonomy and others have called self-reliance or adequacy.

*The Sense of Initiative.* The central problem for the four- or five-year-old is that of developing initiative. Children of this age are beginning to want to come to grips with life. During this stage they try on the roles of the adult. They need to be challenged, not coddled, encouraged to explore, to imagine, to perform at their highest level of ability. They should be allowed to dream, to plan for things they can do when they are older.

*The Sense of Industry.* By the time the child has entered first grade, the fourth stage has already begun; it extends from age six through the next five or six years. Its goal is the sense of industry or accomplishment. Children are eager to learn, to settle down to reality and a realistic way of doing things. During this period, when they are in elementary school, the foundations for citizenship are laid. Some of the responsibilities assumed are the direct result of the demands of society. To challenge the child during this stage is perhaps the greatest opportunity of the school.

*The Sense of Identity.* Although the elementary school is primarily concerned with the stages of development up to and including the fourth stage, teachers must understand the problems arising with the onset of puberty. Stress and strain, conflict and frustration are a part of the life of the adolescent. To be someone, to identify with someone he can admire is his chief problem. To discover his identity and find his role in society is far from an easy task. A child one day, an adult the next — problems face him; difficult decisions must be made. If parents and teachers have done their work well in helping children develop a sense of trust, autonomy, initiative, and industry, this stage too will accomplish its purpose. The youth will be well on his way toward achieving success as a member of society.

At each period the central problem or dominant trait is different. On the basis of evidence from studies of large groups of children, it is possible to identify the major characteristics of each age.

Hurlock recognizes five developmental periods:

1. Prenatal period. The period from conception to birth, approximately 200 days.
2. Infancy. The first two weeks of the child's life.
3. Babyhood. The period from two weeks to about two years. During this period the child develops autonomy, feeds himself, controls his muscles, walks, makes his needs known through verbal usage and play.
4. Childhood. From age two to puberty — from two to eleven, twelve, or thirteen. Whereas the baby sought control of his body, the child at this stage seeks to control his environment in order that he may become a person in his own right. The six-year-old is becoming interested in socialization, the nine to twelve in group activities — the group feeling characterizes the period.
5. Adolescence. From the onset of puberty (eleven to thirteen) to maturity (twenty to twenty-four).[14]

The fifth period is frequently subdivided into three shorter periods: (1) pre-adolescence, (2) early adolescence, and (3) late adolescence.

We are primarily concerned with preadolescence, which occurs in girls generally between eleven and thirteen years of age and in boys approximately a year later. It has been described as the time when the nicest children often begin to behave in the most awful way. Living with the preadolescent at home or at school is a complicated matter. The negative phase and the unpredictable behavior are partly a result of rapid biological developments.

Early adolescence is marked by awkwardness, self-consciousness, and clumsiness. Late adolescence is characterized by responsible behavior, independence from adults, and decisions about vocations.

[14] Adapted from Elizabeth Hurlock, *Child Development* (New York: McGraw-Hill Book Company, 3rd ed., 1956), pp. 27, 28.

Upon maturity the developmental cycle is completed — to start all over again as the mature individual establishes a new home. It is essential for the teacher to understand the stages the child passes through, the problems he encounters along the way from infancy to the point where he is legally and socially regarded as a mature adult. All adults, leaders or followers, were once children.

KNOWLEDGE OF NORMAL DEVELOPMENTAL SEQUENCE

Knowing the normal developmental sequence is important for three major reasons:

1. It tells us approximately when to expect a certain type of behavior, growth, and development, so that underestimating or overestimating the capabilities of children at a given age can be avoided.

2. It gives the adult a clue as to when and how much to stimulate. It makes it easier to plan the environment so that when the "teachable moment" arrives for the child the encouragement to achieve is at hand. Significantly enough, the children themselves give evidence of the urge to practice new skills; thus the teacher has a basis for providing the type of experience they are "ready" for.

3. It makes it possible for parents or teachers to prepare the child for imminent changes in his development. Many children are worried about physical changes and new urges and drives that they ought to understand and take in their stride. To be forewarned is to be forearmed. Those who know beforehand something about the experience of entering school for the first time, whether kindergarten or first grade, are likely to make a favorable adjustment. Orientation periods, conferences, and visits to the school are common. Children need to be prepared for experiences that are new — whether academic, social, or physical.

Children must be successful in school. They need to be competent not only in academic achievement but also in getting along in group situations. They need to learn ways of behaving based on integrated personalities with increasing "behavior controls" from within, not on conformity for the sake of conformity. They have a right to a school in which they can practice the skills essential to good citizenship in a democratic atmosphere encouraging respect for the individual, responsibility for behavior, and creativity.

THE DEVELOPMENTAL SEQUENCE IN THE ELEMENTARY GRADES

The following year-by-year summary describes the child's characteristics, needs, and achievements as he makes his foray into an ever widening world. See him at five as he takes the first step up the educational ladder.

*Kindergarten — The Five-Year-Old.* The kindergartner may or may not be a novice at the educational experience. He may have had a year or two of nursery school and be already initiated into the mysteries of education. One sophisticated nursery school graduate surprised his kindergarten teacher by remarking, "I really expected to be bored here, but you have a different approach." Children who have been weaned from their mothers, who enjoy people and are curious about the unfamiliar, are generally very happy in kindergarten, provided there are challenging experiences, pleasant companions, plenty of space, and a teacher who is genuinely interested in them.

By the time the five-year-old comes to school he has already traveled a considerable distance on the road toward maturity. He has become a part of the family, the neighborhood, the community. He has grown physically, socially, intellectually. He has, in general, learned to take care of his physical needs and established desirable routines and attitudes toward eating, resting, toilet habits, and playing with at least one or two other children. If he has had reasonably intelligent guidance he now has a certain amount of independence and stability. If he has been sheltered and dominated by a possessive parent he will find the transition from the home to the school not without hardship.

Kindergarten children are characterized by activity, curiosity, and eagerness to explore. They are people, and people differ; each five-year-old is the product of his heredity and environment. The differences make teaching difficult, but also more challenging.

The kindergartner wants to express himself. He loves to talk. He likes to listen to stories. He does not particularly like to listen to other children, but as the year progresses he learns that listening is often the other side of the coin of speaking. Books interest him, and he often pretends to read. He is interested in solving problems, manipulating materials, dramatizing, and creating. He likes experiences in science, and numbers fascinate him. He knows what he wants to do and with whom he wants to do it. He likes people. He likes to please his teacher. He acts more "grown up" when he is with her than when with his mother. He takes pride in work well done but will crush or crumple his handiwork if it is not his best. The five-year-old is delightful, active, friendly, and appreciative; but before the year is over he is taking on many of the characteristics of the six-year-old.

*First Grade — The Six-Year-Old.* A first-grader is not just a kindergartner grown taller. He is an entirely changed person. Growth is change and change is dynamic, although at times it is imperceptible. There is a sharp line of demarcation when the kindergartner becomes a first-grader. The long day, the pressure to achieve, the repeated caution by the teacher to listen make their demands upon the child. He is more aggressive, more wiggly, and more enterprising than when he was in kindergarten. His vocabulary increases and he likes to try out new words. He shows greater interest in books, organized games, girls, and mathematics. He likes to write to 100, add and subtract, and make use of tools of measurement.

He is interested in science, in space ships and rockets. He likes to watch the jets streak across the sky. He is creative, dramatic, ecstatic, and energetic. The first-grade teacher must provide for his energies and creative abilities. He needs opportunities for self-expression and appreciation, a diversified program of challenging experiences that test his mettle, the opportunity to fumble, stumble, and pick himself up again. A characteristic of the first-grader is his inability to behave consistently. He is in need of an adult who will keep a nice balance between opportunities to develop independence and teacher guidance.

The problem of the first-grader is to cope with both home and school pressures. A certain amount of strain in the adjustment to school is inevitable for most children. The expectations of the culture, the long school day, the physiological instability of this age require that the first-grade teacher be relaxed, friendly, interested, and willing to give attention to six-year-old feelings, comments, questions, drawings, paintings, stories, and problems — and not of one child but of thirty. Flexibility and creativity must be the keynote for the curriculum.

*Second Grade — The Seven-Year-Old.* The aggressive first-grader is quieting down — the calm after the storm. Development at this stage gives the appearance of introspection and reflective evaluation of experience. The average seven-year-old likes to talk with adults, to watch television or listen to the radio. He enjoys reading to himself and having stories read to him. Socially the seven-year-old is aware of and interested in others, not alone as they affect him and his personal drives and satisfactions, but as he affects them. He becomes self-critical and demands of himself perfection in his accomplishments. If he feels he has failed he is unhappy and despondent. He has, however, a persistence, a holding-on quality, that is characteristic of the budding scholar. Many teachers prefer second-graders because they are persistent in their tasks, considerate in their demands, and earnest in their desire to please the teacher. They are respectful, quiet, amenable to suggestions, courteous, and more independent than first-grade children. Routine suits them and they rarely rebel audibly. With understanding and a minimum of adult criticism and disparagement they can exercise necessary self-discipline to gain control over such immature behavior as tattling, alibiing, and griping about "teacher's pets." The second-grader is cooperative, contented, and agreeable much of the time. He is concerned over academic achievement, and he needs opportunity for creative expression, problem solving, experiences in group situations, and discussions of concepts.

Some seven-year-olds appear to be tense, worried, and overly aware of their own shortcomings. They are more apprehensive than are the sixes and dependent upon the teacher for a close personal relationship. It is extremely important, therefore, that the teacher be a person who genuinely likes children — not one who teaches the second grade because it is "easier."

*Third Grade — The Eight-Year-Old.* At this age children are independent; teaching shows results; and ethical values, emotional development, and creative abilities are readily encouraged. Broad interests develop. The third-grader takes enthusiastically to new areas of learning and is challenged by experiences in science and social science. Intellectual growth as well as physical and social development is taking an upward swing. The third-grader is a social creature, less absorbed in himself and his own problems and eager to include his schoolmates. Sex differences are becoming noticeable, from the standpoint of both maturities and interests. Girls are beginning to show weight and height superiority over boys. Girls gang up on boys and vice versa. The role of the teacher is neither that of the confidante nor that of mother hen; it is that of umpire or arbiter. The teacher of third-graders who can umpire the ball game at recess has status with the children and can maintain the role of arbiter when they return to the classroom. Loyalty to the group and need for status with the group become increasingly important during the third grade. It is not that the children like the teacher less; it is simply that they need the approval of the group more.

The eight-year-old may be said to be characterized by a reaching out for independence, diversity of interests, and the development of individual and sex interests. Identification with members of his own sex is a dominant need for anyone in the "group age" and should be considered by the teacher in planning for the group.

*Fourth Grade — The Nine-Year-Old.* Slow, steady growth precedes preadolescence. The rate of growth and learning is increasing. The child has not yet reached the point where he wants to throw off the yoke of adult domination. He takes suggestions from adults and consequently the teacher's delight is the fourth-grader. Growth in height and weight for the nines and tens is normally steady. Games requiring skills and muscular control are enjoyed by both sexes. Practice to become proficient in games requiring skill is common. The ability to excel helps the child gain in peer status. The heart is subject to strain, and physical activity should be regulated to avoid overstrain.

Girls are nearer adolescence than are boys and nearer to the wisdom of adulthood. Sex differences begin to exert a strong influence. Intellectual skills are marked. Self-expression becomes a significant need during this period. To be one of the group is increasingly important.

Many children begin lifelong hobbies through interests in collections such as stamps, butterflies, pins, coins, and the like. They express themselves in writing, art, music, and drama.

The fourth-graders are less susceptible to fatigue and have more skill in activities requiring fine coordination. Approval of peers is taking on more significance than approval of adults. Creativity is at a high point. Loyalty and group cooperation are characteristic of the period. The nine-year-old is intrigued by learning, particularly learning that requires special skills and self-discipline such as studying to play a musical instrument, to work out some pet project, or to drill for the spelling contest.

*Fifth Grade — The Ten-Year-Old.* The ten-year-old is poised, relaxed, and, like the seven-year-old, somewhat reflective. Utilizing group processes is essential for the teacher of this age group. The fifth-grader is an organizer. He likes to plan, to make decisions, to carry out plans and evaluate the results. He likes to be responsible for organizing committees and carrying out creative dramatizations, school programs, and parties. In these activities he shows more skill than the fourth- or sixth-grader.

He appears to have greater self-possession in comparison with children in the other elementary grades. Learnings that have social significance will have real meaning for him. Social science, if taught from the point of view of social problems, will be readily accepted. Emphasis on creativity, communication skills, and social and natural science will make the fifth grade a year of significant growth for children and a year of satisfaction for the teacher.

Differences in maturity rate account for many of the problems which baffle teachers during the upper elementary years. Activities and reading materials should be provided that will take into account these differences.

From the point of view of parents, ten is a comfortable age. The child is agreeable, obeys without undue pressure, and is in general satisfied with his family, his school, and his teacher. The world to him is a pretty nice place. He is, in general, cooperative, friendly, and pleasant. Never again will he show so openly the same whole-hearted and unreserved acceptance of the actions and motives of adults.

In development, however, no year stands by itself. Each one bears a close and dynamic relation to the preceding and succeeding years. Ten is the "golden age" of development, perhaps because the ten-year-old is more relaxed than the nine, more casual, more sure of himself, and may give the appearance of being less ambitious because he is less intense about what he is doing.

The ten-year-old is a joy to his teacher. He likes to learn; he wants a good teacher, one who will keep him motivated and interested in a variety of things. He is normally respectful to the teacher and accepts her word as law, in sharp contrast to the sixth-grader, who is striving for independence. He will make a point of looking well-groomed if his teacher is attractive and well-groomed. He is interested in what the teacher wears. Typical of fifth-graders is the boy who described his teacher as "the one who always wears a blouse and skirt." The more mature fifth-graders may assign undue significance to the comradely behavior of the teacher of the opposite sex.

*Sixth Grade — The Eleven-Year-Old.* During sixth grade almost anything can happen. Some of the nicest children begin to act in the most impossible ways. This period is most disappointing to parent and teacher, a time in which children are difficult to live with and hard to understand.

At eleven it is not easy to maintain a balance between adult and peer demands. As a result, continuous conflict and aggression are never far beneath the surface; in extreme cases outright rebellion against authority may occur. The child is ending one cycle of development, that of childhood, and beginning another, that of the adolescent-adult. He is bewildered by new feelings and new inner needs. He must make choices and decisions. Perhaps one of the greatest challenges of working with sixth-graders is that they have reached the point where they are convinced that their teachers do not know everything, do not have all the answers at the tip of their tongues. This characteristic is actually to the advantage of teacher and child. Instead of giving the answer the teacher can encourage the child to find the answer, to use techniques of research. The teacher had also better use techniques of research in order to speak the same language. In the process, both teacher and child can learn something new, can explore.

The eleven-year-old is not just a bigger ten-year-old. The teacher who has taught fifth- and sixth-graders will bear witness to this. The new forces and undercurrents of development are beginning to make themselves felt and the child is reacting by changed behavior. The physiological changes affect his entire action and behavior pattern. He is growing rapidly, always on the go, talkative, and "starved to death." Moods are changing, too. One day gloomy, one day gay.

The gloom may not last all day — almost anything can chase it away. The desire for independence results in argumentativeness with parents, brothers, sisters, and bosom friends. Creativity, giftedness, maturing talents make themselves evident during this year. The ease, the contentment, the poise of the ten-year-old gives way to "a new self-assertive expansion, restless searchings, and probing thrusts; proud defences; variable moods, dark and gay; flashes of anger and affection; active and effervescent curiosities; eager identifications with home, school, and friends; low moments of discouragement; high moments of desire and aspiration."[15]

Growing up is no easy process — at times child, at times adult, and at times neither child nor adult; wanting desperately to grow up and at the same time fearful of what growing up means; worrying, wondering, anxious, and not willing to admit how lonely, how worried, and how anxious one is. These are some of the clues to the behavior of the eleven-year-old, the sixth-grader. But he can be challenged, motivated, and stimulated to high endeavor by a teacher who is firm but patient, understanding but strict, intelligent but not pedantic.

*The Twelve-Year-Old Among Us.* The child who progresses normally up the educational ladder will, if all goes well, be out of the elementary school by the time he is twelve. However, non-promotion, late entry to school, illness, migratory situations are a few of the reasons we find children in the elementary school who are past the age of puberty. Therefore, the elementary teacher must have a clear picture of the adolescent and his problems.

Girls tend to seek association with older individuals, while boys are still interested primarily in their own age group. Adolescents are concerned with adult standards and judgments. At the same time they face the problem of freeing themselves from adults. They need someone with whom they can confidently talk over problems and work out solutions.

This brief view of the child as he progresses from kindergarten through sixth grade shows each of the phases of growth — physical, social, and intellectual. By the end of the kindergarten year he uses most of the forms of speech and has a vocabulary of nearly 3000 words. His motor skills are well established and he needs opportun-

[15] Gesell, Ilg, and Ames, *op. cit.,* p. 73.

ity to practice them in the primary school. He has, in general, learned to accept himself and others; he is well aware of the physical and social environment around him and of his inner world. He has taken the first steps in living and getting along with people. He is capable of using many of the intellectual operations that adults use. He can remember the past, plan for the future, and enjoy the present to the extent that his experiences and knowledge permit. He has come a long way, but he has a long way still to go.

The elementary school child begins to value achievement in the communication skills and arithmetic. He is increasingly interested in the social skills of living with others and becomes more dependent upon group approval. His dependence upon adults gives way to a need for status with his peers as he approaches the preadolescent or group stage. Identification with an admired adult becomes a motivating force. He shows marked progress in knowledge, general information, and broadened interests. He improves in the ability to deal with abstractions, to solve problems, to participate in group processes, and to develop concepts. He improves in the ability to concentrate and to apply himself to tasks requiring concentration. He is now ready for the next significant stage of development — adolescence — and when he emerges from this stage he is faced with acting the part of a responsible mature citizen.

How the teacher develops insight in understanding the behavior of children from preschool through the elementary years will be examined from the point of view that children behave as they do for reasons that they believe to be sound; that behavior is caused; that it can best be understood in terms of the child's maturation level, needs, and unique developmental pattern.

## Understanding the Behavior of Children

Daniel, a husky oversized five-year-old, hurries up the stairs to his kindergarten room brushing aside the children in his way. Steve gets pushed aside, Johnny trips, and then chaos begins. Steve and Johnny's friends gang up on Daniel and soon the teacher arrives. The same old story. Every day there is trouble, and the children say, "It's all Daniel's fault."

Edith Jones, the first-grade teacher, is sitting at her desk com-

| LEVELS | GROWTH STAGES | GROWTH CHARACTERISTICS | NEEDS | | |
|---|---|---|---|---|---|
| | | | Personal-Social | Bio-logical | Inte-grative |
| KINDERGARTEN | Infancy | Most rapid period of growth. The child is mainly concerned with satisfying his basic needs. Learning to trust others in his world. Establishing habits of eating, sleeping, and elimination. | Need for achievement, security, and recognition. | Need for food, air, liquid, clothing, shelter, rest, activity, physical safety, and space. | Need for creative expression, self-realization, and self-direction. |
| KINDERGARTEN | Early Childhood | Motor coordination gradually developing. Learning by touching, tasting, and feeling. Improving in motor control. Mastery of walking, running, climbing, jumping, skipping; learns to use tricycle. Dresses self, brushes teeth, and laces shoes. Large muscles better developed than small ones. | | | |
| PRIMARY | Middle Childhood | Language now a useful tool; uses most of the basic language structures. Body begins to lengthen. Permanent teeth begin to appear. Heart is growing rapidly. Most motor skills are established; needs practice now. Better use of small muscles. Large muscles continue to develop. Permanent teeth continue to develop. Arms lengthening; hands growing. Poor posture may develop. | Need for affection, belonging, and acceptance. | | |
| INTERMEDIATE | Middle Childhood | Eyes ready for near and far vision. Slow physical growth continues; girls develop more rapidly than boys. Plateau preceding pre-adolescent growth. Eye-hand coordination good. Enormous appetite. Secondary sex characteristics developing. Uneven growth in different parts of body. | | | |

| DEVELOPMENTAL TASKS | EDUCATIONAL IMPLICA |
|---|---|
| Learning to walk, eat, and communicate, to control and eliminate waste. | Guidance in developmen and social experiences, based on children's needs and provided in an educational setting, is advantageous for young children.<br><br>Experience can help the child lessen his tensions, anxieties, and frustrations. |
| Forming simple concepts of social and physical reality.<br>Learning to relate oneself emotionally to parents, siblings, and others.<br>Learning to tell right from wrong; developing a conscience.<br>Learning sex differences and sexual modesty.<br>Achieving physiological stability. | Well-directed kindergarten programs provide social and educational experiences which meet the needs of children for activity, creativity, exploration, and problem-solving.<br><br>The child of four or five will develop a sense of initiative if adults provide him with challenging experiences and responsibilities. |
| Learning physical skills necessary for ordinary games.<br><br>Building wholesome attitudes toward oneself.<br><br>Learning to get along with age-mates.<br><br>Learning a sex role.<br><br>Developing skills in the three R's.<br><br>Developing social concepts needed for everyday living.<br><br>Further development of conscience; development of a scale of values and morality.<br><br>Achieving personal independence.<br><br>Developing attitudes toward social groups and institutions. | The period from about age six to age twelve is characterized by the child's will to achieve and to accomplish. The child needs to come to grips with real tasks. It is at this stage that he will acquire knowledge and the skills of the basic school subjects; he will also learn to cooperate, to work and play with others, to leave the shelter of the home and begin his initiation into the world of adult reasoning and concepts, communication, symbolism, and mastery of tasks involving purposeful endeavor. To the school goes the chief responsibility for giving instruction that will help him solve problems and prepare him to be a contributing member of society with a sense of industry and achievement. |

pletely exhausted. Today the elements as well as the children have contrived against her. Indoor recess, voices raised to shrill levels, laughter that shattered her nerves, and the day is only half over. Without realizing it she found herself shrieking, "Stop talking and put your heads on your desks for twenty minutes! I can't stand another minute of it!"

The door of another kindergarten room is open. Miss Orange is conferring quietly with her class. Everyone appears to be interested in the discussion about plans for planting seeds in the garden outside the kindergarten room. The children are eager to begin planting but they are courteous as they contribute to the discussion. Soon they will go out and spade the garden; later they will plant the seeds. Here are the results of teacher-pupil planning, cooperative action, and challenging activities.

Down the hall the sixth-grade teacher is shouting. "Didn't I tell you to have that assignment ready by today? Can't you understand plain English? Do you think I talk just to listen to my own voice? Do you? Well! *Do you?*"

To understand and guide the behavior and development of children the teacher must first of all understand himself. He must recognize the basis for behavior, whether in the child or in himself. If the teacher is harsh or unsympathetic the child reacts by withdrawing into a shell or by striking back in a variety of undesirable ways. The child who sees all around him disapproval, dissatisfaction, hostility, and negativism will tend to react in a similar manner. It will be difficult for him to learn anything better.

Even where the home has provided a happy environment, the child cannot be immune to sarcasm and harshness from the teacher. Jersild quotes Sullivan in this connection: ". . . Harsh, cruel teachers . . . may affect the child from a happy home who has been taught to expect friendliness and a receptive and inquiring attitude, may teach him gradually, by reiterated pain and humiliation, that the world into which he has moved is an unfriendly and cruel world."[16] On the other hand, the child who is accepted, welcomed, and appreciated, if given the opportunity to learn and guidance in harmony with his developing needs and abilities, will confidently approach new experiences.

[16] Arthur T. Jersild, *In Search of Self* (New York: Bureau of Publications, Teachers College, Columbia University, 1952), p. 94.

Certain principles emerging from the study of children are important for the teacher's understanding of behavior:

1. All behavior of children has a causal explanation.
2. Children's activity is directed toward satisfying needs.
3. Problems of adjustment occur when these needs cannot be satisfied.
4. Children try to meet problems intelligently.
5. Children's behavior is influenced by the maturation level.

*Causal Explanation for Behavior.* There is a reason for everything a child does. Each activity is affected by heredity, maturation, the particular situation of the moment, the degree to which it satisfies his needs, and the experiences he has had in a similar situation. When the child fights or otherwise displays violence toward teacher or children, steals, destroys property, uses undesirable language, fails to comply with assignments, lies or cheats, plays truant or carries dangerous weapons, he is telling the adults around him that he is unable to satisfy his basic needs in an acceptable way. A teacher interested in helping the child develop social and emotional maturity will take an inventory to see whether or not he is providing an educational environment and curriculum in which his biological, social, and personal needs can be effectively met.

*Activity and Need Satisfaction.* Needs are an important consideration in promoting desirable classroom behavior. Unmet, unfulfilled, neglected, or ignored, they form the basis of patterns of misbehavior. They are the source of daydreaming, brooding, withdrawing, as well as the aggressive behavior exhibited by Daniel. If not corrected, the situation may result in delinquency or neurotic tendencies. The *biological* or *physiological needs* include need for air, food, shelter, clothing, warmth, and a proper balance of activity and rest. The activity of the infant centers largely around the satisfaction of biological needs — food, warmth, elimination, and a rhythm of rest and activity. He is trying to gain control of his body before he takes on the task of gaining control of the physical and social environment. Success in satisfaction of biological needs results in a feeling of well-being; equilibrium is restored, tensions are reduced. The adult must recognize that the child's activity is not random or haphazard. It makes sense to him and is directed toward a goal. Creating an environment in which all his needs can be satisfied is a responsibility of the adults in the life of the young child.

Social needs — for love, acceptance, security, status, and identification with peers — develop only through experience with others. The baby learns about people by coming in contact with them. The home is the first training ground for the child's social experience. He begins to feel the need for affection and wants to trust adults and be accepted by them. His personality is shaped by what he sees around him. A well-adjusted personality is neither too self-assertive nor too dependent on others. It maintains a balance between self-effacement and self-assertion. As the individual matures, social needs become increasingly important. A democratic classroom in which opportunity is provided for participating in group processes and developing a sense of responsibility for decisions is necessary for the satisfaction of social needs.

An essential of mental health is that the individual accept himself — accept his limitations as well as his strengths. Creativity, spontaneity, imagination, exploration, and self-realization are *personal* or *psychological needs* that must be satisfied. Children require experiences that help them understand the forces operating in their world. They must also have experiences that bring inner contentment and personal satisfaction. Expression in the arts is a means to such satisfaction. The creative teacher will provide the time, the space, the materials, and a social environment in which ideas flow freely and are expressed spontaneously.

*Adjustment Problems and Satisfaction of Needs.* All children have problems. They try to find ways to satisfy their needs but for various reasons may be unsuccessful. When the pattern of non-success becomes established they resort to some other means of satisfaction, or they withdraw from reality and thus ignore the problem.

Many teachers recognize such symptomatic behavior as lying, cheating, stealing, or aggressiveness but overlook behavior with just as serious connotations: withdrawing and daydreaming. The teacher must be alert to all types of behavior indicative of unsatisfied needs. He must try to discourage whatever causes the lack of satisfaction. It may be in the relationship of the child with his age-mates or adults, or in failure to achieve academically. "Early childhood is the period of life predominantly concerned with the origin of neuroses."[17] The child's adjustment in these early years is tremendously significant, since the infant portends the child, the child the youth, and the youth the man.

*Adjustment and Intelligence.* One of the evidences of normality is the capacity for intelligent behavior. The intelligent child soon recognizes his power to control the adults around him. He observes, accepts, resists, rejects what he meets in his environment on the basis of the approval he receives. If certain actions bring approval he learns this response. If certain behavior brings attention from adults he repeats it. For him such behavior is intelligent.

When a parent enrolls a five-year-old in kindergarten and says, "I hope Jim doesn't give you any trouble, but he has temper tantrums when he doesn't get his way," Jim smiles broadly as if to say, "What a big boy I am." Jim is due for a shock. This behavior that gets him everything he wants at home is very certain *not* to impress the teacher. In fact, it is highly probable that an intelligent lad like Jim will soon discover that what "works" at home does not necessarily "work" at school. The more intelligent he is the sooner he will learn to substitute a new behavior at school. Jonathan, an aggressive first-grader, informed his teacher, "My mother is scared of my pouting and sulking. Last year it was my temper tantrums. I just go into my room and sulk and then she lets me do what I want to. What are you scared of?" Such a child should be helped to find a better way of meeting his needs. One evidence that a child is maturing is his willingness to adopt more mature behavior that takes into consideration the rights and feelings of others.

*Maturation and Behavior.* Maturation is the total developmental process and includes the physical, motor, sensory, and mental growth. How a child reacts to different situations and experiences depends to a great extent on his maturation rate. How well he performs at certain skills, how he meets new situations, how he responds to academic requirements, how he expresses himself are influenced by his maturation pattern. The teacher must understand each child well enough to know from the signs he displays that he is ready for new experiences, for children's activity always gives a clue to the type of

[17] Catherine Landreth, *The Psychology of Early Childhood* (New York: Alfred A. Knopf, Inc., 1958), p. 6.

experiences for which they are ready. To have the greatest effect on the child, the teacher ought to have the opportunity to guide his growth and learning for longer than the traditional one-year term.

## The Responsibility of the Teacher

It is the teacher's responsibility to seek the causes of undesirable behavior and try to modify or remove them, or change the environment if possible. He should try to improve the conditions within the classroom so that the symptomatic behavior does not become more acute or more disturbing to the child or group. He should help the child find more acceptable, socially approved, and individually satisfying ways to meet his needs. The task is to provide an environment in which a wholesome personality can emerge, one which finds its greatest satisfaction in constructive, cooperative endeavor, its greatest joys in individual creativity, and its ultimate aim in service.

Children need and seek guidance from adults. The controls can gradually be lessened and withdrawn only as the child assumes greater responsibility for his actions and develops an increasingly mature attitude toward the rights of others. While he is in the process of developing more mature concepts he should be encouraged in self-direction and independence.

As teachers work with children one of their goals should be to help children develop adequate controls from within. "The way to controls from within is amply paved with incidents of controls from without."[18] In a learning environment in which the child's basic needs are met with a maximum amount of satisfaction and a minimum amount of frustration, desirable behavior will be a by-product.

The road toward mature behavior is filled with rich living, with failures as well as successes. Emotional maturity means the "degree to which the person has realized his potentiality for richness of living, and has developed his capacity to enjoy things; to love wholeheartedly; to laugh; to feel genuine sorrow; to feel anger when faced with the thwartings that would rile the temper of the sensible person; to experience fear when there is occasion to be frightened."[19]

[18] Fritz Redl and David Wineman, *Controls from Within* (Glencoe, Ill.: The Free Press, 1952), p. 8.
[19] Jersild, *In Search of Self*, p. 21.

## *Conclusion*

We have looked at the elementary school child and his world. We have examined ways of knowing him through the totality of his environment, as a growing organism, an emerging personality in the home, society, and school in which he grows as a contributing member. We have examined the basic principles of development, the developmental tasks children face, the developmental sequence from kindergarten through the elementary school, and the psychological bases for understanding the behavior of children as they move through infancy, early and middle childhood, and into adolescence.

We have pointed out repeatedly that understanding children in general through the use of norms does not relieve the teacher of the necessity of knowing each child in the classroom. Norms are valuable in orienting the teacher to the children of various age levels and will give a knowledge of what may be expected of the children in a particular grade. However, the norms may be harmful unless each child is considered as a unique individual with a peculiar design for development. Behavior is best understood from the viewpoint that the individual himself provides its basis, in terms of needs and of genetic and environmental factors.

Tables citing height, weight, mental age, motor coordination, academic achievements, growth, and behavior characteristics for large groups of children in the elementary school give the teacher some idea of what to expect of an "average" child in a certain age group. They do not, however, give data concerning a particular child. A study of growth patterns of boys and girls will reveal wide differences in all phases of development at any given chronological age. They will vary not only in physical, social, emotional, and intellectual development but also in attitudes, aspirations, sense of values, aptitudes, and interests. Only by knowing each child individually will the teacher be able to help him attain his maximum potential. Only then will the teacher be equipped to plan a curriculum that will have meaning for each child individually and for the group as a whole.

## ACTIVITIES AND QUESTIONS

1. How does an understanding of growth and behavior of children aid the elementary teacher?

2. Visit an elementary classroom and determine which principles of development are applied by the teacher.

3. In the same classroom which of the developmental tasks listed in the text were the children working on? Did you see any evidence of help from the teacher in accomplishing these tasks?

4. How would a knowledge of developmental tasks as defined by Havighurst and an understanding of the problems at each stage of development as outlined by Erikson aid the teacher of the kindergarten child? The teacher of the twelve-year-old in the elementary school?

5. Normative studies conducted by Gesell and his associates have been widely used by teachers and parents in an effort to gain a better understanding of children. What recommendations would you make to a parent to help him to better understand his children? What recommendations would you make to a parent on the use of these studies?

6. Summarize the main principles for understanding the behavior of children. Which ones in your opinion seem to be of most significance?

7. Organize a role-playing situation in which three primary teachers are meeting with the principal to set up minimum standards for achievement in reading. One is a former nursery school teacher, one taught kindergarten for five years, the third prides herself on having been a first-grade teacher for fifteen years.

8. Miss Jameson, a student teacher, is fascinated with child study. She is so interested in studying an individual child that she forgets to guide the group in learning experiences. What concrete suggestions would you have to help her sense her responsibility to the group?

9. Visit a classroom of six-year-olds and observe individual differences in height, language facility, social skills, creative ability, motor coordination, achievement in reading and numbers. Observe a class of eleven-year-olds. What conclusions do you draw concerning individual differences in the two classes? Formulate in your own words a generalization that applies to this situation.

# BIBLIOGRAPHY

Almy, Millie. *Child Development*. New York: Henry Holt and Company, 1955.

Almy, Millie. *Ways of Studying Children*. New York: Bureau of Publications, Teachers College, Columbia University, 1959.

American Council on Education. *Helping Teachers Understand Children*. Washington, D.C.: The Council, 1946.

Breckenridge, Marion, and Vincent, E. Lee. *Child Development*. Philadelphia: W. B. Saunders Company, 1950.

Carmichael, Leonard (ed.). *Manual of Child Psychology*. New York: John Wiley and Sons, 2nd ed., 1954.

Caswell, Hollis L., and Foshay, Arthur W. *Education in the Elementary School*. New York: American Book Company, 3rd ed., 1957.

Cunningham, Ruth, *et al. Understanding Group Behavior of Boys and Girls*. New York: Bureau of Publications, Teachers College, Columbia University, 1951.

Erikson, Erik H. *Childhood and Society*. New York: W. W. Norton and Company, 1950.

Forest, Isle. *Child Development*. New York: McGraw-Hill Book Company, 1954.

Foshay, Arthur. "Educational Goals," *Educational Research Bulletin*, 36: entire issue, February 13, 1957.

Foshay, Arthur, *et al. Children's Social Values*. New York: Bureau of Publications, Teachers College, Columbia University, 1954.

Frank, Lawrence K. *Individual Development*. Garden City, N.Y.: Doubleday and Company, 1955.

Freud, Sigmund. *An Outline of Psychoanalysis*. New York: W. W. Norton and Company, 1949.

Garrison, Karl C. *Growth and Development*. New York: Longmans, Green and Company, 1952.

Gesell, Arnold, and Ilg, Frances L. *Child Development*. New York: Harper & Brothers, 1949.

Gesell, Arnold, and Ilg, Frances L. *How a Baby Grows*. New York: Harper & Brothers, 1945.

Gesell, Arnold, Ilg, Frances L., and Ames, Louise Bates. *Youth: The Years from Ten to Sixteen*. New York: Harper & Brothers, 1956.

Havighurst, Robert. *Developmental Tasks and Education*. New York: Longmans, Green and Company, 2nd ed., 1952.

Havighurst, Robert. *Human Development and Education*. New York: Longmans, Green and Company, 1953.

Hurlock, Elizabeth. *Child Development*. New York: McGraw-Hill Book Company, 3rd ed., 1956.

Ilg, Frances L., and Ames, Louise Bates. *Child Behavior*. New York: Harper & Brothers, 1955.

Jersild, Arthur T. *Child Psychology*. New York: Prentice-Hall, Inc., 4th ed., 1954.

Jersild, Arthur T. *In Search of Self*. New York: Bureau of Publications, Teachers College, Columbia University, 1952.

Landreth, Catherine. *The Psychology of Early Childhood*. New York: Alfred A. Knopf, Inc., 1958.

Lane, Howard A., and Beauchamp, Mary. *Understanding Human Development*. Englewood Cliffs, N.J.: Prentice-Hall, Inc., 1959.

Lee, Jonathan Murray, and Lee, Doris May. *The Child and His Development*. New York: Appleton-Century-Crofts, Inc., 3rd ed., 1960.

Loomis, Mary J. *The Preadolescent: Three Major Concerns*. New York: Appleton-Century-Crofts, Inc., 1959.

Martin, W. E., and Stendler, C. B. *Child Development*. New York: Harcourt, Brace and Company, 1953.

Midcentury White House Conference on Children and Youth. *A Healthy Personality for Every Child*. Raleigh, N.C.: Health Publishing Institute, Inc., 1951.

Millard, Cecil V. *Child Growth and Development in the Elementary School Years*. Boston: D. C. Heath and Company, rev. ed., 1958.

Millard, Cecil V. *School and Child*. East Lansing, Mich.: Michigan State College Press, 1954.

Mitchell, Lucy (ed.). *Know Your Children in School*. New York: The Macmillan Company, 1954.

Moustakas, Clark E. *Children in Play Therapy*. New York: McGraw-Hill Book Company, 1953.

Moustakas, Clark E. *The Teacher and the Child*. New York: McGraw-Hill Book Company, 1956.

Olson, Willard C. *Child Development*. Boston: D. C. Heath and Company, 2nd ed., 1956.

Prescott, Daniel. *The Child in the Educative Process*. New York: McGraw-Hill Book Company, 1957.

Prescott, Daniel. *Emotion and the Educative Process*. Washington, D.C.: American Council on Education, 1938.

Redl, Fritz, and Wineman, David. *Controls from Within*. Glencoe, Ill.: The Free Press, 1952.

# 3 Oh,

I know
Such a lot
Of things, but as
I grow I know I'll know
Much more.

ANN AND PAUL RAND

# Helping the child to learn

What motivates a six-year-old? An eight-year-old? A ten- or twelve-year-old? How does learning occur? What types of learning take place in school? When does a child begin to learn effectively in a group? How can the teacher help the child learn? Is the learning process different for the five-year-old and the twelve? How can the teacher tell if the child is "ready" to learn? Are some learnings more significant at certain times? What is the relationship between the child's attitude toward his teacher and his willingness to get his lessons?

57

One of the most difficult tasks of teaching "comes in helping boys and girls who don't know what they want to learn, to establish clear purposes, and in helping pupils who have undesirable social purposes to re-examine those purposes and begin to want to learn the things that will make them effective citizens in our society."[1]

A persistent task of the teacher is to help *all* boys and girls learn — the eager, the indifferent, the antagonistic. The teacher who is successful in motivating pupils must have certain knowledge and skills, certain attitudes toward learning. He must understand what catches and holds the interest of the child in order to help him develop the self-drive needed for success in learning.

## The Learning Process

There have been numerous definitions of learning. The tendency at the present time is to define it as changed behavior. Munn defined the process in these terms: "Learning may be said to occur whenever behavior undergoes . . . modification of a more or less permanent nature as a result of activity, special training, or observation."[2] Hilgard called it "the process by which an activity originates or is changed through reacting to an encountered situation, provided that the characteristics of the change in activity cannot be explained on the basis of native tendencies, maturation, or temporary states of the organism (e.g., fatigue, drugs, etc.)"[3]

Theorists vary as to the number of types of learning. Most frequently found are (1) conditioned responses (as a result of conditioning), (2) autogenous responses (as a result of self-initiated activity), (3) sociogenous responses (as a result of social stimulation or direction), (4) incidental learning (as a result of repeated exposure to a set of stimuli or to a single stimulus), and (5) insightful learning (as a result of seeing relationships or reorganizing perceptions). These different types do not necessarily involve the same

1 Kimball Wiles, *Teaching for Better Schools* (Englewood Cliffs, N. J.: Prentice-Hall, Inc., 1957), p. 21.

2 Leonard Carmichael (ed.), *Manual of Child Psychology* (New York: John Wiley and Sons, 1946), p. 370.

3 Ernest R. Hilgard, *Theories of Learning* (New York: Appleton-Century-Crofts, Inc., 2nd ed., 1956), p. 3.

basic processes. However, they are not wholly dissimilar and the same factors or circumstances may operate in each of them.

Cantor points out that the central problem of education is self-discipline. The learner must freely accept responsibility for his decisions, his successes, his failures. "This cannot be 'teached' but it may be learned. Significant learning stems from the self-directed motivation of the learner who wants something positive and creative for an unexpressed or unfilled need of his."[4] It is the school's task to give the stimulus required to set off this process of self-education. It is also the school's task to provide time for learning, time for reflection, time for study, time for developing ideas and concepts, time to read, to think, and to discuss ideas.

Inherent in such a concept of the task of the school is the conviction that the school should do well what it does, that it should not attempt to do too much, and that it should select the most significant tasks and perform them effectively. It assumes further the sharing of the responsibility of educating the nation's children with the home and the community. If respect for learning is present in home and community, conditions for learning will be much more favorable. "What a nation honors it will cultivate," Plato said. American communities must be concerned to upgrade educational expectations, to actively support excellence in achievement, and to make it evident to the learner that learning should be respected not alone for its material values but for the personal satisfaction it brings.

Parents need to set an example of respect for learning, for study, and for the discussion of ideas. Much of the child's attitude toward learning, much of his interest and curiosity about his world, stems from the attitudes of those closest to him — his family, his friends, and members of his community. To meet our obligation for improving society we must place education at the top of the value scale. Instead of complaining that the school expects too much of their children, that assignments are too difficult, and that more time should be allowed for social activities, extracurricular events, and entertainment, parents might do well to examine their own role in the education of their children as they ask the age-old question, "What did you learn in school today?"

[4] Nathaniel Cantor, *Dynamics of Learning* (Buffalo, N.Y.: Henry Stewart, Inc., 1946), pp. xiv, xv.

## The Four Essentials of Learning

All learning must serve the purpose of satisfying some drive, some urge or desire. An individual will select from the experiences offered him at home, at play, at school, or at work what is of value to him in the light of his ability to comprehend, assimilate, enjoy, and use.

Dollard and Miller[5] have suggested four significant elements in the learning process: *drive, cue, response,* and *reinforcement* or *reward.* The *drive* is the stimulus that thrusts the individual into action. The *cue* is the stimulus that guides his action. The *response* is the action. The *reinforcement* or *reward* is the result of the action.

The child who is learning, then, is involved in these steps: wanting something, paying attention to something, doing something about it, and receiving a reward. Let us look in on John, a fifth-grader, as he illustrates the steps in the learning process.

Observe what occurred as he read the story he prepared for the "read and share it" period on Friday. John went to the front of the room wearing a confident smile, a new suit, and a new bow tie. He began in capital style and then got "caught" on the word *biography.* He tried to sound it out but failed. The teacher wrote it on the board, dividing it into syllables with the diacritical markings. Then she asked John to pronounce it. He did. When the word came up again near the end of the story he didn't even falter. John had learned the word.

An analysis shows that four learning elements were present:

1. The child wanted something. There must be a *drive* or desire to learn. Without such a drive or need for satisfaction the learning will not take place. In John's case the drive was there. He wanted to read for the group. The need for help to reduce the state of tension was sensed by the teacher as John stuttered, colored, and fidgeted. She understood his need and helped him by dividing the word into syllables for him to pronounce.

2. The child noticed something. The *cue* the teacher gave was the syllabification of the word. John picked up the cue as soon as he noticed it and related it to his past knowledge of similar words.

---

[5] J. C. Dollard and N. E. Miller, *Personality and Psychotherapy* (New York: McGraw-Hill Book Company, 1950).

3. The child did something. The *response* was necessary in order to learn the word. Had John merely stood there tongue-tied or returned to his seat, learning would not have occurred. As it was, he did something. He figured out the word on the basis of the markings and syllables and pronounced it. Because he had had training in word analysis he was successful.

4. The child got something. *Reward* must follow response. John received the approval of the teacher and of the group. The next time John meets a similar situation he will tend to respond in a positive manner. Consistent repeated reward of behavior sets the pattern of reinforcement.

Along with the learning of new skills and knowledges come other learnings that have to do with attitudes. The concept of conditioning helps explain children's attitudes toward some of their subjects, their teachers, or their age-mates. Unfortunately, many children learn to respond with fear instead of with confidence to the learning situation. If, for example, the teacher had shouted, "John, I'm tired to death of having you come up here unprepared. Why didn't you take that book home last night and learn to read it before you came here and made a monkey of yourself in front of our visitor? I never did have anybody in the fifth grade before who is as poor at figuring out new words as you." Such an experience repeated many times would condition John against wanting to read. His tension would mount, he would dislike school, and he would blame the teacher for his failures.

A good teacher uses positive motivation and is alert to the types of cues the children are picking up. He provides the drill needed and arranges the classroom environment so that positive attitudes and healthy emotional responses are established. Success leads to success and nothing is more satisfying to the child than to know his teacher is there to help him help himself.

## *Principles of Learning*

It is impossible to understand the behavior of children without knowing something about the principles of learning. It is impossible to teach the child without knowing something about the conditions under which learning takes place.

Frequently student-teachers and teachers who have only a theoretical knowledge of basic principles of learning have a problem in translating the theory into action in the classroom. They understand the principles but under the pressure of large classes, crowded quarters, and personal anxieties they fail to put them into practice. Principles of learning frequently disregarded include the following factors:

*Maximum Satisfaction and Understanding.* Larry dawdled through the entire period with his basal reader. When Miss Jones called on him to tell the most important part of the story he stumbled and finally came out with "I don't know." He apparently was not getting either satisfaction or understanding from his study. Here is a problem for the teacher. She must try to develop in him a desire to learn, to feel the satisfaction that comes from a task well done, a problem solved, a skill mastered. This can be the beginning of a love for learning. Children enjoy activities in which they can perform well.

*Relation to the Pupil's Goals.* "I can't see any sense to that assignment" is an indictment that may show the teacher does not know his group, does not provide adequately for individual differences, or hasn't explained it fully. "Learning takes place more readily if the child accepts as useful and important the activities in which he is expected to engage."[6] Knowing children includes knowing their goals, aspirations, and abilities. In planning the assignments and learning experiences it is well to remember that the child participates in the activity with more enthusiasm if he sees in it some relation to his goals. Watch him as he dashes down the stairs to the gymnasium. Then follow him as he drags back to music class (if he is a monotone or in the stage where his voice is neither soprano, alto, nor bass).

Children are not always clear about their purposes or sufficiently mature to define them. It is the teacher's privilege to help children establish goals and clarify hazy purposes; by using their interest, arousing their curiosity, and expanding their horizons he can bring the goals of the children and the objectives of the school into closer harmony.

[6] Virgil Herrick *et al, The Elementary School* (Englewood Cliffs, N. J.: Prentice-Hall, Inc., 1956), p. 107.

*Concrete Situations Preceding Abstract Concepts.* Children learn best through real-life experiences. They learn about the world through direct contact with people in the home, school, and community. They learn also through movies and television. The concrete materials and experiences are the foundation for abstract symbols. Children bring their past experiences, knowledge, creative thinking, and insight to bear on the solution of problems. Excursions, science experiments, gardening, care of pets, cooking, sewing, and woodworking help them understand life and provide them with an experiential background for academic subjects.

*Learning and Readiness.* It is up to the teacher to determine the child's readiness for a particular learning activity. Mental, physical, social, and experiential development has direct bearing on readiness, as the observant teacher well knows. Interest, if matched by the mental and physical maturity required, gives a strong "go-ahead" signal. The teacher should provide the facilities and opportunities for learning activities deemed essential.

*Correlation of Instruction, Practice, and Maturation.* Evidence from experiments shows the relation between learning and maturation in skills,[7] in concept formation,[8] in social adjustments,[9] in emotional reactions,[10] and in types of thinking.[11] Forcing learning before the required maturation, the teachable moment, is as useless as it is unwise. In an experiment in which identical twin sisters were taught to climb a stairway it was demonstrated that one twin made greater progress in a two-week period of training at the age of fifty-three weeks than the other twin made in a period of six weeks at the

[7] W. C. Olson and S. I. Davis, "The Adaptation of Instruction in Reading to the Growth of Children," *Educational Method*, 20:71–79, November, 1940.

[8] Frederick A. Pistor, "How Time Concepts Are Acquired by Children," *Educational Method*, 20:107–112, November, 1940.

[9] Stephen M. Corey, "The Developmental Tasks of Youth," in Hollis L. Caswell (ed.), *The American High School: Its Responsibility and Opportunity.* Eighth Yearbook of the John Dewey Society (New York: Harper & Brothers, 1946), pp. 70–99.

[10] Arnold Gesell and Frances L. Ilg, *The Child from Five to Ten* (New York: Harper & Brothers, 1946).

[11] Jean Piaget, *The Language and Thought of the Child* (New York: Harcourt, Brace and Company, 1932).

age of forty-six weeks. The superiority of the first twin is attributed to the maturation process.[12]

*Uniqueness of Rate of Learning.* There is a growing awareness of the necessity for providing for individual differences in children. Various plans have been tried and are being tried to help the teacher meet individual needs. In an average classroom difference in ability may range from three to six years. Each child has his own rate of learning, which is fairly well established by the time he comes to school. Plans must take into consideration the use of teaching procedures that permit the child to work at his level of ability in individual and group activities.

*Continuity of Learning.* Learning, like growth, is continuous. The child has been growing and learning from infancy, assimilating new ideas and integrating them with what he knows. He tries to relate out-of-school experiences to those the school provides.

What he learns at any point is based on his previous learnings. He must always be understood in terms of his experience, his present stage of growth, and his ambitions for further learning. The teacher must challenge him, so that he won't feel school is just the "same old grind." Every day must bring new concepts and new discoveries. The four-year-old asks 400 questions a day. He learns by asking questions, by exploring, by experimenting, by creating, by touching, tasting, and smelling. He learns by thinking about what he sees, hears, feels, and touches. The six-year-old is able to deal with some problems on the level of ideas. He can handle symbols without having the concrete materials always present.

*Learning and Interaction with Environment.* Learning does not occur in a vacuum. It is an active process which the learner involves himself in. It is multi-sensory and requires the utilization of all types of stimuli. The child who is in an environment filled with interesting things and experiences is in a much more advantageous position for learning than one who is allowed to "vegetate."

The teacher must arrange the environment so that it provides stimulating situations and challenges each learner at his particular stage of development.

---

[12] Arnold Gesell, "The Developmental Psychology of Twins," in Carl Murchison (ed.), *Handbook of Child Psychology* (Worcester, Mass.: Clark University Press, 1931), pp. 158–203.

*The Learner's Self-Image.* The learner who has a confident attitude toward himself, his task, and the circumstances under which the learning takes place is likely to succeed. In recent years a number of psychologists, including Carl Rogers, Gordon Allport, Abraham Maslow, and Erich Fromm, have concerned themselves with defining the adequate personality. Combs suggests that a truly adequate personality takes an essentially positive view of himself. "People who see themselves as liked, wanted, acceptable and able, people of dignity and integrity, constitute the well adjusted people of our society."[13]

Children who have a positive self-image are challenged rather than threatened by new learning situations. Indeed, one job of the teacher is to find ways of challenging children without threatening them. The child who sees himself positively has little need to be on the defensive; as a result he is able to think more clearly, sense relationships more accurately, and use his imagination freely. He meets problems courageously and faces life with confidence. He takes learning as he takes all experiences — in stride, secure in the knowledge that he can achieve, that he can be effective. Hence the importance of helping the child learn a positive view of self. If there is a chance for him to have at least a measure of success in the endeavor he will gain self-confidence and a feeling of worth. The role of the teacher is to help him develop the courage to try and the perseverance to take on increasingly challenging and satisfying tasks.

## The Role of Motivation in Learning

The experienced teacher will make use of the child's natural urges:[14] the urge to satisfy curiosity, to communicate, to engage in dramatic play, and to create. These urges represent an open-sesame to learning for many children in the classroom and in the home.

[13] Arthur W. Combs, "Personality Theory and Its Implications for Curriculum Development," in Alexander Frazier (ed.), *Learning More About Learning* (Washington, D. C.: Association for Supervision and Curriculum Development, NEA, 1959), p. 16.

[14] Ernest R. Hilgard and David H. Russell, "Motivation in School Learning," Chapter II in Nelson B. Henry (ed.), *Learning and Instruction*, Forty-Ninth Yearbook of the National Society for the Study of Education, Part I (Chicago: University of Chicago Press, 1950).

Motivation — the purposes, ambitions, drives, and values of a person — enables one to take advantage of learning experiences, to develop and use his abilities. It can be influenced by a propitious environment, favorable attitudes, and challenging experiences. Motivation has also been termed drive, urge, impulse, and reaction tendency stemming from biological, social, or personal needs.

Some writers believe that motivation consists primarily of the desire to reduce tensions (escape from hunger, pain, anxiety, or fear). But more positive incentives such as curiosity, exploration, creativity, or the arousing of positive (pleasurable) effects are also involved. According to the holders of this view, primary rewards or reinforcements are those leading to tension reduction through satisfying drive conditions, as when hunger tension is reduced by feeding, or thirst tension by drinking. Secondary or acquired rewards are those that derive their power through prior association with primary rewards. This theory asserts that there is no learning except as aroused drives are somewhat satisfied by rewards.[15]

DeHaan and Havighurst[16] suggest four psychological elements of motivation that occur in various combinations among gifted children — need for achievement, valuing achievement, intrinsic motivation, and social motivation. In addition they believe that health and constitutional factors, biological factors, influence the drive to achievement, and affect the learning of all children.

A high aspiration level is associated with a basic unconscious need to achieve at peak performance in anything one attempts. Closely related to this drive is the high value some individuals place upon achievement. Intrinsic motivation is related to the deep desire to engage in an activity for the joy or pleasure the activity brings. This is particularly evident in the pursuit of art, music, dance, drama, and research activities in which the reward is the activity itself, not the material reward. Social motivation operates as the child accomplishes particular objectives because of the expectations of his family, his friends, or his teachers.

The predominant view of motives today, according to Deese, is that "human motivation stems from either a small number of basic

[15] This view is associated with the names of Clark L. Hull, Neal E. Miller, John Dollard, O. H. Mowrer, and K. W. Spence. An introduction to their ideas may be found in Hilgard, *op. cit.*
[16] Robert F. DeHaan and Robert J. Havighurst, *Educating Gifted Children* (Chicago: University of Chicago Press, 1957), pp. 9, 130–132.

The *intermediate child changes
rapidly from gay to pensive moods.*

*The intermediate child, as he strives to achieve, needs peer acceptance.*

*A broadening of interests and development of abilities characterize the child in the intermediate grades.*

*The preschool child develops basic motor and communication skills.*

*During the primary years the child learns new skills and becomes part of a broader world.*

## UNDERSTANDING THE ELEMENTARY SCHOOL CHILD

A panoramic view of children as they progress from the preschool through the years of middle childhood reveals the need for understanding and effective guidance. Although every child has his own design, he normally progresses through several predictable stages of development. A dominant trait, a leading characteristic, a peculiar pattern marks each stage. The rate of development and the time required to complete each stage varies from child to child; for every child certain traits develop more rapidly, certain qualities stand out more conspicuously, certain needs are more pronounced.

During the preschool years the child establishes most of his basic motor and communication skills. He becomes part of a broader world as he enters the primary school. Here he learns new skills that are essential in achieving recognition and approbation. He discovers the importance of getting along with others in a complex world.

The intermediate child, too, is faced with problems unique to his stage of development. Achievement and peer acceptance become increasingly important. He enjoys games that require prowess and muscular control. His interests broaden rapidly. His struggle for independence is evidenced by a fluctuation between inner restlessness and outward rebellion. Moods are fast and fleeting.

urges or even one basic urge, and that all of our concern for family, money, prestige, social status, security, etc., comes from an elaboration of the basic urge or urges through experience and maturation."[17] It is generally believed, too, that goal relationships have to be learned — that most of the rewards and punishments in life acquire their positive or negative value through learning. The child's motives thus change as he interacts in various relationships with parents, siblings, and peers.

Such incentives as grades, verbal rewards, and reproofs have been studied intensively. The conclusions appear to be that, although these factors operate less upon learning itself than upon performance, they are powerful techniques in the control of performance level. Because of differences in individuals as they respond to these incentives it is not always easy to evaluate the effects of specific rewards and punishments.

The teacher must know the individual child well in order to influence his learning. He must discover what each child's particular motivations are, what arouses his interest and sustains it until he accomplishes his goal.

The following principles may help the teacher to motivate pupils constructively:[18]

1. Motivation is based essentially upon the particular values held by the individual. By knowing the characteristics of children of a given age or grade level, by being familiar with basic drives, the teacher can plan learning experiences that will arouse the interest of the majority of children in the group. However, in order to be certain that each child is learning, he must observe each individual response and plan assignments accordingly. Many times a child shows no interest because his background for comprehending is inadequate or because he does not see the relationship between a particular activity and the ultimate goal. The teacher must use ingenuity in helping him see the need for learning the task in order to realize a future goal. Learning is an individual matter, dependent upon what the learner believes is significant.

2. Motivation is more effective if the relationship between a learning activity and a specifically defined goal is clearly perceived. For

---

[17] James Deese, *The Psychology of Learning* (New York: McGraw-Hill Book Company, 2nd ed., 1958), p. 114.

[18] The authors have drawn upon material from Hilgard, *op. cit.*

example, if children are doing a research project in order to put on a play for an assembly program they are more likely to work hard to discover all the details if they are interested in the project and see a reason for all the work involved. When they are merely expected to answer questions written on the board day after day they lose interest, and the caliber of work decreases as the term progresses. When one type of assignment is used consistently, children tend to slacken effort. They look for something that arouses their interest and gives them a chance to explore and solve problems.

3. Motivation is more effective if children are involved in goal setting. If children begin in the kindergarten to set standards for work and play, to do their best at all times, it is not so difficult to motivate them in the higher grades. Young children are readily led to set goals for desirable behavior — on excursions, for example. Staying in a group, asking questions about what they see, listening to the guide, looking for something interesting to report on when they return to the school, and enaging in desirable safety behavior — these standards are much more effective if they are planned by teacher and pupils together. A group of sixth-graders engaged in a social studies unit about their state formulated questions about the state capitol and listed specific items they wished to investigate before they made a trip to visit it. Third-graders interested in learning about their community find that planning what to see and what specific problems to explore results in more effective learning. Teacher-pupil planning will be discussed in detail in a later chapter.

4. Individuals should be encouraged to set goals for themselves as well as group goals. The idea of "togetherness" has been emphasized to the neglect of developing individual initiative, creativity, and abilities. Children need time to plan and carry out individual projects based on individual goals.

5. Negative motivation is usually ineffective. Motivation that is based on pain, fear, or anxiety may be accompanied by such distracting emotional states that efforts to learn are hindered. The motivation that results from pleasurable drives will, on the whole, elicit more effective response. However, such motivation as occasional competition is frequently enjoyed by pupils if they are in a group in which differences in ability are not too great.

## Implications for the Teacher

Since the problem of motivation is so important in learning, the teacher must give particular attention to the question of rewards and punishments, feelings of success and failure, knowledge of progress, and the use of the positive drives of curiosity, exploration, and creativity as desirable motivations for learning. "If it is katydid nature to scrape, frog nature to croak, warbler nature to warble, it is human nature to play *Air for G String* on a Stradivarius. To reply that the last named of these is a learned activity whereas the others are innate is not relevant, because the whole question is what sorts of things does any species tend to learn; what are the lines of development which it follows when it does what it wants to do?"[19]

In all too many classrooms the children are required to do specific assignments on the basis of extrinsic rewards and punishments. In all too few is a learning situation set up in which children are interested in finding out, in creating, in problem solving. Failing to take advantage of such powerful motives as social approval, creativity, and curiosity, some teachers rely on punishment and rewards to keep the class under control. But this system has the disadvantage that as the years go by both rewards and punishments have to be increased. If in the first grade the children are promised a treat of candy or a party at the end of the week if they behave well when the parents visit, they will look for a similar reward for good behavior as they reach the higher grades. If they are accustomed to receiving gold stars for perfect work in the primary grades they will expect to be rewarded more amply for good work by the time they are in the intermediate school. A more effective procedure is to structure a classroom organization wherein interests, curiosity, exploration, problem solving, and social approval are the natural motivations. Children are usually eager to cooperate, to achieve without threat of punishment and without extrinsic rewards.

*Knowledge of Progress.* "How am I doing?" "What do you think of this?" Knowing how he is getting along, discovering his progress toward a goal, developing skill in assessing his own record

[19] Gardner Murphy, "A Cosmic Christmas Carol," *Saturday Review*, 41:50, December 13, 1958.

is related to a child's success. The capacity for self-appraisal is a mark of maturity. Knowing how far he has to go to reach a goal helps the child direct his energies and focus on achieving it. The teacher should help him set realistic goals and become aware of his weaknesses and strengths in order to improve his performance.

Children — even first-graders — can evaluate their own progress by keeping a record of their work. It is surprising how skill in self-appraisal grows if the opportunity is presented to know where one is going, and if there is an incentive to move forward.

*Positive Motivation.* Children are naturally curious. What arouses their curiosity, what catches their interest influences their conduct and changes their behavior. Mr. Ahrens, an intermediate grade science teacher, makes use of the curiosity of children to motivate learning. When he enters the class he brings in the materials for the science lesson — anything from the model of a dinosaur to the liquids needed for an experiment in physics — places them on his desk, walks over to the middle of the room, and begins to talk. The natural curiosity of the children is aroused to the point where they literally beg him to tell them what they are going to do. Through curiosity he has caught their attention and he is ready to teach. The group is ready to respond.

Closely related to curiosity is the desire to explore. All of us have the urge to look for aesthetically satisfying experiences because of the pleasure they bring. Watch the child who has become interested in an exciting project. As he explores the situation he frequently becomes involved in creativity in one form or another. The desire to satisfy curiosity, to explore, to create are innate drives and powerful incentives to learning.

Creative impulses are often associated with motor activity: painting, dancing, drawing, and dramatizing. In a class in which children's drives are considered in planning the learning experiences, adequate space, variety of materials, and flexibility are in evidence.

*Motivation and Instructional Devices.* Certain mechanical devices such as the teaching machines advocated by Skinner[20] are being tried

[20] B. F. Skinner, "The Science of Learning and the Art of Teaching," in W. Fullager, H. Lewis, and C. Cumbee (eds.), *Readings for Educational Psychology* (New York: Thomas Y. Crowell Company, 1956), pp. 44-56.

to help pupils learn the responses needed for acquiring skill in the elementary subjects. Skinner argues that "the free use of such devices ... would free the teacher to do what she is best suited for — dealing with the socialization of the individual child." [His thesis that] "the personal control of reinforcement by a teacher is too erratic and irregular"[21] has led to the construction of the teaching machines.

*Teaching Machines.* "Actually a teaching machine does not teach. What it does is simply to bring the student in contact with the person who composed the material it presents."[22] In essence it works by feeding facts and questions in doses that the learner can assimilate and master. Questions may be given in the form of uncompleted sentences, e.g., "A candle is hot. It is a (an) ........................ source of light." (Answer: incandescent.) The sentences are exposed to the learner through an opening and a roll of paper is provided on which the learner makes his responses. (He fills in the blank.) When he has finished he lifts a flap on the teaching machine, exposing the right answer. At the same time his own response is locked into place and cannot be changed.[23] The questions are organized in such a way that the learner will almost certainly get the right answers. The sequence of questions on the same subject is designed to "reinforce" him. If he makes mistakes on the first try, he will do better the second for he has been exposed to the right answers. He keeps at the task until he has learned to answer all the questions correctly. He works at his own rate and finishes one step before he can proceed to the next.

The Skinner Machine consists of sets of separate presentations or "frames" of visual materials stored on disks or tapes. One frame is presented at a time, the adjacent frames remaining out of view. Not until he correctly completes the first step does the student proceed. He participates actively in the learning experience. Since he must comprehend a given point before he can move on, only material for which he is ready is presented. He is helped to come up with the correct answer through hints, suggestions, promptings, and the orderly organization of the material. The teaching machine capitalizes on immediate feedback and reinforces the students for every

[21] Deese, *op. cit.,* p. 329.
[22] B. F. Skinner, "Teaching Machines," *Science,* 128:971, October 24, 1958.
[23] "Professor Skinner's Teaching Machine," *Fortune,* 58:195, October 1958.

correct response. "So far, concern has mainly been with practical problems in the design and the use of the machines and with testing and revising sample programs.[24]

An attempt at evaluation of automatic teaching was made at a Conference on the Art and Science of the Automatic Teaching of Verbal and Symbolic Skills. Among the papers read was one by Kendler of New York University pointing to the value of the teaching machines, At the same time Kendler was concerned with the possibilities of making them even more effective; there are still problems: the ability of the students to transfer what they learn; how simple verbal responses develop into abstract ones; the implication of a mass, standardized educational program that will be the logical outcome of the teaching machines and a serious threat to creativity. "Ultimately we have to develop better theories of behavior, particularly those of transfer and symbolic processes, in order to make the best use of teaching machines."[25]

Porter[26] reports on an experiment carried out in teaching spelling to elementary school children by the machines. Teaching machines used were of maximum simplicity for economic and mechanical reasons. Teaching materials printed on conventional 8½" × 11" sheets were fed past two windows in the machine. Students wrote their responses directly on the sheets through the lower window. Operation of a lever moved the written response to the upper window and exposed the correct response in the lower window. The student checked his response with the correct one and scored his answer. The operating lever was again moved, and the next item appeared. Teaching materials were prepared to parallel the standard lesson materials prescribed by the school and used by the control group. The programing of the materials required the following sequence of response: identification of the spelling words in a meaningful sentence context; matching the correct word to a specific definition; matching several words on the basis of letter formation; and writing the missing letters in words presented in a sentence con-

[24] Skinner, *op. cit.*, p. 975.

[25] Howard H. Kendler, "Teaching Machines and Psychological Theory," in Eugene Galanter (ed.), *Automatic Teaching: The State of the Art* (New York: John Wiley and Sons, 1959), p. 184.

[26] Douglas Porter, "Some Effects of Year-Long Teaching Machine Instruction," in *ibid.*, pp. 85–90.

text. No oral instructions were given. The following[27] is a sample of program material:

1. Underline these words: *thunder, steady, soaked, frightened*

   I hadn't gone halfway when thunder rolled and rain came down in a steady pour. I was soaked. I made a dash for an old horse shed. And there was Wolf. Crouching in the shadow, he looked so like a wolf that for a moment he frightened me.

   frightened     steady     thunder     soaked

2. Circle the word that rhymes with *ready*:
   thunder     steady     pour     soaked

           steady

3. Circle the word that means *firm, regular,* or *not shaking*:

   steady     thunder     umbrella     southern     sweeping

   steady

4. Write the missing letters:

   Then rain came down in a s......ea......y pour.
           steady

5. Write the missing letters; they are all the same:

   Ragged clouds were sw...... ...... ping the south......rn sky.

         sweeping      southern

6. Write the missing letters:

   Without thinking of an umbre...... ......a, I set out.

         umbrella

7. Write the missing letters:

   Halfway to the store thu...... ......er rolled.

         thunder

8. Write the missing letters:

   Then rain came down in a s......ea......y pour.

         steady

[27] *Ibid.,* pp. 86, 87.

9. Write the missing letters:

Brushing, moving quickly, s ... ee .....ing.

sweeping

Both the sixth and second grades were taught twenty-two out of the thirty-four weeks of spelling instruction by the machine and compared with the control group. At the sixth-grade level seventeen pupils preferred machine teaching as compared with twelve who preferred the teacher and two who had no preference.

At both the second- and sixth-grade levels spelling achievement as measured by standardized tests was significantly superior for the experimental group. In the sixth-grade experimental group there was a positive relationship between the number of responses required per lesson and consequent achievement, but no relationship between the number of errors made in each lesson and achievement.

> Sixth grade: Lesson material available on a regular week-by-week basis, but experimental group studied only about one-fourth as much as the control group.
> Second grade: Lesson materials available on an *ad libitum* basis for twelve weeks during which time the range of materials worked on by pupils was spread over nine lessons.

The author of the experiment concluded: "These high rates of responding are due in part to the release of better students from the usual constraints of group study, but in addition, the machine and/ or program seems to generate rapid responding."[28]

In this day of crowded classrooms, curriculum demands, and overworked teachers, the use of devices to monitor pupil practice, supply immediate feedback, and enable self-evaluation to proceed has caught the imagination of some and evoked the opposition of others. Among the advantages cited are the saving of the teacher's time and effort, individualized instruction, and providing for individual differences.

The fear that machines will replace teachers has been expressed by some. However, the teaching machine is not intended to replace the teacher. It is admittedly no real substitute for classroom discussion, but for getting ideas and information across to students

[28] *Ibid.*, p. 90.

Skinner believes it is efficient and economical. "The sequence of questions, from simple to complex, forces the student to think through his material at every step; it encourages him to the end; it conditions him to getting things right. Students do not learn, he says, by being tricked and baffled; they learn by solving problems successfully, and when they acquire the habit of doing that, they develop a more wholesome attitude toward the entire educational process."[29]

Motivation is without question a constant challenge to the teacher. He must keep broadening his understanding of the children he teaches and helping them to understand their own drives and desires. As he plans learning experiences that are profitable, he must always be aware of the importance of his role in motivating children through materials, people, and situations.

## Concept Development

Many concepts held by children are erroneous and confusing, and the learning experiences provided for them often do not help them increase their understanding of the world. In social sciences there are democracy, nation, senator, interdependence, feudalism, and justice. In a certain classroom some children thought "justice for all" meant "just us for all." In science there are concepts of osmosis, cell, magnetism, gravity, air pressure, conservation, erosion. In arithmetic there are weight, fraction, ration, percentage, equivalent, time, distance, length, multiplication, subtraction, set. In language arts there are words, sentences, punctuation.

The world of the child is full of ideas, experiences, and sensations. In order to deal with them we must cut them down to the size of our mental processes. In a way we can do this is by categorizing and assigning names to the categories. Deese defines concept formation as the "process of categorizing so that all the infinite variety of the external world may be dealt with by our mental processes and language."[30] Evans states that "when an intellectual effort is needed . . . to abstract some quality (such as roundness or redness) from its

---

[29] "Professor Skinner's Teaching Machine," *Fortune*, 58:195, October, 1958.
[30] Deese *op. cit.*, p. 291.

existence in material objects, the idea that results is called a concept."[31]

The ability to help children develop concepts is essential in successful teaching. Learning new concepts is perhaps the most important kind of learning the child must master. When he enters school he has some ideas of the world about him, but many of them are vague, fragmentary, and misconceived. True, he knows his father works and makes some money — that his new shoes have to wait until daddy brings home his check. He knows that food comes from the store, but how it gets there and what would happen if it didn't get there is a conundrum to him. If he discovers that milk comes from cows instead of containers he may not want to drink it. He is interested in the physical world, but much of it is a mystery to him. Helping him expand his knowledge, correct his misconceptions, broaden his ideas about life is the challenge to the teacher.

In order to help the child build concepts the teacher must provide him with a rich foundation of firsthand experiences. What the child has actually felt is the foundation upon which the teacher must build. The greater the chasm between the experience and the concept the more difficult learning will be. One of the reasons teachers of primary children begin the early reading experiences with trips to the zoo, the store, the fire station, the farm, the dairy, the library, and the post office is to assure the firsthand knowledge essential to an understanding of the concepts they will meet in their reading. If teachers better understood the qualities of concepts and were aware of how children form concepts they might be more successful in aiding the process.

## QUALITIES OF CONCEPTS

*Concepts as Experiences.* The learner needs experiences that give both horizontal (enriching the meaning) and vertical (increasing the number) extension of concept development. In addition to firsthand experiences, visual aids and classroom discussions will help develop concepts.

*Concepts Not "Given" to Students.* Each learner must develop his own concepts. The teacher can provide experiences that will

[31] Bergan Evans and Cornelia Evans, *A Dictionary of Contemporary Usage* (New York: Random House, 1957), p. 230.

help the child formulate useful concepts. He can also rephrase or restate concepts for the child.

*Variation in Difficulty.* Young children learn object concepts more readily than class concepts. Concepts of causal relationships increase with age, IQ, education, and adequate vocabulary and communication skills. Obviously concepts that involve concrete elements are the easiest to learn. In working with four- and five-year-olds, the writers have discovered that the ability to classify and categorize is related to experience, training at home and school, and the ability to express ideas in fluent language. Children whose parents were interested in educational experiences were superior because of added experiences and increased vocabulary.

*Variation in Kind.* A concept may refer to a class, a category, a group of things, a process, relationships, or principles.

*Complexity.* Concepts have dimensions. In their development they move along various lines of change. Concepts gain in clarity, specificity, and abstractness as the meaning is increased in these senses. As the learner deals with a concept he branches out beyond the limits of the original narrow class or system of ideas. He discovers common qualities of the concept or actions or events of the class to begin with and then extends use of the concept into new relationships of which he was previously unaware. "Since concepts are the results of continuous changes with experience, each may be expected at different times in its development to be at various points on the continuum of meaningfulness."[32]

*Concepts as Abstractions.* A concept as an abstraction may not relate to anything which a child can immediately and directly use. He can read the word "charity" or recognize it in conversation, but the concept of charity may not mean anything to him until he is twelve or thirteen years old.

How Concepts Are Formed

The young child forms a concept by taking the common elements from a number of objects, situations, or phenomena that he meets or

[32] W. A. Brownell and Gordon Hendrickson, "How Children Learn Information, Concepts and Generalizations," in Nelson B. Henry (ed.), *Learning and Instruction,* Forty-Ninth Yearbook of the National Society for the Study of Education, Part I (Chicago: University of Chicago Press, 1950), p. 109.

observes. Concepts are meanings attached to words, symbols, and their relationships. For example, the young child who is forming the concept of softness might have a number of experiences that would help him attach meaning to the category "soft." He might listen to a soft voice as contrasted to a loud voice, or soft music as contrasted with loud music. He might hold a baby chick and feel the softness of its feathers or put his head on a pillow made of feather down and sense its softness. He might eat fresh bread which is soft and dry bread which is hard. He might have an ice-cream bar right out of the dry-ice pack and observe how it softens. Some of the problems that concern teachers in guiding concept formation are the following: What are some concepts generally held by children today at various maturity levels? How do children learn? On what maturity levels do they learn certain concepts? What is the teacher's role in helping them develop concepts?

## SEQUENCE IN CONCEPT DEVELOPMENT

One of the most significant concepts children must learn in this age is a concept of space. The following sequence relates to concepts of space that develop from preschool through the elementary school years.

The child is aware of space before he is aware of time. It is an external experience. The preschool child is space-minded. See him race down the street on his tricycle with a cape thrown over his shoulders to give him the feeling of flying in space. In our age someone may achieve space flight, going into orbit and returning safely to earth. Perhaps the space-minded youngster in the next block will land on the moon and establish an outpost for scientific exploration.

When a child enrolls in the kindergarten his spatial experiences are increasing as he goes alone into the neighborhood, to the store, and to school. He likes to tell about the trips he takes to other states by car or airplane, and he writes to his friends at kindergarten saying, "I'm having a wonderful time in Florida at the beach. We hear you had a blizzard. I'll tell you more when I come back. P.S.: The swimming's fine." If he stays home he crosses the streets and one day brings a note from home saying, "Johnny can go home by himself now."

The *six-year-old's* space continues to expand. Now he makes more extensive excursions into the community as well as in the neighborhood and to school. He reads street signs and has his own familiar landmarks. "I turn right at Higg's Market and cross Stringtown Road." He likes to tell the names of streets and to locate major points of interest on his jaunts. He can tell his left hand from his right hand, but his spatial concepts are still hazy.

*Seven* has discovered that there is a place in the world of space for him. He shows interest in the objects in space, types of airplanes, stones, waterfalls, fire, the earth's crust. He is fascinated to discover that oil comes from the earth, heat from fire, and power from water. He is interested in places far away as well as near and delights to describe trips he has taken to other cities, states, or countries.

*Eight* is on his way toward becoming at home with space. He enjoys a bus trip alone if the plans are well made, or a ride home from school in a taxi. He likes to visit museums, wanting to go every week, to the dismay of his mother and father. He likes to go to the zoo or park and loves geographical games and maps. He might enjoy a telescope, a compass, or a space helmet for Christmas. He is beginning to tell directions and to know the points of the compass. He thinks he wouldn't get lost because "moss grows on the north side of a tree." He can distinguish left from right without confusion.

*Nine* likes the feeling of independence in handling space. He goes to his violin lesson or to the dentist's office on his bicycle, the bus, on foot, or by taxi. He thinks about the trip, makes specific plans concerning the mode of transportation, and speculates about the interesting events that may occur.

*Ten* relates space to air. He may try to define it by saying, "Space is a part of something bigger." "Space is an empty piece of something." "Space is what you fly in." "Space is where things are." Outer space takes on new meaning. "Outer space is a place to explore." "There's more air up there."

*Eleven*, in keeping with the restlessness of his spirit, is acquiring a more dynamic feeling about space. He handles the practical aspects of space well. He goes to town alone on the bus or streetcar and keeps an appointment book to help him remember. He likes to travel by plane, train, or boat and is not too obviously excited. He changes trains, studies schedules, and helps plan the trip. The eleven-year-old is finding a variety of definitions of space. He recognizes numerous possibilities: "Space is the room." "Lots and lots of space." "Space is where the universe is."

*Twelve* experiences as well as expresses space. He is impressed with the vastness of space as he travels by air or streamliner. Seeing a mountain for the first time a twelve-year-old said in wonder, "Whe-e-e, that's big." Another, in more poetic language, said, "If you could touch the top of the clouds and by some trick of magic float on them, you could stay up there for years and years and one day you'd find the cloud you could come back to earth on."

Twelve is capable of getting around on his own. He can shop or go to the movies by himself, and if he is in a strange place he feels quite secure about asking a policeman for directions. He is sure that when he gets a job he will do his traveling by plane. "It gets you there in better shape." Twelve is fascinated by speed, by space, and by exploration of space — especially outer space. He likes to read science fiction and will read authentic accounts of space travel and exploration.[33]

Perhaps the most significant task of the teacher of young children is to help them to form accurate concepts. These are the tools with which they will have to work as they go about the process of learning and solving problems.

## Role of the Teacher in Guiding Concept Development

As the child matures he constantly revises his concepts in the light of new experiences and added knowledge. The concepts he has already formed before coming to school will have to be further developed. Teachers will find useful the following guiding principles for this task:

1. Determine the concept to be developed and list the generalizations surrounding the concept.

2. Arrange the learning situation so that children experience a drive to solve a problem in order to satisfy the existing need.

[33] Material on space concept adapted from Arnold Gesell, Frances L. Ilg, and Louise Ames, *Youth: The Years from Ten to Sixteen* (New York: Harper & Brothers, 1956), p. 40.

3. Provide concrete experiences so that the children will discover the external cues that will help them arrive at categories.

4. Provide opportunities to test the concept by responding to a variety of situations to see if it applies under different circumstances.

5. Show approval of correct responses through approving behavior.

6. Provide for a satisfactory reward to the basic drive that set off the problem originally.

*Implications for the Teacher in Guiding Concept Formation.* Concepts may be much poorer and much more inaccurate than the teacher suspects. In order to guide concept formation adequately the teacher must understand the child's environment and experiences.

Firsthand experiences are more conducive to accurate concept development. They should be varied and meaningful.

Analysis and synthesis are the basis of concept formation. The problems the teacher presents to the children must be meaningful.

Concept formation may be aided by stimulating and guiding the child's natural curiosity and interest.

The reaction of the teacher to the concepts of children plays an important role.

*Organizing the Learning Situation Effectively.* The teacher sets the stage and thereby opens the door to self-directed motivation of the learner who wants something positive, something creative for an unexpressed or unfulfilled need.

| THE LEARNER | THE SETTING FOR LEARNING |
|---|---|
| 1. The learner's behavior follows the pattern of growth of all human beings. | 1. The teacher arranges the classroom in terms of what he knows about the development of learning as growth. |
| 2. The learner is a unitary, integrating whole. | 2. The effective setting provides for learning experiences which give the child opportunity for integration of thinking, feeling, exploring, and creating. |
| 3. The learner reacts to a field of stimuli. | 3. The setting must counteract the distracting stimuli in the |

THE LEARNER

THE SETTING FOR LEARNING

environment by making use of motivations that in themselves are intense and positive enough to catch and hold the child's interest.

4. The learner is unique. Each has his own tempo and rate of learning.

4. The setting must allow for activities and assignments in keeping with the range of abilities at each maturity level, and with the differing rates of development and learning.

5. The learner is motivated by the urge to explore, create, act, and grow.

5. The setting must provide freedom to explore, create, construct, solve problems, and seek new ways of working and learning. Freedom ends where the rights of others are jeopardized.

6. The learner seeks a goal: to satisfy his drives and needs.

6. The teacher will use the motivating forces which impel the children to learn. The effective organization for learning will include goals, set up by teacher and pupils, which challenge their best efforts.

7. The learner brings to his task his character structure, goals, and social habits.

7. The value system and the goals of the learner must be considered as well as his socioeconomic and family background. Experiences should be planned to help him raise his sights in harmony with his capacity.

8. The learner is both an individual and a social being and needs experiences to develop both sides of his nature.

8. In view of the fact that individual contributions are needed in our society, the child must be allowed to work alone on projects vital to him as well as to partici-

THE LEARNER

THE SETTING FOR LEARNING

pate in group processes. Overemphasis on learning to adjust to and cooperate with the group may hinder the development of inner resources and creativity.

9. The learner learns his behavior. Learning is a process of growth, maturation, differentiation, and insight.

9. Children *learn* to behave in a certain way as they learn to read, write, swim, or skate. The teacher will observe the point at which a child has arrived in his learning and will provide experiences which challenge him.

10. The learner learns through seeing relationships. Parts have meaning only because of their relationship to the whole.

10. The child should learn to see relationships, to form generalizations, to develop insights and reasoning as he works on skills as a part of and in connection with meaningful activities rather than in isolation. He should first have an understanding of the whole process before he begins drill on specific parts.

11. The learner learns facts and skills in connection with activities of which they are an integral part.

11. Isolated drill on facts and skills is not a part of efficient learning instruction. The child should not have drill on phonics as an isolated exercise apart from reading but should practice word-recognition skills as an integral part of his reading lesson. Correct, regular practice in connection with the activity is of more value than prolonged erratic practice in isolation.

THE LEARNER

THE SETTING FOR LEARNING

12. The learner must perfect skills through motivated purposeful practice and teacher guidance.

12. Practice does not make perfect; it makes permanent. Therefore it is essential that the child be motivated to practice correct procedures in order to become proficient in reading, writing, or arithmetic. The amount of drill assigned should vary with the need of the child for the particular practice. Not all children benefit from a particular drill. Other activities should be planned for the child who has no need to practice a particular skill.

13. The learner is entitled to the materials of instruction which facilitate the specific learning activity and maturity of the learner.

13. The materials should be determined by the ability and maturity level of the children.

a. Materials which stimulate the senses are valuable in teaching.

b. A variety of materials provide for originality; e.g., in art paints, chalk, clay, crayons, water colors, charcoal, etc., are superior to any one of these alone.

c. Materials should be available to meet differences in range in ability.

d. Community resources, both physical and personnel, should be utilized.

e. Supplementary materials in the form of readers, library books, audio-visual aids, and pictures are essential.

THE SETTING FOR LEARNING

    f. The room should give the child the feeling that school is a challenging place, somewhat of a cross between a laboratory and a home, a place where learning is inevitable because the environment is stimulating, the activities are challenging, the teacher is encouraging, and the experiences are purposeful.[34]

Most teachers have generalized information similar to that just listed. However, the ability to apply knowledge about the learner and the classroom setting is too often taken for granted. In the following report of visits to two different kindergartens the reader will observe how the teachers applied their knowledge of the learner and the learning situation.

Miss Ensign invited us into her room where thirty kindergarten children were sitting quietly at their tables. There were five children at each table listening to a record that one of the children had brought from home. The teacher explained that they had just last week completed their project on Easter so the room was bare and there wasn't anything very interesting going on. From the looks on the faces of the children this seemed all too true. When the record was finished (it was an LP record of popular music and the entire side was played) Miss Ensign suggested that the children bring their chairs and sit in rows to watch some film strips on science.

The children immediately moved their chairs and did the teacher's bidding, but surreptitiously several came over to tell us about important events: a new tooth, a new baby, a birthday, an Easter party, a tornado warning the previous evening and the exciting storm with its rain and flooded basements. This went on during the showing of the film strip "Signs of Spring." The teacher read the captions on each strip and "taught" about spring and the birds, the flowers, and the butterflies. The children recognized most of the

[34] Adapted from William H. Burton, "Basic Principles in a Good Teaching-Learning Situation," *Phi Delta Kappan*, 39:248, March 1958.

strips. There was a great deal of wiggling, running back and forth to the bathroom, and excursions across the room to report on happenings. When the second film strip was over Miss Ensign obviously was at a loss to know what to do next, so it seemed a good time to take our leave. The children seemed reluctant to have us go, but they were obedient and went back to their tables to wait for the teacher to tell them what to do next.

Around the room there were materials that suggested that many exciting activities could be going on. However, this day they were on the cupboard shelf and from the general reaction apparently this was not unusual.

At another school the same day Miss Carpenter, also a kindergarten teacher, invited us into the room where eighteen children were busily engaged in a discussion of the garden they were getting ready to plant. They had their seeds carefully lined up in labeled cups. The tools for the digging, raking, and planting were all laid out on the low shelves underneath the windows. Excitement ran high as they decided where they would plant the various types of seeds. In the doll house a four-year-old spent the time taking care of her household, oblivious to the discussion.

After a while the children took their equipment and with the teacher and a student teacher went out to the garden to plant and dig and rake. Whether all the seeds planted would grow was an important point of speculation among several of the children. Everyone showed a real interest in the activity and participated eagerly. The children and their teachers returned to their room for orange juice and a story. During the story some of the children moved away from the group to rest but most of them seemed to enjoy hearing the story "The Carrot Seed."

Getting ready to go home the children commented, "This has been the big day. We planted gardens." "I'd say spring is here." "I think the seeds will grow." Not only the seeds but also the boys and girls in this classroom environment will grow. In a discussion after the children had gone Miss Carpenter pointed out, "I try to arrange an environment in which all children can grow, an environment in which all children can learn."

Much of the concern of the teacher has to do with arranging the physical and social environment so that there is motivation to learn. The learning situation is good or poor depending on the extent that

(1) it helps a learner establish goals that are clear and meaningful to him; (2) it helps him select from the environment what he considers relevant to the accomplishment of his goals; and (3) the teacher challenges the learner to use all his resources to reason and solve problems and to discover himself as an achiever of ever expanding goals.

In a setting such as that described above, the teacher can challenge children by taking into consideration each learner's abilities and needs, by providing activities to meet growing interests and abilities, by making experiences meaningful and significant, and by the wise use of instructional materials and procedures for making drill and practice sessions profitable. A child can then accept the responsibility for learning assignments because he understands them, because they have meaning for him, and because of the nature of the relationship he has with the group and the teacher. The teacher has neither demanded, coerced, nor punished him. He has set him on the way to self-direction, self-motivation, self-discovery, and self-education. He has given him a glimpse of the rewards of learning because he understands the joys as well as the nature of learning. In such an environment work becomes not a task to be avoided, a necessary ill in order to be socially accepted, but a personal satisfaction.

## Key Concepts in Learning

The capacities of the learner and his character structure should influence the method as well as the content of the learning experience. He should have practice in setting goals that are realistic. If his goals are too high he will be frustrated and if they are too low he will be bored; in neither case will there be satisfactory progress. Learning is most effective when the child is in good health, both physical and mental, and is surrounded by a stimulating environment, where learning is active and curiosity can be satisfied. Evaluation should be a part of the learning process. Knowing one's weakness, strengths, and the results of past performance helps the learner reach his goals. Active participation is more effective than passive participation — in proposing, planning, executing, and evaluating the learning experience.

The motivated learner learns more readily than the unmotivated. The young child, the handicapped child, the retarded child, the insecure child — all are in particular need of much encouragement and praise. Motivation is most effective if it is not too intense. Distracting emotional conditions may accompany fear, anxiety, or pain and thus hinder the learning process. Intrinsic motivation is preferable to extrinsic motivation, and learning motivated by reward is usually more effective than learning under threat of punishment. Providing a shock absorber for failure can best be accomplished by insuring a backlog of success.

Assignments that the learner comprehends are more easily mastered than those which are not meaningful or understood. Correct repetitive practice is essential in overlearning certain skills such as memorization of music or unrelated items. Spaced recall is helpful in fixing materials that must be remembered over a period of time. Transfer to new tasks and situations will be improved if, in the learning process, the learner sees relationships for himself and applies the principles to a variety of tasks and situations.[35]

## Conclusion

Many questions remain unanswered: How does the child select from among the tasks presented to him? Why does he relish some and leave others half-done? What particular type of learning skills does he employ? What are the motives that guide him? In applying learning theories and principles the teacher must take into consideration the dynamic factors of the pupils. Since motivation influences behavior, and behavior is what we learn, we have given considerable attention to the role of motivation in learning.

The young child as well as the infant is subjected to drives of great intensity — partly because he is so dependent upon others. Drive reduction is a basic and powerful element in controlling the behavior of young children.

As the child matures, other motives such as identification with others become strong factors in reward or reinforcement. The teacher should recognize that the child must have help in finding

[35] Adapted from Hilgard, *op. cit.*, pp. 485, 486.

ways to satisfy his needs that are in harmony with his maturing personality.

The good teacher will help the child realize that to be free of frustrations, to be disencumbered of problems, to be rid of irritations is not the sole purpose of living. An individual struggles to gain something, to learn, to achieve, to utilize his powers and innate capacity for thinking, experiencing, creating, and sharing with others his findings. In such a concept life takes on new meaning and learning becomes a way of life. In realizing his potential for living as well as for learning one develops his capacity to enjoy, to love, to laugh, to sorrow, to live life, not by submitting to it, but rather by contributing to it, "by becoming himself in the noblest and deepest way."[36]

## ACTIVITIES AND QUESTIONS

1. Discuss the learning process and explain how purposeful learning would take place in the following activities: swimming, driving a car, preparing a research project in social studies, preparing a lesson plan, teaching a lesson in music to fifth-graders.

2. Observe in a primary grade and note application, if any, of the principles of learning discussed in this chapter. Give specific evidence and cite principles operative.

3. Visit an intermediate classroom and observe the types of motivation the teacher used; the extent to which children had a part in setting their goals; the way the children's interests were used in motivation; the provisions made for children to evaluate their progress toward a specific goal; the ways in which the teacher provided for differences in ability and maturity levels.

4. Factors other than native abilities are reflected in performance. Motivation is important in determining performances as well as learning. Many times you have heard such remarks as "Johnny could learn that if he wanted to." What factors would need to be considered in evaluating the truth of this statement?

5. The teacher sets the stage for self-directed learning through his knowledge of the learner and the learning process. In the reports of

---

[36] Albert Schweitzer, "The Evolution of Ethics," *The Atlantic*, 202:73, November 1958.

visits to two kindergartens the difference in the concept of the learner and the setting for learning is illustrated. From the behavior of the children and teacher described in each classroom what underlying beliefs about child development and learning are evidenced?

# BIBLIOGRAPHY

Association for Supervision and Curriculum Development. *Continuity in Learning.* Washington, D.C.: The Association, NEA, 1957.

Association for Supervision and Curriculum Development. *Creating a Good Environment for Learning.* Washington, D.C.: The Association, NEA, 1954.

Association for Supervision and Curriculum Development. *Learning and the Teacher.* Washington, D.C.: The Association, NEA, 1959.

Association for Supervision and Curriculum Development. *Learning More About Learning,* Alexander Frazier (ed.). Third ASCD Research Institute. Washington, D.C.: The Association, NEA, 1959.

Brogan, Peggy, and Fox, Lorene. *Helping Children Learn: A Concept of Elementary School Method.* Yonkers-on-Hudson, N.Y.: World Book Company, 1955.

Burton, William H. *The Guidance of Learning Activities.* New York: Appleton-Century-Crofts, Inc., 1952.

Cantor, Nathaniel. *Dynamics of Learning.* Buffalo, N.Y.: Henry Stewart, Inc., 1946.

Cronbach, Lee J. *Educational Psychology.* New York: Harcourt, Brace and Company, 1954.

Crow, Lester, and Crow, Alice. *Human Development and Learning.* New York: American Book Company, 1956.

Deese, James. *The Psychology of Learning.* New York: McGraw-Hill Book Company, 2nd ed., 1958.

Dollard, J., and Miller, N. E. *Personality and Psychotherapy.* New York: McGraw-Hill Book Company, 1950.

Educational Policies Commission. *Contemporary Issues in Elementary Education.* Washington, D.C.: NEA, 1960.

Fry, Edward. "Teaching Machines: the Coming Automation," *Phi Delta Kappan,* 41:28–31, October 1959.

Galanter, Eugene (ed.). *Automatic Teaching: The State of the Art.* New York: John Wiley and Sons, 1959.

Hilgard, Ernest R. *Theories of Learning.* New York: Appleton-Century-Crofts, Inc., 2nd ed., 1956.

Hull, C. L. *A Behavior System*. New Haven, Conn.: Yale University Press, 1952.

Kingsley, Howard L., and Garry, Ralph. *The Nature and Conditions of Learning*. Englewood Cliffs, N.J.: Prentice-Hall, Inc., rev. ed., 1957.

Koch, Sigmund (ed.). *Psychology: A Study of Science*. New York: McGraw-Hill Book Company, 1958, Vols. I and II.

Lewin, Kurt. *A Dynamic Theory of Personality*. New York: McGraw-Hill Book Company, 1935.

Lumsdaine, A. A., and Glaser, Robert. *Teaching Machines and Programmed Learning*. Washington, D.C.: Department of Audio-Visual Instruction, NEA, 1960.

Martin, William E., and Stendler, Celia Burns. *Child Development: The Process of Growing Up in Society*. New York: Harcourt, Brace and Company, 1953.

McClelland, David C., Atkinson, John W. *et al*. *The Achievement Motive*. New York: Appleton-Century-Crofts, Inc., 1953.

McGooch, John, and Irion, Arthur. *The Psychology of Learning*. New York: Longmans, Green and Company, 1952.

Miel, Alice (ed.). *Continuous Learning*. Washington, D.C.: Association for Childhood Education International, 1951, Bulletin No. 87.

National Society for the Study of Education. *Learning and Instruction*. Forty-Ninth Yearbook, Part I. Chicago: University of Chicago Press, 1950.

Phi Delta Kappa Commission on Research. "What Research Says About Teaching and Learning," *Phi Delta Kappan*, 39: entire issue, March 1958.

Prescott, Daniel A. *Factors That Influence Learning*. Pittsburgh: University of Pittsburgh Press, 1958.

Skinner, B. F. "The Science of Learning and the Art of Teaching," in W. Fullager, H. Lewis, and C. Cumbee (eds.), *Readings for Educational Psychology*. New York: Thomas Y. Crowell Company, 1956.

Skinner, B. F. "Teaching Machines," *Science*, 128:969–977, October 24, 1958.

part two

# The Curriculum Design

4    There is an unreal quality about
these arguments about returning to an earlier
or more restricted curriculum. It is somehow
as if the twentieth century had failed to exist.

BYRON S. HOLLINSHEAD

# Planning the curriculum

How can the school present what children must learn in such a
way that children will want to learn it? How can the teacher translate this material into a specific plan that reaches out and touches boys
and girls so that behavior is changed, skills are strengthened, and
understandings are deepened? For every teacher the central problem
is how to organize learning experiences that are academically worth
while, socially significant, individually challenging, and universally
applicable. This involves a knowledge of curriculum planning, principles of curriculum organization, types of curriculum, and interrelationships of the component factors of the curriculum. It involves
seeing the correlation among children, teacher, staff, physical situation, materials, resources, parents, and community. It also involves
organizing instruction in such a way that these elements all contribute to the total educational process.

Most children come to school eager to learn. The school has the task of offering a curriculum that will challenge them to become equipped to communicate, to solve problems, to take their places as responsible members of society. It is not enough, however, for the child to be challenged. The teacher, too, must be stimulated to put forth his best efforts, to be creative in his approach to teaching, and to become increasingly skillful in helping each child attain his highest and most excellent goals.

*What Is Curriculum?* Curriculum has been defined in a variety of ways. Prescott defines it in terms of the individual child: "The curriculum of a school for an individual child is everything that he experiences in and around the school — physical conditions, inter-personal relationships, peer-group structure and dynamics, cultural expectancies and demands in operation in the school, textbooks, assignments, drill and practice periods, committee work, participation in discussions and in evaluative work."[1] From this point of view what the child learns, the particular meanings and skills he acquires, is the effect of the learning activities as he perceives them in terms of his unique background of experience, his image of himself, and his orientation toward the world.

Ragan conceives of the curriculum as including "all experiences of children for which the school accepts responsibility."[2] He believes, however, that it exists only in the experiences of children, "not in textbooks, in the course of study, or in the plans and intentions of teachers."[3]

Kyte defines curriculum briefly as consisting of "the totality of learning experiences essential for the maximum development of the individual as a useful member of a changing democratic society."[4]

The school is charged with the responsibility of teaching children the things they will need to know in order to take their places as effective citizens in society. To this end "A sequence of potential experiences is set up in the school for the purpose of disciplining children and youth in group ways of thinking and acting. This set

[1] Daniel A. Prescott, *The Child in the Educative Process* (New York: McGraw-Hill Book Company, 1957), p. 346.
[2] W. B. Ragan, *Modern Elementary Curriulum* (New York: Henry Holt and Company, rev. ed., 1960), p. 3.
[3] *Ibid.*, p. 4.
[4] George C. Kyte, *The Elementary School Teacher at Work* (New York: The Dryden Press, 1957), p. 171.

of experiences is referred to as the *curriculum*."[5] Their purpose is to teach boys and girls to communicate, to solve problems, to think critically, to contribute toward the solution of the problems faced by the society of which they are a part.

## Cooperative Planning

Planning the curriculum should be a cooperative enterprise in which the school community comes to a general agreement on its philosophy of education. "The first goal is to frame a philosophy which will express the quality of living which the community aspires to have for its children and youth. It should include such items as the established function of education in our republic, the relation of education to children's behavior and growth, and the place of the school in the local community. If the necessary study and resulting statement are effectively achieved, the outcome should be a philosophy of the school's work which all community members can understand. Formulated in a democratic manner, it should become a unifying factor around which the school and the community may build their educational program."[6]

The curriculum is a reflection of what the people believe, think, feel, and do about education. When teachers, administrators, supervisors, consultants, parents, and other lay members of the community work together to define the purposes of the school and to use resources effectively, the curriculum becomes a true expression of the people whom it directly affects.

In the cooperative attack upon the problems of curriculum planning lies to a great extent the secret of success in the educational enterprise. The following are the common tasks of curriculum planning:

1. The identification, definition, and use of objectives to provide direction, scope, and emphasis to learning and to provide the teacher with one of the important bases for selecting desirable learning experiences and adequately evaluating them.

[5] B. Othaniel Smith, William O. Stanley, and J. Harlan Shores, *Fundamentals of Curriculum Development* (Yonkers-on-Hudson, N.Y.: World Book Company, rev. ed., 1957), p. 3.

[6] Herold C. Hunt and Paul R. Pierce, *The Practice of School Administration* (Boston: Houghton Mifflin Company, 1958), p. 38.

2. The selection of learning experiences of educational significance.
3. The organization and development of these experiences so that all essential educational elements are considered; the experiences have foci that are sufficiently comprehensive to include children, ideas, materials, plans, activities, and evaluations; and the relationships among these elements are seen and used to predict future behavior. Proper organization and development of learning experiences are concerned with adequate breadth, useful perception of relationships, and effective continuity of learning.
4. The evaluation of the products of learning so that their bearing on objectives is perceived, their adequacy of development at that time is determined, and their consequence for future improved behavior is examined.
5. The formulation and carrying out of plans which include the important people of the teaching-learning enterprise — children, teachers, staff, parents, and other adults — at their proper points of responsibility and in relation to their respective functions in insuring and developing a desirable educational program.[7]

An examination of these tasks shows that they are interrelated and interdependent. They do not occur in the teaching-learning process in a 1, 2, 3, 4, 5 order. The key tasks upon which the others hinge and to which they contribute are selection, organization, and development of the learning experiences. These indicate the decisions that must be made and give a clue to the way teaching tasks may be performed, but they do not say when and how. The latter questions are answered through understanding the principles of curriculum organization, types of curriculum, the role of curriculum design, and principles for improving the curriculum.

## Principles of Curriculum Organization

*Pupil Participation in Planning.* After the general outline of areas to be studied has been completed by the school community, children can help in planning learning activities for their particular group. The skills of the democratic process are not learned in a vacuum. They must be practiced under the guidance of a teacher who is versed in the procedures.

---

[7] Adapted from Virgil E. Herrick *et al., The Elementary School* (Englewood Cliffs, N.J.: Prentice-Hall, Inc., 1956), pp. 133, 134.

*Development of Basic Skills and Knowledge.* In an effort to make education palatable some schools have organized the curriculum in such a way that there is little time for drill or the development of the fundamental skills. Promotion takes place whether or not the children have the necessary skills to profit from the next year's instruction. Direct teaching of certain complex skills is necessary.[8] Many children who have tried to learn to read or to compute solely in an activity program have been unsuccessful. A good curriculum affords time for group processes, for development of social skills, the creative arts, but it does not exclude time for drill in the fundamentals required for effective participation in a society in which literacy is essential.

*Continuity in Learning.* Curriculum experiences must be planned so that the child can move from the simple to the complex and master increasingly effective skills of communication. He will move naturally from the concrete to the abstract. However, in the development of social concepts he need not wait until he is in the sixth grade to understand children who live in other countries. He can learn about the world across the ocean while he is learning about his home and his own community. He need not move from home to school to neighborhood to community and finally to more remote regions. Concepts of interdependence, tolerance, and democracy are of a spiral nature. He learns about them as he uses them in his own living and thinking. The point at which he is ready for a particular concept or mastery of skills is dependent upon his own design of development, background of experiences, and ability to comprehend. Minimum grade standards, annual promotions, heterogeneous grouping, lockstep educational practices do not necessarily achieve continuity in learning. They merely achieve continuity in content to be taught. In order for skills and concepts to be developed through the years the curriculum must provide a continuing opportunity for their practice. This suggests that over a period of time in the elementary school children will have a chance to deal with the same

8 Paul R. Hanna, "Opportunities for the Use of Arithmetic in an Activity Program," *Teaching of Arithmetic,* Tenth Yearbook, National Council of Teachers of Mathematics (New York: Bureau of Publications, Teachers College, Columbia University, 1935), pp. 85–120. This study points out that skills must be taught; they cannot be learned satisfactorily solely through an activity program.

types of skills and the same concepts at a higher level of complexity as they progress.

*Sequence of Learning Experiences.* Each successive learning experience must build upon the preceding one and delve more deeply into the content. Sequence refers not to repetition or duplication of learning experiences but rather to increased depth and breadth at each higher grade level.

The curriculum worker has to arrange learning experiences so they will coincide with the individual's ability to adapt to his environment and learn to control it for his own welfare. Several sequences have traditionally been used in determining the order of materials of instruction: *chronological order, logical order, difficulty,* and *geographical expansion.* Leonard points out that "The sequence of learning experiences should be based upon the development of the individual as changes in his maturing personality require the acquisition of knowledge, skills, and principles. He is affected by his abilities, his drives, and the pressures of his environment."⁹

*Orientation to the World.* It is no longer enough for the child to learn the three R's; he must learn the important skills of human relationships. He must do more than understand the traditional subject matter; he must do more than understand social problems. He must be helped to "project [his] thinking into the future, to conceive the kind of social ends and relationships it is possible to build within the bounds of basic social trends. . . ."¹⁰ In order to improve society, conserve natural resources, better living conditions, and develop intercultural understandings the child must study the needs and existing conditions of his own community through organized learning experiences.

*Integration in Learning.* Learning is more effective if the pupils see some relationships between the various subjects studied. In some schools separate subjects are taught at specified times. In others there are long, uninterrupted periods of planning and developing unit activities using subject matter from various fields. Integration

⁹ J. Paul Leonard, "Some Reflections on the Meaning of Sequence," in Virgil E. Herrick and Ralph Tyler (eds.), *Toward Improved Curriculum Theory,* Supplementary Educational Monographs, No. 71 (Chicago: University of Chicago Press, 1950), p. 71.

¹⁰ Smith, Stanley, and Shores, *op. cit.,* p. 317.

occurs when subject-matter areas are related normally and naturally as they are needed by the group in the study of the problem. The curriculum organization in many schools provides both for the teaching of subjects at regular periods and for long blocks of time to work on projects and challenging problems.

*Balance of Activities.*   There should be time for work on signifi-cant problems in units that cut across subject-matter lines as well as for systematic study and drill. Group experiences should be a part of the program, but time should also be allowed for developing individual interests and creative expression. Achieving balance in the curriculum must be a consideration both in long-range and in daily planning.

When the interests of the pupils are considered in organizing and developing learning experiences it is not too difficult to schedule the daily program so that periods of strenuous activity are followed by quiet group experiences; activities contributing to creative indi-vidual expression are balanced by those in which group standards are met; and group studies or units or problems are balanced by systematic drill as it is needed.

## Types of Curriculum Organization

Many terms have been applied to different patterns of curriculum organization. Separate subjects, broad fields, activity, areas of living, social functions of living, problems of living, integrated, experience, emerging needs, core — all have had their ardent supporters and staunch foes. In spite of local autonomy in education, relatively few curriculum types have survived.

Herrick, Eberman, and Goodlad[11] identify the following types as centers for selecting and organizing learning experiences: subject matter, persistent problems of living, and felt needs of children. Beck, Cook, and Kearney[12] identify four types: the separate-subjects curriculum, the correlated curriculum, the broad-fields curriculum,

[11] Herrick *et al., The Elementary School,* p. 147.
[12] Robert H. Beck *et al., Curriculum in the Modern Elementary School* (Englewood Cliffs, N.J.: Prentice-Hall, Inc., 2nd ed., 1960), pp. 193–197.

and the developmental-activity curriculum. Hunt and Pierce[13] identify four types: subject-field organization, activity curriculum, functions -of-living pattern, and experience or "needs" curriculum. Smith, Stanley, and Shores[14] focus on three patterns: the separate-subjects curriculum, the activity curriculum, and the core curriculum.

## SEPARATE-SUBJECTS CURRICULUM

The separate-subjects curriculum is based on traditional ways of classifying knowledge. It is usually characterized by formal information and skills taught within the framework of precise time allotments, daily lesson plans, and subjects organized in narrow slices or discrete fields. The child may study as many as fifteen subjects in the elementary school during a single school term. Among the subjects observed in a one-teacher school organized on this basis were reading, writing, spelling, oral language, artithmetic, geography, history, civics, physiology, hygiene, nature study, music, art, manual training, and cooking. Each subject was studied independently and the learning experiences took place within its boundaries.

There is a trend in the separate-subjects curriculum organization to correlate two or more similar subjects. For example, music and art are often correlated.

The type of organization influences the teaching method. In the subject-centered curriculum the textbook is usually the most important teaching tool. The chief teaching procedures are lectures, discussions, questions and answers, written exercises, oral reports, term papers, and so forth. Activities such as construction, modeling, designing, and dramatization are conspicuous by their absence.

However, there is no reason to believe that good teaching is impossible under the restrictions imposed by this organization even though it de-emphasizes the interests and activities of children, tends to result in fragmentary or compartmentalized learnings, and often limits teacher-pupil planning. The teacher who is dedicated to helping children learn will find means to stimulate critical thinking, wider reading, group discussion, and creative expression. Such a

[13] *Op. cit.*, pp. 83, 94.
[14] *Op. cit.*, pp. 225–385.

teacher may find the practice of broadening the subject fields to permit the wider, more realistic use of materials and procedures a step toward greater creativity in teaching.

## Broad-Fields Curriculum

The broad-fields curriculum is a modification of the separate-subjects curriculum. It cuts across subject-matter boundaries, substituting a few comprehensive categories for the multiplicity of separate subjects. In place of the fourteen subjects, five or six broad areas are organized. To these new content is added. The school day is divided into larger blocks of time for language arts, social studies, science and health, and arts and crafts. The language arts, or communication skills as they are frequently called, are used in practically every school activity. Children use reading in their study of social studies, science and health, arithmetic, and the creative arts. They use speaking, listening, and writing skills as an integral part of learning. Not only do they have opportunity to practice the language arts in relation to other activities; they learn to develop their skills in activities designed specifically for the purpose of improving listening, speaking, and writing. Spelling is usually taught in a separate period, as is reading.

The social studies area includes learnings from history, geography, sociology, civics, anthropology, and related fields having to do with the study of man and his relationship to man and environment. The use of themes such as interdependence, conservation, and others contributes to greater flexibility, continuity, and integration in learning. For example, in a study of the local community the theme of interdependence might be stressed as the children learn of the history, the pioneers of the region, and the manner in which people worked together to build a community.

Science and health form another division of the broad-fields curriculum. Children learn the scientific bases for health practices. In the process they find out something about physiology, anatomy, biology, and chemistry. The use of the scientific method in teaching health counteracts superstition and practices which contribute to ill health. "It is probably accurate to say that this broad-fields plan, combined with an activity approach within the fields (and especially in the social studies) is the typical organization used in American elementary schools."[15]

*Daily Program in a Broad-Fields Curriculum.* In the following schedule the classes in social studies meet three days a week, science and health two days, language arts every day, music and art on alternate days, and reading, arithmetic, and physical education every day.

| | |
|---|---|
| 9:00– 9:15 | Planning the day's activities |
| 9:15–10:15 | Reading groups |
| 10:15–10:45 | Outdoor play |
| 10:45–11:15 | Arithmetic |
| 11:15–11:45 | Music and art on alternating days |
| 11:45– 1:00 | Lunch |
| 1:00– 2:00 | Language arts |
| 2:00– 2:30 | Physical education |
| 2:30– 3:15 | Social studies, alternating with science and health |

From this illustration it is evident that, in spite of the greater flexibility compared with the separate-subjects organization, the fundamental considerations and concepts in the broad-fields curriculum are basically those underlying the separate-subjects curriculum. It is subject centered — not society or child centered.

## CORE CURRICULUM

Because many educators are not completely satisfied with the broad-fields curriculum in providing for integration in learnings they have attempted to organize the curriculum not around subjects or combinations of subjects but around social problems that involve concepts from many different areas. The core curriculum focuses on persistent problems of living or social functions that man has faced in the past and continues to face today. The specific areas selected for study vary from school to school, but a fairly representative list includes:

Maintaining good health.
Making a living.
Conserving our natural resources.
Living in our communities.
Transportation.
Home and family living.

[15] Hollis Caswell and Arthur W. Foshay, *Education in the Elementary School* (New York: American Book Company, 3rd ed., 1957), p. 262.

Life in other lands.
Preserving, distributing, and consuming goods and services.
Recreation and playing.
Communicating.

Content is drawn from the types of activities common to all people regardless of the culture into which they are born and in which they develop.

The social-problems core places emphasis on the study and solution of problems. The elements of the core curriculum are organized into social categories based upon major areas of social activities. These categories may be conceived in terms of social functions such as maintaining health or conserving natural resources, or in terms of "needs" of individuals in social adjustment such as those arising from face-to-face relationships or from individual-social problems.

Once the categories have been determined the staff must decide on the aspects of each category to be developed at each educational level. This brings up the problems of sequence.

Sequence is influenced by maturity, experiential background, prior learnings and interests, and difficulty of content. It is determined largely on the basis of sociological strands of life in the expanding community — the home, the school, the neighborhood, the community, the region, nation, and world. These strands must be integrated at each grade level and from grade to grade.[16]

### *Examples of Sequence in the Curriculum*[17]

Kindergarten:   The home and the school.
                Adjustment to school life.
                Making the transition from home to school.
                Relating one's self to the expanded peer group.
Grade 1:   The home.
           The school.
           The neighborhood.
Grade 2:   The immediate community.
Grade 3:   The human resources in the community.

---

[16] A comprehensive discussion of the areas-of-living curriculum design is found in Florence B. Stratemeyer *et al.*, *Developing a Curriculum for Modern Living* (New York: Bureau of Publications, Teachers College, Columbia University, 2nd ed., 1957).

[17] University of Wisconsin Summer Laboratory School, 1950.

Adjustment of the various culture groups in the community.

Background and contributions of these groups.

Grade 4: The community in its metropolitan area and geographic region.

The manner in which natural and controlled environmental factors influence and contribute to community living.

Grades 5 and 6 deal with the areas of human living in Wisconsin and its relation to living in our community; the present in relation to the past (Grade 5); human living in the United States and its relation to living in our community (Grade 6).

In schools that organize learning experiences around a core, children may study the same problems at each grade level, but the concepts to be learned become increasingly complex.

The following daily schedule illustrates the effort to integrate learnings. There are longer blocks of time and fewer divisions of subject matter than in other curriculum patterns discussed.

9:00–10:30    Major problem to be studied. Content from the social, physical, and biological sciences as needed to solve the problem. Activities include planning, finding information, writing reports, experimenting, working on art projects and so forth.

10:30–11:00   Outdoor recess.

11:30–12:00   Communication skills. This period is designed to meet individual and group needs in communication and study skills as revealed in the major problem area.

12:00– 1:00   Lunch and relaxation.

1:00– 1:35    Arithmetic.

1:35– 2:30    Music and physical education.

2:30– 3:15    Free reading. This is largely an individualized reading period. The aim is pleasure in reading.

Basing instruction and materials on functions of living is the distinguishing characteristic of the areas-of-living or problems-of-living curriculum. The major social functions of living are analyzed into their essential activities and form the basis for organizing the learning experiences. The advantage of this curriculum pattern is that it provides for both the needs of the children and the demands of society. It does not do away with subject matter; it emphasizes problems of social living and uses subject matter in defining and solving them. It is neither subject centered nor child centered. It is society centered. The interests of children are not overlooked, but they do *not* form the primary basis for selecting and organizing learning experiences.

The core curriculum demands a high type of staff *esprit de corps*, community backing, and cooperative planning and development to be successful. It requires, too, a willingness to regard the school as an agent for cultural renewal and improvement of society.

## EXPERIENCE OR ACTIVITY CURRICULUM

This curriculum organization has also been called the project or emerging-needs curriculum. Its dominant characteristic is without question its focus on the essential interests of children. "It is only as interests are expressed and grow into purposes — that is, intended courses of action, which have been accepted only after their probable consequences have been reviewed — that they are acceptable as the basis of an educational program."[18] The source for learning experiences is neither the organized fields of knowledge as in the subject organization, nor the problems of social living as in the core curriculum, but the shared interests and purposes of children. Special interests are met through cocurricular and extra-class activities in which creative expression is encouraged and utilized.

The activity program makes use of conventional subject matter through books, audio-visual aids, and other forms of organized bodies of knowledge. A variety of subject matter is required, and a broad reference library is essential. Reading, discussion, study, and critical thinking are important in this type of curriculum. The criticism has been made that the activity program and subject matter are incompatible. As a matter of fact the activity motivates study of skill subjects. Children turn to studying reading and arithmetic, for example, because they need them to carry out their projects. Books and other supplementary materials are used for the real purpose of answering questions that arise as children learn about their environment and select specialized projects for study.

[18] Smith, Stanley, and Shores, *op. cit.*, p. 271.

The following example[19] illustrates the way in which the activity program emphasizes individual and group activities in the daily program:

9:00   (Monday through Friday) Informal greetings, reports, observations, rhymes, music, events of current interest, informal activities designed to create a mental set conducive to a happy, profitable day.

9:15   *Arithmetical Enterprises*
(Monday through Friday) Playstores, banking activities, handling of school supplies, etc. Although rich in arithmetical content through which the child is trained in skills and abilities, such units also yield abundantly in group and individual situations which develop initiative, responsibility, and co-operation. The flexible period provides opportunity for individual instruction.

10:00  *Healthful Living Enterprises*
(Monday through Friday) Physical education activities, free play, the nutrition program, and adequate relief periods are provided for daily; units of work such as: "the study of milk," "a balanced meal," etc., provide enterprises which have healthful living as a center of interest but provide situations developmental of social and civic attitudes as well.

10:50  *Language Arts*
(Monday through Friday) Oral and written composition, spelling and writing develop from activities rich in opportunities for expression, as the writing of a play to be presented in the auditorium period, puppet shows, the school newspaper, etc. The period should provide opportunity for literary discrimination and original expression; the long period provides for concentration of effort and attention according to individual interest and need.

12:00  (Monday through Friday) Lunch, rest and directed playground activities.

1:00   *Avocational Activities*
(Monday) Music; activities, music appreciation, rhythm, harmonica, band, orchestra, etc.
(Tuesday) Nature Club, school museum, aquarium, gardens, terrarium.

[19] *Teachers' Guide to Child Development: Manual for Kindergarten and Primary Teachers,* prepared under the direction of the California State Curriculum Commission, Ruth Manning Hockett (ed.) (Sacramento: California State Department of Education, 1930), pp. 355, 356.

(Wednesday) Creative art and constructive activities in pottery, weaving, painting, drawing.
(Thursday) Use of auditorium for music, dancing, dramatics, projects, stagecraft, related to class activities.
(Friday) Civics Club committees responsible for various phases of school life.

1:50   (Monday through Friday) Recreation and rest.
2:00   *Reading Groups: Library Activities*
(Monday through Friday) Group organization on the basis of reading ability provides opportunity for remedial work with children having reading deficiencies and library guidance to superior readers. The quiet reading period may contribute to the development of information needed in the class activities related to social science, avocational, or health interests.
2:50   (Monday through Friday) Recreation and rest.
3:00   (Monday) Social studies activities.
(Tuesday) Social studies activities.
(Wednesday) Free creative work period.
(Thursday) Social studies activities.
(Friday) Shop enterprises.

Unlike the separate-subjects and core curricula, the activity program is not planned in advance. However, the teacher does not sit with folded hands waiting for the children to take over the responsibilities of the curriculum and instruction. His tasks in planning are exceedingly important:

1. To work with individuals and groups to discover the children's interests.
2. To guide them in evaluating their interests and selecting those which appear to have the most value in terms of criteria set up.
3. To help the individual or group plan, organize, and develop activities required in pursuit of these interests.
4. To guide the individual or group in evaluating what has been accomplished.

This program requires that the teacher gain skill in teacher-pupil planning, make a study of children's interests, and learn to use the problem-solving method. It calls for provision for children's specialized interests — music, art, and others. It requires the teacher to have a broad general education with special training in child development, guidance, discussion skills, and project methods of teaching. It demands physical facilities that encourage many activities — multi-purpose rooms, general-purpose rooms, much space for projects and experiments and outdoor doings. An activity curriculum requires flexibility in scheduling, grouping, and administering the program.

Inherent in this curriculum is the conviction that the felt needs of children are significant, that children learn to solve problems by dealing with them, and that they learn to take care of future needs by handling present problems. Learning centers around the activity or experience. Knowledge and skills are taught in response to the needs of children as they pursue their interests.

Critics of the activity curriculum do not believe that children's interests provide a sound basis for curriculum organization. They fear that following these interests will lead to a sterile educational program with huge gaps in basic knowledge, and to the neglect of important processes. They are concerned that sequence and balance will be ignored.

Under the direction of a superior teacher, however, the experience curriculum can be exciting and rewarding. Children are self-motivated to learn, since they see the relation between their goals and the learning experiences they are having in school. Teachers are freed from the restrictions of the more highly structured curriculum.

In the following discussion Wingo suggests some minimum essentials of a worth-while and effective activity program.

1. . . . activities must provide for the continuity of experience in young children. Activities must emerge from the interests, capacities, and conscious needs of children.

2. . . . subject matter, whether it comes from the teacher, from printed matter, or from some other source, must be functional in relation to actual problems. Its function is to serve as the data of thought. . . . skill subjects . . . should be developed in action, in the process of inquiry and not in isolation from experience. . . .

3. Above all else, an activity must provide for reflective thinking and for testing ideas. Children must have the leading part in identifying and planning situations to be dealt with. The children must collect the data, originate the ideas, and check facts and ideas against each other. The children must evolve the hypotheses which are to direct the attack on the doubtful situation. And it is the

children who must carry out the overt activities which change the situation.[20]

Obviously when these things are done, the activity program is neither futile, aimless, haphazard, nor teacher imposed and directed. It is instead an educative learning experience. At the elementary school level the activity curriculum emphasizes individual and group activities that provide rich opportunities to develop initiative, social skills, personal competence, and cooperation. Time is provided for practice in communication skills, music, and arithmetic. There is time for play, lunch, and relaxation. Flexibility is an essential in such a program.

Hopkins succinctly cites the differences between the subject-oriented and the experience curriculum in the following lists[21] showing the extent of the chasm between the most widely and the least used forms of curriculum organization.

| SUBJECT CURRICULUM | EXPERIENCE CURRICULUM |
|---|---|
| 1. Centered in *subjects*. | 1. Centered in children. |
| 2. Emphasis upon teaching subject matter. | 2. Emphasis upon promoting the all-around growth of children. |
| 3. Subject matter selected and organized prior to the teaching situation. | 3. Subject matter selected and organized cooperatively *during* the learning situation. |
| 4. Controlled by the teacher or someone representing authority external to the learning situation. | 4. Controlled and directed cooperatively by those directly involved in the learning situation. |
| 5. Emphasis upon teaching facts, imparting information, acquiring knowledge for its own sake or for possible future use. | 5. Emphasis upon meanings which will contribute immediately to improved living. |
| 6. Emphasis upon teaching specific habits and skills as separate and isolated aspects of learning. | 6. Emphasis upon building habits and skills as integral parts of experiences. |
| 7. Emphasis upon improving the | 7. Emphasis upon understanding |

[20] G. Max Wingo, "A Theoretical Basis for the Activity Program," in Herrick and Tyler, *op. cit.*, pp. 98, 99.
[21] Adapted from L. Thomas Hopkins, *Interaction: The Democratic Process* (Boston: D. C. Heath and Company, 1941), p. 20.

| Subject Curriculum | Experience Curriculum |
|---|---|
| methods of teaching subject matter of specific subjects. | and improving the process of learning through experience. |
| 8. Emphasis upon uniformity of exposures to learning situations and in so far as possible uniformity of learning results. | 8. Emphasis upon individual differences. |
| 9. Education as conforming to the curriculum organization. | 9. Education as individual development. |
| 10. Education as schooling. | 10. Education as growth. |

## The Role of Curriculum Design

"Curriculum design," according to Herrick, "is a statement of the pattern of relationships which exist among the elements of curriculum as they are used to make one consistent set of decisions about the nature of the curriculum of the child."[22] The bearing of curriculum design on the improvement of the educational program can best be seen in the light of its functions (1) as a definer of the elements and their pattern of relationships in curriculum development, (2) as a statement of the basis for selecting and organizing learning experiences, and (3) as an indicator of the role of teachers and children in curriculum planning.

The chart on page 114 reveals that the attempts to achieve the overall objectives of education are influenced by such factors as beliefs about the development of children, the nature of learning, democracy and its processes, and the concept of the school's function. The school organization and the initial focus will also influence the quality and type of learning experiences, as will the way in which the elements of the curriculum are combined and the extent to which the curriculum design allows the teacher to make important decisions. Although the learning experiences are initially focused on either subject, society, or child, these foci are not mutually exclusive. The good teacher will find a way to relate all three. The manner in which the curriculum is organized can help the good teacher do a

[22] Virgil E. Herrick, "The Concept of Curriculum Design," in Herrick and Tyler, *op. cit.*, p. 37.

better job; it cannot guarantee that a weak teacher will do a good job. The teacher should be familiar with each curriculum type not only in order to select, organize, and develop learning activities that will enable the children to make the greatest possible progress toward the desired objectives but also in order to contribute to curriculum improvement in the school in which he teaches.

The curriculum design should provide for organizing a series of learning experiences in which children can participate in selecting problems that challenge them, that are significant, and that utilize worth-while subject matter. The curriculum that permits a part of the day to be centered on broad issues has the advantage of bringing together the interests of children and the problems of society in such a way that they can come to grips with them. However, it is essential for part of the day to be spent in working on particular skills. Fundamental skills must be learned and specific provision must be made for them. Motivation for such learning should come from a need to use these skills on important problems and projects.

## *Organizing Learning Experiences*

Goodlad defines organizing centers for learning experiences as catch-hold places for moving forward educationally. He suggests that they are fruitful to the extent that (1) they are adequately comprehensive, include a certain breadth of ideas, allow different children to come to grips with them in their own way, account for high and low levels of performance, and so forth; (2) they have organizing capacity — that is, they allow children, ideas, materials, and so forth to merge in an integrative fashion that adds to what has been before and prepares for what is to follow; (3) they have capacity for movement — intellectual movement from facts to generalization to application, social movement from culture to culture, or person to person, geographic movement from one place to another.[23]

In deciding on organizing centers the teacher must take into con-

[23] Adapted from John I. Goodlad, "Three Dimensions in Organizing the Curriculum for Learning and Teaching," in Vincent J. Glennon (ed.), *Frontiers of Elementary Education, III* (Syracuse: Syracuse University Press, 1956), p. 13.

# A Proposed Curriculum Design

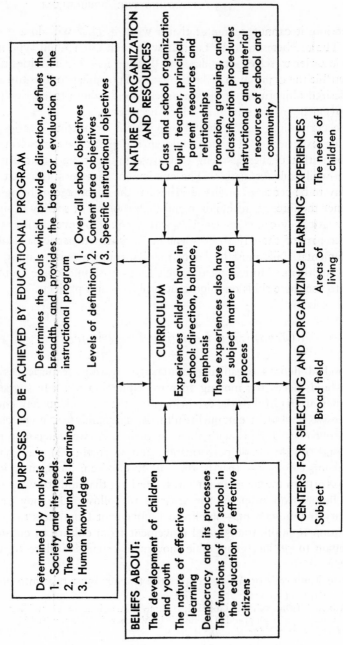

## PURPOSES TO BE ACHIEVED BY EDUCATIONAL PROGRAM

Determined by analysis of

1. Society and its needs
2. The learner and his learning
3. Human knowledge

Determines the goals which provide direction, defines the breadth, and provides the base for evaluation of the instructional program

Levels of definition {
1. Over-all school objectives
2. Content area objectives
3. Specific instructional objectives

## NATURE OF ORGANIZATION AND RESOURCES

Class and school organization

Pupil, teacher, principal, parent resources and relationships

Promotion, grouping, and classification procedures

Instructional and material resources of school and community

## CURRICULUM

Experiences children have in school: direction, balance, emphasis

These experiences also have a subject matter and a process

## BELIEFS ABOUT:

The development of children and youth

The nature of effective learning

Democracy and its processes

The functions of the school in the education of effective citizens

## CENTERS FOR SELECTING AND ORGANIZING LEARNING EXPERIENCES

| Subject | Broad field | Areas of living | The needs of children |

Source: Virgil E. Herrick and Ralph Tyler (eds.), *Toward Improved Curriculum Theory*, Supplementary Educational Monographs, No. 71 (Chicago: University of Chicago Press, 1950), p. 43. Copyright 1950 by the University of Chicago.

sideration children, content, and the learning process. Each is important in creating a curriculum structure that will enable children to develop the behaviors deemed essential for successful living in and out of the classroom. Beginning with the kindergarten child the organization of learning experiences is a vital consideration.

## The Curriculum in the Kindergarten

The discovery and development of the capacities of each child so that he may become a responsible member of society is the central responsibility of the kindergarten. Here he has many stimulating experiences and opportunities for socialization denied him at home. Although he grows and learns at home, in kindergarten there is someone specifically trained to guide his growth and learning, and other children with whom he can associate and share his experiences. He is at a most impressionable and plastic age. He is curious and eager about his world, and if he has the chance he will discover many interests as his horizon expands. He will learn to work and play in groups, develop new concepts and clarify old ones, develop creative abilities and increase his powers for critical thinking and problem solving.

The learnings of the familiar curriculum areas in the elementary school — reading, writing, speaking, science, art, music, and arithmetic — are firmly rooted in the kindergarten. The children increase their understanding and appreciation of the physical and social world and develop better ways of working and planning together.

The kindergarten child is intensely interested in himself, his environment, and the people around him. For him a curriculum that is child centered, socially oriented, and teacher guided is satisfactory. Creating, manipulating, exploring, communicating are the bases of the curriculum. His interests are at first personal, individualistic, and fleeting. But as the year progresses he becomes more social-minded, persistent, and interested in more things. He wants to explore beyond the neighborhood. He wants to learn about the world outside the home and school. He is able to concentrate on an area of interest and enjoys venturing to the library, the store, the post office, the zoo, the fire station. He is interested in the ways people travel and how they live. During the kindergarten year the child learns how to get along with others. Through excursions, observations, and stories his horizons are broadened, his knowledges extended, and his understandings deepened. Through rhythms, games, and art his aesthetic nature is fostered; through science his interest in the world about him is aroused. His communication skills are increased as he has time to plan, evaluate, discuss, and converse. By observing the interests and needs of children the teacher can find organizing centers around which to plan the kindergarten curriculum.

### THE CURRICULUM IN THE PRIMARY AND INTERMEDIATE GRADES

By the time the kindergarten child has become a primary school child he is ready for a more highly organized curriculum. Learning experiences can be built around more complex centers of interest, problems of living, people and places, and vital ideas.

*Centers of Interest.* Centers of interest in the room, such as a library, a science area, an arithmetic center, a work center (tools and workbench), an art center, a music center (rhythm instruments, piano, water glasses, etc.), stimulate creativity, exploration, manipulation, and experimentation.

*Problems of Living.* The problems of living — living in our community, transporting goods, making a living, communication, transportation, conservation of natural resources, maintaining good health, life in other countries, getting along with other nations — provide excellent organizing centers.

*People and Places.* People in the school, the community, and our country as well as people in other countries of the world make effective organizing centers at every level in the elementary school. Out of the study of people can develop some of the best social understandings and appreciation of other cultures which in turn lead to world understanding. The effort should be made to emphasize the ordinary, not the exotic, characteristics of the people and the culture, and to discover the likenesses as well as differences in the cultures. For example, many school children have the erroneous idea that all Mexicans wear serapes and large sombreros and spend the afternoon taking a siesta.

Places, too, offer experiences worthy of time and effort. From the playground, the school environs merging into the neighborhood, to the shops, market, zoo, farm, post office, harbor, airport, terminal, bank, mill, factory, courts, and other civic institutions — all can become centers for organizing learning experiences.

*Vital Ideas.* Ideas become increasingly important organizing centers as the child progresses through the elementary school. Consider the challenging activities that can evolve as he begins to discover the implications of the concepts of man and his environment, man and his place in the universe, custom and convention, democracy, liberty, time, wisdom, oligarchy, quality, quantity, duty, government, constitution, opinion, mind, progress. "Like each individual star, every idea is a source of life and light which animates and illuminates the words, facts, examples, and emotions that are dead — or deadly — and dark without them."[24]

Schools vary in the centers they use for curriculum organization and the kind and quality of learning experiences they provide. Some schools limit the learning experiences to the confines of the classroom; activities are selected that can be carried on only in the school itself. Others accept an enlarged concept of curriculum which includes community enterprises, excursions and field trips, and camping; they emphasize the importance of social learnings, attitudes, and skills as well as subject-matter areas. One of the useful tools for helping the teacher understand the particular educational situation of a school is the curriculum guide.

*The Curriculum Guide.* A curriculum guide presents objectives, content, outlines, suggested references, teaching-learning activities, and instructional resources. Some suggested activities and experiences are indicated, with their desired outcomes. The curriculum guide should contain a statement of evaluation procedures to be used to determine the extent to which the defined objectives are achieved. To be of maximum help to the teacher the good curriculum guide should include information about the following:

1. Needs, interests, developmental tasks of children.
2. Needs of the community.
3. Educational philosophy of the school.
4. Theory of learning which guides the thinking.
5. Objectives in terms of outcomes.

[24] Mortimer J. Adler, "What Is an Idea?" *Saturday Review,* 41:13, November 22, 1958.

6. Variety of learning experiences.
7. Some experiences with illustrations of how the learning experiences contribute to the objectives.
8. Instructional materials.
9. Continuity, sequence, integration, and balance in learning experiences, with illustrations.
10. Organizing centers to be used.
11. Evaluation procedures and devices used in harmony with the objectives.

## Curriculum Improvement

More and more the teacher is being involved in efforts to improve the school curriculum. He is asked to serve on curriculum commissions, curriculum planning and development committees, curriculum organization committees. All too frequently he fails to realize the possibilities of such cooperative effort because he does not understand the principles basic to curriculum improvement, which are as follows:

1. Planning the curriculum instructional program should be a cooperative enterprise shared by representative members of school and community personnel.

2. The concept of the total child — his nature and growth characteristics — should be the main focus of curriculum planning and practice.

3. Consideration of the total educational program is essential to balanced, well-rounded teaching and learning.

4. Organization for curriculum-instructional planning should be based chiefly on the group process, with a representative curriculum council and constituent committees comprising a basic element of the organizational framework.

5. The chief administrator, whether superintendent or principal, must provide in person the professional leadership of curriculum planning and action.

6. Community agencies and personnel should be enlisted and the chief spheres of their contributions indicated for participation in the educational process.

7. The philosophy and objectives of an educational program should be suited to the needs of the community and made the basis of teaching and learning procedures.

8. The activities of successful American living, arranged under major functions of living, according to stages of pupil development, should be made the foundations of courses of study and units of learning.

9. Curriculum planning should begin with the existing situation and proceed only as fast as understanding and acceptance of school and community personnel are developed.

10. The classroom, enlisting the assistance of parents and key citizens, provides the guidance of living and learning in school, home, and community.

11. The results of curriculum-instructional planning must be evaluated in the light of curriculum-instructional objectives, and with the aid of pilot studies and experimentation.[25]

Simply changing the design of the curriculum does not necessarily improve the program of the elementary school. Certain essential features must be present: superior teachers, good physical facilities, excellent and varied instructional materials, progressive leadership, good curriculum design, harmonious community relations and participation, and an administration that supports the teachers.

It is important for both administrator and teacher to consider the factors that contribute directly and indirectly to curriculum improvement. Whether or not a teacher is receiving personal satisfaction from his job, for instance, will greatly affect his behavior and contribution to the school organization.

In an effort to determine the sources of job satisfaction a systematic analysis was used to aid a researcher in collecting and analyzing data.[26] Using this analysis, Eash and Chasnoff identified nine types of satisfactions which teachers seek from their work and which have implications for curriculum improvement:

1. *Doing something worthwhile.* Teachers want to feel that they are doing work which makes a difference and which leads to a goal.
2. *Having trust in leadership.* Teachers want to feel their leaders have their interests at heart and understand how they feel.
3. *Doing one's share.* Teachers want to feel they are carrying their

[25] Hunt and Pierce, *op. cit.*, pp. 53, 54.

[26] Robert Saltonstall, "What Employees Want from Their Work," in Edward C. Bursk (ed.), *Human Relations for Management: The Newer Perspective* (New York: Harper & Brothers, 1956), p. 332.

fair share of the burden, but are not receiving an unjust number of duties.

4. *Counting for something.* Teachers want to receive recognition for their work, and to feel they have status with their colleagues as well as with the administration.

5. *Making a decent living.* Not only do teachers need to feel they are receiving adequate wages, but, also, that leadership is concerned with the problems of wages.

6. *Having a chance to get somewhere.* Teachers want to feel that there is opportunity for continuing professional growth — both for improving the quality of present work and for possible promotion.

7. *Looking to a safe future.* Teachers want to feel that they are secure in their personal status with the school system. They want to know where they stand, and they want protection in case of sickness, accident or early retirement.

8. *Knowing what's going on.* Teachers want to be informed of events in the school system, especially those affecting them. Suspicion multiplies when information is spread by rumor.

9. *Enjoying conditions of work.* Teachers want to feel that the school system is making an attempt to provide an environment which will stimulate better teaching.[27]

The teacher is still the key figure in instruction. To the extent that he is satisfied with the job, well qualified to teach, has a broad educational and cultural background, is adequately paid for his professional services, has a normal class size, good physical facilities, excellent materials and teaching aids, respect from the community, personal freedom, and pleasant working conditions — to this extent will the education of the children he teaches be superior. The curriculum is simply a vehicle for providing the school with an educational program. It can be improved through cooperative effort of those concerned.

Educators are agreed that curriculum improvement involves changes in behavior on the part of the individuals directly concerned with promoting the objectives of the school. The teacher must be aware of the goals the school seeks to achieve. However, this is not enough. He must also feel that the proposed action for

[27] Maurice J. Eash and Robert E. Chasnoff, "Framework for Effective Curriculum Improvement," reprinted with permission from the March 1960 issue of *Overview* Magazine. Copyright 1960, Buttenheim Publishing Corporation.

curriculum improvement will afford him greater personal satisfaction in his teaching. He must see clearly the purposes which underlie curriculum organization and curriculum improvement. Only as he accepts the school's goals and finds satisfaction in seeking them will he be effective in the process of curriculum improvement.

## *Conclusion*

The organization of the curriculum varies with the community. In some communities it embraces the learning experiences confined within the four walls of the schools; in others it includes any learning experiences which the child has under the guidance of the school, including excursions, camping, and other so-called "cocurricular" activities.

The curriculum is more likely to be effective when it is planned cooperatively by staff, administrators, supervisors, parents, and lay members, and when provision is made at some point for teacher-pupil planning. The curriculum should stress problems of social significance, assure development of basic skills, and provide the continuity, balance, and integration in learning. The subject matter should be functional — related to the problems studied. The children should have an opportunity to participate in problem solving. There should be a balance of activities and continuous evaluation.

In spite of local autonomy in regard to curriculum development in our country there is considerable uniformity among schools, and relatively few types of curriculum organization have evolved. In many schools the curriculum organization is based on the separation of man's knowledge into discrete subjects. In this separate-subjects curriculum academic subjects characterized by formal knowledge and skills are taught with daily lesson plans in precise class periods. A modification is the broad-fields curriculum, in which more liberal procedures and more comprehensive materials of instruction permit cutting across compartmentalized subject-matter lines.

The core program is based on broad social problems, or functions of living. The major social functions of living are analyzed into their essential activities and form the content of the curriculum. This type of organization cuts across subject fields and is concerned with the demands of society and the needs of youth. Inherent in the plan is the improvement of society through a study of the problems that society and the individual learner face.

The activity or experience curriculum is characterized by its focus on the essential interests, activities, and felt needs of children and youth. It is a far call from the formally organized body of subject matter and deals specifically with the present needs and pursuits of the child. It is characterized, too, by the problem-solving method and teacher-pupil on-the-spot planning, in contrast to the preplanning of the other types of curriculum organization. Although this plan has possibilities for great educational worth, the requirements of master teachers, staff planning, excellent facilities, superior materials and resources, and flexible administration make this the least widely used curriculum design.

Even when planned cooperatively by staff, administration, and lay personnel, the curriculum is interpreted and actualized by the teacher, upon whose skill, knowledge, insight, and experience rests the major responsibility. Together with the children, it is the teacher who translates the design of the curriculum into a pattern for daily living in the elementary school.

## ACTIVITIES AND QUESTIONS

1. Why is a knowledge of principles of curriculum organization important for the teacher?
2. What are the distinguishing characteristics of the separate-subjects, the broad-fields, the core, and the activity curricula? Visit in an elementary school and determine which of these types is used.
3. How does the planning in the activity curriculum differ from that of the other curriculum types? The orientation?
4. If you were given the choice, under which type of curriculum design would you prefer to teach? Why?
5. How is the content of the activity or experience curriculum determined? The core? The broad-fields?
6. Organize a role-playing situation in which a principal has called a meeting to inform his teachers of an impending change from the broad-fields curriculum to the core curriculum.

7. Compare the role of the teacher in separate-subjects, the broad-fields, the core, and the activity curriculum.

8. A survey of units of a fourth grade reveals the following: Maintaining Health, Beautifying Our Community, The Life of Helen Keller, The U.N., Magnets, How People Travel, Life in the East Indies, Spending Money Wisely. From this information what curriculum organization would you assume is being followed? Evaluate the selection of topics.

9. Examine several curriculum guides and evaluate them in terms of the criteria for a good curriculum guide suggested in this chapter.

10. Discuss the relationship between job satisfaction and curriculum improvement. Interview several teachers and try to determine whether the view advanced in this chapter appears to hold.

# BIBLIOGRAPHY

American Association of School Administrators. *The High School in a Changing World*. Washington, D.C.: National Education Association, 1958.

Archer, Clifford P. *Elementary Education in Rural Schools*. New York: The Ronald Press Company, 1958.

Association for Supervision and Curriculum Development. *Guidance in the Curriculum*. Washington, D.C.: National Education Association, 1955.

Association for Supervision and Curriculum Development. *A Look at Continuity in the School Program*. Washington, D.C.: National Education Association, 1958.

Association for Supervision and Curriculum Development. *The Modern Community School*. Washington, D.C.: National Education Association, 1953.

Association for Supervision and Curriculum Development. *Research for Curriculum Improvement*. Washington, D.C.: National Education Association, 1957.

Beauchamp, George A. *Planning the Elementary School Curriculum*. Boston: Allyn and Bacon, Inc., 1956.

Beck, Robert H., *et al. Curriculum in the Modern Elementary School*. Englewood Cliffs, N.J.: Prentice-Hall, Inc., 2nd ed., 1960.

Caswell, Hollis, and Foshay, Arthur W. *Education in the Elementary School*. New York: American Book Company, 3rd ed., 1957.

Crewson, Walter. "Involvement of the Lay Community in the Development of Curriculum," in Vincent J. Glennon (ed.), *Frontiers of Elementary Education*, IV. Syracuse: Syracuse University Press, 1957. pp. 69–74.

Goodlad, John I. "Three Dimensions in Organizing the Curriculum for Learning and Teaching," in Vincent J. Glennon (ed.), *Frontiers of Elementary Education*, III. Syracuse: Syracuse University Press, 1956, pp. 11–23.

Gwynn, J. Minor. *Curriculum Principles and Social Trends*. New York: The Macmillan Company, 3rd ed., 1960.

Herrick, Virgil E., *et al. The Elementary School*. Englewood Cliffs, N.J.: Prentice-Hall, Inc., 1956.

Herrick, Virgil E., and Tyler, Ralph W. (eds.). *Toward Improved Curriculum Theory*. Supplementary Educational Monographs, No. 71. Chicago: University of Chicago Press, 1950.

Hopkins, Thomas L. *Interaction: The Democratic Process*. Boston: D. C. Heath and Company, 1941.

Hunt, Herold C., and Pierce, Paul R. *The Practice of School Administration*. Boston: Houghton Mifflin Company, 1958.

Hurley, Beatrice Davis. *Curriculum for Elementary School Children*. New York: The Ronald Press Company, 1958.

Krug, Edward A. *Curriculum Planning*. New York: Harper & Brothers, rev. ed., 1957.

Lambert, Hazel. *Teaching the Kindergarten Child*. New York: Harcourt, Brace and Company, 1958.

Leavitt, Jerome E. (ed.). *Nursery-Kindergarten Education*. New York: McGraw-Hill Book Company, 1958.

Lee, Jonathan Murray, and Lee, Dorris May. *The Child and His Curriculum*. New York: Appleton-Century-Crofts, Inc., 3rd ed., 1960.

Macomber, Freeman Glenn. *Principles of Teaching in the Elementary School*. New York: American Book Company, 1954.

Miel, Alice, *et al. Cooperative Procedures in Learning*. New York: Bureau of Publications, Teachers College, Columbia University, 1953.

National Society for the Study of Education. *The Integration of Educational Experiences*. Fifty-Seventh Yearbook, Part III, Nelson B. Henry (ed.). Chicago: University of Chicago Press, 1958.

Parrish, Louise, and Waskin, Yvonne. *Teacher-pupil Planning for Better Classroom Teaching*. New York: Harper & Brothers, 1958.

Passow, A. Harry, *et al. Training Curriculum Leaders for Cooperative Research*. New York: Bureau of Publications, Teachers College, Columbia University, 1955.

Ragan, William. *Modern Elementary Curriculum*. New York: Henry Holt and Company, rev. ed., 1959.

Rudman, Herbert C. "Patterns of Textbook Use — Key to Curriculum Development," *Elementary School Journal,* 58:401–407, April 1958.

Shane, Harold, and McSwain, E. T. *Evaluation and the Elementary Curriculum.* New York: Henry Holt and Company, 1958.

Stendler, Celia B. *Teaching in the Elementary School.* New York: Harcourt, Brace and Company, 1958.

Stratemeyer, Florence, *et al. Developing a Curriculum for Modern Living.* New York: Bureau of Publications, Teachers College, Columbia University, 2nd ed., 1957.

Tyler, Ralph W. *Basic Principles of Curriculum and Instruction.* Chicago: University of Chicago Press, 1950.

Warner, Ruby H. *The Child and His Elementary School.* Englewood Cliffs, N.J.: Prentice-Hall, Inc., 1957.

# 5

The sign post says three miles to town,
But not come on or keep away
Or how a stranger fares; . . .

JOHN V. HICKS

# Organizing for instruction

The ability of educators to teach and children to learn is influenced by the organizational and instructional pattern in the school. Only as the school becomes a laboratory for learning in which the child is challenged to improve living, and to make life outside the school coincide with the values, knowledges, and aims gained from the classroom, will education accomplish its goals.

That pattern of organization would appear to be best which makes the greatest use of personnel and facilities. Although the organization on grade levels is still the most common pattern, it has met with serious objection on psychological grounds; experimentation has shown that the elimination of grade lines helps children achieve their maximum potential. "It is literally true that any plan that can be proposed has been tried, sometime, somewhere, by someone. Grouping for instructional purposes has been viewed typically as an organizational problem."[1]

Among the numerous plans for organization that have been initiated, discarded, modified, and gradually accepted, Shane cites ungraded groups, primary-intermediate groups, grade grouping, heterogeneous grouping, homogeneous grouping, XYZ grouping, vestibule grouping, cooperative group plan for teachers, Winnetka Plan using self-instructional materials, Dalton Plan or "contract plan," multiple-track grouping, platoon grouping, Woodring Plan (modified multiple-track plan), social maturity grouping, organismic age grouping, nongraded primary and intermediate groups, split grades, inter-classroom grouping, intra-classroom grouping, departmental grouping, self-contained classroom, interest grouping, self-selection grouping, extracurricular activity grouping, special group for the gifted, opportunity room for the slow learner or mentally handicapped, self-realization room for the gifted, and ungraded four- and five-year-old kindergarten. He concludes on the basis of his study that "As American elementary education stands on the threshold of the 1960's the matter of grouping children continues to be characterized by: (1) problems of terminology, including overlapping terminology and conflicting interpretations of terminology, (2) insufficient comprehensive research data, and (3) appreciable differences in both practice and opinion."[2]

## *Plans of Organization*

### THE GRADED SCHOOL

"It is the function of the school, among other things, to accept and enroll the child, to classify and assign him to a teacher and group, to take stock of his growth, and to regulate his progress month by month and year by year. In discharging these functions, the school

[1] Willard C. Olson, "Implications of the Dynamics of Instructional Groups," in Nelson B. Henry (ed.), *The Dynamics of Instructional Groups*, Fifty-Ninth Yearbook of the National Society for the Study of Education, Part II (Chicago: University of Chicago Press, 1960), pp. 272, 273.

[2] Harold G. Shane, "Grouping in the Elementary School," *Phi Delta Kappan*, 41:314–318, April 1960.

either profits or suffers from the kind of administrative machinery that exists to govern each child's advancement."[3]

Back in the era of the one-room school, the problem of organization was simple. It was taken for granted that a teacher would teach all children, all subjects, all day. Beginners through eighth-graders studied, recited, sang, played, and worked together. However, as city schools grew into multiple units the problem of organization became acute. Today most elementary schools classify children by grades. The work for a particular grade, a year of progress, and a chronological year in the life of a child are treated as the basis for comparison in the eyes of the school. The teacher is faced with pressures to bring the child up to the grade-level standard in spite of the fact that he knows that individual differences are great and continue to increase as the child progresses. The teacher in the elementary school is generally responsible for one class or group, most commonly composed of one grade level, although there are interesting variations of this plan in many systems.

The six-year elementary school, with the kindergarten struggling to become or remain an integral part of the program, is the basic organizational plan. Variations within this structure depend on the willingness and ability of the community to support multiple units, to enrich facilities, to provide special teachers, to recruit instructional resources, to modernize supervision and administration, or to modify the traditional classroom setup.

The type of classroom in which a single teacher has the major responsibility for the children for the entire day has persisted through innovations in classroom organization. This arrangement is often referred to as the self-contained classroom.

*The Self-Contained Classroom.* In the self-contained classroom the work of a particular class or group is carried on under one teacher. Among the advantages cited by those who see in it a setting in which teacher and children can live and work together in a laboratory atmosphere are the following: it allows the teacher to study children and plan adequately for individual needs and abilities; it permits a flexible daily schedule in which the unexpected, temporary interests of children can be met; it offers an opportunity to

[3] From *The Nongraded Elementary School* by John I. Goodlad and Robert H. Anderson, © 1959, by Harcourt, Brace and Company, Inc., p. 61.

plan and develop a curriculum in which broad problems and basic school subjects and skills can be integrated; it provides a setting in which a teacher can experiment with curriculum design. If the teacher wishes, he can call in available specialists, parents, and resource personnel in the community to enrich the experiences of boys and girls.

An advocate of the self-contained classroom sums up the values by stating, "The self-contained classroom is home base for organizing, evaluating and intellectualizing experiences. It is the place where learners hang their hats if their job can be done there or can be organized and planned there."[4]

The disadvantage of the self-contained classroom frequently cited is that one teacher is not necessarily skilled in art, music, and physical education; nor is he always equally skillful in teaching science, social studies, language arts, and arithmetic.

Ackerlund[5] found that elementary teachers have some definite attitudes about the self-contained classroom. On the basis of his survey he made the following observations: the self-contained classroom provides teachers with opportunities for emphasizing or de-emphasizing certain subjects on the basis of their likes or dislikes; it offers a teacher less opportunity for choice of areas in which to teach; it demands a higher degree of knowledge, particularly in the upper elementary grades. The strongest support for the self-contained classroom appears to be in kindergarten and Grades 1 and 2 with increasing opposition from teachers of Grades 3, 4, 5, and 6.

Ackerlund concludes that the basic philosophy of the self-contained classroom is excellent and should probably be continued. He feels that the advantages of the self-contained classroom — provision for a closer teacher-child rapport, greater flexibility in the daily schedule with improved correlation and integration of subject matter, and avoidance of forcing the child to adjust to more than one teacher — are worthy of preservation. However, he believes it is possible to retain the unity of the self-contained classroom and combine it with team teaching, in which two to five teachers work together with a group of children.

[4] Alice Miel, "The Self-Contained Classroom: An Assessment," *Education Digest*, 23:26, April 1958.
[5] George Ackerlund, "Some Teachers' Views on the Self-Contained Classroom," *Phi Delta Kappan*, 40:283–285, April 1959.

Regardless of one's attitude toward this type of classroom organization, it is evident that there are advantages that should be retained and serious weaknesses to be overcome. A former enthusiastic supporter of the self-contained classroom, after a year of teaching sixth grade under the plan, made this observation:

> Before I started teaching in the self-contained room, I was all for it. I was so sure that the most important consideration was the close teacher-pupil relationship and the opportunity to integrate learnings. I thought, "I can check on reading skills in all the classes. I can help pupils with their speech during the whole day. I can make sure that their writing is legible in all written work." Now that I have to teach everything, including music, art, physical education, I've changed my mind. The youngsters are bored with having to take all their work from me, and I have little time to plan. I'm doing an excellent job in social studies, but a poor one in language arts and arithmetic. I'm looking for a position in a departmentalized program next year. Other teachers in my building feel the same way. I think the self-contained classroom is better for the primary grades where the youngsters need the security of being with one teacher.

*The Departmentalized Plan.* In contrast to the self-contained classroom, in which one teacher directs the learning experiences of the children, in the departmentalized plan several teachers are responsible. Children may be in their homeroom for certain specific areas of instruction such as language arts, social studies, science, and/or arithmetic. Special teachers in charge of music, physical education, and art work with children from several different classrooms while the homeroom teacher may work with only one group.

In some schools the teacher is in charge of only one area — social studies, language arts, science, or arithmetic. He teaches children from several grades in a specific area and is in charge of a homeroom and guidance period for a particular group of children daily.

The main advantages of the departmentalized plan are that the teacher trained in a special field is usually more competent in that specialty than the classroom teacher, and the instructional materials and special room or equipment such as the art room, the science laboratory, the music room, or the gymnasium can be scheduled for the most efficient use by all the children.

The limitations of the plan are the necessity of adhering to a strict schedule, the need for children to adjust to several teachers instead of one, the fear that special teachers are interested in the subject and not the child, and the possibility that instruction cannot always be effectively integrated. If the homeroom teacher is willing to cooperate and accept the contributions of the special teacher, and if the latter can recognize the homeroom teacher as a competent, qualified, worth-while individual, these limitations may be overcome.

*The Platoon System.* The platoon organization is actually a modification and extension of the departmentalized organization. Large cities find it useful, particularly if the school-plant facilities are limited. The platoon assumes separate subjects as the foundation of the elementary school curriculum.

The unique feature is the division of the school into platoons or groups of pupils and the curriculum into two distinct parts — the academic and the special subjects. Each homeroom teacher is responsible for two platoons, and sometimes three. The pupils in a single grade are divided into two, four, or six platoons depending on the enrollment. The academic subjects are taught in the homeroom during half of the day, and the special subjects are taught by special teachers the other half of the time. The groups rotate, one platoon remaining in the homeroom studying academic subjects while the other platoon is taking special subjects. For the other half of the day the platoons reverse. The platoon system may be used with all grades beyond kindergarten but is less successful in the primary grades.

The chief advantages cited by proponents of the platoon plan are that every classroom is used every period of the day, instruction is in terms of discrete subjects in a fixed schedule, classrooms are equipped for the particular subject to be taught, and teachers are specialists in the subjects they teach. Since the platoons make possible full use of the facilities of the school the entire time, the services of specialists are available without an increase in the teaching staff.

The daily schedule of a school with nine platoons appears below. Each homeroom teacher is responsible for three platoons and works with each for three periods daily. While one platoon is with the homeroom teacher, the others are with one of four different teachers. Time is available during the day for the children to participate in special interests such as orchestra, art, library, and group councils.

Limitations of this plan include the difficulty of the staff in understanding the problems and needs of the individual child, and the difficulty of integrating the learning experiences.

PLATOON ORGANIZATION,
DENVER PUBLIC SCHOOLS, 1954–1955

| | Mrs. M. | Miss W. | Miss S. | Mrs. S. Art, Soc. St., Lang. | Mrs. B. Art, Soc. St., Lang. | Miss J. Art, Soc. St., Lang. | Mrs. D. Library | Mrs. W. Music | Mr. & Mrs. S. Phys. Ed. |
|---|---|---|---|---|---|---|---|---|---|
| 9:00– 9:30 | 1 | 4 | 9 | 2 | 6 | 8 | 3 | 7 | 5 |
| 9:30–10:00 | 1 | 4 | 9 | 2 | 6 | 8 | 5 | 3 | 7 |
| 10:00–10:30 | 1 | 4 | 9 | 2 | 6 | 8 | 7 | 5 | 3 |
| 10:30–11:00 | 2 | 5 | 7 | 3 | 4 | 9 | 1 | 8 | 6 |
| 11:00–11:30 | 2 | 5 | 7 | 3 | 4 | 9 | 6 | 1 | 8 |
| 11:30–12:00 | 2 | 5 | 7 | 3 | 4 | 9 | 8 | 6 | 1 |
| 1:15– 1:50 | 3 | 6 | 8 | 1 | 5 | 7 | 2 | 9 | 4 |
| 1:50– 2:25 | 3 | 6 | 8 | 1 | 5 | 7 | 4 | 2 | 9 |
| 2:25– 3:00 | 3 | 6 | 8 | 1 | 5 | 7 | 9 | 4 | 2 |
| 3:00– 3:15 | 1 | 4 | 9 | 2 | 6 | 8 | 3 | 7 | 5 |

*Platoons 1 and 2 are Grade 3; 3 and 4 are Grade 4; 5, 6, and 7 are Grade 5; 8 and 9 are Grade 6. Each platoon is with the same teacher for the first and last period each day. The first six teachers work three platoons daily; the last three with all nine platoons daily.*

Source: Herbert J. Klausmeier, *et al.*, *Teaching in the Elementary School* (New York: Harper & Brothers, 1956), p. 125.

*Ability Grouping.* Ability grouping is not new. It is one way to provide for individual differences. In this plan the children are divided according to ability and the curriculum is arranged on varying levels of difficulty. Among the factors that are considered in the groupings are intelligence, social and emotional maturity, and similarity of interests. Intelligence and personality tests play an important part in the grouping process. In addition, teacher observation and staff planning help determine the particular group in which the child is placed.

There are arguments on both sides of the case for ability grouping. The belief that it is undemocratic to separate children on the basis of ability has for a number of years been strong enough to largely discourage this type of organization. However, the present tendency is to accept responsibility for helping each child develop his maximum potential and ability grouping affords one way to do it. If it is democratic to provide for the slow learner and the handicapped child, it is also democratic to provide opportunity for the gifted and accelerated child.

## The Nongraded School

*The Primary School Plan.* A type of organization that appears to have merit in meeting the needs of individual children is that of the ungraded primary block. In defining an ungraded primary school Anderson states, "An *ungraded primary school,* or simply *primary school* as it is often called, is an arrangement within an elementary school whereby children below the fourth grade level are grouped together in classes which have no grade designation."[6] Kelly, a pioneer in the movement in Milwaukee, defines it as "a place whereby children of similar chronological age and social and emotional maturity are kept together when administratively possible."[7]

Anderson points out that some school systems prefer the term "primary school" without the "ungraded" because of the existence of "ungraded classes" in connection with the handicapped, opportunity rooms, or other centers dealing with atypical children. However, except for the problem such a connotation might create in public relations, he sees "no reason to shun the word ungraded because . . . the philosophy which operates in such special classrooms is essentially the same wonderful philosophy which prompts us to be interested in

[6] Robert H. Anderson, "The Ungraded Primary School as a Contribution to Improved School Practices," in Vincent J. Glennon (ed.), *Frontiers of Elementary Education,* II (Syracuse: Syracuse University Press, 1955), p. 29.

[7] Florence C. Kelly, "Can Promotion Practices Give Security to Children?" *The Primary School: Stop! Look! Evaluate!* Bulletin No. 61, Association for Childhood Education International (Washington, D.C.: The Association, 1952), p. 31.

the elimination of grade labels and grade-level thinking in all other classrooms."[8]

Children from kindergarten through the primary school (the third grade) are grouped on the basis of physical and emotional maturity and readiness for learning. The groups progress in their learning at rates related to their maturity levels, capacities, and readiness. The child who can move ahead at a faster pace does so, while the child who needs four or more years to complete the primary school program can take them without the feeling that he has failed. The grouping is flexible and the child may work in several different groups during a given period. Since groups are not graded, no status is lost if he shifts to another group. The teacher may or may not stay with the group throughout the primary block.

A child with ability may complete the three years' work in two and move into the intermediate school. The child who is transferred into the slow-learning group feels no chagrin because promotions are not stressed. Each teacher becomes well acquainted with children in her group. Transfer ahead or back to a slower group is made in consultation with parents and in terms of the child's individual design of growth and learning. The flexible organization of the school, the study of children, careful attention to records, and conferences among members of staff and parents are some of the distinguishing characteristics of the plan. The elimination of administrative labels — "first grade," "second grade," "third grade" — removes the threat of failure at the end of each school year. The teacher has no grade-level expectations against which to pace himself; his only obligation lies in helping children move along as fast as they are capable of moving. At the end of the school year when the child takes home his final progress report, no mention is made of a grade assignment for the following year. "The parent is simply advised that the child will continue in primary and pick up in September where he left off at this point in June."[9]

The primary or nongraded school comes to grips with individual differences on the basis of each child's design for development and academic attainment. When it is not necessary to preserve the conventions of the lock-step graded school, a greater variety of opportunities and possibilities for grouping and achieving is offered.

[8] Anderson, *op. cit.,* p. 29.

[9] Robert H. Anderson, "Ungraded Primary Classes," *Education Digest,* 21:50, November 1955.

In this type of organization evaluation as a continuous process is a reality. The particular day of decision, to promote or not to promote, poses a problem only at the end of the primary school. Children who do not meet the requirements are kept at any one level for an additional year. The membership remains fairly constant. However, as individual children master the levels assigned they are shifted to another classroom if the group no longer provides the best possible learning situation for them.

Although reading has been the most common basis for the ungraded primary grouping, the other curriculum areas — the other language arts, the social studies, science, creative arts, and physical education — should also be concerned with providing for continuity in learning experiences.

Among writers expressing enthusiasm for and citing examples of nongraded primary groupings are Anderson,[10] Kelly,[11] and Polkinghorne.[12] Goodlad and Anderson conclude that the nongraded school motivates improved instruction and improves mental health of children. They cite three organizational advantages of the nongraded school over the traditional graded school:

> First, the nongraded school provides a single, unbroken learning continuum through which pupils progress. No longer are the school years divided into several parts of equal length, each with its own content and own requirements to be met. There are no predetermined barriers.
>
> Second, the nongraded school encourages continuous, individual pupil progress. Bright children do not mark time at grade barriers, waiting for their slower classmates to catch up. Slow children do not struggle in frustrated desperation to reach barriers that lie beyond their capabilities. Such artificial but nonetheless consequential hurdles have been removed.
>
> Third, the nongraded school encourages flexibility in pupil grouping. Billy is placed in a group not out of respect for artificial grade standards but out of respect for Billy. He is placed in the setting thought to be best suited to his abilities, attainments, and

[10] Robert H. Anderson, "Ungraded Primary Classes: An Administrative Contribution to Mental Health," *Understanding Children*, 24:66–72, June 1955; and same article, *Education Digest*, 21:47–50, November 1955.
[11] Florence C. Kelly, "Ungraded Primary School," *Educational Leadership*, 18:79–81, November 1960.
[12] A. R. Polkinghorne, "Parents and Teachers Appraise Primary Grade Groups," *Elementary School Journal*, 51:271–78, January 1951.

general maturity. He is moved when it becomes apparent that another setting would be even better suited to Billy's needs and abilities.[13]

*Examples of the Nongraded School.* One of the programs in the ungraded primary systems is that in the Linda School District, Marysville, California.[14] In this plan the work of the primary grades is divided into eight levels, based on the reading books of each grade. The first year is composed of Levels 1, 2, 3, and 4; the second grade is replaced by Levels 5 and 6 and the third grade by Levels 7 and 8. Plans call for other curriculum areas to correspond sequentially to the prescribed levels. Cursive writing follows manuscript writing at Level 6. In arithmetic, children can add and subtract figures to the total of ten by Level 6, and in Levels 7 and 8 they learn the higher combinations in addition and subtraction, and multiplication by 2's and 3's. The social studies and other areas of the curriculum harmonize with the levels plan.

Another experiment in a "levels" plan in University City, Missouri, is designed to define more rigorously the major learning skills to be mastered in the period normally encompassed by Grades 1 through 3. Under the new program each child will move at his own pace. A few rapid learners will be assigned to the fourth grade after two instead of the customary three years if they are sufficiently mature, physically and emotionally. The fast learners will not "skip" any work. The slow learners who take four years will not "repeat" any of the work.

*The Dual-Progress Plan.* In the dual-progress plan designed by Stoddard which is replacing the grade-level program all pupils progress along the sequence of understandings and skills at their own rate. There are no grade-level restrictions or demands. Gifted students may learn in the course of a single year what the slow learner takes two or more years to master. Pupils are assigned to classes with other students of the same general ability and level of achievement without regard to grade placement.

[13] Goodlad and Anderson, *op. cit.,* p. 212.
[14] Annual report published by Linda School District in 1956. In 1958–1959 an intermediate and senior high school ungraded block was added. The fourth grade is designated as Level 9 and the fifth through eighth grades form the next two ungraded blocks.

Two tracks in the curriculum are offered. In the nongraded track in mathematics, science, arts and crafts, and music the pupil receives forty minutes daily of instruction in mathematics and science and forty minutes on alternate days in music and crafts. In the language arts, social studies, and physical education he follows the usual grade structure. All the teachers are specialists in teaching their particular subjects.[15]

"Without any prearranged signal, schools scattered across the nation are seriously examining and changing, not just valves and buttons but basic machinery."[16] This they are doing in an effort to break the lock step of the graded school.

*Multigraded Grouping.* Any consideration of the attempt to achieve an improved method of organizing and staffing a nongraded structure is incomplete without a reference to the multigraded pattern. Behind this plan is the belief that groups should have a wide range of ages, cutting across several grade lines, so several levels of maturity are represented as they are in real-life situations in which groups are established.[17]

This plan is in operation in the Walteria School, Torrence, California.[18] Four classes in the Walteria School were organized experimentally as primary multigrade classes and three classes as intermediate multigrade classes. Each contained approximately thirty-three children — eleven from each of the three grade levels. The major objective was to make a scientific study of the amount of learning that took place in such areas as reading, language, arithmetic, personal and social adjustment, behavior, and attitudes toward school compared with that of pupils in the regular classes from first through sixth grades. Parent, teacher, and principal attitudes were

[15] Glen Heathers and Morris Pincus, "The Dual Progress Plan in the Elementary School," *Education Digest*, 25:46, April 1960.

[16] John I. Goodlad, "Pattern of Change," *Elementary School Journal*, 59:17, October 1958.

[17] Howard Lane and Mary Beauchamp, *Human Relations in Teaching* (Englewood Cliffs, N.J.: Prentice-Hall, Inc., 1955), pp. 283–303.

[18] J. H. Hull, Superintendent, in collaboration with Warren Hamilton, "The Little Red School House Has Something." Mimeographed. Warren Hamilton and Walter Rehwoldt, "By Their Differences They Learn," *The National Elementary Principal*, 37:29, December 1957. Walter Rehwoldt and Warren Hamilton, "An Analysis of Some Effects of Interage and Intergrade Grouping in an Elementary School," mimeographed final chapter of a doctoral dissertation at the University of Southern California. Available from authors.

also studied. With but two exceptions in a total of forty-eight statistical comparisons the multigrade pupils showed greater gains in personal and social adjustment, social maturity, and behavior characteristics; their attitude toward their school work, their school, their peers, was superior to that of the regular grade pupils; they achieved more academically. Parents have requested that the school add an eight and ninth class, thus showing their support of the plan. Teachers, too, are enthusiastic about it.

*Team Teaching.* Team teaching is often used in the nongraded school. This approach "capitalizes on the possibilities for improved teaching and learning that are created when more children and more teachers of varied interests and competencies take part in the planning."[19]

An example of a pilot experiment in team teaching in Flint, Michigan, is cited by Goodlad.[20] Three teachers working as a team at the same grade level in an elementary school planned a curriculum for ninety-nine pupils. Teacher A and Teacher C were experienced teachers, and Teacher B was a liberal arts graduate who had not taught but wanted to qualify for teaching.

The pupils were placed in three adjacent classrooms on the same side of the corridor with connecting doors. The children in the three rooms were regarded as a unit, as if they were in a self-contained classroom. This homeroom type of arrangement was kept throughout the year, but groupings were flexible and changed from day to day and during the day as the teachers worked out the program. At the beginning of the year the children were divided between Teacher A and Teacher C, leaving Teacher B free to carry out activities planned by the trio in regular sessions.

The arrangement permitted the grouping for reading into five groups distributed among the three teachers. The range in reading achievement was narrower than is ordinarily the case because the total spread was divided into five instead of three groups. In spite of the fact that groups were larger they were more homogeneous. With fewer groups to work with the teachers could use their abili-

[19] John I. Goodlad, "News and Comment," *Elementary School Journal,* 59:17, October 1958.
[20] *Ibid.,* p. 11.

ties and time more effectively. Their skills in the arts, social studies, and other fields could be utilized more constructively. More time was available for planning, studying children, and guiding subgroups. In certain activities the ninety-nine could work as a group. At other times a teacher would work with about a third of the pupils while the other sixty-six worked in small groups or individually. Sometimes one of the teachers had a free period while the other two worked with the children. Sometimes all three moved from one small group to another, guiding and helping in projects and study. This plan has the advantages of the self-contained classroom with the added advantage of enrichment afforded by the utilization of trio talent.

In Englewood, Florida, a teaching team consisted of a woman with a third-fourth-grade combination and a man with a fourth-fifth-grade combination. The typical day for this team began with a planning period of fifteen to twenty minutes in which each group discussed with the teacher the plans for the day including individual and group activity. For the next hour and a half each teacher worked with from two to four reading groups composed of children of similar reading achievement levels from both rooms regardless of their grade placement.

Morning juice was followed by a combined physical education period. This period was planned together and one teacher had the responsibility for the whole group while the other took a break, collected materials, evaluated the work of the children, etc. Following the physical education period the sixty-five children in the combined groups remained together for music, art, or a story period. The teacher who had had charge of the physical education now had a break while the other teacher took full responsibility. Between the end of the story time and lunch each teacher worked with two arithmetic groups organized on the basis of achievement.

After the lunch period, the program varied. There might be a project in which the two classes combined. Special interests and competencies of the teachers often determined the class leadership. In such activities as a major unit on electricity the groups worked together with the man assuming the major responsibility for planning, gathering materials, and teaching. The woman member of the team functioned as an aide, helping individuals and small groups.

Later, during a unit on space the teachers reversed their roles.[21] Social studies, science, music, and art were integrated although they were sometimes taught as separate subjects.

"These descriptions are not as important as the fact that the staff has shown that professionally trained teachers, given freedom to develop practices, rise to the occasion and modify traditional practices in line with their educational beliefs."[22]

The basic advantage of team teaching is that it pools teacher resources so that several groups of children may be combined and regrouped for specific purposes. Replanning of space, with removal of partitions and doors, may facilitate such regrouping.

There is no way of grouping which of itself will guarantee success. However, an understanding of the bases for grouping is important. In the graded schools attempts are made to modify rigid grade lines by ability grouping according to achievement in reading, interest grouping, age grouping, social grouping, or random selection.

Exponents of the nongraded organization endorse a combination of grouping procedures accompanied by various evaluative devices. They are convinced that *planned* flexibility in grouping is a key to maximum pupil growth. They recommend that

1. Each nongraded classroom be organized around achievement groups, interest groups, and work-study skills simultaneously; planned heterogeneity in some areas such as social studies is as important as planned homogeneity in others such as reading and arithmetic skills.
2. Formal and informal evaluative techniques be used so that each child's progress can be readily seen. The use of visual aids such as charts and graphs facilitates evaluation.
3. Grouping which cuts across class lines be considered on the basis of whether certain desired learnings can be effected in this way rather than according to the teacher's whim. Team teaching, yes — but not indiscriminately.[23]

In the nongraded arrangement grade-to-grade and class-to-class barriers become insignificant until they finally disappear in the wake of a creative approach to the age-old problem of providing for individual differences in the classroom.

[21] John M. Bahner, "Grouping Within a School," *Childhood Education,* 36:354–357, April 1960.
[22] *Ibid.,* p. 356.
[23] Adapted from Goodlad and Anderson, *op. cit.,* pp. 99, 100.

## Utilizing Resources of the
## School and Community

A proposed plan for administrative organization at the elementary school level designed by Stoddard[24] should be cited before we leave the subject of organizational schemes. This plan suggests ways of organizing 600 pupils so that every resource of the school is fully and effectively utilized.

For part of the schoolday half of the children are assigned to regular teachers in smaller than normal classes. These teachers are responsible for teaching the usual subject matter in the usual manner. To begin with, until more is known about what kind of teaching best fits what kind of learning experiences, such subjects as English, reading, writing, arithmetic, social studies, and the drill and technique sides of art and music might be assigned to the regular teacher. Clerical or other assistance should be provided to relieve him of non-teaching duties, freeing him to concentrate on the essential phases of teaching.

The other half of the children are having learning experiences (1) in a "resource room," utilizing television programs and other instructional aids, (2) in the auditorium, library, music room, or theater, or (3) on the playground or in the indoor playroom or gymnasium.

The two schedules are reversed after lunch so the same teachers carry on the same activities the second half of the day as they did in the morning.

Such a plan, according to Stoddard, requires the following personnel: 12 regular class teachers; 3 special teachers; 4 aides: resource room, auditorium, playground, and general; 1 curriculum coordinator; and possibly ½ music teacher and ½ secretary.

The possible advantages of the plan include:

1. The improvement of instruction in the regular subject areas because of the smaller classes during an uninterrupted three-hour period.
2. The teacher's ability to become a specialist in certain phases of the curriculum.

[24] Alexander J. Stoddard, *Schools for Tomorrow: An Educator's Blueprint* (New York: Fund for the Advancement of Education, 1957), pp. 44–48. (Adapted.)

3. The reduction of the number of subjects required of the regular teacher.
4. The use of specialists in such areas as art, music, physical education, library, foreign languages, and academic subjects where specialists are needed.
5. The need for fewer trained teachers since many of the chores could be carried on by assistants, releasing funds for the employment of teacher aides, curriculum coordinators, and secretarial help through a task-force approach to education.
6. The reduction of the number of classrooms needed, making possible without additional cost the construction of resource rooms and provision of television facilities.
7. The possibility of more effective education through utilization of the special abilities of the teachers on the staff.

"Possibly it will be found that education is like many other types of services in that the task force of specialists may prove to be more effective than the general practitioner who attempts to carry on all the processes involved in a self-contained basis."[25]

In initiating any new plan success is dependent upon a number of considerations. A few suggestions will be helpful to a school on the brink of considering a change.

*Preparing the Way.* Before acting on a plan prepare the way. Develop understanding and cohesiveness among the staff, the administration, and the community. Spend some months or even a year or two in studying the proposed plan.

*Taking a Step at a Time.* People are not anxious to try something they are not familiar with. To help teachers shed old ideas and routines in teaching, for example, a modified approach to nongrading can be used, such as having the teachers move along with the pupils into the next grade, before a primary unit is established.

*Planning for Firsthand Observation.* A delegated committee made up of staff, administration, and lay members should have an opportunity to observe a system in which the plan under consideration is meeting with success. Seeing is often a prerequisite to believing. Some enthusiastic supporters are important if the plan is to succeed.

*Making Some Concrete Changes.* When the plan for the primary and intermediate units is adopted, be sure to change the door signs.

[25] *Ibid.*, p. 48.

In place of "Miss Jones, Grade Three," and "Miss Sullivan, Grade Four," new signs reading "Miss Jones, Primary" and "Miss Sullivan, Intermediate" should be substituted.

*Keeping Methods with Which Teachers Have Been Successful.* If teaching methods are sound, if teachers are secure with materials which are effective, do not change them merely for the sake of change. Nongrading is not an instructional device; it is an organizational plan.

*Continuing the Plan of Continuous Evaluation and Testing.* The nongraded plan calls for careful, continuous evaluation and testing as does every good plan of organization.

*Keeping an Open Mind.* Do not allow the plan to crystallize at the level of techniques or organization. Any program needs a willingness to continue to experiment, to modify, to see what is required in order to move ahead to the next step of improving education. One of the best opportunities to use the democratic process comes when a staff and a community plan a program cooperatively and evaluate the results continuously.

## The Challenge of School Organization

An examination of various types of organization makes it obvious that no one scheme offers a panacea. In choosing its organization pattern the school community must not lose sight of its basic challenge:

1. To develop procedures whereby the creative abilities of teachers, parents, and pupils are released in the cooperative planning of the curriculum.
2. To develop procedures whereby the school becomes an integral part of the community it serves.
3. To develop a school organization in which individuality and achievement are always respected and fostered.
4. To develop staff cohesiveness to the point where teamwork is the hallmark of the school.
5. To experiment with a variety of procedures for dealing with individuals and for using the teaching resources more effectively.
6. To give attention to the curriculum as a whole; to try to achieve optimum teaching in all phases of the program.
7. To make a concentrated effort to improve classroom instruction

by creating a physical setting rich in resources for motivating learning experiences.

8. To prepare the pupils for each successive level in the educational ladder through a program of good relationships among personnel in various educational units, through visits in the units to which they will be promoted, and through a guidance program that acquaints them with the procedures at the next step in the program.

## Characteristics of Effective Class Organization

In evaluating the effectiveness of his class organization the teacher should be guided by standards of flexibility, independence, and control. "*Flexibility* permits change as conditions in the classroom and purposes of instruction demand. *Independence* provides for individual initiative and action on the part of the teacher and pupil. *Control* is essential for the smooth and orderly functioning of any plan for grouping."[26]

Flexibility is essential so that the teacher can adjust the grouping to emerging needs and unforeseen situations. It is desirable to use more than one basis for grouping. Special-interest groups, specific instructional groups, ability groups, reading groups, and friendship groups can all be used. Indeed, if the teacher is concerned with providing for individual differences he will be ever alert to improve grouping procedures.

Independence, too, is essential if children are to gain from individualized instruction. Children should learn early in their school experience to be self-reliant, to use self-teaching devices and evaluation techniques. They must be taught research techniques that will enable them to explore and solve problems independently. Some of these techniques will be taught to the class as a whole; others to individuals or small groups as the need arises.

Control is another essential feature of effective classroom organization. The social climate created by the teacher in his relationships with children, parents, and staff influences the control he exerts. The quality of these relationships is dependent upon the genuine

[26] J. Wayne Wrightstone, "What Research Says About Class Organization for Instruction," in Marvin D. Alcorn and James M. Linley (eds.), *Issues in Curriculum Development: A Book of Readings* (Yonkers-on-Hudson, N.Y.: World Book Company, 1959), p. 257.

interest the teacher has in the children, the security he feels in the job, and his teaching ability. The personality, personal traits, attitudes, and interests of the teacher influence the emotional and social climate of the class. Effective human relationships are a product of a well-ordered classroom, which in turn is a product of a well-organized school.

## *Relationships in Curriculum Organization*

Many of the problems of organizing the school and the class for instruction must be handled by the administration; others are the specific responsibility of the staff; still others fall in the province of the teachers and pupils in a classroom setting. In the design for curriculum that follows, the teacher has an opportunity to see the relationships among the various elements involved in the smooth functioning of the school organization, and so to carry out his responsibility effectively. How he formulates objectives, plans experiences, and develops and evaluates activities as children progress toward defined goals depends upon his convictions about child growth and learning, the role of the school in society, the role of the teacher, and the way the curriculum should facilitate optimal learning for each child.

### DESIGN FOR CURRICULUM

| *Convictions about* | *Objectives* | *The school organization must plan effectively for:* |
|---|---|---|
| How children grow and develop | Must be significant | A flexible daily schedule |
| Why children behave as they do | Determine content | Material and personal resources |
| How children learn effectively | Assure sequence | Grouping and promotion procedures |
| The role of the school | Maintain balance | Continuous evaluation |
| The role of the teacher in teaching children | Define scope | Self-contained, departmental, platoon, level, nongraded, or cycle patterns of instruction |
| | Provide continuity | |
| | Achieve integration | |

*Types of Curriculum*

Subject-matter    Broad-fields    The core    Activity or experience

## Planning the Daily Program

Miss Geller is about to begin what she hopes will be a career in teaching. She has given careful consideration to the tasks she will face. She is not alarmed by the problem; she is challenged by the opportunities. There are, however, a few questions which keep recurring and which she has tried to push back to the far recesses of her mind. In a sense, they are not serious, but they keep coming back to trouble her. She is well prepared, she believes, to teach in a primary grade. She prefers working with young children. She enjoyed student teaching and now she has a contract to teach in a kindergarten in a nearby city. She is not sure just how to plan for the first day — or for the succeeding days. When she did her practice teaching she did not plan to teach in kindergarten. Now she needs help in deciding what activities to plan, when to plan them, and how to be sure she has a balanced daily program.

Miss Miller, too, has a problem. She will be assigned to a first grade for her first teaching experience. When she did her practice teaching in the first grade the children were well along in the year and she is not sure how to begin the activities in September. Should she plan for a period similar to a kindergarten work period? When should she begin to teach reading? What hour of the day should she schedule reading? Since the curriculum design is based on a broad-fields approach should she have a certain time for reading or just work it into the language arts period?

Mrs. Bland also has a problem. She has been teaching sixth grade for a number of years, but her school is moving from a separate-subjects curriculum into a broad-fields approach. She has been teaching reading, writing, language, and spelling as separate subjects with a specified time for each. Now she wonders what she can do to assure the children's learning the essentials in spelling, writing, grammar, and reading skills. She is afraid that with the freedom of a broad-fields curriculum the temptation to concentrate primarily on literature will be too great to resist. There it is again — the problem of planning.

Mrs. Aldem is back teaching after fifteen years away from the classroom. She took a concentrated course to prepare her to teach again, but she can't understand the terminology the teachers are using. "They don't speak my language," she says. "I'm not sure I know how to plan the daily schedule using this 'function-of-living' approach. I studied about it in the courses I took, but it is still vague in my mind. If I hadn't been so timid I would have admitted I didn't understand the underlying assumptions. I am eager to try it the classroom, but I feel the need for help in making specific plans."

These teachers have one thing in common. They know they need help in making important decisions. The quality of the learning experiences they provide for children will be determined in part by the measure of security they feel about the decisions they make. These should be based on a knowledge of a curriculum that is academically sound, socially significant, individually stimulating, and universally applicable.

The daily schedule will reflect the type of curriculum design the school follows: subject centered, society centered, or child centered. It is important, however, for the teacher to realize that although the initial focus is on one of the three — the subject, the society, or the child — they are not mutually exclusive. A good teacher will find ways of bringing the three elements together. Under some types of curriculum design integration is more readily achieved. The task of the teacher is to select and develop those learning experiences which help the pupil to communicate effectively, to think for himself, to draw his own conclusions, to develop his creative abilities, to interpret his social and physical environment, and to assume responsibility as a contributing member of society.

*The Daily Schedule in the Kindergarten.* Although there are wide variations in individual programs, the following time allotments may serve as a tentative basis for a kindergarten program. As she becomes acquainted with her children, the physical plant, and curriculum design the teacher may modify or reconstruct the initial program.

| | |
|---|---|
| 60 minutes | Work period |
| | Discussion of work |
| | Further plans |
| | Cleanup |

60 minutes   Outdoor play
             Rest
             Midmorning juice or milk
60 minutes   Creative experiences — singing, rhythms, rhythm
             band, storytelling, dramatizations, excursions,
             science experiences

How this time allotment is translated into a kindergarten daily program based on the broad-fields curriculum is shown below:

9:00–10:00   Social living
             Arrival; morning inspection as each child arrives
             Roll call
             Work period — including blocks, doll corner,
             workbenches, puzzles, apparatus, easel painting,
             clay modeling, toys, looking at books, manipula-
             tion
9:30–10:00   Swimming: boys Tuesday, girls Thursday
10:00–10:40  Routines
             Bathroom, 10 minutes
             Juice, 10 minutes
             Resting on rugs, 20 minutes
10:40–11:10  Outdoor play
                or
             Excursions (science)
                or
             Indoor Games
                or
             Rhythms
11:10–11:45  Creative experiences
             Monday — singing
             Tuesday — rhythms and singing games
             Wednesday — rhythm band
             Thursday — dramatization
             Friday — library or listening to records
11:45–12:00  Cleanup time
             Dismissal

*The Separate-Subject Curriculum.* An example of a fourth-grade schedule under the separate-subjects curriculum follows:

9:00– 9:05   Opening exercises
9:05–10:00   Reading
10:00–10:15  Recess
10:15–10:45  Spelling

10:45–11:15  History
11:15–11:45  Geography
11:45–12:15  Music, gym, auditorium[27]
12:15– 1:00  Lunch
 1:00– 1:45  Arithmetic
 1:45– 2:15  Science first semester, health second semester
 2:15– 3:00  English and writing
 3:00        Dismissal

*The Broad-Fields Curriculum.*  In the following schedule for the second grade the curriculum is organized around the broad fields:

 9:00– 9:30  Health inspection, class routines, planning
 9:30–10:40  Social studies, science, health and safety
10:40–11:40  Reading groups and related activities
11:40–11:45  Dismissal
11:45–12:45  Noon intermission
12:45–12:50  Rest
12:50– 2:25  Language arts, reading, related activities, spelling, writing
 2:25– 2:45  Supervised play
 2:45– 3:05  Arithmetic
 3:05– 3:25  Creative arts
 3:25– 3:30  Dismissal

*The Core Curriculum.*  This schedule for a first grade is based on the core program:

 8:45– 9:00  Arrival of children, hanging up wraps, collecting milk money, caring for plants or pets, checking on plans for work period
 9:00–10:15  Work period relating to the current problems group is working on (A variety of activities may be going on. The time allotted for individual, small group, and entire class work varies with the problem and the interest of the children. Activities may be directly concerned with the major center of interest or with an individual interest or skill.)
10:15–11:00  Lunch, rest, outdoor play if weather permits; rhythms and games if weather is inclement
11:00–11:45  Basic skills — reading, writing, numbers, speech
11:45–12:45  Lunch
12:45– 1:45  Work period (This may be an extension of activities

[27] Art is correlated with other subjects. Music is on Wednesday and Friday, gym on Monday and Thursday, auditorium on Tuesday.

carried on in the morning or it may be related to a second area of concern. Frequently this period is used for an excursion.)

1:45– 2:00 Outdoor play or game, depending on the needs of the children

2:00– 3:00 Creative experiences — singing, using musical instruments, listening to phonograph records, painting, clay modeling, dramatization, puppet plays

3:00– 3:15 Evaluation; planning for tomorrow

In the fourth grade the integrated nature of the core program is reflected in this daily schedule:

8:45–10:15 Work period, devoted to the major problem area (The area is defined by the staff and the particular problem is decided on by the teacher and children. During this period the children engage in such activities as planning, reading to find out, writing reports, working on creative projects, or experimenting in science. Children work in groups or as individuals. The content is taken from the persistent problems of living.)

10:15–10:45 Organized instruction in a skill area (This period is used to develop both group and individual skills. The teacher determines which skills children need work on and the period is flexible in order to meet the needs of specific children.)

10:45–11:00 Recess (On Monday and Thursday this period is extended from 10:30 to 11:00 to provide time for rhythms or movement.)

11:00–12:00 Science (This period includes time for planning, carrying out an experiment, reference reading, making reports, oral or written, and evaluation.)

12:00– 1:00 Lunch

1:00– 1:45 Open period in which children work on their interests, either in their own classroom or with another teacher; special help provided for those who need it

1:45– 2:45 Discussion; working on reports (This period is also used for individual reading and may be interchanged with the work period in the morning.)

2:45– 3:25 Special problems (This period is concerned with short-term interests of the group, such as special plans for an auditorium program, some special local problem, or an interview with a consultant or visitor.)

Evaluation of the day's activities; plans for the next day

*Time Allotments in Terms of Subject Areas.* It is interesting to note average percentages of time devoted daily to particular subject areas. The following table indicates the proportionate emphasis given to various areas of study from kindergarten through the sixth grade in one community.[28]

| Per Cent of Time | Subject Areas | Grades K, 1, 2, and 3 |
| --- | --- | --- |
| 50 | Language arts | Reading, language, spelling, writing |
| 10 | Fine and industrial arts | Music, rhythms, arts, crafts |
| 10 | Mathematics | Mathematics |
| 10 | Health | Physical education, nutrition, health services, recreation |
| 20 | Social-content area | History, geography, science, citizenship |
| | | *Grades 4, 5, and 6* |
| 35 | Language arts | Reading, literature, oral and written expression, spelling, and writing |
| 10 | Fine and industrial arts | Music, dramatics, arts and crafts |
| 20 | Mathematics | Mathematics |
| 10 | Science | Natural, physical, general science |
| 10 | Social Studies | History, geography, character education |
| 15 | Health | Physical education, nutrition, health education, recreation |

[28] *Program of Studies for the Elementary Schools*, Evansville Public Schools, Evansville, Ind., 1953, pp. 4, 5. The time allotment is computed in percentages instead of minutes because the length of the school day varies in different schools.

## WHAT A TYPICAL DAY LOOKS LIKE

Daily schedules are empty shells until they are filled with the children for whom they are planned. Let us see what a day in the fourth grade is like.

Thirty-two of the thirty-five fourth-graders in Miss Englewood's class came in at nine o'clock, went to their tables, and were ready for roll call. Miss Englewood had appointed captains for each table to check attendance. When she got the attention of the group she said, "I think we'd better plan the work for today. Those of you who are in Myra's group may want to go on with your research on industry in our community; those in Eddie's group are planning to work on the frieze showing the location of the original civic and cultural institutions in our city; those in Jim's group were planning to write original stories about the early settlers in the community. John, what was your group planning? That's right, I had forgotten that you wanted to work with the others on the map which will help explain the frieze Eddie's group is working on. Remember, you have until 10:15 to work. If you need to get your groups together to discuss your plans, this will be a good time to get started. I will come around and see if you need any help."

The dispatch with which the groups organized bore evidence of the fact that there had been a great deal of experience in planning. The children were able to carry on and develop plans with much less overt guidance than some groups would need. Among the activities observed during this work period were: planning, reading to find information related to the problem of living in our community, writing reports, working on the frieze, writing original stories, and working on individual large maps which were to be used in connection with an explanation of the frieze. Three boys appeared to be in no group and were at the arithmetic center working with some of the number games. The teacher went from group to group, giving advice as needed and guiding the groups in the solution of problems they were unable to handle alone.

At 10:15 the children formed four new groups for arithmetic. They were divided according to ability in arithmetic skills. The advanced group was working on more difficult skills, while the slow groups had time to work with the arithmetic games at the arithmetic center, or with simple addition and subtraction combinations. The three boys who had been at the arithmetic center now went to the library center and looked at books. This period, too, was character- ized by flexibility. The teacher went to each group in turn to see that they understood what they were to do, then let them work on their own. The slower group seemed to demand and get the most attention.

At 10:45 the children had recess. They got their wraps on and went outdoors without the teacher. Outside they divided into groups — this time according to sex. The boys played ball and the girls played hopscotch and jumped rope.

At 11:00 the children came in, and it was obvious from their en- thusiasm that they looked forward to science. They had brought in bulbs to study. The teacher wrote a problem on the chalkboard that a child suggested: "How can these bulbs grow without soil?" There were several "guesses." Mary said, "The food is probably stored in the bulb." The teacher asked if there was any way of prov- ing that Mary was right. The children said there were several ways of finding out. "You could look it up in a book." "You could cut the bulb in half and see if what the books says is right." "If you didn't want the bulb cut up, you could experiment with an onion."

"How would you know," asked Miss Englewood, "if what you see inside is food?" "We could cut one onion that has sprouted and one that hasn't started to grow yet. Then we could — er — might know," said John.

Miss Englewood waited for more suggestions. None was forth- coming so she suggested they summarize on the chalkboard what they planned to do. This is what she wrote:

1. Cut the bulbs in half to see how they look. Make a diagram for the science notebook.
2. Look up the information in the science book.
3. Cut a bulb that has sprouted to see if some of the bulb is gone.
4. Check to be sure an onion is a bulb.

"Now," said Miss Englewood, "there are four things to do. Divide into four groups and go to work to find the solutions. When you have finished with your project we'll meet and come to some conclusions." The children divided into four groups, but not the same groups they had been in before. There was apparently some pre-agreed-upon way of organizing for this science lesson. When each group was through with its phase of the project they assembled as a whole to report on their findings. One pupil in each group had been selected to be the spokesman for the group. These children were not only developing science concepts but were getting experience in the use of the scientific method.

At 12:00 about half of the children went home and the other half went downstairs to the cafeteria. Here for twenty-five cents they purchased a lunch consisting of fish cakes, mashed potatoes, peas, milk, and chocolate cake.

The class resumed with a roll call at 1:00 o'clock. During this first period of the afternoon the children were free to work on individual interests either in their own classroom or in the music or art room. Many of the children were working on reading skills. The teacher gave help where it was needed.

The 1:45 period was used for reading and related activities. The children were divided into three groups and given assignments in connection with the unit. They had been studying about pioneer life in their major problem area. Preceding the reading there was a discussion about life in pioneer days. Miss Englewood tried to get the children to imagine what the people in the pictures illustrating the story were doing. They read the subtitles of the story, pronounced the word list on the chalkboard, looked up meanings of the words in their glossary. Following the reading they discussed the story. Children who were not reading were drawing pictures depicting typical scenes of pioneer life, with captions explaining the pictures, and making a model of a covered wagon and a pioneer fort.

From the running account of the reading lesson it is evident that the group who read were much interested in the topic of pioneer life and absorbed in the discussion and reading.

TEACHER: We've been talking about pioneer people and their travel. Yesterday we read about something scarce. Does someone remember what it was?

CHILD: A needle.

TEACHER: Yes, it was a neighborhood needle because needles were scarce in the pioneer days. Today we're going to read about hasty pudding. What do you think that is?

CHILD: Some sort of food.

TEACHER: What kind of food?

CHILD: Butterscotch pudding.

CHILD: Hasty means hurry, so it must be something they made in a hurry.

TEACHER: Yes, they must have done it in a hurry. Well, we'll have to read the story to find out. The family is the Barker family and they have three children. Their names are Betsy, Tom, and Martha. (*Writes names on board.*) They lived on a lonely farm about thirty miles from Trader's Point. Do you think thirty miles is a very far distance?

CHILD: It was in those days.

TEACHER: Can you think of any place around here that's about thirty miles away?

CHILD: New Harmony.

TEACHER: Well, we'd say we could get there in a hurry, but in those days how long do you think it would take?

CHILD: Around two days in a covered wagon.

TEACHER (*talking about the pictures connected with the story*): What do you think the people are doing?

CHILD: Hitching horses.

CHILD: They might be telling the older children to put the younger ones to bed early.

CHILD: They might be warning them not to go too far from home.

TEACHER: Well, let's read the story and find out. This story is divided into parts. What do we call these parts?

CHILD: Subtitles.

TEACHER: What is the first subtitle?

CHILD: Betsy in Charge.

TEACHER: The second?

CHILD: An Unexpected Guest.

TEACHER: And the third?

CHILD: Tom's Bright Idea.

TEACHER (*putting list of new words* — loft, awkwardly, comical, beams, bar — *on chalkboard*): Let's see if we can say them. (*Children pronounce them. They also look them up in glossary.*)

TEACHER: Now let's read the first part and let's keep these two questions in mind: What happened at the Barker home? Find a paragraph that tells how to make hasty pudding. (*Writes questions on chalkboard.*) (*Children read section silently.*)

TEACHER: Why were Mr. and Mrs. Barker going to Trader's Point?

CHILD:   To get their corn ground into meal so they could trade it for cloth.

CHILD:   They were going to trade some for a hoe.

CHILD:   They were going to trade bacon for something else. It was easy to get bacon because they had pigs. They traded it for things they didn't raise themselves.

TEACHER:   It seems strange that they would trade it. What would we do?

CHILD:   Buy it.

TEACHER:   Why did they trade?

CHILD:   Money was scarce.

TEACHER:   What were some of the things that happened after the mother and father had gone?

CHILD:   The children fed the chickens and milked the cows. Betsey started to make the pudding.

TEACHER:   Let's read the part that will tell us what part of the day it was.

(*Child reads that portion of the story.*)

TEACHER:   Was that the same day as when the mother and father left?

CHILD:   Yes, the same day.

TEACHER:   Did you find the part of the story that told how they made the hasty pudding?

(*Child reads that portion of the story.*)

TEACHER:   Can you think of something that we eat that would be similar to hasty pudding?

CHILD:   Cream of wheat.

CHILD:   Oatmeal.

TEACHER:   What were some other things that the children were going to have?

TEACHER:   I think we're kind of anxious to find out about the unexpected guest. Let's read and find out.

(*Children read the second part silently.*)

TEACHER:   Let's see if we can find out who the unexpected guest was. (*Writes on board:* Who was the unexpected guest? Why did they let him stay?)

TEACHER:   Did you find who the unexpected guest was?

CHILD:   Big bear.

TEACHER:   How did he get in the house?

CHILD:   The children forgot to bar the door and the wind blew it open.

TEACHER:   Why did they let the bear stay in?

CHILD:   If they tried to get him out he would have eaten them.

CHILD:   He was looking for food. The children thought he was comical and so they let him stay.

TEACHER:   Well, we'll want to see what happens next, but we'll save the rest of the story for later.

The last period of the day, 2:45–3:35, was spent making special plans for a program to be given for the school assembly at the culmination of the social studies unit, Living in Our Community. Among the suggestions the children made for the program were: writing an original sketch of life among the pioneers in the community and life in our community today, explanations of the early institutions in the community pointing out the locations on the large map, use of the large frieze as a background to give atmosphere to the program, plans to ask the music teacher to help them sing several songs that were in vogue during the pioneer days. The children discussed the phases of life that showed the greatest contrast between horse-and-buggy days and the modern era.

Just before the discussion was ended, Miss Englewood suggested that they might talk over the plans with their parents and get additional information which they might contribute tomorrow. The room cleanup committee spent the last few minutes quietly attending to room housekeeping — watering plants, arranging the science materials, making the classroom tidy.

At 3:25 the dismissal bell rang and the children started for home, taking their readers and spelling and arithmetic books with them. Miss Englewood was not yet ready to leave. She was checking reports, looking at plans, and writing out the last suggestions the children had made for the assembly program.

Although the children appeared to participate in activities planned there was a certain sterility in the approach of the teacher not quite in keeping with the apparent interest and enthusiasm of the group.

### APPROACH TO MAKING THE DAILY SCHEDULE

Examination of the daily schedules, time allotments, and account of a day in the fourth grade reveals the orientation of the curriculum. In some of the schedules the program shows evidence of being subject oriented, in others socially oriented, and in still others needs-of-children oriented. Where the program is socially, child, or experience oriented, the daily schedule is characterized by longer periods to provide for unit teaching; it is more flexible, and fewer periods come within the restrictions of the bell. Teacher and pupils share in the planning, the development of activities, and the continuous evaluation. The extent to which the teacher is free to plan the daily schedule with the children is determined by the curriculum design and class organization of the particular school. In an effort to plan for unified programs the day is frequently divided into two parts — one in which units of work are based on problems of living or centers of interest, and the other devoted to direct teaching of skills in arithmetic, social studies, science, health, language arts, and creative arts. The daily schedule and long-range planning are both concerned with providing time to teach the fundamental skills and to give opportunity for unit work periods of sufficient length and flexibility to permit the definition, solution, and evaluation of problems.

The following suggestions have helped teachers in planning the daily schedule in harmony with an integrated program of learning experiences:

1. Plan for a balance of activities. Provide time for skills and time for unified experiences.

2. Set aside time for individual projects as well as for group participation in activities. Children need opportunity to work independently on constructive activities.

3. Reserve large blocks of time to permit work on a major topic or problem of living.

4. Allow flexibility in the program for the development of temporary interests and use of consultants who may be available.

5. Plan for enough sameness in the program with young children so that they will feel secure about what happens next. Have a few fixed points in the program.

6. Make effective use of consultants. Plan to have the music teacher, the art supervisor, the physical education teacher help enrich and coordinate the program.

7. Take into consideration such factors as the nature of the children, the maturity of the group, the size of the group, the length of the day, the physical plant, the local conditions, the climate, seasonal changes, the time at which the services of special teachers, supervisors, or consultants are available, the time at which the gymnasium, auditorium, or playground is free, the time at which children can get their midmorning snack, the time at which lunch is scheduled.

## *Conclusion*

In organizing a class or planning a daily schedule the important concern is not so much what design of curriculum is used, what type of organization is planned for the classroom, or how the daily program is set up; it is rather whether or not the structure of organization permits learning experiences which carry out the objectives of the school.

All good programs are designed to foster citizenship and develop each child to his maximum potential. All programs include learning experiences which have both content and process. All programs place responsibility for the actual teaching upon the teacher. It is he who with his group must select, develop, and evaluate learning experiences which are academically worth while, socially significant, individually challenging, and universally applicable. In each curriculum design there are three bases for defining objectives and making decisions about the curriculum — subject matter, society, and child. Each design uses all three. The initial focus and the emphasis varies with the type. The ultimate objective is to put together the three in such a way that educational experiences are integrated.

In the following chapter we will look at ways of so integrating the learning experiences of boys and girls that each student is challenged to reach his optimum development to discover his strengths and weaknesses as well as his aptitudes and interests, and to prepare himself to make his best contribution and find his place in a changing society.

## ACTIVITIES AND QUESTIONS

1. Observe a primary grade in an elementary school. What type of organization did you see? What, if any, special resources did the teacher have at her disposal?

2. Observe in an intermediate grade. What type of classroom organization was used? For which areas of teaching was the teacher responsible?

3. What criteria did you use in evaluating the effectiveness of classroom organization?

4. Arrange a debate on the topic "*Resolved,* That a nongraded plan is a more effective way of organization than the traditional graded school in meeting the problem of individual differences."

5. What is the purpose of school organization? Of curriculum design? What criteria would you use in determining adequacy of each?

6. Compare the daily schedules organized for three types of curriculum design discussed in your text. Evaluate them in terms of the objectives of the elementary school.

7. What value does a typical daily schedule or time allotment chart hold for a prospective teacher? For a teacher of experience in a new situation? For a parent visiting in the school? For a supervisor?

8. Select a type of curriculum design under which you would like to teach. Select a grade of your choice and design a daily schedule in harmony with the type of curriculum design you choose.

9. Observe in an elementary grade of your choice. Try to determine the guiding principles used in planning the daily schedule. Compare them with the guiding principles suggested in this chapter.

10. Study the chart for the Hunter College Elementary School program. Explain the interrelationships among the various tasks in teaching, using this chart as an aid.

11. How would you define this curriculum design? What instructional pattern of organization of classes does it assume?

## A Typical Day at the Hunter College Elementary School

| TIME | AGE 4-5 (KINDERGARTEN) | AGE 6-7 (GRADE 2) | AGE 8-9 (GRADE 4) | AGE 11 (GRADE 6) | REMARKS |
|------|------|------|------|------|------|
| 9:00 | Free play | Planning | Gymnasium[1] | Audio-visual room | [1]Two classes at same time. |
| 9:45 | Music room / Stories | Mathematics | French room / Music room | Citizenship education[2] | [2]Social studies. |
| 10:15 | Creative expression | Science lab / Music room | Language arts | German / Written English | [3]Reading, spelling, and penmanship. |
| 11:00 | Outdoor play | Language arts[3] | Trips[4] | Mathematics | [4]More time given for longer excursions. |
| 11:30 | Juice; rest | Citizenship education | Lunch[5] | Lunch[5] | [5]Lunch brought from home. Milk and juice purchased at school. |
| 12:00 | Dismissal | Lunch[5] | Library | Pupil participation[6] | [6]Routine; housekeeping. |
| 12:30 | | Group reading[7] | Art room / Shop | Music room / Science lab | [7]Only eight pupils remain. Others dismissed at 12 o'clock. |
| 1:00 | | Creative expression | Citizenship education[2] | Boys' gym / Girls' gym[8] | [8]Separate instruction. |
| 1:30 | | Outdoor play | Language arts[9] | Language arts | [9]Education and planning. |

*The program is flexible and is arranged to give time for each group to engage in the varied units and activities in the school building, the campus, and the neighborhood.*

Source: *Gifted Children "As We See Them"* (New York: Hunter College Elementary School, n.d.), p. 17.

# BIBLIOGRAPHY

Adams, Joseph J. "Achievement and Social Adjustment of Pupils in Combination Classes Enrolling Pupils of More Than One Grade Level," *Journal of Educational Research,* 47:151–155, October 1953.

Anderson, Robert H. "The Ungraded Primary School as a Contribution to Improved School Practices," in Vincent J. Glennon (ed.), *Frontiers of Elementary Education II.* Syracuse: Syracuse University Press, 1955. pp. 28–39.

Association for Childhood Education International. *Grouping . . . Problems and Satisfactions.* Reprint Service Bulletin No. 26. Washington, D.C.: The Association, 1954.

Association for Childhood Education International. "Grouping," *Childhood Education,* 36: entire issue, April 1960.

Association for Supervision and Curriculum Development. *Research for Curriculum Improvement.* Washington, D.C.: National Education Association, 1957.

Brogan, Peggy, and Fox, Florence K. *Helping Children Learn.* Yonkers, N.Y.: World Book Company, 1955.

Case, Roscoe D. *The Platoon School in America.* Stanford, Calif.: Stanford University Press, 1931.

Caswell, Hollis L., and Foshay, Arthur W. *Education in the Elementary School.* New York: American Book Company, 3rd ed., 1957.

Cummins, Evelyn Wood. "Grouping: Homogeneous or Heterogeneous?" *Educational Administration and Supervision,* 44:19–26, January 1958.

Daly, Ronald P. "The Daily Program in the Elementary School," *Education Digest,* 23:46–47, November 1957.

Educational Policies Commission. *Contemporary Issues in Elementary Education.* Washington, D.C.: National Education Association, 1960.

Foshay, A. Wellesley. "Interage Grouping in the Elementary School," Unpublished doctor's project, Teachers College, Columbia University, 1949.

Goodlad, John I. "Illustrative Programs and Procedures in Elementary Schools," in Nelson B. Henry (ed.), *The Integration of Educational Experiences.* Fifty-Seventh Yearbook of the National Society for the Study of Education, Part III. Chicago: University of Chicago Press, 1958, pp. 173–193.

Goodlad, John I., and Anderson, Robert H. *The Nongraded Elementary School.* New York: Harcourt, Brace and Company, 1959.

Goodlad, John I. "News and Comment," *Elementary School Journal,* 59:1–17, October 1958.

Goodlad, John I., *et al.* "Reading Levels Replace Grades in the Nongraded Plan, *Elementary School Journal*, 57:253–256, February 1957.

Hagman, Harlan L. *The Administration of American Public Schools.* New York: McGraw-Hill Book Company, 1951.

Herrick, Virgil E., and Tyler, Ralph (eds.). *Toward Improved Curriculum Theory.* Supplementary Educational Monographs No. 71. Chicago: University of Chicago Press, 1950.

Hopkins, L. Thomas. "Curriculum and the Future," *Educational Leadership*, 15:298–302, February 1958.

Hopkins, L. Thomas. *Integration: Its Meaning and Application.* New York: D. Appleton-Century Company, 1937.

Hopkins, L. Thomas. *Interaction: The Democratic Process.* Boston: D. C. Heath and Company, 1941.

Hunt, Herold C., and Pierce, Paul R. *The Practice of School Administration: A Cooperative Professional Enterprise.* Boston: Houghton Mifflin Company, 1958.

Hunter College Elementary School, *Gifted Children "As We See Them."* New York: Hunter College Elementary School, n.d.

Krug, Edward A. *Curriculum Planning.* New York: Harper & Brothers, rev. ed., 1957.

Mehl, Marie A. Mills, *et al. Teaching in the Elementary Schools.* New York: The Ronald Press Company, 2nd ed., 1958.

Miel, Alice. "The Self-Contained Classroom: An Assessment," *Education Digest*, 23:23–26, April 1958.

Miel, Alice, *et al. Cooperative Procedures in Learning.* New York: Bureau of Publications, Teachers College, Columbia University, 1952.

National Society for the Study of Education. *The Dynamics of Instructional Groups.* Fifty-Ninth Yearbook, Part II, Nelson B. Henry (ed.). Chicago: University of Chicago Press, 1960.

Otto, Henry J. *Elementary School Organization and Administration.* New York: Appleton-Century-Crofts, Inc., 3rd ed., 1954.

Reavis, William C., *et al. Administering the Elementary School.* New York: Prentice-Hall, Inc., 1953.

Reeder, Edwin. *Supervision in the Elementary School.* Boston: Houghton Mifflin Company, 1953.

Roff, Rosella. "Grouping and Individualizing in the Elementary Classroom," *Educational Leadership*, 15:171–175, December 1957.

Saylor, J. Galen, and Alexander, William M. *Curriculum Planning.* New York: Rinehart and Company, 1958.

Shane, Harold G. "Grouping in the Elementary School," *Phi Delta Kappan*, 41:314–318, April 1960.

Shane, Harold G., and McSwain, E. T. *Evaluation and the Elementary*

*Curriculum*. New York: Henry Holt and Company, rev. ed., 1958.

Shane, Harold, and Yauch, Wilbur. *Creative School Administration*. New York: Henry Holt and Company, 1954.

Sligh, Charles R., Jr., *et al.* "The Public School Curriculum," *Harvard Educational Review*, 27:239–309, Fall 1957.

Stoddard, Alexander J. *Schools for Tomorrow: An Educator's Blueprint*. New York: The Fund for the Advancement of Education, 1957.

Strang, Ruth. *Group Work in Education*. New York: Harper & Brothers, 1958.

Stratemeyer, Florence, *et al. Developing a Curriculum for Modern Living*. New York: Bureau of Publications, Teachers College, Columbia University, rev. ed., 1957.

Wagner, Guy. "A Present Day Look at the American School Curriculum," *Education*, 78:328–334, February 1958.

Wiles, Kimball. *Supervision for Better Schools*. Englewood Cliffs, N.J.: Prentice-Hall, Inc., 2nd ed., 1955.

Wiles, Kimball, and Grobman, Hulda. "The Role of the Principal in Curriculum Development," *Educational Administration and Supervision*, 44:10–14, January 1958.

## ORGANIZING THE CURRICULUM

One of the broadest and most significant tasks of educators is to organize the instructional program in a way that will develop individuals who can think critically, respond creatively, and develop habits of perseverance and integrity. The curriculum pattern inevitably reflects, to a greater or lesser degree, the values of society, the needs of children, and the concept of the nature of learning held by a given school community. To the extent that these concerns are central in the selection and organization of learning experiences, methods of teaching, and techniques of evaluation will the schools achieve their purposes.

To the extent, too, that curriculum planning involves the cooperative participation of all who influence the child's learning will the school achieve the goal of helping each child reach his highest potential.

The curriculum should stress problems of social significance, assure development of basic skills, and provide continuity, balance, and integration in learning; the staff should select those learning experiences that help children develop academic, social, creative, and physical skills essential for effective living.

*Television and teaching machines are modern aids already integrated into many elementary school programs.*

*A good program provides for physical development.*

*Children need time in the daily program to practice skills.*

*Today's curriculum reflects the importance of science in the modern world.*

*Excursions into the community augment the elementary school program.*

*Group problem solving develops critical thinking.*

*Time for rest is an important part of the primary program.*

# 6

. . . the child may deepen concepts, gain a greater concern for certain social values, and acquire increased skill in study. The foregoing elements are suggested threads for the weaving; but the teaching of it will involve the closely woven fabric.

RALPH TYLER

# Integrating learning experiences

One of the most difficult tasks of the teacher is that of integrating learning experiences in a plan that is challenging and effective for the learner and practical for the teacher. "Since the focus of integration in learning experiences is the pupil, the effectiveness of curriculum organization in facilitating integration depends upon the extent to which it aids the student in perceiving relationships among phenomena and ideas, in sensing the meaning and significance of his feelings and in developing abilities, skills, and courses of action which are guided by comprehensive knowledge and through and by disciplined feelings."[1]

According to Tyler, "The term learning experience refers to the interaction between the learner and the external conditions in the environment to which he can react. Learning takes place through the active behavior of the student; it is what *he* does that he learns, not what the teacher does."[2]

What the teacher must do is create an environment and structure the situation so as to evoke the desired response. He must find an integrating thread or organizing center by which he helps children tie together two or more areas of the curriculum. Tyler identifies three common elements that may serve as threads — concepts, values, and skills. For example, the frequently used concept of interdependence is one that runs throughout the social studies curriculum. The kindergarten child learns that he is dependent upon other children as they help him find his wraps or set the table for lunch. They in turn are dependent upon him. He knows he is dependent upon the grocer, the milkman, and the postman. They in turn are dependent upon others. As he matures this concept of interdependence widens until ultimately it reaches the peoples of the world in all their complex relationships.

An example of a value that has meaning at every level of development is the dignity and worth of the individual. Consideration for every individual regardless of nationality, race, occupation, or income may be fostered in the nursery school as well as throughout the elementary and secondary school years.

An example of a skill that carries through the elementary school is the ability to collect and organize data. Even young children can learn to observe carefully and listen attentively for facts; to select dependable sources of information; to read charts, graphs, tables, and maps; and to distinguish between important and unimportant facts as they organize the data. As they mature they should be taught to become more critical in the evaluation and more discriminating in their search for information. Not only do these common

[1] Ralph Tyler, "Curriculum Organization," in Nelson B. Henry (ed.), *The Integration of Educational Experiences*, Fifty-Seventh Yearbook, National Society for the Study of Education (Chicago: University of Chicago Press, 1958), p. 105.

[2] Ralph W. Tyler, *Basic Principles of Curriculum and Instruction* (Chicago: University of Chicago Press, 1950), p. 41.

elements provide continuity and sequence to the learning experience; they also weave a more integrated curriculum.

Bloom conceives of an integrating thread as "any idea, problem, method or device by which two or more separate learning experiences are related. The relation may be perceived by the students and/or the instructor."[3]

## *The Unit of Work*

One of the most widely used and most effective methods for securing integration, individualization, critical thinking, creative expression, and enrichment of learning experiences is the unit of work.

"What is a unit of work?" asked Miss McKim, the intermediate supervisor.

"That's what I'd like to know," Miss Redly said with a perturbed expression on her usually smiling face. "I thought I knew about units. Now I'm not so sure. We had a discussion in faculty meeting yesterday after school. I never heard so many ideas expressed and so many ways of expressing them. We talked about units — all kinds and varieties of units: resource units, cultural units, experience units, activity units, science units, subject-matter units, social studies units, process units, topic units, units of adaptation, teaching units, and group studies. Finally we decided we'd better try to find some common ground for discussion and get a definition of the term. We agreed that a unit is a way of organizing learning experiences and information around a core, central theme, problem, or purpose, and is developed cooperatively by the teacher and the class.

"Cooperative planning by the teacher and the class caused some controversy because there were those who felt that the pupils might take advantage of an unskilled or inexperienced teacher. When we finally got past that hurdle it wasn't quite so difficult to define types of units, characteristics of units, and advantages offered by this organizing structure. I'm working with a group to formulate a framework which we might use as a guide in experimenting with a unit of

[3] Benjamin Bloom, "Ideas, Problems and Methods of Inquiry," in Nelson B. Henry (ed.), *The Integration of Educational Experiences*, Fifty-Seventh Yearbook, National Society for the Study of Education (Chicago: University of Chicago Press, 1958), p. 91.

work in our classes. I think, maybe, we're on the way. At least we're working on it."

*Types of Units.* The experience of Miss Redly illustrates the extreme differentiation in the literature concerning units. However, there are basically two kinds — *subject-matter* or topical, and *experience* or activity. Both types have certain elements in common. All units have content, utilize activities, provide experiences, and foster creativity. The distinction between the subject-centered and the experience-centered unit is chiefly one of emphasis. The subject-centered unit focuses on the subject matter, whereas the experience-centered unit emphasizes experiences. The significant element in the unit is the degree to which it provides learning experiences which are socially significant, academically worth while, individually challenging, and the "degree to which it can combine subject matter and experience in a way valuable to the learner";[4] i.e., aid him in continually integrating his behavior.

The content or type of planning involved may be understood from the name. For example, the *foreign culture unit* is concerned with life in a foreign culture; the *activity unit* lists the projects which children can carry on in connection with the unit; the *resource unit* outlines the information, materials and sources, and resources available in the school, the library, and the community to be used in developing the unit. These are all planned and written down in advance. The resource unit frequently contains (1) a title and grade or age level to be covered, (2) an introductory statement, (3) a statement of objectives, (4) a content guide or list of concepts and generalizations to be taught, (5) pupil activities, (6) materials and resources for teachers and pupils, and (7) evaluation procedures. Working out a resource unit is helpful to the pre-service and beginning teacher as a prerequisite to planning a *teaching unit* which is not too different from it. The teaching unit, however, is limited to the activities, concepts, materials, and evaluation techniques the teacher will actually use, in sequence, in the class.

The point at which the pupils enter the planning depends upon

---

[4] William H. Burton, "Implications for Organization of Instruction and Instructional Adjuncts," in Nelson B. Henry (ed.), *Learning and Instruction*, Forty-Ninth Yearbook, National Society for the Study of Education, Part I (Chicago: University of Chicago Press, 1950), p. 219.

several factors including the curriculum design, definition of pupil participation, flexibility of the daily schedule, and ability of the teacher to guide group processes. The teaching unit must be flexible enough to consider individual interests and abilities of the children and at the same time structured enough to serve as a useful guide. It must fit the needs of the teacher and the particular group. The following is a framework for a unit.

### The Form for a Unit

1. Introduction to the unit
   a. Topic of the unit
   b. Age and grade level
   c. Time involved
2. Objectives to be attained
   a. Important concepts and generalizations
   b. Basic skills
   c. Interests, appreciations, and attitudes
3. Content guide
   a. Subject-matter content
   b. Problems to be solved
   c. Projects to be carried out
4. Pupil activities
   a. Initiatory activities
      (1) Motivating factors including instructional materials, excursions, films, resource personnel
      (2) Approximate time for the suggested activities
   b. Developmental activities
      (1) Activities essential to acquire understandings, skills, and attitudes listed in the order in which learning will be facilitated
      (2) Approximate time required for these activities
   c. Culmination of the unit
      (1) Summation or group of activities to which the entire class can contribute, and to which they direct effort in developing the unit; individual interests and abilities considered
      (2) Approximate time required for these activities
5. Materials and resources
   a. Audio-visual aids, materials for experimentation, demonstration, displays, printed materials, creative arts materials which contribute to the development of the activities planned

  b. Facilities outside the school
  c. Excursions, and interviews with people in the community
6. Evaluation
  a. Determining where pupils are when the unit begins
  b. Self-evaluation by pupils throughout the unit
  c. Final evaluation of pupils in terms of growth in knowledge, understanding, skills, and attitudes

Any predetermined framework will generally need modification when applied in a particular situation.

### SAMPLE UNIT FOR INTERMEDIATE SOCIAL STUDIES[5]

1. Title: "Our City — Past and Present"
   Grade level: Fourth — thirty-three children
   Time: Five weeks, one hour a day (longer periods for excursions)
2. Introductory statement: The fourth-grade social studies theme centers around understanding our community, the development of our city, and its relation to the state and nation. The social studies curriculum begins with a unit "Our City." This is followed by a unit on the state and one on the regions of the United States. This unit includes four major problems:
   a. How do people in a community meet the problem which living in a particular area presents?
   b. How does life in our city today differ from that of early pioneer days?
   c. How do people make a living and plan a way of life?
   d. How is the development of our city affected by the Ohio River?
3. Objectives
   a. Understandings
     (1) Understanding of the social and physical setting of the city
     (2) Understanding of how the early settlers obtained food, clothing, shelter, medical services, education, transportation, and communication services
     (3) Understanding that life in our city today is the result of the social and geographical features of our city and the contributions of the civic-minded citizens
     (4) Understanding of the relationship between the city, the child, the state, and the nation

[5] Activities in this unit were developed by Ruth Holtz, fourth-grade teacher at Scott Township School, Evansville, Indiana.

b. Skills. Each child develops skills in the following areas:
   (1) Social studies — reading social studies books and supplementary materials, using tables of contents, indexes, glossaries, maps, illustrations, graphs, charts, etc.; reading maps, locating places on an outline map, using the city map, interpreting historical and geographical facts in early history and present-day literature of our city; taking trips to places of significance and relating present conditions to historical beginnings
   (2) Language arts — increasing ability to report, to record, selecting material to read, organizing, evaluating and summarizing data, reading for enjoyment, listening to reports of others, dramatizing situations and historical events, writing letters, inviting the fifth grade to an assembly program
   (3) Problem solving — recognizing and defining problems, collecting and evaluating information, finding and applying solutions
   (4) Arithmetic — developing skills in connection with problems involved in the unit

c. Attitudes: developed by
   (1) Working cooperatively with classmates
   (2) Recognizing the right of people to be different in their manner of living
   (3) Using a more objective approach to understanding why people live and act as they do
   (4) Acquiring a wholesome outlook

4. Content guide
   a. Geographical features such as location, size, principal river
   b. Location and activities of the early settlers
      (1) Indians
      (2) Early explorers
      (3) Early settlers
      (4) Development of the area
         (a) Agriculture
         (b) Manufacture
         (c) Schools
         (d) Religions
      (5) Building the city
         (a) The first courthouse
         (b) The first public school
         (c) The first post office
         (d) The first church

c. Life and activities
  (1) Development of transportation
    (a) Growth and services of railroads in the community
    (b) Roads and highways
    (c) Airlines
    (d) Bus transportation
    (e) Growth of river transportation
  (2) Development of the city
    (a) Civic services
    (b) Cultural organizations
    (c) Industries
    (d) Parks and recreational facilities
  (3) Our city as it is today
    (a) Economic life
    (b) Cultural life
    (c) Social life
    (d) Civic life

5. Activities
  a. Initiatory activities — first week
    (1) Arranging the environment in the classroom; pictures, maps, charts, pamphlets, products of local industries, movies, and film strips showing early and contemporary life in our city
    (2) Talks on life in early days — by long-time residents
    (3) Field trips to points of interest
    (4) Plans for a display of materials and pictures of life in early and present day
    (5) Outline for gathering information to answer questions formulated by group
  b. Developmental activities — second week
    (1) Re-examining study guide and planning activities for the week
    (2) Class interviews of four civic leaders to obtain certain facts about the city
    (3) Chart to show products of the area, postcard collection, collection and display of snapshots of city
    (4) Map of city showing Ohio River and public parks
    (5) Period for individualized reading
    (6) Dramatizations of events and situations in pioneer days
Third week
    (1) Study guide, reading, questions, and class discussion
    (2) Film, "Balance Point U.S.A.," discussion on it.

(3) Locating points of interest on a city map: high schools, grade schools, industries, parks, libraries, post office, fire stations, police stations, health department, courthouse, hospitals, water works, museum

(4) Interviews of a judge, policeman, fireman, librarian, and the mayor's representative; taped recordings played in the classroom

(5) Thank-you note to the men who were interviewed

Fourth week

(1) Study of the different types of industry in the city

(2) Display of products of as many industries as possible

(3) Preparation for dramatization of special events in the development of the city

(4) Continued work on maps and charts to use for final reports

(5) Sightseeing tour of the city

(6) "Quiz programs" based on questions in the study guide

c. Culminating activities — fifth week

(1) Invitation to the fifth grade for a program: "Our City"

(2) Panel discussion; reports on "Our City — Its Past and Present, Life and Customs" by committee

(3) Display and explanation of a map of the city

(4) Dramatization of special events in the development of the city

(5) Letters to parents about the activities most enjoyed in developing unit

6. Materials and resources

(This would include books for the teacher and the children, recordings, films, and school and community resources. However, since the study is a locally oriented one the materials available would be those limited to the local area.) Books, articles, pamphlets, newspaper items, chamber of commerce reports and maps

7. Evaluation

a. Pre-unit evaluation of children's present knowledge of city

b. Informal evaluation of children's contributions to the initiation and development of the unit at the end of the first week

c. Teacher evaluation of the pupil's work — the questions he suggested for the study guide, his participation in class discussion, his map study, panel and individual reports, dramatization, interviews, letter to parents, contributions to culminating activity, conduct on trips and excursions

    d. Self-evaluation by pupil: questions in the study guide checked as he answers them; criticism of committee work

The children in Mrs. Holtz's fourth grade worked exceptionally well in this particular unit. They were interested in learning more about their city, its historical beginnings, its development, and its present status. Interest led to a unit on "How Can We Improve Our City So That We May Attract Industry?" In other schools, activities which were not suggested here might well be used, as could other resources of a personal and material nature. Additional suggestions for social studies activities and materials for various grades from kindergarten through the sixth grade will be discussed more fully in a later chapter.

### CHARACTERISTICS OF A UNIT OF WORK

*Content.* A unit of work is organized around a center which is educationally worth while. Teachers use concepts, vital ideas, problems, topics, experiences. The aim is to select a unit which has worth-while content, lends itself to development, and invites further exploration of related problems after it is ended.

*Time.* A unit of work is planned for longer than a day or single class period. It requires a large block of time in the school day and extends from a week to several weeks or even several months. The length of time is determined by the curriculum design and the daily schedule, the maturity of the group, their experimental background, their abilities and interests as a group and as individuals, the availability of instructional materials and resources, the possibility for excursions and experiments, the complexity of content to be studied, concepts to be developed, the degree to which other activities are correlated with the unit, and the skill of the teacher in pacing activities and sensing the psychological time at which the unit should be culminated.

*Comprehensiveness.* A unit of work cuts across traditional subject-matter lines. If the problem is comprehensive it will encourage research, stimulate wide reading and experimentation, foster creativity, and motivate basic skills. It is not necessary, however, to correlate the unit activities with all the subjects. To correlate for the sake of correlation may result in a situation similar to the one related by John. "Sure I like to learn about Eskimos, but I think taking the class to the drugstore to buy Eskimo Pies is silly; not that I don't appreciate ice cream. We haven't had a reading class for weeks. But you should see our igloo. That took time. I built a little one at home, but it melted the day the sun was so hot."

*Cohesiveness.* A central core around which learning experiences cluster is essential. If integration is to be achieved the subject matter, the experiences, the content, the instructional resources, the experiments must be related to the core of the unit. One of the values of the unit is that it provides for many types of learning activities — reading, experimenting, exploring, taking trips, bringing in resource people, constructing, problem solving, and creating.

*Practice in Skills.* A unit of work provides time for teaching basic skills. One of the criticisms of the unit of work is that it ignores the basic skills of communication and calculating. However, it is recognized by teachers who employ this method of integrating learning experiences that time must be provided for learning and practicing the basic skills. Although units stimulate learning the basic skills, they do not always afford the time for the teacher to teach them or the pupil to practice.

The successful teacher copes with this problem by careful planning. Preplanning, daily planning, long-term planning, and teacher-pupil planning are all involved in providing a balanced program.

## DAILY PLANNING

The unit has the advantage of a flexible schedule. Rigid time barriers make the integration of learning experiences more difficult. For example, in the unit "Our City" such activities as a tour of the city require more time than is ordinarily provided for a social studies class in a subject curriculum. Flexibility allows for adjusting learning activities to the abilities and needs of children, for utilizing material and personal resources effectively, and for teacher-pupil planning and problem solving. The constant pressure to finish the lesson by the time the bell rings limits discussion, planning, and problem solving.

In the unit the teacher must make sure of two types of planning —

the daily plan that outlines the work to be accomplished on a particular day and the long-range plan that covers an extended period. Even teachers who have taught successfully for years find it essential to have a plan to help them maintain teaching at a high level. Those who are inexperienced in the classroom need an outline to "keep them on the track." As one beginning teacher expressed it, "I get so involved in watching the children I sometimes forget what I am supposed to be teaching. A plan, a skeleton outline is a real help to me." The following outline may be adapted to meet specific needs of a teacher at any grade level in the elementary school.

### OUTLINE FOR A DAILY PLAN

1. Type of lesson
2. Purpose
   a. Children's purpose
   b. Teacher's purpose
3. Relationship to preceding lesson in the unit
4. Content to be developed
5. Materials needed
6. Sequence of activities
   a. Motivation
      (1) Opening statement
      (2) Teacher's responsibility
      (3) Children's responsibility
   b. Activity period
   c. Evaluation
      (1) Did I orient the class to the learning experience?
         (a) Review of what has gone before
         (b) Establishing the purpose of the lesson with the group
      (2) Did I make the assignment carefully?
         (a) Written on the board for reference
         (b) Adjusted to the abilities of the group
      (3) Did all the children understand what to do?
         (a) What to read
         (b) How to record findings, etc.
      (4) Did I provide for individual need for guidance?
      (5) Did I provide opportunity for participation of pupils in discussion, critical thinking, individuality, creativity, group and individual evaluation?
      (6) Did I guide the discussion so that everyone had some satisfaction from it?

(7) Have I set the stage for further learning?
(8) Have I clinched the learnings so children will utilize their knowledge?
(9) Have I motivated the class to look forward to tomorrow's activity?

In a carefully prepared plan the following essentials are readily identified:

*Materials.* All the materials to be used by the teacher in motivating the activity, as well as the materials the children will need, are included.

*Objectives.* This means both teacher's and pupils' purposes. They should be attainable and concise.

*Time Schedule.* The estimated time allotment for motivation, pupil activities, summary, and evaluation, are set down.

*Procedures.* Motivation and specific activities to be carried out by the group are clearly explained. The procedures and related materials to motivate the children, develop purposes, and suggest possible activities are listed. Activities are arranged in order; questions, illustrations, and specific directions for individual and/or group activities are given.

*Evaluation.* Procedure for evaluating pupil learning is outlined. Sometimes this is included under procedures, because it is a part of the teaching-learning experience.

## Long-Range Planning in the Unit

Long-range planning is essential for the integration of learning experiences, whatever they are called: unit of work, group study, problem solving, or teaching unit. The teacher must choose the problem to be studied; formulate the concepts and generalizations to be learned; select the activities to be carried out; initiate, develop, and culminate the activities; locate materials and resources; and determine the methods of evaluating what has been learned. Each of these will be discussed briefly to point out the responsibility of the teacher in each area.

*Choosing the Problem or Unit to Study.* The selection of the unit is determined on the basis of the curriculum guide provided by the school, or the scope and sequence chart, if there is one. In the absence of any guide from the school, the teacher, or the teacher and children, make the selection — on the basis of the children's experiential background, previous units studied, complexity of subject matter involved, needs and developmental level of children, availability of materials and resources, and possibility for activities needed to carry on the unit. Criteria such as the following may be used: (1) The unit must be sufficiently complex to allow varied experiences and to require many children to make contributions, according to their abilities. (2) It must be socially significant as well as academically worth while. The study of the unit must broaden the outlook and social understandings of the group. (3) It must have an ongoing quality that leads to related units of significance. (4) It must foster children's creative ability, nurture their physical health, and promote their mental well-being. (5) It should motivate the learning of the fundamental skills. Once the unit is selected the teacher and children or the teacher alone formulates the list of problems to be solved.

*Formulating Concepts and Generalizations for the Content Guide.* From the wide variety of possible ideas the teacher must decide on the significant concepts and generalizations the children should gain from the unit. Experiential background and development level of the group are prime considerations. Through units the child can increase his knowledge of the world in which he lives, broaden his understanding of others, gain skills in problem solving, develop creativity, and integrate his learning activities. In the content guide the teacher includes the subject matter needed to develop concepts and generalizations, the problems to be solved, and the activities to be carried out.

*Selecting the Activities.* Units begin in various ways. The teacher may simply announce a new unit or problem for study. Or the teacher may raise a specific question, bring in materials, or plan an activity that catches the interest of the children. Again, an incident in the classroom or a visitor to the class may give the lead to initiate the unit.

In some classes units have their origin when one or two children become interested in a particular problem and request time to explore it. During the process of exploration other children in the room become interested and before long the time is ripe for defining the problems to be solved by the group as a whole. Sometimes two interest centers or problems exist simultaneously. The teacher and pupils decide which is to receive the major emphasis. Teachers have the responsibility of helping children determine which problems or units are significant. If the teacher feels that the suggested problem is not worthy of intensive study by the group, it can be developed as a minor interest or an individual project rather than eliminated. Teachers may fail to find the needed resources for certain units. There is no reason for a teacher to feel guilty about rejecting, selecting, or initiating a unit.

In some situations children are given the choice of units or a choice of alternative units from a list drawn up by the staff or teacher. In such cases the initiative lies with the children. Even when children originate the study, the teacher is responsible for guiding, implementing, and planning the next steps with the children.

*Developing the Unit.* The activities carried out in the development of the unit are determined by the abilities, interests, and needs of the children; the accessibility of material and personnel resources; and the opportunities for experimentation, creative expression, and field trips or excursions. Constructing, making murals, drawing, making maps and graphs, creative writing, dramatizing, and evaluating are possible activities. Some teachers make an effort to balance the activities of the unit by planning experiences in the creative arts, the language arts, science, and construction. As the unit develops, the suggested list of activities may be modified if it seems necessary, to harmonize with the demands of the situation.

*Culminating Activities.* When the unit of work has reached the point where the problems have been solved, the interest of the children has been satisfied, and a consensus indicates that the unit is completed, the children and teacher may plan a culminating activity: a program to be presented before another grade or the whole school, a series of reports on their findings to be read to parents, or an original play based on dramatic incidents of the unit. In a unit on nutrition the culminating activities may be planned specifically for the pupils in the classroom and may center around planning and eating a balanced meal. Such an activity would effectively summarize the knowledge acquired.

*Teaching Materials and Resources.* In planning for the unit the teacher locates and collects all the materials he expects to use. The modern classroom has a wide variety of instructional materials: projectors, films, slides, film strips, study prints, art reproductions, dioramas, recording devices, globes, maps, charts, models, games, exhibits, pictures, radio and television, teaching machines, and flannel boards, in addition to textbook materials, encyclopedias. and dictionaries.

In selecting materials the teacher should keep in mind that children learn through the senses. The concrete precedes the abstract. Instructional materials which help the child see and hear at the same time make learning more concrete.

Teaching machines help the child evaluate his own progress. Manipulation of materials such as the counting frame, the abacus, and the fraction wheel help him discover important concepts in the development of number comprehension. One of the reasons children are provided with opportunity and materials for manipulation is to help them grasp the abstract, the symbolic, and the general. Children can teach themselves concepts through deduction if they have the materials with which to work. Flash cards, games, workbooks, and flannel-board exercises are important steps in the learning process and provide the drill essential for learning and retaining certain skills and knowledge. The instructional materials of this type catch a child's interest and hold it as well.

The prospective teacher can profitably begin the collection of instructional materials, organized in a filing system that is practical and efficient. The in-service teacher, too, needs to check materials periodically in order to retain only the most useful. Many times teachers become attached to materials which have long since lost their value.

Textbooks are used far more widely than other teaching aids in the elementary schools. Many schools no longer adopt a single text for a grade but use a tri-basal or co-basal reading series supplemented by trade books and others available from libraries and administrative offices. Some schools buy small quantities of several different series so children have greater choice in the selection of reading materials without additional expenditure. Still other schools are experimenting with a completely individualized program in reading; as many as 200 books may be used in a single grade.

*Achieving a Balanced Program.* The balanced curriculum will include mathematics, science, social science, language arts, creative arts, and, for some, foreign language. It will provide time for teaching specific skills apart from the unit.

Besides continuous planning for unit activities and those not related to the unit, daily planning helps keep the activities in balance, and integrated. Even the teacher who is skillful in selecting, organizing, and developing units which have significance for children and in discovering the activities, resources, materials, teaching methods, and evaluation techniques which meet the needs of the group must continue to plan. Only then can he approach each teaching day with expectancy, secure in knowing that not all the aspects of teaching are unknown quantities. An understanding of ways of organizing learning experiences to help children learn more effectively together with a knowledge of what a balanced program should contain will help him teach with confidence.

*Methods of Evaluation.* To be effective, evaluation of learning experiences must be continuous, have as a basis objectives the teacher and pupils understand, involve cooperation of teacher and pupils, be focused on the individual pupil's progress as well as the progress of the group, and make use of a variety of techniques — oral examinations, written examinations, interviews, questionnaires, observations, reports, and discussions.

Evaluation should be an integral part of the teaching-learning process taking place day by day, hour by hour. The results of continuous evaluation supply the motivation for reorganizing and redirecting learning experiences. They lead to a critical examination of previously defined goals, of methods used by the teacher and group to move toward these, and of the adequacy of the evaluative techniques themselves.

The chief concern of evaluation is to determine the extent to which the behavior of children has changed. It is not enough for children to acquire certain information and give it back to the teacher in a recitation or test. The facts must be incorporated into their experience and make a difference in their patterns of thinking and acting.

Unless evaluation instruments identify the strengths and weaknesses of the learning experiences in relation to the development of children they are ineffective. Evaluation is useful also in individual guidance. It is as important for the child to grow in the ability to determine his progress toward defined goals as it is for the teacher to know the child's background. It is as important for the teacher to know about the child's achievement of various kinds of objectives as it is for the child to be aware of the basis upon which the evaluation is being made. Such information will be forthcoming if evaluation procedures determine that changes are taking place in the children.

### ADVANTAGES OF THE UNIT METHOD OF TEACHING

1. It enables each pupil to work at his own rate and level. With its broad areas of interest the unit provides freedom for exploration, research, creative expression, problem solving, and integration of learning activities.

2. It permits him to work alone in areas of special interest and creative ability and also to work with others on group projects.

3. It allows for individualized assignments and permits him to advance at his own rate of learning.

4. It makes use of firsthand experiences, observation, experimentation, and creative expression, which furnish a broad background for developing concepts, formulating generalizations, and reaching conclusions.

5. It provides opportunity to develop skills in leadership and group participation and develops individual initiative and creativity.

6. It enables the pupil to become more proficient in the skills of communication and calculation needed in solving problems related to the unit. It provides for the functional use of skills.

7. It satisfies the innate drives of children to be physically and mentally active, to communicate, to manipulate and construct, to explore, to satisfy curiosity, to create, to experiment, and to dramatize.

The unit of work organizes learning experiences around important centers. Its wide acceptance stems from the nature of learning experiences, the nature of the learning process, and the nature of children.

It gives opportunity for certain learnings, attitudes, and skills to be developed by the entire class. But it also provides for the organization of the class into groups or committees to explore social phases of the problem and for individual pupils to pursue related interests. All available instructional materials and community resources may be used. A variety of experiences including communication skills, experimentation, construction, and creative expression related to the solution of the problem are involved in the unit, as well as understandings, facts, knowledges, skills, attitudes, and ideals. Learning must be balanced and integrated. The unit motivates and vitalizes the basic skills, but separate daily instruction and practice are needed in most cases.

Evaluation and planning are continuous. In the culminating activity the learnings of the unit are summarized, reviewed, tested, applied, and frequently expressed in some creative activity.

The good teacher maintains a balance between unit activities and separate systematic instruction in skills, recognizing that only as the experiences become a part of the learner will they function for him.

## *The Textbook*

"As a source of information, as a sequential, logical development of ideas within the covers of a single book, the textbook is planned to help the student to organize and to intellectualize, that is, to make meaningful his experiences."[6]

In the modern school the textbook is a very useful tool, an excellent instructional aid, a good source of information. There are textbooks in arithmetic, the social studies (geography, history, civics), language arts (reading, spelling, writing, language, literature), and science and health. They are used not only in the subject-centered curriculum but also in the experience- or society-centered curriculum. However, the pattern of textbook use varies with the type of curriculum design, the organizing center, and the philosophy of the staff concerning the primary focus of the learning experiences.

Teachers often feel a certain security in the knowledge that the textbook is available; they need "a blueprint that is geared to the realities of school situations. The textbook and its use supplies a key

[6] Ralph W. Tyler, "The Place of the Textbook in Modern Education," *Harvard Educational Review*, 12:338, May 1941.

to a realistic appraisal and modification of existing educational practices."[7]

## PATTERNS OF TEXTBOOK USE

One of the interesting things about the textbook is the variety of ways in which it is used. Some elementary schools have a textbook per child per subject studied. In others one may look in vain for a "set" of textbooks, even for reading.

Miss Grant has been a fourth-grade teacher for a number of years in schools in which the textbook was more than an instructional aid. It was the course of study. It determined the content to be studied, the skills to be learned, and the sequence in which these skills were to be taught. There were textbooks for arithmetic, reading, science, health, geography, history, language, and music. Weekly plans consisted of little more than writing down page numbers for each subject to be taught. "The textbook relieved me," Miss Grant said, "of making any real decisions. After years of teaching I found myself modifying my teaching only when the school changed textbooks. Teaching was not difficult; neither was it creative. Then I became aware that the way you use the textbook determines in a large measure the actual curriculum of your classroom. The more I studied the problem the more I realized that in a sense the textbook was no longer a servant; it had become the master of my classroom. I discovered upon careful research that there were at least three major emphases on the use of the textbook: (1) as the determiner of content, skills, and sequence, (2) as the determiner of skills and sequence; and (3) as supplementary material."

*Pattern I: The Textbook as the Determiner of Content, Skills, and Sequence.* In this pattern the source of activities, the content to be studied, the skills to be practiced, and the order in which they are to be practiced are given. Content takes precedence over the interests of children. The textbook dominates the program, determining what will be studied and when it will be studied.

There are three advantages to this pattern. It provides a complete course of study; it presents the teacher and pupils with a logical, well-articulated over-all plan for developing skills throughout the elemen-

[7] Herbert C. Rudman, "Patterns of Textbook Use: Key to Curriculum Development," *Elementary School Journal*, 58:406, April 1958.

tary and secondary schools; and it may permit some freedom in using instructional aids and experiences, group processes, committees, audio-visual aids, resource people, research techniques, and art activities.

The chief disadvantage is that the children's intellectual horizons may be limited by the predetermined content to be studied.

*Pattern II: The Textbook as the Determiner of Skills and Sequence.* In this approach the textbook is not solely responsible for determining what children are taught. It is used only to determine skills to be practiced and the sequence in which they will be taken up. The content is derived from the interests of the children, the nature of the community in which they live, and the demands placed upon them by society. The teacher selects the content to be studied at a particular grade level on the basis of these elements. "In this pattern only the teacher uses a textbook. The children use other printed materials — trade books, pamphlets, brochures and many materials of instruction of a non-verbal nature."[8]

Advantages of this design are that the curriculum is geared to the needs of children in a particular community setting, the sequence of skills development is retained throughout the school year by use of the textbook, and the content may be more closely related to interests of children than is the predetermined content of textbooks. This pattern is a step in the direction of integrating learning experiences more effectively.

The chief disadvantage is that the interests of children might become the only basis for determining the selection of learning experiences.

*Pattern III: The Textbook as Supplementary Material.* Under this plan content and skills are determined by the teacher and the school in accordance with the needs and interests of children and the demands of society. Skills are developed as they are called for by specific projects. Children are free to explore the environment and broaden their intellectual horizons. The teacher has a real opportunity to integrate learning experiences and uses textbooks as supplementary material.

This pattern demands a superior teacher with a broad cultural and

[8] *Ibid.*, p. 403.

professional background and skilled in group processes. He is guided by his professional judgment concerning the content to be studied.

Pattern III requires a high degree of cooperative planning — by the staff, administrators, supervisors, teachers, pupils, and community. Too few schools, unfortunately, provide an optimum setting for such a curriculum; few teachers, supervisors, administrators, and community members are free to participate in the time-consuming meetings and conferences required; few teachers have the ingenuity, knowledge, and skills to put the program into action. However, where teachers are challenged to use their best creative efforts, integration in learning experiences is more readily achieved.

Teachers can make more effective use of textbooks and other instructional materials if they understand the limitations of the textbook.

1. The textbook alone cannot be expected to provide generalizations about significant ideas, nor can it, in itself, develop all of the necessary skills. These are the functions of the teacher and children.

2. The textbook alone cannot organize and develop the concepts, relationships, and important ideas in a subject field or relate this configuration of ideas to the concerns of a group of boys and girls.

3. The textbook alone should not determine what children are to be taught. As a guide, resource, or teaching aid it is a singularly valuable tool.

4. The textbook alone cannot pace the learning of the individual child, in terms of the content to be studied and the purposes he may have in studying it. This, too, is the responsibility of the teacher and the group with whom he works.

5. The textbook alone cannot evaluate, and learning, to be effective, must be evaluated and utilized in the learners' activities. Textbooks are no substitute for good teaching.[9]

## EVALUATING INSTRUCTIONAL MATERIALS

Teachers' committees frequently set up criteria to use in evaluating textbooks. Without some criteria they may be unduly influenced by the physical structure of a book to the exclusion of the content. For example, one of the finest reading series was rejected by a state

---

[9] Adapted from Virgil E. Herrick *et al., The Elementary School* (Englewood Cliffs, N.J.: Prentice-Hall, Inc., 1956), pp. 135–136.

committee because some of its members thought the books so large they would crowd the desks. In evaluating instructional materials the teacher may make use of the following criteria:

Are the means stimulating? Integrative?

Are the means self-directing, self-teaching, self-testing?

Are the materials readily comprehensible, readable, hard enough to challenge but not to frustrate?

Do the means economize the teacher's time, avoid putting an undue burden of effort on her?

Do the means promote self-discovery?

Do the means avoid mere imitation, do they emphasize the *why* as well as the *how?*

Do the means promote thinking?

Do the means promote explicit and transferable generalizations?

Do the means promote a mood of mutuality, of sharing? A good emotional climate?

Do the means permit growth at desired levels and at a pace suitable to the rhythm and tempo of the learner?[10]

Other useful criteria for the selection of textbooks and reference materials are found in the bibliography at the end of the chapter.

The teacher in today's school must increase his knowledge of instructional materials and resources, select carefully, work out an efficient system of storing and cataloguing materials, make appropriate use of the school's audio-visual department, make materials easily accessible to pupils, and set up standards for their use and care.

The key task of the teacher is to organize and integrate learning experiences in a meaningful, practical way. We have seen how he may use the unit and the textbook. We will discuss now the teacher-pupil compact — a method that provides for individual differences in learning.

## *Teacher-Pupil Compact: An Individualized Approach*

"Integration does not necessarily take place because of any particular organization of the curriculum. It is a process which must occur

[10] Edgar Dale, "Educational Means," *Educational Research Bulletin*, 36:43, 44, February 1957.

in the mind of the learner."[11] Learning experiences should provide the individual with an opportunity to grasp the interrelationships among the various areas of knowledge, to understand the basis of our culture, to think creatively about the universe and man's role in it. The school tries to help the individual "to understand and judge the integrations proposed by others. . . . All of this is but a means to an end — that the individuals begin to organize their own experiences. The task is to whet, not satiate the integrative appetite."[12]

Individualizing instruction is not new. From time to time under various names there have been attempts to challenge the individual to attain his highest potential. Experimental programs have had as objectives one or more of the following:

1. To challenge each child to attain his maximum potential.
2. To help each child select activities of special interest to him.
3. To help each child proceed in his tasks at his own pace.
4. To permit each child to move from task to task and grade level to grade level on the basis of readiness for learning.
5. To assure the individual child a balance of creative experiences and basic skills and drill, while utilizing effectively space, equipment, materials, and people.

Such plans as dual tracks or multiple tracks (in which a child could shift from track to track), or level plans (in which he could move from level to level at his own rate), or acceleration (in which he could "skip" a grade on reaching a certain level of achievement) were criticized for placing undue emphasis on academic achievement rather than on growth in areas of behavior, particularly the social learnings.

Well known among the efforts to use an individualized approach to teaching were the Winnetka and Dalton plans. Washburne abolished grade promotion and failure per se in the Winnetka Plan; studies were divided into individual and group activities, the former being subdivided into specific tasks. Social learnings were taken care of by providing two periods a day for group and creative activities, and two periods a day for individual instruction in fundamental skills. In the Dalton Plan, devised by Helen Parker, formal recitation was

[11] Taylor Morse, "Administrative Procedures," in Nelson B. Henry (ed.), *The Integration of Educational Experiences*, Fifty-Seventh Yearbook, National Society for the Study of Education (Chicago: University of Chicago Press, 1958), p. 170.
[12] Paul Dressel, "Integration: An Expanding Concept," in *ibid.*, p. 259.

replaced by the conference. Classrooms took on the aspect of laboratories. Each child accepted a "contract," which he completed at his own rate with the aid of several teachers instead of a single homeroom teacher; each contract covered a designated amount of work. He could work on the contract and complete the assignments or work sheets as rapidly as his interest and ability permitted. The nonacademic learnings were undertaken by the class as a whole.

Chief criticism of the Dalton Plan centered around two factors: the pupils were under pressure to complete the contracts, and the contracts tended to become highly compartmentalized. They were, however, an attempt to modify the ill effects of the graded structure and to allow pupils to move ahead at their own rate unimpeded by uniform grade restrictions. As happens so frequently with a motivating spirit behind the idea, the form crystallized and what was left was the technique; the creative idea died.

Individualized instruction is possible either in the graded structure of the departmentalized and self-contained classroom or in the more fluid organization of the nongraded school. The chief problems center around developing contracts or compacts with the students in all subjects and creating a learning environment that has both a resource center and a resourceful teacher. It calls for better-qualified teachers, better utilization of teacher time, effective use of technological equipment and materials, and more individualized activity.

The core of the program is a resource center, where pupils spend a third of the time in listening and/or viewing booths. Here they study the appropriate lessons in English, social studies, mathematics, or science by dialing the particular lesson needed on closed-circuit television.

The teacher meets with students for small-group discussion of problems encountered in the lessons that have been televised or taped. If the pupil needs to rehear the lesson or parts of it in order to solve problems, this is possible. Group discussion extends old concepts and promotes the expression of new concepts.

Evaluation of individual lessons is made through the use of testing machines. The student takes the appropriate test, receives the scoring, and restudies as the scoring indicates. One-third of the student's day may be spent at his desk with his own books and in the laboratories, shops, libraries, and project rooms doing individual work.

In order to carry out such a program effectively the teacher must be free to spend about 50 per cent of the time in group sessions with students, 25 per cent in preparation, viewing, committee meetings, and staff planning, and 25 per cent in individual conferences with students and conferences with parents to discuss children's progress. Close personal contact with each pupil supplies essential motivation, but group processes and communication skills are not neglected.

In such types of instruction as teacher-pupil compacts or contracts, individual projects, independent research activities, unit plans, self-instructive materials, and self-evaluative devices are necessary. Individual instruction is a method of meeting the needs of children who (1) are motivated to participate in special projects in which they can proceed at their own rate, (2) are able to carry on independent research, and (3) respond well to long-range assignments that require ability in organizing, developing, and evaluating material and progress toward predetermined goals. Through the teacher-pupil compact the teacher can adjust learning experiences to cope with individual differences.

Organizing and developing a program which emphasizes individualized instruction is dependent upon skill in teaching children to work alone. "Children need to learn to work independently in many ways with many materials. Being able to do this involves knowing how to proceed independently with an assignment and how to follow systematically from one activity to another. This, in turn, requires the ability to understand and follow directions, as well as such study and library skills as locating needed books, using reference materials, finding information, and taking notes."[13]

The teacher-pupil compact challenges the teacher as well as the pupil. The course or subject is organized into a major work project, a research project, or a series of assignments which the student agrees to complete as rapidly as possible, at his own rate, working out the problem in his own way. If one teacher is responsible only for the language arts, he plans that course of study himself. Another teacher may be responsible for social studies and still another for arithmetic or science. In order to provide for individual differences in ability teacher-pupil compacts may be organized on three levels

---

[13] J. Wayne Wrightstone, "What Research Says About Class Organization for Instruction," in Marvin D. Alcorn and James M. Linley (eds.), *Issues in Curriculum Development: A Book of Readings* (Yonkers-on-Hudson, N.Y.: World Book Company, 1959), p. 257.

of difficulty to permit the gifted, the average, and the slow learner not only to proceed at their own rate but to achieve on their own level of ability.

This plan has the advantage of allowing the pupil to advance as rapidly as possible. His progress is based solely on his ability to learn. He must complete one assignment before moving on to the next. The gifted child is not penalized by having to wait for others in the class to catch up with him; he is not assigned to teach the slow learners, or to relieve the teacher of such chores as monitoring other students, passing out paper, conducting reading classes, helping children with workbooks, or tidying up the room because he has finished his work early. As for the slow learner, he proceeds at his optimum rate and is not threatened by failure.

Schools experimenting with individualized instruction may begin with compacts in one or two areas at first — reading, language arts, music, science, or mathematics.[14] In one such program the pupils spend a half-day with a homeroom teacher responsible for language arts and social studies. The rest of the day they have separate classes in science, mathematics, art, and music with a specialist teaching each class. Progress in the language arts and social studies is still based on traditional grade-level system corresponding roughly with the students' chronological ages. However, in the other subjects they progress at their own rate.

When teachers become skilled in planning projects and contracts which children can work out, when they learn to organize material around topics or problems requiring the completion of specific assignments, when they discover ways of allowing children to evaluate their own work objectively, more experimentation with teacher-pupil compacts is likely to follow.

Dual- and triple-track curricula can be adapted to the elementary classroom in order to provide for individual differences in learning. The teacher must provide for two or three levels of materials as well as two or three levels of assignments to make such a plan effective. As soon as the teacher begins to experiment with individualizing instruction he opens up a new world of organizing learning experiences for children through teacher-pupil compacts and flexibility in facilities, schedules, materials, and assignments. The use of dif-

[14] "NYU School of Education Tries Dual Progress Plan," *Phi Delta Kappan*, 40:36, October 1958.

ferentiated assignments, differentiated texts, differentiated laboratory work allows each child to work at his own rate. The teacher-pupil compact offers the teacher a challenge, although it means additional record keeping, testing, a greater variety of materials and books, and frequent interviews with children.

The advantage of this method is that it places more responsibility for integrating learning where it rightly belongs — on the individual. Its disadvantage is that it makes unusual demands upon the teacher: — keeping individual records of progress, formulating individual compacts, and planning and evaluating with the students as they work out their projects.

Trump[15] suggests that the secondary school of the future will be organized around three kinds of activities: large-group instruction, individual study, and small-group discussion. Such activities would also be challenging to elementary school children. Serious consideration should be given to more flexibility in grouping. Problem solving and discussion require small groups. On the other hand, music and art may be carried on in larger instructional groups. And reading, arithmetic, and handwriting may well call for individualized teaching. Once a staff starts to re-examine its practices the possibilities are endless.

## *Problem Solving*

Faced by a problem the solution of which appears important, children are motivated to respond to the question "How can we find a solution?" If they are to improve their ability to solve problems they must be encouraged to experiment, observe, read, discuss, inquire, and make use of all available resources. The problem may grow out of the child's own perplexity or it may come from the teacher, the textbook, or a curriculum guide. Whatever the source, the pupil's need to find a solution will influence his learning.

The terms "problem solving," "critical thinking," and "scientific method" are often used interchangeably. In any case, these are the

[15] J. Lloyd Trump, *Images of the Future: A New Approach to the Secondary School* (Urbana, Ill.: Commission on the Experimental Study of the Utilization of the Staff in the Secondary School, 1959).

primary steps in the process: (1) recognizing and defining the problem; (2) clarifying the problem through definition of terms, distinguishing between facts and assumptions; (3) collecting and organizing data; (4) formulating possible solutions or explanations (hypotheses); (5) selecting one or more promising hypotheses for testing and verification; and (6) stating tentative solutions.

Research studies indicate that the acquisition of scientific methods and attitudes is facilitated by direct teaching. Teaching subject matter alone does not measurably train in the scientific method.[16]

Problem solving is also used as an integrating thread in organizing learning experiences. Developing skill in problem solving helps the student to find relationships. He encounters a problem as he tries to reach a specific goal; he needs to solve the problem in order to move ahead; in the process of solving it, he learns.

Group problem solving, too, is an important skill. How can we improve our health? How can we plan a profitable summer? How can we organize a school newspaper? How can our city attract industry? How can we get ready for junior high school? These problems challenge not only the individual but the group as a whole. At times the group study begins with a personal concern. At other times it begins with a group concern. When used as the element for integrating learning experiences, the over-all problem is analyzed and subproblems are formulated which require solution of the over-all problem and use of the problem-solving technique.

The questions facing the teacher are: How do children learn to solve problems? Why do children need the problem-solving skills? What specific steps does problem solving involve? How can the teacher help children to use the scientific method? How can the teacher help children improve in critical thinking skills?

Teachers have the responsibility of helping children live successfully in their world by facing and solving problems as they meet them. Problem solving is an essential prerequisite to citizenship in the larger community into which the child will move. He has his

---

[16] George Wessel, "Measuring the Contribution of Ninth-Grade General Science Courses to the Development of Scientific Education," *Science Education*, 25:336–339, November 1941. John Dewey, *How We Think* (Boston: D. C. Heath and Company, rev. ed., 1933). Francis D. Curtis, "Some Values Derived from Extensive Reading in General Science," doctoral dissertation, Teachers College, Columbia University, 1924. Oreon Kesslar, "The Elements of the Scientific Method," *Science Education*, 29:273–278, December 1945.

apprenticeship for adult citizenship by living in a classroom in which the democratic process is an integral part.

"Everything we know about environmental forces in personality development points to the assumption that the individual *who is emotionally capable* of utilizing critical-mindedness and reasonable judgment in attacking problems will have these powers developed and made more effective by years of practice in situations which may require them."[17]

Problem solving provides the pupil with still another means of tying together many different experiences and organizing and inter-relating new experiences. The student who learns with a network of integrative threads can select a specific learning experience out of many and bring it to bear on his current problem so that it will have meaning and aid him in future learning. Students skilled in the problem-solving technique can apply definite procedures in unfamiliar situations.

Unless the teacher himself is skilled in problem solving it is difficult if not impossible to arrange a classroom environment in which the technique is used. The outline for a problem-solving sequence which many elementary teachers have used successfully includes the following steps:

1. Phrase the problem as a question.
   a. Question may concern a matter of fact.
   b. Question may concern a matter of policy.
   c. Question may concern a matter of value.
2. Define the problem.
   a. Set up the objectives.
   b. Define all terms.
   c. Reach an agreement upon acceptable definitions.
3. Determine the extent of the problem.
   a. Explore the scope of the problem.
   b. Limit the scope to the ability of the group.
   c. Limit the scope to the time available.
4. Set up tentative solutions to the problem.
   a. Begin with known information.
   b. Locate the possible sources of information.

[17] John H. Niemeyer, "Education for Citizenship," in Nelson B. Henry (ed.), *Social Studies in the Elementary School*, Fifty-Sixth Yearbook, National Society for the Study of Education, Part II (Chicago: University of Chicago Press, 1957), p. 226.

    c. Collect additional information needed.
    d. Organize material into tentative solutions.
    e. List the possible solutions.
  5. Choose the best solutions.
    a. Analyze and interpret all solutions, checking each against the objectives.
    b. Choose the solutions which best meet the objectives.
  6. Carry out or recommend the chosen solutions.

Once the teacher understands the process of scientific thinking and uses it in his approach to problems he cannot stand by and expect the children to absorb it. He has a threefold responsibility: (1) to arrange the classroom environment in such a way that teacher-pupil planning and evaluation are possible, (2) to accept each child as a worth-while individual and create a climate in which children are free to discuss their problems, (3) to develop skill in problem-solving techniques and in leading discussions. Many teachers would like to give children the opportunity to participate in the problem-solving, but they have neither the technique nor the skills required. Children need guidance. They sense their own lack of maturity in defining and solving problems and realize that the process should be a vital part of their educational experience. If a teacher feels guilty about the time spent in discussion of problems, if he believes the child should be taught to read, write, or calculate every minute of the day, he will be unsuccessful in creating the atmosphere in which problems can be defined, discussed, and solved. If he is convinced, however, that an education is what you have left when you have forgotten specific facts, then he will see the value in helping children solve problems and will realize that the more responsibility the child takes for integrating his own learning the more able he will be to move forward in his development after he has left the classroom.

Under the guidance of a wise teacher skilled in the techniques of problem solving, children will learn to gather facts and base their conclusions on them. The kindergartner who looked at a new rectangular aquarium insisted, "That won't be good for guppies because the bowl should be round so the fish can swim round and round." The teacher listened as several other children expressed their points of view. Finally she said in a matter-of-fact voice, "Are you sure about your facts or are you just guessing?" She suggested that they find out how to build a balanced aquarium and test their opinions. In the fact-finding sessions that followed, the children learned something about the difference between a fact (what is really true on the basis of sound evidence) and opinion (what one believes from hearsay or incomplete information). As children test their ideas to find out when they are using opinions or hunches and when they are using fact they progress in discussion skill and critical thinking.

Youngsters who learn to gather data before arriving at conclusions become more discriminating and quicker to detect false claims in advertising or other persuasive techniques. They are less likely to fall prey to propaganda. They may learn to demand data as evidence for a statement more promptly than does the average adult.

"Instead of submitting to mass pressures, poor choices, smooth talk and no-time-to-think attitudes today's children can be guided to acquire the skills needed to think straight and thereby live more honestly and satisfyingly."[18]

*Evaluation of a Problem to Be Solved.*   Questions for the teacher:

1. Have we defined the problem clearly?

2. Is the problem one for which the children see a need for solution?

3. Does the problem have several possible solutions?

4. Will it motivate children to help in planning, collecting, evaluating, and organizing the data?

5. Will it necessitate a variety of ways of obtaining and reporting the data?

6. Will it require teacher guidance and participation in seeking solutions or drawing conclusions?

7. Will it provide the children opportunity to utilize the solution in the situation from which the problem arose in the first place?

8. Will it assure the possibility for moving ahead once it is solved?

[18] Roma Gans, "Teaching the Child to Think Straight," in Vincent J. Glennon (ed.), *Frontiers of Elementary Education,* IV (Syracuse: Syracuse University Press, 1957), p. 24.

CYCLE OF ACTIVITIES IN PROBLEM SOLVING

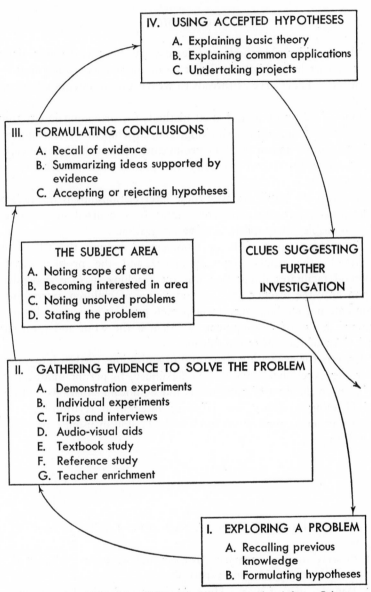

**IV. USING ACCEPTED HYPOTHESES**
   A. Explaining basic theory
   B. Explaining common applications
   C. Undertaking projects

**III. FORMULATING CONCLUSIONS**
   A. Recall of evidence
   B. Summarizing ideas supported by evidence
   C. Accepting or rejecting hypotheses

**THE SUBJECT AREA**
   A. Noting scope of area
   B. Becoming interested in area
   C. Noting unsolved problems
   D. Stating the problem

**CLUES SUGGESTING FURTHER INVESTIGATION**

**II. GATHERING EVIDENCE TO SOLVE THE PROBLEM**
   A. Demonstration experiments
   B. Individual experiments
   C. Trips and interviews
   D. Audio-visual aids
   E. Textbook study
   F. Reference study
   G. Teacher enrichment

**I. EXPLORING A PROBLEM**
   A. Recalling previous knowledge
   B. Formulating hypotheses

Source: Contributed by Phillip G. Johnson to the Atlanta Science Curriculum Committee. Used in Annie Sue Brown, "Unlocking Doors of Understanding," *The Delta Kappa Gamma Bulletin*, 26:55, Summer 1960.

## *Conclusion*

Ideas, problems, methods, and devices have been used as organizing centers that help children relate two or more separate learning experiences. They serve as threads to weave a more integrated curriculum.

One of the most widely used methods for providing integration, individualization, critical thinking, and enrichment of learning experience is the unit of work or group study, in which basic concepts, skills, and values serve to unify the pupil's understanding of his environment.

To help the pupil discover these interrelationships is the task of education. Learning experiences must be organized in a manner which enables the pupil to achieve integration.

An understanding of the development of the unit, the role of the textbook, the teacher-pupil compact, and the problem-solving method facilitates integration but the teaching itself is dependent upon how the teacher uses his knowledge of children, curriculum, content, and methodology to help each pupil as he weaves his own unique design of development. Content is the woof and creativity the warp of the integrated fabric.

Criteria for evaluating structural organizations used in integrating learning experiences involve (1) flexibility, to permit modification of plans in the light of pupil needs and significant situations, (2) ease of planning sequence and effective integration relationships, (3) contribution to pupil motivation, and (4) skill in using a particular curriculum design.

## ACTIVITIES AND QUESTIONS

1. Observe in an elementary classroom and see what method is used to integrate the learning experiences.

2. Define a unit of work. How many types of units did you find in your reading of the text and references suggested at the end of the chapter? What characteristics distinguish the types?

3. In your opinion, should all teaching in the elementary school be carried on by the unit method? Why or why not?

4. What problems must be taken into consideration in planning and developing a unit of work or group study?

5. What advantages do you see in the teacher-pupil compact as a way of organizing learning experiences? What disadvantages?

6. Set up a role-playing situation in which you, a third-grade teacher, are planning to introduce a new unit on Indians. You are about to begin when one of the children interrupts with the statement "Oh, we studied Indians in the second grade where I came from." How will you resolve the situation?

7. Arrange a role-playing situation in which you are helping a beginning teacher to plan a daily schedule which provides for unit teaching plus time for basic skills. In the middle of your session, in walks a senior teacher who is opposed to the whole idea of units as so much "play" and interrupts your discussion.

8. Make use of the steps in problem solving in a discussion of the role of the textbook as the determiner of skills to be learned and the sequence in which they are to be learned.

9. What criteria would you use in selecting a problem as an organizing center? A method? A concept?

10. Examine a subject-matter unit and an experience unit. Which appears to you to be more effective in integrating learning experiences? Cite your reasons.

11. Plan to debate the topic "*Resolved,* That the beginning teacher is more likely to succeed in a subject-matter than in an experience approach to a unit of work."

12. Evaluate the following in terms of your reading in this chapter and selected references.

   One of the outstanding characteristics of the American public school system is the local autonomy in the matter of education for children. When one goes into a foreign country to observe in the schools or when foreigners observe in our schools, the question of a centralized educational program is a very real issue. One of the surprises visitors from abroad have is the wide variety in education programs and curriculum designs.

   A proposal by Hanna[19] of a design for a curriculum to serve the ends of our national community suggests the replacement of local

---

[19] Paul Hanna, "Design for a National Curriculum," *Education Digest,* 24:1, December 1958.

school boards and state educational commissions by an agency of the national government to determine curriculum design. This proposal would seek to attain educational objectives through a nationwide administration of a single curriculum design controlled by federal action.

# BIBLIOGRAPHY

"Audio-Visual Supplement," *The Instructor*, 67:59–90, June 1958.

Bathurst, Effie G., Blackwood, Paul, *et al. The Place of Subjects in the Curriculum*, U.S. Office of Health, Education and Welfare, Bulletin No. 12. Washington, D.C.: Government Printing Office, 1949.

Brown, James, Lewis, Richard B., and Harcleroad, Fred. *Audio-Visual Instruction: Material and Methods*. New York: McGraw-Hill Book Company, 1959.

Brown, James I. "Two with One Stone," *College Composition and Communication*, 8:41, 42, February 1957.

Burton, William H. "Implications for Organization of Instruction and Instructional Adjuncts," in Nelson B. Henry (ed.), *Learning and Instruction*. Forty-Ninth Yearbook of the National Society for the Study of Education, Part I. Chicago: University of Chicago Press, 1950, pp. 224 ff.

Campbell, Ronald F. "Articulating Elementary and Secondary Schools," *Elementary School Journal*, 58:257–263, February 1958.

Clark, Carl A. "A Look at Some Class Teaching Methods," *Chicago Schools Journal*, 19:65–69, November–December 1957.

"Curriculum Planning and Development," *Review of Educational Research*, 27:237–304, June 1957.

Dale, Edgar. "Improved Teaching Materials Contribute to Better Learning," in Harold Shane (ed.), *The American Elementary School*. New York: Harper & Brothers, 1953, pp. 233–234.

Dale, Edgar. "Educational Means," *Educational Research Bulletin* 36:43, 44, February 13, 1957.

Dallmann, Martha. "Bulletin Boards of the Month," *Grade Teacher*, 75:54, May 1958.

DeHaan, Robert F. and Havighurst, Robert J. *Educating Gifted Children*. Chicago: University of Chicago Press, 1957.

Dorff, Joseph A. "In-Service Improvement of School Bulletin Boards," *Educational Research Bulletin*, 36:267–272, November 13, 1957.

*Educators Guide to Free Films,* Mary Foley Horkheimer and John W. Diffor (eds.). Randolph, Wis.: Educators Progress Service, 18th ed., 1958.

*Educators Guide to Free Slidefilms,* Mary Foley Horkheimer and John W. Diffor (eds.). Randolph, Wis.: Educators Progress Service, 1958.

Fulton, W. R., and White, Frederick A. "What Constitutes Teacher Competence in Audio-Visual Communication?" *Phi Delta Kappan,* 40:158–160, January 1959.

Hanna, Lavone A., Potter, Gladys L., and Hagaman, Neva. *Unit Teaching in the Elementary School.* New York: Rinehart and Company, 1955.

Hanna, Paul R. "Design for a National Curriculum," *Education Digest,* 24:1–4, December 1958.

Harrison, Raymond, and Gowin, Lawrence. *The Elementary Teacher in Action.* San Francisco: Wadsworth Publishing Company, 1958.

Heffernan, Helen. "No Mean Hut," *Childhood Education,* 34:112–117, November 1957.

Herrick, Virgil E. "The Concept of Curriculum Design," in Virgil E. Herrick and Ralph W. Tyler (eds.), *Toward Improved Curriculum Theory.* Supplementary Educational Monographs No. 71. Chicago: University of Chicago Press, 1950.

Hunt, Herold C., and Pierce, Paul. *The Practice of School Administration.* Boston: Houghton Mifflin Company, 1958.

*Instructional Materials for Elementary Schools.* Thirty-Fifth Yearbook of the Department of Elementary School Principals. Washington, D.C.: National Education Association, 1956.

Keliher, Alice. "Creative Classroom Management," *Grade Teacher,* 75:101, May 1958.

*Kindergarten Resource Handbook,* Kindergarten Curriculum Guide. Appleton, Wis. Public Schools, n.d.

Laing, James M. "The Role of the Curriculum Co-ordinator," *Education,* 78:87, 88, October 1957.

*Lesson Plans Using Audio-Visual Materials in Teaching on Three Grade Levels: Primary, Intermediate, Junior-High.* Macomb, Ill.: Western Illinois University Bulletin No. 37, 1958.

Mackenzie, Gordon N. "What Should Be the Organizing Elements of the Curriculum?" in Virgil E. Herrick and Ralph W. Tyler (eds.), *Toward Improved Curriculum Theory.* Supplementary Education Monographs No. 71. Chicago: University of Chicago Press, 1950, pp. 51, 52.

Miel, Alice (ed.). *Continuous Learning.* Association for Childhood Education International, Bulletin No. 87. Washington, D.C.: The Association, 1951.

National Society for the Study of Education. *Education for the Gifted.* Fifty-Fourth Yearbook, Part II, Nelson B. Henry (ed.). Chicago: University of Chicago Press, 1958.

National Society for the Study of Education. *The Integration of Educational Experiences,* Fifty-Seventh Yearbook, Nelson B. Henry (ed.). Chicago: University of Chicago Press, 1958.

Parrish, Louise, and Waskin, Yvonne. *Teacher-Pupil Planning for Better Classroom Learning.* New York: Harper & Brothers, 1958.

Ragan, W. B. *Modern Elementary Curriculum.* New York: Henry Holt and Company, 1960.

Rice, Arthur H. "ASCD Defends Balanced Curriculum," *The Nation's Schools,* 61:80–89, April 1958.

Suttles, Patricia Horkheimer (ed.), with John Guy Fowlkes, Educational Consultant. *Elementary Teachers Guide to Free Curriculum Materials.* Randolph, Wis.: Educators Progress Service, 14th ed., 1957.

Tyler, Ralph W. "How Can Learning Experiences Be Organized for Effective Instruction?" *Basic Principles of Curriculum and Instruction.* Chicago: University of Chicago Press, 1950, pp. 54–67.

Tyler, Ralph W. "How Can the Effectiveness of Learning Experiences Be Evaluated?" *Basic Principles of Curriculum and Instruction.* Chicago: University of Chicago Press, 1950, pp. 68–81.

Tyler, Ralph W. "The Organization of Learning Experiences," in Virgil E. Herrick and Ralph W. Tyler (eds.), *Toward Improved Curriculum Theory.* Supplementary Educational Monograph No. 71. Chicago: University of Chicago Press, 1950, pp. 59–67.

part three

Curriculum Areas

# 7

... Language is the tool by means of which the child tries to do the great bulk of his thinking, whether that thinking be concerned with building an idea, making a judgment, drawing a conclusion, or solving a problem.

PAUL MCKEE

# Teaching the communication skills

The ability to talk over problems, to sit around a conference table and discuss varied points of view, to settle differences by means of tongue and pen — not the fist or the sword — is the hallmark of civilized man. As the ability to communicate becomes increasingly significant in this interstellar age, schools must assume greater responsibility for teaching children the arts of listening intelligently and critically, expressing ideas effectively through the spoken and written word, and thinking clearly and honestly. "Effective communication at home and abroad is the chief means by which men will find a way of living together around the world in harmony with our belief in the inherent dignity of man and the worth of the individual."[1] Only as individuals learn to use the language arts to understand, analyze, and improve the world in which they live can they be said to be truly educated. To the school is assigned the task of "releasing the individual's language potential, of cultivating his talents, of correcting his imperfections and of developing in him an attitude favorable to future growth."[2]

## Children and Communication

In many homes there is a constant bombardment of sounds from the television set, the radio, the phonograph, and assorted voices. Children adapt to this confusion by giving only halfhearted attention to what they hear. They engage in fringe listening, selecting only those sounds that appeal to them at the moment. They are easily distracted, quickly bored, and unwilling to concentrate for any length of time. They adopt the careless speech they hear around them. They need to be taught to listen and to speak as well as to read and to write.

From the moment a child is born he is dependent upon the adults in his environment to teach him to speak correctly, to ask questions, and to evaluate the answers. "The kind of world a youngster gets inside his head depends upon the questions the child asks and the answers his elders give him."[3] The young child is a living question mark. He wants to know why; he wants to know how; he wants to know what; he wants to know where. The four-year-old asks hundreds of questions a day as he explores his world.[4] For him speech is a continuous activity during the waking hours. What happens to

---

[1] Commission of the English Curriculum of the National Council of Teachers of English, *The English Language Arts* (New York: Appleton-Century-Crofts, Inc., 1952), p. 271.

[2] *Ibid.*, p. 273.

[3] Wendell Johnson, *Your Most Enchanted Listener* (New York: Harper & Brothers, 1956), p. 8.

[4] *Ibid.*, p. 9.

this quest for knowledge when he enters school depends upon the opportunities he is given for practicing and developing the language arts.

Parents are the first teachers of the language arts. "A six-year-old child is pretty well integrated into the language used by his family and friends. . . . The facts of nature, human life, and human society which act so as to channel, restrict, or encourage conversation are the primary shapers of speech."[5]

Parents who value the significance of communication skills make an effort to help children develop these skills before they reach school age. However, many parents through ignorance, indolence, or indifference fail to assume this responsibility. "At least a third of our school children live in homes where reading is not a normal daily activity. . . . Fully half the children never see writing done in the home. A large segment of the school population literally believes that reading and writing are school tasks rather than daily duties."[6] For such children the opportunity to learn effective oral and written expression must be provided by the school. For these children, too, the experience of hearing a cultivated voice may be limited to listening to a teacher who sets an example of good speech.

## *Teachers and Communication*

"There is no question in my mind about the importance of communication and my responsibility in helping children develop skills in language. My problem is not *why*. My problem is *how*. I try hard enough to get my children to talk, but they just sit there and look at me. I bring up interesting subjects for discussion, but I get absolutely nowhere. I don't know what to do." As Miss Miller, a primary teacher, sighed, Miss Johnson broke in with "You don't know how lucky you are. I wish mine would keep quiet long enough to listen to the assignment. When I'm trying to teach

[5] Donald J. Lloyd and Harry R. Warfel, *American English and Its Cultural Setting* (New York: Alfred A. Knopf, Inc., 1956), pp. 42, 43.

[6] Harry R. Warfel, "Structural Linguistics and Composition," *College English*, 20:209, 210, February 1959.

reading children keep coming up and interrupting the class to ask me what they are supposed to do next. Why weren't they taught to listen?"

Mr. Russell, the intermediate teacher, spoke up. "Mine talk and listen, but they can't write. If they don't learn to write, what good will talking and listening do?" Mr. Brown, who had been unusually quiet, voiced his concern. "The supervisor dropped in last Friday to listen to the reading class. That was fine. They read well and carried on an interesting discussion in connection with the unit on Brazil. When it came to the spelling period I was embarrassed. I don't find much time to teach spelling and apparently they didn't do too much with it in the fourth grade. I wish we could spend some time in faculty meetings in trying to improve our teaching in this area."

## Principles for Teaching the Communication Skills

*Integrated Experiences and Separate Teaching of Skills.* Activities should include both integrated experiences and separate teaching of the five basic skills of listening, speaking, reading, writing, and spelling. The average child develops these skills in sequence; he listens before he speaks, speaks before he reads, usually reads before he writes, and writes before he spells. Not all children follow this pattern, but all do use the skills interrelatedly according to their interests, needs, and abilities.

*Emphasis on Communication Skills as Tools.* Through communication children extend their knowledge. "When the school teaches a child to read, his ability to learn is immeasurably enlarged, since reading . . . is the key to the rich storehouse of human experience."[7] The development of the language arts as useful tools for future learning is a significant development in today's schools.

*Concerted Attack on the Common Language Difficulties.* Every teacher should be a teacher of English and should help children in

[7] Guy T. Buswell, "Helping Children Learn How to Live," *Learning and the Teacher*, 1959 Yearbook of the Association for Supervision and Curriculum Development (Washington, D.C.: National Education Association, 1959), p. 146.

his group to be at home with correct forms of usage and to improve their vocabularies through experiences in which the common difficulties in the language arts are solved. Because they learn largely through imitation children are entitled to hear correct speech throughout the school day and to receive specific help in improving their own communication skills.

*Planning Activities in Terms of Individual Students.* Children differ as much in communication skills as they do in other abilities. Kindergarten children range from those like Alvin, who has not yet learned to speak, to those like Stephen, who expresses himself freely and effectively on every possible occasion. During a sharing period in kindergarten Stephen made the following contribution: "We went to Notre Dame over the week end. We stayed at the hotel and my brother Daniel was with us. He is studying medicine. Then he can take care of us when he isn't too busy with other patients."

*Insistence upon Attainment of a Level of Proficiency in Each of the Five Skills.* The level of proficiency should be consistent with the level of the child's development. The teacher should keep in mind each child's design of development, his need for a particular skill at each level, and his ability to improve in the skills through informal and formal experiences.

The teacher should be familiar with the key concepts pertaining to each of the communication skills. He must also know how to select, organize, develop, and evaluate learning experiences and find effective ways of fostering creativity in the process of teaching.

# Listening

In the years ahead it seems certain that we shall be influenced even more by the things we hear than by the things we read.

RALPH G. NICHOLS AND
THOMAS R. LEWIS

Schools have always accepted responsibility for teaching reading. Listening, however, was taken for granted on the assumption that when a teacher stands in front of the class and speaks the child automatically listens; that he needs no specific training in learning to listen, or in listening to learn. Recently, however, there has been a move to teach the aural skills of listening and speaking as well as the visual skills of reading and writing. One of the tenets underlying the interest in listening is that in the school we should teach those skills which we are going to use most frequently throughout our lives. An early study by Rankin[8] points out that 70 per cent of our waking day is spent in verbal communication — 45 per cent of this time in listening, 30 per cent in speaking, 16 per cent in reading, and only 9 per cent in writing.

An even higher percentage of classroom time (57.5 per cent) was

[8] Paul T. Rankin, "The Importance of Listening Ability," *English Journal* (College Edition), 17:623–630, October 1928.

spent in listening, according to Wilt,[9] whose observation of children in classrooms reveals that most of them listen for an average of more than two and one-half hours out of a typical five-hour day. It can be assumed that much of this time they are listening to the teacher and participating in listening and speaking activities.

Other writers, including Anderson,[10] Beery,[11] Brown,[12] and Nichols and Stevens,[13] have emphasized the fact that of all the communication skills listening has received the least amount of attention. Markgraf[14] made a study of listening pedagogy among the 411 colleges and universities of the American Association of Colleges of Teacher Education. Responses from 839 educators in 406 of the institutions indicated that 44.5 per cent included a unit on the methods of teaching listening. Three schools, 0.7 per cent, offered a specialized course in listening. To the question "Do you believe that high school and elementary school teachers should endeavor to teach listening?" the replies were Yes: 84.3 per cent; No: 5.9 per cent; Other: 9.8 per cent. Obviously theory is in advance of practice.

With the advent of television the amount of time spent in listening increased. Witty[15] reports that children now average somewhat more than twenty hours a week with television. In addition they give considerable time to the radio and other activities that involve listening. Accordingly, it is imperative that greater emphasis be placed on teaching and guiding listening.

## Key Concepts in Listening to Learn

*Learning Through Listening and Reading.* The ear is as important an organ for learning as the eye. In fact, listening involves the

[9] Miriam E. Wilt, "A Study of Teacher Awareness of Listening as a Factor in Elementary Education," *Journal of Educational Research*, 43:626–636, April 1950.

[10] Harold Anderson, "Teaching the Art of Listening," *School Review*, 57:63–67, February 1949.

[11] Althea Beery, "Listening Activities in the Elementary School," *Elementary English*, 23:67–69, February 1946.

[12] James I. Brown, "Why Not Teach Listening?" *School and Society*, 59:113–116, February 12, 1949.

[13] Ralph G. Nichols and Leonard A. Stevens, *Are You Listening?* (New York: McGraw-Hill Book Company, 1957).

[14] Bruce Markgraf, "A Survey of Listening Pedagogy in American Teacher-Training Institutions," master's thesis, University of Wisconsin, 1960.

[15] Paul A. Witty, "What Children Watch on T–V," *The Packet* (Boston: D. C. Heath and Company), Winter 1959–60, pp. 1–15.

assimilation of aural and visual clues. It requires motivation, attention, concentration, previous acquaintance with the material, and guided, graded practice.

Children absorb an impressive amount of their information and ideas from non-written sources. It is listening, not just reading, that has given them information or misinformation about themselves, their communities, and the world in which they live. "For every fact which a student can trace to a book, there are more that can be traced to the spoken word."[16]

*Efficiency of Listening and Reading as Media of Learning.* "Experiments make it clear that learning can take place effectively through listening and through reading — in many situations, perhaps with equal success through either approach. Any difference in learning efficiency may be traced not to the visual or to the auditory presentation, but instead, to factors such as the difficulty or nature of the material to be learned, the way in which it is presented, and its suitability in terms of the experience and interests of the group studied."[17] What is needed is direct teaching in both listening and reading.

*Listening: A Combination of What We Hear, What We Understand, and What We Remember.* When the teacher says to a six-year-old, "Write your name at the bottom of the page and hand it in when you are finished," she should not be surprised if some of the children turn the paper in without a name at all, some turn it in with the name in the usual place (at the top of the right-hand corner), and a few follow the instructions to the letter. The teacher cannot be certain that every child will do what he is asked. Telling is not teaching. There is no guarantee the child has really listened in the sense that he heard, understood, and recalled the directions. The teacher must remember that listening is a combination of hearing, understanding, and remembering.

White makes this distinction between hearing and listening: "A person 'hears' if he is conscious of having received the sound waves produced by the speaker. A person 'listens' if, in addition to being

[16] Joseph Mersand, "Developing Competence in Listening in Secondary Schools," *The Speech Teacher*, 7:289, November 1958.

[17] Paul A. Witty and Robert A. Sizemore, "Studies in Listening: III. The Effectiveness of Visual and Auditory Presentation with Changes in Age and Grade Level," *Elementary English*, 36:138, 139, February 1959.

aware of such stimuli, he attaches appropriate meanings to them. Hearing is a passive process, listening an active one."[18]

*Formal Listening as a Group Activity.* In most cases listening activities are planned for the group as a whole. The child listens to the teacher's instructions as a part of the group. He listens as the teacher talks; he listens during the socialized recitation or the group discussion; he listens as members of the group give talks or speeches. Some schools provide a listening laboratory where individuals as well as groups are allowed to go at whatever times of the day are convenient for them. They use the facilities available and keep a record on individualized progress charts. Tests before and after a series of listening exercises contribute to the effectiveness of such training.

*Adjustment to the Pace of the Speaker.* The listener has to adjust to the rate of the speaker, and he must concentrate because the speaking word-rate is slower than the thinking word-rate. The difficulty comes when the listener uses the differential between these in daydreaming and woolgathering. Teaching the child to concentrate, to listen for the main thought, to try to recall what the speaker said in sequence takes careful, persistent work and requires time for practice.

*Relationship of Listening and Reading.* Several important interrelationships exist between reading and listening. (1) The first instruction in reading comes to the child through the spoken word of the teacher, and his ability to listen and comprehend is vital. (2) Listening is the prime means of verbalized learning throughout the primary grades. Listening comprehension continues to be superior to reading comprehension in the primary grades. (3) Telling pupils to be quiet and listen attentively is useless without specific instruction in listening skills. (4) Children with limited listening vocabularies tend to have difficulty in reading. (5) Poor auditory discrimination is associated with poor reading and may be a contributing factor. (6) Listening helps the child get main ideas. (7) The young child retains what he learns through hearing longer than what he learns through reading.

*Types of Listening.* Appreciative listening is that which is in response to any kind of stimuli that is gratifying to the listener. Critical listening is that which evaluates the speaker's argument or

[18] Eugene E. White, *Practical Speech Fundamentals* (New York: The Macmillan Company, 1960), pp. 189–190.

evidence. Discriminative listening is that which has as its purpose the comprehension of ideas.

*Teaching of Listening.* Without trained listening there is only about 25 per cent recall.[19] Listening must be taught through specific graded exercises. It cannot be left to chance. Primary children prove to be the best listeners in terms of mental age. They are eager to set up and follow standards and participate in listening exercises.

Training in listening skills brings about decided improvement.[20] Perhaps the best statement of the reasons for instruction in this neglected phase of communication skills is that by Brown, one of the pioneers in listening research.

1. Listening is the most frequently used of the language arts.
2. Critical listening is more difficult than critical reading.
3. The most important affairs of this country are carried on around the conference table.
4. We cannot excuse ourselves by saying that people automatically and without effort learn how to listen effectively.
5. We cannot claim that in every respect except listening there are individual differences which must be taken into consideration in planning and conducting education experiences.[21]

The kind of listening teachers hope to help their pupils achieve has been defined by Hook as "the conscious, purposeful registration of sounds upon the mind, and it leads to further mental activity."[22] A more comprehensive definition given from the point of view of the teacher is that of Baird and Knower. "Profitable listening requires more of the listener than his presence. He must recognize the ideas presented, evaluate the ideas presented, discover relationships among them, and select from what he hears those ideas he finds worth remembering. If a listener makes his listening a thoughtful process, he controls his own thinking; if he does not listen critically, he is little more than a sponge, and often not a very good one."[23]

---

[19] Alice Sterner *et al.*, *Skill in Listening* (Chicago: National Council of Teachers of English, 1944), p. 4.

[20] Kenneth O. Johnson, "The Effect of Classroom Training Upon Listening Comprehension," *Journal of Communication*, 1:57–62, May 1951.

[21] Brown, *op. cit.*, p. 116.

[22] J. N. Hook, *The Teaching of High School English* (New York: The Ronald Press Company, 1950), p. 216.

[23] A. Craig Baird and Franklin H. Knower, *General Speech* (New York: McGraw-Hill Book Company, 1949), pp. 281–282.

*Relationship of Listening and Speaking.* The best speakers in the class are usually the best listeners. They recognize the value of good listening as they talk, and in turn give careful attention to other speakers. Courteous listeners become attentive audiences. Communication is a two-way process. It requires a listener as well as a speaker to communicate and share ideas.

## MISCONCEPTIONS ABOUT LISTENING

Because listening is so important to learning, the question is often raised: Why isn't listening taught in all schools? One of the main reasons has been that many people have misconceptions about listening. They believe:

1. That listening ability is largely a matter of intelligence. (Actually, we listen more with our experience than with our intelligence.)
2. That listening ability is closely related to hearing acuity. (Only 3 to 6 per cent of the school population suffer hearing defects serious enough to impair learning in the classroom situation.[24] Many times children feign hearing loss because they are bored and consequently do not "pay attention.")
3. That daily practice eliminates the need for training. (Children do not automatically learn to listen because the teacher tells them to "pay attention." A study in the Nashville public schools showed that "individual variation in listening comprehension at any single grade appears to be as great as variation in reading comprehension and that developing ability in listening is a curriculum problem."[25]
4. That to learn to listen, we need only to learn to read. (Research indicates that the effective way to develop any skill is through direct training designed to improve the skill. Studies by Blewett,[26] Brown,[27] and Johnson[28] support this generalization.)

[24] Ralph G. Nichols and Thomas R. Lewis, *Listening and Speaking* (Dubuque, Iowa: William C. Brown Company, 1954), p. 8.
[25] Ralph G. Nichols, "Factors in Listening Comprehension," *Speech Monographs*, 15:155, June 1948.
[26] Thomas Blewett, "Experiment in Measuring Listening," *Journal of Communication*, 1:50–57, May 1951.
[27] James I. Brown, "Can Listening Be Taught?" *College English*, 15:290–291, February 1954.
[28] Kenneth O. Johnson, *op. cit.*

5. That learning to read is more important than learning to listen. (People listen three times as much as they read. Listening influences the behavior of people to a marked degree, as witness the psychological methods used on the air to get people to buy things they neither need nor want.)

## Learning Through Listening in the Kindergarten and Primary Grades

What listening skills should be taught in kindergarten and the primary grades? What activities will develop the needed skills? How does the teacher go about setting up standards for teaching these skills?

A teacher who was faced with a large kindergarten gradually developed these standards for listening through discussion with her children:

We listen when someone else is talking.
We wait for children to be ready.
We stop what we are doing and pay attention.
We listen with our ears.
We do not interrupt the speaker.
We listen when the teacher speaks, signals, or "talks with her eyes."
We listen to the whole thing.

A good listener in kindergarten exhibits the same characteristics as a good listener in the upper grades. Basic skills are essentially the same. They expand with maturity.

In making plans the teacher should determine the types of listening skills he wishes to develop, organize activities which will help develop them, and decide on evaluation procedures. Listening skills and activities may be organized into three categories: listening for directions, listening for information, and listening for enjoyment.

I. Listening for directions
   A. Objectives
      1. Putting distracting materials out of sight
      2. Lending an ear from the beginning
      3. Listening actively to learn who — when — where — what

B. Techniques
1. Waiting until everyone is attentive
2. Speaking simply, with clear-cut phrases
3. Organizing material so it is brief, systematic, explicit
4. Making use of visual aids to support the auditory experience

C. Activities
1. Listening to directions and announcements
2. Playing games such as
   a. "Do this": Initiate a game by tapping a nursery rhyme on the table and ask the child to repeat the action.
   b. "Follow directions": Have a child respond to a direction, such as "Hop over to the door and say 'Good morning.'"
   c. "Listen and tell": Have children close eyes and identify sounds.
3. Learning to stop activities when announcements are made and listen courteously
4. Distinguishing signals for fire drills, storm shelter drills, end of class periods, and others

D. Evaluation
1. Did the speaker wait until the children were ready to listen?
2. Did the children listen when someone was speaking?
3. Did they stop what they were doing and pay attention?
4. Did they remember what was said?
5. Did they distinguish the signals and know what to do?

II. Listening for information
A. Objectives
1. Interest in subject or project
2. Desire to share experiences with others
3. Listening actively to understand what is said
4. Noting sequence of ideas
5. Evaluation of relative importance of ideas
6. Holding the thread of a discussion in mind
7. Watching for transitional phrases and change of subject
8. Courtesy, even when one disagrees
9. Intelligent and pertinent observations
10. Reserving judgment while listening to different points of view

B. Activities
1. Sharing period — show and tell, conversation

    2. Discussing, planning, and evaluating

    3. Working in groups and committees

    4. Oral reading, storytelling

    5. Telephoning

    6. Raising and answering questions in connection with a problem

    7. Giving a summary of what has been said

    8. Giving a summary of a story read aloud

  C. Evaluation

    1. Did the children remember the information?

    2. Did they act on the information?

    3. Did they use the information in productive ways?

    4. Did they work independently on the basis of the information?

    5. Did they discuss and evaluate on an increasingly mature basis?

III. Listening for enjoyment

  A. Objectives

    1. Developing the ability to enjoy good music, drama, literature (stories well told or read), choral speaking

    2. Value of the numerous sounds around us

  B. Activities

    1. Listening to good vocal and instrumental music, literature, drama, and poetry

    2. Responding rhythmically to music

    3. Planning original ending to a story

    4. Arranging instrumentation for rhythm band

    5. Perceiving the sounds around us

    6. Listening to selected radio and television programs

  C. Evaluation

    1. Did the children grow in their ability to enjoy the creative arts?

    2. Did they grow in their ability to appreciate literature, music, and rhythms?

    3. Did they grow in ability to listen appreciatively to programs given in the school auditorium or one of the classrooms?

    4. Did they grow in ability to listen with discrimination to programs on radio and television?

If teachers organize activities to include experiences in listening discriminatingly, critically, and appreciatively from kindergarten throughout the elementary grades the children will have learned one of the skills essential to successful living. Learning to listen cannot be left to chance. Listening must be taught.

The teacher should provide for balanced activities which give the children opportunities for each type of listening skill; he should appraise the listening skills on the basis of levels of listening attained; and he should plan for individual and group experiences and social growth in listening. The individual experiences include: listening as children tell about week-end excursions and parties; showing and telling about possessions; listening to directions, messages, telephone conversations, stories, and rhymes. Group experiences give children opportunity to develop discussion and evaluation techniques as they plan a class party; discuss a problem of interest; plan an experience chart; work on committee assignments; evaluate a program, a play, or the day's activities; or summarize the unit of work. Social growth in listening deals with progress in listening courteously when anyone is speaking, developing both sides of the conversation (listening and speaking), sensing the propriety of occasions when talking is out of order, such as in libraries, churches, or theaters, during rest periods, and when an adult is speaking.

Children in the primary grades benefit from listening for information and for appreciation to regularly scheduled radio and television programs devoted to music, stories, and plays. Experiences of this type require preparation before the broadcast and follow-up activities after the broadcast.

Time should be provided for specific instructions in listening to directions, with checkups to see if the children understand them. Then there is listening during the news or sharing period, and listening during assembly programs. For the latter, the children can explore the behavior expected of audiences through role playing, and evaluate the program upon returning from the auditorium, emphasizing the quality of listening as well as the quality of the program.

Specific things to listen for on a trip to the fire station, for example, might include the following:

Listen to the directions of the teacher.
Listen for sounds of birds.
Listen to identify the noises around us.
Listen to the fire chief who explains the duties of the firemen.
Listen to the sounds of the siren, the voices of the firemen.

Listen to one another during the discussion which follows the trip.

Other audience situations include listening to stories and poems read or told by the teacher and pupils, listening to the science program on radio or television, listening to stories told by the librarian, recognizing words that rhyme, listening for words beginning with the same sound.

## Learning Through Listening in the Intermediate Grades

One of the most challenging responsibilities of the intermediate teacher is to get children to listen without wasting a great deal of time. Unless they have been building up skills of attentive and active listening it may be necessary to start with the fundamentals. One fourth-grade teacher used the line "Friends, Romans, countrymen, lend me your ears" as her attention getter. It worked like a charm. The children became intrigued with the idea of setting up a code for listening and worked out the following standards:

We listen while another is speaking; we do not interrupt.
We enjoy stories read by the teacher and other children.
We listen attentively to school radio broadcasts and the recording of music and stories.
We listen courteously to class discussions and reports.
We give complete attention to the person who is talking.
We evaluate what we hear.

By the time these children were ready for junior high school they had developed the following listening standards:

We listen with respect to the opinions of others.
We evaluate critically the reports made by other children.
We listen carefully to the school radio and television programs.
We listen appreciatively to literature read orally.
We listen actively in order to comprehend, evaluate, and enjoy what we hear.

Typical of the guided exercises that help children develop listening skills is the following excerpt to be read aloud by the teacher of a sixth grade, followed by a written test to check on the ability to understand and remember what was heard.

What queer creatures we would be if we could hear with our eyes and see with our ears! We cannot, of course; however, the bat uses its ears as we do our eyes, to avoid collisions. Watch a bat early some summer evening. How fast he flies! Yet he seldom hits an object. Stretch fine wire between trees. He will not strike the wire as he flies. He does not see the wire either in light or in darkness. He hears it. We look about us as we move rapidly, so that we will avoid obstacles. The bat listens for them. How? As he flies he makes shrill noises rapidly. His ears can hear them, but yours cannot. The bat can tell by the echo where an object is and how close to him it is. Think of all the sights and sounds around you that you never see or hear! Do you know why you cannot?

Observing the bat's method and making use of radar, scientists have invented a small box for the blind to carry. As the blind person approaches an object, his earphones, attached to the box, buzz. The length of the buzz tells him how near to the object he is. Thus, the blind person "sees" with his ears, in somewhat the way a bat does.

1. The text tells how scientists have
    (a) improved upon nature
    (b) applied nature's principles for their own use
    (c) learned little or nothing from nature
    (d) destroyed nature
2. The bat's "blind flying" has been, for most of us,
    (a) mysterious
    (b) understandable
    (c) explainable
    (d) easily interpreted
3. The bat seldom hits an object while he is flying because he
    (a) feels it
    (b) sees it
    (c) hears it
    (d) smells it
4. About how many miles per hour do you think the bat flies?
    (a) 5
    (b) 10
    (c) 15
    (d) 20
5. When the bat "sees" in the dark, what is it that tells him how to avoid objects when flying?
    (a) radar

   (b) echo

   (c) radio

   (d) wind

6. We cannot "see" in the dark as well as the bat does because our

   (a) eyes are not so good as his

   (b) nose is not so sensitive as his

   (c) ears are not so keen as his

   (d) attention is poorer than his

7. The blind are greatly helped to avoid running into things they cannot see by the discovery and use of

   (a) radio and echo

   (b) radium and echo

   (c) radar

   (d) echo

8. What helps to make the blind person "see" in somewhat the same way as the bat does?

   (a) a small box

   (b) earphones and radio

   (c) a small box and earphones

   (d) earphones

9. What is it that tells the blind person how close he is to an object when he is moving about?

   (a) loudness of the buzz he hears

   (b) length of the buzz in the earphones

   (c) vibration of the box he holds

   (d) a small electric shock

10. This invention which aids the blind person to move about safely is the result of

   (a) scientific research

   (b) chemical research

   (c) study of the ear

   (d) study of the eye[29]

## Conclusion

Listening to learn is receiving increased emphasis in our schools. Research shows that children need training in listening, that listening

[29] William A. McCall and Lelah Mae Crabbs, *Standard Test Lessons in Reading* (New York: Bureau of Publications, Teachers College, Columbia University, n.d.), Book E, Lesson 7, pp. 7, 8.

should be taught, and that it should be taught through systematic, planned instruction. Through listening the student experiences satisfactions in hearing beautiful phrases and artistic expression; he enhances his appreciation of poetry, drama, and various forms of literature; he grows more discriminative in evaluating the language he hears and thereby extends and improves his own usage; he becomes better able to recall information and ideas; he learns to react critically and become selective as he learns.

It is through a conscientious application of the guides for teaching listening that the teacher helps the child to develop the ability to understand, retain, and evaluate what he hears. Increased skill in acquiring, retaining, and using information will enlarge the student's opportunities for learning, capacity for friendship, and chances for vocational success. Increased competence in critical evaluation of what he hears can help protect the individual from propaganda, trickery, sham, and high-pressure salesmanship. It can help him remain calm in time of hysteria, and efficient in time of stress.

## ACTIVITIES AND QUESTIONS

1. Observe in a primary grade and try to determine the proportion of time the child spends in listening to the teacher. What types of listening did you observe? What did the teacher do to improve the listening skills of the children? What did she do to evaluate the children's growth in listening?

2. If listening skills are so vital to success in teaching a child to read and to communicate, why isn't more time devoted to this phase of the communication skills in the elementary school?

3. Outline a program for teaching three types of listening skills to a group of intermediate children. Be specific about objectives, activities, evaluation, and methods of teaching.

4. Suggest a bibliography on teaching listening for the use of a primary grade teacher. Limit your selection to five of the books that you have found most helpful.

5. Administer the listening test included in this chapter to a group of

children in an intermediate grade. Determine their ability to listen in the sense that they hear, comprehend, and remember what is read.

# BIBLIOGRAPHY

Association for Supervision and Curriculum Development. *Research Helps in Teaching the Language Arts.* A report prepared for ASCD by Harold G. Shane. Washington, D.C.: National Education Association, 1955.

Barbara, Dominick. "Art of Listening," *Today's Speech*, 7:5–7, February 1959.

Blewett, Thomas. "Experiment in Measuring Listening," *Journal of Communication*, 1:50–57, May 1951.

Brown, James I. "Can Listening Be Taught?" *College English*, 15:290–293, February 1954.

Brown, James I. "How Teachable Is Listening?" *Educational Research Bulletin*, 33:85–93, April 1954.

Caffery, John G. "Auding," *The Review of Educational Research*, 25:121–38, April 1955.

Commission of the English Curriculum of the National Council of Teachers of English. *The English Language Arts.* New York: Appleton-Century-Crofts, Inc., 1952.

Hubbell, Richard. *Television Programming and Production.* New York: Murray Hill Books, Inc., 1945.

Johnson, Kenneth O. "Effects of Training on Listening," *Journal of Communication*, 1:57–62, May 1951.

Johnson, Wendell. *Your Most Enchanted Listener.* New York: Harper & Brothers, 1956.

Lloyd, Donald J., and Warfel, Harry R. *American English and Its Cultural Setting.* New York: Alfred A. Knopf, Inc., 1956.

Mikalson, Elaine. *Listen and Learn* (Records for Children). Children's Music Center, 2858 West Pico Blvd., Los Angeles, n.d.

Neville, Mark A. "Listening Is an Art: Practice It," *Elementary English*, 36:226–233, April 1959.

Nichols, Ralph G. *Are You Listening?* New York: McGraw-Hill Book Company, 1957.

Nichols, Ralph G., and Lewis, Thomas R. *Listening and Speaking.* Dubuque, Iowa: William C. Brown Company, 1954.

Russell, David H., and Russell, Elizabeth F. *Listening Aids Through the Grades.* New York: Bureau of Publications, Teachers College, Columbia University, 1959.

Walker, Lalla. "Nashville Teachers Attack the Problem of Listening," *Education*, 75:345–49, January 1955.

Warfel, Harry R. "Structural Linguistics and Composition," *College English*, 20:208–212, February 1959.

Whyte, William H., Jr. *Is Anybody Listening?* New York: Simon and Schuster, 1952.

Wilt, Miriam E. "A Study of Teacher Awareness of Listening as a Factor in Elementary Education," *Journal of Educational Research*, 43:626–636, April 1950.

Wilt, Miriam E. "What Is the Listening Ratio in Your Classroom?" *Elementary English*, 26:259–264, May 1949.

Witty, Paul A., and Sizemore, Robert A. "Studies in Listening: I. Relative Values of Oral and Visual Presentation," *Elementary English*, 35:538–552, December 1958.

Witty, Paul A., and Sizemore, Robert A. "Studies in Listening: III. The Effectiveness of Visual and Auditory Presentation with Changes in Age and Grade Level," *Elementary English*, 36:130–140, February 1959.

Witty, Paul A., and Sizemore, Robert A. "Studies in Listening: A Postscript," *Elementary English*, 36:297–301, May 1959.

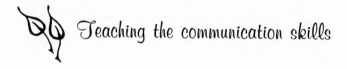 

# Speaking

> It is not enough to know what to say,
> but it is necessary also to know how
> to say it.
>
> ARISTOTLE

People are swayed by words. People are moved to action by the flow of words that sound convincing to the ears. People are lulled to sleep by patterns of speech that have the effect of hypnosis. From the lips of a good man speech is a force for right. From the lips of a demagogue it is a force for evil. Quintilian defined an orator as "a good man skilled in speaking." In a society in which group action is an integral part of the pattern of life, it is essential that all the members recognize the power of communication skill — and recognize, too, that with power goes responsibility for using it to improve society.

As the world shrinks, communication skills become increasingly important. In the life of every individual, the child as well as the man, the ability to communicate is a prerequisite for status in the group. Ability to express ideas clearly and succinctly, to listen courteously but critically, and to evaluate introspectively yet objectively is important in a democratic society. In fact it is to people who develop such skills, and who are able to get along with others, that we look for leadership.

Even preschoolers are unimpressed with the child who cannot express himself intelligibly. They are frank, and although they follow the teacher's lead in helping the child improve, they receive his opinions with less respect. Most children speak before they come to school. Speaking is an avenue through which they learn about their world.

By the time he enters the first grade the "average" child has established his basic speech patterns. "He uses the basic structures and tunes of the language with an expertness that will not be greatly increased — although his range will widen — through a long life."[30]

An important doctrine of structural linguistics holds that speech is a social inheritance which a child masters by the age of six. Early experience with language is usually concentrated. For the first three years the parents make great effort to help the child gain fluency and accuracy in speech. For the next three years they give less attention to his speech, for by this time he is reaching out to play with other children and makes speech his chief occupation. "He reaches out for language with a hunger that often exceeds his physical desire for food. Food he eats occasionally; speech is his ceaseless activity in waking moments."[31]

When he enters school he should be challenged with innumerable opportunities for improving the skills he has already attained. The teacher must be sensitive to the evidences of readiness for new experiences in language expression. He must be sure that his classroom is one in which a child is encouraged to express himself, in which his contributions are appreciated, in which his efforts are valued, and in which his interests, abilities, and needs are considered. In a happy classroom environment teacher and children are constantly discovering new and challenging ideas, and every child is developing communication skills and creative interests.

## *Key Concepts in Speaking to Communicate*

*Experiences.* The child who has experiences can express himself more fluently and listens with greater interest because he has some-

[30] Harry R. Warfel, "Structural Linguistics and Composition," *College English*, 20:209, February 1959.
[31] *Ibid.*, p. 209.

thing to share with others. Experiences in themselves are less valuable to the child's development if he is not encouraged to talk about what he has seen, and given opportunity to clarify his thinking and concepts. Having something to say and wanting to say it is more readily accomplished in an environment in which children are motivated to explore and solve problems.

*Language Ability in Proportion to Opportunity for Practice.* In the school where children were seen and not heard it was difficult for oral language skills to flourish. Children who were told repeatedly "We don't talk here" could not suddenly turn on the speech mechanism when the teacher said, "Will you give us a report about the country you are studying?" In the proper speech environment the children are motivated to develop individual interests and talk over new and exciting ideas.

*Environment and Language Skills.* The child who is in an environment in which correct speech is an integral part of daily living, who participates in discussions, is encouraged to ask questions, and receives intelligent answers, who has many experiences and hears stories, is much more likely to have adequate speech skills and to use them when he is given the opportunity. The child who hears slovenly speech is handicapped when he comes to school. Since children imitate the speech they hear, teachers, too, need to guard against careless speech habits.

*Language and Thought.* Thinking is often described as subvocal speech. Have your speech muscles ever become tired when you have been concentrating for a long time? You think with symbols. If you say, "I know what I mean but I cannot say it," you are telling only a half-truth. You probably have a vocabulary extensive enough to express the idea, but you are not clear enough about the idea to put it into words. As the power to express increases, the power to think also improves. The same skills are needed in organizing thinking as are needed in organizing speech.

*Speech as a Means of Extending Horizons.* Watch a young child as he uses his resources to extend his boundaries. "What's this?" "Why is it?" "What makes it work?" "Why won't it go?" "What will happen if . . .?" "What is that plane in the sky?" What — why — where — how — when — The child learns not alone through observation; he learns by asking and finding answers to questions. Speech helps him to understand himself and to understand the world around him and the people who live in it. Speech helps him to communicate with others.

*Speech and Personality.* The child who is tense, worried, and strained shows it in his voice. As the violin string is tightened to produce a higher tone, so the tightening of the throat muscles produces a high-pitched voice which has an unpleasant effect on the listeners as well as on the speaker. The teacher should keep his own voice low and his throat muscles relaxed in order to help the children in the group relax. A well-modulated voice should be an essential part of the teacher's equipment. Many schools screen out teachers who have problems in diction, articulation, or voice quality. Children imitate not only the pattern of speech but voice quality as well. Unfortunately they seem to imitate poor speech more readily than good speech patterns.

*Speaking as a Social Activity.* A child adapts to his social world through speech; he uses speech to influence others and to participate in group discussions. He learns that he must listen to others if he wants them to listen to him. He tries to speak so he can be understood and talks about things that are interesting to the group. He discovers, too, that he can gain his own ends more effectively through speech than through physical action — that instead of grabbing for the ball one asks for it. True, he finds that some children are not as mature as he is. They still grab. But he likes to hear the teacher say, "Billy asks for what he wants. He doesn't grab." He likes, too, to hear the teacher say, "Let's sit down and discuss it. I'm sure we can come to some agreement about what to do." Speech is significant for communication and is the most important tool for social adjustment.

*Good Speech: Audible, Acceptable, and Agreeable.* The speaker must be heard. Even the preschool child can learn to project his voice so that all can hear. Speech should be acceptable. It is the responsibility of the teacher to understand speech development so that he recognizes when and how to help a child with articulatory and voice problems. The classroom environment should be such that the child feels free to speak without worrying about being laughed at if he has speech difficulties. The teacher's own voice should be agreeable, and free from harshness, nasality, tenseness, shrillness, huskiness, or throatiness in order to set a good model for the child.

*Speech Problems.* If the child's speech is inadequate to meet his communication needs he should be helped to improve his skills. If he says, "Widy div me da wed waddon to pay wi?" or calls for "Dwamma Doddy" the teacher has not written finis to the task when he deciphers the code and recognizes the first as "Will you give me the red wagon to play with?" and the second as "Grandma Coodry." He must help the child communicate more effectively. "A speech deficiency can become a potent factor . . . in contributing to a person's feelings of inferiority, of being different, of not belonging. A serious defect of speech such as stuttering, cleft palate, or a severe articulatory disorder, may effect the individual in a very concrete and far-reaching way."[32]

## *Speech Activities in the Kindergarten and Primary Grades*

Nowhere in the elementary school is the guiding of language experiences more rewarding than in kindergarten and the primary grades. At this stage children develop rapidly in speech skills and vocabulary. The teacher should keep in mind objectives of oral communication as he plans stimulating activities in meaningful situations.

*Share and Tell.* Sharing experiences informally in a show-and-tell period is one of the most interesting speech situations in the daily schedule. Children are eager to tell about things of interest to them — pets, family, trips, holidays, visits, new clothes, new babies, weather, toys, and gifts — though they vary in ability to express their ideas. Some youngsters can hardly wait for an opportunity to share their news. Others find it easier to express themselves orally if they have something to show. They like to bring treasures from

[32] Virgil A. Anderson, *Improving the Child's Speech* (New York: Oxford University Press, 1953), p. 11.

home and show them to the group. At first they may do little more than hold up the object, shyly give the name, and sit down. The teacher must guard against doing all the talking. For example, if Dorothy brings her doll up to show, the teacher sometimes unwittingly launches into a monologue: "Oh, Dorothy, you brought your new doll to school. Is her name Dotty? Where did you get her? Did Mother buy her? Did Santa bring her? What does she do? She closes her eyes, doesn't she?" And Dorothy is gently pushed aside to make room for the next child to "show and tell." Rather, the teacher should encourage the child to tell all she can about her doll. The response may be, "This is Elaine. She is my new doll. Mother brought her from the Baby Shop. She can walk, talk, and dance. She can cry, too." Later children can leave the articles at home and discuss topics of interest, thus developing their language skills without leaning on the crutch of the "show and tell." The period can develop into "share and tell" and can be interesting to children throughout the primary grades.

*Conversation.* Conversation is an art. Children learn to converse through informal talking together which differs from the sharing period. Conversation between two or three people is an important activity in the kindergarten and primary grades. There is time to converse before school begins, during the work period, at recess, and during small group or committee meetings. Children learn to distinguish between the informal activities in which they are free to converse and the more formal discussion and planning period. If the groups are engaged in planning activities the teacher can move from group to group to help children pinpoint the discussion and plan to return to a committee of the whole and report their findings.

*Dramatic Play.* In imaginative play little children relive familiar experiences and explore new ones; they "try on life" and begin to understand people and social relations. Familiar home experiences and imaginary companions are examples. This activity is spontaneous and child centered.

"I'll be the mother. You be the father. You be Jane. You can be the baby."

FATHER: I'm not going to work today. There is a strike at the plant. I am going to sit on the porch and watch the snow and rock. Jane, get ready for school or you'll be late.

MOTHER (*interrupts*): There goes that phone again. (*Picks up receiver.*) Who? Mrs. Lane? How do you like the snow? Just a minute, the baby is crying. She's all right now. Just a minute, Mrs. Lane. Here is my brother at the door. I better see what he wants. Maybe his car wouldn't start.

FATHER (*grumbling to himself*): There goes my day off. That's life for you.

Children also identify with people outside the home — the baker, the grocery man, the pilot, the conductor, or the captain — as they play store, airplane, train, and boat.

*Greetings, Introductions, and Messages.* Children enjoy dramatizing the social situations: how to greet each other and visitors, how to introduce parents and friends, and how to be hosts and hostesses. Such expressions as "thank you," "I'm sorry," "please," "pardon me" should become a part of the child's social vocabulary.

*Telephone Techniques.* If it is possible to have a telephone in the classroom children will make a greater effort to learn the mechanics and manners of good telephone conversation. For example, if you are really answering the telephone you hold it correctly because that is the only way you can hear. A group of children who had a phone of their own in the room became very efficient in the proper procedure. A typical conversation was, "Elementary School, Billie Blank speaking. With whom do you wish to speak? He's with the outdoor group. Please hold the line and Miss Smith will call him to the phone." Fine audio-visual aids for telephone experiences are available through army surplus.

*Giving Talks.* Children enjoy telling about what they did during the work period. They like to explain the process used in making the clay bowl, in building the castle, the store, or the boat. They are often explicit in telling how to get to the post office, the library, or the store. They can describe the standards for a particular activity. They can tell the group about the pictures they painted. They can give talks about trips, hobbies, and activities.

*Planning and Evaluation.* Participation in planning the activities of the day should begin early in the school career. It is a source of security because the children know what will happen next. They can move smoothly from one activity to another without bothering the teacher at each turn. They like to see the daily schedule either posted on a chart or written on the chalkboard. In addition to the few minutes' discussion of the day's plans every morning, the children may plan a program to entertain their parents or they may discuss the plans for a trip and the standards for evaluating their behavior afterwards.

*Interviews.* Primary children are not too young to learn the techniques of interviewing. They need to set up standards so they are poised in the situation and do not act "silly" when interviewing such people as the principal, the nurse, the mailman, the policeman, the fire chief, the custodian, or the zoo-keeper. A group of children in a primary grade set up the following standards:

> Greet the person in a friendly manner.
> Introduce yourself.
> Ask pertinent questions politely.
> Listen courteously.
> Take notes or remember what he tells you.
> Thank the person for the interview.
> Plan to write a thank-you note from the entire group.

## Speech Activities in the Intermediate Grades

Many of the speech activities begun in the primary grades continue in the intermediate grades on a level commensurate with the added maturity, increased skills, broadened interests, and new needs of the children. Although primary grade children participate in such activities as talking before the group, giving informal reports, and engaging in group discussions, older children need more advanced skills, particularly in giving talks, holding group discussions, and conducting meetings.

### GIVING TALKS

Informal speech activities continue, but techniques are refined. The children learn the purposes of speaking, the principles of finding a topic, collecting material, organizing the talk, adapting it to the audience, practicing it, and giving it.

The classroom environment should make the children feel at ease in expressing themselves both formally and informally. Conversational speaking should be encouraged. In fact, the children should understand that a good talk is like good conversation in the essential respects. The purposes for which people give talks are to entertain, to inform, to stimulate, to convince, and to actuate.

The sole purpose in the *speech to entertain* is to get and hold attention. Any information that may be given is incidental. The speech is usually humorous, but it need not be. It may have an exciting story or a ghost story as its basis. Many times the speech starts with "Let's pretend that . . . ," and the speaker is off into the realm of imagination, weaving a spell around his listeners.

In the *speech to inform*, the speaker tells how to do or make something, how it works, what the plans are, or where we are going. It is through the speech to inform that we gain much of our new knowledge. This is the speech most often given.

The purpose of the *speech to stimulate* is to arouse interest in doing what the listeners already know they should do. The belief already exists, but the urge to do anything about it has been lacking. The pep talk to get the student body to back any school project is a common example of the speech to stimulate.

In the *speech to convince*, the speaker is trying to change opinions. The listeners may be indifferent or opposed to his suggestions. He must present reasons that will help them change their minds.

The *speech to actuate*, may be the outgrowth of either the speech to stimulate or the speech to convince. The group goes out to support the team; the majority votes for the candidate the speaker has been electioneering for; the students sign the petition.

In selecting a topic the speaker should choose something with which he and the audience are familiar. The following four factors should be considered: the purpose, the speaker, the occasion, and the audience.

In preparing for the speech the child reviews what he knows about the subject, he reads, he observes, he inquires of authorities, and he evaluates the material to see what he can use. In planning the construction of the speech he includes an introduction, a body, and a conclusion.

*Types of Organization.* Speeches in the elementary school may be organized on any of the following patterns: chronological (time sequence), spatial (space or location sequence), effect and cause, need and plan, personal experiences, visual aid (demonstration), and "string-of-beads."

The *chronological* pattern is one of the easiest for the elementary school child. He relates events in their time order. Describing his vacation trip he tells what happened each day. If he decides to tell the group about his birthday party he may begin with the decision to have the party and then give in sequence the events that led up to the party, the events of the party, and the cleaning up afterward. This type of organization is used most often for the speech to inform.

In the *spatial* organization the child tells what he sees step by step. The near objects are described before the farther ones. Spatial order refers to location. If he is describing his school he will start with the view as he turns the corner and sees it, then the close-up description of the grounds, then the entrance, the entrance hall, and the space sequence of the building as he goes to his room. This is an excellent way to organize the speech to inform.

In the *effect and cause* pattern, commonly used for organizing the speech to convince or actuate, the student states the problem (the effect) and then goes on to tell the various causes that he has found leading up to it. Sometimes the order is reversed and the causes are examined to see what logical effect may be expected.

Children frequently give the *need and plan* type of speech without realizing they are giving a speech. The need may be the class picnic. The need is explained, the type of picnic the class wants, and the plans that will make the picnic a success. Perhaps Edwin wants the picnic at the park where there is a shelter house so they can keep dry in case of rain; the park is near enough, too, to reach in the time they have. He uses the need (the picnic) and the plan (where to have it) as his type of organization. This development is used for the speech to stimulate, convince, or inform.

*Personal experience* may be the basis for some of the other types of organization, but it can also be used as the organization itself. The child usually delights in relating experiences he has had at home, on trips, or shopping. This method is usually used for the speech to entertain or inform.

The speech demonstration or *visual aid* is one the child has opportunity to give often as he demonstrates how the engine works, shows step by step how to make a puppet, or points out on the map the route the family took on their trip to the mountains. This method may be used for the speech to inform or actuate.

The *"string of beads"* is a series of stories or incidents, usually all relating to a single theme — the "string" on which the beads are strung. This is especially good for the speech to entertain.

*Making the Talk.* Once the student has his speech ready he must give it in such a way that the audience enjoys what he is saying, listens, and evaluates it. If he knows what he is talking about, if he is interested in the topic, if he is well prepared, giving the speech is a creative experience. By gestures, voice, posture, and attitude he re-lives the experience, re-creates his ideas, and conveys the meaning to an interested audience.

In setting the stage for communication of this kind the teacher first establishes a setting in which the classroom atmosphere encourages real communication and develops standards with the group. In such an environment there is a two-way communication going on. The audience is looking at and listening intently to the speaker, who in turn is giving a vivid explanation or demonstration which takes careful listening and critical evaluation.

DISCUSSION

Discussion is an integral part of the democratic procedure as children talk over such problems as how to get along, how to get ready for Christmas, how to plan a program for mothers, how to spend the money the Parent-Teacher Association allotted, and others. As was shown in Chapter 6, group discussion involves defining the problem, pooling information, suggesting possible solutions, selecting the best solution, and testing the solution. The teacher must know the techniques in order to help children gain skills in leading and participating in discussion.

*Types of Discussion.* By the intermediate grades children can become skilled in carrying on various types of discussion: round table, panel, interview, symposium, and forum.

The *round table* discussion is used most frequently in the classroom. Children and teacher together plan the activities that are needed to solve a particular problem, arriving at decisions through discussion. They work together to define, analyze, and solve the problem and to evaluate the solution. The round table discussion involves the entire class under the direction of a leader.

In the *panel discussion* four to eight members are chosen to represent the various viewpoints of the group. After careful preparation by reading, interviewing, and studying, they discuss the problem or topic under the direction of a moderator. There are no set speeches. A panel discussion is a conversation that is guided by a tentative agenda prepared by the group or the moderator. The panel members should be the best-informed people of the group. A panel discussion should result in the sharing of knowledge, not the pooling of ignorance.

For an *interview*, the child who has the greatest knowledge of the subject should carefully prepare questions to be asked of the expert who is being interviewed before the group. The questions should give the expert opportunity to talk and should not be used to show how clever the questioner is.

In a *symposium* three to six children give prepared speeches on various aspects of a single subject. Care must be taken to see that each child understands the specific topic on which he is to talk and does not speak on the others' material. Each should have a definite time and be held to it, being allowed neither more nor less than the time set. The chairman introduces each speaker and his topic.

The term *forum* is used to designate the question-and-answer period that may follow any of the above types of discussion. The forum may also be used after a lecture or film. The chairman presides, directing the questions to the various members of the panel or symposium or to the interviewer or person being interviewed. The questions usually are asked from the floor, but they may be written out and handed to the chairman.

Boys and girls are interested in learning to solve problems through the pooling of information. They should learn the techniques of group discussion which facilitate problem solving. The type of discussion and the extent to which the children learn correct forms depend upon the maturity, ability, and interest of the group and the skill of the teacher in sensing their readiness for a particular kind of discussion for a specific purpose.

*Why Use Discussion Techniques?* Discussion has several values: the increased ability to express one's ideas, the promotion of careful, exact thinking on the part of the group, the fostering of interest in solving problems, and the development of better relations among members of a group. Children make an effort to think carefully and express themselves clearly if they are contributing to the group solution of a problem. They learn to evaluate, to distinguish fact from opinion, and to make sure of the source of their authority before making positive statements.

They also learn to cooperate with others in group solutions instead of competing in finding the right answer in the question-answer type of recitation. Each person gets an opportunity to contribute. No one should dominate the discussion. Learning to disagree courteously is an important product of this type of activity. The children learn to develop habits of reflective thinking, to be objective, and to look at the facts before they come to a conclusion.

*Topics for Discussion.* Ogilvie lists certain requirements for discussion: "(1) The discussion topic should be within the range of experiences of the members of the group. (2) It should be concerned with a problem that is important to the group. It may be a problem of the classroom, community or nation. . . . (3) It should be controversial, except where group discussion is used as a technique to impart information to others. (4) It should serve, as far as possible, as a basis for planning the activities of the classroom."[33]

*The Role of the Leader.* "I can't seem to accomplish anything through group discussion. It just seems to turn into a 'gabfest,'" said Miss Eberly, the sixth-grade teacher. "If I knew how to handle it I'd use it more often." The teacher must know the responsibilities of the discussion leader and help him discharge them: keeping the discussion moving ahead, staying with the topic or problem to be solved, and developing desirable attitudes on the part of the participants. It is the function of the leader not only to guide but also to encourage each person to do his best thinking and to contribute to the discussion.

Experiments have shown that at times it is well to seat the entire class in a circle and disperse the members of the discussion panel among the "audience" part of the class. "The device works, apparently, on the principle of social facilitation. At any rate, this arrangement draws many of the 'audience' part of the class into the discus-

[33] Mardel Ogilvie, *Speech in the Elementary School* (New York: McGraw-Hill Book Company, 1954), p. 184.

sion, the panel serving to direct and motivate the discussion as it goes along."[34]

It is the leader's place to see that the discussion is not monopolized by any individual. It is his responsibility to (1) state the problem, (2) get the group to think critically, (3) get everyone to partipate, (4) motivate the acquisition of needed information, (5) handle conflict skillfully, and (6) summarize frequently. Tact goes a long way toward maintaining the atmosphere conducive to cooperative group planning and discussion. An evaluation by the group at the end of a discussion is essential if skills are to be improved. Among the questions that should be considered are the following: Did the members all participate? Did they benefit from the discussion? Did the leader assume responsibility effectively?

## The Problem of Acceptable Usage

Usage presents a persistent problem to the elementary teacher. Children come to school from homes of varying backgrounds in speech habits and of various levels of usage. Those who come with a background of cultivated speech patterns present almost no problems to the teacher, except perhaps the task of keeping them from adopting, consciously or unconsciously, less admirable speech. Other children, however, bring with them speech patterns and habits which are inadequate and may in fact be extremely undesirable. The task of the teacher in this case is far from simple. He must help the child not only to break the undesirable speech habits but to substitute patterns of informal, easy, acceptable English. "No one questions this goal, but opinions differ as to the way to accomplish it."[35]

According to Pooley, the most effective type of usage instruction in the elementary grades at the present time emphasizes direct correction and much oral and written practice. Principles which underlie such instructions are as follows:

    1. The number of items for specific attack will be kept as small as possible.

    2. Only speech forms which are frequent in occurrence, and

[34] Charles T. Brown and John J. Pruis, "Encouraging Participation in Classroom Discussion," *The Speech Teacher*, 7:346, November 1958.

[35] Robert C. Pooley, *Teaching English Grammar* (New York: Appleton-Century-Crofts, Inc., 1957), p. 118.

which are unquestionably outside the limits of informal standard speech, will be attacked.

3. Once an item has been selected for correction, no exception will be tolerated. This means that both teacher and pupil must be alert to catch and correct any lapses from the desired form. . . .

4. Specific oral drill upon desired expressions will attempt to anticipate errors. Practice upon such expressions as *I have done my work, I have seen my friend, he ran to the store, they have gone* will establish familiarity with desired patterns and will provide a positive approach to corrections.[36]

The kindergarten and primary grade teachers have the first responsibility for helping the child establish acceptable social usages. These will vary with the neighborhood and the section of the country. It is not wise for the teacher to attempt to impose standards that are foreign to the group or the area. Rather, he should try to discover the best patterns of the community and insist on these. If the child's speech is changed in school to the point of becoming conspicuous, either the child will reject it or he will be rejected. On the other hand, the teacher must make a determined and concentrated attack on the gross errors that are common to large numbers of pupils.

It is important that the teachers agree among themselves on the errors that should be eliminated at various maturity levels. First, they must be sure that they are setting a good example in their own speech. Then they must be sure that the children understand the usages being introduced and the reasons for the changes. Unless the child accepts as logical the reasons for a change he will resist it. He may conform in school but revert to even poorer usage outside of school to show his protest.

One excellent way to introduce good usage is through the positive approach of structuring social situations. Many children are uncertain of what is expected of them in greeting people, introducing friends or relatives, answering the doorbell or telephone, excusing themselves from the group, interrupting a conversation to give a message, and other such situations. If these are practiced until they become second nature the child gains poise and will usually accept the less tangible standards that the school has agreed are desirable for his age group.

As the child progresses into the intermediate grades he can under-

[36] *Ibid.,* p. 119.

stand better the specific reasons for many of the usages he is asked to accept. Although schools often defer "formal" grammar until junior or senior high school, in those elementary schools that do introduce it there should be a close relationship between the teaching of the formal aspects and the teaching of usage. The child should realize that the study of grammar involves an understanding of *why* our language is structured as it is.

In the elementary school, particularly, the teacher should help the child express his ideas with spontaneity, confidence, clarity, and without embarrassment. If there are corrections to be made, they must be made so that a minimum of self-consciousness results. Keeping in mind always the worth of each individual as he learns to communicate effectively will help the teacher improve the usage of boys and girls in the classroom.

## *Conclusion*

To teach speech effectively the teacher must first of all possess a voice that is clear, resonant, well pitched, emotionally warm, and that gives evidence of precise articulation. Such a voice encourages communication in others, particularly the withdrawn and timid. Closely related is an awareness of the speaking voices of the pupils. It is up to the teacher to require and help children develop clear, pleasant, and articulate speech in recitations, discussions, reports, and oral reading.

In addition, the teacher must consciously create an atmosphere in which communication skills can flourish. This means the "creation of an audience by teaching students how to listen. Of prime importance here is the teacher's own voice and classroom manner. . . . A pleasant, well-modulated voice accompanied by a gracious and dignified manner can draw out the most timid. . . . The manner is ideally that of the host in his own living room; confident of his leadership, but aware of his responsibility to avoid dominating the conversation while seeing that all participate."[37] In the interplay of the arts of speaking, listening, and writing we can see beyond question that effectiveness in teaching speech rests with the teacher in the final analysis.

[37] Robert C. Pooley, "The English Teacher's Preparation in Speech," *The Speech Teacher,* 5:189, 190, September 1956.

## ACTIVITIES AND QUESTIONS

1. What can a teacher do to improve the quality of speaking in the primary grades?

2. Nursery and kindergarten children frequently talk as they work with art media. Observe a situation in which a child expresses himself in speech while he is painting a picture, drawing, modeling, or building with blocks. What does the teacher do to encourage this verbalizing or to discourage it? What effect does her behavior have on the child?

3. Discuss with a first-grade teacher the relative significance of form and content in oral communication. Discuss the same problem with an intermediate teacher. What differences do you find in the viewpoints expressed? How do you account for these differences?

4. Observe in a primary grade, other than the first grade, what the teacher does to motivate the children to use the correct forms of expression throughout the school day.

5. Observe in an intermediate classroom to determine how seriously the teacher takes the adage that "every teacher is a teacher of English."

6. How can the elementary teacher integrate communication skills in a subject-centered program? What in your opinion is the most effective way to integrate communication skills with other curriculum areas — in the kindergarten, the primary grades, the intermediate grades?

7. What courses in speech are required for elementary teachers in your state? What suggestions for improvement could you make?

## BIBLIOGRAPHY

Akin, Johnnie. *And So We Speak.* Englewood Cliffs, N.J.: Prentice-Hall, Inc., 1958.

Anderson, Virgil A. *Improving the Child's Speech.* New York: Oxford University Press, 1953.

Baker, Zelma W. *The Language Arts, the Child, and the Teacher.* San Francisco: Fearon Publishers, 1955.

Barbara, Dominick. *Your Speech Reveals Your Personality.* Springfield, Ill.: Charles C. Thomas, Publisher, 1958.

Carroll, Ann. "How to Conduct a Class Discussion," *The Grade Teacher*, 46:47, September 1956.

Childs, Dorothy. "Public Speaking Begins in the Grades," *The Instructor*, 68:56, April 1959.

Francis, W. N. "Linguistics and Composition," *Phi Delta Kappan*, 61:336–341, May 1960.

Greene, Harry A., and Petty, Walter T. *Developing Language Skills in the Elementary School*. Boston: Allyn and Bacon, Inc., 1959.

Hatchett, Ethel L., and Hughes, Donald. *Teaching Language Arts in Elementary Schools*. New York: The Ronald Press Company, 1956.

Johnson, Wendell. *Your Most Enchanted Listener*. New York: Harper & Brothers, 1956.

Jones, Daisy M. "So You Have Something to Say!" *Elementary English*, 36:248–252, April 1959.

*Language Arts for Today's Children*. National Council of Teachers of English Curriculum Series, Vol. 2. New York: Appleton-Century-Crofts, Inc., 1954.

Micken, Ralph. *Speaking for Results*. Boston: Houghton Mifflin Company, 1958.

Mowrer, O. H. "Hearing and Speaking: An Analysis of Language Learning," *Journal of Speech and Hearing Disorders*, 23:143–152, May 1958.

Ogilvie, Mardel. *Speech in the Elementary School*. New York: McGraw-Hill Book Company, 1954.

Pooley, Robert C. "The English Teacher's Preparation in Speech," *The Speech Teacher*, 5:189–194, September 1956.

Pooley, Robert C. *Teaching English Grammar*. New York: Appleton-Century-Crofts, Inc., 1957.

Ralph, David C. "The Flannel Board as an Aid in Teaching Parliamentary Procedure," *The Speech Teacher*, 8:15–22, January 1959.

Rasmussen, Carrie. *Speech Methods in the Elementary School*. New York: The Ronald Press Company, 1947.

Raubicheck, Letitia. *Choral Speaking Is Fun*. New York: Noble and Noble, Publishers, 1955.

Robinson, Edward R. "What Can the Speech Teacher Do About Students' Stage Fright?" *The Speech Teacher*, 8:8–15, January 1959.

Rubenstein, Ben O. "Some Comments about Stuttering for Teachers," *Educational Administration and Supervision*, 45:162–168, May 1959.

Sarett, Lew, Foster, William T., and Sarett, Alma Johnson. *Basic Principles of Speech*. Boston: Houghton Mifflin Company, rev. ed., 1958.

Siks, Geraldine Brain. *Creative Dramatics: An Art for Children*. New York: Harper & Brothers, 1957.

Smith, Raymond G. *Principles of Public Speaking*. New York: The Ronald Press Company, 1958.

"Special Journal Feature — Speech Education" (a symposium), *NEA Journal*, 49:21–36, November 1960.

Sturgis, Alice F. *Learning Parliamentary Procedure.* New York: McGraw-Hill Book Company, 1953.

"A Symposium of Speech for Elementary Schools," *The Speech Teacher*, 9:276–303, November 1960.

Torrence, E. Paul. "Creative Thinking through the Language Arts," *Educational Leadership*, 18:13–18, October 1960.

Van Riper, Charles, and Butler, Katherine G. *Speech in the Elementary Classroom.* New York: Harper & Brothers, 1955.

## IMPROVING COMMUNICATION SKILLS

The need for improved communication skills has never been greater, the need for constructive use of mass media never more urgent. Today's teacher must be aware of the sequence in which the child develops the communication skills, show him how these skills can be used to influence his environment, and teach him to use them for worthy ends. It is through the language arts that the child expresses his personality and his ideas. The importance of communication cannot be overestimated. The determination of the adequacy of each child rests largely on the ability of the child to communicate effectively what he comprehends.

Communication skills, social learnings, and other academic knowledge should develop simultaneously. The school that emphasizes each of these through a wide variety of experiences meets its obligations to the child, to the community, and to society.

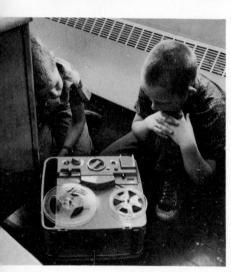

*Listening may be taught in a variety of ways.*

*Curiosity is a prerequisite for reading.*

*Good teaching relates reading to the child's interests.*

*The study of phonics contributes to independence in reading.*

*Handwriting expresses individuality.*

*Student participation vitalizes spelling instruction.*

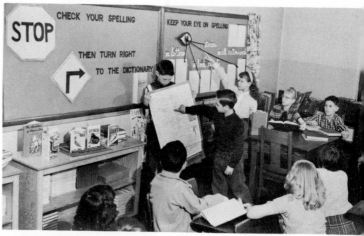

*Group discussion increases verbal facility and stimulates thought.*

# Reading

> Through books we can put on the
> shoes of swiftness, sense the power of
> subduing the elements, discover the
> secret virtues of minerals, sail the seas,
> fly across the mountains on a magic
> carpet.
>
> NAGOL

Few experiences bring greater satisfaction or stimulation, contentment or exhilaration, than reading. Reading is a way of communicating with the great minds of all ages; a way of expanding horizons, increasing understandings, and developing insights. "Reading is something we do, not so much with our eyes as such, as with our knowledge, our interests and enthusiasms, our hatreds and fondnesses and fears, our evaluations in all their forms and aspects."[38]

"The tricks and whimsies of the sky, . . . the creeping vines of ivy and wild grape, . . . the ways of snow, rain, drizzle, sleet, the visitors of sky and weather coming and going hour by hour — he tried to read their secret."[39] The quotation is from Sandburg's description of Lincoln's early schooling. As young Lincoln walked to and from

---

[38] Wendell Johnson, *op. cit.,* p. 123.

[39] Carl Sandburg, *Abe Lincoln Grows Up* (New York: Harcourt, Brace and Company, 1926), pp. 94, 95.

school he observed the oak, the elm, the sweet gum, and the syca-
more. He listened to the birds on the trail that led to the small school-
house of hewn logs. Long before a child reads in the sense of translating symbols, he has been "reading" the meaning of things he
experiences.

Every child needs a rich and varied experiential background,
opportunity for developing skills in oral language, a degree of emotional, social, physical, and mental development, and a desire to read
before he is ready for the complex process of reading the printed
page. The eager pupil and the skilled teacher are still the best combination for teaching reading.

## Key Concepts in Reading

*Reading as a Communication Skill.* A child's reading skill and his
total development are closely related. The teacher should know how
communication skills develop; as pointed out earlier, the child usually
listens before he speaks, speaks before he reads, and reads before he
writes. A substantial vocabulary, fluent expression, skill in discussion
and evaluation are prerequisites to reading with confidence.

*Reading Rooted in Experience.* The initial focus must be on experiences. The child gets meaning from the printed page only as he
brings meaning to it. Broad experiences and reading go hand in
hand. The task of the teacher and parents is to provide the experiences — some of them firsthand and concrete, others vicarious.

*Reading as Responding.* Reading is responding to stimuli. Children respond at several levels: the surface level of recognition and
word calling; the comprehension level of deriving explicit meaning
from a sentence, paragraph, passage, or chapter; the creative level of
discovering new and personal or individual meanings. Teachers
strive for the third level, where "images, memories, identification or
fresh and creative thoughts"[40] are stimulated. They should not be
satisfied to have children plod along laboriously one word at a time,

[40] David H. Russell, "Personal Values in Reading," *The Reading Teacher*,
12:3, October 1958.

word calling, "droning," and "word thumping" without giving any thought to the meaning behind the words. Motivating children to read at the third level is a persistent and challenging task.

*Reading as a Socializing Experience.* Reading becomes creative when the individual identifies with the characters of the writer's imagination, relives their experiences. Through books children's lives are enriched and they gain broader understanding of others. Those growing up in isolated areas can emerge from their limited environment and become part of a broader society.

*Contagion of Enthusiasm for Reading.* A desire for reading, a recognition of need to interpret the symbols, is something that the child acquires much as he catches the measles or a cold, "by being exposed to someone who already has it."[41] He is most likely to catch it from a parent, a teacher, or even a favorite relative who loves to read and who reads stories to him. Once he has the desire, nothing will suffice until he learns to break the code. He will then use his own resources in much the way he learns to ride a bicycle, skate, play ball, or play the piano. Reading then becomes an exciting experience.

*Reading as a Developmental Process.* Most people do not fully realize how long it takes to learn to read. It takes a lifetime — and even then the goal is not wholly achieved. Reading development progresses year by year, not in a series of separate steps but in patterns which merge almost imperceptibly as one moves from stage to stage. The teacher's task is to understand the child *and* the reading process — to determine when the child is ready to move ahead, when he needs to work on a particular skill for a longer period, and when a certain method should be modified and improved or discarded in favor of a more effective one.

*Complexity of Reading.* Anyone who has taught reading realizes that it involves physical, psychological, intellectual, and emotional responses. In the physical realm there are sensation and perception; in the psychological, abstract symbols are clothed with meanings; in the intellectual, critical thinking is a major goal; and in the emotional there is the nature and intensity of the reaction to the material presented by the writer. The reading process involves perception

41 Wendell Johnson, *op. cit.,* p. 123.

(seeing the words clearly), recognition (recognizing each word and its meaning), comprehension (understanding words, sentences, and paragraphs and seeing relationships among the ideas), interpretation (making an accurate analysis of the meaning of the material read), evaluation (determining the adequacy of the ideas in the light of predetermined criteria), and utilization (using the ideas for a purpose).

There was a time when children in the primary grades were expected to learn to read, in the intermediate grades they were expected to read to learn, and in junior high school they were expected to read to evaluate. Now we emphasize learning, interpreting, evaluating, and utilizing the content from the early stages of reading. "The fact is that every child at every level of reading . . . needs to have the gamut of skill experiences on the level appropriate to his development. Whatever is omitted in one grade becomes a millstone around his neck in another."[42]

## Stages of Development in the Basic Reading Program

Reading is a developmental process. Each child has a particular developmental pattern and achieves his potential in the reading skills according to his abilities, his interests, and the effectiveness of the teaching. There is no sharp line of demarcation between one stage and another. The following stages, educational levels, and statements of achievement are given merely as general indexes of development: prereading, beginning reading, initial stage of independent reading, transition, intermediate, and advanced.[43]

*1. The Prereading Stage.* In the prereading stage the child has his first association with things, people, and processes. He learns to understand oral language and to speak. He develops a number of the abilities and skills in auditory perception and visual discrimination

---

[42] Ruth Strang, Constance McCullough, and Arthur Traxler, *Problems in the Improvement of Reading* (New York: McGraw-Hill Book Company, 2nd ed., 1955), p. 90.

[43] William H. Burton *et al.*, *Reading in Child Development* (Indianapolis: The Bobbs-Merrill Company, 1956), pp. 162–163.

so essential in learning to read. He learns to interpret pictures, observe sequence in telling about events, follow simple directions, identify colors, and coordinate muscular activities. He learns to "read" people, places, and things in his environment. During this period he discovers that expressions on faces and in voices mean something. He learns to discriminate words in the flow of sound. He finds that he can use his voice to communicate his needs and wants. Next he begins to use words to control his environment. He develops a general readiness for reading.

*II. The Beginning-Reading Stage* (First Grade). Most children have their introduction to reading during this stage. They learn to use context clues, phonetic clues, and word-form clues. They acquire the specific skills of deriving information from pictures, discriminating between both letter forms and word forms, discriminating between initial sounds of spoken words, using oral context to supply a missing word, using an initial sound together with oral context to supply an unknown or missing word, listening for specific purposes, and reading from left to right.[44] Even in this period emphasis is on reading for meaning, not for word recognition.

The challenge of teaching beginning reading is to maintain a fine balance between helping children recognize words, understand words, and read with "expression" — that is, read as they speak. The greatest weakness in teaching during this stage is that of allowing children to plod along word by word, in a way that meaning is completely lost.

*III. The Initial Independent-Reading Stage* (Second Grade). Children now develop an increased desire to read, an interest in a variety of materials, and independence in word recognition, comprehension and interpretation. This is a critical period, requiring skillful adaptation of materials and the pace of learning to the child's development. "Continually in a room which is plentifully supplied with reading materials, children face fresh proof that it is important to learn to read. Interesting messages await them. Information which they need is at hand. Records of their most exciting experiences are available for them to reread for their own pleasure or share with

[44] Adapted from Paul McKee *et al., Jack and Janet,* Teacher's Edition, The Reading for Meaning Series (Boston: Houghton Mifflin Company, rev. ed., 1957), p. 23.

their friends. Beginning readers start their activities in an atmosphere which is a rich source of stimulating opportunities to learn to read."[45] Independence in reading thrives in such an environment; it grows as children learn to read for a greater variety of purposes, adapt their techniques to different purposes, take steps in locating materials, and develop skills in unlocking unfamiliar words.

*IV. The Transition Stage* (Third Grade and Early Fourth Grade). During this period many children show greater enjoyment in reading. They take more responsibility for reading on their own. They read longer units which demand more mature skills of word recognition and comprehension: word-attack techniques, change of rate, comprehension (noting detail, getting main ideas), predicting outcomes, ascertaining organization of ideas, grouping significant ideas and supporting data. The transition stage requires a shift of emphasis from reading short thought units to reading longer and more complex materials.

Because many schools are no longer concerned with specific accomplishments at a particular grade level from kindergarten through primary school, it will perhaps be valuable to consider some of the accomplishments of the children who have progressed through primary school. In general, the children will exhibit a wide range in reading abilities, various types of materials are read, reading groups undertake a variety of activities in which reading is an integral part, and recreational reading provides increased satisfaction.

*V. The Intermediate Stage* (Fourth to Sixth Grades). During this stage many children are expected to develop the skills that they will use in reading the rest of their lives: comprehension, reading for various purposes at various speeds, ability to shift approach or method according to the demands of the materials, reading in the content fields, reading for retention, reading for enjoyment. Specialized skills such as skimming, outlining, summarizing, relating ideas in sequence, and giving book reports should be learned by the time the child completes the sixth grade.

The classroom teacher will find that children in the intermediate grades need specific help in five general areas:

[45] Margaret G. McKim, *Guiding Growth in Reading* (New York: The Macmillan Company, 1955), p. 146.

1. Further training in phonetic analysis.
2. Continued development in structural analysis of words, emphasizing prefixes, suffixes, and roots.
3. Additional training in using verbal context to increase comprehension.
4. Training in the more mature use of pictures, graphs, etc., as an aid in solving problems in other content areas.
5. Further training in the use of the dictionary for pronunciation, word meanings, and extension of vocabulary.[46]

*VI. The Advanced Stage, or the Stage of Expansion* (Junior High School and Beyond). Children vary in the reading skills they have acquired by the time they leave the elementary school. (Some intermediate children will be reading at this advanced stage.) Schools, too, vary in the programs they offer in reading. Some junior high schools continue a program whereby the pupil learns to read more rapidly, with greater comprehension and discrimination. The child in need of remedial work is helped to improve in the specific skills he has failed to develop prior to this time. Other schools make no attempt to teach reading in junior high school, on the assumption that the child is on his own as far as techniques of reading are concerned. They believe that he should now be ready to read for a variety of purposes, using a number of skills. He should know how to read to study, to gain pleasure, to get information, and to share material. He should have developed criteria for selecting materials suitable to a specific purpose. He should read with comprehension, interpreting and evaluating what he has read. Reading should be an essential part of his everyday living, and he should read independently, effectively, eagerly, and with appropriate techniques.

The stages of reading development are presented, not as infallible guides for every child at any given level, but to indicate the points at which the majority of children appear to be ready for certain attainments and experiences in reading.

Stage I. Readiness for reading is attained.
Stage II. Children begin to read.
Stage III. Children progress in basic reading habits, attitudes, and initial skills in word recognition.

[46] Adapted from Paul McKee, *The Teaching of Reading in the Elementary School* (Boston: Houghton Mifflin Company, 1948), pp. 365–367.

Stage IV. Children consolidate some of the gains they have been making in independence in reading.

Stage V. Children develop the skills they will use in reading throughout adult life.

Stage VI. Children expand and refine their reading purposes, skills, and taste in literature.

The stages have been related to specific grade levels only for the convenience of the reader. The teacher is aware of the fact that at any given level some children will be in the stages above or below. Children differ in reading as they do in all other activities, and the program should be planned accordingly.

Knowledge of the process of development in reading implies an understanding of the objectives of reading, of the sequential development of skills in the process, and of providing for individual differences in achievement, abilities, skills, habits, and attitudes. In the elementary school the teacher will find children at all stages of development as they progress toward the goal of maturity in reading. Only if he recognizes landmarks on the way to maturity in reading will he be able to offer skillful, creative, efficient, and intelligent guidance. Only then will he avoid the pitfalls evident in the following all-too-frequent scene.

## *Motivation for Reading*

"I don't like first grade at all. I liked kindergarten. They let you do lots of things there. We played in the dollhouse, built with blocks, went on trips, played games. Sometimes we sang songs, and every day we painted pictures or played with clay. We even had a slide in our room. All they talk about this year is reading — reading — reading! Why do I have to read? I don't know how."

Susan was a very unhappy six-year-old. She saw no reason for reading. Her family looked at television every evening. Reading was limited to the daily news and a few magazines in her home. Life had been interesting and satisfying in the kindergarten. Now everything had changed. She was a first-grader and she was expected to read. Her question "Why do I have to read?" needed an answer. Why *do* people read?

Adults and children have two basic reasons for reading. They read for information and they read for enjoyment.

*Reading for Information.* Adults read to find out what is happening in the world, for general information, to solve a problem, to find specific information such as how to bake a cake, build a boat, or make a dress. The popularity of the "do-it-yourself" books is convincing evidence that adults read for information.

Children, too, read for information. They want to know about the world in which they live. One of the best motivations in teaching beginning reading is children's desire to learn more about what interests them in their immediate — and remote — environment. If they see that reading serves the purpose of giving them information about the things they are interested in, they will be much more inclined to reach for the key that unlocks the door.

Adults and children also read to evaluate and to check on the validity of information.

*Reading for Enjoyment.* When children begin to sense the exhilaration, the wonder, the adventure in books, the problem of motivation ends and the problem of finding the right book begins. The ability to select books which have interest and meaning, to become discriminating in one's literary tastes, to find ways of sharing books with others, and to attain a richer personal development must be cultivated by parents and teachers.

The teacher often sets an example of reading for personal enjoyment through the practice of reading aloud at designated times each week or each day. He can demonstrate his enthusiasm for reading, share in creative activities, and show that reading helps to develop ideas and viewpoints. Arousing the desire to read is his responsibility. Through providing for participation in such activities as book clubs, choral speaking, dramatic groups, and sharing periods he can do much to stimulate reading for enjoyment. Suggesting radio and television programs in which children can hear literature well presented is also helpful.

Librarians play a prominent part in helping children develop interest in books and taste in their selection. Whether a child wants to read about the everyday world or the world of interstellar space, the world of the past or of the future, he should find a teacher, a librarian, or a parent who can introduce him to it.

In the final analysis it is not reading to acquire information, to solve problems, to understand ideas, to develop viewpoints, to evaluate what is read, or to think critically that gives us our greatest satisfaction; it is reading for sheer pleasure, to appreciate better the world in which we live, and to participate in creative activities.

## Reading in the School Program

Reading to find the answer to questions raised in the unit or problem, carrying on research projects, giving book reports or book reviews, dramatizing stories read, reporting on topics studied in the unit — these are activities which relate reading to the total school program.

In schools in which part of the day is devoted to unit activities integration of learning experiences is facilitated. When there are many interesting activities going on, when the environment is stimulating and children are challenged to find answers to problems, there is added incentive to read.

In subject-centered schools children can of course also read to find out more about their world. Here teachers make use of direct and vicarious experiences related to the child's interests and the topics of study predetermined by the curriculum. Among the activities which can be used to motivate reading are: direct experiences, vicarious experiences, dramatizations, demonstrations, excursions, pictures, exhibits, television, movies and film strips, recordings, radio, discussions, reports, and sharing of oral reading.

To understand the reading program at a particular stage or grade is not enough. In order to teach reading effectively the teacher must recognize the factors that determine success in reading for each child from the readiness stage throughout the elementary school. The following section will discuss providing adequate reading-readiness activities at home and in school, developing prereading skills, devising methods for initiating beginning-reading activities, selecting aims of instruction, and developing independent reading. Illustrations of teacher guidance in classroom reading experiences will show how teachers help children reach their maximum potential in reading achievement.

# Reading in the Kindergarten and Primary Grades

*Reading Readiness at Home.*  Readiness for reading begins in the home, as soon as the child develops an awareness of the world in which he lives and his relation to that world.  It is determined by his experiential background, his physical, social, and emotional maturity, and his mental endowment.  It is influenced, too, by the attitudes and example of the adults in his environment.  If his parents read widely, if his early experiences with books have overtones of warmth and affection, if his preschool years include memories of being read to by parents — if they include the sound of his father's voice, the comfort of his mother's nearness as he listens to the story and matches the pictures in the book with the words as the story moves along — the probability is that he, too, will enjoy books.  If in addition he is encouraged to explore the world outside the home, he will be eager to participate in any challenging experience he meets.  This is the heritage parents can give to their children.  But unfortunately many parents do not.

Mrs. Holhausen, a parent, is not sure of her responsibility for helping June to read.  She is concerned, as are other parents, by the conflicting reports of the effectiveness of reading instruction in our schools today.  She is puzzled by the terminology of educators as they discuss reading.  She is worried about June, who will enroll in kindergarten in September.  She is determined that June will learn to read.  Jimmie didn't read until he was in the third grade.  This time she would do something about the problem before it started.  She would buy a phonics book, or maybe she would teach June the alphabet.  She had heard that some schools were going back to teaching the ABC's and phonics.

For parents such as Mrs. Holhausen orientation conferences explain how a parent can help a child bridge the gap between home and school.  They make it clear that readiness for learning is not confined to reading, and that readiness for reading is not confined to the kindergarten or first-grade classroom; it is an ongoing process.  Teachers or administrators point out that parents can facilitate readiness for school by providing the child with experiences outside the home, by reading to him, by listening to him as he talks about the things he sees and his little adventures.  They show that the motivations operating in the life of the child are not haphazard, but instead are significant in the learning process. If the parents do not take take time to read to the child, if they use a limited vocabulary, the child is certain to be handicapped in his initial experiences in reading. If he lacks varied contacts with his world he cannot bring much meaning to the printed page.

Fortunately, Mrs. Holhausen attended an orientation conference in which these facts were discussed. She left with a lighter heart. She did not have to try to teach phonics or the ABC's, or to pressure June into reading. She had learned that most kindergarten children have neither the physical nor the psychological readiness for reading or writing; nor do they yet have the motivation for learning these skills. She had learned, too, that varied and wide experiences, language facility, good relationships between parents and child, and between teacher and child, are as important in learning to read as are mental age, interest, temperament, and intelligence. She had found out that factors which contribute to reading failure include intellectual and emotional immaturity, social inexperience, emotional blocks, sight defects, and frequent or prolonged absence from school at critical periods in the learning process. The importance of good health and the responsibility of the parents in maintaining the health of their children were emphasized. Readiness for reading was more meaningful to her now.

*Reading Readiness in the Kindergarten.* The kindergarten program is not a reading program, but it is reading oriented. Kindergartners are provided with an opportunity to extend their knowledge, deepen their concepts, broaden their horizons, investigate their world, improve their communication skills, develop creativity, and build an experiential background which leads naturally into reading in the primary grades. They manipulate, experiment, and solve problems. In terms of curriculum areas the learning experiences relate to language arts, social studies, science, numbers, and the creative arts. Those specifically reading oriented are: listening to the teacher as she reads a favorite story, browsing at the library table, "reading" a favorite book to a friend, dictating experience stories to the teacher and watching her print them on the chalkboard, telling a story in sequence, creating imaginative stories, and dramatizing stories, poems, and songs.

The responsibility of the kindergarten in the reading program is to supply a rich and varied experiential background, help children develop social and emotional maturity, and provide activities which expand oral language facility. The emphasis is on general readiness.

Typical of specific materials for developing reading readiness in kindergarten are the following: (1) labels on objects around the room — the cupboard, chalkboard, crayons, blocks, toys, (2) signs such as "Come and See," "Come and Read," "Come and Play," (3) plans for the daily schedule, (4) standards for activities, (5) notices on the bulletin board such as "Today we go to the fire station," "Today we go to the gym," "Our new teacher is coming on Monday. Her name is Miss Miller," "The nurse is coming tomorrow."

Specific activities include the following: (1) bringing in objects for "show and tell" time, (2) talking about and caring for a pet at school, (3) taking trips in the community and around the school, (4) listening to stories and seeing movies, (5) dramatizing songs, poems, and stories, (6) planning, discussing, and evaluating experiences, (7) looking at pictures and interpreting them, (8) playing matching games of all kinds, (9) using art media, (10) recognizing likenesses and differences, (11) creating rhythms, games, and stories, (12) dictating experience stories, and (13) doing science experiments.

*Reading Readiness in the First Grade.* Specific prereading skills include interpreting pictures, following the sequence of the story, remembering the central idea, developing auditory and visual discrimination, observing details and making associations, "reading" from left to right, "reading" from top to bottom, turning pages and handling books properly, and answering questions based on some phase of the story. The prereading period involves many organized experiences designed to lead into reading from books. Some teachers develop their own materials. Others use the prereading books available from publishers. Children continue to participate in experiences related to other phases of the communication skills while they focus on specific prereading activities that help them understand sequence, story continuity, and picture interpretation.

How long the prereading program continues in the first grade depends on the abilities, skills, and experiential background of the children, and the skill, insight, and ingenuity of the teacher in determining the psychological moment when they are ready to read from books or other printed material. Although there are many tests available for measuring readiness, no single guide is infallible. The teacher may use observation, informal tests, a check list, or a commercially prepared readiness test to help him determine the time at which a relatively smooth transition can be made from informal language experiences to preprimers or charts and other simple stories used in beginning reading.

The reading readiness check list on page 259 may be useful in planning the transition from informal experiences in the language arts to reading.

*Reading-Readiness Tests.* Many teachers feel more secure about grouping children for beginning reading if they have the evidence of a reading-readiness test in addition to observation and informal tests. Since the readiness tests measure specific prereading skills, the teacher can use the results not only to determine readiness for reading, but also to group children and diagnose their specific strengths and weaknesses. The directions must be followed closely in administering the tests.

Among the problems that teachers must be aware of are the following: (1) Some children are unduly disturbed at the thought of taking a test; (2) others are fatigued before the test is completed; (3) some are tempted to look at another's work. However, if the teacher is acquainted with the children, has their confidence, and administers and interprets the test wisely, he will have an additional basis for deciding when and how to organize the beginning reading. He will have evidence of the skills needed for reading: language facility, ability to remember the sequence of ideas, ability to detect likeness and difference in symbols and pictures, muscular control in copying, recognizing and writing numbers, and drawing a man. Some of the widely used tests are listed below.

> *Gates Reading Readiness Tests.* Picture directions, Word matching, Word-card matching, Rhyming, Reading letters and numbers. Bureau of Publications, Teachers College, Columbia University, 1958.

> *Harrison-Stroud Reading Readiness Profiles.* Using symbols, Making visual discriminations, Using the context, Making auditory discriminations, Using context and auditory clues. Houghton Mifflin Company, 1956.

# Reading Readiness
## Check List for the First-Grade Teacher

| Name of Child | | |
|---|---|---|
| | *Teacher's Comments* | *Dates* |
| 1. He enjoys picture books. | | |
| 2. He asks questions about the printing below the picture. | | |
| 3. He listens with comprehension to the story read. | | |
| 4. He can tell the story in sequence. | | |
| 5. He can "read" the titles of a number of books. | | |
| 6. He has developed motor coordination and can handle books with ease. | | |
| 7. He sees a relationship between oral and written words and can associate ideas. | | |
| 8. He shows evidence of a desire to find out what the marks on the page or chalkboard mean. | | |
| 9. He has developed ability in auditory and visual discrimination. | | |
| 10. He has mastered the specific prereading skills required for success in beginning reading. | | |
| 11. He shows evidence of social, emotional, physical, and intellectual maturity and general readiness. | | |
| 12. He gives evidence of wanting to read and eagerly asks questions about reading. | | |
| 13. On the basis of teacher observation, informal tests, language facility, and records, readiness is highly probable. | | |
| 14. On the basis of any good reading readiness test he is in the category predicting success. | | |

*Metropolitan Readiness Tests.* Reading readiness, Number readiness, Total readiness. World Book Company, 1950.

*Murphy-Durrell Diagnostic Reading Readiness Test.* Auditory discrimination, Visual discrimination, Learning rate. World Book Company, 1949.

## BEGINNING READING

Reading-readiness and prereading activities merge in the initial experiences in reading. The first-grade classroom is designed to encourage children to read. Centers of interest, a library table, pictures, games, puzzles, materials for dramatic play and storytelling, captions on materials and apparatus, interesting experience reading charts, and a flexible schedule in which children plan, discuss, develop, and evaluate activities stimulate interest in reading. The children have been pretending to read ever since they were in kindergarten. Many of them are now ready and eager to read.

Three of the best-known methods used in introducing children to printed materials are (1) the direct book approach, in which children are introduced to reading through books (usually a basal series); (2) the experience-reading approach, in which children gain their introduction to reading via the "experience chart"; (3) the combination experience-book approach, which merges the other two methods.

*The Direct Book Approach.* The basal reading series sequence consists of a readiness book, several preprimers, a primer, and readers of graded difficulty. Supplementary readers are provided according to the need and the availability of materials. Basal readers still form the foundation of reading instruction in most schools. The chief advantages of this method of instruction appear to be the following: (1) The teacher has a supply of ready-made material of sequential difficulty, well illustrated and attractive to the reader; (2) the sequence of vocabulary development and basic reading skills is well planned; (3) the children enjoy having a book of their own (they get a great deal of pleasure from reading a book small enough to handle easily); (4) there is usually an accompanying workbook which checks on children's comprehension, vocabulary, and ability to work independently; (5) a set of complete and thoughtfully planned manuals usually comes with the series.

The children are divided into ability groups, in which each child proceeds at his own rate.

The teacher plans the objectives for the reading groups to include (1) giving the children an opportunity to talk about the experiences on which the story is based; (2) allowing the children to look at the pictures in the story and discuss them prior to the actual reading; (3) reading the story aloud to the children and encouraging them to follow along in their books; (4) discussing the story afterward; (5) following the story with related activities such as drawing a picture of part of it or creating a dance or game related to it. Teachers make use of aids such as phrase cards, pictures, sentences, and words printed on the chalkboard.

Critics of the direct book approach point out that the content and vocabulary used in the books are at times removed from the experiences of some children. However, most teachers are successful in teaching children to read from basal series.

*The Experience Approach.* An experience chart is simply a record — an individual or group-directed composition. As children express themselves on some topic, the teacher records what they say. Experience charts are most used in primary grades prior to reading from the first book.

In the direct book approach the reading materials are the core of the reading program; experiences of the children are secondary. In the experience approach the opposite is true; experiences of the children form the reading materials. Children and teacher together develop charts based on their experiences. One problem is the selection of words which are both in the experiential background of the children and in their oral vocabulary. Teachers who use the experience chart must be aware of the advantages and disadvantages involved. Typical reading experience charts in the first grade give some basis for evaluation.

### Our Program

Our mothers are coming tomorrow.
We will dramatize *Snipp, Snapp, Snurr and the Red Shoes.*
After the play we will serve refreshments.
We baked the cookies today.
They are peanut butter cookies.
The punch, we will make tomorrow,
It is really grape-ade,

*Our Octopus*

We have an octopus in our room.
He lived in the ocean — the Pacific Ocean.
He isn't living anymore.
He is preserved in formaldehyde.
John wanted to know what he eats.
He doesn't eat anything — any more.

Drawing up experience charts for reading requires the teacher to be able to select a controlled vocabulary, provide breadth in content, develop a good literary style, understand the sequence of reading skills, and possess ample time. To the average overworked teacher laboring with the average overcrowded schedule this additional time-consuming responsibility is not always welcome.

For the teacher who has the time, the necessary skills, and the interest, experience charts prove effective in stimulating language expression. The children enjoy creating stories about themselves and cooperating in reading them, for the materials are their own. The charts provide an easy transition to reading from books.

*The Combination Experience-Book Approach.* Betts,[47] for one, considers strict adherence to a basal series to be less effective than a combination approach to reading. This combines the best features of the two preceding methods. It introduces children to printed materials sooner than is possible in the experience approach and provides more readiness activities than the direct book approach. In the first few days of school children build up a background for reading through talking about their experiences, carrying on activities related to the content of the story they will be reading from the basal reader, and utilizing communication skills. As they show evidence of readiness for reading from books the teacher groups them for beginning-reading experiences. This approach is successfully used by many elementary teachers.[48]

[47] E. A. Betts, *Foundations of Reading Instruction* (New York: American Book Company, 1957), pp. 388–433.

[48] Gates reported that 99 per cent of the classrooms in America have a program built around the basal reader, supplemented by a variety of materials on the children's reading level. In many such cases the combination experience-book approach is used to introduce reading to children. Arthur I. Gates, "Improvements in Reading Possible in the Near Future," *The Reading Teacher,* 12:83–86, December 1958.

*Introducing the Preprimer.* One of the most exciting events in the life of the child is receiving his first book. The teacher must "step into the shoes of the child" to appreciate what it means to him. The procedure to be used in presenting the book should be carefully planned, for the child's initial response colors his attitude toward reading. Teachers have found the following suggestions helpful:

Before they receive their books let the idea of "we will be reading from books soon" be a source of pleasant anticipation.

Have a book for each child and if possible use new and attractive books.

Give children time to handle the books, to look at the pictures, to get the "feel" of the books, and in general to express appreciation.

Take time to discover the parts of the book together. Talk about the title, the table of contents, the division of the book into sections, the page numbers, the format, the illustrations, and the characters.

Set up standards for caring for books. Keep the books in a special place and collect them at the end of each period.

Provide interesting supplementary reading materials for the children to read during free time. (Keep the basal series for the reading period.)

Take time to bring out the "magic" of books. Enthusiasm is important in every reading class but especially during the first reading experience.

## Aims in Reading Instruction in the Primary Grades

Miss Kohlman, who was to be graduated in January, had a problem. "I have a chance to teach a second grade next semester. I'm not worrying about anything but reading. I'll have about thirty-five children. My practice teaching was in the kindergarten and first grade. What shall I teach them and how much can I expect of them by the end of the year?"

Fortunately such situations are rare. Most beginning teachers have more understanding of the children they will teach and the nature of the reading process.

By the beginning of second grade many children have reached the early stage of independent reading. The simpler study skills have been mastered.

During the third stage of development the teacher tries to provide a balanced reading program for informational, functional, developmental, and recreational reading; to help children adjust their reading rate according to the purpose for which they are reading; to increase their skills in accuracy and independence in word recognition and increase their speed of reading with comprehension; to promote skills in oral reading that will help them interpret the author's meaning; to acquaint children with the techniques of using the library more efficiently.

At the end of the third stage of development the pupils should read independently the materials designated for the second grade; interpret correctly the materials related to the content areas; find materials related to their interests, hobbies, and projects; make strides in gaining wholesome and varied reading interests; read silently more rapidly than they read orally; read at sight materials suited to this stage of development; adjust their rate according to the purpose for which they are reading; and show increasing skill in combining the use of context clues with visual and auditory clues in unlocking unfamiliar words.[49]

This list of pupil attainments will serve only as a guide. Some children will have mastered these skills before entering the first grade; others may not be proficient in them by the time they leave the elementary school.

At this level some children are enthusiastic about all types of reading. They become completely absorbed in reading and interpret the material in a variety of ways. They show increased ability to acquire new words through the use of context and analysis clues. They read with comprehension in many areas and use the information gained. They listen to others and share their reading by telling stories and reviewing books read. Reading for enjoyment is characteristic of this stage.

Many teachers have found the following method effective in developing reading in the primary grades.

### DIRECTED READING

*1. Preparation.* In this step of the reading lesson the stage is set, the pupils are introduced to the story and any new concepts are

[49] Adapted from Burton *et al., op. cit.,* p. 161.

clarified, and the meaning of new words is explained. The children use the vocabulary which is found in the story.

*2. Reading and Discussion.* Three activities occur in this step: silent reading, discussion, and oral reading. The purpose for reading the story is stated; reading to answer questions, reading to find general meanings are typical purposes. In discussion, the purpose is checked and the teacher makes sure the children have comprehended the material. Oral reading provides a further check on comprehension. Pupils may read aloud a favorite section, a line or lines that give specific information. Oral reading should be used for an audience situation in sharing materials, not merely for diagnosis of reading ability.

*3. Word Analysis and Reading Skills.* At this point exercises in word recognition, phonetic analysis, and certain reading skills are provided to develop independence in identifying strange words and in recognizing familiar ones with greater facility. Exercises and drill should be used according to the specific needs of the children. Drill and practice in skills must be motivated, challenging, brief, and well planned to be effective.

*4. The Extension of Experiences.* This is one of the most interesting phases of reading. The children discuss related material. They search for additional material about characters in the story. They are interested in the original from which the excerpt in their book has been taken. They find stories with a related theme or setting, or with similar characters. Some teachers think of this step as enrichment and plan it only for the most promising students. However, *all* students can benefit from the extension of experiences such as drawing, painting, and constructing in follow-up activities. Observation of actual reading experiences in the classroom will show how the teacher develops a reading lesson.

Observation: Third grade, Glenwood School, Evansville, Ind.
Teacher:  Miss Mundy
Observer:  Kay Jennings
Materials:  Basic reader
Method:  Direct book approach
  1. *Preparation.* The subject for the reading lesson was the story "Bread and Jam," based on an incident in a country school. Some wasps had found their way into the classroom. Through the de-

vice of getting the wasps to follow one of the children who en-
ticed them with jam sandwiches, the wasps were led back into the
woods where they wouldn't harm the children or Sarah Best's
pony, Dusty.

In preparation for the reading, interest was built up through a
discussion of schools based on the children's own experiences —
how the country school differs from the city school; how, in
country schools, all the classes are sometimes held in one room;
how children of all ages are in the one room. The discussion logically turned to the name of the school in the story, the people
the children would meet in the story, which of these people they
had met before, etc. The children were then shown a picture of
the school in the story and asked what the people around the school
would be doing. After a discussion, the teacher told the children
that this story was about somebody who came to school, but who
hadn't been invited.

2. *Reading and Discussion.* New words found in the story were
pronounced and the meanings discussed. A list of the new words
had been printed on the chalkboard prior to the reading lesson.

Throughout the actual reading use was made of the pictures in
the story. For example, the first picture showed Betty Jane and
Don in front of the school. Suggested ways of getting to school
were also shown (this was in conjunction with part of the actual
reading matter). The teacher asked the following questions:

TEACHER: How many ways can you see for people to get to
school?
CHILD: Horse, car, bicycle, bus, walking.
TEACHER: This page tells exactly what Betty Jane and Don are
doing. Can you read it to yourself?

After the page was read silently, the material was discussed for
meaning. The page was also read aloud. The procedure for the
remainder of the reading was as follows:

a. A question about material to be read.
b. Silent reading of the page.
c. Discussion of what had been read.
d. Oral reading of the page (children took the part of characters in the story).

3. *Drill.* Practice in recognizing new words through the use
of phonetic skills was introduced in the preliminary-to-reading
discussion.

4. *Follow-up Activities.* Drawings were made about the indi-

vidual stories. Friezes depicting a series of related stories were created.

The following is a running account of the reading lesson.

The preliminary discussion about schools in general was based on the children's own experiences. Then:

TEACHER: You're going to be interested in the name of the school in the story. (*Points to words "Maple Grove School" printed on the chalkboard.*) What does "grove" mean?

CHILD: Where lots of trees are.

TEACHER: Can you think of another name for grove?

CHILD: Woods.

T (*showing children picture of school*): Do you suppose the children at Maple Grove School have as much fun as we do?

C: I think they do.

T: Do you know who the people in the picture are? We've met them before. What could they be doing?

C: They're walking to school.

C: I think they're playing.

T: This story tells how somebody comes to school who isn't invited. (*Points to word "wasps" on chalkboard. Children pronounce it.*) Do you know what wasps are?

C: Like bees.

T: What do they do that we don't like?

C: Sting.

The phonetic analyses of the other new words of the story were then discussed. For example: the *j* like the sound in *jam;* difference between *ride* and *rid;* vowel sound in *draw;* long *i* sound in *sight.* Some letters, it was pointed out, are silent.

T: I think we're ready to read our story. Let's be sure to look at the table of contents. How many stories are in the group we are reading?

C: Eight.

T: How many of the stories have we read?

C: One.

T: How many more are left to be read?

C: Seven.

T: How many ways can you see for people to get to school? (*Picture on first page of story.*)

C: Horse, car, bicycle, bus, walking.

T: This page tells exactly what Betty Jane and Don are doing. Can you read it to yourself?

(*Children read silently.*)

T:  Who was Betty Jane waving at?
C:  Sarah Best.
T:  Who can read where it tells how the children came to school?
C:  (*Reads aloud from reader.*)

*Second Page of Story*

T:  Let's read to ourselves and see what sounds the children heard at school.
(*Children read silently.*)
T:  What was the first sound?
C:  A bell.
T:  What did the children do in their school?
C:  Wrote stories.
C:  Drew pictures.
T:  Whom did we meet that we didn't know before?
C:  Tom.
T:  Who is Tom?
C:  Sarah's brother.
T:  What did Tom do?
C:  He killed the wasps and threw them out the window.
T:  What was he doing before that?
C:  He was drawing a picture of himself on a horse.
T:  That gives us a clue to what Tom might have been doing during the summer.
C:  Visiting his grandmother where he learned to ride horses.
(*Children read second page aloud.*)

*Third Page of Story*

T (*talking about picture on page 3*):  Who is standing by the window?
C:  Don.
T:  Why is he so excited? Let's see if this page tells.
(*Children read third page silently.*)
T:  Who else was excited.
C:  Sarah, because Dusty, the pony, was afraid of the wasps and started running toward the woods.
(*Child reads this portion aloud.*)
T:  What did Don Burns say?
C:  (*Reads this portion of the story.*)
T:  These next two pages tell about a very clever plan. Who thought of the clever plan?
C:  Don.

On reading the above pages orally, the children took the parts of the characters in the story. This procedure was used throughout the reading lesson, ending with the portion of the story that dealt with the actual carrying out of the plan.

T: This part is so good, let's save it for this afternoon.

Ordinarily, the entire story would have been read silently during the morning period, with discussion and oral reading following in the afternoon.

## WORD-RECOGNITION SKILLS, THE KEYSTONE TO PRIMARY READING

An effective primary reading program must provide for specific instruction in word recognition. Word-recognition skills include: a sight vocabulary in which the child recognizes a familiar word just as he recognizes a familiar friend — by the way it looks; use of context clues — inferring meaning from context; use of word-form clues; phonetic analysis; structural analysis; and use of a dictionary.

*Building a Sight Vocabulary.* At the preprimer level, children read by recognizing as a whole the printed forms of words they fully understand. The basic stock of sight words thus built up is the cornerstone for acquiring language understanding, word recognition, and word-attack skills. The teacher must plan carefully, sequentially, building always from the known to the unknown. Sight words are the known. As each sight word is presented it is discussed in an informal situation in which it has the same meaning as in the story to be presented. It may be written on the chalkboard during the discussion as it is pronounced. The child who has experienced the word makes a direct association of sound and meaning with the symbol. This, of course, is only the introductory step in word recognition. Unfortunately, some teachers rely on this method for the development of vocabulary long after the child needs more advanced ways of looking at a word he has never seen and deciphering it for himself.

*Context Clues.* Both picture and verbal clues are helpful in figuring out an unfamiliar word from the context. This calls for meaning — not merely word calling. The word has to make sense in the context in which it is used. However, meaning clues are limited. The child needs more technical skills for learning new words.

*Word-Form Clues.* These, too, have their limitations. They help children distinguish some words by configuration. Length, striking details, height, and over-all pattern or shape of the word serve as distinguishing features. Only in the early stages of sight reading are such clues useful. They lead to guessing, and if used at all should soon give way to more scientific ways of word recognition. If the shape of the word has striking details — as in *elephant* or *giraffe* — the child may find the method helpful, but in many words which look very much alike the word-form clues are inadequate.[50]

*Phonetic Analysis.* An adequate understanding of the science of sounds is essential for teacher and child. Relating the phonetic analysis to the reading lesson — not spending time in isolated drill — makes this method meaningful. The phonetic principles children learn should derive from the sounds they hear in words which they use and recognize at sight. In phonetic analysis the child perceives sound elements within the word — beginning letters, phonograms, consonant blends.

Phonetic analysis is primarily a process of associating the appropriate sounds with the printed word forms. The child who makes use of this skill can more readily figure out the pronunciation of many printed words the first time he sees them. Then he associates with the printed symbol the meaning or meanings that he has heretofore associated with the sounds of the spoken word.

In order to use phonetic analysis successfully as an aid to word recognition, the child must identify the sounds that are used in our language and associate these sounds with the letter symbols that represent the sounds. Some forty-three separate and distinct phonemes, or sound units, are used in general American speech. Each of these is either a consonant or a vowel sound. The twenty-six letters of the alphabet are the written symbols that represent them. The difficulty lies in the fact that we have more sounds in our language than we have symbols. Therefore certain symbols are used to represent more than one sound. Each of the vowel symbols represents several vowel sounds. For example, the letter *a* represents a different vowel sound in *age, all, after, ago, bar.*

[50] See Harold D. Rivkind, "Development of a Group Technique in Teaching Word Recognition to Determine Which of Four Methods Is Most Effective with Individual Children," doctoral dissertation, University of Florida, 1958.

". . . The wise teacher will develop and maintain phonetic understandings and patterns of analysis that will be permanently useful. She will develop knowledge of phonetic elements and promote understandings on the basis of the child's experience with words. She will provide phonetic analysis by a carefully planned program in which the child applies his understandings to new words as he goes along."[51]

The wise teacher, too, will make use of research findings to improve his teaching. Research indicates that it would be difficult to support either a program of all phonetics or one of no phonetics. "By using a combination of common sight words plus some phonetic analysis for other words whose meanings are already known through use in speech, the school may develop a very workable method. However, the case for phonetics should not be dismissed, and better research on the problem is certainly warranted."[52]

Even before 1895 teachers were warned that "Mere recitations about the sounds of letters are of no practical value. . . . Notwithstanding children usually possess the same sense-organs, owing to the differences in their environments, wide differences exist in their ability to learn . . . and also in the kinds of knowledge, and in the amount, which they possess then. Consequently, the work of the teacher should be more directed to ascertaining the degree of development . . . than to training them."[53]

Children who have no need for certain types of training and are able to work out their own system of word recognition often are stymied in their development in reading because of an overzealous or misguided teacher who believes in a single "method" for all.

*Structural Analysis.* Structural analysis clues help children recognize (1) the large number of words composed of basic roots to which endings such as *s, ed, ing,* and various prefixes and suffixes have been added, (2) compound words and contractions, and (3) words of more than one syllable which must be divided into pronunciation units before "sounding out" is possible.

[51] William S. Gray, *On Their Own in Reading* (Chicago: Scott, Foresman and Company, 1948), pp. 93, 94.
[52] Guy T. Buswell, "The Process of Reading," *The Reading Teacher,* 13:112, December 1959.
[53] N. A. Calkins, *How to Teach Phonics* (Chicago: Beckley-Cardy Company, n.d. — Calkins died in 1895), pp. 3, 4.

In order to use structural analysis effectively the child must develop a variety of specific abilities. He must recognize words formed by the addition of inflectional endings to root forms, and associate varied meanings with such endings. He must recognize words formed by adding prefixes and suffixes to root forms, and associate varied meanings with these structural elements. He must recognize syllables in words and use them as aids in pronunciation. He must combine simple known words to form compound words, and reverse the procedure.

As the child studies a new word he should make a visual survey of the entire word, looking for units within the word which have meaning for him — the root word, a prefix, or a suffix. If he identifies a root word as a meaningful unit, or if he identifies syllables of the word as pronunciational units, he has analyzed the structural pattern of the word and is ready to pronounce it.

"Efficient reading involves ability not only to hold in mind the wholeness of a word, phrase, or sentence (that is, to perceive the larger relationships both mechanically and ideationally), but also to attend to individual words and, at times, to parts of words. Perceiving in a general way the whole, but not discriminating clearly among its component elements (letters, words, phrases) may cause as much difficulty in reading as does concentrated attention on word-analysis and word-calling."[54]

*The Dictionary.* Many children are ready to make good use of the dictionary in the primary grades if it is adapted to their grade level, if it is easy to manipulate, and if the information can be located without too much difficulty. Teaching the use of the dictionary should be preceded by specific dictionary-readiness skills. The children must learn the alphabetization rules, and how to select the appropriate meaning for the sentence with which they are concerned. They must know how words fit the context, and understand the structure of the word and the association of sounds and symbols.

Every teacher must realize the importance of independence in word attack. Recognizing words is not reading; but without recognition reading is impossible. Each new learning builds on earlier learnings.

[54] Jean Turner Goins, "Relation of Visual Perception to Reading," *Education Digest,* 24:44, September 1958.

## At the End of the Primary Grades

By the end of the third grade most children have moved from a stage of complete dependence upon the teacher to a marked degree of independence. They read for a variety of purposes. They have learned to locate information, to work with many types of materials, and to unlock unfamiliar words with comparative ease.

Many of them have adequately met the standards of achievement implied in the following questions:

Does the child read basal and supplementary reader selections and story books for himself with interest and comprehension?

Does he show a growing confidence in the ability to attack and solve problems by means of reading?

Can he interpret material he reads in a variety of ways?

Is he growing in independence in using books for information — to find answers to questions and simple facts in what he reads?

Does he ask intelligent questions, carry on discussions, and evaluate what he reads?

Is he independent in attacking most unfamiliar words?

Is he increasing his vocabulary?

Does he set up standards in reading and evaluate his progress toward the goals he sets?

Does he read for enjoyment?

Does he like to share reading orally with members of the class?

Is he establishing habits of recreational reading?

Is he motivated to read on his own and anxious to improve his skill?

Does he make use of the library facilities?

Does he show improved taste in literature he selects to read on his own?

By the end of the primary grades many children will be able to achieve the above goals; some will be reading at sixth-grade level and others will still be at the beginning level.

## Reading in the Intermediate Grades

Providing the child with the basic reading techniques in the primary grades is only the beginning. When he has developed techniques of word attack, of getting information, of making simple inferences, he is reading only in the narrowest sense. "At best, this is a superficial kind of reading, as shallow as it is narrow, a mechanical act. The mechanics are important, . . . but the mechanics are only the beginning."[55] From the earliest possible stage, the mechanical and nonmechanical skills of reading go hand in hand. To shift entirely to nonmechanical skills in the intermediate grades on the assumption that the mechanical skills have been fully developed in the primary grades is unwise. In the majority of cases the intermediate teacher must continue to help children develop skills of phonetic analysis, structural analysis, and the use of verbal context, pictures, graphs, and the dictionary. There are four types of guided reading periods: (1) periods in which the basal reading materials are used, (2) periods involving recreational reading, (3) periods devoted to reading in content areas, (4) periods in which children share oral experiences.

## AIMS OF INSTRUCTION IN THE INTERMEDIATE GRADES

In the intermediate grades children read for a greater variety of purposes. They develop more skill in adapting techniques to the purposes; they are better able to locate information independently; they increase their ability to handle the technical difficulty of the material; and they become more independent in recognition of words. They need time to read for enjoyment, select books at the library, share books with the class, develop reading skills, develop techniques for reading in content areas, carry on research projects in connection with units or class topics, discuss ideas and information gained in reading, and engage in remedial activities as needed.

Guided practice is necessary in such specific skills as getting the main thought from a paragraph or selection; locating and remembering significant details; locating material in encyclopedias and other reference books; reading from several sources to obtain information; making outlines of material read; adjusting reading rate and technique to purpose and type of material; evaluating material read; interpreting maps, charts, and graphs; using the dictionary as a tool in pronunciation and selection of word meanings; extending vocabu-

---

[55] R. Jean Hills, "Reading and the Art of Thinking," *Elementary School Journal*, 60:215, January 1959.

lary; developing versatility in attacking words; and reading aloud effectively. It is at this point that reading becomes a tool for thinking and problem solving as the child learns to read critically, evaluate, and summarize material read. He becomes skilled in using reading to answer questions, using reference materials independently, and obtaining various types of information. He reads purposefully in the content subjects, and his taste in selecting books for enjoyment and creative experience becomes refined.

## PROBLEMS IN THE INTERMEDIATE READING PROGRAM

Problems in this stage of reading development center upon (1) reading in the content areas, (2) providing for individual differences, and (3) organization.

*Reading in the Content Areas.* When the primary-grade child becomes a fourth-grader he is frequently presented with difficult reading material in the content areas and may be stumped by such problems as technical vocabulary, new and undefined concepts, complicated explanations, a multiplicity of facts, and inadequate progression of difficult material.

Teachers can aid the pupil by providing materials of high interest and low reading difficulty. They can make use of films, televised experiments, field trips, lectures, and biographical and fictional accounts of topics to be studied.

*Providing for Individual Differences.* The better the teaching, the wider the differences in achievement. In a typical fourth grade the teacher finds children who are of average ability in reading, those who are well above average, those who are reading at primary level, and a few nonreaders. The range in reading ability may be as much as seven years. In some schools where there are several rooms of the same grade level, children are evaluated at the beginning of the year for general intelligence and reading achievement. The reading groups are then organized on the basis of ability grouping: (1) above average, (2) average, (3) below average, and (4) children with problems in reading. Those who have mastered a basic sight vocabulary, who have acquired word-recognition skills, and who are able to read in content areas are placed in the average and above-average reading groups. Those who are unable to help themselves are placed in the below-average reading group and those with reading problems of various types are assigned for reading classes to a teacher who is skilled in remedial reading techniques. Even where there is provision for ability grouping the teacher must cope with differences which exist within the groups.

The use of units is especially helpful in providing for the great range of individual differences within a single classroom. Reading to solve problems raised in the unit of work provides an incentive for reading at varying levels of ability. Students read to find answers to problems much more eagerly than they do for a specific reading lesson. The teacher supplies reading material on the topic of the unit ranging from easy primary material to upper-level material to challenge the gifted student.

Individualized reading, to be discussed later in this chapter, offers another possibility for handling reading differences.

The teacher may consider the following suggestions for providing for individual differences in reading:

1. Evaluate reading achievement continuously.

2. Keep complete and accurate information on each child as he is promoted from grade to grade.

3. Use unit-type instruction for part of the reading program.

4. Provide a program using a variety of required reading materials so each child will have appropriate material at graded levels of difficulty.

5. Develop a variety of supplementary reading and art and construction activities related to children's interests.

6. Utilize audio-visual teaching aids which can be used by the entire class at one time.

7. Organize field trips and excursions which interest all children.

8. Plan exhibits, collections, scrapbooks, friezes, dramatizations, discussions, choral speaking, role-playing activities.

9. Differentiate assignments according to ability to achieve.

10. Base assignments on individual teacher-pupil compacts.

11. Keep the groups flexible, evaluating continuously.

12. Allow children to form interest groups, skill groups, invitational groups.

13. Use team grouping to allow children of similar abilities to work together.

14. Conduct conferences with parents in which the parents can discover how to help the child.

15. Outline the objectives on which children are to be evaluated so they may understand the goals toward which they are working.

16. Provide worth-while activities for the pupils who finish work quickly so they may broaden their experiences rather than have more of the same activities.

Whatever method the teacher uses, every child is entitled to progress at his maximum rate and to receive the amount of attention and help which is in harmony with his abilities to profit from instruction and makes him feel the teacher is interested in seeing him succeed.

*Grouping for Instruction.* Classrooms differ widely in the degree to which stability in reading groups is maintained. The teacher may schedule three groups — high, average, low. He may divide the time between those who can handle the grade-level materials and those who are having difficulty in reading. He may use individualized reading instruction or a modified group-individualized program. He may spend an entire reading period with one group one day and another the next day, while the other groups are engaged in unit reading activities or independent work.

Some teachers divide the children into groups on the basis of standardized tests. Others regroup after each reading test. Still others maintain inflexible basal-series reading groups but allow other types of grouping such as interest grouping, self-chosen grouping, invitational grouping, drill or skill grouping, and recreational reading in addition.

*Interest groups* are brought together regardless of ability. The interest serves as a motivating factor. It may center around a specific story, a research project, a construction project, or manual activity. The chief advantage of such groups is that children are already motivated to read before they join the group. The teacher will do well to provide reading material of varying difficulty on the subject of interest so that the differences in ability will not cause a problem.

*Self-chosen groups* may be formed when a child invites several children to read together during a free reading period. They also may be motivated by the teacher when he introduces the children to the material to be read by each reading group. For example, the teacher might describe briefly the three or four books to be used by the group, giving a preview of the books and an idea of the

## Suggested Week's Program, Three-Group Plan

| Day | Min. | Group I (High) | Group II (Average) | Group III (Low) |
|---|---|---|---|---|
| **Monday** | 20 | Direct teacher guidance: new material | Work on individual problems: solo-team | Free reading: individual interests |
| | 20 | Committee work: planning of book reports | Direct teacher guidance: reading from text | |
| | 20 | Free reading | Reaction to story in art, drama, or writing | Direct teacher guidance: new story, guided reading |
| **Tuesday** | 20 | Free reading: individual interests | Direct teacher guidance: discuss story or answer specific questions | Independent activities, work-study, games |
| | 30 | Direct teacher guidance: presentation of oral reports, dramatization | Committee work, individual work | Free reading, work on skills |
| | 10 | All-group activity: choral reading, story, dramatizations, etc. | | |
| **Wednesday** | 25 | Reading related to unit of work | Work on individual needs: team, solo reading related to unit of work | Direct teacher guidance: silent-oral reading, work on skills |
| | 25 | Direct guidance: new story | Reading related to unit of work | Reading related to unit of work |
| | 10 | Help to the children from different groups who have a common need to practice a specific skill; others continue their activity | | |
| **Thursday** | 20 | Silent reading and reaction to story | Direct teacher guidance: discussion related to stories, planning of activities | Reading related to stories: help by pupil assistants |
| | 20 | Direct teacher guidance: discussion, oral-silent reading, work on skills | Developing activities related to reading (committee work, etc.) | Reading related to stories: help by pupil assistants |
| | 20 | Individual guidance on book selection for free reading, for unit reports, etc.; use of library aids | | |
| **Friday** | 40 | Free reading | Work on individual needs: team, solo; committee work; reading related to unit, etc. | Direct teacher guidance: discussion; plans for sharing with class |
| | 20 | All-group activity: library, dramatizations, storytelling, etc. | | |

WEEKLY LESSON SUMMARY, FOUR-GROUP PLAN

| Group and Reading Range | Monday | Tuesday | Wednesday | Thursday | Friday |
|---|---|---|---|---|---|
| GROUP 1 5.1–6.2 | *Word Study*, Part 1 | *Exploring Today* | *Practice Exercises in Reading*, Book 5, Types A, B, C, or D | Basal reader, Grade 4 | Basal reader workbook |
| GROUP 2 4.0–4.9 | *Practice Exercises in Reading*, Book 4, Types A, B, C, or D | Basal reader, Grade 4 | Basal reader workbook | *Eye and Ear Fun*, Book 3 | *Adventure Trails* |
| GROUP 3 3.1–3.9 | *Scottie and His Friends* | *Practice Exercises in Reading*, Book 3, Types A, B, C, or D | Basal reader, Grade 3 | Basal reader workbook | *Eye and Ear Fun*, Book 3 (half period) Recreatory reading, Grade 2 (half period) |
| GROUP 4 2.3–2.9 | Basal reader, Grade 2/2 | Basal reader workbook | Sound charts and sheets | *Red Deer* | Recreatory reading, Grade 1 (half period) *Eye and Ear Fun*, Book 2 (half period) |

relative difficulty of each. Each child is then free to join the group reading the book of his choice.

In *invitational grouping* one or two children may invite a few others to join them in reading a story for a particular purpose, such as getting the story ready for a dramatization or puppet show. Children who are free to work in groups often find this type of grouping a very rewarding motivation and a satisfying experience.

| Group and Reading Range | Monday | Tuesday | Wednesday | Thursday | Friday |
|---|---|---|---|---|---|
| GROUP 1 5.1 to 6.2 | 3-min. speed drill, *Standard Test Lessons*, Book C Basal reader workbook | *Digest Reading Skill Builder*, Book 6, Part 1 or 2 | 3-min. speed drill, *Standard Test Lessons*, Book C *Compton's Treasure Hunt* | Practice reader, Book I (Motiv. to Speed) | 3-min. speed drill, *Standard Test Lessons*, Book C Basal reader, Grade 4 |
| GROUP 2 4.4 to 4.9 | 3-min. speed drill, *Standard Test Lessons*, Book B Dictionary exercises | "Phrase-O-Game" | 3-min. speed drill, *Standard Test Lessons*, Book B Basal reader, Grade 4/2 | Basal reader workbook | 3-min. speed drill, *Standard Test Lessons*, Book B *Reading Adventures*, Book B |
| GROUP 3 4.0 to 4.3 | 3-min. speed drill, *Standard Test Lessons*, Book B Word wheels | Basal reader, Grade 4/1 | 3-min. speed drill, *Standard Test Lessons*, Book B Basal reader workbook | *Digest Reading Skill Builder*, Book 4, Part 1 or 2 | 3-min. speed drill, *Standard Test Lessons*, Book B *Phonics We Use* |
| GROUP 4 3.1 to 3.9 | 3-min. speed drill, *Standard Test Lessons*, Book A Basal reader, Grade 3/1 or 3/2 | Basal reader workbook | 3-min. speed drill, *Standard Test Lessons*, Book A *Digest Reading Skill Builder*, Book 3 | *Phonics We Use*, Book D | 3-min. speed drill, *Standard Test Lessons*, Book A *Adventures in Wordland*, E and F |
| GROUP 5 2.3 to 2.9 | 3-min. speed drill, *Standard Test Lessons*, Book A *Phonics We Use*, Book C | *Reading Adventures*, Book A | 3-min. speed drill, *Standard Test Lessons*, Book A *A Trip Through Wordland*, C, D | Basal reader, Grade 2/2 | 3-min. speed drill, *Standard Test Lessons*, Book A Basal reader workbook |

## Weekly Lesson Summary, Six-Group Plan

| Group and Reading Range | Monday | Tuesday | Wednesday | Thursday | Friday |
|---|---|---|---|---|---|
| GROUP 1 5.5 to 6.2 | Basal reader workbook | *Tom Trott* | Practice reader, Book 2 | Building Reading Skills, *Space Ship Book* | Basal reader, Grade 4 |
| GROUP 2 4.7 to 5.2 | Basal reader workbook | Practice reader, Book 1 or 2 | Recreatory reading, Grade 4 or 3/2 | Building Reading Skills, *Atomic Gyro Book* | Basal reader, Grade 4 |
| GROUP 3 4.1 to 4.5 | Building Reading Skills, *Rocket Book* | Basal reader, Grade 4 | Basal reader workbook | *Uncle Ben* | Dictionary exercises |
| GROUP 4 3.6 to 4.0 | *Uncle Funny Bunny* | *Assembly Line Helpers* Balance: recreatory reading, Grade 2 | Basal reader, Grade 3/2 | Basal reader workbook | Building Reading Skills, *Jet Plane Book* |
| GROUP 5 2.9 to 3.5 | Basal reader, Grade 3/1 | Basal reader workbook | Building Reading Skills, *Jet Plane Book* | Reading games | *Uncle Funny Bunny* |
| GROUP 6 2.3 to 2.7 | *Nicky* | *Assembly Line Helpers* | Building Reading Skills, *Jato Car Book* | Basal reader, Grade 2/2 | Basal reader workbook |

Rittenhouse[56] refers to Hester's concept of reading by invitation, in which the children are told during the planning period preceding the reading classes that they are free to join any or several of the reading groups. They are not assigned to any specific group but must be motivated by the teacher to visit one or all of the three read-

[56] Gloria G. Rittenhouse, "An Experiment in Reading by Invitation in Grades One Through Four," *The Reading Teacher*, 13:258–261, April 1960.

ing groups. A child may be invited to join a group either by the teacher or by one of the children. Children who are too immature for a directed reading lesson are free to participate in centers of interest. Once a week a vocabulary test is given, and each child may tell a story he has read or read a story from the chalkboard which lists the new words introduced that week.

In *drill or skill grouping* the children who need practice in certain skills are brought together by the teacher for special help. The teacher observes the children who need to improve their skills in reading and finds time to give group and individual help as required.

*Recreational reading* is almost always an individual activity in which children engage primarily for pleasure. They are free to select books that appeal to them on the basis of their hobbies or interests. Recreational reading differs from the interest group in being an individual rather than a group experience. It may develop into a group experience if the child decides to prepare the story for sharing it orally with the group.

Providing for individual differences is not solved entirely by the three-reading-group plan. There must still be some individualized instruction to discover particular strengths and weaknesses. Children vary in specific skills and attitudes toward reading as well as in general ability. In a typical third grade some children will be reading at the preprimer level while others can read sixth-grade material with comparative ease. In the usual sixth grade the range of reading abilities is normally about six or seven grades. Grouping must therefore be flexible enough to allow transfer from group to group as the need arises, and to allow a child to work in different groups for different purposes. For example, in a single day a child might read as a member of the entire class, as an individual, as a member of a small committee, and in his subgroup. Among the types of grouping identified by McCullough are achievement grouping, special-needs grouping, team grouping (two without aid of the teacher), tutorial grouping (one student helping another who does not know a certain technique), research grouping, and interest grouping. It is in achievement grouping that the teacher provides a systematic year-long instructional program, reviewing and developing important skills.[57]

[57] Constance McCullough, "About Practices in Teaching Reading," *English Journal*, 66:484, November 1957.

The following[58] is an illustration of how a set of scores may be used as a basis for grouping three different ways for reading instruction.

| *Four-Group Plan* | *Five-Group Plan* | *Six-Group Plan* |
|---|---|---|
| 6.2 Group 1 | 6.2 Group 1 | 6.2 Group 1 |
| 5.7 | 5.7 | 5.7 |
| 5.5 | 5.5 | 5.5 |
| 5.2 | 5.2 | |
| 5.2 | 5.2 | 5.2 Group 2 |
| 5.1 | 5.1 | 5.2 |
| | | 5.1 |
| 4.9 Group 2 | 4.9 Group 2 | 4.9 |
| 4.9 | 4.9 | 4.9 |
| 4.9 | 4.9 | 4.9 |
| 4.8 | 4.8 | 4.8 |
| 4.7 | 4.7 | 4.7 |
| 4.7 | 4.7 | 4.7 |
| 4.5 | 4.5 | |
| 4.5 | 4.5 | 4.5 Group 3 |
| 4.4 | 4.4 | 4.5 |
| 4.4 | 4.4 | 4.4 |
| 4.3 | | 4.4 |
| 4.3 | 4.3 Group 3 | 4.3 |
| 4.2 | 4.3 | 4.3 |
| 4.2 | 4.2 | 4.2 |
| 4.1 | 4.2 | 4.2 |
| 4.0 | 4.1 | 4.1 |
| 4.0 | 4.0 | |
| | 4.0 | 4.0 Group 4 |
| 3.9 Group 3 | | 4.0 |
| 3.9 | 3.9 Group 4 | 3.9 |
| 3.8 | 3.9 | 3.9 |
| 3.7 | 3.8 | 3.8 |
| 3.7 | 3.7 | 3.7 |
| 3.6 | 3.7 | 3.7 |
| 3.6 | 3.6 | 3.6 |
| 3.5 | 3.6 | 3.6 |
| 3.4 | 3.5 | |
| 3.1 | 3.4 | 3.5 Group 5 |
| | 3.1 | 3.4 |
| | | 3.1 |

[58] Evansville College Reading Clinic.

| Four-Group Plan | Five-Group Plan | Six-Group Plan |
|---|---|---|
| 2.9 Group 4 | | 2.9 |
| 2.9 | 2.9 Group 5 | 2.9 |
| 2.7 | 2.9 | |
| 2.5 | 2.7 | 2.7 Group 6 |
| 2.3 | 2.5 | 2.5 |
| | 2.3 | 2.3 |

An examination of the schedules on pages 278–281 will show that "grouping itself is a method of individualizing, not a way of escaping responsibility."[59]

### INDIVIDUALIZING READING INSTRUCTION

Because some teachers are convinced that grouping in itself is fraught with many difficulties, and because they believe that individualizing the reading process is an answer to many problems, this method has become popular in some circles. If one keeps in mind the fact that no one method is a panacea, it will be of interest to look in on a classroom using an individualized reading program. The following account tells of an experiment in a third grade:

"I devote one hour and a half per day to reading during the year. All the children read their own choice of books during the first half hour and spend the remaining hour on seatwork. I usually take the first ten minutes of the day before reading time to explain the seatwork for the day and then I interview about ten children a day during the ninety minute reading period. Each of the ten children gets about seven minutes apiece of personal attention on a one-to-one basis. The other twenty minutes are spent answering questions from children in their seats; I also designate reading helpers to help individual children during the time I am holding individual conferences.

". . . I have found it best to divide the class into three families so that good readers can be placed in each of the three sections to help the slower ones. I use a child's desk and two chairs for the reading conference table. These are placed in one corner of the room away from the three families so as to insure as much privacy as possible. We also have an 'on-deck' chair where the next reader

[59] Strang, McCullough, and Traxler, *op. cit.*, p. 111.

can sit while waiting his turn to read. The children come up to read voluntarily although I sometimes call up certain children who need extra help.

"A library of over two hundred books is stored in four orange crates in another corner of the room, easily accessibile to the three families. In an effort to have as many children as possible with their books ready for the next day's reading period, I have instituted a 'book check' time just before the end of the school day. Before the children leave the room, they show me the book they are going to read the next day.

"During the interview I take notes on a chart made from a large manila folder. It contains twelve columns headed with the following titles: Name of child; initial sounds, middle sounds, ending sounds; word meaning; word pronunciation; skimming; main idea of story; main idea of paragraph; details of story; anecdotal remarks; and reading conference dates."

. . . The teacher is teaching reading skills, recording weaknesses, checking on comprehension, forming temporary groups based on immediate needs, becoming perceptive to children's reading interests, and using all the other techniques necessary for stimulating reading growth.[60]

A widely discussed trend in the teaching of reading is that of individualized reading. Everywhere elementary teachers are asking about this "new" approach. As a matter of fact, although the surge of interest is relatively recent, Stauffer[61] indicates that the underlying principles were advanced by the National Society for the Study of Education as early as 1932. Washburne[62] in 1937 encouraged teachers to individualize instruction in reading, beginning in the second grade. In the 1938 Yearbook of the Department of Elementary School Principals[63] this practice was advocated.

Opinions vary on this method. Although scientific studies seem to indicate that self-selection alone is not the answer, the enthusiastic

[60] Alice Miel (ed.), *Individualizing Reading Practices*, Practical Suggestions for Teachers, No. 14 (New York: Bureau of Publications, Teachers College, Columbia University, 1958), pp. 47, 48.

[61] Russell G. Stauffer, "Individualizing Reading Instruction — A Backward Look," *Elementary English*, 36:335–341, May 1959.

[62] Carleton W. Washburne, *Adjusting the School to the Child* (Yonkers-on-Hudson, N.Y.: World Book Company, 1937).

[63] Marie R. Conroy, "Using Individual Reading Materials Instead of Sets of Class Readers," *New Practices in Reading in the Elementary School*, Seventeenth Yearbook (Washington, D.C.: DESP, 1938).

advocates point to unusual success with the plan. McCullough[64] warns that children who are free to follow their own whims are naturally happier than those who receive intensive instruction. Witty,[65] in reviewing the literature, concludes that an adequate reading program must include the best features of both individualized and group instruction, and Gray[66] and Harris[67] concur.

The important characteristics of the individualized approach are elimination of the basal reader as the core of the reading program, self-selection of materials by the pupils, and individual conferences between the pupils and the teacher. The program capitalizes on pupil interest, and Olson's[68] principles of self-seeking, self-selection, and pacing are often quoted in support of this. Teachers and children alike respond with enthusiasm, and for this reason the plan is strongly favored in some quarters.

On the other hand, certain disadvantages appear: (1) the possibility of losing the real values of group learning through a completely individualized reading program; (2) the great demand made upon the teacher's time in procuring books, holding conferences, and keeping records; (3) the tendency for certain needed reading skills to be partially or even totally ignored.

In this approach the teacher's role is changed and he is faced with new problems as well as new opportunities. He must now find time to work alone with each of the thirty or forty youngsters in his class. Teacher ingenuity, willingness to experiment, technical skill, cooperative effort of the total school, and favorable over-all school climate are essential if the program is to be effective.

The teacher must provide challenging activities for those not reading with him at any given time. Where team teaching is used, classes can be combined for certain types of learning experiences, so that one teacher is left free for reading guidance. This type of

[64] Constance McCullough, "Opinions Differ on Individualized Reading," *NEA Journal*, 47:163, March 1958.

[65] Paul Witty *et al.*, "Individualized Reading — A Summary and Evaluation," *Elementary English*, 36:401–412, 450, October 1959.

[66] William Gray, "Role of Group and Individualized Teaching in a Sound Reading Program," *The Reading Teacher*, 11:99–104, December 1957.

[67] Albert J. Harris, *How to Increase Reading Ability* (New York: Longmans, Green and Company, 1956), pp. 116–121.

[68] Willard C. Olson, "Seeking, Self-Selection, and Pacing in Use of Books by Children," *The Packet* (Boston: D. C. Heath and Company), Spring 1952, pp. 3–10.

reading program requires careful planning, vivid imagination, genuine enthusiasm, and grim determination, but advocates feel that ". . . once the vision is caught, the problem can be surmounted."[69]

Jenkins, who has written a great deal on individualized reading, has presented some evaluative results:

> The individualized groups met with the teacher on a daily basis. Each child had his "special time" with the teacher for individual instruction. His particular reading problem was brought into sharp focus and reading skills were reviewed, developed and refined at the time of immediate need. A detailed reading record card was kept for each child. Daily reference was made to this record in order to ascertain whether the difficulties of yesterday had been mastered or if they still persisted. . . .
>
> Control groups were set up for use in comparing growth in the reading skills. In the control groups instruction was given to three groups based on reading ability. Books to be read were selected by the teachers from series available. . . .
>
> The results of standardized reading tests showed that self-selection produced significantly greater gains than did the conventional reading methods in the areas of reading vocabulary, reading comprehension and total reading.
>
> The control group averaged 1.14 years in total reading gains while the experimental group averaged 1.41 years. . . .
>
> In vocabulary growth the control averaged 1.09 and the experimental 1.96 years. In comprehension 59 per cent of the experimental group gained two years or more, while 24 per cent of the control group scored in this range.[70]

Such illustrations may show that when the individualized method is used in teaching reading the enthusiasm and interest on the part of the teacher and the novelty of the situation for the children influence the end result.

A survey of a well-managed individualized reading program shows that several highly desirable features are present. Individual conferences stimulate the student and appear to have therapeutic value for the slow learner. They also tend to give the teacher insight into

[69] Ruth Rowe, "Individualized Reading: As a Principal Sees It," *More About Reading*, Reprint Service Bulletin No. 29 (Washington, D.C.: Association for Childhood Education International, 1959), p. 20.

[70] Marian Jenkins, "Self-Selection in Reading," *The Reading Teacher*, 10:84–90, December 1957.

the child's strengths and weaknesses. Individualized instruction reduces much of the pressure found in the school program. It is in no sense, however, a panacea. It is most successful if there are fewer than fifteen in a classroom, and not many classrooms can meet this restriction. The following suggestions may serve as guideposts.

1. A wide selection of books based on the child's reading level, interest, and need is imperative. At least 100 books per grade level, including textbooks, trade books, supplementary texts, realistic fiction, and folk tales are needed. Bookmobiles and libraries should be used. Three or four copies of one title of the basal reader are sufficient.

2. Systematic instruction in the skills is essential.

3. The teacher must plan, evaluate, and check to see if the children are reaching goals. Children learn to work independently. Individual motivation and peer motivation characterize the reading.

4. Records of progress should be kept by both the teacher and the children. The teacher must have a record of the book, page, and comment on each child's reading. There should be space for remarks on his progress in reading skills and needs. Names of children who will read on a particular day may be listed on the chalkboard.

5. Readiness activities are important in individualized reading.

6. Reading is integrated with other phases of the curriculum. The other language arts, the social studies, and the creative arts furnish motivation for reading.

7. The audience situation is real. Children listen to a story when one child is ready to read it for the group. The story is new to most of the children.

8. Evaluation of progress in individual instruction is carried on through observing retention after the summer vacation; continuous appraisal of comprehension and word-attack skills; use of a tape recorder to check on fluency, phrasing, and enunciation; use of reading tests at the end of units.

The proponents of individualized reading cite these advantages: "(1) it allows the child to select books for reading on the basis of his needs and purposes; (2) allows him to read books at his own comfortable reading level; (3) allows him to read at his own rate of speed; and (4) gets rid of the status problems associated with directing children into slow, average, and fast reading groups."[71]

[71] Miel, *op. cit.*, p. 43.

In sharp contrast to the extreme views of the proponents of individualized instruction comes the recommendation of Sartain.[72] In a carefully designed and controlled study of individualized reading in the Roseville public schools in St. Paul, Minnesota, Sartain advised that the basal plan be continued, but that the individual conference be used with supplementary reading material. He further suggested that able readers might profit from individualized reading after they had mastered the work of their respective grades. Or they might divide their time equally between the two approaches. He recommended that the strengths of the individualized approach be incorporated into the basal program.

The good teacher is not dependent on *a* method. He discovers the best features of each method, works out a way of teaching that is superior to any one method, and adapts the reading program to the children in the group.[73]

## At the End of the Intermediate Grades

By the end of the sixth grade many children will have acquired considerable power in reading. A few will have attained the highest skills they will reach. They are mature readers. To the degree that they are taking on the characteristics that distinguish the mature reader they are progressing in reading ability.

## The Mature Reader

According to Gray and Rogers,[74] the mature reader has enthusiasm; reads widely and intensively; comprehends and interprets

[72] Helen M. Robinson, "News and Comments. Individualized Reading," *Elementary School Journal*, 60:418–420, May 1960. Harry W. Sartain, "The Roseville Experiment with Individualized Reading," *The Reading Teacher*, 13:277–281, April 1960.

[73] "While there is no evidence at this time that individualized reading will become widely accepted as the total approach to the teaching of reading, it is clear that this approach has already made a real impact and that some phases of it will be incorporated into programs utilizing basal readers." Leo Fay, "Trends in the Teaching of Elementary Reading," *Phi Delta Kappan*, 41:347, May 1960.

[74] William Gray and Bernice Rogers, *Maturity in Reading* (Chicago: University of Chicago Press, 1956), p. 56.

words, ideas, moods, and feelings; makes use of ideas gained in reading; reads critically and evaluates the material; integrates ideas gained in reading with previous experiences; adjusts pace to the occasion and the demands of interpretation; and discriminates in the selection of material and interpretation of the selection.

This description gives the teacher a guide for determining whether or not the children in his classes regard reading as an avenue for gaining a greater understanding of themselves and their world and for reliving the experience of great literature. "Through literature, the voices of mankind's most searching imaginations remain alive to all time. No man is half-civilized until those voices have sounded within him. . . . What one learns from those voices is his own humanity. . . . Until he has heard those voices deeply within himself, what man can have any sizable idea of himself? . . . The reader . . . *becomes* the poet and relives the experience of the poet's imagination."[75]

## *Recreational Reading*

"The more you read of exciting things the less words you have to skip." Johnny's eyes were shining as he spoke these words of wisdom to his second-grade teacher. He had found the secret of reading — reading for enjoyment! "Children are stimulated to read more when they know of the many exciting avenues into which books may lead them."[76]

Teaching children the mechanics of reading, keeping them at work until they are able to help themselves, is only one side of the coin in teaching reading. Paralleling reading to learn is reading for enjoyment, which has as significant a place in the reading program of boys and girls as in the lives of adults.

Many children find television a spur to reading; many others take weekly trips to the library to check out books they want to read. Where teachers, librarians, and parents encourage it, recreational

[75] John Ciardi, "Literature Undefended," *Saturday Review*, 42:22, January 31, 1959.

[76] Harold Postel, "Reading the Entire Book: An Experiment in Sustained Reading," *Elementary School Journal*, 58:390, April 1958.

reading is an integral part of the child's life both outside and in school. Many schools have libraries and others are located close to libraries. In some places bookmobiles deliver books to the schools at the invitation of the teachers. Use of the free-reading period, book reports, book reviews, and book clubs spur children on to wider reading. The teacher should be aware of children's abilities and interests in reading at various levels of maturity.

## *Children's Reading Interests*

A teacher of many Septembers said recently, "I had a course in children's literature so long ago I don't know any of the books outside of the fables and the fairy tales. I want to find out what there is for boys and girls today."

There is research[77] available on the reading interests of children in various stages of maturity. However, it must be remembered that tastes vary with sex, individual interests and hobbies, and ability to read the material. Some of the findings and recommendations from research and observation are as follows:

1. The typical boy and girl enjoy easy narrative reading mingled with adventure, fun, humor, and imagination — hero stories, stories about children like themselves and children who are different.

2. Boys like adventure, action, humor, suspense, and comical incidents. They do not like romance or sentimental stories. (Girls become interested in romance before boys do.) They are interested in people. They like humor and fun with some suspense mixed in.

3. Girls are more interested in home life, romance, schoolgirl stories, fairy tales, and animals. They also like stories of cowboys and adventure. (Boys are more interested than girls in sports, adventure, science, and violent action.)

[77] Herbert C. Rudman, "The Informational Needs and Reading Interests of Children in Grades IV through VIII, *Elementary School Journal*, 55:502–512, May 1955. Margery R. Bernstein, "Relationship Between Interest and Reading Comprehension," *Journal of Educational Research*, 49:283–288, December 1955. S. M. Amatora and S. M. Edith, "Children's Interests in Free Reading," *School and Society*, 73:134–137, March 1951. Fannie Wyche Dunn, *Interest Factors in Primary Reading Materials* (New York: Teachers College, Columbia University, 1924).

*Kindergarten and Primary Grades.* Children in the kindergarten and primary grades are interested in stories about other children, animals, and science activities and in folk tales, legends, and a few fairy tales. Among the perennial favorites are *Peter Rabbit*, the *Snipp, Snapp, Snurr* stories, *Ping, Wait for William, The Golden Egg, Three Billy Goats Gruff, The Three Bears*, and *Millions of Cats*. The bibliography gives sources of best-liked books to help the teacher stimulate wide reading. These stories have action, rhythm, and plot and are easily read.

*Intermediate Grades.* For children in the stages of independent reading, ages eight to eleven, adventure stories, animal stories, fanciful tales, legends, hero stories, biography, stories of home and family life, stories of other countries and of games and sports, books of information, folk stories, and stories of everyday experiences are demanded. Science becomes very important to children at this time as they want to find out more about rockets, space ships, jets, snakes, turtles, and dinosaurs.

Jacobs[78] suggests the following categories of literature for these years: animals, folk tales, American heroes, modern magic, machines and gadgets, contemporary life, historical fiction.

Arbuthnot[79] suggests Mother Goose stories, ballads and story poems, fairy tales, fables, fanciful tales, here-and-now stories, stories of other times and places, animal stories, biography, and informational books.

The Johnson, Sickels, and Sayers anthology[80] has been widely used by teachers for many years as a basis for presenting children with a rich selection of the best-loved books. To have at one's finger tips the right story or poem at the right moment is essential for the teacher in today's schools. This anthology meets the need most effectively.

*Bringing Children and Books Together.* The teacher in the kindergarten and primary grades is responsible for helping children develop the desire to read for pleasure as well as for information.

[78] Leland Jacobs, "Children's Experiences in Literature," Chapter 9 in Virgil E. Herrick and Leland B. Jacobs (eds.), *Children and the Language Arts* (Englewood Cliffs, N.J.: Prentice-Hall, Inc., 1955).

[79] May Hill Arbuthnot, *Children and Books* (Chicago: Scott, Foresman and Company, rev. ed., 1957).

[80] Edna Johnson, Evelyn R. Sickels, and Frances Clarke Sayers, *Anthology of Children's Literature* (Boston: Houghton Mifflin Company, 3rd ed., 1959).

By creating a classroom environment in which reading is valued, by providing a library table, a library corner, or a bookcase in which interesting books are displayed, by making use of available resources for keeping the library well stocked with at least two books per pupil, the teacher can set the stage for reading for fun. Book fairs, book reviews, celebration of Book Week by dramatizing story-book characters — these are ways to stimulate interest in recreational reading.

*Free Reading at School.* There is a growing trend toward setting aside at least one period a week for free library reading. In the modern elementary school the library is the heart of the educational program. It is the core of the free reading program and the source of supply for materials needed in connection with units of study in various curriculum areas.

The library, in addition to providing fiction and non-fiction on a variety of reading levels and a wealth of subjects, may also be a central storehouse for audio-visual materials. The librarian serves not only as a consultant for teachers and pupils, but frequently acts as a coordinator of materials: filmstrips, slides, recordings, pamphlets, pictures, sound films, and clippings.

Class library periods, during which children are free to browse, to study, to exchange books, or carry out research activities, are an integral part of the child's educational experience. A variety of activities are carried on according to the needs of a particular class: story-telling, book reports, library instruction (Dewey decimal system, card catalogue, encyclopedia use, etc.), plus individual guidance in book selection, and conferences between teacher and librarian in regard to materials for the classroom. The school library has come out of the "book corner" to become a vital, dynamic, and exciting center for learning.

In many schools, too, children may choose books from the reading table when they have finished their work and are encouraged to browse until they find just the right one. As early as kindergarten, many a child will select a book and "read" it to a group of playmates or to himself.

The following practices may be used to motivate free reading in the classroom:

Placing a tree on the bulletin board on which children display replicas of the books they have read. The children may share the introduction of a book with the class but they should never tell the entire story — just enough to whet the appetite of other readers.

Providing books and stories that are of varying length and difficulty.

Planning varied activities in free reading for different days of the week. On one day the children will share favorite passages with the class, on another day there will be poetry, on another choral speaking, reading club meeting, book reports, etc.

Allowing the children to reread books they particularly enjoy. Adults do.

Listening to children when they tell about their favorite stories.

Taking time to discuss the free reading with the children.

Giving children help with words they are uncertain about — if they request it.

Providing books for everyone, checking the reading difficulty and seeing that there are some books for the nonreaders and for the accelerated readers as well.

Recreational or free reading is one of the best ways to develop extensive reading in and out of school. Among the specific objectives it serves are:

1. To develop a love of books through a carefully planned program designed to lead to reading as a leisure-time activity now and later.
2. To improve general reading ability.
3. To broaden interests and refine tastes in literature by providing a wide selection of good books in each classroom.
4. To improve the language-arts program as a whole through the use of library books and reporting.
5. To develop library skills.
6. To help parents select better books and set an example of reading at home.
7. To help teachers improve techniques in the area of wide reading.
8. To provide a bond between parents, children, teachers, and librarians.

## *Evaluation Procedures in Reading*

Any teaching-learning process requires the teacher and pupils continually to appraise progress in terms of specific objectives set up cooperatively. Evaluation begins before the teacher enters the classroom in September, when he decides on objectives of instruction and appropriate teaching materials. It continues as he gets acquainted with the children and discovers their reading abilities, interests, and needs. It does not end until he and the children evaluate the year's program in the light of each child's progress toward the goals.

In evaluating pupil progress it is important to recognize that both skill and disability in reading are the result of many factors and must be analyzed in terms of all the information the teacher can assemble concerning the home environment and the child's health, social and emotional adjustments, maturity, and intelligence.

Effective evaluation of reading involves the following:

1. Observation of the children's language facility, vocabulary development, speech and usage in class discussion, conferences, and informal conversation.
2. Observation of oral reading of text material in an audience situation.
3. Discussion of the meaning the class gets from silent reading of the basal series and supplementary materials in content reading.
4. Checking on comprehension of story content through the use of paper-pencil tests, standardized reading-readiness tests in late kindergarten or early first grade, standardized achievement tests in reading at every level, and tests for mental maturity, vision, and hearing as needed.
5. Records children keep of books read, poems enjoyed, new words learned and used in oral and written assignments.
6. Checking on children's skills in using the dictionary, using library resources, and using research techniques as required in unit and text activities. (Postel[81] has pointed out in a recent study that "textbooks have their place in reading classes.")

To be effective, evaluation must consider vocabulary development, comprehension, study skills, ability to analyze words in and out of context, critical thinking, appreciation of literary style, reaction to content, reading interests, reading habits, shifting gears in reading rate, and record keeping as the student appraises his own progress toward group and individual goals.

Elementary teachers may ascertain progress through the use of

[81] *Op. cit.,* p. 390.

anecdotal records, work samples, observations of personal development, incomplete-sentence tests, and counseling interview notes, as well as the standardized-test results.

Children in the elementary school can write critiques, and usually enjoy this activity. Even the primary child is ready to tell what he hopes to accomplish in reading and to evaluate his progress toward his goal. The teacher may record his comments.

Excerpts from case histories, work samples, and samples of the pupils' writing will give the teacher a picture of development as the child grows in expressiveness, in insight, and in comprehension and interpretation skills.

Evaluation rewards the teacher by presenting in tangible form the achievements of the children and the extent to which cooperatively planned goals have been reached. It reveals the strengths and weaknesses of the children, the achievements of the group, and the problems yet to be solved. It brings into focus the extent to which the instructional program is effective and suggests the points at which improvement is called for. A planned program of continuous evaluation cannot be overestimated.

## *Conclusion*

Effectiveness in teaching reading depends upon the teacher's skill, what he knows and believes about children, what he believes about the significance of reading in the lives of individuals, and what he knows about evaluation procedures and techniques.

Whatever his approach to reading — whether it be the direct book approach, the experience-chart method, or a modified approach — the teacher in the primary grades must help every child develop a readiness for reading, acquire a stock of sight words, become increasingly independent in the acquisition of basic skills and habits. He must help him use context clues, word-form clues, phonetic analysis, structural analysis, and the dictionary in unlocking new words. He should relate the reading experience to the total school program and see its role as one of the communication skills. At every stage of development he must recognize readiness, promote learning through meaningful experiences, and encourage reading for a variety of purposes.

In the intermediate grades the teacher will continue the program of refining skills in reading comprehension, word recognition, and interpretation and utilization of ideas gained from the material read. Children will still need help in developing mechanical skills in reading, but they must also learn to interpret, to think critically and to evaluate. "Such skills as interpreting the main ideas, recognizing emotional reactions of characters, making inferences, anticipating outcomes, generalizing, seeing relationships, organizing and summarizing ideas, reacting to mood, identifying elements of style, interpreting the thoughts and ideas of the characters, and comparing and contrasting and evaluating ideas are stressed in the reading program."[82] Reading materials must be challenging and thought provoking, so that each child will learn to use books to enrich his experiences, extend his horizons, broaden his understandings, develop his insights, and unlock the door to learning. Growth in reading is a continuous process.

## ACTIVITIES AND QUESTIONS

1. Formulate your own definition of reading.
2. List the key concepts concerning reading which will be most helpful to the kindergarten teacher, the primary teacher, the intermediate teacher.
3. What is the purpose of attempting to describe stages in the development of reading? What value can you see for the teacher, the parent, the supervisor?
4. What elements of readiness for reading does the teacher appraise through observation? Through the use of readiness tests? Distinguish between general and specific readiness.
5. Observe in a kindergarten and a first grade. Try to determine whether the teacher is concerned with general readiness for reading or specific prereading skills. What evidence do you find in your observation and reading to support your answer?
6. Three approaches to the teaching of reading in the first grade are presented in this chapter. Distinguish among them. Evaluate them in terms of the aims of instruction in beginning reading. Which approach was used in the first grade you observed?

[82] Strang, McCullough, and Traxler, *op. cit.*, p. 127.

7. Examine a guide for teaching word-recognition skills in the first grade you observed and one for the fifth grade. What differences do you find?

8. Arrange a debate: *"Resolved,* That all children would learn to read if they were taught only by the phonics method."

9. Observe in a primary or intermediate grade and determine what provisions are made for individual differences in reading achievement.

10. Arrange a role-playing situation in which a primary teacher is telling a parent that her child in the third grade is still reading at primer level. One in which a sixth-grade teacher is telling a parent that her child is reading at the eleventh-grade level. Be sure to include concrete evidence of the achievement of each child.

11. Describe the methods used for providing for individual differences. For integrating reading with the entire instructional program. Which seem to be the most practical? Why?

12. Discuss activities which help pupils in a given grade read for a variety of purposes.

13. Observe children in and out of school. From their interests what books might be valuable to help them read to gain information and enjoyment?

14. What books would you recommend for each of the elementary grades in a school in which the budget allowed only ten books to be purchased from school funds? Defend your selections.

15. What are the advantages of the three-group plan? The four? The five? The six? What problems can you see in trying to plan for more than three subgroups in reading? Which of the suggested plans would be feasible for a first-year teacher to use? Why?

It is possible that a set of reading achievement scores for a particular grade will not allow the three-group plan. Referring to the examples on pages 283 and 284, show how a given set of scores may be grouped three different ways — in a four-group, five-group, or six-group plan.

# BIBLIOGRAPHY

Anderson, Irving H., and Dearborn, Walter F. *The Psychology of Teaching Reading.* New York: The Ronald Press Company, 1952.
Arbuthnot, May Hill. *Children and Books.* Chicago: Scott, Foresman and Company, rev. ed., 1957.

Association for Childhood Education International. *More About Reading*. Reprint Service Bulletin No. 29. Washington, D.C.: The Association, 1959.

Bond, Guy L., and Wagner, Eva Bond. *Teaching the Child to Read*. New York: The Macmillan Company, 3rd ed., 1960.

Burger, Victor, *et al*. *Bringing Children and Books Together*. New York: Library Club of America, Inc., 1956.

Burton, William H., *et al*. *Reading in Child Development*. Indianapolis: The Bobbs-Merrill Company, 1956.

Calkins, N. A. *How to Read Phonics*. Chicago: Beckley-Cardy Company, n.d.

"Classroom Organization: Differing Viewpoints," *The Reading Teacher*, 11: entire issue, December 1957.

Dawson, Mildred A., and Zollinger, Marian. *Guiding Language Learning*. Yonkers-on-Hudson, N.Y.: World Book Company, 1957.

DeBoer, John J., and Dallman, Martha. *The Teaching of Reading*. New York: Henry Holt and Company, 1960.

*Developing Reading Procedures for the Beginning Reader in the Third Grade*. Language Arts Bulletins, Nos. 2–6. New York: Division of Elementary Schools, Board of Education, May 1955–March 1956.

Durrell, Donald D. *Improving Reading Instruction*. Yonkers-on-Hudson, N.Y.: World Book Company, 1956.

Gates, Arthur I. "Improvements in Reading," *The Reading Teacher*, 12:83–86, December 1958.

Gates, Arthur I. *Teaching Reading: What Research Says to the Teacher*. Department of Classroom Teachers and the American Educational Research Association, NEA. Washington, D.C.: The Association, 1953.

Gray, W. S., and Larrick, Nancy (eds.). *Better Readers for Our Times*. International Reading Association Conference Proceedings, Vol. 1. *Scholastic Magazine*, 1956.

Gray, William, and Rogers, Bernice. *Maturity in Reading*. Chicago: University of Chicago Press, 1956.

Harris, Albert J. *How to Increase Reading Ability*. New York: Longmans, Green and Company, 1956.

Hester, Katherine. *Teaching Every Child to Read*. New York: Harper & Brothers, 1955.

Hildreth, Gertrude. *Teaching Reading*. New York: Henry Holt and Company, 1958.

Hill, Archibald. *Introduction to Linguistic Structures*. New York: Harcourt, Brace and Company, 1958.

Hunnicutt, C. W., and Iverson, William J. *Research in the Three R's*. New York: Harper & Brothers, 1958.

*Individualized Reading, Interim Report.* Survey in Selected Schools, 1956–57. New York: Bureau of Research, Board of Education, 1957.

Jacobs, Leland B. (comp.). *A Bibliography of Books for Children.* Washington, D.C.: Association for Childhood Education International, 1953.

Jacobs, Leland B. "Children's Experiences in Literature," Chapter 9 in Virgil E. Herrick, and Leland B. Jacobs (eds.), *Children and the Language Arts.* Englewood Cliffs, N.J.: Prentice-Hall, Inc., 1955.

Jewett, Arno, *et al. Literature for Life.* Boston: Houghton Mifflin Company, 1958.

Johnson, Edna, *et al. Anthology of Children's Literature.* Boston: Houghton Mifflin Company, 3rd ed., 1959.

Karlin, Robert. "Research in Reading," *Elementary English:* 37:177–183, March 1960.

McKee, Paul. *The Teaching of Reading in the Elementary School.* Boston: Houghton Mifflin Company, 1948.

McKim, Margaret C. *Guiding Growth in Reading.* New York: The Macmillan Company, 1955.

Miel, Alice (ed.). *Individualizing Reading Practices.* Practical Suggestions for Teachers, No. 14. New York: Bureau of Publications, Teachers College, Columbia University, 1958.

*Reading, A Symposium.* Bulletin No. 98, Association for Childhood Education International. Washington, D.C.: The Association, 1956.

*Reading for Today's Children.* Thirty-Fourth Yearbook of the Department of Principals, NEA. Washington, D.C.: The Association, 1955.

Robinson, Helen M. (ed.). *Promoting Maximal Reading Growth Among Able Learners.* Chicago: University of Chicago Press, 1954.

Smith, Nila B. "What Research Tells Us About Word Recognition," *Elementary School Journal,* 55:440–445, May 1955.

Strang, Ruth, and Bracken, D. K. *Making Better Readers.* Boston: D. C. Heath and Company, 1958.

Terrell, William B. *Standards for Survey Reading Material in Public Schools* (Including Survey Score Form). Houston, Tex.: Commission on Instructional Materials, Gulf School Research Development Association, 1958.

Wrightstone, J. Wayne. "Research Related to Experience Records and Basal Readers," *The Reading Teacher,* 5:5, 6, September 1957.

Yoakim, Gerald A. *Basal Reading Instruction.* New York: McGraw-Hill Book Company, 1955.

# Handwriting

A child's eyes should be filled with print before writing starts.

HARRY R. WARFEL

"A child should not begin writing unless he has mastered the pencil as an instrument of drawing, has perfected the skill of forming small loops and other marks needed in writing, and knows how to put similar forms on a line from left to right. . . . When writing is assigned too early, a distaste for it is often generated."[83]

If the child is pushed into writing too soon, before he gains some competence in speaking, listening, and reading, his task has no real meaning for him. Just as listening precedes speaking, and speaking precedes reading, so should reading precede writing. "Until a child has an awareness of the patterns of print, he cannot visualize the patterns of writing."[84] He must be comfortable with language if he is to succeed in writing, because writing is in its muscular activity not a language skill but a form of drawing. Even when he arrives at the point where writing has meaning for him, where he sees a need

[83] Harry R. Warfel, "Acquiring Helpful Attitudes Toward Writing," *College Composition and Communication* (National Council of Teachers of English), 9:220–221, December 1958.

[84] *Ibid.*, p. 221.

for it, he should understand what he is writing and should know that writing has its basis in speech. Writing is for reading; writing is for communicating; writing is for expressing.

Handwriting is more than a tool; it is an expression of individuality. "No two individuals have the same carriage, the same stride, the same stance or the same handwriting."[85] Individual differences exist in the ability to coordinate the skills needed to write legibly. Formerly these were ignored and every child was expected to imitate the model exactly. This he learned to do through systematic, formal, isolated drill. First he practiced on separate strokes, then whole letters, and finally words. He wrote laboriously in his copybook, slavishly copying line after line with as much precision as he could muster.

Educators more recently believe that children should be taught to write by writing and that they should begin with whole, meaningful words which they use in daily communication. They agree that learning to write is best accomplished not by motor imitation, but by expressing ideas graphically. The visual images of whole words are more readily retained by the child when they express ideas that are meaningful to him.

Research concerning the mechanics of teaching handwriting gives evidence that the best approach is to have children write rather than trace or practice handwriting motions. In an early study Gates and Taylor[86] concluded that children did twice as well with less practice by learning to write by writing rather than by tracing. Mercer[87] substantiated the superiority of the functional approach to handwriting. Hertzberg[88] reported that after an initial liking for mechanical procedures children preferred direct writing after the first three weeks of instruction. A survey[89] of practices indicated

[85] James F. Magary, "The Psychologist Views School Language Activities," *Elementary School Journal*, 59:284, February 1959.

[86] Arthur I. Gates and Grace A. Taylor, "The Acquisition of Motor Control in Writing by Young Children," *Teachers College Record*, 24:459–468, November 1923.

[87] Iva A. Mercer, "An Experiment in Handwriting in First Grades," *Journal of Educational Research*, 22:361–368, December 1930.

[88] Oscar E. Hertzberg, *A Comparative Study of Different Methods Used in Teaching Beginners to Write*, Teachers College Contributions to Education, No. 214 (New York: Bureau of Publications, Teachers College, Columbia University, 1926).

[89] Ada Polkinghorne, "Current Practices in Teaching Handwriting," *Elementary School Journal*, 47:218–224, December 1946.

that about two-thirds of handwriting instruction is carried out with the aid of a commercial handwriting system.

As handwriting became a tool rather than an art, emphasis shifted from writing a beautiful hand to writing a legible hand. However, a beautiful hand and a legible hand are not mutually exclusive.

Today teachers are primarily concerned with helping children develop two aspects of skill in handwriting — legibility and fluency. How to teach children to write legibly and fluently in a minimum amount of time is the problem that faces the school. Among the factors involved are key concepts about handwriting, readiness for instruction, a knowledge of manuscript and cursive writing, materials of instruction, and methods of evaluating children's handwriting.

## Key Concepts

An examination of the studies of handwriting and the recommendations for developing the skills reveals some key concepts that should prove of value to the teacher.

1. The child is the focus for deciding the best and most effective methods of handwriting. There are many good systems for teaching children to write. It is the responsibility of the teacher to help the child adapt the system and recommendations to his own needs.

2. The goal in handwriting is legibility and ease of writing. Simplicity of letter formation, economy of time, and comfort in writing position and movement are main considerations.

3. Handwriting is more a drawing problem than a language problem. It involves interrelationships of motor coordination, letter forms, words, symbols, and ideas in effective quality-speech patterns.

4. Most children are introduced to handwriting through manuscript writing. Later cursive writing is introduced. The time when the transition is made varies, but in general the change takes place in the second or third grade.

5. The emphasis should be on learning to control and adapt writing techniques to a variety of writing assignments, a variety of speed requirements, and a wide variety of qualities of excellence.

6. Handwriting is a tool rather than an art.

7. The example the teacher sets in his own handwriting and his

understanding of the development of handwriting and its relation to the other language arts are important factors in the teaching of this skill.

8. Quality of handwriting is not significantly related to intelligence. Children will improve in quality as they are motivated to study and diagnose their own writing needs and evaluate their own progress.

## Readiness for Instruction

Interest in informal manuscript writing may begin when the child feels the need to write a letter, to identify his own work at school, or to take a note home to Mother. Teaching children writing skills before they are ready is futile. The majority of preschool children are not ready for instruction in handwriting because they have not developed the muscular coordination required for such a refined skill, nor have they the desire to learn to write. The average nursery and kindergarten child is happy at scribbling, drawing, painting, modeling, constructing, and other related activities that develop the muscles of his hands, fingers, and arms. Using paints, clay, chalk, and crayons not only contributes to the child's creative expression, but serves to communicate ideas and feelings and to develop the muscular coordination essential to writing at a later date. "A considerable (though indeterminate) part of the maturity required for the ability to write comes from previous training. The relation between transfer and mental maturity plays an important role in the concept of readiness."[90] No teacher should try to force readiness for an activity. Beery[91] concluded on the basis of research studies pertinent to readiness for writing that a child can safely be taught manuscript writing if the following conditions of readiness obtain:

1. He has spontaneously shown an interest in learning to print his own name.
2. He has developed facility in the use of scissors, crayons, the paint brush and the pencil in a variety of informal activities.
3. He can copy simple geometric or letter-like characters. . . .

[90] James Deese, *The Psychology of Learning* (New York: McGraw-Hill Book Company, 2nd ed., 1958), p. 235.
[91] Althea Beery, "Readiness for Handwriting," in *Readiness for Reading and Related Language Arts*, a research bulletin of the National Conference on Research in English (Chicago: National Council of Teachers of English, 1950).

4. He has established a dominant hand.
5. He has participated in composing and sending written messages.
6. He senses a personal need to learn to write.
7. He can be introduced to a writing program geared to his level of maturity.

Some children exhibit these signs of readiness in the kindergarten and are ready for such activities as writing their names in manuscript, copying from dictation on the board, and progressing from left to right on writing paper or on newsprint. Individual differences exist in writing interest and ability and children often are not ready for formal instruction in writing until late in the first grade.

## Manuscript and Cursive Writing

Manuscript writing has distinct advantages in introducing writing. It can be learned quickly and can easily be used for communication while it is being learned. Boy and girls are intrigued with the simple letter forms, composed of circles and straight lines, which are easy for them to form and copy. They can draw each stroke of a letter separately and need not be concerned with joining the letters to form the words. Many children in kindergarten enjoy writing their names or the alphabet and copying poems and plans from the chalkboard in an informal situation in which there is no formal instruction in handwriting as such. In the first grade, as more children are ready for handwriting, systematic instruction brings more satisfactory results than merely incidental and informal handwriting experiences alone. The teacher must make clear the purpose for writing — to communicate ideas or to practice to improve handwriting skills. Although much learning can take place incidentally, planned sequential exercises in which words and letters are selected on an advancing scale of difficulty probably give the greatest gain in a given time. However, it should be remembered that children need much opportunity to write to communicate ideas as well as to practice letter formation and other handwriting skills.

Many teachers look upon manuscript writing as a functional tool that can be used for expressing ideas. They find manuscript style is easier to teach; children get good results with less effort than with cursive writing.

Values and disadvantages of both manuscript and cursive writing have been alleged. Houston[92] found in an experiment with two first grades each having thirty-one children that manuscript writing was mastered more readily than cursive. Gates and Brown[93] in an earlier study carried on in the first six grades in a New York public school reported that children learned manuscript writing a little more rapidly the first year and were speeded up to the norms for cursive in Grades 3 to 6 by intensive practice, and that primary children especially liked manuscript and preferred it for many purposes. In the intermediate grades cursive writing seemed more rapid and adults considered it almost as legible as manuscript.

Turner,[94] on the basis of a study of specimens in Grades 2 to 6, recommended manuscript writing for both legibility and speed. Thomson[95] found that with increased speed cursive writing tends to become a scribble, that manuscript writing deteriorates less under pressure. In summarizing the arguments for changing to cursive writing in the upper grades Herrick[96] points out that cursive is the socially accepted form.

READINESS FOR CURSIVE WRITING

Herrick and Jacobs,[97] Strickland,[98] and others warn of the danger of teaching children cursive writing before they have mastered manuscript. Among the signs of readiness for cursive writing suggested by Parke and Bristow[99] are the following:

1. A desire on the part of the child to write in cursive style.

[92] Harry Houston, "Manuscript Writing and Progress in Reading," *Elementary School Journal*, 34:116–118, October 1939.

[93] Arthur Gates and Helen Brown, "Experimental Comparison of Manuscript and Cursive Writing by Young Children," *Teachers College Record*, 24:459–468, November 1928.

[94] Olive G. Turner, "The Comparative Legibility and Speed of Manuscript and Cursive Writing," *Elementary School Journal*, 30:780–786, June 1930.

[95] George L. Thomson, *Better Handwriting*, Puffin Picture Book No. 96 (Middlesex, England: Curwen Press, Ltd., 1954).

[96] Virgil E. Herrick, "Children's Experiences in Handwriting," Chapter 12 in Virgil E. Herrick and Leland Jacobs (eds.), *Children and the Language Arts* (Englewood Cliffs, N.J.: Prentice-Hall, Inc., 1955).

[97] *Ibid.*, p. 273.

[98] Ruth Strickland, *The Language Arts in the Elementary School* (Boston: D. C. Heath and Company, 2nd ed., 1957), p. 362.

[99] Margaret B. Parke and W. H. Bristow, *Practices and Problems in Handwriting* (New York: Board of Education, 1947).

2. Adequate physical development so that there is coordination of muscles of the arm, hand, and fingers.
3. Ability to write all the letters of the manuscript alphabet from memory.
4. Ability to read simple passages written in cursive writing.
5. Ability to copy a selection in manuscript at a rate varying from 25 to 45 letters per minute and to maintain quality of 35 to 50 on the Conrad Scale or an equivalent on another scale.

### Transition from Manuscript to Cursive Writing

Investigators[100] have found that most schools begin to teach manuscript writing before the end of the first grade and make the transition to cursive writing during a year and a half period prior to the fourth grade. Surveys show that in the cities of 10,000 and above the prevailing practice is to make the change in Grade 3.[101] Reasons are that second-grade children have not developed sufficient muscular skills to make cursive writing easy and the time spent in learning it at this stage is excessive, and also that children in the second grade are just beginning to enjoy manuscript writing as a tool and to use it for functional and creative writing.

Those schools which make the change from manuscript to cursive in the second grade do so (1) in order to lighten the heavy curriculum load in the third grade, (2) because there is an advantage in having the teacher who teaches manuscript make the change, (3) in order to prevent children from making the change on their own, (4) in order to prevent the manuscript habit from becoming fixed, and (5) because some children are eager to write like their parents. However, any decision should be made on the basis of the best interests of the children in a particular grade. The program should be flexible to allow for individual variation, muscular coordination, desire to change, and willingness to apply oneself in the task.

That there are serious problems involved in changing from manuscript to cursive writing seems not to be substantiated by available

[100] Polkinghorn, *op. cit.* Frank N. Freeman, "Survey of Manuscript Writing in the Public School," *Elementary School Journal*, 46:375–380, March 1947. Gertrude Hildreth, "Manuscript Writing After Sixty Years," *Elementary English*, 37:6, January 1960.
[101] Frank N. Freeman, "The Transition from Manuscript to Cursive Writing," *Elementary English*, 40:366–373, October 1958.

research. Several independent studies found that if the change is made beyond the second grade it created little difficulty and had little effect on speed or quality of writing.[102] Whether the change should be made at all is still a moot question. It is certainly true that individual teachers have difficulty helping children make the transition. Turmoil, frustration, and tears are a by-product for slow learners or immature and sensitive children who are just beginning to feel secure in manuscript and are upset by the changeover.

If children in the intermediate grades are permitted to retain manuscript they still need practice. They need help with alignment, spacing, and letter formation and the development of a slight slant to give a more interesting appearance to the writing. Teachers should become thoroughly familiar with this style and do it well themselves in order to provide a good example.

Parents must be taken into the planning if manuscript writing is to continue throughout the elementary grades. In schools where this style is continued through the upper grades the cooperation of the parents has been important in successfully carrying out the program. Instruction in manuscript writing through the years in Brookline, Massachusetts, and the Bronxville, New York, schools has made it clear that this style of writing is effective and serviceable for use in and out of school and can result in attractive, legible script. The children are encouraged to develop a rapid manuscript style and to retain it in high school. Some children develop and retain both styles.

## INDIVIDUAL DIFFERENCES IN HANDWRITING

Examples of children's writing clearly show the wide variations in ability. As children become ready to write and show evidence of being successful, the teacher can begin with informal individualized instruction and move gradually toward a more formal practice period of from ten to fifteen minutes. School systems teach children the handwriting skills by various methods: in the order and sequence developed by the commercial system used, in terms of the specific situation or need, or in correlation with spelling and reading

---

[102] *Research Helps in Teaching the Language Arts,* a report prepared by Harold G. Shane for the Association for Supervision and Curriculum Development (Washington, D.C.: National Education Association, 1955), pp. 36–38.

lists. Most schools expect children to master the handwriting symbols by the end of the primary grades.

The teacher must allow the slow writer more time to finish an assignment, or give him a different assignment. Children who are accelerated in handwriting abilities may proceed at their rate, may participate in extra creative-writing experiences or in writing activities requiring greater skill and quality such as making posters, writing for the school paper, writing thank-you letters on behalf of the class, and writing captions for the bulletin board.

*The Left-Handed Child.* The kindergarten or first-grade teacher is responsible for observing the child's hand dominance. If the child is ambidextrous he should perhaps be encouraged to use his right hand. However, if he is left-handed he should be allowed to continue to use that hand for writing activities. The following are suggestions for the left-handed child which have been helpful both to children and to teachers:

1. The child's seat and desk should permit free use of the left hand in writing.
2. The light should come from the right.
3. The child should have considerable freedom in slanting letters, with the slant more to the right, and considerable freedom in selecting the instrument for writing.
4. The child should be given individual instruction so that excessive pressure is not put on him to develop speed.[103]

Examination of the literature indicates that percentages of left-handed children range from 5 per cent to 10 per cent. The preference of a child for one hand over the other is conditioned and influenced by many factors. Koch[104] cites instruction, example, convenience, previous habits, the specific nature and familiarity of particular tasks, hand strength, and genetic factors. Carrothers[105] reported that environmental left-handedness reveals a relative as well as actual increase over a generation ago.

[103] Herbert Klausmeier *et al., Teaching in the Elementary School* (New York: Harper & Brothers, 1956), p. 294.

[104] H. L. Koch, "A Study of the Nature, Measurement and Determination of Hand Preferences," *Genetic Psychology Monographs*, 13:117–218, February 1933.

[105] George Carrothers, "Left-Handedness Among School Pupils," *American School Board Journal*, 114:17–19, May 1947.

## Materials and Devices for Instruction

Teachers are constantly looking for new devices to help children develop handwriting skills. Among the most commonly used are tracing, copying, rhythmic writing, exercises and drills, manual guidance, and blackboard practice. Forming letters in the air, and push-pull and oval exercises still carry over in today's practice sessions. Hertzberg[106] found that direct copying of the teacher's model was the best of four methods. Tracing with the pencil was slightly superior to the groove and finger tracing methods. Gates and Taylor[107] concluded from their study that tracing and writing are quite dissimilar functions although they have some common elements. Experienced teachers have found that practice is important in teaching handwriting, but that the amount of practice needed varies with the interest and abilities of the children in writing and with the extent to which writing is an integral part of the curriculum.

In a typical elementary school the materials for writing instruction usually include crayons, chalk, beginner's pencils, adult pencils, speed-ball pens, fountain pens, pen and holder sets, 8 by 11½ sheets of lined paper with lines 1 inch, ¾ inch, and ⅜ inch apart, unlined paper, writing easels, typewriters, and chalkboard. Writing instruments noted in the Wisconsin survey, in the order of frequency of use, are as follows:

| | |
|---|---|
| Kindergarten | Crayons, beginner's pencil, chalk. |
| Grade 1 | Beginner's pencil, chalk, crayon, adult pencil. |
| Grade 2 | Adult pencil, chalk, beginner's pencil, crayon, mechanical pencil. |
| Grade 3 | Adult pencil, chalk, mechanical pencil, beginner's pencil, crayon, ball point pen, fountain pen, pen and holder. |
| Grade 4 | Adult pencil, fountain pen, ball point pen, mechanical pencil, pen and holder, chalk, crayon, beginner's pencil. |
| Grade 5 | Fountain pen, adult pencil, pen and holder, ball point pen, mechanical pencil, chalk, crayon. |

[106] *Op. cit.*
[107] *Op. cit.*

Grade 6      Fountain pen, ball point pen, adult pencil, pen and holder, mechanical pencil, chalk, crayon.[108]

There appears to be little support for some of the materials used in the primary grades. Available evidence favors use of the adult pencil rather than the larger beginner's pencil. Blackboard and easel writing has value as an opportunity for free, large writing but in no way substitutes for the kind of writing most individuals will do the rest of their lives.

## *Evaluation*

As handwriting skills improve throughout the elementary grades teachers are concerned not alone with legibility and fluency but with style of writing as well. They consider the two most important factors in good writing to be those having to do with the relationships and uniformity of letter formation (size, alignment, line quality, proportion, spacing, endings) and those having to do with body and proper positions and arm movement. Handwriting scales[109] often use letter formation, spacing, alignment, slant, and quality of line for measuring quality of handwriting.

Some schools are now making use of the typewriter.[110] With the interest young children have in actively exploring the possibilities of yet another instrument for communicating, and the need of the student to prepare reports and essays, more and more schools are offering children instruction in typing along with other forms of written expression. As schools seek a broader and more realistic approach to materials of instruction, research is needed to determine the best

[108] Virgil E. Herrick *et al.*, *Handwriting in Wisconsin: A Survey of Elementary School Practices* (Madison: School of Education, University of Wisconsin, 1951), p. 114.

[109] *American Handwriting Scale* (New York: A. N. Palmer Company); *Ayers Measuring Scale for Handwriting* (New York: Russell Sage Foundation); *Handwriting Measuring Scale* (Columbus, Ohio: Zaner-Bloser Company); *Normal Handwriting Scale* (Columbus, Ohio: Zaner-Bloser Company); Gertrude Hildreth, *Metropolitan Primary Manuscript Handwriting Scale* (Yonkers-on-Hudson, N.Y.: World Book Company). (New forms of these scales are printed periodically.)

[110] Bertis E. Capehart, *Does the Portable Typewriter Stimulate Learning in the Elementary Classroom?* (New York: Education Department, Hill and Knowlton, Inc., 1959).

writing instruments for elementary school children as well as the value of one over another at a specific time.

In evaluating growth in handwriting it is important that the child recognize whether he is writing to improve his skill in handwriting or to express ideas. Each purpose is legitimate. When the purpose is to improve his skill, he is evaluated on the basis of words and letters selected on an advancing scale of difficulty. He should progress from the easy to the difficult and concentrate upon one difficulty at a time. When the purpose is to express ideas, the teacher evaluates his growth on the basis of how effectively he solves the difficulties he encounters as he writes. Although incidental learning does take place, the child needs planned exercises and directed teaching in order to make the greatest gain over a given period of time. Emphasis on good handwriting in the final draft of expository writing — compositions, reports, and the like — gives practice in careful writing. Such activity forms an excellent basis for self-evaluation.

## ACTIVITIES AND QUESTIONS

1. Discuss the reasons for teaching manuscript writing in the primary grades. What specific advantages do you see in this plan? What objections may be raised by parents? By children?

2. What are the most significant objectives for which the primary teacher should work in the teaching of handwriting?

3. Observe in a primary grade and try to determine what methods the teacher uses for providing for individual differences in handwriting abilities.

4. Collect samples of the best and poorest handwriting in a primary grade. Try to evaluate the handwriting in terms of objectives you believe to be the most significant.

5. How would you go about helping the child who is the poorest writer to improve?

6. What procedures would you use to improve the quality and speed of writing in the intermediate grades? How would these differ from those used in the primary grades?

7. How would you provide for individual differences in handwriting in the primary grades? In the intermediate grades?
8. What do you consider the place of the typewriter as a communication tool in the elementary school?

# BIBLIOGRAPHY

Beery, Althea. "Readiness for Handwriting," in *Readiness for Reading and Related Language Arts*. Research bulletin of the National Conference on Research in English. Chicago: National Council of Teachers of English, 1950.

Capehart, Bertis E. *Does the Portable Typewriter Stimulate Learning in the Elementary Classroom?* New York: Education Department, Hill and Knowlton, Inc., 1959.

Covert, Sidney J. "An Evaluation of Handwriting in Certain Iowa Schools." Doctoral dissertation, State University of Iowa, 1953.

Freeman, Frank N. "How to Deal with Left-Handedness," *NEA Journal*, 49:12–14, January 1960.

Freeman, Frank N. "The Transition from Manuscript to Cursive Writing," *Elementary English*, 40:366–373, October 1958.

Freeman, Frank N. *What Research Says to the Teacher. Teaching Handwriting*. Washington, D.C.: National Education Association, 1954.

Furness, Edna L. "Diagnosis and Remediation of Handwriting Defects," *Elementary English*, 32:224–228, April 1955.

Herrick, Virgil E., *et al. Handwriting in Wisconsin: A Survey of Elementary School Practices*. Madison: University of Wisconsin, 1951.

Herrick, Virgil E. "Handwriting and Children's Writing," *Elementary English*, 37:248–258, April 1960.

Hildreth, Gertrude. "Manuscript Writing After Sixty Years," *Elementary English*, 37:3–13, January 1960.

Hunnicutt, C. W., and Iverson, William J. (eds.). *Research in the Three R's*. New York: Harper & Brothers, 1958, pp. 263–285.

"Just Where Do We Stand in Handwriting?" *Instructor*, 63:57, January 1954.

McKee, Paul. *Language in the Elementary School*. Boston: Houghton Mifflin Company, 1939.

Magary, James F. "The Psychologist Views School Language Activities," *Elementary School Journal*, 59:282–285, February 1959.

Parke, Margaret B. "Composition in Primary Grades," *Elementary English*, 36:107–122, February 1959.

Parke, M. B., and Bristow, W. H. *Practices and Problems in Handwriting.* New York: Board of Education, 1947.

Swenson, Ima. "An Analytical Study of Illegibilities in the Handwriting of Third Grade Children During the Transition Period from Manuscript to Cursive." Master's thesis, University of Texas, 1956.

Templin, Elaine M. "Research and Comment: Handwriting — The Neglected 'R,'" *Elementary English,* 37:386–389, October 1960.

*Transition Unit: Manuscript Writing for Primary Grades to Cursive Writing for Upper Grades.* Columbus, Ohio: Zaner-Bloser Company, 1954.

# Expository and expressive writing

> . . . selection from the chaotic form-
> lessness of experience, and the record-
> ing of the fragments selected in a
> sequence that makes sense.
>
> ARCHIBALD MACLEISH

Most children talk before they are two, but few children write
before they come to school. There is no need. When they enter
school, however, they need to identify their personal belongings and
their papers, to keep a record of daily plans, to write about their
experiences, to write messages to take home. The initial emphasis in
teaching communication in writing is on selecting from the child's
own experiences the things which are important to him to preserve.

## *Teaching Expository Writing*

The teacher must (1) create an environment in which there is
both need and opportunity for writing, (2) provide firsthand experiences in and out of the classroom, (3) develop additional back-

ground for writing through literature as experience, (4) help children establish purposes for writing, (5) help children evaluate their progress in writing, (6) provide time for writing, and (7) direct children in the development of skills.

*Creating an Environment for Writing.* Children communicate in a stimulating environment. Where many activities are going on, where children are encouraged to manipulate, construct, explore, experiment, create, and discuss ideas, they have something to write about. New experiences develop new ideas, increase vocabulary, broaden concepts, and extend horizons. Children participate in making plans, listing activities, keeping records, dictating stories, recording weather, and writing invitations. Teachers are guided by the principle that "Writing begins with the need to say something; it does not begin with the workbook, the spelling exercise, the vocabulary drill, the sentence diagram, the identification of speech parts, or even the ingratiating study of the nature of language."[111]

*Providing Firsthand Experiences.* The extent to which the child uses writing depends upon the number of ideas he has to express, his willingness to communicate them, and his opportunity to see, taste, smell, touch, hear, experiment, and experience. Before he is ready to write he dictates the ideas gained through group experiences within and outside the classroom. He observes as the teacher translates his ideas into meaningful symbols on the chalkboard. He discusses excursions. He participates in dramatic play and games and creates the dialogue for his stories, which he illustrates with pictures. He composes stories, poems, and riddles as writing becomes part of his daily program.

*Developing Background for Writing Through Literature.* As the child listens to stories and poems, he forms vivid pictures in his mind. Later, "the printed words excite images, and the images, if they are sufficiently vivid, produce attitudes (dispositions to act) in the reader."[112] He writes from experience. Not all experience need be his very own, however. Many unrelated, half-remembered fragments — some from real life, others from literature — are brought into play.

[111] Carl G. Wonnberger, "Writing — A Way of Life," *English Journal,* 48:66, February 1959.

[112] Wallace A. Bacon and Robert S. Breen, *Literature as Experience* (New York: McGraw-Hill Book Company, 1959), p. 25.

*Establishing Purposes for Expository Writing.* If a child knows that his writing will be read, if he writes to communicate something that is significant to him, he will try to write with clarity, with correctness, and with logical organization. Children can be taught that notices, invitations, thank-you notes, reports, and business and social letters must be well organized and carefully written. In expository writing clear and logical organization of ideas is important. Outlining and developing ideas in sequence should be stressed.

*Evaluating Progress in Writing.* Most children are eager to improve. They want to know whether they are making progress and if not, why not. Progress must be measured in terms of objectives for the type of writing to be evaluated. Keeping samples of written communication in a folder and periodically checking on individual progress is a frequently used method of appraisal. ". . . Folders of written products are considered the most useful measure of progress in composition and handwriting since growth in sentence power appears to be the best single measure of developing maturity in expression."[113]

*Providing Time, Direct Teaching, Guidance, and Encouragement.* Children need time to grow, time to experience, and time to write. They should not be hurried, harassed, or pressured. Tension and good writing are antagonistic. The child is most likely to become interested in writing through someone who is interested in it. "He is most likely to 'catch it' from parent or a teacher or favorite uncle who loves to read or else quite by himself from an author who loves to write and who lets the prepositions fall where they may."[114]

## Developmental Steps in Written Communication

As children learn to write they progress through several steps: (1) composing and dictating stories or group experiences to the teacher, (2) dictating and copying, (3) learning skills through direct practice, and (4) developing confidence in writing to communicate.

[113] Margaret B. Parke, "Composition in the Primary Grades," *Elementary English*, 41:111, February 1959.
[114] Wendell Johnson, *op. cit.,* p. 123.

*Composing and Dictating to the Teacher.* Children are eager to talk about exciting experiences. The teacher knows this and encourages them to tell their experiences as he acts as a scribe. Plans, responsibilities, experiences, and stories are organized and developed step by step as a class project. The teacher first finds a topic of interest to the group, then asks questions that stimulate thinking and encourage the expression of the children's own thoughts.

*Dictating and Copying.* Children are soon eager to begin copying from the script on the board or newsprint. Often kindergartners ask the teacher to write "Happy Birthday," "To Mother," "I love you," "Thank you," "P.T.A. tomorrow," "No school Thursday," "Happy Easter," "Merry Christmas," "Happy anniversary," and so forth, so that they may copy the words.

The teacher continues to act as a scribe and helps them record their ideas while they are learning the mechanics of writing. Even as they compose stories they are gaining skills in organizing ideas and expressing them clearly, logically, and fluently.

*Direct Practice.* Once the teacher sees that a child is ready to learn the mechanics of composition (punctuation, spelling, and capitalization), he must give specific help. He calls attention to such items as placement and capitalization of the title, capitalization and punctuation for each sentence, margin, spelling of difficult words, and the formation of letters. The mechanics are stressed, and the children pick up the needed skills according to their readiness and ability. Practice is geared to the needs of individual children for specific training.

*Independence in Writing.* Dawson and Zollinger suggest the following techniques for motivating the beginning writer:

*The unfinished story* (developed cooperatively by the group and written by the teacher, leaving the last sentence for each child to complete as he chooses).

*An unfinished letter* (composed by the class, written on the board by the teacher. The last part is left incomplete for individual response.)

*Writing captions* (either titles or sentence descriptions of pictures).

*A series of pictures which tell a story.* The teacher folds a large sheet of paper and divides it into six or eight sections which outline the space for each picture. Captions at the bottom of the page tell the story briefly. The beginning, the sequence, the ending are emphasized in the picture sequence.[115]

## Activities for Written Communication

Because some children develop skills far beyond those required in the activities usually planned for the primary grades, while others are not able to succeed in even the simplest activities, provision should be made for individual differences in ability, interest, and need for written expression. Many meaningful opportunities for using written communication, as well as for practicing written usage forms based on correct oral usage, should be provided in the classroom if the children are to be motivated to sharpen the tools for writing. The following activities challenge children to develop the mechanics of writing and improve the level of language usage:

Group activities
　Composing group stories or experience charts.
　Selecting captions for pictures and pictures series or movies.
　Writing letters, invitations, and thank-you notes.
　Keeping a record of daily plans, weather charts.
　Formulating problems for a unit of work.
　Planning and listing questions to be answered during an excursion.
　Listing names of characters and scenes for dramatizations.
　Listing room duties, committee assignments, books read.
　Outlining plans for a program, games to be played, rules for the game.
Individual activities
　Signing name, writing captions and labels for objects.
　Writing tags for gifts.
　Writing brief notes, greetings, and letters.
　Observing and recording daily temperatures.
　Writing stories of daily news items.
　Keeping records of lunch money, attendance, library reading.
　Writing numbers for pages of books, for a monthly calendar, for arithmetic games.

[115] Adapted from Mildred A. Dawson and Marion Zollinger, *Guiding Language Learning* (Yonkers-on-the-Hudson, N.Y.: World Book Company, 1957), pp. 316, 317.

Framing questions for interviewing people: the nurse, custodian, policeman, librarian, fire chief, postman.

Keeping a personal spelling list.

Making a dictionary.

Writing original arithmetic problems.

Composing original poems, stories, songs, riddles, plays.

Group and individual activities

Using correct manuscript form, correct margins; heading papers according to prescribed plan.

Using capital letters correctly; forming upper- and lower-case letters correctly.

Capitalizing the names of people, the school, first word of a sentence, "I," names of months, days, holidays, titles of stories, poems, pictures.

Capitalizing names of towns, states, streets.

Capitalizing heading and closing of letters.

Capitalizing Dr., Mr., Mrs., Miss.

Using correct punctuation:

Period at end of sentence, initial, or abbreviation.

Question mark in ending sentences asking a question.

Apostrophe in simple contractions, in possessive case.

Comma between towns and states, after greeting in friendly letter, between connected words in a series.

Exclamation mark at end of sentences that show strong feeling.

Quotation marks at beginning and end of the direct words of others.

*Using Words Correctly.* The school must take responsibility for helping the child develop the ability to communicate on the level of standard English usage. Examples of standard English to be emphasized and mastered by the end of the primary grades are: *saw, seen; did, done; went, gone; come, came; ran, run; eat, ate; wasn't, weren't; has, have; hasn't, haven't.*

In the primary grades, while the basic conventions of written expression should be taught and practiced, children should also be motivated to express themselves freely and at some length in writing without undue attention to form. They should recognize that a written unit begins with a capital letter and ends with a terminal mark appropriate to the particular idea expressed. In the intermediate grades children can be increasingly directed to the sense of completeness within word units, beginning with the incomplete, rather than the overcomplete, statement.

*Developing Vocabulary.* In all of the elementary grades children are faced with the problem of acquiring a rapidly expanding vocabulary. Some suggestions for helping them are:

Increasing vocabulary through new experiences.

Using new words appropriately.

Choosing words that are colorful, descriptive, vivid, clear, and precise.

Recognizing differences in meaning for the same word.

Explaining the terminology used in written communication such as *sentence, capital letter, small letter, period, question mark, comma, heading, greeting, body, closing* and *signature, indent, paragraph, apostrophe, contraction,* and *command.*

*Developmental Activities.* Copy work (from chalkboard) can include announcements, lists, labels, a cooperative story or letter, a picture story, an individual story, and invitations. Practice in writing correctly from dictation is valuable, particularly for the observation of mechanics. When a pupil indicates readiness for independent writing he may compose experience stories, thank-you notes, invitations, greetings, and letters. Learning to fill out records of library books and library forms is an important activity. There are always bulletin-board announcements to be written. News stories or news letters can be written individually or by the group. For proofreading, models from textbooks or samples of work can be used as guides.

Most primary children are ready for the basic fundamentals of written expression if they are provided opportunity for oral practice and are encouraged to apply their knowledge in meaningful situations. Even first-graders can be taught the use of capital letters at the beginning of a written unit and periods at the end. As children show a readiness for more mature experiences in writing, attention can be given to the feeling of completeness within word groups.

Young writers can be educated to regard with dissatisfaction such fragments as:

By the end of the day
All the teachers and children
While the rain was falling
Since I was unable to go[116]

[116] Pooley, *Teaching English Grammar,* p. 123.

Good oral usage is the keystone to developing good written communication. The child begins to sense the incompleteness in fragments like those above, particularly when they are presented orally. Perhaps more than anything else, children need to build written communication skills upon good oral skills. The child who is accustomed to saying "We was there" will probably write "We was there." Workbooks and practice sheets have little value unless accompanied by practice in correct oral usage of the same material. Remember, the child must not only think of the way he should write the phrase but also labor with the problems of penmanship. In order to write correctly, he should acquire correct speech habits by daily practice in both oral and written forms. Children learn correct speech by speaking correctly. They learn to write by speaking and writing correctly.

## Evaluation of Expository Writing

Children want to know the basis on which they are being evaluated. They want to participate in the evaluation process. They can help evaluate their progress in writing if they know the specific objectives for each phase of writing and if they have some guides or models to check progress against. Teachers can help children evaluate their writing in the following ways:

Keeping folders of written products over a period of time.
Comparing previous products with present ones to determine growth.
Comparing the work with a model from a textbook or other reliable source.
Reserving a place on the bulletin board for work that shows improvement as evaluated by the child and teacher as a team.

## Expository Writing in the Intermediate Grades

Expository writing in the intermediate grades is stimulated primarily by a need to express ideas in a form in which they can be preserved. Many situations demand writing. Children have to write to invite, to express, to record, to explain, and to keep in touch with friends who are ill or on trips. Teachers should be constantly alert to opportunities for having children write social and business letters and make written explanations. The writing must meet high standards of form and organization because it is meant to be read by others.

*Goals for Written Expression.* Perhaps the most important task of the intermediate grade teacher is that of helping children establish goals and evaluate their progress. Individual children in the intermediate grades can work to

Establish goals which are attainable.
Write well when there is a reason for writing.
Write for pure enjoyment.
Write clearly, logically, and intelligibly.
Project themselves into their writing.
Improve their writing by rewriting.
Evaluate their own work.
Recognize and appreciate good writing of others and themselves.

Individual children and groups will differ in the extent to which they realize these or similar goals. However, the good teacher plans activities in terms of the needs, abilities, interests, and past experiences of the group; provides a climate in which expression is stimulated; gives time, encouragement, and guidance; and challenges children to use writing to communicate ideas. It is his responsibility to motivate each child to loftier efforts and more satisfying experiences in both expository and expressive writing. In the section on speaking many types of activities which stimulate oral expression were presented. Practically all of them can also be used to stimulate motivation for written expression. Activities that have their origin in social situations, or situations with social implications, serve initially to motivate children to write.

As they develop the mechanics in expository writing, as they learn to organize ideas, to use correct sentence forms, to spell the words, they apply their knowledge in expressive writing. The emphasis in expository writing is on the product. The communication must be easily read and correctly written in a socially acceptable style for the benefit of the reader.

In expressive writing the emphasis is on expressing what one has an intense desire to say. "It is personal, individual, imaginative and highly perishable."[117] Such matters as mechanics, appearance, spelling, penmanship are kept subordinate to the ideas, the feelings, and the imagination of the writer.

# Expressive Writing

"We are all poets as children, and my whole effort in teaching is to recover some of the creativity that is lost in childhood."[118] Within each child is a creative spark, an imaginative power waiting for something to release it. All children are waiting for someone to kindle the flame or fan it into action. This creative urge is expressed in dance, song, art, or writing. Some express it quietly, not caring to share it; others come running with a poem and ask the teacher to read it.

## THE NATURE OF EXPRESSIVE WRITING

A creative work is the child's own. It is original in content and in style. "Words used . . . are as colors used by the painter. . . . The form grew out of the materials of the tale and the tellers' reaction to them."[119]

In expressive writing as in art, music, or the dance the whole point is the expression of the idea, imagination, and physical response of the individual. It is spontaneous, and here the teacher stands by as the child creates. There is no doubt that there can be spontaneity in expository writing, that a child may write a letter spontaneously, but it is still expository writing if it has a utilitarian motive. Creative writing is free expression, motivated by one's own inner drive or urge.

For writing to be truly creative it must have the following characteristics:

1. *Originality or spontaneity*, in the sense that it is an expression of the individual's own ideas, feelings, and imagination. The ideas

[117] Alvina T. Burrows *et al.*, *They All Want to Write* (Englewood Cliffs, N.J.: Prentice-Hall, Inc., 1952), p. 194.

[118] Rochelle Girson, "A Trio's Intents and Methods," quoting Theodore Roethke, *Saturday Review*, 42:23, March 14, 1959.

[119] Sherwood Anderson, *A Story Teller's Story*, quoted in Hughes Mearns, *Creative Youth* (Garden City, N.Y.: Doubleday, Doran and Company, 1925), p. 10.

may not be new, but they are expressed in a way that is new to him. The ideas come and he puts them on paper, not because he is told to do so but because he feels the need to write what he has to say.

2. *Necessity or need*, in the sense that the child is drawn to express himself in this art medium as surely as he feels compelled to express himself in the dance, in song, in drama, or with the brush. He is largely self-motivated but the urge can be fostered by a creative teacher who understands what is required to bring forth such expression.

3. *Sparkle or vividness*, reflecting the imagination, thought, and personality of the writer. To be truly creative the individual stretches his imagination and as he starts to write he follows where fancy leads. The mere act of sitting down and starting to write is in itself a motivating factor.

Expressive writing differs from expository writing both in nature and in the purposes it serves in the development of the child. Expressive writing is concerned with artistic self-expression; expository writing with functional communication.

Children must have faith in the power to express themselves creatively. They need encouragement in writing honestly, in expressing what they believe needs to be said. Writing of this type is motivated by an inner urge which stirs the imagination, develops ease in putting words on paper, and stimulates the desire to make words say what one wants to say. Such expression is an exhilarating experience and can be motivated by an interested teacher. "There is such a thing as contagion of mind, spirit acting upon spirit; it is an important instrument of education; perhaps it is the only important one."[120]

### The Purpose of Expressive Writing

The child is not confined to any one art medium. He tries his hand freely at several modes of expression. However, in the medium in which he finds the greatest personal satisfaction and enjoyment he is likely to make repeated efforts. Expressive writing has values which are akin to the values of expression in other creative media: it gives the child a sense of satisfaction that comes from expressing himself creatively, and it gives him a release from pressures and tensions.

[120] Hughes Mearns, *The Creative Adult* (New York: Doubleday, Doran and Company, 1940), p. 208.

The child who writes something which others appreciate has the satisfaction not only of having created the expression but of receiving the approbation of the group. He is stimulated to try again. He may find that the joy that comes from others' appreciation of the product is the motivating factor at the outset. However, if he is to increase his ability to express himself creatively in this form he must sooner or later write for the reward it brings him personally.

Children live among tensions, problems, and fears which more often than the adult realizes make a deep impression on them. Expressive writing provides a way of releasing tension acceptably.

The teacher who understands children will make every effort to help them express themselves in this medium. He should know what he can do as well as what he cannot do to stimulate them. He will above all remember that the significant thing in this as in every form of self-expression is the process, not the product. What expressive writing does for the child is of greater significance than what the child does in expressive writing.

## THE ROLE OF THE TEACHER IN EXPRESSIVE WRITING

What can the teacher do to get a child started? His responsibility lies in providing worth-while, vital experiences which will give the child something to write about, an environment in which creativity can flourish, free exchange of ideas, concrete help in expressing his ideas, time for self-motivated writing, and an encouraging audience.

*Providing Vital Experiences.* Experiences which will give a child something to write about may range from trips into the community to television programs in the school; in fact, they include any activity that will broaden his outlook, clarify and extend his concepts, and increase his awareness of the world around him.

The creative experience in writing is transforming impressions into thought and articulated feelings. "We live and we learn, as much by unconscious absorption and assimilation as by systematic effort. The impact of life around us is continually affecting us in countless ways of which we are unconscious. We are endlessly noticing things, responding to things, remembering things, and forming impressions, then storing them away somewhere in our minds and hearts — for future reference, if we but learn to tap this hidden reservoir."[121]

[121] Luella B. Cook, "Writing as Self-Revelation," *English Journal*, 48:250, May 1959.

Creativity rarely seeks expression unless there is a background of experience behind it. The child who has just had his first train ride or airplane trip — his first *anything* inside or outside the classroom — is much easier to guide into writing about it than the child who spends much of his time sitting or repeating the same experiences.

Applegate points out: "Only a dolt could fail to gain enrichment from the exciting goings on in today's classrooms: the world of many books, excursions, hikes, radio, television, magazines, wonderful pictures, talks by travelers, exhibits, letters from pen pals, free materials from business houses, maps that do everything but talk, music from every land, folk dances that make one feel other folks through his feet, historical museums alive with dioramas. . . . Almost any child can be stimulated to write if he is first stimulated to *Read, Look,* and *Listen.* . . ."[122]

*Providing Literary Experiences.* The teacher who brings literature and children together does much to encourage expressive writing. Fiction, biography, hero tales and legends, as well as the stories of modern times, will help develop greater sensitivity to people, situations, and periods of history. The teacher should plan to read regularly to the group from the wealth of literature that is available for every age level. The wide variety of children's books today enables youngsters to become more familiar with the heroes of yesterday than yesterday's children were with their own heroes.

*Providing for Exchange of Ideas.* Not all children have an equal talent for writing. Some have only to be given time, freedom, and encouragement and they are off; others can't write more than a few sentences, even if they are pressured; and the largest group do surprisingly well if stimulated and guided by a creative teacher.

The noncreative child gets his ideas from others. The teacher should recognize the importance of the exchange of ideas in motivation. Applegate suggests the following procedure in carrying out the stimulation and guidance phase of the program.

> Let's pretend that the whole class is to write adventure stories of cowboys, or gauchos on the pampas of Argentina. The stimulation via books, movies, pictures, and exhibits has been provided. The next step is the exchange of ideas. . . . Ask children for idea

[122] Mauree Applegate, "After All, Mrs. Murphy —," *When Children Write*, Bulletin No. 95 (Washington, D.C.: Association for Childhood Education International, 1955), p. 25.

seeds or starters such as for a cowboy adventure story. If the stimulation and the information have been provided, ideas will come
faster than you can write them on the blackboard. Some children
may suggest that a cowboy was hunting stolen cattle and came
upon the rustlers unaware. . . . Another may suggest that a cowboy
got caught in a storm with his cattle, another that a baby calf be
rescued from wolves. . . . If the class runs out of ideas, add a few of
your own. . . . By this time, all those children filled with ideas . . .
will be ready and all the teacher needs to do now before writing
time is to work with words. Why stimulate children to write, why
let them exchange ideas for stories and then give them no tools of
expression — words?

From the children's study of pictures and books they may suggest words to describe. the great plains of Argentina; the rich
stretches of the pampas grass flowing in the wind like a sea; the
mahogany faces of the cowboys from long living with the winds
and the sun; the easy way the gaucho rides his horse and the long,
easy lope of his steed. . . ."[123]

It is in using the words and phrases imaginatively that a teacher
can help children in the re-creative aspect of expressive writing —
helping them to observe, to feel, and *then* to write.

*Helping Children Express Ideas.* The teacher may help children
improve their writing through a program of *vocabulary development*. Children usually lack the words to express shades of meaning
or to put things vividly. They need to form the habit of finding
the exact word for what they want to say.

To help children increase the pool of words from which they may
draw in writing the teacher may

1. Keep a list of colorful phrases and descriptive words on the
   chalkboard.
2. Have a descriptive file box or file folder to which children
   have access.
3. Make a point of calling attention to literary techniques such
   as alliteration, rhyme, onomatopoeia, metaphor, and simile.
4. List on a chart various categories of words such as "colorful,"
   "tranquil," "gay," "angry," "sad."
5. Use a wide vocabulary in his own speaking and writing, being
   careful not to talk down to children.

[123] *Ibid.,* pp. 11, 25, 26.

6. Play word games in which pupils hunt for words that establish different moods.
7. Define common terms; describe everyday occurrences in interesting ways.
8. Keep a list of trite words, such as "good," "nice," "pretty," "swell," "gorgeous," "grand," "terrific," and find substitutes for them.
9. Correlate the foreign-language lesson with writing and make use of foreign phrases and words that are more descriptive for particular purposes.
10. Pantomime the shades of meanings of words.

*Encouraging new ideas* is a prime responsibility of the teacher. Children and teachers often get bogged down talking about the same ideas in the same old way. If a child comes up with a unique way of expressing something he should be commended for it. Originality is worthy of praise, and children should be encouraged to read widely, discuss what they have read, and evaluate the effectiveness with which they speak and write.

*Suggesting interesting topics* is part of the teacher's job. Some teachers keep a list of interesting topics on the chalkboard or in a "treasure box" which give children ideas for writing. There are children in every group who are not self-starters. They need specific motivation before they feel free to express themselves. If topics are available so children can work with them at their leisure, the results are much more likely to be satisfactory than if the teacher suddenly tells the children to "write a story."

Greene and Petty[124] suggest the following topics:

How I Feel in the Dark
What I Do First Thing in the Morning
How Our Back Yard Looks Today
Troubles I've Had Baby Sitting
What I Love to Touch (See, etc.)
Seeing the Earth from a Space Ship

A group of children will think of many more interesting subjects that will stimulate the non-self-starter.

[124] Harry A. Greene and Walter T. Petty, *Developing Language Skills in the Elementary School* (Boston: Allyn and Bacon, Inc., 1959), p. 358.

*Providing Time for Self-Motivated Writing.* Without question the most rewarding writing, both in satisfaction received from the activity and in quality of writing, is not assigned writing but the individual writing done completely on one's own. This is the truly creative type — the expressive writing. All the teacher need do here is to scratch the match; the potential flame is already there. The creative child needs little more than time. He enjoys the stimulation of discussion, playing with words, vocabulary development, and word study — but the real reward comes from writing and perhaps sharing what he has written.

*Sharing Written Work.* Many children want to share their creative writing when they have finished their story or poem. The decision to share or not to share the work should be the child's own. Work that is highly personal or confidential should be the private property of the author.

When the children are ready to read their stories to the group, the stage must be rather carefully set. Creative listening, not merely courteous listening, characterizes the sharing period and helps make it meaningful.

The teacher's role during this experience is that of appreciative encourager. He is not a critic. He makes a positive comment about each work in the early sharing periods — "That was a lively bit of action," "What a delightful sense of humor you have," "You wrote about a curious incident," "You have a genius for invention," "You are an artist with words" — which stimulates the child to release his creative gifts, to become more confident, and to be eager for the next writing time. As children gain in self-confidence, as they learn to express ideas with increasing ease, as they develop the skills that make stories come alive, the teacher spends less time in commenting and more time in encouraging listening. He seeks to open the channels through which thought and language flow. His best allies in fostering creativity in writing are the children themselves. "When a few youngsters have grown excited about a group of lively characters or a new pattern of writing, their enthusiasm spreads throughout the group until most of the class gets caught up in the story-making activity. Contagion is one of the most effective means we have yet discovered."[125]

[125] Burrows *et al.*, *op. cit.*, p. 92.

## Initiating Story Writing

Experience suggests some important guides for initiating creative writing. The significance of getting off to a good start by a warming-up process in the intermediate grades cannot be overestimated. Included in this process are (1) establishing the rapport necessary to happy, easy writing; (2) whetting love of writing to the point of action — this may take from a month to a whole semester of "breaking the ground" before writing gets under way; (3) inviting the group to write when the time seems ripe; (4) providing a time for writing in the regular class schedule — those not caring to write may turn to other self-chosen quiet activities such as reading, drawing, painting, working on unit activities, and so forth; (5) giving approval to those who choose to write, but not attaching any stigma to the non-writers; (6) encouraging those who want to write, but, if they can't seem to get started even with suggestions from the teacher, suggesting that they wait until another day; (7) encouraging children to write about characters drawn from life or from literature, or make-believe; (8) emphasizing getting ideas down on paper, not neatness or correctness of mechanics in this writing — as children develop skills in expository writing they will transfer many of them automatically; (9) writing words they ask for on the chalkboard to facilitate writing; (10) not necessarily requiring titles for stories at the outset — concentrating on a title may inhibit the embryonic writer. Freedom to wander where the story leads is an essential.[126]

## Principles for Guiding Expressive Writing

*Learning to Write by Writing.* It is only by writing and rewriting that the channels of communication remain open to allow thinking and feeling to come through spontaneously. It is not the product but the process that is of prime importance in the writing of the elementary school child. Not many of the products at this stage of life will be preserved for posterity. However, the satisfactions that come from having something to say and saying it as effectively as possible will lead to growth.

[126] Adapted from *ibid.*, pp. 88–90.

*Philosophy of Creativity and Guidance.* The teacher's philosophy of growth and creativity is the essence of guidance in expressive writing. Such a philosophy is implied by Mearns in the following words: "You have something to say. . . . Something of your very own. Try to say it. Don't undervalue it. Don't let the fear of what others may think prevent you from saying it. . . . You have something to say, something no one else in the world has ever said in just your way of saying it."[127]

*Motivation and the World's Literature.* Exposure to fine literature in the home as well as in the school improves the child's ability to express himself. Reading a variety of good stories and poetry not only helps him develop understanding, insight, and vocabulary but gives him ideas out of which writing evolves. He assimilates and weaves into his own design of living what he reads and it becomes an integral part of that design.

*Spurs to Creative Activity.* Weather, seasons, stars and night, birds, fish, streams, the seashore, fire — any of these, and countless others, may stir a response. The following examples show how some children responded to these stimuli.

By a fifth-grade child:[128]

> The snow falls
> Softly
> From heaven,
> Cloaking the waiting earth
> With beauty.
> Softly it comes down
> Like fairies
> On fragile
> Crystal wings.
>
> NANCY

By a five-year-old:

> In the wintertime I like to go out and play
> And make a great big snowman every single day.
>
> JONATHAN

[127] Hughes Mearns, *Creative Power* (Garden City, N.Y.: Doubleday, Doran and Company, 1929), quoted in Winifred Ward, *Playmaking with Children* (New York: Appleton-Century-Crofts, Inc., 1957), p. ix.
[128] Katherine Koch, "Kindling the Imagination," *The Packet* (Boston: D. C. Heath and Company), Fall 1956.

By an eight-year-old:

> The scent of apple blossoms in spring
> And burning leaves in autumn
> The sound of footsteps in the snow
> And sand that slithers through my hand — in summer.
>
> GRETA

By six-year-olds:

> There is springtime sitting on the hill
> With the sun on the point of the hill.
> The sun is going down
> The moon will soon be up
> And there'll be darkness all around.
> Where will springtime sit?
>
> SCOTT

> The rains of Spring are coming down
> On roofs of houses in the town;
> When I say "Rain, rain, go away
> So I can go outdoors to play,"
> My mother says in her way
> "It's typical spring weather."
>
> JON

> There is a bird on a tree top
> His song is so wonderful
> Tweet, tweet, tweet.
> I love him, I love him,
> I wish I could catch him
> I wish — I wish — I wish.
>
> JOHN K.

By seven-year-olds:

> I saw some fishes in the lake
> They popped right out with a shake, shake, shake.
> They wiggled and waggled and flipped and flapped
> And then they swam off with a flip, flap, flap.
>
> GLENDA

> Oh the snow, the beautiful snow
> Filling the sky and the earth below;
> Over the house tops — over the street
> Over the heads of the people you meet:
> Dancing
> Flirting

> Skimming
> Beautiful, beautiful snow.
> PAMELA

By a nine-year-old:

> In wondering about the stars
> That shed their glimmering light
> I'd like to be up there with them
> And stay out once all night.
> JANE

By twelve-year-olds:

> I look into a valley
> And see a sparkling stream.
>   It runs so clear and beautiful
>   Its beauties are like a dream.
>
> That stream, I know its magic
> Made by a fairy's beam.
>   And every time I see it
>   I want to dream, and dream, and dream.
> ANITA

> There before my very eyes,
> Billowing smoke curled toward the skies.
>
> I stood frozen, and in a daze,
> Far across the valley was a blaze.
>
> The great forest I once knew
> Now was desolate and black,
>   A colorless hue.
>
> A twisting, twirling mass of flame,
> What — who — for this is to blame?
> LUCINDA

*Writing as Self-Portraiture.* Each individual's writing is the expression of his experience, personality, and ability. Style, phrasing, tempo, content, and method alike express his uniqueness. An example of self-portraiture at an extremely early age is that of five-year-old Klaus, who came from Germany and composed a few weeks after his arrival:

> In the country where I lived, there was no Shoppers' Fair.
>   But there were woods and trees and flowers everywhere
>     In the country where I lived way, way over there.

Would you like to go with me to that other land?
There are no roses at the door and all alone I stand
Waiting for Rosemary and Lee — in the country where I lived.

There were woods and trees to see —
But only one of me.

KLAUS

EXAMPLES OF EXPRESSIVE PROSE

The following examples illustrate the preceding principles. The spelling in each story is the child's own.

### The Six-Inch Monster

Once there was a monster that was about six inches high. If you got a ruler and measured him you would find that he was exactly six inches high.

And you could measure him because he is very polite. That is, if you could ever find him. I know where he lives and I visit him sometimes. He has a lot of money that he has hid somewhere. He digs holes and puts it in. He has a lot of holes with money in it. Because he is so little and couldn't handle very much at a time. He told me where a pot of gold was but that little monster had just dug it up to give it to someone for helping him. That monster is really just an overgrown fairy. I've been calling him a six inch monster because he plays so many tricks.

Once I went to visit him to get some butter. When I knocked at the door I listened for a while. And all I heard was that little monster trying to teach his dishes how to sing. Then I knocked again and he opened the door and gave me some butter right in the face.

He said, "That is what you wanted, isn't it?" So I never tried to borrow anything from him again. And once I lost my purse and I told the little six inch monster about it and then the next day I went to visit him. He came out with a big thing (anyway it was big to him) on his back.

I asked him what it was and he said, "It is your purse." I took it off his back and it was my purse. He said he took a long walk but it was just a few steps away. He said he had to cross an ocean, but it was really just a little puddle. He said it was too long to go around. But the funny thing about it was he had fun.

PHYLLIS ORMAND, third grade, age 8

*Little Bear Finds Honey*

Once upon a time there was a little Bear. He want some honey. But he didn't want to sting his nose. He asked his mommy if his daddy could get some honey for him. "There is daddy! Daddy could you get me some honey." "Why yes little bear. I love to get honey. Why didn't yeo get honey yourself?" "Daddy I sting my nose eveay time I tiy to get honey." "Hi little Bear." "Hi Peter." "Little Bear do you want to get some honey." "Know thanek you Peter." "Why?" "Well I sting my nose eveay time I try it." "Oh Little Bear I didn't know it." "Peter how do you get honey without stinging your nose." "It's easy Little Bear. All you do is stick your hand in the hole and take your hand out and run down the tree and that is how you get honey." "But Peter, didn't you forget that I'm littler than you?" "Little Bear it doesn't matter how big you are and it doesn't matter how little you are." "Peter is it all right if daddy goes along?" "Why it will be allright little Bear." "Sniff-sniff, I smell honey." "Where?" "Right here in this tree." "Oh! Please may Daddy and I go up to the honey in the tree? Daddy let me get the honey." "OK little Bear?" "I got it Daddy. I got it Daddy. I got it Peter. Let's go home Daddy." "OK little Bear. "I got it mommy and that's how little Bear got honey.

KATHY SHANE, second grade, age 7

In the primary grades the teacher is concerned with providing children with experiences that help them become aware of their environment and helping them express their feelings and ideas. In the intermediate grades experiences are still important, both firsthand and vicarious. The teacher is aware of the role motivation plays in children's writing.

## What Research Says About Expressive Writing

Smith[129] made an extensive study of procedures for encouraging creative writing involving some 17,941 pupils and 508 teachers in 40 elementary schools. He defined as creative "any writing in which the pupil is free to choose the time of composing, the subject matter,

---

[129] E. E. Smith, "Procedures for Encouraging Creative Writing in the Elementary School," doctoral dissertation, Northwestern University, 1943.

and the length and form of the composition." The following procedures proved most effective:

1. Providing attractive classrooms, rich in materials.
2. Encouraging pupils to write from their own interests and needs.
3. Providing rich experiences about which a child can express himself.
4. Developing sensitivity to good writing which in turn helps a child improve his own experience.
5. Using real needs of children or helping them develop new ones.
6. Providing freedom from fear and helping pupils gain confidence in their ability to create.
7. Providing abundant time and opportunity for writing in many areas and many forms.
8. Developing skill in mechanics without sacrificing spontaneity.
9. Sharing the end products of writing.
10. Evaluating the writing in terms of the total growth of the child.

Creed[130] suggests three approaches to creative writing (1) preparing yourself for writing (pick a favorite word and explore its meaning), (2) exploring what to write about, and (3) keeping at it.

Treanor[131] described an approach which involved listening before writing. The children listened and discussed sounds they would normally hear in familiar situations — for example, the circus. Three times a week oral lessons were held. The listening provided "ideas" for composition and fourth-graders found this technique helpful in their writing.

Littwin[132] reported three methods of developing imagination in children's writing:

1. The pupils looked at a picture, discussed it, then each pupil took one look at it and wrote for ten minutes.
2. The pupils studied picture-making words, wrote them and discussed how the author made pictures, and then wrote for a ten-minute period.
3. Pupils were given visual and audio motivation; for example,

[130] E. D. Creed, "What'll We Write About?" *Elementary English*, 33:24, January 1956.
[131] H. H. Treanor, "Listen Before Writing," *Elementary English*, 30:209, April 1953.
[132] M. F. Littwin, "Three Methods in Developing Imagination in Pupil Writing," *English Journal*, 24:660, October 1935.

they took a piece of fruit, felt it, smelled it, looked at it, tapped it, and tasted it. Then they were asked to describe it in ten minutes.

The experimenter concluded that firsthand experiences are more effective in developing imagination than vicarious ones. The best results in imaginative stories were obtained first through sense training, second by models, and least by picture study.

Witty and Martin[133] found that children can use derived experiences as a basis for writing. Their study dealt with the potential of silent films to build interests and to create a reservoir of feeling. The film used, *The Hunter and the Forest*, has no dialogue, but it has a musical background and sound effects marking the entrance of birds and animals. At the end of the film children were asked to write stories about the film experience. Criteria for judging the composition were (1) expression of genuine feeling; (2) sensitivity of particular words, phrases, and larger language units; (3) response to the film makers' intent and to the materials presented; (4) use of correct and appropriate English.

In comparing the stories and poems of primary and intermediate grades Witty and Martin described the work of the intermediate children as more detailed and imaginative than that of the primary children. They had mastered the basic art of writing by the time they were in the sixth grade and were able to express themselves with imagination and artistry. They evidenced originality of expression and made more use of metaphor and original language. The study has two values: it suggests the possibility of using the silent film (1) as a motivating device in creative writing and (2) as a means of identifying pupils talented in expressive writing.

## Evaluating Expressive Writing

The child is usually eager to improve his own writing. He senses when he has done good work but he doesn't always know why it is good. He should know, too, that the teacher expects him to do his best work, and that he is not satisfying anyone when his work is poor. Child and teacher can work together in evaluation. If he shares his creative work with others and appraises it in terms of some

133 Paul Witty and W. Martin, "An Analysis of Children's Composition Written in Response to a Film," *Elementary English,* 34:160, March 1957.

criteria he is far more likely to keep on going than if he merely writes without any attempt at evaluating. Applegate has set forth the criteria for good writing so clearly that an intermediate grade child can answer the questions in terms of his own product.

### For the Child

1. Did it hold your attention? Did you enjoy it?
2. Is it fresh and a bit different?
3. Does it make use of the senses?
4. Are the verbs specific and the adjectives pruned?
5. Has it imagery and comparison and rhythm?
6. Is it convincing? Does it ring true? Is it your own thinking?
7. Are the mechanics a help, not a stumbling block?[134]

### For the Teacher

1. Do I judge the child's work on the basis of growth — not the product?
2. Do I put comments on his work, rather than a grade?
3. Do I note the needs of each child and plan for his success in some phase of the writing?
4. Do I direct children to a growing awareness of the world?
5. Do I encourage children to use imagery, synonymns, and other literary devices?
6. Do I provide vital experiences that give them something to write about?
7. Do I use imagery, the senses, audio-visual stimuli to motivate them in writing?
8. Do I use art media to motivate writing?
9. Do I treasure each child's work as a gift to be shared when he is ready?
10. Do I provide a time, a place, and an environment for expressive writing, sharing, and evaluating?
11. Do I encourage expression in the creative arts as an integral, vital part of teaching?
12. Do I try to develop my own skill in expressive writing?

## Conclusion

Children cannot be forced to create, but they can be motivated through a stimulating environment, a creative teacher, and a variety

[134] Adapted from Mauree Applegate, "Let's Write" (Madison: University of Wisconsin, Wisconsin School of the Air, 1954–55), p. 29.

of experiences and stimuli. An exciting experience — a trip, a flower, a beautiful sunset, falling snow, burning leaves, rhythmic movement in response to winds — gives children the desire to write. Some of them respond to beauty in nature, others to the sound of music. Children motivate each other to try writing for expression. Creative teachers inspire them to write through the environment they fashion, their awareness of beauty in everyday things, their lively imagination, colorful, vibrant personalities, and their personal interest and warm encouragement.

There are some children who are self-starters and will create in the medium of writing without specific motivation. Others need stimulation and guidance, which can be supplied in a variety of ways.

Creating an atmosphere in which children are eager to express, setting a mood, and motivating the children who need additional impetus before beginning to write is the responsibility of the teacher. He may read a poem, discuss a topic, play a recording, show a film, tell a story, take the children on a trip, provide a sensory experience, give help in selecting appropriate and colorful words and getting thoughts down on paper.

The mere act of writing often leads to unforeseen results. "Not until we begin to write, often, do we know what we are going to say. Once started, however, once over those strange inhibitions that impede the flow of thought, we are likely to find that we know more than we thought we did; that we *do* have an idea after all; that words *do* come to mind, in spite of our fears."[135]

## ACTIVITIES AND QUESTIONS

1. Keep a record of the number of experiences in written expression you observe in a primary grade over a period of one week. When does the teacher act as a scribe and when do pupils write independently?
2. Try one of the following activities in a college class:
   a. Have the class compose an experience story and print it on the board as the pupils dictate it to you.

[135] Luella B. Cook, "Writing as Self-Revelation," *English Journal,* 48:249, May 1959.

    b. Teach an unfinished-story experience.

    c. Teach a lesson in copying dictation from the board.

    d. Teach a picture-series-story lesson.

3. Examine a group of stories written in a primary grade. Which would you characterize as expressive writing? Discuss the best and poorest samples in the set. What factors contributed to the wide range of individual differences?

4. Distinguish between expository writing and expressive or creative writing. Be specific.

5. In what ways can a child share his writing with others, in school and outside of school? (Observe in an intermediate classroom and see how many ways the children have of sharing their writing or "publishing" it.)

6. How does guiding creative writing in the classroom differ from teaching expository or practical writing?

7. Plan and teach a lesson in expository writing to a class of an intermediate grade in which you use as motivation objects the students bring from home — kite, camera, telescope, bat and ball, kaleidoscope, and so forth.

8. On the basis of your reading determine which of the following activities motivate expressive writing. Which motivate expository writing. Give reasons for your decisions.

    a. Writing "Our News" each day. The teacher does the writing with the children contributing news items at the beginning of the term; later the children take turns doing the writing.

    b. Writing experience stories together. At first there is a conversation period, then some of the things related are written down.

    c. Children read or listen to expressive writing by adults.

    d. Children read or listen to expressive writing by children.

    e. Sharing time for the children's poems, stories.

    f. Field trips around school and in the community.

    g. Keeping a room diary.

    h. Arousing interest in words by using vocabulary and rhyming games.

    i. Writing about specific days — holidays, school affairs, etc.

    j. Writing about usual or unusual happenings.

    k. Writing about experiences — home, travel, church, party, sports, and so forth.

    l. Use of the flannelgraph or flat pictures.

    m. Reading or telling part of a story and letting the children write the ending.

    n. Showing a movie without words and letting children write their interpretation.

    o. Children write stories about their own pictures.

    p. Displaying creative work on bulletin boards.

    q. Sharing the best productions with other rooms.

    r. Using creative poetry in choral reading.

    s. Dramatizing children's original stories or poems.

    t. Writing notes or letters to parents, relatives, friends, pen pals, absent pupils.

# BIBLIOGRAPHY

Anderson, Arline C., *et al.* "Lesson Plans to Stimulate Beginning Creative Writing in Grades Three to Five." Group master's thesis, Boston University, 1958.

Applegate, Mauree. *Helping Children Write.* Evanston, Ill.: Row, Peterson and Company, 1954.

Applegate, Mauree. "Inventors Extraordinary," *The Grade Teacher,* 76:41, 96, March 1959.

Applegate, Mauree. "To Write Creatively," *The Grade Teacher,* 74:44–45, October 1956.

Applegate, Mauree. "What Do You Mean Language Arts?" *The Grade Teacher,* 74:40, September 1956.

Association for Childhood Education International. *When Children Write.* Washington, D.C.: The Association, 1955.

Baciagalupo, Edwin C., *et al.* "Language Vocabulary Test Results in Relation to Written Composition in Grade Six." Group master's thesis, Boston University, 1958.

Berry, Eloise. "Films and Creative Expression," *Elementary English,* 35:383–386, June 1954.

Board of Education of the City of New York. *Developing Children's Power of Self-Expression Through Writing.* Curriculum Bulletin 1952–53, Series No. 2. New York: Board of Education, 1953.

Brown, James M. "Communicative Effectiveness of Expository Prose," Faculty research, North Texas State College, 1959.

Burrows, Alvina T. *Teaching Composition.* Washington, D.C.: National Education Association, n.d.

Burrows, Alvina T., *et al.* "Children's Written Composition," *Elementary English,* 41:106, February 1959.

Burrows, Alvina T., *et al. They All Want to Write.* Englewood Cliffs, N.J.: Prentice-Hall, Inc., 1952.

Callahan, Frederick L. "Exercises for Developing Organization in the Writing of Children in Grades Five and Six." Doctoral dissertation, Boston University, 1959.

Christopherson, Merrill G. "The Necessity for Style in Oral and Written Argument." Post-doctoral study, University of South Carolina, 1958.

Cook, Luella B. "Writing as Self-Revelation," *English Journal*, 48:247–254, May 1959.

Dawson, Mildred A. *Teaching Language in the Grades*. Yonkers, N.Y.: World Book Company, 1951.

Dawson, Mildred A., and Zollinger, Marian. *Guiding Language Learning*. Yonkers, N.Y.: World Book Company, 1957.

Edmund, Neal R. "Writing in the Intermediate Grades," *Elementary English*, 36:491–502, November 1959.

Francis, W. Nelson. *The Structure of American English*. New York: The Ronald Press Company, 1958.

Halvorsen, Gladys. "The Effects of Emphasis on Mechanics on Children's Writing." Doctoral dissertation, University of California, in progress.

Herrick, Virgil E., and Jacobs, Leland B. (eds.). *Children and the Language Arts*. Englewood Cliffs, N.J.: Prentice-Hall, Inc., 1955.

Hill, Jeraldine. "Fostering Creativity," *Elementary English*, 37:23–26, January 1960.

Hill, Mary Evelyn. "Creative Writing: First Steps," *Elementary School Journal*, 60:433–436, May 1960.

Kelly, Chenault, and Richards, Bertrand. "Grammar Is Not a Purple Turtle," *English Journal*, 48:199–206 April 1959.

Larom, Henry V. "Sixth Graders Write Good Short Stories," *Elementary English*, 37:20–23, January 1960.

Logan, Lillian M. *Teaching the Young Child*. Boston: Houghton Mifflin Company, 1960.

McIntire, Rose Emogene. "The Development and Evaluation of Creative Writing in the Second and Third Grades." Master's thesis, Indiana State College, 1958.

Mackintosh, Helen, and Hill, Wilhelmina. *How Children Learn to Write*. Reprint Bulletin No. 2. Washington, D.C.: Government Printing Office, 1954.

Malmstrom, Jean. "Linguistic Atlas Findings Versus Textbook Pronouncements on Current English Usage," *English Journal*, 48:191–199, April 1959.

Mearns, Hughes. *Creative Power*. Garden City, N.Y.: Doubleday, Doran and Company, 1929.

Mearns, Hughes. *Creative Youth.* Garden City, N.Y.: Doubleday, Doran and Company, 1925.

Moore, Robert H. *Effective Writing.* New York: Rinehart and Company, 1955.

Parke, Margaret B. "Composition in the Primary Grades," *Elementary English,* 41:107–122, February 1959.

Pooley Robert C. "What Grammar Shall I Teach?" *English Journal,* 47:327–333, September 1958.

Porter, Eleanor. "The Problem: To Say What You Mean," *Elementary English,* 40:388–390, October 1958.

"Special Journal Feature — English Composition," *NEA Journal,* 49: 17–30, December 1960.

Strickland, Ruth. *The Language Arts in the Elementary School.* Boston: D. C. Heath and Company, 2nd ed., 1957.

Tidyman, Willard F., and Butterfield, Marguerite. *Teaching the Language Arts.* New York: McGraw-Hill Book Company, 2nd ed., 1960.

Ward, Winifred. *Playmaking with Children.* New York: Appleton-Century-Crofts, Inc., 2nd ed., 1957.

Warfel, Harry R. "Structural Linguistics and Composition," *College English,* 20:209–213, February 1958.

Willis, Benjamin C. *Teaching Guide for the Language Arts.* Chicago: Chicago Public Schools, 1957.

Wilt, Miriam E. "Words Are the Colors on My Palette," *Creativity in the Elementary School.* New York: Appleton-Century-Crofts, 1959.

Wise, Harold L. "Independent Writing in Grades One, Two, and Three." Master's thesis, State University of Iowa, 1958.

Witty, Paul. "Some Values of Creative Writing," *Elementary English,* 39:157, March 1957.

Witty, Paul. "The Use of Films in Stimulating Creative Expression and in Identifying Talented Pupils," *Elementary English,* 33:340–344, October 1956.

Wonnberger, Carl G. "Writing — A Way of Life," *English Journal,* 48:66–74, February 1959.

# Spelling

> The candidate for a new job is judged
> by the spelling in his dossier no less
> than by the polish on his shoes.
>
> GERTRUDE HILDRETH

To many businessmen literacy and the ability to spell are synonymous. Parents usually recognize this and try to impress upon their offspring the importance of correct spelling. Pressures build up and the schools are criticized for failing to teach children to spell. "Within the framework of the school system, placing responsibility for failure to teach spelling . . . follows this pattern: the college teacher blames the high school teacher, the high school teacher blames the elementary teacher, the elementary teacher blames the mother, and the mother says, 'He's just like his father.' "[136]

Finding a scapegoat does not solve the problem. Finding ways of vitalizing spelling instruction does. Spelling was once an activity filled with excitement and drama as characterized by the spelling match. In recent years it has become a kind of draft horse assigned to haul a heavy load. In the jet age a draft horse is out of character; it holds no challenge.

Teachers can do much to restore the adventure in spelling. "Be a

---

[136] Edna Furness and Gertrude Boyd, "335 Real Spelling Demons," *College English*, 20:292, March 1959.

spelling magician," he can say, writing the word *all* on the board and asking the children to see how many other words they can make by putting different consonants in front of it. How quickly they can compose some ten or fifteen words they use in writing! Playing spelling games, grasping a principle, finding ways of working independently, using words they have just learned to spell in purposeful writing, working out anagrams, having spelling matches — these are just a few activities that make spelling fun for children.

Teachers can make spelling challenging by looking to research for new ways to improve the spelling program, by integrating spelling with the other language arts, the social studies, and the creative arts, and by making use of the excellent new textbooks in the field.

*What We Can Learn from Research.* Spelling in the modern school is learned and practiced as an integral part of the program in written expression in the content subjects as well as in the language arts. "Children need spelling as they write of science interests and interests that fall into the social studies realm and even in their arithmetic work. Any material that is to be read by others must follow conventional patterns of spelling."[137]

In most cases spelling is taught as a skill which serves the child's needs in written communication. Helping the child develop habits of independence, increasing skill in the use of the dictionary, and ability to evaluate spelling in all written work is the responsibility of the teacher.

Learning to spell is largely an individual matter. Spelling research for the past half-century has indicated that few children learn to spell by the identical method. It has indicated, too, that needs in spelling vary widely. Some children require 300 times as many words as others to tell their experiences. In addition to the "unit" words, each child needs his own spelling list. Effective methods of learning to spell, then, vary from child to child.

Dupee[138] found that the large amount of time saved, together with the efficient use pupils make of the time saved, is sufficient evidence that the self-study method has great possibilities for meeting individ-

[137] Strickland, *op. cit.*, p. 373.

[138] C. W. Dupee, "Self-Study in Spelling," quoted from C. W. Hunnicutt and William J. Iverson (eds.), *Research in the Three R's* (New York: Harper & Brothers, 1958), pp. 301–303.

ual needs. Guiler and Lease[139] compared upper intermediate children; an experimental group was given preliminary diagnostic help and systematic instruction while the control group followed a routine of study-test procedures, recommended systematic diagnostic procedures, and individualized remedial help. Fernald's[140] research revealed that overemphasis on visual methods was a detriment to those who learn best through auditory or kinesthetic approach to words.

Porter found that the opportunity for individualized instruction through the use of the teaching machine brought improvement at the second- and sixth-grade levels. In his opinion, "These high rates of responding are due in part to the release of better students from the usual constraints of group study, but in addition, the machines and/or program seem to generate rapid response."[141]

Dolch, Fitzgerald, Horn, Strickland and others hold that a multisense approach should be used in learning to spell.

Horn[142] believes that children should learn the *ways*, not the *way*, in which each sound is spelled; emphasis should be placed on word patterns, syllables, word positions, meaning, the addition of suffixes, and adjacent influencing sounds that show considerable consistency. He believes, moreover, that children should develop the ability to draw generalizations regarding these characteristics for themselves.

While researchers continue to explore, teachers are faced with three basic problems: to determine readiness for spelling instruction, to select the words that should be taught in various grades, and to develop appropriate methods of teaching.

## *Readiness for Spelling*

Some children can spell a few words before they come to kindergarten. At home they have scribbled on writing paper and sent a

---

[139] W. S. Guiler and G. A. Lease, "An Experimental Study of Methods of Instruction in Spelling," *Elementary School Journal*, 43:234–238, December 1942.

[140] Grace M. Fernald, *Remedial Techniques in Basic School Subjects* (New York: McGraw-Hill Book Company, 1943).

[141] Douglas Porter, "Some Effects of Year Long Teaching Machine Instruction," in Eugene Galanter (ed.), *Automatic Teaching: The State of the Art* (New York: John Wiley and Sons, 1959, p. 90.

[142] Ernest Horn, "Phonetics and Spelling," *Elementary School Journal*, 57:424–32, May 1957.

letter to Grandma. When they get to kindergarten, they want to put their names on their work, write messages to Mother, and spell out their names and the names of their best friends. Many of them learn to print during the year. A number of them become interested in spelling games: "How do you spell ———?" "I see a little girl whose name is M-a-r-y." "Will J-o-h-n go to the desk and bring me a b-o-o-k?"

Formal instruction, however, must wait until a child evidences certain specific abilities related to spelling — mental maturity, auditory and visual discrimination, muscular coordination, perceptual readiness, and social and emotional control. A basic program of instruction in beginning spelling will (1) help the child recognize that words are made up of sequences of individual sounds blended together and that in the written form of our language each such sound is represented by one or more of the letters of the alphabet; (2) help him hear, speak, and think these sounds clearly so that he may distinguish adequately between them; (3) help him develop an automatic association of a written letter with each of those sounds which is very commonly represented by a single letter; (4) help him develop skill in manuscript writing so that he can form those letters legibly.

Early in the first grade, children write their own names, write labels and signs, compose stories and announcements, and write invitations to parents and friends. Interest in using spelling as a tool for writing is keen. When the child associates letters with the sounds he hears in words, when he reads words with comprehension, when he writes legibly, formal instruction in spelling can begin.

Hildreth[143] suggests that systematic teaching of spelling should begin when the pupils have achieved

A mental age of 7½ years or more.
A speaking vocabulary of some 5000 words.
The ability to enunciate words distinctly.
Ability to recognize and pronounce 300–400 of the commonest words met in reading.
A beginning in phonics — the commonest letter-sound combinations.
The ability to write the letters of the alphabet correctly.
The ability to copy simple words correctly.
The ability to write a few simple words from memory.

[143] Gertrude Hildreth, *Teaching Spelling* (New York: Henry Holt and Company, 1956), p. 50.

Initial experiences in spelling should be based largely on words that are familiar to children in their speaking and listening vocabularies and are spelled in a phonetically regular manner. Words of high service value that are not spelled in a phonetically regular manner should also be introduced but kept to a reasonable minimum.

Spelling activities may include the cooperative compilation of a class dictionary containing words used in speaking, names of children in the group, days of the week, and months of the year. Individual and group lists are important in early experiences in spelling. As instruction progresses, increasing attention is given to structural and phonetic analysis (in the second and third grades) to facilitate spelling independence. In the intermediate grades independence grows as children follow a sequence of study, participate in varied writing activities, and engage in oral communication in which pronunciation and enunciation are emphasized.

## Selecting Words to Be Studied

Three widely used practices for selecting spelling words are (1) selection on the basis of graded word lists in a basic spelling series or course of study, (2) making up individual word lists based on the child's own needs in written expression, and (3) combining these two.

Because of crowded classrooms and busy schedules many teachers find the first method easiest. However, they recognize the advantage of using the child's needs to supplement a graded list. Modern spelling texts are planned with careful consideration for graded lists of words which the child will need. The teacher should make it a point to be familiar not only with the spelling textbooks in his school but with other series in order to supplement spelling lists.

The second method is somewhat limiting unless the teacher motivates the child to extend his need for writing material and so to build an increasingly useful vocabulary.

In the third method the teacher observes the words with which the child is having difficulty as he writes, and helps him develop his own list, in addition to teaching him the basic graded list. Developing group and individual lists for each of forty children is difficult for many teachers. For this reason selection on the basis of a spelling series plus the individual word list finds considerable favor.

## Methods for Teaching
## Spelling in the Primary Grades

Although variations exist, the steps generally included in learning to spell a word are: looking at the word, listening to the pronunciation, pronouncing the word, using it in a sentence, visualizing it, saying the letters in sequence, determining the hard spots, and writing the word.

Hanna[144] suggests this six-step sequence:

1. Look at the word and say the word. Be sure to say it correctly. See how the word looks. Hear how it sounds.

2. Say the word and the letters in the word. See what letters stand for the sounds you hear.

3. Look at the word. Say the word and write it with your fingers.

4. Look at the word. Say the word and write it with your pencil. Look to see if you spelled it right. If you made a mistake, correct it.

5. Cover the word and the copy you made in Step 4. Say the word and write it without looking at it.

6. Look at the word you wrote in Step 5. Did you spell it correctly? If you did, go on to the next word. If you made a mistake, go back to Step 1.

Most teachers find that following some type of weekly organization plan facilitates the teaching-learning process. A widely used plan — the study-test plan — is presented here.[145]

Monday

1. Discuss spelling principles that will be needed in the week's work.

2. Broaden children's understanding of the new words and their uses.

---

[144] Paul R. Hanna and Jean S. Hanna, *Building Spelling Power*, a basal spelling series, Grades 2–8 (Boston: Houghton Mifflin Company, 1956–60).

[145] Recent research involving methods of studying spelling has been supplemented by attention to test-study *vs.* study-test which indicates the superiority of the test-study approach in Grades 2 and 3. Gladys Hibles, "The Test-Study Method Versus the Study-Test Method of Teaching Spelling," Study I, master's thesis, University of Texas, 1957. Margaret A. Montgomery, "The Test-Study Method Versus the Study-Test Method of Teaching Spelling in Grade II," Study II, master's thesis, University of Texas, 1957. Bernice K. Ledbetter, "The Test-Study Method Versus the Study-Test Method of Teaching Spelling in Grade III," Study III, master's thesis, University of Texas, 1959.

3. Pronounce each word correctly. Have children listen and then pronounce the words in unison.

Tuesday

1. Give the pretest today.
   a. This test provides for individual differences.
   b. It helps children discover which of the spelling words they already know and which they need to study.
2. New words should be used in writing sentences, stories, or descriptions.

Wednesday

1. Introduce word study — supervised study of new and review words.
   a. Children should study review words, words missed in tests, and words misspelled in written work.
   b. Keep track of misspelled words in stories, letters, reports.
2. Encourage use of the accepted procedure in studying words previously misspelled.
3. Let children study word meanings and usage in exercises.

Thursday

1. Build spelling power.
   a. Show how to use what has been learned to spell new words.
   b. Teach something new to help in future spelling needs.

Friday

1. Give a final test on the spelling words.
   a. Check words missed.
   b. Write words missed under "Word Study" for next week.
2. Motivate the child to use the newly mastered words by
   a. dictation.
   b. news items.
   c. letters.
   d. announcements.
   e. other projects.
3. Use these games and activities:
   a. crossword puzzles.
   b. missing-word puzzles.
   c. spelling matches.
   d. spelling battles. (The child who misspells a word must go over to his opponents' side and spell against his own team.)

## SUGGESTED GAMES FOR SPELLING

*Card Game.* A "deck" consists of "books" of related words, one to a card, e.g., *like, likes, liking; talk, talks, talking, talked.* (These may be used as a card game in a group, or the children may underline known parts of new words as they draw each card.)

*Bingo Spelling Game.* Children fold paper in sixteen squares. They then call out sixteen words, which the teacher writes on the board. A child who mentions a word for the teacher to write must spell it. The children write any four of these words on their papers in the sixteen squares in any order. A child comes to the front of the room, turns his back to the board, and spells the words which the teacher selects for him from those on the board. Any child having that word puts a disk on his paper. The one who first fills a row or diagonal calls "Bingo."

*Dictionary Game.* A boy whose name begins with A writes it on the blackboard, then a girl whose name begins with B, and so on through the alphabet. This game is varied by using other categories, such as fruit, vegetables, or animals, for each letter of the alphabet.

*"Tea Kettle."* One player leaves the group. The group chooses a word. The player is called back and members of the group use the word in sentences, substituting the word *tea kettle* for the correct word. For example, "I have a new *tea kettle* of shoes" (pair). The player is to guess the word and spell it correctly.

*"Can You Guess the Word?"* A list of words to be reviewed is written on the board. A child stands near the list and silently chooses a word. The other children raise hands and the leader calls on one, who says, for example, "Judy, are you thinking of the word *climb, c-l-i-m-b?*" Judy answers, "No, I am not thinking of *climb.*" The game continues until the word is guessed.

*Take-a-Chance Game.* Words written on separate slips are placed in a box. Each pupil draws a slip but does not look at it. He hands it to the leader, who pronounces the word for the pupil to write. The pupil keeps the slip if the word is spelled incorrectly. Pupils who have no slips at the end are the winners.

*"Erase the Word and Spell."* The teacher places review words on several blackboard spaces. Then she asks, "Who can find, erase, and spell *neighbor?*" A variation is, "Who can pick out and spell all the words which mean something to wear? To eat? To do?"

REVIEW LESSONS

Well-planned reviews are essential to an effective spelling program. What a child learns is soon forgotten if it is not used. Practice makes permanent, but review must be based upon a systematic plan.

By the end of the primary grades children have developed considerable independence in spelling. They have memorized several hundred words which they need and frequently use in written work. They take increasing pride in spelling correctly and have developed spelling power. They have learned to locate needed words in the dictionary, have mastered systematic spelling procedures, and have learned the most regular representations of the common English phonemes. They have formed the habit of noticing and remembering unexpected spellings — and have learned some basic generalizations about spelling. They can discover and correct many of their own spelling errors.

## Spelling in the Intermediate Grades

Spelling instruction in the intermediate grades aims to increase spelling power. Hildreth[146] suggests several aims for instruction:

1. To memorize the spelling of all commonly used words not clinched in the lower grades, and to learn other frequently used words — about 2500 to 3000 in all.
2. To continue to establish the habits that make for self-dependence in writing.
3. To practice spelling as a tool for writing.

To this list should be added the aim of challenging the child to discover the satisfaction that comes from spelling correctly. Students must take more and more responsibility for attacking new words; sensing how words are put together; and developing power in visualizing, hearing, and spelling accurately. They need to get the dictionary habit to check on spelling. Most important to the child is the ability to spell words correctly to the end that communication is improved.

Not until children are stimulated to take pride in words correctly spelled and legibly written, not until they become aware of the

[146] Hildreth, *Teaching Spelling*, pp. 167–168.

significance of accuracy in all written work, not until they sense the "magic" in spelling will the aims of instruction be accomplished. Each teacher must find ways of challenging the children in the class-room. Some methods that have been used successfully are suggested here.

1. Stimulating pride in the pursuit of excellence by having a bulletin board space reserved for well-written papers of children who have made progress.
2. Using purposeful activities of written work to improve children's ability to spell and write correctly; providing many opportunities for letter writing, reports, newspaper articles in connection with interesting projects.
3. Using games, contests, and spelling matches to stimulate interest in spelling accurately.
4. Impressing upon children the social values of correct spelling as well as the utilitarian aspects. As children sense the importance of correct spelling for success in vocational opportunities, some of them are motivated to apply themselves.
5. Individualizing instruction to meet the needs of each child so that he can progress at his own rate.
6. Supplementing basic texts and graded word lists with individual lists and written work geared to individual needs and interests. Spelling series which combine instruction in reading, writing, spelling, and oral communication are especially effective in developing spelling power.

*Promising Practices in Teaching Spelling.* Children in the intermediate grades are ready for formal spelling study. They continue to need much opportunity to practice activities begun in the primary school: spelling-in-context writing, systematic drill on words frequently used by group or individual, continued work with phonetics, word building, and proofreading. Some promising practices that teachers of spelling are using effectively include:

1. Making use of the results of research in teaching spelling and experimenting with new ways of improving spelling in the classroom.
2. Helping the child practice spelling words he cannot already spell correctly and review words systematically.
3. Requiring the child to proofread what he writes and correct misspelled words.
4. Encouraging the child to supplement the standard textbook list with his own spelling list.

5. Emphasizing the development of spelling power.
6. Teaching children to help themselves and make use of self-study materials and automatic teaching devices.
7. Giving more attention to individual differences. Children vary in spelling skills as much as they do in other skills. They should be taught in relation to their readiness and should be encouraged to progress at their own rates.
8. Grouping children for spelling instruction on the basis of observation and test results.
9. Selecting word lists in terms of the basic list and the individual's own list needed for his personal use in writing.
10. Working out more effective ways of caring for routine tasks such as handling of supplies, checking papers, recording errors, summarizing individual and group results.
11. Concentrating on teaching efficient techniques of word study: for memorization, for attacking new words with regular features, for noticing the spelling of irregular words, for finding interrelationships among words and using generalizations which apply in similar situations and circumstances.
12. Recognizing evaluation as a continuous process; using diagnostic studies to help determine the innate capacities for learning, the range of achievement in the class, readiness for new steps, individual difficulties.
13. Including oral spelling in the program as a stimulating supplementary activity for the purpose of motivation, convenience in quick review and checking, revealing errors promptly, saving time in grading papers.

When a child learns that spelling can be mastered, that spelling makes sense, that there is satisfaction in being able to figure out how to spell a new word, he will express himself more freely in writing. As he progresses through the elementary school, spelling correctly tends to become automatic.

# ACTIVITIES AND QUESTIONS

1. What can we learn from research in spelling that will vitalize the teaching of spelling in the elementary school?
2. Observe in an elementary school and try to discover the ways in

which the teacher makes spelling an integral part of the language arts.

3. Bring in examples of children's spelling which illustrate wide differences in spelling abilities. Try to determine whether the child who has the best spelling paper is a high achiever in the other language arts. Do you find evidence of a relationship between abilities in the various language arts?

4. Examine three basal spelling texts. Compare them in the following factors: aids to independent spelling or self-help in study; opportunities for self-evaluation; suggestions for related language arts activities; lists of words for particular grades.

5. Examine and compare two curriculum guides. To what extent are reading, spelling, handwriting, and written expression integrated?

6. Which of the methods of selecting words to be studied would you prefer to use? What are some of the advantages of the graded word list? The individual list?

7. Make up some spelling games and try them out with a class of elementary grade children.

8. Work out a weekly spelling lesson for a third grade in two situations. Assume that the spelling class is integrated with the other language arts. Assume that spelling is taught as a separate subject. Present both lessons to a group of your classmates and have them evaluate the effectiveness of each method in terms of their reading in the chapter, observations, and supplementary reading.

9. Plan a role-playing situation in which an employer is interviewing a candidate who has made two errors in spelling in the letter of application for a secretarial position. In other respects the candidate meets the employer's specifications for the position.

10. Arrange a role-playing situation in which a superintendent is interviewing a candidate for a teaching position. She has misspelled the word *superintendent.* In all other respects the candidate presents superior qualifications and has excellent references.

# BIBLIOGRAPHY

Anderson, P. S. *Resource Materials for Teachers of Spelling.* Minneapolis, Minn.: Burgess Publishing Company, 1959.

Association for Supervision and Curriculum Development. *Research Helps in Teaching the Language Arts.* A report prepared for ASCD by Harold Shane. Washington, D.C.: NEA, 1955.

Blake, Howard E. "Studying Spelling Independently," *Elementary English*, 37:29–32, January 1960.

Breed, Frederick S. *How to Teach Spelling*. Dansville, N.Y.: F. A. Owen Publishing Company, 1930.

Dawson, Mildred A., and Zollinger, Marian. *Guiding Language Learning*. Yonkers-on-Hudson, N.Y.: World Book Company, 1957.

Dolch, Edward W. *Better Spelling*. Champaign, Ill.: The Garrard Press, 1942.

Fitzgerald, James A. *A Basic Spelling Vocabulary*. Milwaukee: Bruce Publishing Company, 1951.

Fitzgerald, James A. "Children's Experiences in Spelling," in Virgil E. Herrick and Leland Jacobs (eds.), *Children and the Language Arts*, Englewood Cliffs, N.J.: Prentice-Hall, Inc., 1955.

Fitzgerald, James A. *The Teaching of Spelling*. Milwaukee: Bruce Publishing Company, 1951.

Fitzgerald, James A. "The Teaching of Spelling," *Elementary English*, 30:79–85, February 1953.

Furness, Edna, and Boyd, Gertrude. "335 Real Spelling Demons," *College English*, 20:292–295, March 1959.

Hanna, Paul R., and Hanna, Jean S. *Building Spelling Power*. A basal spelling series, Grades 2–8. Boston: Houghton Mifflin Company, 1956–60.

Hanna, Paul R., and Moore, James T., Jr. "Spelling — From Spoken Word to Written Symbol." Boston: Houghton Mifflin Company, n.d. Reprinted from *Elementary School Journal*, February 1953.

Herrick, Virgil E., and Jacobs, Leland. *Children and the Language Arts*. Englewood Cliffs, N.J.: Prentice-Hall, Inc., 1955.

Hildreth, Gertrude. *Teaching Spelling*. New York: Henry Holt and Company, 1956.

Hoffman, James D. "A Non-Discriminatory Spelling Game," *Elementary English*: 37:240–243, March 1960.

Horn, Ernest. "Phonetics and Spelling," *Elementary School Journal*, 57:424–432, May 1957.

Horn, T. D. "Research in Spelling," *Elementary English*, 37:174–177, March 1960.

Horn, T. D. *Teaching Spelling*. Washington, D.C.: National Education Association, 1954.

Hunnicutt, C. W., and Iverson, William J. (eds.). *Research in the Three R's*. New York: Harper & Brothers, 1958.

McKee, Paul. "Teaching Spelling by Column and Context Forms," *Journal of Educational Research*, 15:246–266, April 1927.

Picozzi, Adelaide. "Spelling Can Be Fun," *Elementary English*, 36:178, 179, March 1959.

Russell, Karlene V., *et al. Developing Spelling Power.* Yonkers-on-Hudson, N.Y.: World Book Company, 1957.

Strickland, Ruth G. "Utilizing Spelling Research," *Childhood Education,* 32:67–76, October 1955.

Woolf, Maurice D., and Woolf, Jeanne A. *Remedial Reading.* New York: McGraw-Hill Book Company, 1957.

## *Concluding Statement*

The power to think, to express, to interpret, and to evaluate has long been a mark of civilized man. In this fast-moving age in which boundaries are disappearing, barriers are vanishing, and distances are diminishing, the ability to communicate is essential. No one is equipped for living unless he can communicate effectively. The task of the school — the task of the teacher — is to teach each child to listen as well as speak, to read as well as write, and to spell as well as think.

In order to discharge this responsibility the teacher must be aware of the developmental sequence in the communication skills, the interrelatedness of these skills, the basic concepts underlying each, the relationship between having time and opportunity for practice and being able to develop the skills. He must plan for the direct teaching of specific skills in each phase of the program so as to insure maximum growth as well as to integrate the language arts with the whole curriculum.

By listening, speaking, reading, writing, and spelling man communicates and thus influences the course of action in world affairs. Through a developmental sequence of learning to listen, to speak, to read, to write, to spell, the child, too, communicates and makes his wishes, ideas, and beliefs known. Through his efforts to be understood, his growing powers of communication, he, too, can influence the course of action — present and future.

The skills of communication are not separate skills to be learned in isolation; they are interdependent. How he uses these skills influences the total development of the child. They are the tools through which experience is expressed.

Each of the communication skills, however, has a discipline of its own, which must be understood by the teacher if he would teach the child to use these skills wisely. Developing the skills for expressing oneself effectively in oral and written form takes years and requires the guidance, inspiration, and direct teaching of those who sense its importance.

# 8

Anyone who would say now that he was content to master and manipulate the environment without bothering to understand how it worked or what to do with it would show first that he did not know what science was, for science is nothing but organized understanding, and second that he had no grasp of the kind of problems we now confront.

ROBERT M. HUTCHINS

# Interpreting the physical world

What makes the grass green? What makes the sky blue? What's in a cloud? What makes it rain? Where did the water go? Why can't we see the stars in the day? How does the rocket travel? What's a helicopter? What will happen if . . . ?

These are a few of the innumerable questions children ask. They want to know what, they want to know why. They are curious about everything from atoms to zirconium. In this age of rapidly expanding knowledge curiosity is essential for survival. Tomorrow's adult, in order to survive, must extend his knowledge and apply scientific principles in order to solve his problems creatively. He must ask intelligent questions, search for truth, and come to logical conclusions.

## Values of Science

*Relatedness to the Environment.* Science helps children feel a part of their world. In a primitive society it is comparatively simple to develop a feeling of relatedness. In pioneer days, too, psychologically speaking, the world was a small, "secure" place. Families assumed responsibility for providing shelter, food, clothing, learning, and entertainment. They were self-sustaining and roots were deep. Few children today share in the experience of carving a livelihood out of the wilderness. They do not help build the home in which they live, grow the food they eat, harvest the produce, or make their clothes. Born into a society in which physical, social, and intellectual needs are met largely through the efforts of others, they search for some way to feel relatedness with a world of infinite complexity. They need time to explore, to observe, to discover what the universe holds for them. A study of science can help them.

*Building a Scientific Attitude.* Science helps children develop faith in a scientific attitude. The child who studies science systematically does not rely on a rabbit's foot or a four-leaf clover. But development of a scientific attitude cannot be left to chance. It must be carefully fostered. Characteristics of the scientific attitude are open-mindedness, habitual curiosity, careful and accurate observation and investigation, realization of cause-and-effect relationships, and demand for evidence which is corroborated by reliable authority.

Children should be taught the importance of checking information. New knowledge is being added so rapidly that they must know how to look for up-to-date references. They must realize, too, the necessity of checking on the background of a source and of putting faith in careful investigative techniques rather than a talisman.

*Skill in Problem Solving.* Science contributes to growth in the ability to solve problems. The child is confronted early with problems which concern him, his environment, and his relation to the environment. The study of science offers one method for solving them. He learns to define objectively, observe carefully, interpret accurately, record and communicate discriminately, and evaluate critically. He learns to withhold judgment and to test the evidence before he accepts it. Effective teaching helps him to see cause-and-effect relationships, to discover that things happen for a reason — not haphazardly. Even while he chases butterflies he is searching for the security that comes from knowing why and how.

*Universal Challenge.* Science challenges all children. Science is for everyone — the gifted, the average, and the slow learner. There is much about science that is exciting and adventurous. Eager to learn, curious about their environment, children are fascinated by experimenting, observing, taking field trips, making effective use of audio-visual aids, reading to find out, and using group processes. When they are interested in what they are doing, when they have a purpose in mind, when they want to find answers to absorbing problems, they learn. "There is still much to be discovered, much to challenge the alert, skillful investigator. Through a taste of science early in their development children begin to respect this aspect of science, and to realize that much still remains for them to do."[1] Such a point of view is vividly expressed by Douglas, a five-year-old, as he boasts, "I may not be the first to go to the moon, but I'll sure find out what it's like."

But will he find out without a teacher to guide him? If teaching science consists of collecting specimens of rocks, sea shells, bird nests, and mud-daubers and bringing in an occasional fish for the fish bowl, children will be cheated. On the other hand, if teaching science is viewed as more than nature study children will be inspired

[1] Glenn Blough (ed.), *It's Time for Better Elementary School Science*, report of an Association Conference supported by the National Science Foundation (Washington, D.C.: National Science Teachers Association, NEA, 1958), p. 8.

not to stop until they probe the nature of the virus and soar into outer space. Only as teachers, parents, and administrators cooperate to provide an environment in which learning is respected and encouraged and a well-organized science program is supported can the values of science education be realized.

*Finding a Sense of Security.* Science helps children achieve a sense of security. Security comes from knowing what to expect in a given situation, from seeing cause-and-effect relationships, and from being aware of design and predictability in the scheme of things. It is not sufficient for a child to predict with some measure of accuracy the reactions and behavior of people around him. He needs to be able to generalize about things which threaten him — the massive planes, the streaking jets, the exciting rockets, thunderstorms and tornadoes, the ripping wind, the slashing rain — forces which he may be too young to comprehend but which nevertheless give him cause for concern.

Although there is no longer much argument about the value of science in the elementary school, in order to organize and develop an effective science program schools must be willing to take a look at the characteristics of a good program. They must take a further step, however, and help teachers become competent to guide children in science experiences.

## Characteristics of a Good Elementary Science Program

Present science programs "range all the way from a few 'show-share-do-and-tell' items brought in by interested children, shown to the class, and deposited in some selected spot and forgotten, to those programs that have been carefully designed to fit the needs, interests, and abilities of children who live in today's age of science."[2] In far too many schools science is relegated to a corner where a few sea shells, a dead turtle, some milkweed pods, a small magnet, a prism, some narcissus bulbs, and a dying sweet potato vine are allowed to gather dust or fade away. Those who are not content with such a meager science offering may welcome the following suggestions.

[2] *Ibid.,* p. 9.

*A Program for Our Time.* A good science program meets the demands of the scientific age. Today it is not enough to learn a few concepts in science, carry out some well-chosen experiments, and learn terms which may be useful later on in life. Individuals in a scientific age must assume increasing responsibility for making wise choices which require more than a superficial knowledge of science — on such important problems as atomic energy, conservation, pure-food laws, flood control, water pollution, sanitation, and water purification.

Science, too, helps the individual become less resistant to change. Change is inevitable, and people who have a scientific attitude and knowledge of scientific principles can more readily adapt to new situations as they arise.

*Recognition of Importance.* A good science program has a definite place in the curriculum. Incidental science instruction is inclined to be haphazard and inadequate. Good science teaching takes into consideration current pressing problems of children and the current interest in science, but it does not wait until some child brings in a fish, a turtle, or a water snake. Such practice is an inadequate basis for teaching.

Some schools allocate approximately 50 per cent of the science content to science-centered experiences, 25 per cent to incidental experiences, and 25 per cent to social studies integrated with science. Thus there is opportunity for developing a science-centered program while at the same time allowing for incidental interests and integration.

*Scope.* A good science program is comprehensive. In order to insure a comprehensive program it is essential not only that teachers, administrators, supervisors, and principals be familiar with the objectives of the program but that they make effective use of resource people such as junior and senior high school teachers, consultants, and science specialists in the community. In some instances research chemists, physicians, and other specialists devote a portion of their time to teaching in the elementary school, conducting experiments, or serving as consultants. In other school systems high school or junior high school science teachers make materials available and act as consultants to classroom teachers.

*Continuity.* A good science program has continuity. The elementary school child has a right to expect a well-planned, continuous sequence of learning experiences — experiences with living things, the earth, the universe, matter and energy, and man's use of science. A good program provides a firm foundation for the child who goes on to a specialized science program in the secondary school as well as for the child for whom elementary school science is terminal. It must deal with appropriate learnings from every field of science at each level. The over-all objectives of the school determine the specific areas of study. The particular activities are determined by the abilities, needs, interests, and previous experiences of a group, and the competencies of the teacher.

*Balanced Content.* A good science program provides for a balance of content. Science in the elementary school should provide children with experiences from their physical and biological environment. It should help them understand and interpret the universe, the earth, living things, physical and chemical phenomena, ways of controlling the environment, and conditions essential to survival.

*Increased Complexity.* The well-organized science program is spiral in nature. An examination of curriculum guides and textbooks shows that there is considerable flexibility in the selection of content. In general, however, content from each area is included at specific levels such as kindergarten, primary, intermediate. Each succeeding year brings expanded experiences. In kindergarten the science concepts are comparatively simple. "Each time an area of science (such as the universe) is encountered, the new work builds on that previously experienced, adds to and increases in difficulty . . . the generalizations become somewhat more complex as the pupils progress. There is only enough repetition to make connection; not enough to cause pupils to lose interest. . . . On each level pupils should be left with the idea that there is still more interesting material to learn — indeed, that there are still things that scientists themselves have not discovered."[3]

*Early Introduction.* A good science program begins in the kindergarten. "We can with reasonable logic consider children as

[3] Glenn O. Blough and Albert J. Huggett, *Elementary School Science and How to Teach It* (New York: The Dryden Press, 1957), p. 24.

scientists just as we can think of them as artists, musicians, and as social beings."[4] As the young child explores his environment he is constantly tackling problems, setting up tentative solutions, gathering evidence experimentally, and trying things out to see if they work. If they don't he is not discouraged; he tries something else. Innate curiosity, a questioning attitude, imagination, and creative ability should be channeled at the earliest possible time. When can the child more profitably be initiated into the mysteries of his world? His interest is evident; in order to capitalize on it, the science program should be planned carefully. It should be well articulated at the transitional levels and well coordinated throughout childhood and adolescence. The simple experiences of the preschool child should develop into the complex experiences which will challenge the secondary school pupil.

*Evaluation.* A good science program is characterized by continuous evaluation. Appraisal is a part of any good program. In the modern science program it is not limited to tests on the details of content. Other devices include methods of checking progress in problem solving, development of scientific attitudes, and appreciation and interest in learning about the world. Children are evaluated in terms of growth in the ability to participate in varied aspects of the scientific method. The child who experiments as well as reads to find the answer to a problem, the child who raises questions and searches for answers, will fare better in evaluation than the child whose science contributions are limited to reading and carrying on discussions with people. Children must become increasingly competent not only in understanding science concepts but in using them to interpret their environment and in making contributions to scientific investigation.

## Revitalizing Science Teaching

There *are* elementary science programs that are well organized and well executed. The children identify problems, set up experi-

[4] Herbert S. Zim, *Science for Children and Teachers* (Washington, D.C.: Association for Childhood Education International, Bulletin No. 91, 1953), pp. 6, 7.

ments, read to answer questions, hypothesize, and generalize. These children are learning to define problems, look objectively at a variety of facts, and test their findings. In this type of classroom the elementary child is challenged.

Unfortunately "the fact remains that in the same school system, or even the same building, there is likely to be wide variation in how science is taught, if it is taught at all. . . . If science teaching is poor or non-existent in elementary schools, youngsters may make prevocational choices in other fields."[5] Interest has to be created in the elementary school because by the time the students are in high school they have their minds pretty much set about what they like and do not like.[6]

## THE KEY TO A GOOD SCIENCE PROGRAM

The teacher is the key to the quality of science instruction. If he is willing to apply his knowledge and skill to stimulate his students to explore and interpret the physical environment, apply the scientific method, and develop a scientific attitude, his science program will be effective; he will be able to challenge the child to satisfy the curiosity with which he is bursting. The average teacher's attitude toward science must be improved before he will make an effort to increase his knowledge and background in the field or evidence much interest in securing and using adequate equipment and materials for teaching science.

*Improving the Teacher's Attitude Toward Science Teaching.* Today's children are interested in science. Textbooks and other teaching materials are of better quality than ever before, parents are showing a greater interest in science, television is placing emphasis on science in daily living. What about the teacher in the elementary school?

[5] J. Myron Atkin, "Elementary School Science Programs: Appraisal and Recommendations," *Improving Science Programs in Illinois Schools* (Urbana, Ill.: Office of Field Services, University of Illinois, 1958), pp. 38, 39.

[6] There is ample evidence to prove that people are often stimulated to choose science careers before they are twelve years old. In the study of the winners of the Westinghouse Science Talent Search contest Robert MacCurdy found that most of these youngsters made a tentative choice of science for a career before they were out of the elementary school. *Ibid.*, p. 39.

Fortunately, more emphasis is being placed upon the importance of science in teacher education. However, many teachers in the classrooms of today had a meager preparation in science and are afraid of it. For such teachers Blough and Blackwood have this encouraging advice: "If we wait until all elementary teachers feel comfortably equipped to handle science we shall never get started. The most successful teachers of science in the elementary school have said to themselves, 'I believe in the importance of including some science in my work. I don't believe my program is complete without it. . . . I don't mind being asked questions that I can't answer because I know how to help children find answers.'"[7]

These teachers have a positive attitude. They approach the teaching of science with confidence rather than trepidation. They are willing to admit that they do not know all the answers. They let children participate in formulating problems and plans for finding solutions. They are eager to act as a guide and learn with the children.

*Building a Background in Science.*  Once a teacher has faced the problem of teaching science and made the decision to begin he prepares to build an adequate background. He makes use of in-service training through workshops, television courses, extension courses, summer school classes, methods courses, on-campus classes, science consultants, and science specialists in the community. Such experiences are part of his long-range goals.

Immediate needs may be met by following a few simple guidelines.

1. Start on the area in science with which you feel most comfortable. It may be one in which you have a special interest, special knowledge, or available materials and resources.

2. Read some basal science textbooks on the level of the pupils you are teaching. Also be sure to read some advanced books.

3. Perform the experiments before you do them with the class.

4. Try some of the other activities suggested in the books — such as observations, collecting specimens, and taking trips or excursions.

5. Use the teacher's manual accompanying your science textbook as a guide in making plans.

6. Discuss your unit with a secondary or junior high school

[7] Glenn O. Blough and Paul E. Blackwood, *Teaching Elementary Science*, Bulletin No. 4 (Washington, D.C.: Government Printing Office, 1948), p. 10.

science teacher or science consultant and enlist his aid.

7. Encourage the children to bring in materials to supplement those provided by the school.

8. Let the children participate in the experiment. They learn by doing as well as by reading.

9. Develop a science concept file, in which to keep science material, notes on teaching, plans, and equipment for developing a unit so it can be used at a future time.

10. Discuss with other teachers the activities you have found successful and the procedures that work for you. Be ready to share your experience with them and to use information gained from others to improve your own background of knowledge.

11. Cooperate in developing a science resource center in your school.

An examination of the elementary science program will help the teacher understand the importance of teaching broad concepts. For example, the fact that planets revolve around the sun is an important concept; it is not enough to be able to name the planets in the order of their size and distance from the earth.

## *What to Teach in the Primary and Intermediate Grades*

Current courses of study and curriculum guides reflect variation and modification of the science content to meet the needs of particular school systems and groups of children. There appears to be no uniformity in the selection of content. As a matter of fact flexibility in the selection of specific experiences in science seems to be the rule. The task is to provide activities which develop concepts built on previous learning.

Frequently teachers ask, "What science concepts can be successfully taught in the primary grades?" A considerable amount of research indicates that children can have profitable experiences at every grade level in any broad science area: living things, chemistry, electricity, weather, geology, astronomy.[8] The limiting factor in the elementary school is the complexity of the science concepts taught.

[8] Milton O. Pella, "Development of Concepts in Elementary Science," doctoral dissertation, University of Wisconsin, 1948.

Children in the sixth grade could study electricity and so could first-graders. The first-graders, however, would investigate simpler concepts.

Young children can deal successfully with the following science concepts:

*Animals and Plants.*   Living things are either plants or animals. Non-living things have very few characteristics of living things. Plants and animals are dependent upon each other. Animals differ in many ways but are alike in some respects. Some make good pets. Plants need air, water, food, and sunlight in order to grow. Some plants are produced from seeds; others grow from bulbs. Plants are adapted to their environment. Man is dependent upon plants either directly or indirectly for his food. Conservation of living things is essential.

*Magnets.*   Magnets attract and hold things made of iron or steel. Magnets differ in strength as well as shape. They attract through most materials. Magnets are stronger at the poles; they have north- and south-seeking poles. Like poles repel, and opposite poles attract. The needle of a compass is a magnet. Magnets are used in everyday life — in telephones, motors, radio, telegraph, and television. Magnets must be protected if they are to retain their magnetism. The earth is a magnet.

*Electricity.*   Electricity works for man. It is a form of energy. Electric current is produced by generators and cells. Static electricity is produced by friction. Lightning is the discharge of static electricity. Electric current is a stream of electrons that flow through a conductor. Some materials are good conductors of electricity; others are not.

*Energy.*   The sun is the source of nearly all energy. Energy exists in various forms. It cannot be destroyed. Plants and animals require energy to grow. Man requires energy to work. Change of energy from one form to another results in the production of heat.

*Health.*   The healthy child has good health habits; for example, he covers his mouth when he coughs or sneezes. The healthy child needs a variety of foods at regular intervals. He needs active outdoor play all year. He has a wholesome attitude toward rest and sleep. He is clean; he takes frequent baths, brushes his teeth, washes his hands before meals and after toileting. The healthy child maintains good posture. He has regular checkups at the doctor's and dentist's and does not resist taking his shots. The healthy child uses adequate lighting for study and reading.

*Safety.* Safety rules are essential for care of ears, eyes, and body. Safety rules are essential in the use of electrical appliances, electrical wires, and fuses. Safety rules should be observed on the playground, on the street, in the home, and in the community to avoid injury to others and self. The safe child controls sound so that nervous tension is not increased by sudden loud noises.

## Science in the Kindergarten and Primary Grades

The following outline suggests ways to broaden the child's understanding of his physical environment, help him more effectively solve pressing problems of living, and develop in him a scientific attitude which becomes habitual.

Since young children are so interested in living things we shall begin with concepts and activities in that area.

### Life Science
*General Concepts and Activities* (C denotes concept, A denotes activity)

C  There are many kinds of animals.

> A  Observe in the neighborhood and see how many kinds of animals you find.

C  Some animals can be kept in the schoolroom.

> A  Discover the reasons some animals can be cared for in school and others cannot.

C  Animals differ in general physical characteristics and may be classified accordingly.

> A  Have the children look at birds to observe that their bodies are covered with feathers; they have two legs and two wings.

> A  Have them note the way birds are fitted for flight. Observe the different kinds of tails, mouths, feet, feathers, and colors.

> A  Learn to distinguish their songs, discover the food they eat, the type of nests they build, how they protect themselves.

    *A*  Have the children observe that insects have six legs and two antennae or feelers.

    *A*  Make a collection of insect specimens, have someone bring in a collection, or take a trip to a museum to see a collection.

    *A*  Take a walk to observe caterpillars, butterflies, moths, bees, worms, ladybugs, grasshoppers, and other insects.

    *A*  Look for eggs of the monarch butterfly. You will find them on milkweed plants.

    *A*  Have the children observe animals to note the different kinds of teeth, ears, tails, mouths, furs, and colors. Point out that these differences help them protect themselves, get food, and adapt to their environment.

    *A*  Visit the zoo and a farm. Have the children identify the animals and give distinguishing characteristics.

    *A*  Discuss the contributions of the farm animals.

  *C*  Animals vary in the amount and type of parental care they give their young.

    *A*  Observe which animals are cared for by both parents.

    *A*  Observe which animals are cared for only by the mother or left without care.

    *A*  Raise some tadpoles from polliwogs.

    *A*  Watch birds feed their young.

    *A*  Identify the animals you see being fed at the zoo.

  *C*  Some animals are useful to man for food, clothing, and transportation.

    *A*  Discover which animals give us food.

    *A*  Discover which animals give us clothing.

    *A*  If possible observe animals which provide us with transportation.

  *C*  Animals need food to live and grow.

    *A*  Visit a farm and see which baby animals eat the same food as their parents.

    *A*  Which animals get milk from the mother?

    *A*  Build a feeding station and observe the food birds eat.

    *A*  Discuss ways in which an animal deserted by its mother can be cared for.

  *C*  Plants need sunlight, water, and food to grow.

    *A*  Experiment by putting some plants in the dark and others in the light; water some of the plants but not others; provide plant food for some, but not others. Have the children contrast the growth of the plants.

  *C*  Some plants are produced from seeds, others from bulbs.

# DISCOVERING THE WORLDS OF

# SCIENCE AND MATHEMATICS

The child is eager to explore, to observe, to experiment, and to interpret phenomena. The modern school capitalizes on this natural curiosity and innate desire to learn about the world by helping the child to discover scientific principles and quantitative relationships. Science and mathematics have been revitalized. Science has been moved from the "science corner" to a laboratory situation; arithmetic and mathematics from the "ivory tower" to the work table and chalkboard in the elementary classroom. Curriculum guides have been revised in harmony with the need to prepare children for living in an increasingly complex world.

The elementary school child is interested not only in life science; he is interested in the broad areas of earth sciences and mathematics as well. As the child progresses through the elementary school the focus shifts from observation to interpretation in accordance with his growing interests, needs, skills, and experiential background. The teacher has the responsibility for bringing each child to a high degree of competence in problem solving skills. Children learn most effectively through a balanced program in which they are led by teachers to observe, read, explore, experiment, discover, discuss, and evaluate.

*The primary child approaches science through nature.*

*Objective discussion encourages the development of a scientific attitude.*

*Thoughtful reading is a basic tool for the young scientist.*

*Experimentation leads to the discovery of principles.*

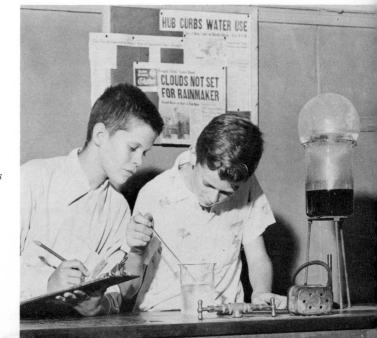

*Excursions to nearby museums broaden the child's knowledge.*

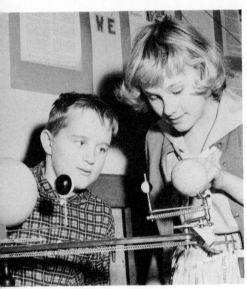

*Creative discovery of fundamental principles is prerequisite to the solution of scientific and mathematical problems.*

*A*   Plant some seeds in the school garden or a window garden; plant some tulip, lily, or onion bulbs. Observe that each plant is produced from one specific seed or bulb.

*C*   There are many different plants; they grow in different ways, in soil or in water.

    *A*   Bring in plants that will grow in soil, in water, in either soil or water.

    *A*   Have children look at plants in the school and on the way to school to discover which grow in soil and which in water.

    *A*   Take a trip to the greenhouse to see the different kinds of plants and the care each type requires.

*C*   Some plants are poisonous.

    *A*   Children should be taught to recognize plants which are dangerous to touch (poison ivy, poison oak) and dangerous to eat.

    *A*   Find pictures of poisonous plants.

*C*   Plants provide food for man.

    *A*   Take a trip to the grocery store to see the fruits and vegetables.

    *A*   Buy some apples and make apple sauce.

    *A*   Make and eat carrot salad or fruit salad.

*C*   Trees have many uses.

    *A*   Take trips to see that birds build nests in trees; trees give shade; trees bear fruit, nuts; trees are used for building, fuel.

    *A*   Bring in leaves and blossoms of trees.

*C*   Trees change their appearance with the seasons.

    *A*   Observe trees in the neighborhood to see the differences at each season.

*C*   There are many different kinds of trees; each tree has a distinctive leaf.

    *A*   Have the children take walks to observe the different types of trees in the neighborhood and identify each leaf they collect.

    *A*   Have them collect fruit from the tree and identify the fruit.

*C*   The tree has a trunk, branches, twigs, and leaves.

    *A*   Have the children become familiar with the parts of the tree through actual observation of trees in the neighborhood.

*C*   Some unusual results are produced by grafting of branches of different trees.

*A* If there is a fruit grower or greenhouse nearby, children may take a trip to observe how grafting is accomplished.

*A* Some children will be motivated to try grafting at home with the permission of parents.

### Physical Science

*Soil*

C Soils differ.

*A* Examine different types of soil.

*A* Make some humus from dried leaves and plant seeds in the humus, in humus and sand, and in sand. Compare the growth of the seeds.

*A* Visit a compost pile in the neighborhood or greenhouse. Find out how it is made.

*A* Use a magnifying glass to observe humus soil.

*A* Make a rock garden. Find out which plants will grow.

*Rocks and Pebbles*

C There are many kinds of rocks and pebbles.

*A* Make a rock collection and identify and label the specimens. Classify them according to three types — igneous, metamorphic, and sedimentary.

*A* Observe the use of rocks (buildings). Find out where the rocks came from.

*A* Visit a quarry if possible or a monument works. Obtain samples for examination.

*A* Walk or climb over rocky places to help children examine rock formations.

*A* Give children opportunity to collect, handle, and identify stones of differing sizes, shapes, and colors.

*A* Make use of stones for drainage in potting a geranium or other plants.

*A* Visit a stream nearby to see the effects of water on rocks.

*A* Visit a museum to see rocks and minerals on exhibit.

*Seasons*

C The seasons follow each other in regular order: autumn, winter, spring, and summer.

*Autumn*

C Animals are affected by seasonal changes.

*A* Read to find out the ways animals adapt to seasonal change.

*A* Take a walk to observe how the squirrel, the rabbit, the insects, and the pets around the school are affected by seasonal change.

C Some animals store food for winter.

   *A* Try to determine which animals you observe are making provision for winter.

C Some birds fly to other places for the winter.

   *A* Observe the migration of flocks of birds in the fall. Which birds leave the area?

C Many animals grow thicker coats as winter approaches.

   *A* Observe such pets as dogs, cats, guinea pigs, hamsters. Which are growing heavier coats?

C Fall brings many changes in plant life.

   *A* Give children experiences with leaves: observe falling leaves, observe the wind blowing the leaves, collect the leaves, play in the leaves, identify leaves on the school ground.

   *A* Plant some hyacinth and tulip bulbs in the school garden and cover them with leaves. Observe them as they grow in the spring.

   *A* Make a seed collection and identify the seeds and nuts.

   *A* Gather ripe fruit and nuts from trees.

   *A* Compare evergreen and deciduous trees.

   *A* Keep a weather chart.

   *A* Record the first frost and observe its effect on plant life.

*Winter*

C Winter weather is cold.

   *A* Watch for the frost on the windows.

   *A* Watch for a milk bottle with a frozen top.

   *A* Feed the winter birds. Skewer an ear of corn on a coat hanger and hang on a branch outside the window.

   *A* On a day below freezing set out a pan of water; how long does it take to freeze?

   *A* Keep a weather chart; record the temperature daily and check the days it snows. Keep a thermometer outdoors.

   *A* Make a snowman.

   *A* Take a walk and observe animal tracks in the snow. Try to determine which animals made the tracks.

   *A* Keep a record of the time the sun sets each day.

*Spring*

C Plants begin to grow in the spring.

   *A* Make a school garden. Plant seeds in the garden.

   *A* Observe people in the neighborhood planting gardens.

   *A* Observe the growth of bulbs planted in the fall.

*A* Plant beans, radishes, carrots, and flower seeds under a glass, on a sponge, and in flower pots.

*A* Bring in a forsythia branch and force it to blossom early.

*A* Take a walk to the greenhouse and observe which of the flowers blossoming there are also in bloom in the school and neighborhood gardens.

*A* Go to a stream and get some polliwogs; watch them grow.

*A* Observe birds building nests. Be cautious so as not to disturb them.

*A* List the types of materials you saw birds using in building their nests.

*A* Arrange a bulletin board display of pictures showing signs of spring.

*Summer*

*C* In summer the days are the warmest of the year.

*A* Keep a weather chart and record the temperature and weather daily.

*A* Record the hour of sunset each day to see that the days are getting longer.

*A* Arrange a bulletin board display of pictures showing summer activities.

*A* Take a trip to a garden in the neighborhood and observe the types of flowers. Name as many as you can.

*A* Keep a record of the birds that come to the bird bath at school or at home.

*C* Direct rays of the sun are hot.

*A* Put an ice cube in the sun and one in the shade. Compare the times they take to melt.

*C* The amount of sun on any place affects the temperature of that place.

*A* Visit a greenhouse and observe that the plants are protected from the direct rays of the sun.

*Energy*

*C* Heat is an important form of energy.

*A* Rub together a number of things and observe how much heat is produced.

*C* Our heating systems make use of three methods of heat transfer: conduction, convection, and radiation.

*A* Visit buildings which are heated by the three methods.

*C* It is possible to regulate the transfer of heat.

*A* Arrange to visit the heating plant of the school and have the custodian explain the utilization of this factor in heating the building.

C  Some materials do not readily transfer heat.

  A  Place a piece of wood and a piece of iron of similar size in hot water. Take them out after a few minutes and determine which one retains the heat longer.

C  Substances conduct heat.

  A  Hold a metal rod, a glass rod, and a wooden rod over a Bunsen burner. Observe which is the best conductor of heat.

C  Liquids, gases, and solids expand when they are heated and contract when they are cooled.

  A  Observe the thermometer indoors on a cold day. Take it outdoors and see what happens to the mercury when it gets cold.

  A  Make a thermometer: Fill a bottle with colored water and use a one-hole stopper through which a clear plastic straw has been passed. The lower end of the tube should not extend inside the bottle. The colored water will rise a certain distance in the straw. Mark this point with a rubber band. Put the apparatus in different hot and cold places and observe what happens to the liquid. When does it rise? When does it fall? What explanation do you have for the phenomenon?

C  Light is a form of energy.

  A  Visit a greenhouse and observe how the soil absorbs radiant energy and converts it into ordinary heat, which the glass enclosure retains.

  A  Check the temperature inside the greenhouse against that outside. Which is warmer? Why?

C  There is "stored sunlight" in coal.

  A  Give reports on the formation of coal and if possible take a trip to see coal mined.

  A  Report on uses of coal.

*Magnets*

C  Magnets attract some materials but not others.

  A  Have the children experiment with different kinds of materials to discover which ones are attracted by magnets. A match, penny, dime, button, thumbtack, safety pin, straight pin, screw, nut, nail, hair curler, and light bulb may be used.

C  The magnet does not have uniform attraction throughout its entire length.

*A* Dip a magnet into a plate of nails (or tacks, or iron filings). Observe to which parts of the magnet the nails cling. Which part has little or no power to attract?

*C* A magnet loses its magnetism under certain conditions.

    *A* Heat a magnet and find out what happens to the power to attract.

    *A* Strike a magnet with a hammer or other heavy object and see what happens.

*Electricity*

*C* Electricity is useful to man.

    *A* Observe the uses of electricity in the home.

    *A* Suggest ways in which children make use of electricity.

*C* The electric current which comes into buildings is extremely powerful. It can produce a dangerous shock.

    *A* Observe the danger signs surrounding high-voltage plants or equipment.

    *A* Discuss the importance of learning the safe uses of electricity.

*Machines*

*C* Man uses machines to work for him.

    *A* Observe machines in the neighborhood which make man's work easier.

*C* An inclined plane makes lifting an object easier.

    *A* Observe demonstration of this principle.

*C* Daily living is facilitated by the use of the lever and the wheel and axle.

    *A* Observe the use of these and determine how daily living is affected by them.

*C* The wheel and axle help us do work.

    *A* Obtain two boxes, same size. Fill with an equal amount of sand. Place one box on a set of wheels and attach a spring scale to one end of the box. Hold the other end of the scale and move the box a distance of one yard. Note the number of pounds indicated by the pointer on the spring scale while the box is being pulled. Attach the spring scale to the other box, without the wheels, and pull it one yard. Note the number of pounds indicated on the scale while this box is being pulled. Explain the difference in the figures.

*Conservation*

*C* Natural resources must be conserved.

    *A* Discuss the uses of such resources as water, soil, trees, minerals, and animals.

*C* Water is one of our most vital natural resources.

    *A* Children should acquire the habit of turning off water faucets when they are not in use.

*C* All materials should be used without wasting them: e.g., one paper towel for drying hands; one sheet of drawing paper at a time. Both sides of writing paper should be used unless the assignment specifically calls for one side only; books should be handled with care; art materials should not be wasted.

    *A* Discover ways in which materials may be conserved.

    *A* Participate in the school paper sale drive.

    *A* Take good care of tools, toys, and play equipment.

*C* Care of clothing is the responsibility of each child.

    *A* Have children or parents label clothing, such as sweaters, galoshes, mittens, painting aprons, rugs, coats, and caps.

    *A* Keep clothing clean and avoid tearing or ripping clothing.

    *A* Discuss the responsibility of making this behavior an integral part of good citizenship.

    *A* Wear rubbers or boots to protect shoes in wet weather.

*C* Our present-day world of electric power and machines depends on natural resources.

    *A* Visit a power plant, a dam, or a conservation reserve.

*C* Animal conservation is aided through wild-life reserves, parks, and zoos.

    *A* Visit a wild-life reserve or a zoo.

*C* Trees should be preserved.

    *A* Visit a nursery and observe how trees are cared for.

*C* Soil needs care in order to avoid erosion.

    *A* Observe the effects of erosion. Discover what can be done to prevent it.

*C* Young trees should be planted to replace trees that are cut down.

    *A* Participate in a tree-planting ceremony.

*C* The woods provide a good home for animals.

    *A* Observe the game laws.

## *Space*

### *The Sun*

*C* The sun is very hot.

    *A* Take a thermometer outdoors and measure the temperature of the air in a sunny place. Measure it in the shade and compare the two readings. Discuss the differences.

    *A* Compare two sets of metal articles — tin cup, tin pan, scissors, and so forth — one of which has been placed in the direct sunlight, the other in the shade. Have boys and girls close their eyes and judge from the warmth of the objects which have been in the sun and which in the shade.

C Sunlight is reflected.

   *A* Use mirrors to reflect the light. Look at the reflection of the sun on the lake, the street, the car or bus.

C The sun is very bright.

   *A* Use sun glasses when looking at the reflection of the sun in a mirror or on the water. Discuss the danger of looking directly at the bright sun.

   *A* Observe the appearance of the sun through a cloud or fog.

C The sunlight gives things color.

   *A* Hold a prism in the sunlight and note the different colors.

   *A* Note the sun shining through a corner of the aquarium.

   *A* Bring in a spectroscope and let children observe its effects.

   *A* Use a glass of water to help find colors.

C The sun makes shadows.

   *A* Observe change in length and position of shadows according to the position of the sun.

   *A* Have the children observe their own shadows in the morning, at noon, and in the afternoon.

   *A* Keep a record of this activity several times during the year to note seasonal changes.

C Sunlight affects growing plants.

   *A* Carry on an experiment in which some plants are placed near the window, some away from the windows, and some in a dark cupboard. After a few days have children notice and record the difference in color and growth.

C Plants grow toward the light.

   *A* Plant seeds in a box. Let them sprout. Place in a light-proof box with a window cut in one end. The only light entering the box should come through the window.

C Sunlight affects health.

   *A* Discuss the beneficial aspects of the sun.

   *A* Discuss the dangers of getting too much sunshine too rapidly.

   *A* Discuss the substitutes for direct sunshine which help maintain health in winter.

*The Moon*

C   The moon is the earth's nearest neighbor.

   A   Compare the size of the moon and stars. Investigate why the moon appears to be large.

C   Sunlight is warm; moonlight is not.

   A   Compare the temperature at night and day.

C   The moon and stars give light at night.

   A   Compare the amount of light when the moon is up and when it is not.

C   The moon moves around the earth.

C   It takes a month for the moon to make all its changes.

   A   Keep a calendar of moon changes.

   A   Examine an almanac to discover superstitions about planting seeds according to the phases of the moon.

*Stars and Planets*

C   Stars are always in the sky.

   A   Investigate why they cannot be seen.

C   Many stars can be seen in the sky at night.

   A   Find the North Star, the Big Dipper, the Little Dipper.

C   The North Star is always in the north.

C   Stars make pictures in the sky.

   A   Give reports to the class on how the constellations got their names.

C   Planets revolve around the sun.

   A   Name the planets.

   A   Collect pictures of planets and stars.

   A   Make a frieze of the heavens.

   A   Visit an observatory or planetarium if there is one in your community.

C   Stars appear to be arranged in groups or constellations.

   A   Read star legends and give reports to the class.

   A   Show constellations on film strips, handmade slides. Find a star map.

   A   Make special reports on telescopes, stars, etc. Make clay ball models of the planets. Set them on large cardboard on which you have drawn the orbits of the planets.

C   Planets and stars help ships and airplanes find their way at night.

   A   Read how sailors and pilots navigate by the stars.

## Science in the Intermediate Grades

As the child progresses through the elementary school he becomes more skilled in the scientific method. He learns to observe carefully, to think critically, and to make judgments on the basis of evidence, not impulse. He learns to solve more complicated problems and to understand more intricate science concepts. Units of instruction can become more complex and broader in scope, as will be evident from the following outlines.

### Magnetism (Grade 4)

C  There are many different sizes and shapes of magnets — the horseshoe, the bar magnet, and the U-shaped magnet.

A  Examine the different types of magnets.

C  A magnet has a field of force which can be demonstrated.

A  Demonstrate.

C  When iron is magnetized, small particles attracted to it are rearranged in such a fashion that the unlike poles are still together, but the lines of force extend in the same direction.

A  Cover a bar magnet with a thin paper. Sprinkle iron filings on the paper evenly. Tap the paper lightly and see how the filings draw together in lines.

A  Put some paper clips on the piece of paper, and move the magnet under the paper. Observe that the clips follow the magnet.

A  Fasten a U magnet to a clamp on a ring stand. Tie a string around the base of the stand and tie a paper clip to the string. Adjust the clamp to allow approximately a quarter of an inch between the magnet and the paper clip. The force of the magnet should pull the clip up so that it is suspended in mid-air when wood, glass, leather, iron, rubber, aluminum, and zinc are passed through the space between the clip and the magnet. Observe that the magnetism passes through most of the substances except the iron.

C  The earth is a natural magnet.

A  Observe how the compass needle always points north.

A  Put a magnet close to the compass to show how the needle turns but always returns to the north when the magnetic field is removed.

C  The needle of a magnetic compass is really a small bar magnet mounted so that it can swing freely around.

*A*  Hold one end of a bar magnet near a compass. What happens? Try holding the other end near the compass and report your findings.

*C*  Unlike magnetic poles attract each other; like poles repel.

*A*  Bring any magnetic toys to school. Explain how they work.

*A*  Make a small magnetic boat by using a cork for the hull, a magnetized darning or sewing needle for the mast, and a piece of paper for the sail. Put the needle through the paper and into the cork. Use a bar magnet to move the boat on the water.

*A*  Hang up a bar magnet by a piece of cord and a piece of tape so it can swing easily. Bring near one of its ends first the north pole and then the south pole of another magnet. What happens?

*C*  Magnetism can be induced. If a piece of iron is brought near a magnet or touches a magnet it is temporarily magnetized.

*A*  Hold a large nail against a magnet. Dip the nail into a box of small tacks so that the nail comes in contact with the tacks. What happens to the tacks? Pull the nail away from the magnet. What happens to the tacks?

*A*  Rub the end of a bar magnet along a knife blade, always in the same direction. Press and move the magnet slowly with each stroke. One stroke will magnetize the blade to some degree, but twenty-five strokes will magnetize it enough to pick up tacks and paper clips.

*C*  Magnetic compasses are useful in finding directions.

*A*  Use the compass on excursions.

*A*  Try to use a compass in a car or bus. Relate what happens.

*A*  Why does the compass that is installed in an automobile work?

*C*  If a magnet is broken, each piece has a north and south pole.

*A*  Bring an inexpensive toy horseshoe magnet to school. Break it. Test the ends of each piece with iron filings, tacks, or a magnet. Relate your findings. Break each piece and compare your findings.

BIBLIOGRAPHY FOR MAGNETISM UNIT

Artley, C. K. *Science Experiences for Elementary Schools.* Practical Suggestions for Teaching Series. New York: Bureau of Publications, Teachers College, Columbia University, 1958.

Atkin, Myron J., and Burnett, Will R. *Electricity and Magnetism.* Elementary School Science Activities Series. New York: Rinehart and Company, 1958.

Blough, Glenn O., Schwartz, Julius, and Huggett, Albert. *Elementary School Science and How to Teach It.* New York: The Dryden Press, 1958.

Branley, Franklyn, and Vaughan, Eleanor K. *Mickey's Magnet.* New York: Thomas Y. Crowell Company, 1956.

Burnett, Raymond Will. *Teaching Science in the Elementary School.* New York: Rinehart and Company, 1957.

Freeman, Mae and Ira. *Fun with Science.* New York: Random House, rev. ed., 1956.

Hubler, Clark. *Working with Children in Science.* Boston: Houghton Mifflin Company, 1957.

Lewellen, John. *The Boy Scientist.* Chicago: Popular Mechanics Press, 1955.

McSpadden, J. Walker. *How They Sent the News.* New York: Dodd, Mead and Company, 1946.

Podendorf, Illa. *The True Book of Science Experiments.* Chicago: Children's Press, 1954.

Sheckles, Mary. *Building Science Concepts.* New York: Bureau of Publications, Teachers College, Columbia University, 1958.

*Neighbors in Space*[9] (*Grade 4*)

Basic Concepts

Man lives in a continually changing world. The vastness of space is being conquered by man's inventions.

Objectives

1. To develop a spirit of inquiry and a desire to learn about outer space.

2. To recognize the possibility of man's traveling outside the atmosphere of this world.

3. To see the earth as a part of a complex solar system.

Initiating the Unit

Motivation will be dependent on current developments in space science. Children are studying elementary astronomy this year and this forms the basis of the science program.

Concepts

1. Other planets, like the earth, travel around the sun.

---

[9] Ruth White, Helen Kalkbrenner, and Clara Howerton, "Science Education for the Elementary Teacher," project for Education 223, Evansville College, Evansville, Ind., 1959.

    a. Some are farther away from the sun than the earth.

    b. Others are nearer the sun than the earth.

2. The members of the solar system we know best are the earth, the moon, and the sun.

    a. The moon is a lifeless ball of rock, without water or air, circling endlessly around the earth.

    b. Sunlight shining on the moon makes moonlight.

    c. The moon is smaller and lighter than the earth. Its gravity is weaker.

    d. The sun is an enormous ball of glowing gas.

    e. Life on earth would be impossible if it were not for the sun.

    f. The gravitational pull of the sun keeps the planets moving in their orbits.

3. To travel in space one would have to get beyond the pull of the earth's gravity.

Activities

Discussion, reading, reports, creating stories and poems, gathering newspaper clippings, bringing in resource people to help clarify concepts. Find out what these scientists contributed: Galileo, Kepler, Copernicus, Herschel, Lowell. Ability to do critical thinking by comparing the different sizes of planets and understanding how gravity affects our lives. Make sky map. Experiments worked out in class.

Evaluations

1. Do the children begin to see their earth as a part of a complex solar system?

2. Do the children show more tendency to check facts before they accept statements?

3. Are the children willing to go to varied sources for information?

4. Have they developed a spirit of inquiry and a desire to learn and has their interest been carried beyond the classroom?

### BIBLIOGRAPHY FOR CHILDREN

Branley, Franklyn M. *Book of Satellites for You.* New York: Thomas Y. Crowell Company, 1959.

Dietz, Davis. *All About Satellites and Space Ships.* New York: Random House, 1959.

Fontany, Elena. *Other Worlds Than This.* Chicago: Follett Publishing Company, 1941.

Freeman, Mae and Ira. *You Will Go to the Moon.* New York: Random House, 1959.

Gallant, Roy A. *Exploring the Planets.* Garden City, N.Y.: Doubleday and Company, 1958.

Heuer, Kenneth. *Adventure in Astronomy.* New York: The Viking Press, 1958.

Hyde. Margaret O. *Atoms Today and Tomorrow.* New York: Whittlesey House, 1959.

Knight, Clayton. *Rockets, Missiles and Satellites.* New York: Grossett and Dunlap, 1958.

Leaf, Munro. *Science Can Be Fun.* Philadelphia: J. B. Lippincott Company, 1958.

Leonard, Jonathan N. *Exploring Science.* Yonkers, N.Y.: World Book Company, 1959.

Lewellen, John. *The Earth Satellite.* New York: Alfred A. Knopf, Inc., 1957.

Moore, Patrick. *The Worlds Around Us.* New York: Abelard-Schuman, 1956.

Nephew, William, and Chester, Michael. *Moon Trip.* New York: G. P. Putman's Sons, 1958.

Newell, Homer E., Jr. *Space Book for Young People.* New York: McGraw-Hill Book Company, 1958.

Ruchlis, H. Y. *Orbit.* New York: Harper & Brothers, 1958.

Watson, Jane Werner. *World of Science.* New York: Simon and Schuster, Inc., 1958.

Zim, Herbert S. *Shooting Stars.* New York: William Morrow and Company, 1958.

Zim, Herbert S. *The Sun.* New York: William Morrow and Company, 1953.

### BIBLIOGRAPHY FOR TEACHERS

Blough, Glenn O., Schwartz, Julius, and Huggett, Albert. *Elementary School Science and How to Teach It.* New York: The Dryden Press, 1958.

Craig, Gerald S., and Urban, John. *Facing Tomorrow with Science.* Boston: Ginn and Company, 1956.

Draper, Arthur. *Wonders of the Heavens.* New York: Random House, 1940.

Frost, George E. *Planets, Stars and Atoms.* Caldwell, Ida.: Caxton Printers, Ltd., 1946.

Goodwin, Hal. *The Real Book About Space Travel.* Garden City, N.Y.: Garden City Books, 1952.

Heuer, Kenneth. *Adventure in Astronomy.* New York: The Viking Press, 1958.

Hurst, Earl Oliver. *The Big Book of Space*. New York: Grossett and Dunlap, 1953.

Hutchinson, William M., and Spielberg, Kurt. *Space Travel*. New York: Maxton Publishers, Inc., 1958.

Levitt, I. M. *A Space Traveler's Guide to Mars*. New York: Henry Holt and Company, 1956.

Watson, Jane Werner. *The World of Science*. New York: Simon and Schuster, Inc., 1958.

White, Terry. *All About the Stars*. New York: Random House, 1954.

### Guarding Your Health *(Grade 6)*

Unit: The common cold

Objectives

1. To develop an intellectual curiosity concerning known facts about prevention and treatment of colds.
2. To accept personal responsibility for avoiding or spreading colds.
3. To recognize unscrupulous advertising for medications.
4. To start an interest in medical experimentation and research.
5. To practice sound health habits that will reduce the incidence of colds.

Concepts

1. The common cold is caused by a virus.
2. The common cold is contagious and can be contracted from persons afflicted.
3. For the common cold there is a definite source of infection.
4. The cold virus multiplies rapidly within the body.
5. Diagnosis and treatment are the province of the physician.
6. White corpuscles in the blood help the body fight the cold virus.
7. Sound personal health and hygiene habits are essential in avoiding the common cold.
8. Scientific research continues to make strides in the control of disease and improvement of health.

Activities

1. Develop a questionnaire to determine attitudes and general knowledge of the children at the beginning of the unit.
2. Visit the health department and perform experiments to observe differences between ordinary cleanliness and bacteriological cleanliness.
3. Make scrapbooks of clippings, charts, graphs, and pictures

about colds gathered from such sources as newspapers, health magazines, health organizations, state and national health associations.

4. Research. Select topics in areas of prevention, treatment, and control of common colds and prepare reports for class — on, for example, health habits, dietary habits, vitamins, medical research.

5. Visual aid. Show movies or film strips dealing with the common cold. Exhibit models or pictures of the respiratory system.

6. Resource people. Invite a physician or public health nurse to the class to discuss and answer questions concerning colds. Invite a bacteriologist to explain immunization.

Evaluation

Repeat the questionnaire developed at the beginning of the unit to determine what changes have taken place in attitudes and knowledge. Observe changes in behavior.

The Common Cold
(an unsigned questionnaire)

Please answer these questions carefully and truthfully. Do not sign your name. The purpose of this questionnaire is to find out what you think about colds.

How many colds have you had in the last twelve months? ...............................

Was this an unusual year in this respect? ...............................

How many colds did the members of your family have? ...............................

When did you have your last cold? ...............................

How did you catch it? ...............................

How long did it last? ...............................

In what ways did it interfere with work or recreation? ...............................

...............................

What did you do for it? ...............................

...............................

...............................

Listed below are some common treatments for colds. Check those that you would recommend, those that you disapprove of, and those you are uncertain about.

| *Treatments* | *Recommend* | *Disapprove* | *Uncertain* |
|---|---|---|---|
| Hot baths | .................... | .................... | .................... |
| Nose drops | .................... | .................... | .................... |
| Aspirin | .................... | .................... | .................... |
| Fruit juices | .................... | .................... | .................... |
| Nose sprays | .................... | .................... | .................... |
| Vitamin tablets | .................... | .................... | .................... |
| Shots | .................... | .................... | .................... |
| Gargles | .................... | .................... | .................... |
| Baking soda | .................... | .................... | .................... |
| Cough syrup | .................... | .................... | .................... |
| Exercise | .................... | .................... | .................... |

In your opinion, what are the causes of colds? Check your point of view in the appropriate column.

| *The Cause of Colds* | *Probable* | *Possible* | *Impossible* | *Not Known* |
|---|---|---|---|---|
| Sleeping with shut windows | .............. | .............. | .............. | .............. |
| Chilling parts of body | .............. | .............. | .............. | .............. |
| Exposure to drafts | .............. | .............. | .............. | .............. |
| Getting feet wet | .............. | .............. | .............. | .............. |
| Tobacco smoke | .............. | .............. | .............. | .............. |
| Fatigue | .............. | .............. | .............. | .............. |
| Overeating | .............. | .............. | .............. | .............. |
| Obstruction in nose | .............. | .............. | .............. | .............. |
| Overheated houses | .............. | .............. | .............. | .............. |
| Contact with someone who has a cold | .............. | .............. | .............. | .............. |
| Changes in weather | .............. | .............. | .............. | .............. |

Individuals learn about the prevention, causes, and treatments of colds from various sources. These sources include physicians, nurses, parents, friends, newspapers, magazines, radio, television, and others. What is your attitude toward these sources? Which do you recommend? Which do you actually use?

...................................................................................................................................

...................................................................................................................................

...................................................................................................................................

...................................................................................................................................

BIBLIOGRAPHY

Barnard, J. D., *et al.* The Macmillan Science-Life Series, Books 4–6. New York: The Macmillan Company, 1959.

Burnett, Will. *To Live in Health.* New York: Silver Burdett Company, 1944.

Callahan, Dorothy, and Payne, Alma Smith. *The Great Nutrition Puzzle.* New York: Charles Scribner's Sons, 1956.

Cosgrove, Margaret. *The Wonders Inside You.* New York: Dodd, Mead and Company, 1955.

Coy, Harold. *Doctors and What They Do.* New York: Franklin Watts, Inc., 1956.

Diehl, Harold S. *Textbook of Healthful Living.* New York: McGraw-Hill Book Company, 6th ed., 1960.

Eberle, Irmengarde. *Modern Medical Discoveries.* New York: Thomas Y. Crowell Company, 1954.

*A Guide for Health Education in Indiana Schools.* Bulletin No. 219. Indianapolis: State of Indiana, Department of Public Instruction, 1956.

Hemming, James. *Mankind Against the Killers.* New York: Longmans, Green and Company, 1956.

Hyde, Margaret O. *Medicine in Action. Today and Tomorrow.* New York: Whittlesey House, 1956.

Ravielli, Anthony. *Wonders of the Human Body.* New York: The Viking Press, 1954.

Report of the Joint Committee of the National Education Association and the American Medical Association. *Health Education.* Washington, D.C., 1948.

Schatz, Albert, and Riedman, Sarah R. *The Story of Microbes.* New York: Harper & Brothers, 1952.

Schneider, Herman and Nina. *Heath Elementary Science,* Books 4–6. Boston: D. C. Heath and Company, 1959.

Schneider, Leo. *You and Your Senses.* New York, Whittlesey House, 1956.

Selsam, Millicent E. *Microbes at Work*. New York: William
Morrow and Company, 1953.

Sever, J. A. *Johnny Visits His Doctor*. Boston: Children's Medical
Center, 1955.

Shippen, Katherine B. *Men, Microscopes and Living Things*. New
York: The Viking Press, 1955.

Turner, C. E., et al. *Cleanliness and Health Protection*. Boston:
D. C. Heath and Company, 1941.

Wilcox, Charlotte S., et al. *Here's Health*. Health Action Series,
Grade 6. Chicago: Benefic Press, 1959.

Zim, Herbert S. *Your Food and You*. New York: William Morrow and Company, 1957.

There are many areas or units of instruction to be developed during the intermediate grades. Children at this age are boundlessly
interested in the world in which they live. The teacher must guide
the learning experiences in science in such a way that their interest
remains keen, their knowledge is broadened, and their skills in the
scientific method are developed. It is not enough to know the
subject matter of science, important as that is; the teacher must
also know how children learn so he can plan effective procedures
for teaching science.

## How Children Learn Science

There are various procedures for helping children learn science:
discussing, experimenting, taking field trips, camping, observing,
using audio-visual aids, and reading. Each will be discusssed briefly.

*Discussion.* Discussion has been examined at length in connection with communication. It is vital to intelligent group action that
children become skilled in defining problems, gathering data, finding
possible solutions, and testing the solution and reaching conclusions.
Such questions as "Is there a problem?" "What are your ideas on
the subject?" "How would you go about finding out?" "Where
did you get your information?" "How do you explain it?" "Is your
source reliable?" will set children off. Discussion is a part of every
science activity and plays a vital role in the experiment, the excursion, observation, and reading.

*Experimenting.* Science experimentation helps develop a scientific attitude which will influence the individual's decisions throughout life. An experiment may be very useful in finding a solution to a problem. However, conclusions must be checked against reliable sources. Children can learn from an experiment which does not succeed if the teacher is effective. But if he takes the attitude of a certain second-grade teacher who said, "The experiments in this book give the answer so we don't have to bother to work any of them out," the children are not likely to learn to use the experimental approach.

A few guideposts for the teacher are as follows:

1. Experiments should be kept simple.

2. The children should know the purpose of the experiment.

3. Experiments must be carefully planned and performed. Materials should be assembled, a plan of procedure must be set up, the plan should be followed carefully, and the children should be taught not to jump to conclusions.

4. Children should have a share in bringing in materials as well as in setting up the experiment.

5. Children should be encouraged to perform experiments which are needed to answer questions set up in the problem under investigation. These experiments should be carried on under the supervision and guidance of the teacher. Experiments which involve the use of fire or other possible hazards should be performed in the science laboratory by the science teacher.

6. Children should be taught to withhold judgment until all the evidence is in; they should not generalize on insufficient evidence. They should learn that results may change with new evidence.

7. At some time during the year each child should have opportunity to engage in the manipulation of materials, setting up the experiment, and performing experiments.

*Taking Field Trips.* To many children, taking a field trip is synonymous with science education. Excursions to help solve problems, to get needed information, and to develop appreciation of the environment are essential in elementary science. The teacher should make a survey of community resources to plan for well-motivated, well-organized, and profitable trips. Among typical excursions are those to a park, a stream, the woodland, the sawmill, the airport, the water purification plant, an apiary, and a greenhouse. The teacher should bear in mind the fact that it is his responsibility to enlarge the child's environment and to help him at every possible opportunity to develop concepts that enrich his life.

In order for the excursion to be successful there should be a purpose, the children should be aware of the purpose, they should have specific questions in mind, they should observe safety rules, there should be sufficient time allotted for the excursion itself, and there should be time for evaluation. Preparation beforehand and evaluation afterward are essential to a successful field trip.

If properly organized and conducted, excursions can vitalize classroom teaching and learning. The teacher helps the child understand and interpret the environment, find ways of answering questions, and find solutions to problems. He assists the children in asking questions of the guide and in making sure they see what they set out to see.

With young children excursions should not be lengthy, either in distance or in time. Nearby gardens, streams, woodland areas, and parks are all valuable sources of learning for children.

*School Camping.* School camping represents an extension of the field trip into a laboratory situation with the raw materials for teaching science. Time is spent before and after the camp experience consolidating the learnings in the classroom. Camping thus becomes an integral part of the school curriculum. Across the country it is perhaps most common at the sixth-grade level.

The problem "Our Health Should Be Safeguarded" is a topic to which school camping makes a real contribution. The children plan their trip in the classroom. Their concern lies in such matters as rest and sleep, cleanliness and sanitation, food and clothing. These provide natural situations for learning about health. Menus are planned with the help of the school dietitian. Facts about nutrition, daily diet requirements, and reasons for the basic requirements are discussed and learned in a functional setting.

The school nurse is often called in as a resource person. She discusses with the children the value of sleep and rest, the need for clean hands at mealtime, the importance of disinfecting sanitary facilities, the need to refrain from spreading germs through coughing and sneezing, and other concerns of similar interest. The values of fresh air, exercise, and proper clothing are also integrated in the camping experience.

Scientific learning begins with curiosity, moves on to problem solving, and culminates in finding solutions to the problems. In school camping learning is effectively integrated with life.[10]

*Observing.* Observation is important in science instruction. Children need to use all the senses in learning — to see, touch, smell, weigh, feel, taste, measure, discover, watch, and listen.

The scientist learns early to observe accurately and to report his observations with care. Reliability is essential to the scientific method. Without it, in fact, an experiment is worthless, an excursion ineffectual.

In order to make more effective use of observation the teacher should consider carefully the possibilities for training children to observe weather phenomena such as rainstorms, freezing weather, a high wind, sleet, or hail and to note the effects of seasonal change upon plants and animals. Since observation involves the use of the ears as well as the eyes, the children should learn to appreciate the sounds in the forest and fields. They should begin to understand how keen are the various senses of animals.

To observe the grace of movement in a darting deer or fleeing fawn, to appreciate the perfect balance of a listening bird or a wild rabbit pretending he isn't there is to retain the capacity for wonder.

*Audio-Visual Aids.* Children learn much through the use of audio-visual aids. Radio, television, films, movies, slides, film strips, pictures, models, exhibits are all useful in contributing to concept development and understandings for the young scientist. Any procedure that makes a science principle or concept more graphic, more interesting, and more alive should be used. Many good programs are available on radio and television, but children must be taught to discriminate between the good and the mediocre, between science and fiction. The teacher can help them to use wisely the media which the modern scientific world is making possible.

*Reading.* Judicious use of science textbooks solves many of the problems of science instruction. In the past, unfortunately, courses have often been merely reading courses. Reading is an effective tool for learning science; but it is only a tool. It should be integrated with other science experiences such as planning experiments, discus-

[10] Jerry Baker, "Extending Science Education Through Elementary School Camping," *Science Education*, 44:141, March 1960.

sions, excursions, and observations. The following factors should be considered:

1. Children should have a definite purpose in mind when they read. Rather than say to the children, "Turn to page 11 in your science reader and read to page 15 and then we'll talk about what we read," it is better to have them read for a specific purpose such as to find information, to find out how to do an experiment, to answer a question, to solve a problem, to check the authenticity of a conclusion, and so forth.

2. Children should read a variety of sources on a given topic in order to gain wider information and to evaluate varying points of view. The teacher should select appropriate reading material which meets individual needs and interests in the classroom.

3. Children should be encouraged to carry on individual research projects, following careful procedures for note taking, outlining, organizing, and presenting an accurate and interesting report to the class. Research offers one of the finest motivations in the science curriculum. Children with a research project in progress come to school the next day eager to get back to it. Children frequently get started *reading* about science and then go on to *doing* science.

## Approaches to the Teaching of Science

Among the commonly used approaches to teaching science are the incidental approach, the integrated approach, and the science-centered approach.

*The Incidental Approach.* Too often the incidental approach is synonymous with accidental teaching. The initiative is left largely to the children. Johnny brings in a pet turtle or baby bunny. If Johnny or the group as a whole is interested in doing anything more than look at the animal, and if the teacher is curious about the general environment and the living things in it, some science may be learned. The spontaneous and voluntary interests of the children are taken care of. With this approach no science is taught until it is instigated by a child's contribution.

*The Integrated Approach.* A number of schools organize their programs around social problems or problems of living and teach science as a phase of this broader curriculum. The persistent problem of health, for example, may be considered, and science is integrated with it as the children find solutions to problems which they select. They explore a problem of living, formulate questions, decide upon ways of solving the problem through group methods, and use science only insofar as it bears on what they have selected for the core of their study. As they search for answers to the problem they may use discussion, experiments, excursions, observation, reading, or visual aids.

*The Science-Centered Approach.* This approach to science teaching assumes a carefully planned, sequential course of study in science just as in any other area of the curriculum. A planned course provides scope, sequence, and continuity of experiences based on children's abilities, maturity, background, needs, and age-level interests. It does much to avoid useless repetition and provides a balance of experiences in the physical and life sciences. It encourages the teacher to broaden his outlook as he works with children to develop an interest in and knowledge of all phases of the environment. It assures, too, that a time will be set aside for science in the curriculum; if science is scheduled it is less likely to be accidental. A well-coordinated series of science experiences begins in the kindergarten and continues through the elementary school, junior high school, and senior high school. Such an approach recognizes the importance of developing simple scientific concepts before complex ones. It does not, however, assume that children in the primary grades are interested only in living things. It demands a teacher who is eager to experiment, willing to explore unfamiliar subjects, and interested in being informed about scientific developments. In this approach science is more than an incidental interest; it is a way of life.

Many teachers use all three approaches. However, as science becomes more and more essential for survival, greater emphasis is being placed on the latter two. The three methods may overlap. In some cases a child's personal interest initiates a unit of study. It is still the responsibility of the teacher to provide the experiences that meet the needs of the child in a society in which literacy in science is imperative. In the examples that follow, the three approaches to science teaching are illustrated.

EXAMPLES OF THE APPROACHES TO THE TEACHING OF SCIENCE

*Incidental Approach, in Kindergarten.* During the share-and-tell period, Dennis, a retiring child, brought in a magnet and came up shyly before the group.

"What did you bring to school today, Dennis?" asked Miss Albert. Dennis replied, "A magnet."

"Do you know what a magnet does?"

Dennis replied, "It picks up things — but not just everything."

TEACHER: Does it pick up paper?
DENNIS: No, not paper.
TEACHER: A screw?
DENNIS: Yes.
TEACHER: A stamp?
DENNIS: No, 'cause it's paper.
TEACHER: Nail?
DENNIS: Yes, and every kid knows that.
TEACHER: Why does it pick up the nail?
DENNIS: 'Cause it's made of steel.
TEACHER: Would you like to demonstrate what the magnet will pick up? (*Dennis demonstrates.*)
TEACHER: Now choose other children to show which things the magnet picks up and which it will not pick up. Let's count them. 1, 2, 3, 4, 5, 6, 7, 8. (*The teacher was concerned with developing number readiness with the kindergarten group.*)
TEACHER: Let's separate the things it picks up and put them on this side of the table.

| *Will pick up* | *Won't pick up* |
| --- | --- |
| hook and eye | dime |
| hairpin | ball |
| nail | light bulb |
| clothes hanger | clothespin |
| screw | penny |
| key | wooden block |
| needle | matches |
| thumbtack | stamp |
| paper clip | walnut |

TEACHER: What did this experiment show us?
PUPIL: Magnets pick up things made of iron and steel.

PUPIL:    Magnets pick up some things.

PUPIL:    Magnetism makes the magnet pick things up that are made of iron and steel.

PUPIL:    Magnets pick up more than one thing at a time.

TEACHER:    Do you see the sailboat I have? (*Teacher presents a boat made of a cork, paper, and a needle.*)
Let's put it on the water and see if it will float.
We'll take a magnet and see if it will make the boat sail.
Why is it moving?

GARY:    Magnetism makes it move.

TEACHER:    What is the magnet attracting?

CHILDREN:    The needle. The magnet attracts the needle on the boat.

ELLEN:    You can make the boat move with the magnet because the needle itself is made of steel.

JANE:    It picks up the boat, too, and it makes it move.

TEACHER:    John, why does the boat move?

JOHN:    The magnetism of the needle attracts the magnet and the magnet makes it move.

PAULA:    I'll explain it. Magnetism is the thing that makes magnets pick up things. The magnet has power even if it isn't touching anything.

HENRY:    I have a question. Will a magnet pick up more than one thing at a time?

CHILDREN:    The answer is yes, if they are made of iron and steel and it's big enough.

TEACHER:    I have a question. What two important facts did we learn today?

CHILDREN:    A magnet attracts and holds anything made of iron. A magnet may pick up more than one piece of iron at a time.

*Integrated Approach.* In this approach science and health and safety, or science and social studies are combined. As a phase of health and safety a group of first-grade children studied health and nutrition. The group listed the following objectives:

For the children:
1. To understand and practice good health habits.
2. To choose a balanced diet.
3. To take responsibility for health habits.
For the parents:
1. To see that children get the right food.
2. To see that children get the proper amount of sleep.

3. To see that children get plenty of fresh air and exercise.
4. To see that they acquire good health habits.
   a. Brushing teeth.
   b. Going to bed early.
   c. Keeping clean.
   d. Eating proper food.

The children participated in activities in connection with the health interest every day over a two-week period.

On Monday there was a general discussion of what they had eaten for breakfast and what they usually ate for lunch and dinner. The children responded eagerly and the discovery was made that three of them had not had breakfast.

On Tuesday there was a brief discussion of breakfast and only two children came to school without eating. Individual charts were passed out so that the children could record what they ate for breakfast every day.

On Wednesday the children saw the film *Lazy Lucy* and commented on whether they wanted Healthier or Stealthier for their friend. They sang some health songs and one group went to the cafeteria with a mother to make jello for the next day's midmorning snack.

On Thursday the food charts were checked; some children reported a breakfast of milk and breakfast food or orange juice and toast. They ate the jello for the midmorning snack and planned a trip to the supermarket for Friday. They formulated standards for behavior on the trip and planned to ask some questions relating to the types of breakfast food most often purchased. They dramatized a trip to the supermarket.

On Friday the group and two mothers went to the supermarket. They planned to purchase supplies for a breakfast they would serve to mothers on the following Friday, the last day of the health unit. Returning from the supermarket they found that Karen's mother had left two guinea pigs for them to observe. She had forgotten that this was the day for the supermarket trip. She had left lettuce, carrots, pellets, and salt for the animals to eat over the week end.

On Monday the children were eager to observe the guinea pigs and took turns caring for them. They wrote a story about the guinea pigs.

> Karen's mother brought two guinea pigs to school.
> The brown one is Porky.

The white one is Skippy.
We are studying about food that is good for you.
We learned about the basic foods.
The guinea pigs eat a well-balanced diet.
They eat carrots, lettuce, celery, and salt.
They eat pellets to get their protein.
They drink water for their health.
They like the pellets best and whenever we feed them pellets, they say, "Squeak, squeak. Thank you."
We could have experimented by not feeding them the right food.
But we wanted to take good care of them because we are learning to take good care of ourselves.

On Tuesday the group made plans for Friday, when they would invite their mothers to be their guests at breakfast. They decided to have committees to be responsible for introducing the mothers, seating them, and serving the food. They planned to serve frozen orange juice, cereal, toast, and milk. This would furnish the essential elements. They felt eggs would be too difficult to manage.

On Wednesday they made place mats in the shape of breakfast foods. They planned to give reports on foods they had studied: Ways We Use Milk; The Importance of Protein; Why We Need Outdoor Play; What Animals Need in Order to Survive; Care of Pets; Cooking Can Be Fun. They planned to sing songs they had learned and to dramatize the story *The Perfect Pancake*.[11]

On Thursday they made final plans for Friday's breakfast and rehearsed their program. A group of children who had shown little interest in the unit asked to make a mural of pictures of good food. This was to be on display for the parents with the names of the children on the mural.

On Friday the children were ready to serve the breakfast to the mothers, a few minutes after school started. When the breakfast was finished the children gave the reports they had planned, read experience charts including the one about Karen's guinea pigs, sang songs, and showed the mural they had made. The program ended with the dramatization of *The Perfect Pancake*.

An evaluation of the unit showed that the children retained their interest in eating a balanced breakfast; they were more careful to

[11] Virginia Kahl, *The Perfect Pancake* (New York: Charles Scribner's Sons, 1960).

wash their hands before and after eating; they brushed their teeth more often; and eleven spent longer hours in bed than before the unit began. That the interest in eating breakfast and balanced meals continued for weeks after the unit ended was observed at home by the parents and at school by the teachers.

Science and social studies can be combined in an integrated approach using aerospace education. The idea of earth in space is no longer a novelty. It is basic to our knowledge about day and night and the seasons to understand the rotation of the earth about its axis and its revolution through space around the sun. As man experiments with thrusts into space he is learning many new things, things that explain conditions on the earth, such as weather and temperature.

Children are interested in the sun, moon, and stars. In the integration of science and social studies this natural interest can be drawn upon. Even kindergartners are eager to learn about airplanes, jets, and other aircraft. Trips to the airport are common in connection with a science-social studies program. As the children move into the intermediate grades they often study a unit of world geography that develops the idea of the world as a sphere. Here they learn about travel routes, continents and oceans, and climatic zones. They learn, too, about airline routes, rocket flights, satellite orbits, and other developments in space.

In geography they study the relationship between man and his environment. They learn about life in desert, tropical, temperate, mountainous, island, arctic, and other environments. Aviation can tie these studies together and become the integrating thread to give a clearer concept of time and space and their interrelations. As children study the United States, the other American countries, and the Eastern Hemisphere, aviation again can become the thread that makes their learning experiences more meaningful.

In an integrated science-social studies curriculum in the elementary school there are innumerable opportunities for developing aerospace understanding. International understanding can also be strengthened through aerospace education. Airplanes, television, and social studies-science experiences help children learn about people and places of the world and the role of aerospace developments in the lives of the people. This theme is an effective avenue for integrating science with social studies.

*The Science-Centered Approach, in Sixth Grade.* A unit on the atom began one morning when the teacher walked into the classroom with an armful of books on atomic energy. The children immediately began looking at the books, and the puzzled expressions and concentrated attention indicated a real interest in the topic. A group of the students soon asked permission to go to the library to get additional materials.

Among the questions which were to be answered during the unit were the following: What are atoms? What are they made of? What characteristics do the parts have? How many kinds exist? What holds atoms together? How is atomic energy produced? How are radioisotopes produced? What is a Geiger counter? What is radioactivity? How do scientists split the atom? Where are atomic energy plants located? What was President Roosevelt's connection with atomic energy? What is the cost of developing an atomic bomb? How is nuclear energy controlled? How can atomic energy be used constructively? What is an isotope? What makes electrons whirl around the center of the atom?

In order to facilitate the study of the atom the children were divided into committees on the basis of interest and skills required for a particular phase of the unit. The children discussed the responsibilities of various committees, which were to work in the following areas: (1) research background on atomic energy, (2) vocabulary needed for understanding the literature, (3) production of atomic energy, (4) uses of atomic energy, (5) problems in controlling atomic energy at home and abroad, (6) display, including bulletin board displays, models and drawings of atoms and their behavior, a map showing the sites of plants, testing grounds, and laboratories engaged in atomic energy projects.

The activities which followed included reading to find out, group discussion, research, interview, demonstration, experiments, and evaluation. Children read books, pamphlets, newspapers, and reports to solve problems. They collected and organized data and prepared reports to present to the committees and later to the class. They discussed their findings not only in committees but in the period in which the groups met together as a committee of the whole.

The children were fortunate to obtain the services of a physics professor from a nearby college, who helped answer the questions to which they had been unable to find answers. Thus they used another technique — the *interview*. The highlight of the unit as far as the children were concerned was the *demonstration* of the Geiger counter by one of the members of the community. There were also *simple experiments* which the children carried out to demonstrate chain reaction. They arranged dominoes upright in a triangular fashion and when the domino at the tip of the triangle was knocked over, the next dominoes in the row fell. They in turn knocked over the dominoes in the next row, and so on until there were no dominoes left standing.

### What They Learned

1. Everything in the world is made up of tiny moving particles called molecules.

2. A significant discovery of modern times is that molecules are made up of smaller particles called atoms.

3. Although there are millions of different kinds of molecules, there are only about 100 different kinds of atoms.

4. Every different kind of atom is called an element.

5. Everything in the world is made up of one or more of these elements.

6. The atom is very small.

7. The atom has many parts — the nucleus, the neutron, the electron.

8. The energy of the atom may be released by splitting the nucleus.

9. In a chain reaction, a neutron is fired at a nucleus, a part of the matter becomes energy, other elements are formed, and excess neutrons are emitted. They bombard other atoms and this action in turn forms more neutrons and frees more energy.

10. Nuclear energy can be controlled in a nuclear reactor, where the speed of liberating energy is slower than in an atomic blast.

11. Radioactivity is the emission of rays or particles from such elements as uranium and radium.

12. The Geiger counter is an instrument which detects the presence of radioactive material.

13. Radioactive materials are dangerous, and precautions must be taken by those who come in contact with them.

14. The discovery of nuclear energy carries with it a responsibility for using it for the best interests of mankind. The Atomic Energy Act is the result of pressure for federal control of atomic energy.

In addition to the specific knowledge gained, the frequent sum-marization and evaluation of experiences was most rewarding. Chil-dren continued an intense interest in this unit and were eager to learn more about the possibilities for participation in such a monumental enterprise. Questions of job preparation, academic requirements, etc., were numerous.

*Comparison of the Three Approaches.* The examples illustrating the three approaches to science teaching reveal a wide variety of practices. In the incidental approach science is not taught as an integral part of the program. In the integrated approach it is taught only as it is needed to solve problems in the unit and if there is time. In view of experience charts, art experiences, excursions, movies, exhibits, etc., there is too often little time for science. In the science-centered approach science is an integral part of the curriculum. It is developed in harmony with a well-coordinated plan from kinder-garten through the elementary school. Science here is given a speci-fic time and place in the curriculum, and children are encouraged to delve deeply into it. Teaching science is so important in this modern age that incidental teaching, or the integration of science with social science, is inadequate.

## Science Materials and Equipment

The lack of proper teaching equipment is a common handicap. "The teachers who are able and do wish to try some science should not have to rely on string, empty milk cartons, and sealing wax as their only equipment for teaching science," cautions Blough.[12] Adequate instructional materials include equipment, community resources, free and inexpensive materials, and basic and supple-mentary books.

*Equipment and Community Resources.* The type of equipment purchased frequently depends upon the budget of the school, the storage space available, and the cooperation of the teachers and principal in organizing a materials center from which the needed

[12] Glenn O. Blough, quoted in "Hit 'N Miss Science Programs Ruinous," *Indiana Teacher,* 103:299, March 1959.

materials can be secured. Many teachers avail themselves of science kits which are especially prepared for elementary science use. These may be used cooperatively by several teachers and moved from room to room in case there is no science laboratory or special science teacher.

Where there is a science teacher, a balanced supply of materials to be used for teaching specific subject units should be selected cooperatively by the science teacher and administration. The elementary school teacher should inquire at the local high school or a nearby college for names of firms which supply scientific materials. Most firms publish a catalogue which the school may secure.

An inventory of available material is essential to the success of a science program. The material and apparatus should, in general, be simple and relatively inexpensive. Homemade and improvised equipment, however, is no adequate foundation upon which to build a science program. Too often teachers feel that *all* equipment should be of the five-and-ten-cent-store variety. Makeshift materials can be used in a science program, but they are usually inferior. Schools should take the responsibility for providing adequate materials and equipment, as well as trained teachers, if they would have a science program worthy of the name.

In order for science to be more than a reading course, then, considerably more money must be provided than has been traditional in too many schools. The administration will need to decide with the help of the teaching staff how and in what quantities equipment and materials will be purchased. However, schools still struggling with the problem of adequately financing a science program will profit from Blough and Huggett's list of materials available from local sources (home, store, ten-cent store, etc.). Some items will be used and returned; others will become a part of the permanent material of the science room.[13]

I. *Living things*
    An aquarium (stocked with fish, snails, water plants, etc.)
    A terrarium (stocked with growing plants, etc., a suitable place to keep a small turtle, a frog, a salamander or small snake)
    Larvae of different kinds

[13] Glenn O. Blough and Albert J. Huggett, *Elementary School Science and How to Teach It* (New York: The Dryden Press, 1951), pp. 62, 63.

Cocoons and chrysalids
Seeds (bean, corn, etc.)
Growing plants (geranium, ivy, begonia, bulbs, cactus, etc.)
An ant observation house

II. *Glassware*

Fruit jars
Milk bottles
Glass tumblers
Small mirrors
Flower pots (various sizes)
Lamp chimneys

Cups and saucers
Piece of window glass which may be cut into small pieces
Mechanical toys illustrating machine principles

III. *Miscellaneous*

Safety matches
Scissors
Teaspoons and tablespoons
Rubber bands
Tin cups
Ball of string
Scraps of different kinds of metal (zinc, aluminum, copper, etc.)
Worn-out dry cell
Electric appliances out of repair (extension cords, hot pad, etc.) for examination
Burned-out light bulbs
Burned-out fuses of various kinds
Candles of various lengths
Sand, clay, loam, humus
Globe and map of the world
Medicine dropper
Hot plate
Needles
Tack puller

Pans of various sizes and shapes
Scraps of different kinds of cloth
Paring knife and table knife
Colored chalk
Blotters
Litmus paper
Balls
Wire — steel and copper
Flashlight
Tongs
Egg beater
Cellophane
Rubber balloons
Pet cages
Yardstick
Chalk boxes
Nutcracker
Broken thermometer (to be examined)
Musical instruments of various kinds
Gummed labels

IV. *Construction materials*

Nails, tacks, screws
Paints and varnishes
Hammer, pliers, file, screwdriver
Glue and paste

V. *Chemicals*

Soda

Starch

Table salt

Lime for limewater

Red ink

Vinegar

Iodine

Dyes

Ammonia

Sugar

Parrafin

VI. *Collections*

Seeds and fruits

Leaves

Shells and other sea life

Local rocks, minerals, fossils

Birds' nests (autumn)

Science pictures of various
  kinds

Insects

The teacher and children may add to this list as their interest in science grows and new materials are needed and become available.

"Community resources" includes far more than assembling items and objects to use for performing experiments and discussion purposes. Every community is unique and must be thoughtfully surveyed by the school and teachers for the resources it offers. A committee of teachers may organize and keep up to date a card file which lists all such resources, including pertinent information: (1) name and address; (2) brief statement of the occupation, business, or institution; (3) specific things to see; (4) person to contact, telephone number; (5) best time to visit — time of year and time of day; (6) number of children easily accommodated; (7) grade level most suitable; (8) transportation — type and time needed; (9) safety factors en route and at destination; (10) time required for excursion; (11) advance preparation; (12) special problems — crowding, noise, odors, etc. In utilizing community resources, careful planning must precede the experience, considerate behavior must accompany it, and critical evaluation must follow.

*Basic and Supplementary Textbooks.* Finding answers to questions takes children not only to the laboratory and out of doors but to books — textbooks, supplementary books, and encyclopedias. There are now hundreds of science books for children. Selecting textbooks for an elementary science program has been a problem, but now most science textbooks are organized both with the developmental level of the pupil in mind and with the objective of providing an expanding view of the physical environment. Some of them are based on units or topics, each of which lists concepts to be developed, experiments to be performed, things to talk about, things to do, and things to find out. Children need supplementary material that encourages them to explore science in depth.

## Trends in Teaching Science

Trends in the teaching of science in the elementary schools are becoming fairly well established. Some of these are as follows:

1. *A movement away* from an emphasis on the "verification" of basic principles of science *and toward* an emphasis on the inductive development of a functional understanding of the principles of science through problem-solving performed by pupils under the guidance of the teacher.
2. *A trend away from* using interesting and practical technologies as the central core of sciences *and toward* the use of these technologies as illustrations and applications of principles of science in everyday living.
3. *A movement away from* teacher demonstration *and toward* pupil experimentation and problem-solving.
4. *A trend away from* simple manipulations directed by detailed instructions and occupying a single class period *and toward* pupil-teacher planned experiments, the performance of which may require several days or weeks and for which apparatus must be left in position for the duration of the experiment.
5. *A trend away from* the requirement that all pupils in a science class perform the same experiments in the same period *and toward* the practice of using a variety of experiments and projects performed at the same time by individuals and small groups.
6. *A trend away from* instruction in basic science only for college-bound pupils *and toward* instruction to develop an understanding of basic science principles, concepts, and methods as a component of education for all pupils in an age dominated by science.
7. *Increased use* of science clubs, science fairs, and other supplementary activities to challenge and encourage the talented in science, and to provide opportunities for all interested students to perform experiments and carry on projects which cannot be done effectively during regular class time.

8. *Increased use* of closed-circuit and broadcast TV in science teaching, especially in connection with motivational and supplementary activities; and *increased emphasis* on planning facilities for the effective use of this medium by pupils and teachers and on designing different types of mock-ups and demonstration equipment for use on-camera and in follow-up learning situations.

9. *A trend toward* flexibility in design and construction of science facilities to permit change in room size and in the location of work surfaces, storage spaces, and teaching aids.

10. *Increased use* of audio-visual aids by small groups of pupils or even by individuals engaged in special projects rather than by entire classes at the same time.

11. *A trend toward* the extension of the science curriculum by the introduction of new units. . . .

12. *A trend toward* the homogeneous grouping of pupils particularly for the basic courses, including science, so that the talented students will be encouraged to progress at their own speed. The teachers assigned to the advanced groups are usually those who have a good background in a broad range of science subject matter and can stimulate pupils to perform experiments and projects not feasible in classes which represent a wide range of abilities. . . .[14]

## *Evaluation*

What are the children learning? What progress are they making in scientific method and problem solving? Are they gaining a better understanding of the physical environment? Are they applying what they learn in science? Are we achieving our objectives? These are typical questions teachers ask. In order to answer them evaluation must be conceived of as an integral part of teaching. It must be considered from the standpoint of objectives set up by the school. Such objectives normally include knowledge of content or subject matter, development of constructive attitudes, growth in problem

[14] W. Edgar Martin, "Facilities, Equipment, and Instructional Materials for the Science Program," in Nelson B. Henry (ed.), *Rethinking Science Education*, Fifty-Ninth Yearbook of the National Society for the Study of Education, Part I (Chicago: University of Chicago Press, 1960), pp. 229–231.

solving, and awareness of the role of scientific principles in everyday living.

Evaluation may be carried on in a variety of ways. The teacher may observe behavior changes, interests, growth in problem solving, and application of scientific principles. He can check the extent to which children apply their new-found knowledge to new situations. For example, if he wished to make sure that the children had understood the concept about air he might ask, "Does air have weight? How do you know that air has weight?" By motivating children to apply their knowledge the teacher not only stimulates interest in science but evaluates learning.

Pupil behavior is also evaluated on the basis of a change in attitude. A kindergarten group had a unit on nutrition. Previously several of the children would not drink their milk because they didn't like the taste of it. After the unit they drank their milk. A group of fifth-graders were motivated to visit the dentist periodically and to brush their teeth regularly after a unit on the importance of care of the teeth.

Judging the ability to use problem-solving techniques effectively is somewhat more difficult. However, teachers who understand problem solving can appraise the ability to define problems, to make careful observations, to keep accurate records, to collect, sift, and evaluate data, and to present oral or written reports to the class.

Teacher-made tests are also useful in testing concepts, skills, attitudes. Objective or essay tests will reveal content knowledge. Multiple-choice, true-false, or completion tests are quick and easy to use. The student should not be limited to this type of test, however. He should have opportunity to express his ideas in an essay test, which necessitates organizing the material and expressing it in a clear and logical manner. Unfortunately teachers often feel the essay test requires too much time to grade, and in consequence many students enter junior and senior high school without experience in expressing ideas.

Standardized tests, too, have their place in evaluation. These should be selected, administered, and evaluated with care. Among the most helpful resources for the teacher on the topic of published tests is *The Fourth Mental Measurements Yearbook*.[15]

[15] O. K. Buros (ed.), *The Fourth Mental Measurements Yearbook* (Highland Park, N.J.: Gryphon Press, 1953).

A useful summary of methods of evaluation most frequently used by teachers of science includes (1) periodic written objective tests; (2) periodic essay tests; (3) oral and written reports of observations, readings, and experiments; (4) standardized tests on specific science knowledge; (5) analysis of pupil's notebooks, drawings, reports, collections, etc.; (6) problem-solving tests to determine ability to use problem-solving techniques; (7) periodic checks on ability to think critically in defining and attacking problems; (8) observational records of pupil behavior in science activities; (9) interviews with parents to determine the child's interest in science; (10) analysis of interest in science objects, specimens, science books, science radio and television programs, science fairs, and pictures on the bulletin board; (11) use of self-evaluation check lists for the pupil; and (12) progress graphs kept by the pupil of activities in science.

Effective methods of evaluating teaching are themselves good learning processes and help individuals to become better teachers. Evaluation should always lead to improvement. With the check list that follows, the individual teacher can appraise his own effectiveness in teaching and working with a particular group of children. The school staff concerned with evaluation of the total science program can use it as a basis for discussion.

*Teacher's Check List in Elementary Science*[16]

Purpose:  To measure the effectiveness of school practices and procedures in teaching science in the elementary school.

I. In my teaching is there opportunity or provision for children to:

|  | None | Some | Much |
|---|---|---|---|
| ( a) Raise questions and problems of importance or interest to them? | ............ | ............ | ............ |
| ( b) Study these questions and problems? | ............ | ............ | ............ |
| ( c) Help plan "things to do" in studying science problems? | ............ | ............ | ............ |

[16] "Evaluating Teaching Practices in Elementary Science," *Education Briefs* (Washington, D.C.: U.S. Department of Health, Education and Welfare. Division of State and Local School Systems. Instruction, Organization and Services, No. 21, July 1959), pp. 3, 4.

(d) State clearly the problems on which they are working? ............ ............ ............

(e) Make hypotheses to be tested? ............ ............ ............

(f) Gather accurate data (information) in a variety of ways:

Through reading on the subject? ............ ............ ............

" taking field trips? ............ ............ ............

" watching demonstrations? ............ ............ ............

" doing experiments? ............ ............ ............

" talking to resource persons? ............ ............ ............

(g) Analyze the data (information) to see how it relates to the problem? ............ ............ ............

(h) Think about the applications of their science learnings to everyday living? ............ ............ ............

(i) Think about science relationships and processes instead of merely naming things and learning isolated facts? ............ ............ ............

(j) Bring science materials of different kinds to school for observation and study? ............ ............ ............

(k) Engage in individual science interests? ............ ............ ............

II. In my teaching do I periodically and systematically check on the children's growth in:

|  | None | Some | Much |
|---|---|---|---|
| (a) Ability to locate and define problems right around them? | ............ | ............ | ............ |
| (b) Acquiring information on the problem being studied? | ............ | ............ | ............ |
| (c) Ability to observe more accurately? | ............ | ............ | ............ |
| (d) Ability to make reports on or record their observations? | ............ | ............ | ............ |
| (e) Ability to solve problems? | ............ | ............ | ............ |
| (f) Ability to think critically? | ............ | ............ | ............ |
| (g) Ability to explain natural phenomena? | ............ | ............ | ............ |

( h) Ability to distinguish between
facts and fancies?          ............    .............    .............
( i) Suspending judgment until evi-
dence is collected?          ............    .............    .............
( j) Being open-minded, or willing
to change belief?          ............    .............    .............
( k) Cooperating with others?          ............    .............    .............
( l) Understanding the cause and ef-
fect relationships of events?          ............    .............    .............
(m) Skill in using some common
scientific instruments (ther-
mometers, scales, rulers, etc.)?          ............    .............    .............

Let each teacher note the warning and recommendation of Gilbert White: "In our earnest concern to prepare young people to live in an increasingly complex world we are in danger of trying to teach them so many facts about the world as it was last year that we will teach them little of the ways of thinking about the world that is becoming. The challenges that lie ahead in the changing dimensions of the world community are in fitting people to think about the immense diversity of that spatially contracting community and to recognize the sobering inequality of conditions that continue in our united efforts to advance the welfare of its two-and-a-half billion members."[17]

## *Conclusion*

It is essential for survival in our modern age that everyone become literate in science. Not only the gifted, the scientific-minded child, but every child in the elementary school should study science. He should be provided with the opportunity to explore and interpret the physical environment, to develop skills in problem solving, to acquire a scientific attitude toward life, and to gain a greater appreciation of the forces and wonders of nature.

Children are naturally curious and interested in their physical surroundings. However, they are not always encouraged to develop this interest. They need teachers who are secure about teaching

[17] Gilbert F. White, "The Changing Dimensions of the World Community," paper given before the Conference on the American High School, October 30, 1957, quoted in "Science and Education," *Bulletin of the Atomic Scientist,* 14:384, November 1958.

science. Many teachers are ill at ease in teaching science because they feel their background in subject matter is inadequate, and often it is. Schools are trying to improve the science program by beginning with the key figure — the teacher. In the final analysis it is the teacher who will make the difference between a good science program and a poor one. To improve their knowledge of science, teachers can take in-service courses in science, get help from science consultants or college personnel who work with teachers on the job, take television or off-campus courses, try to get pre-service experience in science, and participate in workshops where they identify problems, talk over problems, get oriented to teaching science, and study solutions to problems. In order to be successful, in-service programs should deal with concerns of teachers, worth-while subject matter, specific objectives formulated by the group, and science concepts. They should emphasize experiments and utilize observations, field trips, and community resources.

Science teaching will be improved if teachers develop their own background of knowledge of the content and method of science; if they are imbued with a spirit of inquiry and a positive attitude toward teaching science; if they have adequate materials of instruction including equipment, books, visual aids, and community resources; if they have administrators who are interested in helping them grow through workshops, science consultants, in-service and on- and off-campus classes. They need every possible opportunity to plan cooperatively with the staff, to evaluate continuously, and to become more skilled in teaching.

Children should have teachers who know the scope and sequence of science experiences and who are familiar with basic concepts, activities and procedures, and with evaluation techniques. They need teachers who believe that growth in the teaching of science as in every other phase of development is the result of readiness to discover, willingness to accept, and enthusiasm to utilize new knowledge, skills, qualities, and traits and weave them into a design for improved living.

## ACTIVITIES AND QUESTIONS

1. Examine several curriculum guides for the teaching of science. Evaluate them in terms of objectives, activities, methods of teaching, and evaluation techniques.

2. What concepts would you try to develop with a group of fourth-graders who wished to study the solar system? List the activities you would use in helping them develop these concepts.

3. Discuss the ways in which children learn science. Observe in an elementary classroom to see which of these methods are being used.

4. Compare the three approaches to science teaching cited in your text. Observe in primary and intermediate classrooms and try to determine which approach is being used, and how effectively.

5. Plan a science lesson in which you demonstrate either the incidental approach, the integrated approach, or the science-centered approach to teaching science.

6. Excursions are suggested as an excellent method of teaching science. How would you make plans for taking a fifth-grade group to a television station? List the responsibilities of the children and the teacher in preparing for the trip.

7. Arrange a role-playing situation in which you are introducing a unit on magnets to the third grade and wish to make use of the discussion technique, but you discover that the children have had no experience in this method.

8. Suggest ways of sharing information about some topic of science that will challenge the pupil to organize and present his data carefully, creatively, and accurately.

9. Devise a two-part test for an intermediate grade — Part 1 an objective test containing ten items, Part 2 an essay question based on the unit reading. Plan the test to determine the pupil's ability to draw conclusions and to apply the knowledge he has learned.

10. Examine three textbook series at the grade level you expect to teach. Evaluate the organization of the content.

## BIBLIOGRAPHY

Artley, Charles K. *Science Experiences for Elementary Schools.* Practical Suggestions for Teaching Series. New York: Bureau of Publications, Teachers College, Columbia University, 1958.

Asimov, Isaac. "Worlds in Space," *American Junior Red Cross News*, 40:14–17, January 1959.

Black, Max. *Critical Thinking*. Englewood Cliffs, N.J.: Prentice-Hall, Inc., 1952.

Blough, Glenn (ed.). *It's Time for Better Elementary School Science*. Report of an Association Conference, National Science Teachers Association. Washington, D.C.: National Education Association, 1958.

Blough, Glenn O., and Campbell, Marjorie H. *Making and Using Classroom Science Materials in the Elementary Schools*. New York: The Dryden Press, 1954.

Blough, Glenn O., Schwartz, Julius, and Huggett, Albert J. *Elementary School Science and How to Teach It*. New York: The Dryden Press, rev. ed., 1958.

Brandwein, Paul F., *et al. Teaching High School Science: A Book of Methods*. New York: Harcourt, Brace and Company, 1958.

Brown, Lewis, *et al. A.V. Instruction*. New York: McGraw-Hill Book Company, 1959.

Burnett, Raymond Will. *Teaching Science in the Elementary School*. New York: Rinehart and Company, 1957.

Cheronis, Nicholas D., Parsons, James B., and Ronneberg, Conrad E. *The Study of the Physical World*. Boston: Houghton Mifflin Company, 3rd ed., 1958.

Craig, Gerald S. *Science for the Elementary School Teacher*. Boston: Ginn and Company, 2nd ed., 1958.

Daniels, Farrington, and Duffie, John A. (eds.). *Solar Energy Research*. Madison: University of Wisconsin Press, 1955.

Daubenmire, R. F. *Plants and Environment*. New York: John Wiley and Sons, 2nd ed., 1959.

Davis, Adelle. *Let's Have Healthy Children*. New York: Harcourt, Brace and Company, 1959.

Deason, Hilary J., Barrett, Nancy C., and Fisher, Stephen W. *The Traveling Elementary School Science Library*. Washington, D.C.: American Association for the Advancement of Science and The National Science Foundation, 1959.

Denno, Hildegarde Hartig. "Science Fair," *The Instructor*, 67:71–73, June 1958.

Department of Classroom Teachers, Educational Research Association of the National Education Association. *What Research Says to the Teacher — Science in Elementary Schools*. Washington, D.C.: The Association, 1957.

Division of Curriculum and Instruction, Department of Education. *Teaching Science, A Guide to the Problem Approach*. Trenton, N.J.: Department of Education, 1957.

Dunfee, Maxine, and Greenlee, Julian. *Elementary Science: Research, Theory and Practice.* Washington, D.C.: Association for Supervision and Curriculum Development, National Education Association, 1957.

"Education for the Age of Science," Report of the Panel on Science and Engineering Education of the President's Science Advisory Committee. Washington, D.C.: Government Printing Office, 1959.

Fermi, Laura. *Atoms in the Family.* Chicago: University of Chicago Press, 1954.

Fermi, Laura. *Atoms for the World.* Conference on the Peaceful Uses of Atomic Energy. Chicago: University of Chicago Press, 1957.

Gaddum, Leonard W., and Knowles, Harold L. *Our Physical Environment.* Boston: Houghton Mifflin Company, 1953.

Greenlee, Julian. *Better Teaching Through Elementary Science.* Dubuque, Iowa: William C. Brown Company, 1954.

Greenlee, Julian. *Teaching Science to Children.* Dubuque, Iowa: William C. Brown Company, 1955.

Greenlee, Julian. "We Learn How to Move Things," *The Grade Teacher,* 76:16, 63–64, May 1959.

Haag, Jessie Helen. *School Health Program.* New York: Henry Holt and Company, 1958.

Hubler, Clark. *Working with Children in Science.* Boston: Houghton Mifflin Company, 1957.

Loebsack, Theo. *Our Atmosphere.* Translated from the German by E. L. and D. Rewald. New York: Pantheon Books, Inc., 1959.

Mallinson, George G., and Mallinson, J. V. B. (comps.). *A Bibliography of Reference Books for Elementary Science.* Washington, D.C.: National Science Teachers Association, a department of the National Education Association, rev. ed., 1958.

Marcus, Abraham and Rebecca B. *Power Unlimited.* Englewood Cliffs, N.J.: Prentice-Hall, Inc., 1959.

Munson, Howard R. "Toward a New School Science Program," *Elementary School Journal,* 59:22–36, October 1958.

Munzer, Martha E., and Brandwein, Paul. *Teaching Science Through Conservation.* New York: McGraw-Hill Book Company, 1960.

National Society for the Study of Education. *Rethinking Science Education.* Fifty-Ninth Yearbook, Part I, Nelson B. Henry (ed.). Chicago: University of Chicago Press, 1960.

Nelson, Leslie W. *Instructional Aids: How to Make and Use Them.* Dubuque, Iowa: William C. Brown Company, 1958.

Nelson, Leslie W., and Lorbeer, George C. *Science Activities for Elementary Children.* Dubuque, Iowa: William C. Brown Company, 1952.

Rockcastle, Verne R. "Simple Electric Circuits," *The Instructor,* 68:32–33, February 1959.

Rockcastle, Verne R. "Spring Wildflowers," *The Instructor*, 68:18–20, May 1959.

Romer, Alfred S. *The Vertebrate Story*. Chicago: University of Chicago Press, 1959.

Smith, Russell. *Teaching a Unit on Astronomy, Grades 1–9*. New York: Vantage Press, 1958.

"Some Signposts of a Good Science Program." Bulletin No. 2, State Department of Education of Louisiana, prepared by Howard Pierce McCollum and the Advisory Committee on Science, 1958.

Thomas, William L., Jr., *et al. Man's Role in Changing the Face of the Earth*. Chicago: University of Chicago Press, 1956.

Winch, Ralph P. *Electricity and Magnetism*. Englewood Cliffs, N.J.: Prentice-Hall, Inc., 1955.

Zim, Herbert S. *Science for Children and Teachers*. Bulletin No. 91, Association for Childhood Education International. Washington, D.C.: The Association, 1953.

# 9

. . . As man starts reflecting upon himself and his behavior toward others, he gradually realizes that all men are his brothers and neighbors. Slowly he reaches a point where he sees the circle of his responsibilities enlarged to comprise all human beings with whom he comes in contact.

ALBERT SCHWEITZER

# Broadening social relationships

The increasing importance of science should not minimize the importance of human relationships. Broadening our understandings, extending our knowledge, and improving our skills in living with others are as essential as is a knowledge of science.

The child's first experiences in social learnings are in the home. It is frequently in preschool or kindergarten that he is initiated into the broader social world. Experiences are planned specifically to stimulate his curiosity, to widen his interests, to expand his environment, and to increase his desire to learn more about his world. The teacher is there to guide him as he begins to understand the society in which he lives and the responsibilities and privileges which are his in that society. As he progresses through the elementary school he expands his knowledge of the world — its people, its geography, and its history.

## Definition of Social Studies

Social studies is concerned with man and his relationships, with man and his environment. It draws from many fields of knowledge — geography, anthropology, sociology, history, economics, political science, ethics, and allied fields.

Social studies in the early years emphasizes the individual and his relationships in his immediate environment. However, social studies consists of more than experiences in social living. The two terms have been used interchangeably in some quarters, but they are not synonymous. When interpreted in this manner social studies is equated with the social education which takes place whenever a child is in a social situation. It does not refer to a specific area of the curriculum which is a regularly scheduled phase of the daily program and has both content and process. The content involves a study of people, their activities, achievements, interrelationships, and institutions. The process involves an understanding and practice of group dynamics.

## Role of Social Studies in the Elementary School

The purpose of social studies is to help the child understand the society in which he lives, develop the skills and attitudes essential to effective citizenship, and apply this knowledge in daily living. Children do not acquire these concepts, skills, and attitudes in a vacuum.

They learn democratic procedures through experiencing them. They learn to accept responsibility for individual and group action through planned activities. They learn to appreciate the values of a democracy through studying these values and their effects on nations.

The primary objective of social studies is the development of good citizens. A good citizen exhibits certain behavior:

1. He understands the importance of meeting both his own basic needs and those of others.
2. He understands and accepts democratic principles and ideals.
3. He practices human relationships consistent with a democratic society.
4 He recognizes and assists in solving social problems.
5. He assumes responsibility for acquiring and using the knowledge, skills, and abilities which will make him a better citizen.

## Good Citizenship Demands Competencies

### UNDERSTANDINGS

An understanding of the world is essential to intelligent consideration and solution of social problems. Progress toward such understanding must begin early in life. Young children can profit from study of content beyond that of their immediate environment. Social studies in the primary grades should examine social institutions and human relationships to a far greater extent than they now do.

### ATTITUDES

The development of wholesome attitudes toward other people is one of the most important objectives of the social studies. The good citizen respects authority, property, opinions, rights, and contributions of others. He also respects himself.

### SKILLS

The third group of competencies includes skills in social living and group processes, problem solving, and handling the tools of the social studies.

*Social Living.* Group living requires the ability to work and play together, to give and take, to assume responsibility, to respect the rights of others, to take turns, and to develop self-discipline and self-direction. It requires a growing sensitivity to others. But social living is only one phase of the social studies program; it is not the be-all and end-all of the program.

*Problem Solving.* Problem solving involves the following steps: (1) definition of the problem; (2) proposal of possible solutions by members of the class and consideration of them by the group; (3) testing of proposals by known facts, data collected, observation, or experimentation (if needed, new facts are gathered); (4) drawing of conclusions on the basis of the evidence. The problem-solving method skillfully used is one of the most effective classroom techniques.

*Handling the Tools of Social Studies.* Social studies requires general, specific, and creative skills. General skills include gathering and collecting data, interviewing, giving oral and written reports, using reference materials, outlining, summarizing, and evaluating. Specific skills include reading and interpreting social studies textbooks and supplementary materials (maps, charts, graphs, tables, globes), and use of special references such as an atlas, *World Almanac*, encyclopedias, and others. The creative skills include sketching maps and diagrams, carrying on surveys, making murals, and dramatizing incidents.

## Organizing the Social Studies Curriculum

There is considerable agreement on the major objectives of instruction in the social studies. However, the problem of selecting and organizing learning experiences which will help realize the objectives continues to concern teachers. They want to find some framework for organizing the social studies in a way that provides comprehensiveness, depth, and balance.

The predominant patterns of curriculum organization in the

social studies reported by Fraser[1] are fusion and integration. Hodgson[2] surveyed 148 city school systems to determine current organizations and found (1) integration, (2) fusion, (3) correlation, and (4) separate subjects, in that order, to be most common.

A social studies program of breadth, comprehensiveness, variety, and balance should be organized around some important theme or problem. Teachers often need help in setting up a problem in the social studies. In examining the following organizing centers one should keep in mind the possibilities of involving a group of children in identifying and defining a problem, organizing subproblems and subtopics to be explored, and having groups assume responsibility for solving the various phases of the problem. The teacher must find ways of working effectively with different groups while at the same time helping each child develop his own initiative, ability, and creativity as the unit moves ahead. Methods for organizing the learning experiences may focus on major themes, socioeconomic problems, the cultural heritage, and human and physical geography. Each of these will be examined.

*Major Themes.* Here the scope of the social studies is defined in terms of social studies concepts and generalizations as the child progresses from kindergarten through elementary school. The following generalizations may be used as the source of many learning experiences:

1. Our community is a desirable place to live.
2. Man adapts to his environment.
3. Peoples of the world are interdependent.
4. Families are made up of members who help one another.
5. People are basically very much alike. They differ in their mode of living because of geographical and historical factors.
6. Man lives in a continually changing world.
7. Man influences his environment; he, in turn, is influenced by it.
8. Our present civilization is the result of the contributions of many peoples.

[1] Dorothy M. Fraser, "The Organization of the Elementary School Social Studies Curriculum," in Nelson B. Henry (ed.), *Social Studies in the Elementary School*, Fifty-Sixth Yearbook, National Society for the Study of Education, Part II (Chicago: University of Chicago Press, 1957), pp. 129–162.

[2] Frank M. Hodgson, "Classification for Social Studies Organization," *Social Studies*, 47:258–260, November 1956.

9. Community workers in our neighborhood help one another.
10. Man uses the resources in his environment to satisfy his basic needs.

Identifying key concepts and generalizations is an essential first step. The staff must plan the experiences that will be developed at each grade level in harmony with the increasing maturity of the children.

An example of this approach is based on the report of the National Council for the Social Studies proposing "twelve general themes which are phrased as goals or values, but each of which implies concepts and content."[3] A complete analysis of each theme should suggest content for a program on a graduated scale of difficulty as the children advance. A summary of the themes follows:

Theme  1. The reciprocal adjustment of man and nature.
Theme  2. The adaptation of individual and group ideas to an interdependent world.
Theme  3. The recognition of the dignity and worth of the individual.
Theme  4. The use of intelligence to improve human living.
Theme  5. The intelligent acceptance of individual responsibility for personal and general welfare.
Theme  6. Increasing the effectiveness of the family as a basic social institution.
Theme  7. Intelligent and responsible sharing of power in order to attain justice.
Theme  8. The wise allocation of scarce resources in order to bring about the widest material security.
Theme  9. Achievement of adequate horizons of loyalty.
Theme 10. Cooperation in the interest of peace and welfare.
Theme 11. Achieving a balance between social stability and social change.
Theme 12. Widening and deepening the ability to live more richly.[4]

*Socioeconomic Problems.* From time immemorial, socioeconomic problems have been common to all ages and all peoples. Basic to solving these problems are the following activities:

[3] Kenneth J. Rehage, "Educational News and Editorial Comment: On Rethinking the Social-Studies Program," *Elementary School Journal*, 57:12, October 1956.
[4] Adapted from *ibid.*, pp. 10–14.

Obtaining food, shelter, clothing.
Living together as families, tribes, nations.
Protecting life, health and property.
Transporting people and commodities.
Communicating with individuals and groups.
Exchanging services and goods.
Establishing education.
Creating techniques and tools.
Providing recreation.
Expressing æsthetic and religious influences.
Conserving human and natural resources.

In every culture people carry on such activities under varying environmental conditions. Therefore it is imperative that the child explore these activities in the social studies curriculum in order to understand his own society and the society of others.

The socioeconomic problems selected at any level will vary with groups and for individuals within the groups. The responsibility of the teacher is to select those that are of greatest concern to the group and to the individuals in the group.

The children share in the selection and development of the learning experiences. If problems that are persistent and of real importance are chosen, they will provide a unifying factor and give direction, purpose, and continuity to the social studies curriculum.

In a survey made of children's needs, interests, concerns, questions, and problems, the findings were organized into twelve major problem areas, as follows:

Themselves.
Their families.
Their friends and age-mates.
Their school.
Their health, safety, leisure-time activities, and recreation.
Their moral and spiritual values.
Their communities.
Their country.
Other peoples of the world.
Their cultural heritage.
The economic system; money values.
Communication, transportation, travel.[5]

[5] "Elementary Social Studies," a preliminary report (Tallahassee: Florida State Department of Education, 1958), p. 59.

Children need the wisdom of the teacher to help them reach beyond immediate problems. These socioeconomic problems are continuing threads throughout the life of the individual, recurring again and again in his everyday concerns.

### Key Concepts in Understanding Socioeconomic Problems

1. New discoveries in medicine have lengthened the life span of individuals, thus changing the structure of our society.

2. The way man faces his socioeconomic problems is dependent upon conditions in the society in which he lives. Earning a living is becoming more difficult for the unskilled individual.

3. Our energy sources are shifting from man power to atomic power, thus creating a technological and social revolution.

4. The rapid increase in automation in industry is changing the pattern of employment.

5. Mechanization has increased the size of farms and decreased the number of farmers.

6. Technology, transportation, communication, and education help man gain control over his environment.

7. Transportation changes involving the airplane and the automobile decrease distance.

8. People are constantly moving; east to west, north to south, from the country to the city, to the suburbs, and back to the city again.

9. Mass communication and centralized ownership, while greatly increasing an individual's contact with the world, may also increase the uniformity of thought.

10. Increased leisure time carries with it responsibility for using it wisely.

11. Leadership in human affairs requires the capacity to use technology as a powerful instrument for enhancing the quality of our society and for contributing to the solution of the great human problems of our day.

*The Cultural Heritage.* "A nation needs not only a common language; it needs even more, a common past; and a sense of that past."[6] Without a knowledge of the way in which our country developed, of the beginnings of present institutions and values, many of our understandings of life remain vague, many of our questions remain unanswered. We need to help children understand the

[6] Henry Steele Commager, "Noah Webster: Schoolmaster to America," *Saturday Review,* 41:66, October 18, 1958.

present by letting them relive the past in history and literature and recreate it in music, art, and drama; it is thus they discover the greatness of our heritage, the values our civilization affords. They can understand that change and progress are a part of a rising civilization, and that present conditions are the result of previous action. They can discover, too, that lessons are to be learned from history if they are wise enough to learn them. From a better understanding of the past will come a greater appreciation of the present.

If such outcomes are possible through the study of the past, why are they not more often realized? In some classes this phase of study consists largely in memorizing dates and naming military campaigns; the procedure followed is for the most part that of the formal recitation. The study of a period of history should embrace an understanding of its people, customs, dress, language, art, literature, music, education, institutions, and science. It can be one of the most rewarding sources of social studies content.

### Key Concepts in Understanding the Cultural Heritage

1. Present-day civilization is built upon the contributions of past civilizations.

2. Men have lived in groups since early history.

3. Differences between our ways of living and those in pioneer days are the result of changes in meeting the basic needs of life.

4. The cultural development of the nation has contributed to the enjoyment of leisure time today.

5. Various national groups who have settled in our community have contributed to the life and culture of our community.

6. Transportation and communication services in the communities, states, nations, and regions of the world have influenced the growth and development of our civilization.

7. The celebration or observance of special days or holidays emphasizes some contributions of the past which are worthy of note.

8. Famous men and women of other nations have contributed to the development of our country.

9. Traditions, ancestral ties, religious beliefs, and attitudes affect family life and in turn life in the community.

10. Many present-day problems, such as trade problems, immigration, language barriers, have their origin in Old World conflicts and struggles.

11. Man has always struggled to solve his problems of living.

12. The foundations of democracy in our country were established by our forefathers from many lands.

*Human and Physical Geography.* More important than ever before in our history are understandings about geography. Americans are traveling abroad by the thousands. Those who remain at home have increased contacts with people of other countries. In the elementary school geography is receiving stronger emphasis as children learn about man's relation to his environment in various regions of the world. Geographical understandings about their state and nation can be applied to similar entities in distant lands.

As children learn about the peoples of the world they can relate geography to current happenings. For example, when a group of foreign dignitaries visits our country children are motivated to develop units, area studies, or depth studies of a particular country.[7]

The problem selected for study may be geographical or sociologically oriented. In determining sequence the principle of the near to the remote — from the family to the neighborhood, the community, the state, the nation, the region, the world — is usually followed. Content may also be selected in terms of geographical areas. Through the study of contemporary regions and cultures, for example, children learn to understand the contributions other peoples make. They become acquainted with groups both at home and abroad. They learn about their customs, tastes, tools, traditions; about their habits, institutions, and inheritance; about their music, art, literature, and recreation; about their attitudes and values; they learn, too, many times, to speak their language. And they learn about the influences that make them what they are. Such a study should draw upon the social sciences and the natural sciences, focusing on the relationship of man to his environment, the culture of the group, and the effect of climate on culture. In order to understand another it is necessary to have walked in his shoes. A good way of "walking in the shoes" of a person from another culture is to learn all one can about it. Resource people from other lands are usually happy to share knowledge and exchange ideas with children in the classroom.

The community is a miniature world. Many are better prepared

[7] J. D. McCauley, "Current Affairs and the Social Studies," *Social Education,* 23:21–22, January 1959.

to understand the wider world if they compare it with the community of which they are a part. Thus they can grasp the concept that as the institutions of the community are interdependent, so are the countries of the world; as the community population is varied, so is that of the world. Local communities have problems that must be solved; so do world communities.

*Key Concepts in Understanding Human and Physical Geography*

1. Man's natural physical environment helps shape the character of his economic and social life.
2. The physical make-up of the earth, distribution of land and water, weather and climate, distribution of natural resources, and so forth, make some areas more desirable for living than others.
3. The major ways of living, such as farming, manufacturing, hunting, herding, and fishing, are dependent upon differing types of resources and environment. Areas rich in resources are sought after on a competitive basis.
4. A high level of technological development makes for greater diversity in the use of natural resources.
5. Ways of using an area may vary according to changing conditions, technological developments, depletion of natural resources, and so forth. For example, the growth of the aircraft industry and the development of such projects as the atomic energy plants, irrigation projects, TVA, and others have brought changes in man's utilization of the areas involved.
6. Man is dependent upon productive soil and adequate water supply.
7. The wasteful use of natural and human resources — soil, forests, water, gas, oil, iron, other minerals, labor — must be curbed in order to meet the needs of the growing world population.
8. Modern methods of transportation as well as cordial relationships among the nations of the world affect the use of the world's resources and the distribution of its commodities.
9. Geographical factors have influenced to a marked degree the movement of people and their decision to settle permanently in a given place.

DETERMINING SEQUENCE

Sequence refers to when and in what order learning experiences will be provided. Among the factors that should be considered are the experiential background and interests of children, the nature of the content, and the organization of the material.

*Experiential Background.* Children are constantly increasing their knowledge of the world. Certain concepts which were formerly of little concern loom large on the horizon as the children move from stage to stage. People once considered remote in time and place become important. Studies reveal that children are interested, not only in the immediate environment, but also in other cultures, pioneer life, the origin of man, ancient peoples, and a wide range of other topics.

In a recent classroom project a teacher undertook the task of learning the geographical concepts held by her twenty-four second-graders. What she learned should not be surprising. The children's environment had been extended far beyond the immediate locality. These children were acquainted with some twenty cities, twenty-one states, and twenty nations or continents. They were not always clear on ideas of location, how the people lived, or what the climate was like. In fact, they were least interested in climate. They acquired most of their information about cities and states through travel with parents. The information about other lands was largely gained through television. Other sources included friends, relatives, books, and magazines. A realistic view of children in today's world should take into consideration their need for going beyond the sequence of the "expanding community."

Huck[8] studied the information possessed by 115 suburban children in the first grade in regard to certain areas of social studies. She found that direct experience was their most frequent and accurate source of data, and television was the next most frequent but not the next most accurate. She reported that children were actively learning from their culture and urged teachers to utilize all the knowledge children bring when they enter school. She reported that today's environment for children includes much of the adult world and goes beyond the home, neighborhood, and community.

*Nature of the Content.* Another consideration in determining sequence is the nature of the content. A principle that may be followed is that of letting the difficulty of the concept be the determining factor rather than the topic itself. Abstract concepts such as

[8] Charlotte Huck, "Children Learn from Their Culture," *Educational Leadership*, 13:171–175, December 1955.

democracy, justice, and virtue are hard for young children to understand. Concepts about people and places are much easier. For example, a primary child studies the policeman as a community helper. An intermediate child studies the policeman as a law enforcement agent.

Curriculum guides or courses of study frequently prescribe the content to be studied in broad areas for each educational level, and cite some major expected outcomes. Both the content and the outcomes are generally determined by committees who represent the school system as a whole, and are harmonious with the principles of child growth and effective teaching and learning. Such committees take into consideration the over-all planning, the maturation and experiential background of the children, the interest, mental-age level, usefulness, and difficulty of the content to be studied.

Within the broad areas selected for the educational level, the teacher is free to analyze the needs of the children and the possibilities for meeting them. He is free to guide the children through experiences designed to help each one individually and the group collectively achieve the greatest personal and group growth. Within the framework of the social studies program he attempts to achieve the objectives defined for knowledge of geography, history, economics, sociology, and other content areas, as well as the desired skills and attitudes.

*Organization of Content.* In social studies it is necessary for children not only to learn specific skills but also to integrate their new knowledge with what they have previously learned as they progress in their experiences. This means that the teacher must organize the content so that each new concept builds on the concepts that have gone before in a balanced sequence.

## Achieving Balance in the Program

In a balanced curriculum the learning experiences are not all drawn from a single content source. Major themes, socioeconomic problems, the cultural heritage, and human and physical geography should all be included in the sources tapped during the year. To help the teacher achieve balance in the curriculum the chart on page 432 will be a useful guide.

| Content Source | K. | Grade 1 | Grade 2 | Grade 3 | Grade 4 | Grade 5 | Grade 6 |
|---|---|---|---|---|---|---|---|
| 1. MAJOR THEME | | | | | | | |
| 2. SOCIOECONOMIC PROBLEMS | | | | | | | |
| 3. THE CULTURAL HERITAGE | | | | | | | |
| 4. HUMAN AND PHYSICAL GEOGRAPHY | | | | | | | |

*Topics selected for study should be inserted in the blanks. The topics listed below are only examples. The teacher will select topics in terms of the social studies curriculum needs of a particular group of children.*

### MAJOR THEMES

1. Our community as a desirable place to live.
2. Man adapts to his environment.
3. Peoples of the world are interdependent.
4. Families are made up of members who help one another.
5. People are basically much alike. They differ in their mode of living because of geographical and historical factors.
6. Man lives in a continually changing world.
7. Man influences his environment; he, in turn, is influenced by it.
8. Our present civilization is the result of the contributions of many peoples.
9. Workers in our community help one another.
10. Man uses the resources in his environment to satisfy his basic needs.

### THE CULTURAL HERITAGE

1. Holidays and special days.
2. American Indians.
3. Early explorers.
4. Life of the pioneers.
5. Westward movement.
6. The ancients.
7. Medieval life.
8. Community heritage.
9. The development of governments.

### SOCIOECONOMIC PROBLEMS

1. Obtaining food, shelter, clothing.
2. Living together as families, tribes, nations.
3. Protecting life, health, property.
4. Transporting people, commodities.
5. Communicating with individuals, groups.
6. Exchanging services, goods.
7. Establishing education.
8. Creating techniques, tools.
9. Providing recreation.
10. Expressing aesthetic and religious impulses.
11. Conserving human and natural resources.

### HUMAN AND PHYSICAL GEOGRAPHY

1. Life in the local community.
2. Survey of community resources.
3. Community planning.
4. Comparison of types of communities.
5. The homeland.
6. Minority culture.
7. Majority culture.
8. Neighboring countries.
9. Remote countries.
10. Isolated regions.
11. Contemporary societies.
12. International boundaries.

Many social studies programs fail to achieve balance. In kindergarten and the primary grades content is often selected almost exclusively from the categories of socioeconomic problems and processes in the community. In the intermediate grades content is drawn largely from the categories of the cultural heritage and human and physical geography. Primary children, however, are also interested in these topics, and intermediate children are vitally interested in socioeconomic problems and major themes. The teacher should attempt to draw upon many content sources.

*Need for Flexibility.* One of the problems of the classroom teacher is the question of how to achieve a framework for organization that allows enough flexibility to insure successful learning. Only through careful planning will a balance be achieved in content and in the development of skills. Only careful planning on the part of the staff will assure continuity of experiences throughout the elementary school. Only by consistent attention to the findings of research and to strengthening his own knowledge will the teacher be able to create a climate in which children learn effectively.

The design for the social studies curriculum should be clearly understood; the waymarks should be evident; the processes should be outlined. However, flexibility is essential in order to meet the specific needs of the group, to challenge each child within the group, and to let the teacher make the most of his own talent in teaching creatively. Organizing the program in such a way that concepts, skills, and values are interwoven requires knowledge of children, curriculum, social studies content, and group processes.

One of the most useful ways of organizing learning experiences is the unit. How understandings, concepts, social values and study skills are combined to provide continuity, balance, and integration of learning will be seen in the following units that are organized around major themes, socioeconomic problems, the cultural heritage, and human and physical geography.

UNITS OF WORK

*Major Theme: The Reciprocal Adjustment of Man and Nature.* Children need to understand the concept of the reciprocal adjustment of man and nature. First-hand experiences provide one of the finest ways for gaining this understanding. Through a study of farm animals a group of children living in a rural area can strengthen their understandings, increase their knowledge, and gain a greater appreciation of the contributions of their own society. It would be equally rewarding for a group of urban children to study the contributions of manufacturing in their society.

### Farm Animals[9]

This unit grew out of the children's interest in young animals arriving on the farm in the spring. The children were in the first and second grades.

A. Introductory Statement

Man can live better, have better food, more kinds of clothing, with the help of farm animals. In turn, he provides food and shelter for these animals.

B. Objectives: To teach the children that

1. Man is dependent upon animals for food and clothing.
2. Animals depend on man for food, water, and care.

C. Concepts and Understandings

1. To teach the child the correct terminology relating to farm animals and farm activities.
2. To learn the products of farm animals — meat (pork, mutton, beef, veal), milk, cream, butter, cottage cheese, cheese, eggs, and leather.
3. To learn the meaning of such terms as *wool, hair,* and *bristles.*
4. To learn the kinds of food that farm animals require.

D. Skills

1. To share ideas through discussions.
2. To build a vocabulary with which to express thoughts and feelings more effectively.
3. To express ideas creatively through art, dramatic play, music, and rhythm.
4. To develop keen observation, scientific attitudes, and problem-solving techniques.

E. Activities

1. View film.
2. Take a bus trip to a farm.
3. Set up a miniature farm in the classroom.
4. Draw, model, and paint farm animals.
5. Make charts with information about different animals.

[9] Nell Walker, Mt. Vernon, Ind., Metropolitan School System, 1959.

6. Sing songs about animals.
7. Learn poems about animals.
8. Listen to stories about animals.
9. Read and dramatize stories about farm animals.
F. Evaluation

Evaluation involves continuous appraisal as the unit develops. Numerous opportunities for improving skills of communication, group cooperation, and critical thinking present themselves. It provides outcomes that will contribute to larger and continuing educational goals.

G. Culminating Activities
1. Dramatize *Mr. and Mrs. MacDonald's Farm*.
a. The farmer feeds the animals proper foods.
b. The animals make appropriate sounds and movements.
2. Riddles about farm animals.

### REFERENCES FOR THE UNIT

*Books*

Beaty, Betty. *Thumps — Story of a Pig*. New York: The Macmillan Company, 1949.

Beem, Francis. *Three Little Pigs*. Eau Claire, Wis.: E. M. Hale Company, 1949.

Dennis, Wesley. *Flip — A Young Colt*. New York: The Macmillan Company, 1941.

*Grandfather's Farm Panorama*. New York: Platt and Funk Company, 1958.

Lewellen, John. *A True Story of the Farm*. Boston: Houghton Mifflin Company, 1953.

Martin, Dahris. *Little Lamb*. Eau Claire, Wis.: E. M. Hale Company, 1953.

Petersham, Maud and Miska. *The Box with Red Wheels*. Boston: Houghton Mifflin Company, 1955.

*Poems*

*Read Me Another Story*. New York: Thomas Y. Crowell Company, 1949.
"The Cow," by Robert Louis Stevenson
*About Farm Animals*

*Mother Goose*. Eau Claire, Wis.: E. M. Hale Company, 1935.
"Little Bo Peep"
"Little Boy Blue"

*Films and Filmstrips*

*How Animals Help Us* — Coronet Films

*Wool from Sheep to Clothing* — Encyclopaedia Britannica Films
*Farmer's Animal Friends* — Jim Handy Filmstrip
Music and Song
   *The Kindergarten Book*. Boston: Ginn and Company, 1957.
   "Getting Up Song"
   "Mrs. Hen and Little Chick"

DAILY LOG

[This is a running account of how this unit was developed by primary children in a consolidated school.]

## The Cow

April 6
A. Showed film, *How Animals Help Us* — Coronet Film.
B. Set up a farmyard.
C. Plans were made for the next day
   1. to bring pictures of cows to class.
   2. to bring information for discussion about cows.
April 7
A. Discussions
   1. Various types of cows — milk cows, beef cows.
   2. Physical characteristics of cows — four feet, hairy coats, split hoofs.
B. Concepts
   1. Terms: *beef, bulls, heifers, steers, calves.*
   2. Value to man — milk, milk products, meat and leather, cowboy holsters, shoes, boots.
C. Activities
   1. Children imitate mother cow's call to baby calf and calf's call to mother.
   2. "The Cow" by Robert Louis Stevenson.
April 8
A. Activities
   1. The children dictated a story about the cow and calf to the teacher to write on a chart.
   2. Children selected pictures for the chart from those brought from home.
   3. Modeled cows from clay, drew and colored cows.
   4. Added some cows, beef cows, milk cows to the already erected farmyard.

## DEVELOPING SOCIAL UNDERSTANDINGS

The home provides the first experiences in social living. The school builds upon these learnings and introduces the child to a broader social world. New faces, new places, new experiences await him as he takes the first steps on the educational ladder. The school shares the task of teaching the social skills necessary for living together in a democratic society and understanding that society and its institutions. It also shares responsibility for developing understandings that will equip the child to live effectively in a world of broadened international relationships.

The curriculum is planned to develop a clearer concept of the kinship of man with man, and man and his environment, through a series of learning experiences that increase individual responsibility for behavior, broaden understandings, and extend social relationships. These experiences foster growth in social skills and increase the child's knowledge of the world — its people, geography, political science, economics, and history. In a well-rounded social studies program children become aware of relationships between the topography, institutions, and traditions of a country and the way its people live.

*Children interpret the roles of family members through dramatic play.*

*Accepting individual responsibility for the general welfare is a social principle that can be developed in school.*

*A visit to the telephone company provides an excellent opportunity to study communication.*

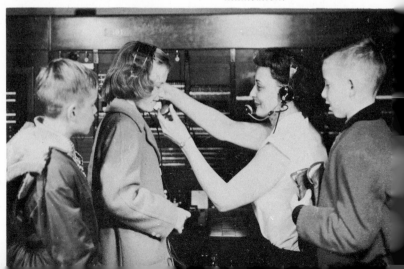

Children study the socioeconomic problems of obtaining foods and exchanging goods and services.

The study of physical and human geography leads to a better understanding of our own as well as other cultures and languages.

5. Plans were discussed for next day. Will study the sheep.
   a. Bring information and materials about sheep.
   b. Plans for trip in school bus to stock farm are started.

April 9

A. Activities
   1. A trip to a pasture to see sheep.
   2. Children played "Little Bo Peep," "Baa Baa Black Sheep."
   3. Sounds of sheep and lamb calls.

B. Concepts
   1. Ram, ewe, lamb, mutton.
   2. Sheep have wool, not hair.
   3. Value to man — meat and wool.

April 10

A. Activities
   1. Children dictated story about sheep.
   2. Selected pictures for story.
   3. Showed woolen articles of clothing.
   4. Listened to story *Little Lamb* by Dahris Martin.
   5. Plans were made for April 13, Monday.
      a. Children plan to gather materials and information about hogs.
   6. Plans for trip to Wayne's father's farm were completed.
      a. Will visit farm in Wayne's father's school bus.

April 13

A. Activities
   1. A trip to a stock farm.
   2. After coming back to school we looked at pictures of different colors and types of hogs.

B. Concepts
   1. Pork is meat of hogs — ribs, sausage, ham.
   2. Hamburgers are not made from ham.
   3. Hide of hog is covered with bristles.

C. Dramatize
   1. Sound of pigs.
   2. *Three Little Pigs.*

April 14

A. Activities
   1. Children dictated story of hogs for chart.
   2. Committee chose pictures for chart.
   3. Children modeled hogs in clay, painted and drew pictures of the farm and hogs.
   4. Children made labels for their models.

5. Listened to story *Thumps*.

6. Plans were made to study horses tomorrow.

April 15

A. Activities

    1. We went to the end of the school property, looked across the road to see a blooded riding horse with its new colt running in a pasture.

    2. On return children looked at pictures of draft horses that do farm work.

B. Concepts

    1. Terms: *stud, mare, colt, farm horse, riding horse.*

    2. Horses are of value to man.

    3. Horses help with farm work.

    4. Horses give pleasure to man.

    5. Leather coats are made from horse hides.

April 16

A. Activities

    1. Listened to story *Flip*.

    2. Children dictated story of mare and colt for chart.

    3. Children selected pictures for the chart.

    4. Added more horses to those in the farmyard.

    5. Modeled horses, painted and cut horses from cardboard.

    6. Plans were made for studying poultry tomorrow — ducks, chickens, turkeys.

April 17

A. Activities

    1. Imitated the noises fowls make.

    2. Modeled, drew, and colored different fowls.

    3. Dictated an experience chart.

    4. Selected best picture for the chart.

    5. Added many more fowls to those in the farmyard.

    6. Sang "Old MacDonald Had a Farm."

    7. Listened to "Mrs. Hen and Little Chick."

B. Concepts

    1. Duck, drake, hen, rooster, chick, gobbler.

    2. Contributions of fowls — eggs, meat, feathers.

    3. Terms: *fowls, poultry.*

    4. Fowls have two legs and are covered with feathers.

    5. Ducks and geese can swim because they have web feet.

    6. Tame fowls cannot fly as wild ones do.

    7. Indians made headdresses of turkey feathers.

C. Discussions
   1. How fowls differ from other animals.
   2. Characteristics of different types of fowls.
April 20   Culminating Activities
   Previously listed (page 435).

*Socioeconomic Problems: A Primary Unit.*   As the child increases his social learnings he acquires an understanding of the specialized interdependent world in which he lives. He learns not only about the people who contribute to his welfare, but he becomes aware of the socioeconomic problems that confront all people. He becomes aware of important factors of our technological age, such as the complexity of the processes involved in producing and distributing material goods and transporting people. He is eager to understand how people utilize natural resources in solving the problems related to transportation and recreation. How one group of children approached the problem of water transportation is illustrated in the following unit.

*How Does Man Use Water for Transportation and Recreation?*[10]

   Many families camp by rivers, lakes, and the ocean where they have opportunity to observe different kinds of boats; some parents have boats of their own for pleasure or fishing. One child told about crossing a river on a ferryboat. Another told about a new boat her father had just purchased. A little boy had seen boats locked through at the dam where his father worked. Another boy told about going to England on a boat. One child's father worked on a boat.
   I. Understandings and Generalizations
      A. Man solves the problem of transporting people and commodities.
      B. Man uses natural resources for recreation.
   II. Objectives
      A. To show the role transporation by boat has played in the development of our country.
      B. To show how boats have improved in size, power, construction, and safety devices.
      C. To show the children what a large variety of boats there are in use today.

[10] Anna Rudd, Henderson, Ky., Public Schools.

D. To interest primary children in boats and the important part they play, and have played, in our lives.

III. Initiation of the Unit

A. Take a trip to see a boat or ferry.

B. Place pictures of all types of boats on bulletin board.

IV. Knowledge

There are different types of boats for various purposes:

A. Barges

1. Have no engine.
2. Towed by small boats.
3. Carry heavy cargoes.
4. Captain and family may have living quarters on board.

B. Ferryboats

1. Usually are flat-bottomed boats.
2. Carry cars, freight, and people across rivers and lakes.
3. Can enter dock either bow or stern first.

C. Tugboats

1. Powerful for their size.
2. Tow heavy barges.
3. Push and pull boats in and out of harbors.

D. Police or patrol boats

1. Can travel thirty-five miles an hour.
2. Patrol the waters to see that traffic regulations are observed.

E. Freighters

1. Carry the heaviest cargoes.
2. Sometimes carry a limited number of passengers.

F. Passenger boats

1. Operate on the Great Lakes, large rivers, and the oceans.
2. Many have luxurious accommodations.
3. The largest carry several thousand people.

G. Tankers

1. Haul oil and gasoline.

H. Dredge boats

1. Pick up sand and gravel from the river bottom for commercial use.
2. Are used to deepen channels in rivers and harbors.

I. Motorboats

1. Outboard — motors at back of boat.
2. Cabin cruisers — larger, and have motors built inside.

J. Excursion boats

1. Make short trips.

        2. Make trips from city to city.

    K. Sailboats

        1. No motor — wind blows the boats.

        2. More difficult to operate.

    L. Rowboats and canoes

        1. Smaller in size.

        2. Use oars or paddles.

V. Vocabulary

    A. Bow — front of boat.

    B. Stern — back of boat.

    C. Hold — inside where goods are stored.

    D. Helm — steering apparatus.

    E. Rudder — blade at back of boat by which boat is steered.

    F. Cabins — rooms in a boat for passengers.

    G. Bridge — elevated platform across deck of boat.

    H. Pilot — one who steers a boat.

    I. Buoys — floating objects to mark the channel or rocks.

    J. Harbors or docks — places where boats can anchor and tie up.

VI. Activities

    A. Formulate questions to be answered in the unit.

    B. Study pictures of different kinds of boats.

    C. Bring in models of boats.

    D. Invite a guest speaker to tell about his boat.

    E. Read books for information.

    F. Discuss what has been read.

    G. Listen to poems and stories about boats.

    H. View films of boats.

    I. Learn boat songs.

    J. Write letters asking permission to view boat anchored in harbor.

    K. Make many kinds of boats with modeling clay.

    L. Make charts of different kinds of boats.

    M. Find out the safety rules that apply to small craft and excursion boats.

VII. Culminating Activities

    A. Make a mural of boats.

    B. Dramatize a boat story.

VIII. Evaluation

    A. Questions.

    B. Reports.

    C. Summary.

IX. Materials
   A. Boat pictures.
   B. Books, stories, poems, and songs about boats.
   C. Modeling clay.
   D. Wallpaper for mural.
   E. Colored chalk.
   F. Poster board.
   G. Films, filmstrips, projectors, screen.

### BIBLIOGRAPHY

REFERENCE BOOKS FOR CHILDREN

Ardizone, Edward. *Little Tim and the Brave Sea Captain.* New York: Oxford University Press, 1955.

Crampton, Gertrude. *Scuffy the Tugboat.* New York: Simon and Schuster, Inc. Little Golden Books, n.d.

BOOKS FOR THE TEACHER

Bishop, C. H., and Wiese, Kurt. *The Ferryman.* New York: Coward-McCann, Inc., 1941.

Hutchinson, William M. *A Child's Book of Ships and Boats.* New York: Maxton Publishers, Inc., 1956.

Lent, Henry B. *Tugboat.* New York: The Macmillan Company, 1951.

Meadowcraft, Enid La Monte. *By Wagon and Flatboat.* Eau Claire, Wis.: E. M. Hale Company, 1938.

*Ships of All Times.* Racine, Wis.: Whitman Publishing Company, n.d.

Smith, Marie Elizabeth. *Ships Come and Go.* New York: Charles Scribner's Sons, 1954.

STORIES FOR CHILDREN

Clark, Florenz. "The Funniest Boat," *The Grade Teacher*, 72:58, May 1954.

Dalgliesh, Alice. *The Little Wooden Farmer.* New York: The Macmillan Company, 1930.

Flack, Marjorie. *The Story About Ping.* New York: The Viking Press, 1946.

Hawkes, Hester. "Policeman of the Sea," *The Instructor*, 44:90, November 1955.

Lenski, Lois. *The Little Sail Boat.* New York: Oxford University Press, 1937.

POEMS

Arbuthnot, May Hill. *Children and Books.* Chicago: Scott, Foresman and Company, 1957. Stevenson, Robert L., "Where Go the Boats." Tippett, James S., "Ferry Boats."

Johnson, Edna, *et al. Anthology of Children's Literature.* Boston: Houghton Mifflin Company, 1959, pp. 1027–1029.

SONGS

*American Singer No. 2.* New York: American Book Company, 1954. "A Boat Race." "My Sailboat." "Rowing."
*I Like the City.* New York: Silver Burdett Company, 1956. "The Little Tugboat."

FILMS

*A Boat Trip*
*Captain Brown — Harbor Pilot*
*Flatboatmen of the Frontier*

*Socioeconomic Problems: An Intermediate Unit.* The problem of communicating with individuals and groups is one of the most vital in our modern age. Learning to communicate effectively, understanding the responsibilities and privileges that go with membership in a democratic society, using the media of communication for recreational and educational purposes, and learning to distinguish the false from the true are among the more important needs of the elementary school child. Teaching the correct use of television can be a vital part of the intermediate program.

*How Does Television Affect Our Daily Living?*[11]

I. Generalizations
  A. Mass communication and its centralized ownership, while greatly increasing our individual contact with the world, may also increase uniformity of thinking.
  B. Leisure time is increasing and should be used wisely.
II. Concepts
  A. Television brings people closer together.
  B. Television, like all public utilities, is regulated by law.
  C. Many people work together to bring television to our homes.
  D. Television can raise the general educational level of the individual.
  E. The general public pays for television programs through buying the products advertised.
  F. Television should be viewed critically.
III. Initiatory Activities
  A. Class discusses televiewing habits, including favorite tele-

[11] Charlotte D. Gelhausen and Pauline Jegley, class project for Education 223E, Evansville College, Evansville, Ind., 1959.

vision programs, why they are liked, comments on commercials, and time spent televiewing.

B. Class writes favorite television programs of each child and reasons for choice on slips of paper. These are saved for later use.

C. Class views movie — *Time for Television*, sd., b and w, 17 min. (Shows how television monopolizes a boy's life, shutting out family, friends, schoolmates, and teacher. Finally, he realizes how much he is losing and works out his own way of letting television take its place as a natural and interesting part of his daily existence.)

D. Class develops criteria for critical viewing of television. Following questions may be included in the discussion:
   1. How can television help us in our schoolwork?
   2. How can television help us in our home and social life?
   3. How can television help us understand our community and the world?
   4. How much time should be spent televiewing for pure enjoyment?

E. Class posts on the bulletin board criteria that are developed.

IV. Developmental Activities
   A. Assign two television programs a week to be viewed critically. Reports to be presented at various times during the unit.
   B. View film — *How Television Works*, sd., b and w, 10 min. (Explains the elementary principles of television, the workings of the television camera, vacuum tubes, the amplifying and receiving systems. Gives the complete cycle of transmission.)
   C. Discuss film.
   D. Interview resource person — perhaps promotion manager of local station.
   E. Question resource person.
   F. Do research in committees to find answers to the following problems:
      1. In what ways do sponsors, networks, and affiliated and independent stations work together?
      2. How does television work?
      3. What are the federal regulations governing television?
      4. What are the jobs of directors, producers, technicians, writers, and announcers?
      5. How do the local television stations arrange their programing in order to make a profit?

G. Invite a resource person to explain programing.

H. Questions and discussion.

I. Give committee reports to the class.

J. Evaluate the reports.

K. Formulate questions to be asked on visit to television station.

L. Visit a television station. Limit group to number required by the station. Call at least two weeks in advance to arrange tour.

M. Evaluate what has been learned from the trip.

N. Write letters of appreciation to the television station.

O. Write to sponsor of a television program expressing appreciation for an exceptionally good program or offering constructive criticism.

P. Make a second survey of favorite television programs and have the children give reasons for their choices.

V. Culminating Activities: "A Day at a Television Station"

A. Invite another class to be guests.

B. Have a panel discussion of the problem "Does television raise the general educational level?"

C. Arrange a quiz show about the things learned during the unit.

D. Write and direct an original play. Design scenery and costumes.

E. Plan a news broadcast about current events.

F. Show slides drawn by children explaining how television works.

G. Exhibit charts made from the two surveys showing changes (if any) in class's viewing habits and give reasons.

H. Explain how television stations cover the United States.

I. Make a chart showing essential parts of a television transmitting station.

VI. Evaluation

A. Evaluation is a continuous process all through the unit.

B. It is based on:

1. Changes in viewing habits.

2. Discussion and summaries of understandings gained through the unit.

3. Specific knowledge gained through the reports.

4. Ways children cooperate in committee work.

C. Write an essay in class on the subject "How Does Television Affect Your Daily Living?"

BIBLIOGRAPHY

Abbott, Waldo, and Rider, Richard L. *Handbook of Broadcasting.* New York: McGraw-Hill Book Company, 4th ed., 1957.

Barnhart, Lyle D. *Radio and Television Announcing.* New York: Prentice-Hall, Inc., 1953.

Barnouw, Erik. *Mass Communication: Television, Radio, Film and Press.* New York: Rinehart and Company, 1956.

Becker, Sam L. and Harshberger, H. Clay. *Television: Techniques of Planning and Performance.* New York: Henry Holt and Company, 1958.

Bretz, Rudy. *Techniques of Television Production.* New York: McGraw-Hill Book Company, 1953.

Busfield, Roger M. *The Playwright's Art: Stage, Radio, Television, and Motion Pictures.* New York: Harper & Brothers, 1958.

Chester, Giraud, and Garrison, Garner. *Television and Radio: An Introduction.* New York: Appleton-Century-Crofts, Inc., 1956.

Field, Stanley. *Television and Radio Writing.* Boston: Houghton Mifflin Company, 1958.

Hyde, Stuart W. *Television and Radio Announcing.* Boston: Houghton Mifflin Company, 1958.

O'Meara, Carroll. *Television Program Production.* New York: The Ronald Press Company, 1955.

Turnbull, Robert B. *Radio and Television Sound Effects.* New York: Rinehart and Company, 1951.

MAGAZINES

Dawson, Marvin. "Where Goest TV?" *Indiana Teacher,* 103:268–270, March 1959.

Frobisher, Mary W. "TV Survey," *Childhood Education,* 35:357–358, April 1959.

"Package Library Briefs," Indiana University, Bureau of Public Discussion, Bloomington, Ind., Vol. 15, No. 7, March 1959.

CHILDREN'S BOOKS

Bendick, Jeanne. *Electronics for Young People.* New York: McGraw-Hill Book Company, 1947.

Bendick, Jeanne and Bendick, Robert. *Television Works Like This.* New York: McGraw-Hill Book Company, 1949.

Blough, Glenn O. (ed.). *Young People's Book of Science.* New York: McGraw-Hill Book Company, 1958.

Gould, Jack. *All About Radio and Television.* New York: Random House, 1953.

Harrington, Ruth Lee. *Your Opportunities in Television.* New York: Medill-McBride Company, 1949.

Hutchinson, Thomas N. *Here Is Television.* New York: Hastings House, Publishers, 1950.

Kaufman, William I. (ed.). *How to Announce for Radio and TV.* New York: Hastings House, Publishers, 1956.

Lewellen, John. *Understanding Electronics.* New York: Thomas Y. Crowell Company, 1957.

Meyer, Jerome S. *Picture Book of Radio and Television and How They Work.* New York: Lothrop, Lee and Shepard Company, Inc., 1951.

Milne, Ruth. *TV Girl Friday.* Boston: Little, Brown and Company, 1957.

Morgan, Alfred. *The Boy's Second Book of Radio and Electronics.* New York: Charles Scribner's Sons, 1957.

Schmidt, Philip S. *Principles of Television — Part 3.* Scranton, Pa.: International Textbook Company, 1953.

Stoddard, Edward. *The First Book of Television.* New York: Franklin Watts, Inc., 1955.

*The Cultural Heritage: An Intermediate Unit.* An understanding of other cultures helps the child appreciate the contributions they make to the American culture. The Christmas season offers an excellent opportunity for the study of foreign customs and traditions. Other holidays are equally suitable for this type of unit.

### *Christmas Symbols in Other Countries*[12]

Basic Understandings
1. Basically people are much alike although they differ in their ways of living because of their cultural heritage.
2. Many people have contributed to our cultural heritage.
I. Objectives
   A. To learn the significance of Christmas symbols.
   B. To increase knowledge of Christmas at home and abroad.
   C. To develop good research habits.
   D. To participate in creative experiences in art, music, and literature.
   E. To cooperate in a group project.
II. Motivation
   A. View films.

[12] Thelma White, Crossville Public Schools, Crossville, Ill.

B. Draw pictures of each symbol.

C. Read stories about Christmas symbols.

D. Look at pictures of Christmas symbols.

III. Activities

A. Locate countries in which various Christmas symbols originated.

B. Learn customs of the people of each country.

C. Learn how the symbols originated and how they were used.

D. Discover the significance and origin of: Christmas tree, bell, holly, ivy, mistletoe, candle, Yule log, hearth, St. Nicholas, wooden shoes, torch, posada, piñata, crèche, wreath, sleigh, reindeer, stocking, and others.

E. Write a story about Christmas symbols.

F. Give reports on the origin of each symbol.

G. Write and illustrate stories and poems about the symbols.

H. Keep a vocabulary list of the symbols.

I. Learn songs and dances about Christmas symbols.

J. Compare dates on the times when the symbols appeared.

K. Arrange a bulletin board with pictures of the symbols.

L. Make a three-dimensional Christmas tree.

M. Make soap sculptures of Christmas symbols.

N. Listen to recordings of Christmas music.

O. Play Christmas songs on bells.

IV. Evaluation

A. What new knowledge have we gained?

B. What new skills in research, reading, writing, and speaking have we gained?

C. What understandings and appreciations about the past did we develop?

D. What progress in individual and group behavior has been made?

V. Culminating Activities

A. Dramatize a play written by the group using Christmas symbols as characters.

B. Invite the parents to the performance.

C. Serve refreshments typical of the Christmas season from the various countries studied.

VI. Instructional Material: films

*Christmas in Many Lands* — Encyclopaedia Britannica Films

*Christmas Through the Ages* — 14 min., color, EB Films

*Christmas in Sweden* — 14 min., color, Audio-Visual Instruction, Westport, Conn.

*Christmas Under the Sun* — 20 min., color, Audio-Visual Instruction, Westport, Conn.

## BIBLIOGRAPHY

BOOKS

Burglon, Nora. *Children of the Soil.* New York: Doubleday, Doran and Company, 1932.

Deucher, Sybil. *Boy of the Northland.* New York: E. P. Dutton and Company, 1946.

Dickhart, Audrey. *Holiday Observances in Social Education of Young Children.* Washington, D.C.: National Council for the Social Studies, 1956.

Gardner, Horace. *Let's Celebrate Christmas.* New York: A. S. Barnes and Company, 1950.

Hooper, Van E. *Christmas Around the World.* Milwaukee, Wis.: Ideal Publishing Company, n.d.

Rothery, Agnes. *Scandinavian Roundabout.* New York: Doubleday, Doran and Company, 1953.

MUSIC

*Songs Children Like: Folk Songs from Many Lands.* Washington, D.C.: Association for Childhood Education International, 1954.

Thompson, Carl, and Nordham, Harriet. *Keys to Teaching Elementary School Music.* Minneapolis: Paul Schmitt Music Company, 1949.

Tooze, R., and Krone, B. F. *Literature and Music for Social Studies.* Englewood Cliffs, N.J.: Prentice-Hall, Inc., 1955.

Wright, Frances. *Song Source Material for Social Studies Units.* New York: Columbia University Press, 1946.

RHYTHMS

Bauer, Lois M., and Reed, B. A. *Dance and Play Activities for the Elementary Grades.* Vols. I and II. New York: Chartwell House, 1951.

Burchenal, Elizabeth. *Folk Dance Source Material.* New York: G. Shirmer, 1947.

*Human and Physical Geography: A Kindergarten Unit.* In order to orient the child to his immediate community and to the larger world community, the school must provide experiences related to the geography of the area in which he lives and the geography of other parts of the world. Although the study of geography per se usually is not included in the curriculum of the kindergarten or primary child, a study of the zoo can provide a fine avenue for learning about his own community in relation to the broader world.

### A Community Study — Our Zoo[13]

I. Introductory Statement

    A visit to the zoo is a valuable firsthand experience as the child studies the community.

II. Basic Understandings

    A. Our community is a good place to live.

    B. Workers in our community help one another.

III. Objectives

    A. To appreciate our zoo and zoo workers.

    B. To understand the nature of the work of the zoo-keepers.

    C. To identify some common zoo animals.

    D. To create an interest in the natural habitat of these animals.

    E. To create an interest in the habits, needs, and care of these animals.

    F. To appreciate the resources of the community.

    G. To discover how people in the community can contribute to the upkeep of the zoo.

IV. Skills

    A. Planning and sharing.

    B. Listening.

    C. Questioning.

    D. Observing.

    E. Using globe.

V. Content

    A. Our zoo.

        1. Our zoo is composed of two main buildings and many outside buildings.

            a. Rails are put in front of cages to keep visitors at a safe distance from the animals.

            b. Some of the animals have two cages — one inside and one outside.

            c. There is one big house for some birds without bars or glass. The birds stay there because they like the light.

[13] Shirley Huber, Evansville Metropolitan School District, Evansville, Ind.

    d. Our zoo has a diet kitchen where animals' meals are prepared.

    e. Our zoo has a hospital room for sick animals.

  2. Our zoo gets animals in different ways.

    a. Some are bought from people who have hunters go to distant countries and catch animals.

    b. Some are exchanged with animals from other zoos.

    c. Some are gifts.

    d. Some are born at the zoo.

B. Our zoo workers.

  1. They take care of the animals.

  2. They keep the zoo clean.

  3. They study about animals so that they can give them good care.

C. Our zoo animals.

  1. The big cats are all dangerous. Babies are called cubs. The zoo-keeper feeds them by poking meat to them through the bars with an iron rod.

    a. The tiger comes from Asia and Malaya. He has stripes and whiskers.

    b. The leopard comes from Africa and Asia. He has spots and climbs trees.

    c. The lion comes from India and Africa. The male has a big mane. The female lion is called a lioness.

    d. The puma is found in the United States.

  2. Monkeys, chimpanzees, and baboons have long arms, and long toes which look like fingers. In their natural habitat they live in trees.

  3. The kangaroo family lives in one big cage. The kangaroos are harmless. A baby kangaroo is called a joey. Joeys are so small when they are born that they must live in their mother's pouches four months until they are bigger. Kangaroos come from Australia. They jump with their long strong back legs and eat vegetables and hay.

  4. Bears hibernate in the winter. Baby bears are called cubs. They can walk either on all four legs or on two.

    a. The polar bear is white and eats only meat. He comes from the far North.

    b. The brown bear eats meat, berries, and vegetables.

    c. The black bear eats only berries and vegetables.

5. The panda comes from Asia. Pandas eat bamboo shoots and move around a lot to get their exercise.
6. Anteaters come from tropical America. They have a long nose and tongue but no teeth. The dietician has to grind up their food.
7. The hippopotamus family stay in the water six or seven hours at a time. They come from Africa. They eat bread, hay, and grain.
8. The rhinoceros is huge and has horns growing on his head which he uses when he fights. He can't see well but has good hearing. He is very short tempered.
9. The elephant has a long trunk which he uses to pick up food which he puts into his mouth. He also sucks in water to put into his mouth to drink or to spray onto his back. A baby elephant is a calf. Calves cannot use their trunks until they are about six months old.
10. The snakes — a boa constrictor and a python — sleep most of the time. Their food is put into their cages alive.
11. Alligators and turtles live in water and on land. They are amphibians.

D. Concepts.

Wild, veterinarian, lioness, calf, cub, joey, stampede, lasso, trap, pit, jungle, cage, bar, hunter, amphibian, dietician, cable, rod, X-ray, skeleton, injections, hibernate, tame.

VI. Activities

A. Planning our zoo trip.
  1. Inviting our mothers to go.
  2. Listing safety rules.
B. Taking the trip to the zoo.
C. Interviewing keeper at each house and the one who visited our class.
D. Discussing zoo-keeper's duties.
E. Finding on the globe the animals' native lands.
F. Playing the game "Animal Charades."
G. Reading stories, books. (fiction and nonfiction)
H. Drawing and painting zoo animals.
I. Making a mural of meat-eating animals.
J. Modeling zoo animals with clay.
K. Making cages out of cheese boxes and straws.
L. Building cages with blocks.
M. Creating poems about the zoo.
N. Singing zoo and animal songs.

O. Listening to records such as "Carnival of the Animals" by Saint-Saens.

P. Creating rhythms typical of zoo animals.

Q. Viewing film strips and films.

VII. Materials

Clay, blocks, records, music, paper, crayons, paint, straws, cheese boxes, globe, pictures, film strips, and films.

VIII. Culminating Activity

A summary discussion and listing things we'd still like to learn about our zoo, zoo workers, and zoo animals. A discussion of the place of the zoo in the life of the community, how a zoo helps make our community a better place to live. The children should see how the zoo-keepers and the visitors have to work together to make the zoo a nice place to visit.

IX. Evaluation

A. Have the children's interest and knowledge of the zoo increased since the initiation of this unit?

B. Do they appreciate the contribution the zoo makes to the community?

C. Did the children behave in a safe and cooperative way during the trip to the zoo?

D. Did the children ask intelligent questions?

E. Are there still questions to be answered?

F. Are new words added to the vocabulary being used correctly?

## BIBLIOGRAPHY

Bauer, Margaret. *Animal Babies*. Chicago: M. A. Donohue and Company, 1949.

Benchley, Belle. *Shirley Visits the Zoo*. Boston: Little, Brown and Company, 1946.

Bridges, William. *Zoo Expeditions*. New York: William Morrow and Company, 1954.

Buck, Frank. *Jungle Animals*. New York: Random House, 1945.

Conway, Hattie. *The St. Louis Zoo Album*. St. Louis: Zoological Board of Control, Forest Park, 1953.

Heffernan, Helen. "Firsthand Experiences in Kindergarten," *The Grade Teacher*, 75:14, March 1958.

Jackson, Kathryn. *Tawny Scrawny Lion*. New York: Simon and Schuster, Inc., 1952.

Leyson, Capt. Burr. *The Zoo Comes to You*. New York: E. P. Dutton and Company, 1954.

Lindquist, Willis. *Animals from All Over the World*. New York: Simon and Schuster, Inc., 1956.

Logan, Lillian M. "The Zoo," *The Grade Teacher*, 73:18, May 1956.

Malter, Morton S. *Our Largest Animals*. Chicago: Albert Whitman and Company, 1958.

Perkins, Marlin. *Zoo Parade*. Chicago: Rand McNally and Company, 1951.

Pitts, Glenn W. *The Kindergarten Book*. Boston: Ginn and Company, 1949.

Semrad, Alberita. *The Zoo*. Chicago: Rand McNally and Company, 1951.

Williamson, Hamilton. *Baby Bear*. Garden City, N.Y.: Doubleday and Company, 1930.

Ylla. *Animal Babies*. New York: Harper & Brothers, 1959.

FILM STRIPS

"Arriving at the Zoo" — Classroom Films, Inc., 1949
"Mealtime at the Zoo" — Classroom Films, Inc., 1949
"Animal Health and Hygiene" — Classroom Films, Inc., 1949
"Animal Habits" — Classroom Films, Inc., 1949

SONGS

Pitts, Glenn W. *The Kindergarten Book*. Boston: Ginn and Company, 1949. "At the Zoo," p. 119; "Guess What We Saw at the Zoo," p. 119; "Lion," p. 120; "Monkey," p. 120; "Giraffe," p. 120; "Elephant," p. 121; "March," p. 121.

*Human and Physical Geography: An Intermediate Unit.* There are several reasons for studying Alaska. As the forty-ninth state to be welcomed into the United States, as an exciting place for colonization by pioneering Americans, and as a rugged country with snow-capped mountains, vast tundras, glaciers, peninsulas, and off-shore islands, it offers rich possibilities for a study of topography, geography, and the impact of civilization on a primitive culture.

*Regions and Cultures — Alaska*[14]

I. Introduction

Alaska in Aleut means "great land." It would cover one-fifth of the mainland of the United States. One of its glaciers alone is larger than all of Switzerland. Its vastness

[14] Wilma M. Bebout and Billie Ann Reyburn, prepared for Education 223E, Evansville College, Evansville, Ind.

is emphasized by its emptiness. Alaska is a land of extremes. The study of the Eskimo is valuable for the contrast it provides between the standard of living we enjoy and that of the people in the frozen lands of North America.

II. Basic Understandings
   A. Man's natural physical environment helps shape the character of his economic and social life.
   B. Geographical factors have influenced to a marked degree the movement of people and their decision to settle permantly in a given place.

III. Motivation
   A. Place on the bulletin board interesting pictures of life in Alaska.
   B. Use totem poles on display table.
   C. Use posters to arouse interest in Alaska.
   D. Listen for questions of children.
   E. Use the pupils' questions to further develop the unit.

IV. Problems
   A. Eskimos
      Why have the 16,000 Eskimos not kept in step with man's progress?
      a. They live far from the lands inhabited by most of the people.
      b. Their struggle to keep alive has been so hard that they have been unable to develop as fast as men in warmer countries.
      c. They lack many of the materials with which to build a civilization.
      2. Upon what do they depend for their food, clothing, and shelter?
      a. They depend upon reindeer, fish, caribou, bear, and sea animals.
      b. They also depend upon dog teams which draw laden sledges.
      c. They have tamed the reindeer and huskies to draw their loads.
      d. They use whale fat to light their houses and for food.
      e. Their food is preserved by hanging it to dry and freeze in the open air.
      f. Eskimos make their clothing from skins of animals.
      g. Most of them wear jackets, hoods, breeches, and long soft boots of fur.

    h. Women sew the garments with the sinews of the reindeer.

    i. An Eskimo man sometimes has more than one wife to do his sewing, cooking, and housekeeping for him.

3. How has the climate affected his mode of living?

    a. In winter some tribes build igloos of blocks of snow.

    b. They line their houses with skins of animals.

    c. They sleep upon piles of furs.

    d. They cook over an open hearth with very few vessels.

    e. They store their harpoons, bows, arrows, and spears in their huts.

    f. In summer they build their houses of stones and twigs.

4. How does the Eskimo make use of his resources and show that a community's wealth lies in developing its natural resources?

    a. There is very little wood and metal.

    b. Wood and metal are secured from white traders whenever possible.

    c. Most tools, weapons, and utensils are made from horn, bone, and skins.

5. What is the religion and culture of the Eskimos?

    a. The Eskimos believe in a spirit world.

    b. They believe that plenty and famine are caused by spirits that watch over the tribe.

    c. People may make the spirits angry by breaking some of the tribal tabus.

        (1) A tabu is a kind of unwritten law forbidding the people to do certain things.

        (2) When the spirits are angry they can be made friendly again if the person who has broken the tabu will confess and make peace with the spirits.

    d. The language of the Eskimos is very difficult, but very beautiful.

        (1) White traders have found the Eskimo language almost impossible to learn.

6. What form of government do the Eskimos have?

    a. The Eskimos have a loosely structured government.

    b. People in the tribe share their huts and their fishing trips with each other.

    c. People keep the things they make.

    d. A man lends his house to whoever wants it while he is away.

    e. There are no chiefs or councils of warriors and hunters.

    f. If a man displeases the tribe, the disapproval of the people is enough to drive him away. It is very difficult to survive alone.

    g. The life of the Eskimos is peaceful and happy.

B. Indians

  1. How do the 14,000 Indians differ in way of life from tribes of Eskimos?

    a. They live on the northern Pacific coast.

    b. They live in permanent homes and get their food chiefly by fishing and by gathering roots and berries.

    c. They are very good seamen.

    d. They are skilled in the fine arts and crafts.

  2. Although they differ in the characteristics of their civilization, what are some of the things they have in common with the Eskimos?

    a. They believe in a spirit world in which the animals play an important part.

    b. They make their tools, weapons, and utensils from stone, wood, clay, bone, and horn.

    c. They never learned to use the sailboat or wheel. They use the kayak.

    d. Like the Eskimo, they own property and land in common.

    e. They fight a great deal among themselves for good hunting grounds, and perhaps for religious reasons.

C. Aleuts

  1. Who are the 4,000 Aleuts?

    a. The Aleuts are a tribe closely related to the Eskimos inhabiting the north coast of the Alaska Peninsula.

    b. Their behavior is like that of the Russian peasant.

    c. They are a mixed race of Russian and Caucasian blood.

    d. They are few in number because of:

      (1) Inhuman treatment by the Russians.

      (2) European diseases.

    e. They are skilled in hunting, fishing, and basket-weaving.

D. New Alaskans
   1. Who are the new Alaskans and where are they from?
      a. Few white people were born in Alaska.
      b. Some came from Europe — particularly Norway, Sweden, and Finland.
      c. The rest came from the United States as seasonal workers during the gold rush, as missionaries, and as teachers.
E. How does the geography and topography affect the life of the people?
   1. The irregular shape of Alaska and the varied physical features of the great area make the territory one of great variety. Since Alaska is very large, its regions are different. As a result the country cannot easily be described as a whole.
      a. There are six main regions.
         (1) Panhandle.
            (a) Shape and location.
            (b) Beauty.
            (c) Capitol.
            (d) Mild and pleasant weather.
            (e) Gold mining and fishing are chief activities.
         (2) South Central Alaska.
            (a) Mt. McKinley.
            (b) Matanuska Valley (famous farming settlement).
            (c) Climate and activities similar to those in panhandle.
         (3) Alaskan Peninsula and the Aleutians.
            (a) "Valley of Ten Thousand Smokes."
            (b) One of the weather kitchens of North America.
            (c) Seals and Kodiak bear.
         (4) Interior Alaska.
            (a) Yukon River.
            (b) Sparse population compared to southeastern Alaska.
            (c) Good farms.
         (5) The Arctic.
            (a) Tundra.
            (b) Land of frozen earth, ice, and snow.
            (c) Sun is not seen for months at a time.

(6) Bering Sea region.
    (a) Seward Peninsula.
    (b) Salmon industry.

F. How does the Alaskan way of life affect the people?
  1. Natural resources.
    a. Mining and mineral resources.
    b. Forests and forest products.
    c. Farming in Alaska.
    d. Lumbering, trapping, and fishing.
  2. Recreation.
    a. Mt. McKinley National Park.
    b. Muldraw Glacier.
    c. Wild life.
    d. Fishing and camping.
    e. Snow skiing.
  3. Education.
    a. Compulsory school age 7–15.
    b. Missionary schools.
    c. One university and one junior college.
    d. Thirty-seven city and town libraries.

G. What contributions does the rest of the United States make to Alaska?
  1. Alaska is dependent on the other states for:
    a. Year-round jobs.
    b. Better transportation (Alaskan Highway).
    c. Tourist trade.
    d. Improved health and educational programs.

H. What contributions does Alaska make to the rest of the country?
  1. Natural resources.
    a. Lumber.
    b. Fish and fish products.
    c. Furs.
    d. Minerals.
    e. Strategic military bases.
    f. Weather observation stations.

V. Concepts
  Kayak, igloo, reindeer, dogs and animals, totem pole, Alaskan bears, tundra, Yukon River. These should be developed and used.

VI. Activities
  A. Locate Alaska on flat map and on globe.

B. Compare location of Alaska with other parts of the world (latitude and longitude).

C. Make a relief map (flour and salt).

D. Color relief map to highlight features and to show contrasts.

E. Make a flat map. Use pictures and specimens to highlight ideas portrayed on maps. Use ribbon or yarn running from the picture or specimen to its location on the map.

F. Use styrofoam to construct miniature igloo.

G. Dress small dolls in Eskimo clothing.

H. Construct an Eskimo summer home of twigs.

I. Construct a miniature dog sledge from cardboard.

J. Use modeling clay to make miniature reindeer and huskies.

K. Make a miniature kayak; use cardboard and cloth to represent wood and skin.

L. Build a scene showing the home life of the Eskimos.

M. Write stories about the Alaskan people.

N. Give oral reports.

| | |
|---|---|
| International Date Line. | Seal. |
| Mt. McKinley National Park | Kodiak bear. |
| Muldraw Glacier. | Caribou. |
| Alaskan Highway. | Walrus. |
| Raising herds of reindeer. | Aleuts. |
| Tundra. | Totem pole. |

O. Compare Eskimo life with that of our civilization.

P. Make a list of the things which your home has and the home of the native Alaskan lacks.

Q. View films on Alaska.

R. Sing songs about Alaska and Eskimos.

S. Discuss similarities of Eskimos to American Indians in regard to
  1. Physical characteristics.
  2. Mode of living.
  3. Activities.
  4. Contributions.

T. Make a scrapbook about Alaska.

VII. Culminating Activity

Invite the parents to visit the social studies class. Have each pupil present something about Alaska. Give reports. Explain how articles on exhibit were constructed. Contrast life in Alaska with that in the children's native state. Show maps, pictures, and scrapbooks which were made during the unit.

VIII. Materials
    A. Pantograph
    B. Poster paper
    C. Flour and salt
    D. Globe
    E. Tempera water paints
    F. Ribbon; pictures or specimens
    G. Styrofoam; knife
    H. Small dolls; fur
    I. Wrapping paper or wallpaper for mural
    J. Cardboard for sledge
    K. Modeling clay
    L. Cloth to represent skin for kayak
    M. Table approximately 30″ × 40″

IX. Evaluation
    A. Have the pupils learned
        1. About climate and scenery of Alaska?
        2. What comprises the Alaskan population?
    B. Have the pupils discovered
        1. How the Eskimo looks?
        2. How he dresses?
        3. How he lives?
        4. What his culture is?
    C. Have the pupils realized
        1. How hard the Eskimo has to struggle for a living?
        2. How simple his life must be for that reason?
        3. How the natural environment has affected his mode of life?
    D. Have the pupils gained an idea of
        1. The contrast between their standard of living and that of the Eskimo?
        2. The contributions of the missionaries to the Eskimo?

### BIBLIOGRAPHY

Altenbernst, T. A. "Alaska: A Radio Script," *Social Education*, 65:7, February 1956.

Baedeker, Karl. *The United States, with Excursions to Mexico, Cuba, Puerto Rico, and Alaska: A Handbook for Travellers.* New York: Charles Scribners Sons, 1899.

Coe, Douglas. *Road to Alaska.* New York: Julian Messner, Inc., 1943.

Corby, Merle Estes. *A Guide to Alaska, Last American Frontier.* New York: The Macmillan Company, 1939.

Dufresne, Frank. *Alaska's Animals and Fishes.* New York: A. S. Barnes and Company, 1946.

Gest, E. "Alaska's Music," *Music Journal,* 71:8, 9, March 1959.

Knoll, G. G. "We Teach on an Alaskan Island," *The Grade Teacher,* 73:41, January 1956.

Koenig, D. W. "World's Most Northern University," *Association of American Colleges Bulletin,* 43:419–421, October 1957.

"Saluting Our New States: Alaska and Hawaii," *The Instructor,* 69:45–51, September 1959.

Shockley, P. E. "Alaska Story," *NEA Journal,* 44:430, October 1955.

"The State of Alaska — One Year After," *U.S. News and World Report,* 47:67–70, July 13, 1959.

"Vast Alaska: Exciting Land of Contrasts," *Michigan Educational Journal,* 36:213, January 1959.

SONGS

"Alaska's Flag," *Voices of America.* Chicago: Follett Publishing Company, 1957.

"The Eskimo," *The American Singer.* New York: American Book Company, 1954.

"Eskimo Baby," *Singing and Rhyming.* Boston: Ginn and Company, 1950.

"The Little Eskimo," *New Music Horizons.* New York: Silver Burdett Company, 1944.

"There's a New Flag," *The Instructor,* 70:32, September 1960.

FILMS

Encyclopedia Britannica Films: "Alaska: A Modern Frontier," 1 reel, color; "Alaska: Reservoir of Resources," 1 reel, b and w; "Alaska's Silver Millions," 3 reels, b and w; "Eskimo Children" (filmstrip)

The foregoing units illustrate the wide variation of format and organization possible in a given unit of work. Each teacher develops the unit within a framework that fits his particular needs and is adapted to the curriculum organization of the school in which he teaches. Some are outlined in great detail; others are less detailed. The units also show evidence of the opportunities for integration of subject areas such as geography, history, economics, civics, science, language arts, and the fine arts. They indicate, too, the necessity for careful planning, wide reading, and diligent searching for information in order to secure an adequate background for teaching the unit. Sometimes the teacher must travel; in addition, he collects materials, surveys community resources, selects those appropriate for the activity, and contacts resource persons who might contribute to the development of the unit.

The teacher may set the stage for the unit by displaying pictures, maps, posters, realia,[15] and reading materials. Or he may use a bare-stage technique and let the children assume the responsibility for bringing materials to the class and exhibiting them. Children enjoy bringing materials related to the unit from home, the library, and other resources in the community.

The creative teacher finds new ways of organizing and developing stimulating learning experiences with children and the unit provides opportunity for wide pupil participation.

## *Characteristics of Effective Teaching-Learning Procedures*

Although there is no magic formula for teaching social studies effectively, certain characteristics are in evidence in a good program.

*Meaningful and Varied Experiences.* If the teacher knows the children, the content, the materials, and appropriate methods of teaching, he will utilize the children's natural interest in their social environment to broaden their social understandings and to help them expand their knowledge and increase their contacts with the world. Under skillful guidance they can develop such concepts as the interdependence of man and the adaptation of man to his society. Through dramatic play, community interests, excursions, and reading, their social relationships are expanded, their social skills increased.

*Favorable Conditions for Learning.* Whatever a child is learning — concepts, behavior, skills, or values — he will learn more efficiently if conditions are right.

1. Children should have a goal in learning social studies.

---

[15] The term *realia* means "real things." It refers here to objects, models, museum items, specimens, exhibits, etc.

2. Children should develop concepts through experiences.

3. Children should have a background for what they are studying.

4. Children should be provided with time and opportunity to practice, review, and apply what they learn.

5. Children should have teachers who stimulate their interest in social studies through providing a variety of methods for arousing and sustaining interest.

Great differences exist in the teaching of social studies. Among effective practices are the selection and definition of objectives, well-planned activities (trips, committee work, dramatics, and so forth), provision for evaluation, guidance in the development of study and research skills, and continuous self-evaluation.

*Varied Instructional Materials.* The teacher who is aware of the significance of his role in challenging children will make use of a variety of articles which interest children — pictures, objects, tools, art materials, musical instruments, maps, globes, etc. The volume of instructional materials is growing every day. In the endeavor to find unusual and unique teaching aids the teacher may overlook the most obvious — textbooks. More and better textbooks are available than ever before. Other sources of instructional materials include reference books, encyclopedias, atlases, almanacs; travel books, biographies, historical novels; pamphlets, periodicals, journals; charts, maps, globes. Audio-visual materials such as pictures, samples of products, models, film strips, and films are also useful in developing correct concepts about life. Children sometimes help in making the instructional materials — a movie of a trip, a dramatization, or a demonstration of a different culture.

Teachers often cooperate in equipping materials centers. However, in addition to finding a place for storing things it is advisable to organize a card file of slides, films, film strips, recordings, and radio and television programs which have been used. Appropriate comments on the cards by those who have used the materials increase their usefulness to others.

Models of various types and exhibits are valuable, too, in the classroom. Among these are specimens, samples, textiles, costumes, instruments, collections, utensils, weapons, products, ornaments, facsimiles, dioramas, puppets, marionettes. The possibilities are endless for the class and teacher who have interest, imagination, and industry as their allies.

*Evaluation of Progress.* Evaluation in the social studies as in other phases of the curriculum is a continuous process. It is not enough that the pupil become socialized; he must be able to make use of the skills he learns in social studies.

## Techniques for Evaluating Progress in Social Studies

Many teachers believe that it is more difficult to evaluate progress in social studies than in science, arithmetic, or spelling because social studies covers a broad area and lacks single direction. Abstract concepts such as liberty, democracy, freedom, trade, government are difficult to teach. There is the added difficulty of knowing when and if the child really understands their meaning. However, if the teacher sees evaluation as "the method or methods used to determine the extent to which previously established goals, objectives, or purposes have been achieved"[16] he will be able to use it successfully.

Because pupil growth is measured in terms of social development, academic achievement, and increasing skills, three sets of "tools" are needed for evaluation. These include devices for studying behavior, for determining information a child has gained from his social studies classes, and for measuring specific skills needed in social studies.

Examples of devices for evaluating social education are the following:

1. Sociograms and social acceptance scales, which help the teacher determine the quality of social relationships within the class.
2. Social maturity scales, which give one index to a child's status in the group at a specific time.
3. Anecdotal records or observations, which provide concrete descriptions of children's behavior and serve as a basis for understanding social and emotional growth over a period of time.
4. Teacher-child-parent conferences.
5. A diagnostic, expository letter reporting on the behavior of the child.

[16] John Jarolimek, *Social Studies in Elementary Education* (New York: The Macmillan Company, 1959), p. 358.

The results of intelligence tests, physical examinations, projective techniques, personality tests, profile charts, and case studies may also be used in appraising both social development and academic progress.

Devices for determining knowledge or information are more widely used and better known to teachers than those used in studying social growth. Commonly used instruments are standardized tests and teacher-made tests. Standardized tests are useful as objective yardsticks for measuring individual academic growth, comparing the class with other classes, measuring specific skills. Teacher-made tests include true-and-false, multiple-choice, completion, and essay-type tests. A good teacher-made test will include the understandings and concepts as well as specific facts and general information gained from the unit or area studied.

No evaluation of the social studies curriculum is complete without an evaluation of what the child has learned about geography, anthropology, sociology, history, economics, political science, etc. Social studies involves not only processes and skills, but also knowledge and understanding of peoples and their activities, achievements, interrelationships, and institutions.

### Knowledges and Understandings

Growing understanding of the American heritage, including a knowledge of the historical development of the United States, an understanding of the principles which have fostered our way of life, and a grasp of the methods by which Americans have solved their social and economic problems.

Increasing knowledge of our form of government and the laws and freedoms under which we live.

Increasing knowledge of the geographical environment in which men live, both in this country and in other countries and areas of the world, and increasing understanding of the growing interdependence of men everywhere in development and use of human and natural resources.

Increasing understanding of the cultures of various peoples of the world and the relationship of those cultures to our own (social institutions, religion, arts, government, resources, ways of making a living, family life, and the like).

Increasing understanding of social concepts, generalizations, and principles through which men seek to control experience. Such concepts, generalizations, and principles may be illustrated from several points of view. In the field of science, for example, the principle of contour plowing is employed in the conservation of soil and water on sloping land; in social science we extend the concept of environment adaptation to include the principle that the movement of peoples is usually in the direction of increased food, water supply, or vocational advantage. In sociological matters one may use to advantage the principle that giving equal opportunity to all individuals is basic to the development of a democratic society.[17]

Finally, in social studies the children should develop specific skills. The following check list will aid in determining their progress. To score, rate the child from 0 to 4. Add the scores and divide by the number of items to obtain the rating of the child.

.......... Studies efficiently at his level of development.

.......... Analyzes problems.

.......... Collects data; is able to listen, to observe, to read critically, to select pertinent and authentic data.

.......... Takes notes.

.......... Organizes and interprets data; outlines, summarizes, interprets, and evaluates.

.......... Interprets material in graphic form — charts, graphs, tables, maps, globes, pictures.

.......... Reports the results of the research.

.......... Presents oral reports.

.......... Writes a well-organized paper.

.......... Prepares a bibliography.

.......... Is able to summarize, and to write a critical book review.

.......... Is able to prepare charts, graphs, tables, and maps and interpret them.

.......... Thinks critically and independently.

.......... Analyzes argument and propaganda.

.......... Participates in group discussion.

.......... Has good work and study habits.

.......... Sees cause-and-effect relationships.

.......... Locates information and uses tables of contents and indexes.

The development of the above skills is the result of careful planning and effective teaching. These skills are cumulative. Some of them begin in kindergarten and others are added as the child progresses through the elementary school.

[17] "The Social Studies Program of the Denver Public Schools" (Denver: Department of Instruction, 1954), p. 3.

Some teachers prefer to keep a single class record consisting of the names of the pupils and an indication of the proficiency of each in specific social studies skills.

## Evaluating the Social Studies Program

Not only must the social studies teacher and the staff be aware of the techniques for appraising progress of individual children in the social studies; they must also develop criteria whereby they can judge whether the school as a whole is making progress toward the defined objectives. The following criteria are suggested to aid in determining a good social studies program.

1. Children are developing personal integrity and gaining an understanding of ethics in human relationships. They are learning that character is the measure of a man — not power or wealth.

2. Children are using the content of geography, history, civics, economics, and sociology in such a way that they are becoming more effective citizens.

3. Children are beginning to take a broader view of the world in which they live. They are becoming aware of and increasingly appreciative of the fact that human achievement, both at home and abroad, deserves recognition.

4. Children are learning the meaning of individual responsibiltiy. They are discovering that with the privileges of a democratic society go duties and obligations of good citizenship. They are learning that what is great about our country is not alone the standard of living but the ideas of freedom — "the ideas that government cannot do certain things to the individual, that his beliefs, his conscience, and his ideas are his own, and it is nobody's business what he thinks."[18]

5. Children are learning the democratic processes by practicing them in an environment in which the dignity and worth of the individual are cherished and the rights of others respected.

6. Children are facing the future with a better understanding of themselves and a growing faith in others. As they mature they realize that their expanding world calls for increased responsibility on their part. They realize that provincialism is antagonistic to progress. Maintaining separate little civilizations, whether the

[18] William O. Douglas, *Education Digest*, 24:5, September 1958.

clique in the schoolroom, the neighborhood, the state, or even the nation, is not the answer to developing effective social scientists, deepening human understandings, and broadening social relationships.

## *Conclusion*

The modern social studies program must help each child not only to become socialized but to acquire the basic knowledge, understandings, and skills that are imperative for living in an interdependent world. Social studies is concerned with human relationships. The responsibility of the teacher is to define the objectives and select, organize, develop, and evaluate appropriate learning experiences. Through these experiences in a classroom in which the worth of the individual is respected, children acquire behavior patterns that aid them in becoming increasingly responsible and contributing members of a society dedicated to safeguarding human progress. They learn essential facts; they develop concepts, values, and understandings; they gain the skills needed in problem solving, fact finding, and concept building.

The teacher who would inspire children to retain their vital curiosity, who would guide them toward greater understanding of and respect for other peoples, must have a broad background in anthropology, sociology, and economics as well as a knowledge of history, geography, and civics. He must not allow his thinking on the concepts, understandings, values, and skills to be taught in the elementary social studies program to become rigid. He must help children link the past with the present, not merely as a series of dates to be learned, but as a background for understanding the world of today. He should explore with them the wide and diversified aspects of culture, attitudes, and values. All the experiences provided in the social studies curriculum should contribute to the improved understanding of oneself, one's neighbor, and one's world.

Evaluation is a continuous and integral part of the social studies program. It is based on objectives which have been formulated by the school staff. The program is successful to the extent that children attain a better understanding of the values of our form of government, the history of our nation, the contributions of other cultures, the rights, privileges, duties, and achievements of citizens in a democracy and a regard for the rights, privileges, and opinions of others.

# ACTIVITIES AND QUESTIONS

1. Define the role of the social studies in the elementary curriculum.
2. Visit in an elementary school and find out the basis for determining scope and sequence in the social studies program.
3. Define and explain three methods for determining scope for the social studies. Observe in a class and determine which source was used in selection of the content of the lesson.
4. Make a chart showing a balanced curriculum for a grade of your choice.
5. Organize a unit of work for a group of third-graders. List the objectives, basic understandings, concepts, activities, materials, and evaluation procedure you would use.
6. Select a social studies concept and tell how you would make it clear to the children.
7. Compare the units illustrated in this chapter on the basis of interest for children, opportunity for social learnings, and provision for academic learnings.
8. Organize a brief unit for primary children around a special day or holiday.
9. Here are some activities suggested by a unit in the fifth grade on the growth of the United States:
   a. Use a large wall map to locate the thirteen colonies.
   b. Locate regions on the map.
   c. Study a relief map of Florida.
   d. Read accounts of the Lewis and Clark expedition and the role played by Sakajawea.
   e. Keep a diary of a journey on the Oregon Trail.
   f. Survey your neighborhoods to see how many different countries are represented among the people.
   g. Make bar graphs showing how states in the Great Plains and Central Plains rank in production of wheat and corn.

h. Decide why only small quantities of corn, oats, hay, and soybeans are sold for cash.

i. Write for materials on your state.

j. Give reports on the industries of the state.

What skills are essential to the successful completion of these assignments?

10. Why should a systematic evaluation of the social studies program be made? Who should be involved in the appraisal? What specific criteria should be used as a basis of the evaluation?

11. Compare the following devices for evaluating learning in the social studies: (1) sociograms, (2) anecdotal records, (3) parent conferences, (4) rating scales, (5) standardized tests, (6) teacher-made tests.

# BIBLIOGRAPHY

Allen, Jack. "Social Studies for America's Children," *Phi Delta Kappan*, 40:277–280, April 1959.

Ambrose, Edna, and Miel, Alice. *Children's Social Learning*. Washington, D.C.: Association for Supervision and Curriculum Development, NEA, 1958.

Association for Childhood Education International. *Social Studies for Children*. Bulletin No. 97. Washington, D.C.: The Association, 1956.

Association for Supervision and Curriculum Development. *Educating for Economic Competence*. Washington, D.C.: National Education Association, 1960.

Bayles, Ernest. *Education for Democracy*. Kansas Studies in Education, University of Kansas Publications, Vol. VIII, No. 2. Lawrence: School of Education, University of Kansas, 1958.

Brower, Robert, and Sternig, John. "Social Living Through Social Studies," *Childhood Education*, 34:209–212, January 1958.

Citizenship Education Project. *Building Better Programs in Citizenship*. New York: Bureau of Publications, Teachers College, Columbia University, 1958.

Cutright, Prudence, and Durand, Loyal, Jr. *Living Together as American Neighbors*. New York: The Macmillan Company, 1958.

Ellsworth, Ruth, and Sand, Ole. *Improving the Social Studies Curriculum*. Twenty-Sixth Yearbook, National Council for the Social Studies. Washington, D.C.: The Council, 1955.

Furst, E. J. *Constructing Evaluation Instruments.* New York: Longmans, Green and Company, 1958.

Hanna, Paul. "Social Studies for Today," *NEA Journal,* 45:36–38, January 1956.

Hill, Wilhelmina. *Social Studies in the Elementary School Program.* U.S. Department of Health, Education and Welfare. Washington, D.C.: Government Printing Office, 1960.

Hill Wilhelmina. "Aerospace Education in the Social Studies," *School Life,* 42:9–11, January 1960.

Hilliard, Pauline. *Improving Social Learnings in the Elementary School.* New York: Bureau of Publications, Teachers College, Columbia University, 1954.

Hogner, Dorothy Childs. *Conservation in America.* Philadelphia: J. B. Lippincott Company, 1958.

Jarolimek, John. *Social Studies in Elementary Education.* New York: The Macmillan Company, 1959.

Lewis, Gertrude M. *Educating Children in Grades Four, Five and Six.* Washington, D.C.: Government Printing Office, 1960.

Martin, Clyde I. *A Venture in International Understanding.* Bureau of Laboratory Schools Publication 9. Austin: University of Texas, 1958.

Michaelis, John U. *Social Studies for Children in a Democracy.* Englewood Cliffs, N.J.: Prentice-Hall, Inc., 2nd ed., 1956.

Miel, Alice, and Brogan, Peggy. *More Than Social Studies.* Englewood Cliffs, N.J.: Prentice-Hall, Inc., 1957.

Moore, Clyde B., *et al. Building Our America.* New York: Charles Scribner's Sons, 1958.

Moore, Clyde B., *et al. Building Our Communities.* New York: Charles Scribner's Sons, 1958.

Moore, Clyde B., *et al. Building Our World.* New York: Charles Scribner's Sons, 1958.

Morphet, Edgar, *et al. Educational Administration.* Englewood Cliffs, N.J.: Prentice-Hall, Inc., 1959, Chap. 18, "Instructional Materials."

National Council for the Social Studies. *A Guide to Content in the Social Studies.* Report of the NCSS committees on concepts and values. Washington, D.C.: The Council, 1960.

National Council for the Social Studies. *New Viewpoints in the Social Sciences.* Twenty-Eighth Yearbook. Washington, D.C.: The Council, 1958.

National Society for the Study of Education. *Social Studies in the Elementary School.* Fifty-Sixth Yearbook, Part II, Nelson B. Henry (ed.). Chicago: University of Chicago Press, 1957.

Nelson, Leslie, and McClusky, F. Dean. *Instructional Aids: How to Make Them.* Dubuque, Iowa: William C. Brown Company, 1958.

Norbeck, Oscar E. *Book of Indian Life Crafts.* New York: Association Press, 1958.

Preston, Ralph. *Teaching Social Studies in the Elementary School.* New York: Rinehart and Company, rev. ed., 1958.

Randolph, Victor, and Samford, Clarence D. *Teaching Elementary School Social Studies.* Dubuque, Iowa: William C. Brown Company, 1957.

Rehage, Kenneth J. "On Rethinking the Social-Studies Program," *Elementary School Journal,* 57:10–14, October 1956.

Rudman, Herbert C. "The Informational Needs and Reading Interests of Children in Grades IV Through VIII," *Elementary School Journal,* 55:502–512, May 1955.

Shane, Harold G. "Evaluating Pupil Growth in the Social Studies," *The Instructor,* 68:6, 67, December 1958.

*Social Studies in the Elementary School; Kindergarten, Grades 1, 2, 3.* Public Schools Curriculum Bulletin 90. Kansas City: Board of Education, May 1954.

*Social Studies in the Elementary School; Grades 4, 5, 6.* Public Schools Curriculum Bulletin 91. Kansas City: Board of Education, May 1954.

Thralls, Z. A. *The Teaching of Geography.* New York: Appleton-Century-Crofts, Inc., 1958.

Wesley, E. B., and Wronski, S. P. *Teaching Social Studies in High Schools.* Boston: D. C. Heath and Company, 4th ed., 1958.

Willcockson, Mary (ed.). *Social Education of Young Children: Kindergarten-Primary Grades.* Washington, D. C.: National Council for the Social Studies, NEA, rev. ed., 1956.

Wittich, W. A., and Halsted, G. H. *Educators' Guide to Free Tapes, Scripts, and Transcriptions.* Randolph, Wis.: Educators Progress Service, 5th ed., 1959.

# 10

Numbers are as abstract as angels. Mathematics is as creative as music, painting or sculpture.

MAX BEBERMAN

# Guiding
# arithmetic experiences

On mathematics depend the future of nuclear science, automation, research in industry, and new approaches to the social sciences. As a subject mathematics "is worth study for itself and its mastery should appeal to some of our best young minds in much the same way that perfecting a drop kick, winning at chess, playing a musical instrument, or running the four-minute mile appeals to others. Mathematics is truly a key to the universe; it has glories all its own."[1]

[1] College Entrance Examination Board, *A Summary of the Report of the Commission on Mathematics* (New York: College Entrance Examination Board, 1959), p. 6.

The possibilities of the creative aspects of mathematics have not been fully explored. Teachers who fail to recognize its potential in the field of original thought deprive children of creative experiences. They too often think of creativity solely in terms of painting a picture, molding a clay object, making a drawing, or composing music. Arithmetic, too, has opportunities for creation and discovery. The child who works out his system for adding double columns or who figures out how to tell time by himself experiences the joy of creation as truly as the one who paints a picture or makes up a poem. Teaching that, instead of stressing skill in computation and problem solving, challenges children to think, to see relationships, and to discover leads to mathematical insight and a better understanding of the processes involved.

It is through the elementary teacher that the child receives his foundation — adequate or inadequate — for later studies of mathematics. The need is to use an approach to arithmetic that will vitalize the teaching.

## *Aspects of Arithmetic*

There are two important and interdependent aspects of arithmetic instruction — one having to do with the "meanings" of mathematical concepts and the other with the "meanings" of arithmetic in daily life. The first of these is often referred to as the mathematical aspect. It deals with the concepts to be learned, the relationships to be realized, the principles to be understood, and the skills to be mastered. The second is referred to as the social aspect, through which the individual appreciates how the quantitative concepts are utilized.

Whether arithmetic is defined as the science of numbers or as the study of the quantitative, the basic structure is the same. What differs is the approach to the subject. Traditionally there has been a conflict as to whether the mathematical or the social aspect should be emphasized. Those favoring the first approach would teach arithmetic as a science or art which might later be applied to the problems of society; those favoring the second approach argue that arithmetic has significance only as it is useful to the individual in daily living. Actually, what is needed is a dual emphasis upon social significance and mathematical meaning, with increasing insight into effective ways of combining the two aspects in a balanced arithmetic program.

*The Mathematical Aspect.* It is through the mathematical aspect that arithmetic concepts become meaningful. The learner must comprehend the mathematical skills and concepts before he can relate them to significant social situations in everyday life and apply them effectively.

With the rise of what has been termed "meaningful arithmetic" the emphasis is placed on the reasons for what is done mathematically. Children learn generalizations from a variety of experiences instead of merely memorizing the words of a formula. For example, $5 \times 3 = 15$ and $15 \div 3 = 5$ are regarded as generalizations. Each individual child, experimenting with concrete materials that show structural relations, will find "that 15 is 5 times as large as 3 and that 3 is only one-fifth of the size of 15; if we divide 15 by 5, each part has the size of 3. . . . If we produce a 3 five times, it amounts to $3 + 3 + 3 + 3 + 3$ — that is, we can refer the process of multiplying back to addition, using equal addends. Similarly, if we subtract one 3 after the other from 15, we find that there are 5 such parts in 15. Thus division is referred back to subtraction, using equal subtrahends."[2] Having discovered that ten 3's are 30, the pupil can locate the middle of the scale: five 3's are half of 30, or 15. The pupil can deduce $5 \times 3$ if he cannot recall the answer. This gives him a way of figuring out what he needs to know rather than being told the answer. Through such experiences children come to possess a functional association of numbers which they can apply in a wide range of situations.

The understandings which the teacher must help the child attain relate to both the mathematical and the social aspects of arithmetic. Those related to the mathematical aspect include the following:

1. Understanding of technical vocabulary.
2. Meaning of number operations and their functions in social situations.
3. Understanding of transformation, set, and regrouping, and the reason numbers behave as they do in basic operations.
4. Understandings of principles, generalizations, and relationships

[2] Catherine Stern, *Children Discover Arithmetic* (New York: Harper & Brothers, 1949), p. 180.

which exist among number facts, numbers operation, and their applications.

Among the emphases that have been predominant in the development of arithmetic are the drill, social, and meaning approaches. Currently all three are recognized, with an attempt to provide for a balance among mathematical rationale, social applications, and meaningful drill. "The modern arithmetic curriculum is a coordinated program providing for the development of vocabulary, skills, progressively increasing maturity in discovering and generalizing, and possession of concepts, information and ability to solve social problems quantitative in nature."[3]

Prior to the 1930's the drill aspect of arithmetic was emphasized above either the mathematical or the social aspect. The psychology of "readiness-exercise-effect" was dominant, and educational practice focused on drill. Processes were analyzed, skills subdivided and memorized.

*The Social Aspect.* During the 1930's, although drill and memorization continued, the child development concept came to the fore. Educators began to insist that children should understand what they were learning and should see sense in what they were doing and how it could be used in daily living. The concept of social utility not only came to be considered important; "In arithmetic the concept of social utility was revered."[4] The curriculum now stressed arithmetic children and adults actually use. Because research findings showed that the only fractions frequently used were halves, fourths, and eighths, the reaction of many teachers was, Why bother to teach what no one normally encounters?

Rightly understood and judiciously used, the social aspect of arithmetic contributes to the significance of numbers in the child's experiences. The social situation may be used as a springboard in the sequence of steps taken to develop mathematical understandings. The alert teacher recognizes the value of the following concepts and understandings included under the social aspect of arithmetic:

[3] John L. Marks, C. Richard Purdy, and Lucien B. Kinney, *Teaching Arithmetic for Understanding* (New York: McGraw-Hill Book Company, 1958), p. 55.

[4] Ben A. Sueltz, "Arithmetic in Historical Perspective," *The National Elementary Principal*, 39:15, October 1959.

1. Basic concepts and understandings in the area of measurements.
2. Understanding and knowledge of the role of money, banks, taxes, stocks and bonds, etc., in the economy.
3. Understanding and ability to interpret charts, tables, spatial relationships, and graphic materials.
4. The role of numbers in science, arts, industry, etc.[5]

In the effort to make use of social aspects of arithmetic some teachers were rather carried away. They believed that meaning in arithmetic comes from everyday situations that require the use of numbers. Academic content and computational skills were taught in a social context through experience units organized around socially oriented problems. Thus children learned arithmetic by playing store, post office, bank, or market. They learned number combinations through social games. In criticizing this approach Kowitz warns: "This bootlegging of learning thrives on the belief that, when the child can see a social use for the material, he will learn it. . . . Nothing could be farther from the truth. . . . Even if the decision to learn is a conscious one, in an age of automatic supermarket check-outs, the general store approach could not meet the requirements."[6]

Buckingham cautions: "The teacher who emphasizes the social aspects of arithmetic does well. But in the sense in which the term is here used, he is not teaching arithmetic. He may, and indeed he should, use a socially significant approach, but his teaching of a given unit is not complete until the goal of mathematically meaningful ideas has been reached. . . . We must, therefore, do two things. We must teach arithmetic as a social study, and we must teach it as mathematics."[7]

Few people today doubt the value of the social aspect of arithmetic. Many teachers, in the primary grades particularly, believe that all arithmetic learning must be taught in a social situation and arise from a social need. The good teacher makes use of the situational

---

[5] Leo J. Brueckner, *Improving the Arithmetic Program: Current Problems in Education* (New York: Appleton-Century-Crofts, Inc., 1957), p. 45. (Adapted.)

[6] G. T. Kowitz, "The Motive to Learn," *Elementary School Journal*, 59:384, April 1959.

[7] B. R. Buckingham, "The Social Point of View in Arithmetic," *The Teaching of Arithmetic*, Fiftieth Yearbook, National Society for the Study of Education, Part II (Chicago: University of Chicago Press, 1951), p. 273.

method of teaching but he also teaches the mathematical aspects of arithmetic. The goal is to interweave the strands of the computational skills, the significant mathematical meanings, and the social situation to the end that the individual can effectively make use of quantitative abilities in and out of the school.

The young child is eager to learn arithmetic when he is first introduced to it. However, much of his initial curiosity falls by the wayside as he progresses through the elementary school. Objectives and methods must constantly be re-examined in the hope that as better ones are found they will be used. The need is not to add topics to the arithmetic program, or to provide more time for drill, or even to assign additional homework. It is to place more emphasis on significant fundamental concepts. The objectives of the arithmetic program should give the teacher a basis for determining what should be taught, how it should be taught, and how it may be organized, developed, and evaluated.

## *Objectives in Teaching Arithmetic*

Brownell has written one of the most comprehensive statements of objectives:

1. Computational skills:
   a. Facility and accuracy in operations with whole numbers, common fractions, decimals, and per cents. . . .
2. Mathematical understandings:
   a. Meaningful conceptions of quantity, of the number system, of whole numbers, of common fractions, of decimals, of per cents, of measures, etc.
   b. A meaningful vocabulary of the useful *technical terms* of arithmetic which designates quantitative ideas and the relationships between them.
   c. Grasp of important arithmetical generalizations.
   d. Understanding of the meanings and mathematical functions of the fundamental operations.
   e. Understanding of important arithmetical relationships, such as those which function in reasonably sound estimations and approximations, in accurate checking, and in ingenious and resourceful solutions.

    f. Some understanding of the rational principles which govern number relations and computational procedures.

3. Sensitivity to number in social situations and the habit of using number effectively in such situations:

    a. Vocabulary of selected quantitative terms of common usage (such as kilowatt hour, miles per hour, decrease and increase, and terms important in insurance, investments, business practices, etc.).

    b. Knowledge of selected business practices and other economic applications of numbers.

    c. Ability to interpret graphs, simple statistics, and tabular presentations of quantitative data (as in study in school and in practical activities outside of school).

    d. Awareness of the usefulness of quantity and numbers in dealing with many aspects of life. Here belongs some understanding of social institutions in which the quantitative aspect is prominent, as well as some understanding of the important contribution of numbers in their evolution.

    e. Tendency to sense the quantitative as part of normal experience, including vicarious experience, as in reading, observation, and in projected activity and imaginative thinking.

    f. Ability to make (and the habit of making) sound judgments with respect to quantitative problems.

    g. Disposition to extend one's sensitiveness to the quantitative as this occurs socially. . . .[8]

## *Meanings Which Teachers Should Develop with Children*

Mathematics gives us a language in which to express, with increasing maturity and refinement, our quantitative ideas. One cannot leave to chance or to incidental teaching the concepts, meanings, or skills which require building step by step in logical sequence.

Organizing the learning experiences in such a way that children develop understandings, see relationships, and increase skills requires careful planning in the arithmetic program. Understandings are an

---

[8] W. A. Brownell, "The Evaluation of Learning in Arithmetic," *Arithmetic in General Education,* Sixteenth Yearbook, National Council of Teachers of Mathematics (Washington, D.C.: The Council, 1944), pp. 231–232.

outgrowth of meaningful learning experiences. Four categories of meanings should grow out of the many and varied experiences provided for the children, as follows:

1. Basic concepts. Children should understand such concepts as numbers, set, symbolism, verification, common fractions, equations, decimal fractions, per cent, ratio, proportion, denominate numbers, divisor, common denominator, addend, etc.
2. Fundamental operations. Children should understand when and how to use addition, subtraction, multiplication, and division. They should understand what happens to the numbers when a given operation is employed.
3. Generalizations. Certain basic laws of mathematics serve the elementary pupil as generalizations which take the place of countless separate statements. For example: commutative, associative, and distributive laws are used to state important principles. The table below[9] summarizes these generalizations.

| *Law* | *Addition* | *Multiplication* |
|---|---|---|
| Commutative | $a + b = b + a$ | $a \times b = b \times a$ |
| Associative | $(a + b) + c = a + (b + c)$ | $a \times (b \times c) = (a \times b) \times c$ |
| Distributive | $a (b + c) = (a \times b) + (a \times c)$ | |

4. Decimal number system. Children should understand the functioning of the decimal system. They also should understand that any number might be used as a base for making a number system. Using a larger number than 10 requires new digits.

*Scope and Sequence in the Kindergarten and Primary Grades.* Children vary in readiness to learn mathematical concepts and computational skills in kindergarten and the primary grades. However, many children are ready for learning arithmetic before the teacher is conscious of their interest. Concepts and skills usually covered include the following:

1. Rote counting. Most children entering kindergarten have little difficulty in rote counting to 10. They do not, however, understand the concept that the number names "1," "2," "3," "4," "5," and so on correspond to something that is being counted. Only

[9] Joseph J. Urbancek, "Effective Arithmetic Teaching Techniques in the New Education," *The Packet* (Boston: D. C. Heath and Company, 1959), p. 8.

through numerous experiences in relating the symbol with something concrete, through matching things one to another, will they understand one-to-one correspondence. Piecemeal counting of single elements does not lead to the understanding of number relations.

2. Rational counting. This is different from rote counting, in which the children merely recite the names of numbers. Now they recognize that when ten children are standing in front of them they can give each a consecutive number and when all have been counted they will have used ten numbers. Teachers can help children grasp the idea that if they have two objects and one more is given to them they now have three objects.

3. Meaning of cardinal numbers. The child needs to learn that there are two types of designation — the cardinal and the ordinal. Cardinal numbers tell how many things are being counted: one, two, etc. Ordinal numbers tell order, sequence, or position: first, second, etc. Playing games such as "Ten Little Indians," "Five Little Chicks," "How Many?" helps children to understand these concepts.

4. Grouping. Before long they learn that two children, two books, two balls, are always the same in number. They learn to sense that when there is a boy and girl or a large ball and a small ball, or a cat and a dog, there are always two. The objects associated with the symbol 2 remain the same in number.

5. Forming subgroups. After the child has learned the preceding concepts and skills he can be taught that numbers or things can be arranged in a variety of ways. Using a counting frame is effective in teaching him how to make subgroupings. Even kindergarten children are interested in learning that the groups of beads on the counting frame can be shifted to make several combinations. For example, the number 6 may stand for 000 and 000, or 00 and 0000, or 0 and 00000, or these may be reversed. The child may even learn, in terms of the four fundamental processes, that putting 0000 and 00 together is addition; taking 00 away and leaving 0000 is subtraction; taking two beads three times, as in 00 00 00, is multiplication; and separating the entire group of six beads into three groups of two each, as in 00 00 00, is division.

6. Sets. Appearing in mathematical literature more and more frequently is the word "set." A set is essentially a collection of things. It is synonymous with collection, aggregate, group, class, family, etc. The habit of thinking in terms of sets is becoming routine for modern mathematicians and for other

scientists. It is generally agreed that all elementary courses should foster the mental concept formed by thinking of several things as a single whole, and should introduce a few of the terms employed in the study of sets.

The mathematician defines an individual set by specifying its members. Some sets which have meaning for the child:

a. The set consisting of the fingers of the right hand.
b. The set consisting of the wheels on an automobile.
c. The set consisting of the corners at the intersection of two streets.
d. The set consisting of the marks / / / /.

The members in the set do not necssarily need to be alike in any way. Numerous exercises may be devised that develop concepts and skills in this context.[10]

7. The four fundamental processes. The basic addition and subtraction facts including carrying and borrowing are taught in the primary grades. However, in teaching the multiplication and division facts there is a wide range of practice.

8. Reading and writing numbers. Children are eager to write the number symbols from 1 to 10 as quickly as they know them. No fixed goal need be set. Some children write the numbers to 31 to make calendars. Others make books and need to write the page numbers. However, by the time they are second-graders they read and write the numbers up to 1000 if they have sufficient time and interest.

9. Concept of place value. If the teacher plans interesting games and uses illustrative material, the child will find the place-value concept fairly easy to grasp. He learns, eventually, that if he has ten and someone gives him five more, the position a number symbol occupies has meaning. In writing 15 he learns that the 1 stands for one 10 and the 5 for five 1's.

10. Roman numerals. By the time the children have progressed through the primary grades they should read and write Roman numerals. As they move ahead into the intermediate grades they will need skills in outlining. An understanding of Roman numerals will be an advantage. Many students arrive in college without being able to read and use this form of number experience correctly.

11. Fractions. Children have had experiences with fractions long before they come to school. They have divided a piece of

---

[10] For further explanation of sets see National Council of Teachers of Mathematics, *The Growth of Mathematical Ideas*, Twenty-Fourth Yearbook (Washington, D.C.: The Council, 1959), pp. 11–17.

cake; they have watched Mother cut a pie; they have seen toys break in two. They can understand the meaning of "half the cookie," "a third of the pie," or "a quarter of an apple." They should understand what it mean by equal parts of a whole or equal parts of a group. They realize that if you want many pieces you have to cut them small. Big pieces make fewer pieces. The more parts a thing is divided in, the smaller the parts become.

12. Measurement. Children are fascinated by measurement. They like to use "tall" and "short" to describe height; "heavy" and "light" to describe weight; "thick" and "thin" to describe depth. The ruler or yardstick gives them reason to use names of units of linear measurement such as inches, feet, yards, half-inch. Play materials and science equipment help them grasp the concepts of pound and ounce as measures of weight; pint, quart, gallon as measures of quantity; and hour, minute, second, day as measure of time. Children vary greatly in their need for and skill in using these concepts of measurement.

13. Money and decimals. Children need to understand money values. They need to be able to read price tags, make change, add and subtract dollars and cents, and compute with dollars and cents in all the processes by the time they leave the primary school. Buying the school lunch, purchasing supplies at the school store, bringing in money for the Red Cross, paying their fare on excursions, and buying tickets for the school play all require the knowledge of computation of money. They learn to recognize pennies, nickels, dimes, quarters, half-dollars, and dollars bills, and to know simple equivalents of coins — for example, five pennies equal one nickel.

14. Solving story problems. Attention is being given to developing skill in problem solving at all grade levels. Verbal problems are included in the first and second grades to give children an opportunity to see relationships between what they want to find and the known facts. Teachers should encourage children to develop ways of solving their own problems and to work out a method of attack on practical quantitative situations. Modern programs in arithmetic make use of story problems to introduce new concepts, to provide practice on concepts which have already been developed, and to evaluate and test those concepts learned.

15. Mental arithmetic. Closely related to story problems is mental arithmetic, or oral arithmetic as it is sometimes called. In all grades beginning in the kindergarten, attention is given to oral

arithmetic, to the development of the ability to estimate, to judge the reasonableness of answers, and to use standard reference units in interpreting quantitative statements. Computations are frequently done without benefit of paper and pencil in daily life and children must learn to compute mentally if they are to use arithmetic to the best advantage.

Children develop concepts slowly. The following chart suggests the usual sequence.

SEQUENCE IN BUILDING NUMBER CONCEPTS TO 10

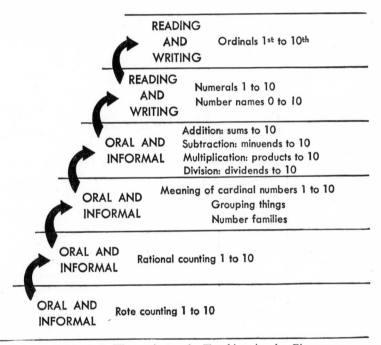

| | | |
|---|---|---|
| READING AND WRITING | Ordinals 1st to 10th | |
| READING AND WRITING | Numerals 1 to 10<br>Number names 0 to 10 | |
| ORAL AND INFORMAL | Addition: sums to 10<br>Subtraction: minuends to 10<br>Multiplication: products to 10<br>Division: dividends to 10 | |
| ORAL AND INFORMAL | Meaning of cardinal numbers 1 to 10<br>Grouping things<br>Number families | |
| ORAL AND INFORMAL | Rational counting 1 to 10 | |
| ORAL AND INFORMAL | Rote counting 1 to 10 | |

Source: Herbert J. Klausmeir *et al., Teaching in the Elementary School* (New York: Harper & Brothers, 1956), p. 310.

Once children are able to read and write numbers from 1 to 10, write the number names, and understand the concepts related to them, they are ready for more complex experiences.

The scope of the child's arithmetical learning and the sequence in which he develops facility with numbers and the notational system are suggested in the following chart. Many children will have achieved the objectives set forth there by the end of the primary grades.

SEQUENCES IN DEVELOPMENT OF FACILITY WITH NUMBERS AND
UNDERSTANDING OF DECIMAL NOTATION THROUGH THE HUNDREDS

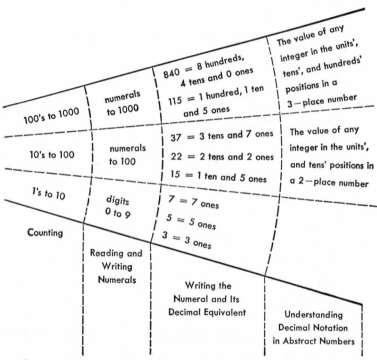

Source: Herbert J. Klausmeier *et al.*, *Teaching in the Elementary School* (New York: Harper & Brothers, 1956), p. 313.

Spitzer suggests the following procedures for developing number facility: the oral solving of problems, the use of diagrams or drawings, writing the number question, pupil formulation of problems, intensive study of number operations, habitually asking oneself questions about the problem, solving the same problem by several techniques, finding new methods of solving problems.[11]

[11] Herbert F. Spitzer, *The Teaching of Arithmetic* (Boston: Houghton Mifflin Company, 2nd ed., 1954), pp. 189–200.

The importance of developing computational skills and number concepts in a logical manner cannot be overemphasized. Pupils must build concept upon concept and skill upon skill. They must be helped to discover the relationships between the processes and to increase their skill in applying word-problem-solving techniques.

The young child proceeds from the concrete to the semi-concrete to the abstract in his development of number concepts. He learns that a number is the symbol for something; that it has a name; that it can represent several different combinations and that he can make groups by shifting numbers around in processes of addition, subtraction, multiplication, and division.

At first he has to handle objects to make sure he has a specific number of things. He has to hold five pennies and count them as he places them on the table to be sure there are five. Learning should proceed steadily, however, to the materials that are semi-concrete. For example, dominoes or dot cards help the child associate the symbol with the actual number of things. The teacher must take care that semi-concrete materials stand for things and not number symbols. A particular configuration of dots showing three or six in a specific manner should not become fixed.

Before too long the child should progress to the level of abstraction, at which the symbols stand for objects and are used in his thought process in lieu of objects, but with a clear understanding at all times of the ideas they represent. By the time the child completes the elementary school he should no longer be dependent upon counting frames or place-value charts.

The teacher must provide the concrete materials to help the child understand the meanings of a number, a numeral, and/or number relationships. At the same time he must help the child progress toward recognizing the abstractions that the concrete materials symbolize.

*Scope and Sequence in the Intermediate Grades.* Intermediate grade children also require careful, sequential building of concepts and skills related to the number system, the computational processes, measurement, fractions, and problem solving. A common complaint of intermediate grade teachers is, "They didn't teach them arithmetic in the primary grades; I have to start from the very simplest concepts and reteach the basic processes." The intermediate grade teacher should realize that the primary child who is promoted needs review for diagnostic purposes and occasional reteaching. He can plan his work on the basis of the former skills and concepts that need to be reviewed and expanded and the new ones that should be introduced. The major emphasis of instruction is on the fundamental processes, measurement, and word-problem solving; and on the decimal system, number relationships, and denominate numbers.

Sequence is carefully planned and experiences are provided for in the basic textbook series on the market today. Examination of existing materials indicates that the following concepts and skills are developed in the intermediate grades:

1. Extension of the four fundamental processes. Practice is provided for adding longer columns of numbers and subtracting numbers up to six places. The basic multiplication and division facts are reviewed; multiplication using two- and three-figure multipliers, and division using two- and three-figure divisors are introduced and practiced.

2. Extension of work on fractions. Pupils review the concept of fraction as part of the whole or quantity. They also learn how to change fractions to equal fractions; change fractions to simplest form; add and subtract like and unlike fractions, and mixed numbers; multiply fractions by a whole, mixed number by a whole, whole by mixed number, whole by fraction, fraction by fraction, mixed by fraction, and mixed by mixed. They learn the ratio and proportion meaning of fractions. They learn that the number of objects in a group can be compared with those of another group by means of fractions (3 in one group as compared with 6 in another, or ½); that the number in part of a group can be compared with the total number in the group (2 out of a group of 6, or ⅓); and that a comparison of size can be made (½ as large). Sequence is as essential in teaching fractions as it is in the four fundamental processes. Textbook series provide a good sequence to follow. They clearly present the meaning of each process and supply problems which develop the computational skills.

3. Extension of measurement. Children use such measures as time, length, weight, temperature, and so forth. The concepts of square, rectangle, and cubic measure are introduced. Area is developed as surface, and volume as the total content of an object. Children use concrete, semi-concrete, and abstract ma-

terials to discover relationships between units for measuring length (linear measure), surface (square measure), or volume (cubic measure). They are fascinated to discover the three formulas for finding perimeter. Linear measurement, liquid measure, and measures of time and weight should be mastered.

4. Decimal fractions. Since decimal fractions are used by most adults they should be a part of a foundation arithmetic program. Children should learn that

a. Decimal fractions are just a selected part of all fractions whose denominators are a power of ten.

b. The denominator of the decimal fraction is determined by place.

c. Decimal fractions are an extension of our decimal number system to the right of a decimal point. Places to the left of the decimal point are read as whole numbers; places to the right are read as fractions. In reading decimals, use the first place to the left of the decimal point as a point of reference — *not the decimal point*. The pupil should remember that one decimal place means tenths, two places means hundredths, three places means thousandths, and four places means ten-thousandths. They must learn that the first place to the right is a tenth, not a unit, and not a 10.

d. The four computational processes are used in working with decimals.

5. Per cents. Children learn the meaning and uses of per cents, fractions, decimals, and per cent equivalents. They develop the concept that per cent means so many out of a hundred more readily if the meaning of decimals is adequately understood. Among experience situations which can be converted to problems involving per cents are the following:

"Per cent of rainy days, sunny days, etc., within a specified period of time.

Per cent of boys and girls in a class, a grade, school register, present, absent.

Per cent of money to be used for various purposes.

Per cent of games won or lost.

Per cent of problems computed correctly and incorrectly.

Per cent of children who participated in an activity on a particular day, in a particular week, etc.

Reading and interpreting social studies data, as per cent of U.S. coal produced in a particular region.

Comparing sales tax on various school supplies purchased."[12]

6. Extension of experiences in problem solving. Primary grade children have had experience in using the problem-solving method in arithmetic as well as in science, social studies, and so forth. They have been solving oral and written problems by a variety of means. Many of the problems have been of the one-step variety. However, as they enter the intermediate grades they encounter more complicated problems. Two-step and three-step problems, problems without numbers, problems requiring estimates for answers, and writing of problems are all used. Children are given experience, too, in solving problems with superfluous data, or missing data, as they increase their power in problem solving.

Intermediate teachers should help improve children's problem-solving technique by having them read carefully to define the problem, gather and organize their information (in terms of the stated problem), and then set up possible solutions, select the correct procedure, and solve the problem.

An illustration of the application of this method is demonstrated in the following problem:

"Mr. Rogers made an automobile trip. When he left his home his odometer read 17,895 miles. When he returned, three days later, it read 18,325 miles. He used 25 gallons of gas. How many miles does his car travel per gallon of gas?

"By re-reading the information in terms of the problem posed it becomes meaningful. Rewriting the same problem and posing the problem first gives this result:

"Mr. Rogers wants to find how many miles he travels per gallon of gas on an automobile trip. When he left home his odometer read 17,895 and when he returned three days later it read 18,325. He used 25 gallons of gas."[13]

This brief overview of arithmetic during the elementary years indicates some of the important concepts and skills to be gained, with some consideration for the underlying mathematical theory. It is not intended to be a description of the entire elementary arithmetic program.

[12] John R. Clark and Laura K. Eads, *Guiding Aritmetic Learning* (Yonkers-on-Hudson, N.Y.: World Book Company, 1954), p. 201.

[13] Peter S. Pierro, "Using the Problem-solving Method," *The Arithmetic Teacher*, 6:160, April 1959.

# *The Role of the Teacher*

The goal of the classroom teacher is to develop the child's mathematical understanding and skills so that he is able to apply them effectively in and out of the school. The following general principles will help to realize this goal:

1. Learning must be meaningful to the child as new steps are introduced.

2. Learning is facilitated when experiences are intrinsically and genuinely purposeful.

3. The discovery of facts, meaning, and generalizations by the learner leads to better understanding.

4. Content should be organized and presented in such a way that relationships can be seen. Drill must be provided in terms of individual need.

5. Sequence of arithmetical processes and concepts should be organized according to the maturing child's abilities, interests, and experiential background. Individual differences must be taken into account by the teacher.

6. A wide variety of learning experiences, materials, and opportunity for practice should be provided in order to help meet individual needs.

7. Learnings should be evaluated in terms of objectives.

## INTRODUCING NEW STEPS

In planning a new step in arithmetic the teacher determines the degree of readiness for learning and the need for the step in solving a problem — either a problem in the classroom or one in the arithmetic textbook. For example, children in the first grade are planning to go to the zoo on the school bus. They need to bring money for the trip and some want to bring enough to ride on the miniature train. They will have to bring a quarter. The teacher will help them develop the concept of the number twenty-five (25). They can use the counting frame to count out five beads "5" times; they can group 10 and 10 and 5; they can count by 1's until they come to 25. They can use the flannel board with disks to represent the amount needed. They can arrange the twenty-five disks or beads into as many groups as possible to discover the meaning of the symbol "25."

Some first-grade children understand when they come to school that one quarter is the equivalent of twenty-five pennies, five nickels, or two dimes and a nickel. When the children understand the concepts about the number 25 they may be given exercises or problems which require them to draw a circle around each group of twenty-five, and to find the number of fives in twenty-five.

In the kindergarten, too, children use concrete materials to help them understand mathematical concepts. For example, if the teacher wants to introduce the concept of fractions she may say: "Jimmie, how can you share your graham cracker so Tommy has as much as you have? Boys and girls, are the pieces the same size?" "No, Tommy's is bigger." "Then," says the teacher, "I will take a cracker and break it into two equal sizes. Now, Tommy, can you try to do it this time?" The children may use pieces of paper which they fold in equal parts. They may divide piles of sticks, beads, or pegs. They may break a stick of clay in half, or divide the blocks equally between two children, or divide a group of children into two equal groups.

In the intermediate grades if children have developed a concept of fractions with the use of concrete and semi-concrete materials they will readily participate in the addition and subtraction of like fractions. Adding one-fourth and one-fourth is no harder than adding one book and one book. The word "fourth" tells the child what he is adding. Expressions such as one-fourth plus one-fourth equals two-fourths, or 1 fourth + 1 fourth = 2 fourths, or $\frac{1}{4} + \frac{1}{4} = \frac{2}{4}$ should be meaningful if the teacher has used concrete materials to help develop basic concepts. Pupils soon discover three convenient ways of dividing a sheet of paper into fourths. They can use vertical lines, horizontal lines, or one vertical line and one horizontal line, as illustrated:

| $\frac{1}{4}$ | $\frac{1}{4}$ | $\frac{1}{4}$ | $\frac{1}{4}$ |
|---|---|---|---|

| $\frac{1}{4}$ |
|---|
| $\frac{1}{4}$ |
| $\frac{1}{4}$ |
| $\frac{1}{4}$ |

| $\frac{1}{4}$ | $\frac{1}{4}$ |
|---|---|
| $\frac{1}{4}$ | $\frac{1}{4}$ |

As opportunities arise fractions should be used in a wide variety of situations. Children may discover the answer to such questions as: How many quarts in a gallon? How many quarters in a dollar?

Thus the children discover meanings for themselves through the inductive method. The teacher sets the stage or structures a situation so they will be motivated to discover for themselves. What he must remember, however, is that in the average classroom there will be some children for whom this procedure is not necessary. They are ready to use the abstract symbols and understand them and are frustrated by what they consider "playing around."

Briefly, the teacher introduces a new step by (1) helping children see the need for learning, through a social situation, a problem presented in the textbook, or one formulated by the teacher; (2) encouraging children who need to manipulate materials to discover relationships and meanings for themselves; (3) demonstrating on the blackboard the relationships in terms of symbols; (4) having children state the relationship they have discovered; (5) providing opportunity for solving similar problems or discovering like relationships under supervision of the teacher; (6) having children work a problem using abstract symbols under the guidance of the teacher; (7) providing drill in the new step, using textbook or workbook material.

HELPING CHILDREN DISCOVER ANSWERS TO PROBLEMS

Teaching is more than telling. Children must do the learning. The function of the teacher is to select, organize, and guide learning experiences in such a way that children discover relationships themselves. The examples below illustrate "teacher-telling" and "child-discovering" procedures.

*Classroom* X
Lesson Procedure:

Mrs. Grayson is speaking: "Today, we are going to learn a new step in fractions. We will learn how to multiply common fractions. Turn in your books to page 145. You will see what happens when a fraction is cut in half. Look, if I divide $\frac{1}{4}$ by 2 I get $\frac{1}{8}$.

"Or I can do it another way: I can say $\frac{1}{2}$ of $\frac{1}{4}$ is $\frac{1}{8}$. I will write it this way: $\frac{1}{2} \times \frac{1}{4} = \frac{1}{8}$. John, you come up and do this problem: $\frac{1}{2} \times \frac{1}{3} =$

"That's right, John. The answer is $\frac{1}{6}$.

"Jennie, you come up and work this problem: $\frac{1}{2} \times \frac{1}{5} = \ldots$."

Jennie writes the answer $\frac{1}{10}$. "Now." says Mrs. Grayson, "you can see that the rule is that you must multiply the denominators in multiplying a fraction by a fraction. Now work the problems on the page. Come up to my desk if you have trouble."

*Classroom Y*

Lesson Procedure:

TEACHER: Today, would you like to start a new topic in mathematics?

CLASS: Yes. (*Various topics were suggested.*) How about multiplication of common fractions?

JOHN: We've been talking about common fractions, and you said that soon we could start multiplication of common fractions. I think I know how to multiply common fractions.

TEACHER: Let us check your ideas about multiplication.

(*Teacher wrote on the board, and the children stated the products as she wrote them*:)

| (a) | (b) | (c) | (d) | (e) |
|---|---|---|---|---|
| 8 | 8 | 8 | 8 | 8 |
| × 16 | × 8 | × 4 | × 2 | × 1 |
| 128 | 64 | 32 | 16 | 8 |

JIM: The multiplicands are all alike, and the multipliers decrease as you go from Example (a) through Example (e).

CONNIE: As you move from (a) through (e), each multiplier grows two times as small and each product grows two times as small.

JIM: And moving from (e) through (a), the opposite is true. Each multiplier becomes two times as large, and each product becomes two times as large as the one next to it. The products vary in the same way as the multipliers.

SUSIE: I think the words *direct proportion* are better than saying *in the same way*. We learned the words when we were studying multiplication the other week.

TOMMY: In the examples on the board, the multiplicands are constant. The multipliers vary and the products vary in direct proportion with the multipliers.

TEACHER: You have expressed the idea very well. Now, let us review the meaning of common fraction expressions. What does ⅓ mean to you, Donald?

DONALD: One divided into three equal parts. One divided by three — just as the numbers and division sign say.

TEACHER: What about the expression ⅚?

GAIL: Five divided into six equal parts. Five divided by 6.

TOMMY: You make the 5 six times as small when you write the division sign and the 6.

HELEN: In the fraction ⅚, the 5 is dividend and the 6 is the divisor.

TEACHER: Let us look at these examples which I am writing on the board.

(*Teacher wrote these two examples*:)

$$
\begin{array}{c}
8 \\
\times\ 1 \\
\hline
8
\end{array}
\qquad\qquad
\begin{array}{c}
8 \\
\times\ \tfrac{1}{2} \\
\hline
\end{array}
$$

TEACHER: The multiplicands of these two examples are the same. The multiplier of the example at the right is how many times as small as that of the example at the left?

JOHN: Twice as small. The product will be 4. The product has to be twice as small as 8 × 1.

TEACHER: That is correct. What about these examples?

(*Teacher added the following two examples so that these four examples appeared on the board*:)

$$
\begin{array}{c}
8 \\
\times\ 1 \\
\hline
\end{array}
\qquad
\begin{array}{c}
8 \\
\times\ \tfrac{1}{2} \\
\hline
\end{array}
\qquad
\begin{array}{c}
8 \\
\times\ \tfrac{1}{4} \\
\hline
\end{array}
\qquad
\begin{array}{c}
8 \\
\times\ \tfrac{1}{8} \\
\hline
\end{array}
$$

BERT: In ¼ × 8, the multiplier is 4 times as small as in 1 × 8. The product would be 2.

EDDIE: And in ⅛ × 8, the multiplier is 8 times as small as in 1 × 8. The product would be 8 times as small as the product of 1 × 8. The product is 1.

HELEN: I see something interesting. Look at our products. They are smaller than the multiplicand when we multiplied by ½ and ¼ and ⅛.

BERT: That sounds strange. Usually our answer was larger than the multiplicand. It has to be when you multiply by whole numbers.

DONALD: That isn't true, Bert, when you multiply by 1. Any number times one is that number.

BERT: Of course, but I meant any number larger than one. And what about zero? A number multiplied by zero is zero.

FRANCES: Is it always true, that your answer is smaller than the multiplicand when you multiply by a common fraction?

TEACHER: Test your ideas with these examples.
(*Teacher wrote on board:*)

$$\begin{array}{ccccc} 9 & 6 & 6 & 12 & 12 \\ \times\,\tfrac{1}{2} & \times\,1 & \times\,\tfrac{1}{2} & \times\,1 & \times\,\tfrac{1}{2} \end{array}$$

MARY: In $\tfrac{1}{2} \times 9$, your multiplier is $\tfrac{1}{2}$ as large as if it were 1. The product will be $\tfrac{1}{2}$ as large as 9. Nine divided by 2 equals $4\tfrac{1}{2}$.

PAUL: In the next two examples, $1 \times 6$ and $\tfrac{1}{2} \times 6$, the multiplicands are the same. $\tfrac{1}{2} \times 6$ will be 3. All you need to do is to divide 6 by 2.

BETH: And in the next two examples, the same is true. $\tfrac{1}{2} \times 12$ is 6.

TEACHER: We can also write the examples this way. Both ways are good, but you will use this way most of the time.
(*Teacher wrote on the board:*)

$$\begin{array}{cccc} 9 & \tfrac{1}{4} \times 9 & 8 & \tfrac{1}{3} \times 8 \\ \times\,\tfrac{1}{4} & & \times\,\tfrac{1}{3} & \end{array}$$

JIM: It is easier to see which is your dividend and which is your divisor when you write the numbers across. That way will be easy.

TEACHER: You have made a good start. Let us end the lesson with your telling what you have discovered to be true about the multiplication of common fractions.

CONNIE: Multiplying by a common fraction is different from multiplying by a whole number. You have to think about division too.

SUSIE: When you multiply by $\tfrac{1}{2}$, you really divide by 2. Multiplication turns out to be dividing.

HELEN: When you multiply by $\tfrac{1}{4}$, you really divide by 4.

BERT: When you multiply by $\tfrac{1}{8}$, you really divide by 8.

TEACHER: If we use $L$ to stand for the value of any given number we want to use, what would the answer to this problem be?
(*Teacher wrote on the board:*)

$$L \times \tfrac{1}{2}$$

BERT: Your answer would be $L$ divided by 2. But that doesn't seem like other work we've had.

TEACHER: What would be the answer to that problem if the value of $L$ is 10?

GAIL: It would be 5. Ten divided by 2 is 5.

TEACHER: What would be the answer if $L$ equals 24?

The lesson continued with several other examples of generalizations concerning a whole number multiplied by a unit fraction.[14]

*Analysis.* In the first of these two lessons, the teacher told the children the answers; they were not taught the meaning of the operation; they were left to discover nothing. The rule was given to them.

In the second illustration the teacher and class participated in the learning experience together. The teacher encouraged the children to think things through, to express their ideas, to generalize, and to summarize the learnings. However, effective procedure in the classroom requires not only guiding children to acquire meanings through the discovery of generalizations which are useful to them, but challenging each child to do his best thinking. Many of these children were not being challenged because no real effort was apparent to provide for individual differences in the group.

## *Providing for Individual Differences*

How can a teacher do justice to a class in which one student is unable to find the answers to such simple problems as: 9 − 0 and 8 × 5 while others in the class are able to compute mentally such problems as: "Find the number of 20-cent pencils I can purchase for $2.80"? Here is one of the most difficult tasks in teaching arithmetic — providing for individual differences.

Teachers are aware of the fact that children in a given grade differ as widely in arithmetic as they do in other areas. In a primary grade, for example, the range of ability may be two or three years, while in the intermediate grades it may be five years. How to teach the slow learner, the average, and the gifted in the same class poses a real problem.

Although many elementary teachers divide the children into three or more reading groups they usually have a single class for arithmetic. They fail to realize that differences in ability to learn arithmetic are as great as those in learning to read. Or if they do realize this they have neither the time, inclination, nor materials to differentiate

[14] Peter Lincoln Spencer and Marguerite Brydegaard, *Building Mathematical Concepts in the Elementary School* (New York: Henry Holt and Company, 1952), pp. 240–242.

the assignments. However, a system of grouping which is flexible, and in which evaluation is an integral part, will help each child devolop to his full capacity. Even where children are grouped according to ability differentiated assignments are still needed. It would be a grave mistake to provide no differentiation of instruction among ability groupings. Rapid learners need much less work with manipulative materials than do slow learners. They move quickly to the abstract level of performance. They are generally capable of greater self-direction and sustained effort. Even in kindergarten they request permission to work abstract arithmetic problems during the work period in preference to building with blocks or using manipulative or art media. As they progress in the elementary school they should be provided with research projects that allow them to move at their own rate and to explore a topic in depth.

Programs providing for individual differences are based on (1) homogeneous grouping or (2) heterogeneous grouping.

## Homogeneous Grouping

Homogeneous grouping of students as an administrative organizational procedure is becoming rather common. One of the most effective ways of providing for individual differences is to divide groups homogeneously when there are two or more groups of children at the same grade level.

The criticism is often voiced that children suffer from such grouping and teachers are unhappy teaching children of average or less ability. However, experience, research, and observation point to the fact that children are less conscious of grouping than are adults, that teachers can do a better job when the range of abilities is decreased, and that the frustration of trying to "bring the children up to grade level" is obviated.

## Heterogeneous Grouping

Many teachers handle the problem of individual differences within a regular classroom by using the same groups for both reading and arithmetic or forming groups on the basis of arithmetic test scores and observation. The problem of more than two groups is tremendous for an inexperienced teacher at first. Later he may plan for three groups — the rapid learners, the average learners, and the slow learners.

*Flexibility*.  Groupings must be flexible in order to allow a child to move from one to another group when the situation warrants it.

*Variety*.  Groupings may change for different purposes. Often the class as a whole may profit from a learning experience; when a new topic is introduced the children can all participate in discovering the concepts underlying it. Once the concepts have been established, however, the children will return to their own groups and differentiated assignments.

*Scheduling*.  Because there are only so many hours in the day a carefully balanced schedule must be worked out to permit sufficient time for an arithmetic class to experience learning. If there are several arithmetic groups they may not have directed teaching every day.

*Assignment*.  In order to provide for the differences in children's ability the teacher may have as many as three textbooks. The pupils may be working on a common topic but at different levels of difficulty. Slow learners need more manipulative materials and drill. Differentiation refers both to scope and to depth.

## Organizing the Class for Arithmetic

Having grouped the children according to a defined criterion the teacher must apply principles which facilitate learning. He must be careful not to spend too much time with any one group. The temptation to concentrate on the slow learners must be resisted; on the other hand, to ignore them in the belief that "they can't learn much anyway" is unfair. The average pupils, too, must be considered; they sometimes are neglected because they are neither gifted nor retarded. The alert teacher will keep the schedule balanced, as well as flexible. Groups in general are organized to meet the needs of three types of pupils:

1. The first group understands concepts as they are explained. The children in this group, in fact, make the discoveries, see relationships, and make applications as soon as they are introduced and

are ready quickly for the next step. The gifted pupil who is ready to move on must not be held back. He does not need the extra drill; he can apply the learning and wants to go on to the next step. The teacher helps this group get started and then is free to give time to the next group.

2. The second group needs no remedial work; but it includes children who must spend more time with concrete materials and who need more opportunity for practice after they do understand the concepts and processes. They need practice under teacher guidance. Unsupervised practice may result in sloppy work and inaccurate learning.

3. The third group needs much opportunity to work with concrete materials in the development of concepts and processes. These children have to have time to explore each concept thoroughly and to be sure of each process involved in the solution of the problems before they are given any drill. A slow, step-by-step development of the basic number understandings and sequence of skills carefully guided by the teacher is essential. Extrinsic incentives have great appeal to this group as well as a liberal sprinkling of praise for good work.

"Does grouping facilitate learning?" Research is still looking for answers to this question. Holmes and Harvey[15] in a study on permanent versus flexible grouping concluded that the method used in grouping the arithmetic classes was not particularly crucial; more crucial were the teacher's personal and professional qualities and methods of teaching.

Weaver[16] discussed the importance of grouping children for instruction on a level-of-learning basis. For example, in the presentation of a problem involving multiplying a fraction by a whole number ($6 \times \frac{1}{2}$) he suggested that some of the group use manipulation of cut-out fractional parts, others draw a diagram, still others use abstract symbols, and some think of the addition process. Still others might recognize the need for multiplication and express the problem as an example to be solved ($6 \times \frac{1}{2}$). He concluded that differentiation in terms of levels of learning has been the most commonly neglected procedure, yet it is one which is extremely valuable and effective.

[15] Darrell C. Holmes and Lois F. Harvey, "An Evaluation of Two Methods of Grouping," *Educational Research Bulletin*, 35:213–222, November 1956.

[16] J. Fred Weaver, "Differentiated Instruction in Arithmetic: An Overview and a Promising Trend," *Education*, 74:300–305, January 1954.

Heathers and Pincus report the effort to meet the needs of all students in arithmetic through the dual-progress plan devised by George Stoddard. They believe that this plan offers a solution to the major shortcomings of current mathematics instruction in the elementary school in that it eliminates the grade-level demands or grade-level restrictions. It replaces the grade-level curriculum in arithmetic with a nongraded program in which all students progress along the defined sequence of understandings and skills at their individual rates. Gifted students move ahead rapidly while slow learners move more slowly than is usually planned in the grade-level program. Not until they have mastered a topic do they move on to the next. Individualized teaching is characteristic of the program. "Crossing the usual age lines occurs whenever the student's level of advancement in mathematics places him behind, or ahead of, other students of his age."[17] Promotion, however, does not depend upon progress in mathematics, but rather on progress in the language arts-social studies area, where the usual grade-level system applies.

Flourney and Otto[18] report the following methods for providing for individual differences:

*Class Organization.* In this method the whole-class organization is used for review and introduction to new topics followed by intraclass grouping to provide for individual needs based on tests, general observation, and daily performance on work sheets and textbook exercises.

*Variations in Time.* The technique of introducing successive topics more slowly to some pupils and allowing others to move more rapidly through the topics of one grade or level into those of the next grade or level is a type of time variation.

*Content Variations.* For the above-average achievers the content is varied through horizontal enrichment, providing more difficult problems and more difficult practice material.

For the below-average achievers the content is varied by delaying the introduction of difficult phases of some topics and some basic facts and providing additional practice exercises with planned repe-

[17] Glen Heathers and Morris Pincus, "The Dual-Progress Plan in the Elementary School," *The Arithmetic Teacher*, 6:302–305, December 1959.
[18] Frances Flourney and Henry J. Otto (eds.), *Meeting Individual Differences in Arithmetic* (Austin: University of Texas Press, 1959), p. 181–183.

tition. The below-average achiever should have enrichment activities involving social and recreational number experiences.

*Variations in Methods and Materials.* Variations in methods and materials should be more fully explored in an effort to meet the needs of all pupils — not merely below-average pupils. The use of concrete materials is frequently seen in teaching below-average achievers. Readiness testing, encouragement to learn by discovery, and varying the test items and testing procedures in order to challenge the thinking of the more able achiever are essential elements in effectively handling individual differences in the classroom.

Brownell predicts that future means of providing for learning differences in arithmetic will go far beyond present methods of class organization, adjusting time, content, methods, and materials. He points out that "in many schools — perhaps most — a great deal can be done in the way of vertical grouping. If arithmetic periods in successive grades were scheduled at the same hour, a slow learner in grade four could move to grade three for arithmetic and the fast learner to grade five. While this plan is a kind of acceleration, it avoids the principal objections to broad-scale, across-the-board acceleration, and it certainly should have the advantage of cutting down the range of learning ability for any given teacher."[19]

## *Providing Practice (Drill) in Arithmetic*

Practice makes permanent; it does not necessarily make perfect. However, motivated practice under supervision is necessary for high-level performance. A guiding principle in the use of drill is that it must be preceded by a thorough teaching program. Practice must follow understanding.

Because in recent years drill has been de-emphasized, suggestions for maintaining a better balance between meaning and skill in arithmetic have been proposed:

1. Give skill in computation its rightful place in arithmetic.
2. Teach essential meanings which contribute to greater skill in computation.

[19] William A. Brownell, "Arithmetic in 1970," *The National Elementary Principal*, 39:44, October 1959.

3. Adjust the amount of drill required for each child to gain mastery of the computation skills.

Spitzer concludes that "Drill should be influenced by several factors other than understanding; pupils should be conscious of the need for drill, and drill should be directly focused on the process."[20]

If practice is to be focused directly on the process, the role of games in drill is questionable; games require attention to more than the process being practiced. The primary purpose of games and similar materials in the drill procedure is to arouse and maintain the interest of the child.

Teachers vary in the way they divide the class period for instruction in arithmetic. Shipp and Deer[21] experimented to determine whether varying the amount of class time intermediate grade pupils spent on "developmental activities" and on "practice work" affected achievement. "Achievement" meant understanding arithmetic, using arithmetic accurately, solving problems, and "total" achievement. The term "developmental activities" referred to those activities of the teacher and class that were designed to increase understanding of the number system, the fundamental processes, and the social aspect of arithmetic. "Practice work" included individual activities in which pupils worked with pencil and paper on assigned computation or verbal problems, exercises, and questions from the text or workbook. The following conclusions were drawn:

1. There was a trend toward higher achievement, measured by a general achievement test, when the per cent of time spent on developmental activities was increased.

2. There was an indication that more than 50 per cent of class time should be spent on developmental activities.

3. The above conclusions apply to all ability levels — upper, middle, and lower.

This study gives strong experimental evidence that it is rewarding to devote more than half of the class time to a consideration of the developmental phase of arithmetic. The good teacher senses *when* and *how* to emphasize understanding and when to provide practice. "Developmental activities included explanations, discussion, and demonstrations by teacher and class; handling, inspecting, and ar-

[20] Spitzer, *op. cit.,* p. 399.

[21] Donald E. Shipp and George H. Deer, "The Use of Class Time in Arithmetic," *The Arithmetic Teacher,* 7:117–121, March 1960.

ranging visual and manipulative materials; and group reading, drawing, construction work, and committee projects. In general, activities of the class as a group were included in developmental activities. . . . In general, individual work on assigned exercises was classed as practice work."[22]

A good rule of thumb for the teacher in regard to the amount and type of drill is to provide for sufficient practice and drill to make arithmetic learnings permanent and readily available when they are needed. Although the words "practice" and "drill" are sometimes used interchangeably, a useful distinction for the teacher is to look on practice as involving variety and drill as being repetitive. Practice implies that the teacher is using a variety of procedures for teaching a given concept or learning and that he accompanies these procedures by demonstrations with materials, oral discussion, explanation, and use of material by the children.

Drill is used when the discovery, exploration, and discussion stages are past; repetition is the method of making permanent the learning. Repetition alone, however, does not help the child move from an immature level, such as that of rote counting, to a higher level, such as that of seeing relationships. Levels of thinking are raised not by mere repetition but by experience and opportunity to respond, to question, to experiment, to explore, to discover, and to give proof. Excessive drill is no substitute for a program filled with varied practice activities. A variety of practice activities that are well planned, teacher directed, and teacher-pupil evaluated will reduce the amount of drill needed to fix the learning.

## Using Instructional Materials and Aids

The success of an arithmetic curriculum depends in large measure upon methods and materials of instruction. The skillful teacher selects both methods and materials on the basis of the objectives to be achieved and the abilities, needs, and interest of the group.

The use of audio-visual material, particularly motion pictures and television, has grown immensely in the last decade, but the possi-

[22] *Ibid.*, pp. 117–118.

bilities have only begun to be realized. Brueckner[23] suggests a check list to determine the adequacy of the instructional materials.

*Kinds of Learning Aids in Arithmetic*

1. Concrete and manipulative materials:
    a. Objects to use to help children to discover number groupings and facts.
    b. Devices to teach meanings of numbers, such as the abacus.
    c. Place-value charts to teach meaning of number system.
    d. Materials used in demonstrating meanings of operations (processes).
    e. Cut-outs to show fractional values and relations.
    f. Instruments of measurement, such as rulers, scales, clocks, coins.
    g. Construction materials, field work, projects.
    h. Mechanical computing devices.
2. Visual aids:
    a. Illustrations that visualize the meanings of operations.
    b. Pictures, photographs, drawings to extend meanings.
    c. Beautiful designs and patterns.
    d. Bulletin board exhibits.
3. Symbolic or abstract materials:
    a. Textbooks, workbooks, practice materials.
    b. Diagnostic tests, progress tests, remedial exercises.
    c. Simplified instructional materials for slow learners.
    d. Advanced material for accelerated pupils.
    e. Charts, tables, graphs, diagrams.
    f. Reference books, pamphlets, bulletins.
    g. Business forms, blanks, bills, checks, receipts.
    h. Clippings, cartoons, maps.
    i. Games.
4. Community resources, field trips, excursions:
    a. Stores, banks, other places of business, markets, governmental buildings.
    b. Health facilities, developmental centers, libraries, weather bureau.
    c. Museums, exhibits.
    d. Transportation centers.
    e. Farms, local construction projects.

Young children gain a better understanding of the number system through the use of such concrete materials as disks and objects to

[23] *Op. cit.,* pp. 93–94.

form groups, the abacus or place-value charts, tickets to show the meaning and use of zero as a place holder, and fractional cutouts of circles to help discover relationships among fractions of different values.

As the child progresses in the elementary school he discards many of these materials. At the higher level of abstract thinking he uses symbolic materials found in textbooks, workbooks, and other printed sources for most of his work. Slow learners make use of concrete and semi-concrete materials for a longer time. Many children in the intermediate grades continue to find manipulative aids useful in performing operations with fractions, decimals, and per cents.

Mechanical devices like the Skinner[24] teaching machine are attempts to motivate the child and to facilitate the learning of arithmetic by putting the burden of learning where it belongs — on the child. The Skinner machine leads the student to *construct* the correct answer in harmony with Skinner's emphasis on "operant behavior," which he defines as behavior without a specific stimulus. Presented with arithmetic problems on the machine, the student responds by moving slides which disclose the right answer. For Skinner, the important role of the teaching machine is to lead the student to emit a response which is progressively brought under the control of the stimuli. He emphasizes the fact that the response should be constructed in a free-choice rather than in a multiple-choice situation.[25]

Zeaman's teaching machine, similar to one of the machines constructed by Skinner, is a special-purpose machine designed for teaching arithmetic to elementary school children. The problem that appears in the window may be of any degree of difficulty from $2 \times 2$ up to advanced problems of square root or long division. The student, after preliminary mental figuring or scratch-paper computation, composes his answer by moving four plungers at the front of the machine. When he is satisfied with his answer, he turns a crank

[24] B. F. Skinner, "The Science of Learning and the Art of Teaching," *Harvard Educational Review*, 24:86–97, Spring 1954.

[25] Norman A. Crowder, "Automatic Tutoring by Means of Intrinsic Programming," in Eugene Galanter (ed.), *Automatic Teaching: The State of the Art* (New York: John Wiley and Sons, Inc., 1959), p. 114.

at the right. If the answer is correct the machine moves to the next problem on the tape. If wrong, he tries again until he gets the correct answer and can proceed.[26]

Calculating machines, hand-operated computing machines, and tachistoscopic presentation of basic facts are also used on an experimental basis.

The creative teacher uses the materials in various ways to improve instruction: to motivate children, to interest them in a new process or step to be mastered, to help them discover meanings as they develop new concepts, to enrich the learning experience, and to illustrate applications of what has been learned. Teacher and children use instructional materials as tools; they never allow themselves to become the tools of the instructional materials.

## *Measuring Growth*

When the kindergarten child holds up five fingers and says, "I'm five years old," the teacher may find out whether the number 5 means something to him. Can he comprehend that 5 is a symbol for five things? Can he go to the counting frame and group five disks, or to the flannel board and put up five ducks beside the number 5, or bring five books to the teacher?

Whether evaluation occurs in the kindergarten or the sixth grade, the teacher must think of it always in terms of the objectives he hopes to accomplish. Such objectives should include the understanding of mathematical concepts and their interrelationships, the ability to compute accurately, and the ability to apply the quantitative skills in solving problems in and out of the classroom. Appropriate techniques for measuring pupil achievement are observation, interview, pencil and paper tests, standardized tests, analysis samples of everyday work, written reports, oral explanations of solutions to problems, demonstration of processes, problem-situation tests, performance tests, interest inventory, self-rating scales, questionnaires, and analysis of reports of methods of study.

[26] A. A. Lumsdaine, "Teaching Machines and Self Instructional Material," *Education Digest*, 25:3, December 1959.

MEASURING PUPIL GROWTH

The methods by which evaluation can be applied to the learner in the classroom are illustrated[27] in terms of four kinds of objectives:

| *Objectives* | *Evaluative Techniques to apply* |
|---|---|
| The student is | |
| 1. Developing meaningful concepts of numbers and of the decimal number system. | Objective tests of understandings. |
|    a. Understands meaning and function of place value. | Observation of daily work. Interview with learner. |
|    b. Uses symbols to express numbers of all kinds. | Anecdotal records about contributions. |
|    c. Understands why numbers "behave as they do." | Demonstration by learner. |
| 2. Becoming skillful in fundamental operations and in ability to apply them in social situations. | Standard tests. Informal tests from textbooks or paper-pencil tests. Observation of student. |
|    a. Has control of basic number facts. | Analysis of daily written work. Interviews to test understanding. |
|    b. Understands the meaning of the four number processes and their interrelationships. | Anecdotal records. |
|    c. Has skill in performing computations. | |
|    d. Can solve problems. | |
| 3. Developing competence in utilizing systems and instruments of measurement and quantitative procedures in dealing with problems of daily living. | Problem-situation tests. Objective tests. Behavior records and ratings. Rating of daily work. Interview. |
|    a. Can read the thermometer. | Analysis of ability to transfer mathematical concepts and skills to other curricular areas. |
|    b. Has skill in using measurement. | |
|    c. Constructs and interpets methods for communicating by graphs and charts. | |

[27] Adapted from Brueckner, *op. cit.,* pp. 25–27.

| *Objectives* | *Evaluative Techniques to apply* |
|---|---|
| 4. Developing effective methods of studying and learning arithmetic. | Tests of effectiveness of learning procedures. Observation of student. |
| a. Makes an aggressive attack on the learning of facts and operations. | Rating of student. Interviews. Record of activities. |
| b. Uses manipulative and visual aids effectively. | Questionnaires. Self-rating tests. |
| c. Practices systematically to develop mastery of skills. | Analysis of reports of methods of study. |

## MEASURING TEACHER GROWTH

"I wonder why certain processes in arithmetic stump my young-sters," said a fifth-grade teacher.

"Could it be," asked Miss Ennes, a veteran teacher, "that we are more competent in teaching certain phases of arithmetic than others? I never did like long division. I never use the process myself if I can help it. My children have never liked it either. I'm convinced that it is the teacher's attitude that helps determine what the children learn."

On the basis of data obtained on the arithmetic ability of 158 prospective elementary teachers Fulkerson observed that too many of the teachers studied had insufficient knowledge of arithmetic to teach the subject effectively. From his experience and other investigations, he believed it likely that comparable deficiencies were general. He concluded that "Good teachers develop in their pupils an enthusiasm for arithmetic, but poor teachers often cause their pupils to have an apathetic attitude toward, or even a pronounced dislike for, this important subject. . . . Poorly prepared teachers are not likely to provide the stimulus which will inspire their pupils to acquire this knowledge and arouse in them the desires to pursue other branches of mathematics."[28]

It is not only what the teacher does with a group of children now, but what was done last week, the week before, and the month before that, and what the preceding teachers did, that help them like arithmetic, see relationships and grasp meanings. "Meanings are not isolated facts. They exist in strands stretching from simple and

[28] Elbert Fulkerson, "How Well Do 158 Prospective Elementary Teachers Know Arithmetic?" *The Arithmetic Teacher*, 7:146, March 1960.

concrete to complex and abstract. The strands themselves are related to each other by cross-strands. Moreover, many strands are continually combining to make fewer strands."[29]

Improvement in arithmetic rests with the already overburdened elementary teacher. Among the ways in which this burden can be lightened are better preparation, in-service programs, and improved teaching conditions.

*Better Preparation.* The first way in which the teacher's load might be lightened is through better preparation in undergraduate years. A significant report by the Educational Testing Service makes this statement: ". . . Let us accept the assumption that a teacher who has a solid understanding of mathematics is more likely than not to develop a similar understanding in his pupils. Where does such an assumption take us? In a vicious circle, apparently, and in reverse — for it has been shown that this 'solid understanding' is frequently absent in teachers. Future teachers pass through the elementary schools learning to detest mathematics. They drop it in high school as early as possible. . . . They return to the elementary school to teach a new generation to detest it."[30]

*In-Service Programs.* In-service programs should be provided for the purpose of giving the teacher a better insight into the nature of the science of numbers and improved ways of teaching it. This can be accomplished through educational television, both on local and national levels, workshops, and the use of arithmetic consultants who supply teaching-learning materials, methods, and research findings.

*Improved Teaching Conditions.* The report cited above had this to say in defense of teachers if not of their teaching: "In any case, the teachers themselves could not be censured for the conditions under which they work. Most of them were struggling with classes of 35 to 40 pupils who sometimes spread over two different grade levels and almost always ranged widely from the bright but bored to the dull and bewildered. It takes more than brains, good will, and a sparkling personality to conquer this kind of situation. It takes a fundamental change in the *conditions* of teaching — a change that

---

[29] Buckingham, *op. cit.*, p. 280.
[30] Educational Testing Service, *Problems in Mathematical Education* (Princeton, N.J.: Educational Testing Service, 1956), p. 16.

only the public, acting through its representatives on school boards, can bring about."[31]

Fortunately there is a trend toward administrative grouping, which places a teachable group of children with similar learning abilities and needs together as a subgroup within a class. This enables the teacher to plan materials and activities that will better meet the needs of the gifted, the average, and the slow learners, as well as the children with special interests.

In the final analysis the teacher is the crux in an improved arithmetic program. He must continue to enrich his own background on the subject matter. He should capitalize on the desire of children to learn. If he plans with them learning experiences that are stimulating and worth while, if he guides them upward on the ladder of development, and if by his own enthusiasm he helps them appreciate the value of arithmetic in their lives, success will ultimately crown his efforts.

## *Conclusion*

The continual rumbling of dissatisfaction with methods of teaching arithmetic, combined with the needs of future scientists, statisticians, engineers, accountants, and housewives, has brought pressure to bear on the arithmetic program in the elementary school. Our citizens need to understand the essential ingredients of arithmetic — the number system and its operations, the basic ideas of quantity and relationships, and the application of concepts and processes. They need to explore the creative aspects of arithmetic and to extend the powers of the intellect as they tackle problems of significance.

The social aspect of arithmetic has been recognized and valued by many. The mathematical aspect has often been minimized or neglected. An effective arithmetic program includes understanding of mathematical concepts, competency in computational processes, and skill in their application. In a good curriculum the teacher guides children in well-defined experiences logically organized in terms of the ability, maturity, and interests of the children and the needs they have for skill in this vital area. The scope and sequence of the

[31] *Ibid.*, p. 17.

program are influenced, too, by other factors — research about the way children learn, the logical and sequential nature of arithmetic, and the clamor at the grass roots for skills and competencies of a higher order.

The teacher guides children in developing number concepts, computational skills, fractional concepts, and skill in problem solving. He selects experiences that extend meaning and help children discover answers. He introduces new steps, provides opportunity for practice, organizes the classroom for dealing with individual differences, and utilizes instructional materials effectively.

The responsibility of the teacher in evaluation rests not alone with appraising progress of the children but with self-evaluation — to determine the adequacy of selection, organization, development, and evaluation of the learning experiences he provides the boys and girls.

## ACTIVITIES AND QUESTIONS

1. What is meant by the mathematical and social aspects of arithmetic? Observe in a classroom and see which of these phases of arithmetic receives the major emphasis.

2. In the same classroom list the ways in which the teacher provides for individual differences among the pupils.

3. Examine three arithmetic textbook series and note the differences in the grade levels in which major emphasis on various computational processes appears.

4. How and when would you teach children decimals and per cent?

5. How would you help children become more competent in problem solving in arithmetic?

6. Organize a sequence for teaching primary children accuracy in linear measurement and plan some activities to which they can apply their knowledge and skill — for example, measuring a table.

7. Examine several curriculum guides to see at what grade level various emphases of instruction appear.

8. Plan a lesson for the grade in which you are most interested and show how you will provide for individual differences. What adjustments in the assignment will you make for the high achievers? The slow learners? What adjustments will you make in the method of teaching? In evaluation? Try to apply the principles found in the text and bibliography.

9. Observe in a classroom and list and evaluate the instructional materials and aids used in teaching arithmetic.

10. Evaluate the techniques suggested in this chapter for appraising understandings, competencies in fundamental operations, and methods of studying arithmetic.

11. Examine two standardized arithmetic achievement tests and determine what each is supposed to measure.

12. Recall your experiences in arithmetic as a child. What shaped your present attitude toward the subject?

# BIBLIOGRAPHY

"Arithmetic in the Elementary School," *The National Elementary Principal*, 39:95–101, October 1959.

Banks, J. Houston. *Learning and Teaching Arithmetic*. Boston: Allyn and Bacon, Inc., 1959.

Baron, Denis, and Bernard, Harold W. *Evaluation Techniques for Classroom Teachers*. New York: McGraw-Hill Book Company, 1958.

Bhargava, Sumitra. "Analysis and Comparison of the Scope and Sequence of the Computational Programs in Selected Arithmetic Textbooks." Doctoral dissertation, Syracuse University, 1956.

Boehm, George. *The New World of Math*. New York: The Dial Press, 1959.

Brown, James W., *et al. A-V Instruction: Methods and Materials*. New York: McGraw-Hill Book Company, 1959.

Brown, Kenneth E. *Analysis of Research in the Teaching of Mathematics: 1955 and 1956*. U.S. Department of Health, Education and Welfare, Office of Education, Bulletin No. 4. Washington, D.C.: Government Printing Office, 1958.

Brueckner, Leo J. *Improving the Arithmetic Program*. New York: Appleton-Century-Crofts, Inc., 1957.

Brueckner, Leo J., Grossnickle, Foster, and Reckzeh, J. *Developing Mathematical Understanding in the Upper Grades*. Philadelphia: John C. Winston Company, 1957.

Buswell, G. T. "The Content and Organization of Arithmetic," *The Arithmetic Teacher*, 5:77–84, March 1959.

Clark, John R., and Eads, Laura K. *Guiding Arithmetic Learning*. Yonkers-on-Hudson, N.Y.: World Book Company, 1954.

Curtin, James. "Arithmetic in the Total School Program," *The Arithmetic Teacher*, 4:235–239, December 1957.

Cutts, Norma A., and Moseley, Nicholas. *Providing for Individual Differences in the Elementary School.* Englewood Cliffs, N.J.: Prentice-Hall, Inc., 1960.

Drews, Ruth H., Mermer, Ada S., and von Boenigk, Winifred P. *Practical Plans for Teaching Arithmetic.* Dubuque, Iowa: William C. Brown Company, 1954.

Dyer, Henry S., Kalin, Robert, and Lord, Frederick M. *Problems in Mathematical Education.* Princeton, N.J.: Educational Testing Service, 1956.

Fry, Edward. "Teaching Machines: The Coming Automation," *Phi Delta Kappan,* 41:29–32, October 1959.

Glennon, Vincent J. *What Does Research Say About Arithmetic?* Washington, D.C.: Association for Supervision and Curriculum Development, NEA, rev. ed., 1958.

Grossnickle, Foster E., and Brueckner, Leo J. *Discovering Meanings in Arithmetic.* Philadelphia: The John C. Winston Company, 1959.

Gunderson, Agnes G., and Gunderson, Ethel. "Fraction Concepts Held by Young Children," *The Arithmetic Teacher,* 4:168–173, October 1957.

Harding, Lowry W. *Arithmetic for Child Development.* Dubuque, Iowa: William C. Brown Company, 1959.

Hunnicutt, Clarence W., and Iverson, William J. (eds.). *Research in the Three R's.* New York: Harper & Brothers, 1958, Chaps. XII, XIII, XIV.

Junge, Charlotte. "The Gifted Ones — How Shall We Know Them?" *The Arithmetic Teacher,* 4:141–146, October 1957.

Kirk, Samuel A., and Johnson, G. Orville. *Educating the Retarded Child.* Boston: Houghton Mifflin Company, 1951.

Larsen, Harold D. *Arithmetic for College.* New York: The Macmillan Company, rev. ed., 1958.

Larsen, H. D. *Enrichment Program for Arithmetic.* Evanston, Ill.: Row, Peterson and Company, 1956.

Marks, John L., Purdy, C. Richard, and Kinney, Lucien B. *Teaching Arithmetic for Understanding.* New York: McGraw-Hill Book Company, 1958.

Mauro, Carl. "A Survey of the Presentation of Certain Topics in Ten Series of Arithmetic Textbooks." Doctoral dissertation, University of Maryland, 1957.

McMeen, George. "Differentiating Arithmetic Instruction," *The Arithmetic Teacher,* 6:113–121, April 1959.

McSwain, Eldridge T., and Cooke, Ralph J., *Understanding and Teaching Arithmetic in the Elementary School.* New York: Henry Holt and Company, 1958.

Merton, Elda L. *Arithmetic Readiness Experiences in the Kindergarten.* Philadelphia: The John C. Winston Company, n.d.

Morton, Robert Lee. *Helping Children Learn Arithmetic.* Morristown, N.J.: Silver Burdett Company, 1960.

Morton, Robert Lee. *Teaching Children Arithmetic.* New York: Silver Burdett Company, 1953.

Mueller, Frances J. *Arithmetic, Its Structure and Concepts.* Englewood Cliffs, N.J.: Prentice-Hall, Inc., 1956.

National Council of Teachers of Mathematics. *The Growth of Mathematical Ideas, Grades K–12.* Washington, D.C.: The Council, 1959.

National Society for the Study of Education. *The Teaching of Arithmetic,* Fiftieth Yearbook, Part II, Nelson B. Henry (ed). Chicago: University of Chicago Press, 1951.

Nelson, Leslie W. *Instructional Aids.* Dubuque, Iowa: William C. Brown Company, 1958.

Provus, Malcolm M. "Ability Grouping in Arithmetic," *Elementary School Journal,* 60:391–398, April 1960.

Rosenquist, Lucy L. *Young Children Learn to Use Arithmetic.* Boston: Ginn and Company, 1949.

Rubenstein, Ben O. "The Role of the Teacher in the Learning Process," *Educational Administration and Supervision,* 45:95–101, March 1959.

Schott, Andrew F. "New Tools, Methods for Their Use and a New Curriculum in Arithmetic," *The Arithmetic Teacher,* 4:204–209, November 1957.

Skinner, B. F. "The Science of Learning and the Art of Teaching," *Harvard Educational Review,* 24:86–97, Spring 1954.

Sole, David. *The Use of Materials in the Teaching of Arithmetic.* Doctoral dissertation, Teachers College, Columbia University, 1957.

Spencer, Peter L., and Brydegaard, Marguerite. *Building Mathematical Concepts.* New York: Henry Holt and Company, 1952.

Spitzer, Herbert F. *The Teaching of Arithmetic.* Boston: Houghton Mifflin Company, 3rd ed., 1961.

Stern, Catherine. *Children Discover Arithmetic.* New York: Harper & Brothers, 1949.

Stern, Catherine. *Structural Arithmetic.* Boston: Houghton Mifflin Company, 1951.

Swain, Robert L. *Understanding Arithmetic.* New York: Rinehart and Company, 1957.

Van Engen, H. "Twentieth Century Mathematics for the Elementary School Child," *The Arithmetic Teacher,* 6:71–77, March 1959.

Weaver, J. Fred. "Research in Arithmetic Instruction — 1958," *The Arithmetic Teacher,* 6:121–132, April 1959.

# 11

Imagination is more important than knowledge.

ALBERT EINSTEIN

# Fostering
## creativity in the arts

Within each child lies the potential for creativity that is waiting to be tapped. Whether the creative urge expresses itself in drama, dance, music, or art is dependent upon the environment, the abilities, the interests of the child, and his opportunities for expression. Children do not create in a vacuum. Arranging an environment which is conducive to creativity requires an understanding of the values of creative expression, the means by which it is fostered, the media through which it is developed, and the activities that bring it to fruition. This is the teacher's contribution to creativity.

## Values of Creative Expression

The average child is surrounded by so many "don'ts" that he is looking for outlets whereby he can express his feelings legitimately. The creative arts offer such a release. If, when tensions build up, he can play them out, express them in color, or poetry, or song, he is able to build inner resources that will become increasingly satisfying as he matures.

Creative expression gives the child a sense of achievement and worth. He needs recognition and praise. Receiving acclaim for an art product is one of the happiest experiences he can have. The teacher who values children will help each child find his hidden talent or gift.

Creative expression helps children make wise use of their leisure time. Increased leisure is making hobbies more important for both children and adults. The problem of longevity is minimized for those fortunate people who in their youth learned to express themselves in a satisfying creative medium. To participate is more rewarding than to view.

Creativity cuts across many disciplines and is an integral part of problem solving. It helps children develop their thinking and stimulates the imagination. Young children are characterized by spontaneity, but this must be encouraged if it is to develop.

Creative expression promotes creative power. Society has placed such value on group participation, togetherness, and cooperative action that individual contributions have often been lost. However, the great achievements in art, literature, philosophy, and science have been the contributions of individuals. Groups cannot invent or create. The individual creates; the group develops.

Creative expression provides opportunities for the operation of social processes through drama, dance, and music groups; scenery and costume making; contributing to school festivals, pageants, and programs. ". . . Concern for creativity should permeate and vitalize childhood education in all its diverse aspects."[1]

[1] Laura Zirbes, *Spurs to Creative Teaching* (New York: G. P. Putnam's Sons, 1959), p. 260.

## *The Role of the Teacher in Creative Expression*

All children are artists; all children have gifts; all children are creative. However, unless the gifts are discovered, cherished, and developed the spark may be forever lost. Where joy is, children create. In an environment in which creativity can flourish there will be found (1) a rich background of experiences, (2) encouragement and appreciation, (3) time to create and evaluate, (4) opportunities and materials for exploration, (5) recognition of each child's contribution, and (6) a teacher who is himself creative. The basis upon which the teacher decides how to encourage, guide, direct, and leave alone will be discussed. The actual creation is the child's own; the teacher stands by.

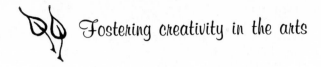 

# Dramatics

Where shall we adventure, today that we're afloat,
Wary of the weather and steering by a star?
Shall it be to Africa, a-steering of the boat,
To Providence, or Babylon, or off to Malabar?

ROBERT LOUIS STEVENSON

Wherever children are they "try on life." They imitate what they have seen or heard. They identify with people, animals, trains, or boats and lose themselves in the role they are playing. They *are* anything their young minds fancy. Teachers who realize the value of this natural interest in make-believe use it in their teaching.

Conversations in the doll house are typical of dramatic play:

"This is a nail file to do your hands. I'll put it on the dresser. I bought it downtown. You really call it an emery board, but filing nails is what it does. Why don't you sit down and do your nails before we go to the party with the Nelsons? Oh, just a minute. There's the telephone now. That's probably them calling. What time will you be ready to go? O.K."

Jim smiles gaily at Ann as he answers the phone. "Yes, Mrs. Nelson, Ann is home, but she's busy filing her nails. I got her a new emery board. *Emery* board — you know, what you use to file your nails with. She likes it fine. Oh, just a moment, she'll be right here to talk to you. Then you two can get together on the time."

*519*

Today Jim is the father, but yesterday he was the little boy. You heard him protesting loudly as his big sister (five-year-old Cindy) was off to school. "Mother! Why can't I go with Cindy? You know Miss Angel wants me to come and visit that school when I can. Don't let Cindy go without me."

"Now, Jim," soothes his "mother" (another five-year-old), "when you're bigger and older and don't cry you can go to school, too. Then you can play in the doll house, or build with blocks, climb the jungle gym, and paint big pictures. And you can drink orange juice and pass the cookies on your birthday, and play games and do lots of grown-up things like they do in kindergarten. And you can be a policeman, a grocery man, a fire chief, and a pilot or a co-pilot or even an engineer."

This is dramatic play — the beginning of creative dramatics.

The younger the child, the less cautious he is about trying something new and difficult. He changes suddenly from one role to another. Teachers learn to get out of the way quickly because a child who only a moment ago was a tree standing in front of the house has suddenly, and without warning, become a jet.

## Definition of Terms

Teachers need to be familiar with the various forms of dramatic activity and the terms used to describe them.

*Dramatic Play.* As has been pointed out, this is the make-believe play of the young child. It is spontaneous, free activity in which there is no plot, no need for an audience. The child tries on the roles of people, animals, and things with which he wishes to identify.

*Creative Dramatics.* Creative dramatics is an activity in which "a group of children make a story come alive by playing it spontaneously, whether it is original or taken from literature, history or current happenings."[2] It differs from dramatic play in having a plot, a definite beginning, a climax, and an ending. Since the dialogue is

[2] Winifred L. Ward, *Playmaking with Children* (New York: Appleton-Century-Crofts, Inc., 2nd ed., 1957), p. 10.

impromptu it is never the same twice. Creative dramatics exists for the children. It is the children's ideas that make it come alive.

*Playmaking.* The term "playmaking" is often used interchangeably with "creative dramatics." It takes in all forms of improvisation in drama, including dramatic play, pantomime, puppetry, and story dramatization. It is impromptu, informal, creative. It may be based on a well-known story in literature or be original in idea, plot, and character.

*Children's Drama.* Children's drama differs from creative dramatics in having a set script. Lines are memorized and spoken as written. The story is written by children or adults for children. The actors are selected from the group on the basis of ability to portray the characters; the settings and costumes are more elaborate, and the audience expects a finished performance.

*Children's Theater.* Children's theater emphasizes the finished performance. It is primarily for child audiences. Players are professional or semiprofessional children or adults. The theater has an obligation to the audience; therefore the emphasis is on the product. Costumes and stage settings are elaborate, and actors able.

In creative dramatics the ideas, experiences, dialogue, and stories are the material out of which children create plays. There are no set lines, no elaborate costumes, no rich settings; the teacher acts as a guide, not a director. The emphasis is on the process, not the product. It is what happens to the child as he participates in creative dramatics that is of paramount importance. "To feel the difference between being generous and selfish, brave and fearful, happy and sad, successful and failing, helps the child recognize the taste of desirable experience, with the result that he seeks more of the same. To some children, vicarious experience provides the only opportunity to experience beauty."[3]

## Creative Dramatics

Creative dramatics is becoming recognized as one of the most valuable activities in the life of the elementary school child. That

[3] Margaret S. Woods, "Creative Dramatics," *NEA Journal,* May 1959, p. 53.

dramatic play is important to the young child has long been generally realized. Erikson[4] emphasizes the value of "playing it out" as the most natural auto-therapeutic measure childhood offers. Isaacs[5] points out that play is not only the means whereby the child discovers his world but the activity that brings him equilibrium in the early years. The value of creative dramatics is epitomized by Winifred Ward: "Creative play is one of the strongest motivating forces in learning. . . . It promotes better understanding of peoples and places and, as no dialogue is written, the creative drama provides an excellent framework for expression and imagination."[6]

*Providing a Legitimate Emotional Outlet.* Creative dramatics offers the child opportunity for emotional development through (1) expressing his problems, (2) releasing his tensions, (3) trying on new roles, and (4) cooperating in group activities.

*Providing a Means of Self-Expression.* Every individual needs to achieve emotional satisfaction and to gain approbation. Creative dramatics affords an excellent opportunity for children who are not necessarily high achievers in academic subjects. Here they are free to portray the characters as they choose. There are no lines to memorize, and they can work out their own pantomime. They can use their talent for making scenery that is not elaborate and yet contributes to the over-all effect. Imagination can take wing and go as far as it will. Imagination is the essential ingredient in creative dramatics. The time to develop it is in the years before inhibitions have been imposed or it has become dormant because of disuse.

*Helping the Child Develop Awareness of the World.* Santayana pointed out that "many of us look for the miracle in the unusual, and the philosopher and poet see the miracle in the usual." Children especially, see the miracle in the everyday world, and through creative dramatics they engage not only in self-expression but in self-dis-

---

[4] Erik H. Erikson, "Studies in the Interpretation of Play," *Genetic Psychology Monographs*, 22:561 (1940).

[5] Susan Isaacs, *Social Development of Young Children*, quoted in Ruth Hartley *et al.*, *Understanding Children's Play* (New York: Columbia University Press, 1952), p. 17.

[6] Winifred Ward, "Dramatics — A Creative Force," *The School Executive*, 69:54, August 1950.

covery. By exploring, experimenting, observing, and reacting to relationships they get to know themselves and to form concepts of the world. Gradually everything in the environment falls into place, and meaningful experiences are later re-created in dramatic play. For example, a group of children may be studying transportation. They take a train ride to a neighboring city, a boat trip across the lake, or a bus trip to the station or dock. They purchase tickets, board the train, find their seats, give the tickets to the conductor, have dinner in the diner, and finally leave the train. Experiences of this type lead to further learning and broader interests.

*Giving the Child Experiences in Social Understanding and Co-operation.* Creative drama allows children not only to learn about other people and cultures but to portray what other people are feeling by actions and words. Such portrayal of character calls for growing sensitivity to another's feelings.

Closely allied to increased understanding and awareness of others is the experience of working with others to make the whole play or dramatization a success. No one tries to "steal the show," always get the leading roles, or make all the contributions. By working together as a team with the interest of the play uppermost children learn to accept responsibility for group achievement, to work with others for a common purpose, and to achieve a common goal while at the same time having the delightful creative experience that drama brings.

## Sources for Creative Dramatics

Children's everyday experiences serve as valuable sources for dramatizing. A second source includes rhymes, poems, stories, folk lore, fairy tales, and legends. A third involves pantomime of situations, objects, or character as the starting point. Examples have already been given of everyday experiences as sources of creative dramatics.

*Poetry and Rhymes.* Children are fascinated by dramatizing Mother Goose rhymes: "Sing a Song of Sixpence," "Old King Cole,"

"Jack and Jill," "Little Boy Blue," "Mary Had a Little Lamb," "Little Jack Horner," "Little Miss Muffet," and others. They are eager to play the different characters and show originality in their expression. They give different interpretations to the same rhyme. For example, in dramatizing "Mary Had a Little Lamb" one lamb may be frisky and kick up his hind legs as he follows Mary to school; perhaps he lingers occasionally to nibble at some grass, then hurries to catch up with Mary. Another lamb may very sedately follow Mary all the way to school and bleat pitifully outside the door until the teacher comes out to turn him away.

Poetry, too, serves as an excellent basis for creative dramatics. "Imaginings" and "Someone" are intriguing to the young child who likes to pretend. "The Butterbean Tent" and "Red Rooster" offer possibilities for characterization. For older boys and girls ballads and narrative poems are favorites — "The Raggle Taggle Gypsies," "The Highwayman," "The Pied Piper of Hamelin," and "Barbara Frietchie." Any number of poems found in anthologies inspire dramatization with a group of children who have learned to enjoy poetry with a creative teacher. It is an axiom that before anything significant can be accomplished in creative activity with children the teacher must be a creative individual, in which case he will have a spontaneous, fresh approach to the old as well as an eager, enthusiastic approach to the new.

*Stories.* Children love to make plays out of such favorites as "The Three Bears," "The Three Little Pigs," "The Gingerbread Man," "The Three Billy Goats Gruff," "The Bremen Town Musicians," and "The Elves and the Shoemaker." The successful teacher balances the old with the new, broadens horizons, extends interests, and develops literary appreciation.

## MATERIALS FOR THE KINDERGARTEN AND PRIMARY GRADES

A creative teacher gives children an outlet for feelings as well as ideas. Teachers of young children realize the importance not only of dramatic play but of the playing out of rhymes, poems, and stories. Among the best-liked stories, rhymes, and poems that children in the lower grades enjoy dramatizing are the following:

| *Stories* | *Nursery Rhymes* | *Poems* |
|---|---|---|
| Ask Mr. Bear | Hickory Dickory | The Crimson Bal- |
| This is the Way the | Dock | loon |
| Animals Walk | The Queen of | The Elf and the |
| The Carrot Seed | Hearts | Dormouse |
| Caps for Sale | Ride a Cock Horse | Galoshes |
| The Cap That | Daffy Down Dilly | Fancy Dress |
| Mother Made | Little Nancy Etti- | Choosing Shoes |
| The Good Shepherd | coat | I'm an Engine |
| The Little Lamb | Jack Be Nimble | The Squirrel |
| Little Black Sambo | Mistress Mary | The Night Was |
| The Little Rabbit | This Little Pig | Creeping |
| That Wanted | Went to Market | Behind the Water- |
| Red Wings | Pussy Cat, Pussy | fall |
| The Little Engine | Cat | Doorbells |
| That Could | Baa, Baa, Black | The Elf Singing |
| Little Duckling | Sheep | Feet — Hands |
| Tries His Voice | Humpty Dumpty | The Wonderful |
| The Tale of Peter | Rub-a-Dub-Dub | Weaver |
| Rabbit | The North Wind | Roads |
| Cinderella | Doth Blow | A Bell for Ursula |
| Jack and the Bean- | Little Bo-Peep | I Saw a Proud |
| stalk | I Had a Little Pony | Mysterious Cat |
| Make Way for | Diddle, Diddle, | Bantam Rooster |
| Ducklings | Dumpling | The City Mouse |
| Benjie's Hat | I Saw a Ship Sailing | Little Snail |
| Timothy Turtle | Six Little Mice | The Little Turtle |
| Wait for William | Wee Willie Winkie | The Swing |
| The Little Wooden | Lavender's Blue, | My Shadow |
| Farmer | Diddle, Diddle | Pretending |
| Snipp, Snapp, Snurr | Simple Simon | Circus |
| and the Red Shoes | One Misty, Moisty | Radiator Lions |
| Mike Mulligan and | Morning | Song of the Train |
| His Steam Shovel | This Is the House | Buckingham Palace |
| A Boat for Peppe | That Jack Built | Twinkletoes |
| The Old Market | The Knave of | The Four Friends |
| Woman | Hearts | Brownie |
| The Sleeping | Dame, Get Up and | Nursery Chairs |
| Beauty | Bake Your Pies | At the Zoo |
| Rumpelstiltskin | Lady Bug | Missing |
| Pinocchio | The Goblin | Hoppity |
| The Three Wishes | A Farmer Went | Halfway Down |
| The Nativity Story | Riding | Teddy Bear |

| Stories | Nursery Rhymes | Poems |
|---|---|---|
| Yertle the Turtle | Goosie Gander | Some One |
| Many Moons | Hey Diddle Diddle | Hiding |
| How the Robin's | Jack and Jill | Fireflies |
| Breast Became | One, Two, Buckle | Good Morning |
| Red | My Shoe | Mud |
| Down, Down the | Little Boy Blue | My Funny |
| Mountain | Little Jack Horner | Umbrella |
| The Biggest Bear | Little Miss Muffet | Crescent Moon |
| Roger and the Fox | Lucy Locket | The Dandelion |
| Snow White | Tom, Tom, the | The Snowman |
| Little Wild Horse | Piper's Son | Snow |

### STORIES FOR OLDER CHILDREN

Teachers of older children do not always realize that the love of the dramatic and the need for expression go far beyond the primary grades. Intermediate children, too, must satisfy the creative urge. Some creativity will be spontaneous and on-the-spot, when the fifth-grade teacher says, "You had better check to see that you have a bathing suit in your luggage because we board the plane for Hawaii at one o'clock tomorrow at the Municipal Airport." Of course she might have said, "Find Hawaii on the map and turn to page 83 to read what it says about the occupations and recreational activities of the people."

There are many excellent stories for intermediate children to dramatize. Some of the perennial favorites are:

| | |
|---|---|
| The Emperor's New Clothes | The Little White Horse |
| Homer Price | The Bishop's Candlesticks |
| Roller Skates | The Strawberry Girl |
| The Bailiff's Wonderful Coat | Amahl and the Night Visitors |
| Caddie Woodlawn | The Boy Knight of Rheims |
| The Christmas Nightingale | The Egg Tree |
| The Nutcracker of Nuremburg | A Christmas Promise |
| Robin Hood | Pandora |
| The Sorcerer's Apprentice | Saint Francis and the Wolf |
| Stone Soup | Heidi |
| The Miser and His Monkey | Tom Sawyer |
| Tyll Eulenspiegel's Merry | The Nuremburg Stove |
| Pranks | Why the Chimes Rang |
| Our Lady's Juggler | Adam of the Road |

The Legend of the Black Madonna
The Three Sillies
Stories from Shakespeare's plays
The Singing Shoemaker
Treasures of the Medranos
Tricky
Tuffy
Monty
Sleigh Bells of Windy Foot
Coarse Gold Gulch

The Page of Count Reynard
Rip Van Winkle
Wind in the Willows
Peterkin Papers
Song of the Pines
Golden Conquest
He Went with Marco Polo
The Hobbit
Banner in the Sky
Patterns on the Wall
Charlotte's Web

*Pantomime.*  Pantomiming situations and characterizations is one of the most interesting modes of dramatic expression. Pantomiming situations requires skill and is a challenge to intermediate grade children particularly. Some situations allowing for a variety of interpretation and creativity are the following:

Activity in a train station
Watching an exciting movie
Getting ready to go out with your parents when you'd rather see your favorite television program
Trimming the Christmas tree
Having fun in the snow
Riding on a crowded bus carrying a very large package
Watching a parade

Watching a Western on television
Gathering flowers on a spring day
Playing baseball and striking out when the bases are loaded
Playing basketball and being pulled out of the game on a foul when the team is one point behind
Getting ready for an important date

As children develop in this skill they may wish to add dialogue. However, for those who are shy about creating dialogue the teacher may wish to use the technique of substituting the letters of the alphabet for words and showing by voice expression the emotion, feeling, and action they wish to portray.

## Guiding Creative Dramatics

From the foregoing discussion it is apparent that there is a wealth of material for children to use in dramatics — rhymes, poems, stories, situations suggested by activities in the home, school, and play-ground, and by seasons or holidays. Children are eager to create. However, they need encouragement. The teacher must be able to motivate and guide them in such a way that their experiences have value. Many times he must give help in selecting and adapting a story that has dramatization possibilities for the particular maturity level, interest, and needs of the children, and in delineating the characters.

Those children are fortunate who have a creative teacher. How-ever, experience of the authors with teachers has shown that many of them, too, have potential for creativity that they have never tapped. A basic essential for success in encouraging children in this area is an environment that is permissive but organized. The teacher needs to know how to guide children, yet allow them to develop their own ideas. Guidance involves insight and skill in motivating the group, presenting the material, adapting the story, planning characters and action, playing the story, and evaluating the activity.

*Motivating the Group.* How teachers motivate children to dra-matize depends upon the interests of the group, the skill of the teacher, and the possibilities in the environment. Rhythm is in-triguing to young children. Stories or poems that have action appeal to them. Sometimes the teacher begins with "Why couldn't they put Humpty Dumpty together again? Why do you think he fell? How would you feel if you were sitting on the wall?" Or he appeals to the children's senses. Listening to the music of Saint-Saëns' *Carnival of the Animals* might well suggest to children drama-tizing a story about "The Three Bears," "The Story About Ping," or "Wait for William," in which the elephant is an important char-acter.

Listening to the sounds in the environment is an excellent way to motivate children to creative play. Bird calls, animal noises, balloons popping, airplanes overhead — all can be used to stimulate interest. Sometimes the sounds may be imagined:

One spring day eighteen four- and five-year-olds were sitting in a circle. The teacher said slowly, "I see as many clocks as I see boys and girls. Each clock makes a sound. When this clock strikes one I want to hear the sound the clocks makes."

"Tick tock, tick tock, it's one o'clock." (Children clap once.)

"Tick tock, tick tock, it's two o'clock." (Children clap twice.)

TEACHER: Listen. Are there any other sounds the clock makes?

CHILD: The little mouse who scampered to get some cheese and then heard the sound the little clocks were making.

TEACHER: If you were as frightened as the mouse who heard the clock strike when he went to get the cheese, what would you do? Let's all be that little mouse getting ready to come out of the tiny hole. Use both eyes and ears before you get that cheese.

The children tried different ways of being the little mouse. Since the space was limited only one mouse went at a time. While the mouse was going after the cheese the third time one of the children chanted:

> Hickory Dickory Dock
> The mouse ran up the clock.
> The clock struck one,
> The mouse ran down,
> Hickory Dickory Dock.

TEACHER: That was very good. I hadn't thought to do just that one, but it's good. What did Jenny do that really looked like a mouse that was warily creeping to get the cheese?

CHILD: She went softly on her toes.

CHILD: How do you know a mouse has toes?

CHILD: I liked the way she came back slowly, slowly on her toes.

JIMMY: I want to scamper up the clock and down the clock, Hickory, dickory, dock.

Jimmy and three other boys were given the opportunty to be the mouse while the group chanted. The children pantomimed the actions of the mouse, or in some cases the clock, and the teacher concluded the session.

TEACHER: That was *nice*. Was it fun to be mice? Was it fun to be clocks?

CHILDREN: Yes! Yes! Yes!

Poems, music, rhythms, riddles, jokes, seasonal activities, the world of nature, all offer rich opportunities for creative play. Teachers often use pictures to motivate creative expression. For example, a picture of the Three Bears might suggest a plot or setting different from the one the children usually play. Both mood and action of the story to be dramatized are important. The teacher is responsible for establishing the mood as he presents the story to the group.

*Presenting the Story.* From the wealth of literature available the teacher may select the stories and poems that he himself enjoys and that he knows the group will enjoy too. The work finally chosen for dramatization should be one with which the children are familiar.

As the teacher reads the story aloud he imparts feeling through his interpretation, gestures, voice, and attitude. A famous teller of tales points to the significance of this step when she states, "The one immutable law of story-telling is to see with your inner eye everything of which you speak."[7] This calls for knowing the story well, having a vivid imagination, and a voice of flexibility, variety, color, and richness.

*Adapting the Story.* With the young child, the play's the thing. He does not want to be weighed down with prolonged discussions, lengthy details, and elaborate settings. He wants to move quickly through planning the scenes, characters, and setting. Once the mood is established, he is ready to select the characters, decide on the scenes, introduce the story, move it forward, and build the climax. Older children enjoy spending more time on each step. Many stories can be adapted to playmaking at various age levels.

*Choosing the Characters.* Trying on characters is one of the most exciting parts of creative dramatics. Everything has been building up to this point. The children may be asked to pantomime the actions that appear to be suitable to a character. They may discuss the traits of a particular character; they may work on characterizations singly or in groups. The teacher can guide them by asking, "What does the character look like? What is he wearing? How does he walk? How does he talk? Why is his disposition the way it is?" When the group is ready to select a person for a particular role they will keep in mind the characteristics they have discussed. They will evaluate characterizations and select the most suitable. Suggestions for improvement may come from the group; characters are not static. Each time the story is played a different character may be chosen.

*Planning the Scenes.* Unless the children and teacher limit the scenes to be included and the events to take place in each scene, the play is likely to fall apart. Some of the questions that help children

---

[7] Edna Johnson *et al., Anthology of Children's Literature* (Boston: Houghton Mifflin Company, 3rd ed., 1959), p. 1086.

get started are: "How should we begin our play? What happened first that would be important to portray? What happened next? How will the dialogue work in to tell that part of the story? How can we plan the next scene?"

After the children decide on the scenes they can play, preplanning the scenes and the dialogue helps get the story off to a good start. It may not be possible to play the entire story in a single period the first time. For example, if they were playing the story of "Snipp, Snapp, Snurr and the Red Shoes" they might play only the scene where the boys are discussing the coming birthday of their mother and get permisison to go out and play. Later scenes could include their attempt to get the money from their bank to buy the gift she wanted, the scene where they seek and find work, the meeting at the end of the day in the shoemaker's shop, and the final reunion at home with the mother.

*Building the Climax.* Every story should have a high point. Sometimes the climax is obvious. At other times one must read between the lines. In such a case the teacher asks, for example, "What could have happened to Katherine at the court of King Arthur? Was she frightened by the strange environment? What did she do? How can you show us that she was frightened?" Questions such as these help children portray the climactic action of the story.

*Planning the Scenery, Costumes, and Properties.* Once the children have decided on the characters, the scenes, and the way to move the story along, they plan what scenery, properties, and costumes they want. Actually, in creative dramatics they need very little. They can imagine the scenery and use just a suggestion of costume for the actors — a bushy tail for the squirrel, long ears for the rabbit, a trunk for the elephant. They may have the mother wear a long dress and an apron and have the farmer carry or wear an old straw hat. Sometimes, however, they may have the urge to paint scenery, make costumes, and assemble more elaborate properties. Remember that the process is the important thing. Good creative dramatics requires little in the way of equipment except the imagination of the children.

*Evaluating the Activity.* One of the most profitable phases of creative dramatics takes place when the play is over and the players return to their seats. The children in the audience evaluate the performance:

"I think the King was very good. He looked and acted pompous and that fit his role."

"The Queen did her part so you could see she was happy. She kept rocking her baby and smoothing the covers on the cradle and smiling as she sang a lullaby. But when Rumpelstiltskin came her expression changed fast."

"The fairies looked and acted like good fairies and were so graceful in their movements. But the wicked fairy, I didn't like the way she looked, but it was good for the part she played."

When the children finish their comments about how good the play was, they may turn to the subject of improving it. "How could we make it better if we played it again?" Children quickly learn to give and take constructive criticism when it is directed, not at a child, but at the character. The teacher is there to see that they are fair, and not unduly harsh in criticizing any role. He emphasizes the fact that evaluation is for the purpose of improving the play next time. Unless the standards are raised as the year proceeds, creative dramatics can degenerate into shoddy, unsatisfying experiences. The teacher's role is to guide and make specific contributions. According to Ward, "Just as we should see to it that good work from every child is commended, we need to supplement the suggestions if they are not vital. . . . Usually, a question is all that is necessary to bring out the point from the children themselves, even to the suggestion of what might be the subjects of conversation in a scene that had been stilted or unnatural, or a point of ethics that had been questionable."[8]

Teachers frequently find it useful to keep in mind questions about each phase of the dramatization: story, characters, conversation, action and blocking, climax, cooperation, pacing, voice, audience reaction, and time spent in getting ready.

> *The story.* If you had not been familiar with the story would you have been able to get the thread from the scenes that were portrayed? Did the climax serve as the high point? Did the story move along?
>
> *Characters.* Did the people stay in character? Did they make

[8] Ward, *Playmaking with Children*, p. 137.

you feel the way they themselves were feeling? Did they capture the personalities they tried to portray?

*Conversation.* Did the conversation seem real for the characters? Did it fit the locale and period of the story? Did the dialogue move the story along?

*Action.* Did the pantomime and business help the story to unfold? Did the groups seem to be doing things that were natural for the story?

*Blocking.* Did the grouping aid the story? Was the "picture" always kept in mind?

*Climax.* Could you tell where the high point came? Did it seem significant enough? How could we improve it?

*Cooperation.* Did the characters help each other? Did anyone try to steal the show? Did they interact with one another?

*Pacing.* Did the play move at a good pace? Did it get anywhere? Was it too fast or too slow? How can we improve the pacing?

*Voice.* Could you hear the players? Did they project throughout the play? Did they talk with their backs to the audience? How can they improve their voices and diction?

*Audience reaction.* Did the audience react at the right places? Did they support the characters by listening courteously? Did they show their appreciation in the accepted manner at the end?

*Time spent in getting ready.* Did we spend enough time on this story to become well acquainted with the background, the characters, and the dialogue? Did we spend so much time on it that we were bored when the time came to play it?

*Principles of Drama.* If the teacher or leader in creative dramatics is acquainted with the elements of drama construction he will feel more secure about trying this activity in the classroom.

1. The story selected should be of literary merit and suitable for creative drama.

2. The elements of a play are plot, characters, and dialogue. There should be a problem, a conflict, complications, and a solution.

3. The story should start at the outset. Action is important. The beginning should get the attention and hold the interest of the audience. The story, once started, should never be interrupted. It must move along.

4. Exposition or explanation of the situation and the characters is given mainly by dialogue and action. The best technique is to use conversation rather than soliloquy.

5. Episodes or incidents are the happenings that make up the plot. Some are main events, others minor. They should be clearly delineated in working out the scenes. For example, in "The Sleeping Beauty" the main events are: The curse, the pricking of the Princess' finger, and the awakening. The minor incidents include the christening, the lessening of the blow by the twelfth fairy, the roaming in the palace by the princess when she is fifteen years of age, the fate of the people of the palace, their awakening, and the marriage. Episodes should be few in number and variety and should have suspense, complications, and a crisis.

6. The climax or high point of the story must be strong.

7. The characters must be understandable. Children "try on" characters in order to portray them vividly. Discussion of the characters helps the children better understand motives.

8. Dialogue should be short and simple. Don't tell it if you can show it. Conversation should be in keeping with the characters.

A working knowledge of the principles of drama will be useful in helping children create if such knowledge is combined with what the teacher knows about children and the values of creative expression. Although creative dramatics is concerned primarily with the process, not the product, there are times when children want to give a play for another group, for an assembly program, or for parents. Occasionally, too, teachers of creative dramatics are called upon to help with children's theater plays, and the knowledge makes them better directors.

## Children's Drama

Although elementary children participate in creative dramatics much more often than in children's drama, both experiences can be creative. The purpose is the determining factor. In creative dramatics all the children can create. They all get a chance to be characters and portray them as they choose, to create their own dialogue, and to develop the stories according to their imagination. Children's drama, on the other hand, challenges the able boy and girl to learn, act, and speak lines that have real literary quality, perform for an audience, and achieve satisfaction in a polished artistic performance. Both creative dramatics and children's drama have value and a place in the elementary school.

## Problems in Children's Drama

*Selecting the Play.* In selecting a play (1) the script, (2) limitations of the stage, (3) the players, and (4) the audience must be considered.

The *script* may be written by a professional playwright or by the children themselves. It should have literary merit; students should not be forced to memorize lines that have no literary value. It should hold the interest through rehearsal; it should have universal appeal. It should be chosen by the teacher and group on the basis of a predetermined criterion.

*Staging limitations* — the size of the stage, the lighting equipment, and the resources for designing and building scenery — must be taken into consideration. With the interest in circle theater little attention need be given to staging or scenery and yet an effective performance may be presented. If children are talented in art and there is time to build scenes, fairly elaborate settings can be designed which enhance certain plays — for example, *Heidi* and *The Emperor's New Clothes.*

An extremely important consideration is the talent, number, and availability of the *players.* There are plays that hinge upon the talent of a single player — a ballet dancer, a singer, or an emotional actress. If there is no such individual available it is well to select another play. The number and sex of actors available must also be determined. If there are few children who can rehearse after school, and that is the only time possible, it will be necessary to choose a play with a small cast. If only one or two boys can stay after school the play chosen will have to have a predominantly feminine cast.

The final factor to consider is the *audience.* The director should select plays that the viewers will find interesting.

Children can be brought into the play selection group and given an opportunity to read, evaluate, and vote on the play to be selected — under the guidance of the teacher.

*Organization.* The creative director knows what he wants the play to say; but he guides the children into understanding the roles they interpret, through discussion. He does not show them how to interpret. Directing is not telling. It is getting the player to understand and interpret the role as he "lives" it. He *is* the character.

If the play is complicated the director needs an assistant. He also needs committees to take care of business, staging, lighting, prompting, costuming, properties, ushering, and scenery. The director organizes and coordinates the functions of these committees.

Frequently the treasurer or business manager of the school is chairman of the business committee. His job is to manage the printing and sales of tickets, the designing and printing of the programs, the payment for costumes, make-up, royalties, advertising, and other items. He keeps a careful record of all expenditures and receipts and makes a full account to the class after the play.

The staging committee takes care of the scenery shifts. The properties committee is responsible for all hand props, on stage or off. The costuming committee gets the clothing, rented or borrowed, and helps to see that all players are ready on time. The make-up committee obtains and applies the make-up in plenty of time before curtain. The lighting committee plans with the director all light changes and handles them during the play. The stage manager is responsible for the over-all direction of the stage committees, of all personnel on and off stage, and the curtain.

Children usually are not mature enough to get along without a prompter. At every rehearsal a prompter is responsible for helping the cast pick up cues promptly. He also cues in the sound effects, an important job — nothing is more ludicrous than to hear the telephone ring *after* the person has answered it. Sometimes the prompter understudies and plays a role in case of sudden illness in the cast.

Members of the class giving the play may usher, or members of a club or interested students may be invited to usher. The usher greets the members of the audience with a friendly smile, checks reservations or asks their preference if there are no reservations, and escorts them to their seats. He presents enough programs to the last person entering in the group if the programs are not given out at the door.

*Casting.* The director, or the director and a committee, casts the players. Usually the time for tryouts is posted and those interested come at the prescribed time and read lines from the play. Players are chosen on the basis of ability for the part, reliability, cooperation, and willingness to work hard, take criticism, and work with the other members of the cast for the success of the play.

*Rehearsals.* Everyone must know what is expected of him, what is to be accomplished by the group, and how the director hopes to accomplish it.

The director must be thoroughly familiar with the play before rehearsals start. He studies the setting, the historical and geographical background, the meaning of the lines, the life of the author, and the subtleties and allusions in the play. He discusses the characterizations with the pupils. Then they read through the lines to get an idea of the voices they will use. At a later rehearsal they will "walk through" the lines holding their scripts, and block out the action. The characters mark the general action on their scripts so that they can memorize action and lines together.

## Guides for Acting

1. The actor should stay in character at all times.

2. The actor should not move on someone else's lines unless the move is a definite part of the action.

3. The actors must react to each speaker.

4. The actors should not turn their backs to the audience unless the action demands their doing so.

5. The actors should project to the back row of the auditorium but sound as if they were talking to someone on stage.

6. Exit lines should be delivered usually as the actor reaches the door or exit.

7. The actor should remember that the stage is a picture and try to keep the "picture" in balance at all times.

There should be at least two *dress rehearsals* with lights, make-up, costumes, and properties. If possible, a small audience should be invited. In every way the dress rehearsal should be a performance. The director should not interrupt to give instructions. He should keep notes for the conference following the rehearsal.

*Scenery* helps establish mood. It can range from simple draperies to more elaborate settings. Line and color help create the mood. Tall, vertical lines suggest majesty; horizontal lines, tragedy; curved lines, comedy. Light colors suggest gaiety; drab colors, gloom. Red denotes danger; purple, nobility; black, tragedy; yellow, comedy; and soft green, calm and peace.

Building sets and designing scenery offer outlets for the creative urge. The purpose of the scenery is to enhance the dramatic art, not overpower it. Questions used in evaluating the scenery are: Did the scenery carry out the idea of the story? Did it evoke the required response? Did it show when and where the story takes place? Did the line and color help express the story? Was it too difficult to build? Did it take an undue amount of time?

*Costumes* help orient the audience to the period and locale of the story. They may be made of inexpensive materials such as crepe paper, tarlatan, or paper cambric if they are to serve only a temporary purpose. However, if there is a plan to build up a costume supply they should be made of durable material.

Little *make-up* is necessary for children unless they are playing character parts. Max Factor and Stein pamphlets and make-up kits are useful.

*Properties* help move the action of the play. Students should use the properties early in rehearsals to feel at ease with them.

*Lighting* is essential in some plays; it is helpful in all. It serves not only to enhance the stage but to highlight certain parts of the play. It creates atmosphere, indicates the time of day, and gives meaning to the story.

Here, as in creative dramatics, *evaluation* is important. The cast is always anxious to discuss what went well, what went badly, and how the play could be improved. When several performances are given, it is usual for the second and third to pick up tempo, to become more polished, and to present a more unified performance. Evaluation takes into consideration all phases including performances of the players and effectiveness of costumes, make-up, lighting, and scenery. The business manager reports on the state of the budget, and expenditures are checked. It is customary to express appreciation to those who have helped in the performance, listing the names of the cast and others who helped in the printed programs or announcing the names from the stage.

## Conclusion

In the elementary school children participate in two types of dramatic activity — creative dramatics and children's drama. Each can be a creative experience although the purpose of each is different. In creative dramatics the children all participate, acting out their own experiences, poems, rhymes, and stories. There is no set dialogue; teacher and children create the experience, decide on the scenes, keep the story moving. Scenery, lighting, and costuming are not important. The emphasis is on the process, not the product. Individual development is the goal, group enterprise is the method.

In children's drama, too, the children benefit from group performance. Those who participate develop emotionally and creatively. The play is selected on the basis of literary value and of requirements in terms of actors, staging, and the preference and interests of the audience. The director follows the traditions of the theater for acting, staging, and rehearsal procedures. He helps the children understand the lines, the characters, and the meaning of the play. Each child *becomes* the character he is playing. Scenery, costumes, properties, and lighting are used in children's drama.

Both of these types of activities have a place in the elementary school *if* the teacher keeps in mind the purposes of each, if he remembers that each can be a creative experience. Logically, creative dramatics is used more extensively. However, "it is worth while for children to see a finished, artistic performance by their peers, for it sets goals for dramatic activities in the classroom."[9]

Not every elementary teacher will be responsible for directing a play. However, it is as well to understand the values in such an activity as it is to appreciate the values of creative dramatics. Creativity expresses itself in many forms, and children's drama is one of them.

# ACTIVITIES AND QUESTIONS

1. Distinguish between the following terms: playmaking, dramatic play, children's drama, creative dramatics, and children's theater.
2. In planning creative dramatics in the elementary school how does a

[9] Mardel Ogilvie, *Speech in the Elementary School* (New York: McGraw-Hill Book Company, 1954), p. 38.

teacher go about motivating the story, presenting the material, planning the scenes, trying out the characters, developing the play, and evaluating the performance?

3. What value does creative dramatics hold for the child? Children's drama?

# BIBLIOGRAPHY

Andrews, Michael F. *A Bibliography on the Nature of Creativity.* Syracuse: Syracuse University Press, 1958.

Brown, Corrine. *Creative Drama in the Lower School.* New York: Appleton-Century-Crofts, Inc., 1929.

Burger, Isabel. *Creative Play Acting.* New York: A. S. Barnes and Company, 1950.

Cole, Natalie R. *The Arts in the Classroom.* New York: The John Day Company, 1942.

Durland, Frances D. *Creative Dramatics for Children.* Yellow Springs, Ohio: Antioch Press, 1952.

Fitzgerald, Burdette S. *Let's Act the Story.* San Francisco: Fearon Publishers, 1957.

Hagga, Agnes, and Randles, Patricia. *Supplementary Materials for Use in Creative Dramatics.* Seattle: University of Washington Press, 1952.

Lease, R., and Siks, G. B. *Creative Dramatics in Home, School and Community.* New York: Harper & Brothers, 1952.

Lewis, Roger. *Puppets and Marionettes.* New York: Alfred A. Knopf, Inc., 1952.

Mearns, Hughes. *Creative Youth.* New York: Doubleday, Doran and Company, rev. ed., 1960.

Merrill, John, and Fleming, Martha. *Play-Making and Plays.* New York: The Macmillan Company, 1930.

Richmond, Arthur. *Remo Bufano's Book of Puppetry.* New York: The Macmillan Company, 1950.

Siks, Geraldine Brain. *Creative Dramatics: An Art for Children.* New York: Harper & Brothers, 1958.

Slade, Peter. *Child Drama.* London: University of London Press, 1954.

Viola, Ann. "Drama with and for Children: An Interpretation of Terms," *The Speech Teacher,* 5:305–308, November 1956.

Ward, Winifred. *Playmaking with Children.* New York. Appleton-Century-Crofts, Inc., 2nd ed., 1957.

Ward, Winifred. *Stories to Dramatize*. Anchorage, Ky.: The Children's Theatre Press, 1952.

Woods, Margaret S. *Creative Dramatics*. Washington, D.C.: National Education Association, 1959.

Woods, Margaret S. "Learning Through Creative Dramatics," *Educational Leadership*, 18:19–23, 32, October 1960.

Zirbes, Laura. *Spurs to Creative Teaching*. New York: G. P. Putnam's Sons, 1959.

# Rhythms and the dance

> But let the woodwind flutes begin
>   Their elfin music, faint and thin,
> I sway, I bend, retreat, advance,
>   And ever more — I dance, I dance!
>
> ARTHUR KETCHUM

Our heartbeat, our every physical activity — running, walking, skipping, jumping, swimming, dancing — is rhythmical. We respond to rhythm in dance, music, poetry, and art. Expression through spontaneous bodily movement is as natural as breathing.

The earlier a child's rhythmic sense is developed, the better will be his preparation for activity in and appreciation of all the arts. For rhythm is basic to them all: the drama, the dance, music, and the graphic arts. The young child is uninhibited as he expresses himself creatively. He responds rhythmically to the joy of living. All children should be encouraged to use this medium of self-expression.

## *The Role of the Teacher*

Teachers should be conscious of the child's need to express himself in rhythmic movement and of the possibilities for developing creativity in it. They should provide a favorable environment and activities that encourage this art. One has only to observe a group of elementary children to see the value inherent in movement. Andrews points out that "When a child is given an opportunity to use movement, it is as expressive for him as it was for primitive man. Through this medium the child can react to the world about him, use it as a means of communication, and express the thoughts and feelings which are deep down inside. . . . Movement is the child's universal language."[10]

## CREATING THE ENVIRONMENT

Creativity requires a receptive atmosphere, time to create, space for movement, and teacher guidance.

*Receptive Atmosphere.* Even young children, who are eager to let themselves go and enter into the spirit of creating rhythms and dances, must be assured that they will not be laughed at, that their contributions will be accepted, and that originality, not imitation, is the highest achievement.

*Time to Create.* Art is long; life is short. Children need time to create. They cannot be forced into a schedule in which they must dash to the gym for fifteen minutes to be creative and then rush back to the room. Children are often moved to create rhythms shortly after an experience. If they return from a trip to the zoo they may want to respond to music suggesting animal rhythms then and there instead of waiting a couple of days for the special teacher to come for the gym class.

If, however, because of space limitations and scheduling difficulties the creative rhythmic activities must be scheduled at a specific time, the special teacher should be aware of the experiences the children are having that can be utilized in the gym or playroom.

Creativity cannot be hurried. It takes time to experiment, to create, to plan, to discuss, and to evaluate.

*Space for Movement.* Using the body as an instrument of self-expression requires space. Young children need some fifty square feet apiece, and many groups have thirty or forty children. The

---

[10] Gladys Andrews, *Creative Rhythmic Movement for Children* (Englewood Cliffs, N.J.: Prentice-Hall, Inc., 1954), p. 25.

picture of a gymnasium usually comes to mind when teachers think of space for movement. However, the gymnasium may be too large; teacher and group may lose the feeling of rapport that is established if the space is "just right." At times a playroom, large classroom, or kindergarten may be right for such activities as galloping, jumping, leaping, flying, and dancing. Space, too, is needed for children to divide into groups and work out cooperative interpretations. The resourceful teacher will find space for the rhythm program even if he has to use the classroom, the halls, the stage, the auditorium, the kindergarten, the tennis court or portable units. One teacher in a schoolroom with forty screwed-down desks where there should have been tables for twenty-five still found it possible to have the children engage in rhythmic activities and to dramatize singing games.

## TEACHER GUIDANCE

The teacher who recognizes the value of creative rhythmic activity, who is not afraid to explore and experiment, and who is willing to learn how to guide this expression will gain in understanding of children.

*Setting the Stage.* It is not enough to create a receptive environment. Teachers must enter into the spirit of the activity, trying a few exploratory movements and asking leading questions such as "How can I take myself across the room in the least amount of time?" They get the group started and give encouragement where it is needed, help children think through problems of interpretation, pick up cues from the children, and challenge them to higher endeavor.

It is a good idea to mention several children who are responding differently so there will be little encouragement to imitate. The beauty of creative activity is that there is no one best way. If it is creative it is unique; if it isn't unique for the individual it isn't creative. The emphasis here, as in creative dramatics, is on the process, not the product. The value is not what the child produces in the way of a dance or rhythmic expression. It is what happens to him in the process.

*Initiating Rhythmic Activity.* How the teacher initiates the rhythmic program is not the most significant factor. The important thing is that he get started. The children themselves, the needs of the group, the maturity, interests, and experiential background influence the approach he takes.

However, as one teacher expressed it, "I'm ready and willing, but I don't know what to say to them after I get them out on the floor." Here are a few suggestions:

How can we move from where we are to some place else in the room?

How high can you go?

Could you gallop around the room?

Can you walk fast — faster — faster yet?

Can you show us how your body bends and stretches?

Can you show me how the animals in the zoo move?

Can you be birds sweeping across the summer sky?

Can you make yourself tiny and put yourself in a little box?

Can you stretch and stretch and stretch some more?

Can you think of a new way to stretch and bend your body?

Can you get across the room with a leap, a gallop, a skip, or a walk?

Can you stretch like an accordion, rubber band, gum, smoke?

Can you skip and move your arms at the same time?

Can you move while you are sitting at your desks?

Can you be ponies racing around the track?

Can you be horses carrying heavy loads?

Is skipping ahead the only direction you can go?

Why does Jon lift his head so high when he's a high-stepping horse?

When you are beating the drum can you move another part of your body?

How can we get from this spot to the door without running?

*Developing Rhythmic Activities.* A look at the above questions makes it clear that there is no one approach in getting started. Once the group has started, the teacher can participate in the activity in a variety of ways. He may beat the drum, play the piano, tap the rhythm sticks, tap the rhythm with his feet, or clap his hands.

In case some children do not respond he may make definite suggestions: "Everyone who would like to be a tree swaying in the wind may come over to this part of the room. Those who would rather be birds resting in the tree may stay where they are." This gives the shy child a chance gradually to get into the activity without feeling he is contributing nothing.

There is no particular sequence for developing the rhythm experience. How it is introduced, how various elements of movement are combined, depends upon the teacher and a given group of children. The teacher studies the children and selects those experiences that stimulate them. Andrews suggests various ways of combining movement to make the experience more effective:

1. Start a run of moderate tempo. Increase tempo and run in place. Go around the room and decrease tempo. Suggest the children go higher and higher and cover more distance on each stride until the run becomes a leap. It helps to make some suggestions as going over puddles of water or over hurdles.

2. Start with an ordinary gallop (combination of walk and leap, two sounds of uneven rhythm). By changing the tempo, vary the gallop — fast and slow, smooth, low and high. Gallop changing directions as forward, backward and all around. Gallop in place. . . . Have the group think of different animals that gallop, and let each child be the animal he suggests.

3. The skip, gallop, and slide are alike in that all three have two sounds of an uneven rhythm, include the walk, or are a combination of locomotor movements. . . . They are different, in that the gallop and slide are made up of a *walk* and *leap* but the skip is a *walk* and *hop*. In the gallop and in the slide the same foot is always in the lead and the walk always comes on the lead foot. In the skip the leading foot changes from one to the other. Have individuals, small groups, or large groups, develop five ways to vary the skip, the slide, or the gallop. The variations may be slow and fast, low and high, smooth or bumpy.

4. Sitting at desks or on a floor in the classroom, have children discover various ways they can move different parts of their body by asking questions or by using such a dance song as follows:

> I've got a head
> You've got a head
> I can shake my head
> That's what we can do.

> I've got two feet
> You've got two feet
> I can tap my feet
> That's what we can do.

I've got hips
You've got hips
I can twist my hips
That's what we can do.

(Suggested tunes: "Farmer in the Dell," "I've Got Rhythm")

5. Have the group sitting down, pushing and pulling forward and back with their feet and legs. Have the group discover other ways they can push with their feet besides out and back. . . . Ask: "What pulls? What does it make you think of while pushing?" Have each individual or small group work out the action of something which pushes and pulls.

6. Start the group with the hop suggesting that they let the other leg go where it will. Same with the other foot. Add turning. Add hopping high and low. Add other . . . movements. Have individuals, small groups, or large groups work on combinations using the hop. (Exploration may result in a schottische, an Indian step, and many others. This may be the time to develop any of these steps or patterns with the entire group.)

7. Have children, either individuals or small groups, go across the room with a leap, a gallop, or any of the locomotor movements [walk, hop, run] with any of the body movements [swing, bend, stretch, push, pull, twist, strike, dodge, shake, bounce].

8. Explore such possibilities of the swing with the group as swinging one arm, two arms, one leg, entire body, and so on. Vary swings by changing tempo, changing levels and range, and so forth. Individually or in small groups, work out combinations of the swing with a locomoter movement. . . .[11]

*Using Ideas to Stimulate Rhythmic Response.* A child can close his eyes and *hear* the ticking of a big grandfather's clock and translate it into movement. He can swing his body as if it were a pendulum. Or he can close his eyes and visualize the clock and decide what kind of clock he wants to be. How he *visualizes* the clock and how he *feels* as he is the clock will determine the movement or rhythm he creates.

Children very frequently are stimulated by the idea of airplanes. They can talk about types of airplanes, functions of airplanes, and before long they can move out into groups and *be* airplanes. This sort of thing gives the child an opportunity to create a rhythm

[11] *Ibid.,* p. 83.

either as an individual or as a member of a group. What children do with the suggestions, the cues, the ideas, depends on their experiential background, the ability of the teacher in creating a receptive atmosphere, motivating children to be creative, and developing ideas with the children.

## Types of Rhythmic Activities

Natural rhythmic activities, animal rhythms, mechanical rhythms, transportation, folk dancing, playing singing games, and creating original rhythms all appeal to elementary children.

*Natural Rhythmic Activities.* Walking, skipping, running, hopping, jumping, and leaping are all natural rhythmic activities. So are galloping, marching, tiptoeing, trotting, swinging, stretching, bending, and the side step. Children enjoy such play activities as bouncing balls and other physical-education-oriented rhythms.

*Animal Rhythms.* Children like to respond to music and pretend they are animals: the lumbering bear, the heavy-treading elephant, the graceful gazelle, the leaping antelope, the galloping zebra, the light-footed tiger, the stealthy leopard, the playful seal, the proud lion, the long-necked giraffe, the waddling duck, the lithe cat, the laden horse, the high-stepping police horse, the trotting race horse, the slow-footed turtle, the vain peacock, the strutting rooster, the arrogant goose, the haughty turkey, and the timid mouse.

*Mechanical Rhythms.* Transportation vehicles from mule pack to streamliners, from the balloon to the jet; automobiles from the old Model T to the latest sports car; and boats: fishing boats, sailboats, freighters, passenger ships, cattle boats, speedboats, lifeboats, canoes — these all illustrate mechanical rhythms, as do spinning tops, bouncing balls, and mechanical toys of all types.

*Folk Dances and Singing Games.* Since these are discussed in the chapter on health and physical education they will not be examined here. Children enjoy folk dances and singing games increasingly as they mature and as social experiences become more meaningful to them.

## GUIDING CREATIVE ACTIVITIES

All children are creative. They express themselves in drama, dance, music, or art as the spirit moves them. The spark of creativity, however, must be kindled, fostered, and nurtured if it is to develop to its full potential. In an environment where children are cherished, self-expression is valued, stimulating experiences are planned, and guidance is provided, creativity will flourish.

The value of creative expression lies not so much in the product as in the process — not so much in what the child does with the media as what happens to him as he expresses his feelings, ideas, experiences, and reactions. The actual creation is the child's own; the teacher provides an encouraging atmosphere and guides the child as he responds with increasing confidence to the dictates of the creative urge.

*The child needs
time to create.*

*Working with puppets
can provide the timid
child with an effective
medium for creativity.*

*Creative rhythms pro-
vide an outlet for the
expression of ideas.*

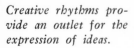

*The child needs appreciation
and encouragement in his creative activities.*

*Under proper guidance, appreciation
of art can become contagious.*

*Creative activities can be related to other areas of the curriculum. Here the children are making African masks as part of a geography class.*

*The child's imagination is challenged in many ways as he acts in and stages a play.*

*Creating Original Rhythms and Dances.* Not only the young child but intermediate boys and girls, too, enjoy creating in response to music. They express their own ideas and the music enhances, rather than prescribes, the response.

In the intermediate grades the rhythmic activity begun in the kindergarten and carried along through the primary grades should still be part of the experience of the children. Skipping, hopping, running are utilized in the more complicated rhythms of this age level. The experiences now become broader in scope as the interest of the group turns more to expression in dance form, making better use of their growing understanding of mood, tempo, interpretation, rhythmic patterns, and so forth.

## Types of Relaxation Activities

Children require a balance of activity and rest. Many times in the effort to accomplish a great deal teachers forget that growing boys and girls require relaxation as well as activity. Some commonly used relaxation exercises are given here. These may suggest others to the teacher:

### Snowman[12]

Ho, Ho, Ho, Hum, Hum, Hum,
You disappear by the minute,
There's one arm gone, now two arms gone.
And plop there goes your head.
Your middle bends, your knees bend, too.
You're littler by the minute.
Ho, Ho, Ho, Hum, Hum, Hum.
Snowman's gone; all gone.
All but your funny hat.

### Readiness[13]
Close your eyes, head drops down,
Face is smooth, not a frown.

[12] *Ibid.,* p. 154.
[13] Louise Binder Scott and H. J. Thompson, *Talking Time for Speech and Speech Improvement* (St. Louis, Mo.: Webster Publishing Company, 1951), p. 19.

Roll to left, head is a ball;
Roll to right, now sit tall;
Lift your chin, look at me;
Deep, deep breath, one, two three;
Big, big smile, hands in lap.
Make believe you've had a nap.
Now you're rested from your play;
Time to work again today.

### *Floppy, Floppy Rag Doll*[14]

| | |
|---|---|
| I'm a floppy, floppy rag doll | (Wave arms loosely) |
| Drooping in my chair | (Relax) |
| My head just rolls from side to side | (Roll head from side to side) |
| My arms fall through the air. | (Let arms swing loosely) |

### *Autumn Leaves*[15]

| | |
|---|---|
| Falling down, falling down, | (Hands held high above head fall slowly and gently to lap) |
| Floating down, floating down, | (Hands above head move gracefully back and forth as they fall to lap) |
| Leaves all yellow, red and brown. | |
| Whirling round, whirling round | (Hands above head, whirl from wrists, fall in lap) |
| Now all quiet on the ground. | |

### *Raggedy Ann*[16]

Raggedy Ann is my best friend.
She's so relaxed; just see her bend.
First at the waist, then at the knee.
Her arms are swinging, oh, so free.
Her head rolls around like a rubber ball.
She hasn't any bones at all.
Raggedy Ann is stuffed with rags;
That's why her body wigs and wags.

[14] *First Presbyterian Nursery School Collection* (Evansville, Ind., n.d.).
[15] *Ibid.*
[16] Scott and Thompson, *op. cit.*, p. 21.

*Yawning*[17]

I yawn and yawn and yawn,
As sleepy as can be.
You, too, will yawn if you will watch
To catch the yawn from me.
Yawn
    Yawn
    Yawn.

With younger children, as can be seen from the above, the power of suggestion is used. This has been termed the *ideational* approach. It helps children relax and gets the group calmed down after they have been moving around the room vigorously. The teacher sets the mood for relaxation by tone of voice and manner, and each child reacts to the suggestion or description of the words in the poems. Andrews suggests for the primary grades such activities as "becoming balloons slowly deflating, elastic bands shriveling up, faucets dripping, salt pouring from a shaker, icicles melting, bubbles getting smaller, . . . sodas fizzing, and ice cream cones melting."[18]

With older children, taking time to talk things over, or getting ready to start a new activity gives a logical break. They also enjoy exercises for relaxation such as those listed below.

*Relaxation Exercises for the Intermediate Grades.*

1. Let the body hang from the waist and let your arms swing freely.
2. Stand in a relaxed position and roll your head around on your neck as if it were a ball.
3. Tense each muscle as hard as possible and then relax it. Do these one at a time, beginning at the toes and working up to the head.
4. Take several deep breaths, relaxing after each.

## Evaluation

How can a teacher tell whether the children are growing in ability to express themselves creatively? How can he tell when they are

[17] *Ibid.,* p. 22.
[18] Andrews, *op cit.,* p. 152.

learning to appreciate formal and creative rhythms? Among the questions he may try to answer are the following:

Am I helping the children enjoy expressing themselves creatively in movement and rhythm?

Am I helping them develop skill in creating rhythms and rhythmic responses?

Am I encouraging them to release tensions and strong feelings through movement?

Am I helping them to use dance as a bridge between strenuous exercises in movement and imagination?

Am I helping them find in rhythm a satisfying and creative art medium for the rest of their lives?

Am I creative in my approach to selecting, planning, and guiding rhythmic experiences for the children under my guidance?

Am I creating an environment that encourages creative expression, not alone through rhythm and dance activities, but in all the arts?

Do I recognize that there is no single method, no single system, that will insure a positive answer to each of the above questions?

Do I have a broad vision, creative imagination, a spirit of adventure and experimentation, and the wisdom to consider the process, not the product, as the ultimate end in guiding creative activities?

Am I in tune with the child who knows that by closing his eyes and using his imagination he can make pumpkins turn into coaches and rats into well-fed coachmen?

Do I relate the experiences in rhythmic expression to the physical education program planned for the school?

## ACTIVITIES AND QUESTIONS

1. Observe in a primary or intermediate grade and make a list of the opportunities children have for participating in rhythmic experiences.
2. Did the teacher you observed use any of the questions suggested for initiating a rhythmic or movement experience? How did he motivate the children to participate, develop the lesson as the period went along, provide for relaxation, and evaluate the experiences with the group?
3. Observe children engaging in rhythmic activity on the playground. What activities or experiences could be capitalized on in the school program?

# BIBLIOGRAPHY

Andrews, Gladys. *Creative Rhythmic Movement for Children*. Englewood Cliffs, N.J.: Prentice-Hall, Inc., 1954.

Geri, Frank H. *Games and Rhythms for Children*. Englewood Cliffs, N.J.: Prentice-Hall, Inc., 1955.

Kuhn, Jacqueline. *33 Rhythms for Children*. New York: Bregman, Vocco and Conn, Inc., 1956.

La Salle, Dorothy. *Rhythms and Dances for Elementary Schools*. New York: A. S. Barnes and Company, 1951.

Mooney, Gertrude X. *Mexican Folk Dances for American Schools*. Coral Gables, Fla.: University of Miami Press, 1958.

Mukerji, Rose. "Creative Expression in Rhythms and Dance," *Childhood Education*, 34:15–17, September 1957.

Mukerji, Rose. "Music, Dance and Fine Arts," *Childhood Education*, 35:350, April 1959.

Murray, Ruth Lovell. *Dance in the Elementary School*. New York: Harper & Brothers, 1953.

Rogers, Carl R. "Toward a Theory of Creativity," in S. I. Hayakawa (ed.) *Our Language and Our World*. New York: Harper & Brothers, 1959.

Scheon, Elizabeth, and O'Brien, Emma. *Rhythm in the Elementary School*. New York: A. S. Barnes and Company, 1951.

Shafer, Mary, and Mosher, Mary Morgan. *Rhythms for Children*. New York: A. S. Barnes and Company, 1938.

Sheehy, Emma Dickson. *Children Discover Music and Dance*. New York: Henry Holt and Company, 1959.

Sheehy, Emma Dickson. *There's Music in Children*. New York: Henry Holt and Company, rev. ed., 1952.

*Teachers Guide to Education in Later Childhood*. Sacramento, Calif.: Bureau of Elementary Education, State Department of Education, 1957.

White, Betty. *Betty White's Latin-American Dance Book*. New York: David McKay Company, 1958.

Winslow, Robert W., and Dillin, Leon. *Music Skills for Classroom Teachers*. Dubuque, Iowa: William C. Brown Company, 1958.

# Music

> All deep things are song . . .
> See deep enough and you see musically;
> the heart of nature being everywhere music
> if you can only reach it.
>
> ANON.

Music is rhythm, melody, harmony, and tone color; but it is far more. Music is what awakens in the individual when he is stimulated by the rhythmic and tonal patterns he hears. The urge to respond is universal. Children react spontaneously to music. They dance, they sing — not merely when they are happy but when they are sad, too. They respond early to lullabies, crooning, to the tones of the mother's voice. They respond to humming, to music on the radio, and to sounds and rhythms about them.

Music affords a satisfying outlet for the creative urge throughout life. But musical responsiveness is not automatic. "The potential power lies within the creator, but the switch that releases it is thrown by some influence from without."[19]

Music contributes to the joy of self-expression through singing and playing instruments, through creating songs and dances, through its emotional appeal, through an understanding of its form, and through awareness of all that makes performance artistic.

[19] Lillian Mohr Fox and L. Thomas Hopkins, *Creative School Music* (New York: Silver Burdett Company, 1936), p. 22.

## *The Role of Music in a Changing World*

Change is an inevitable part of life. However, children need a certain amount of stability in their lives to give them security. They need avenues for self-expression as they grow and learn to express their feelings and emotions. They need an environment in which the innate desire to create, to explore, and to respond to music is carefully cultivated and wisely guided and which serves as a springboard for richer experiences in musical growth. They sense that singing, dancing, playing, and listening to music are as essential to their well-being as are eating, drinking, resting, and exercising.

## *The Role of the School*

Providing an environment in which the child can express himself in the creative arts is one of the most important tasks of the school. Whether this is translated to mean special music teachers, consultants, and supervisors of music or that the responsibility falls solely upon the classroom teacher is an administrative problem. It is the classroom teacher, however, who is the vital factor in causing creativity to flourish. This he may do with assistance from specialists, supervisors, and administrators.

Music should be an integral part of daily living. In such an environment the child with musical talent is discovered and motivated; the child with meager talent is encouraged to try his wings. In such an environment children grow up to like music rather than remembering only *do, re, mi, fa, sol, la, ti, do* in later years.

## *The Role of the Teacher*

The teacher who would develop musical responsiveness and music appreciation in children must (1) value the aims of music in the school; (2) identify the musically talented; (3) establish basic competency in music; (4) organize musical activities into a well-balanced program; (5) offer experiences in music through singing and playing instruments, listening, creating songs, musical organizations; and (6) evaluate growth in musical expression.

### AIMS OF SCHOOL MUSIC

Understanding the aims of music in the elementary school is basic to building a balanced program that meets the needs of all children. The creative teacher knows that what children enjoy they will do. The over-all objective of music for the elementary school child is the development of appreciation and enjoyment of music as an integral part of daily living. Among the specific aims are the following:

*1. To Develop Creativity and to Awaken a Sense of Beauty.* First and foremost, children sing for enjoyment. They are interested in singing because it is fun, because there are so many different phases of music to explore: tone, rhythm, melody, form, and harmony. There are songs that are gay and light, somber and heavy, songs that allow them to express the whole gamut of human emotions. As they sing they should gradually develop taste and appreciation.

*2. To Provide a Means of Recreation Now and in Later Life.* It is becoming increasingly evident that to maintain good mental and physical health there must be time for work and for play. Recreation and the wise use of leisure time are becoming problems as working hours and weeks are shortened. The hobbies and recreational pursuits individuals develop as children continue into adult life. The child who enjoys singing in the school choir or playing in the orchestra or band is very likely to continue his interests in these organizations when he grows up. Participation in musical organizations serves as a safety valve during the trying years of preadolescence and adolescence, when youngsters need satisfying outlets for their feelings and energies.

*3. To Develop Discrimination in Music.* "The best music is reminiscent of a delightful adventure; it rears itself head-and-shoulders above the prosaic, and memory of it lingers . . . long after its sounds have been forgotten."[20] To change a person's taste after

[20] Grant Parks, *Music for Elementary Teachers* (New York: Appleton-Century-Crofts, Inc., 1951), p. 8.

many years of living with music which does not have inherent quality or beauty is not easy. A wider exposure to music and opportunity to listen to and perform great music can develop the individual's musical taste as no amount of intensified training later will do.

*4. To Develop the Imagination.* Music is a powerful stimulant to the imagination. Much is being said about the need for developing the full potential of man's creativity. This resource has scarcely been tapped. Music affords opportunity for fostering the imaginative powers in interpretation, in creating compositions, and in using the skills needed in artistic performance. The significance of any musical experience, whether creative or recreative, lies in the stimulation of the imaginative responses and the degree to which each activity helps the child develop and refine the creative talents he possesses. All children are creative to some degree, but they need encouragement if the creativity is to reach its fruition.

*5. To Provide the Child with Musical Skills.* Enjoyment in music activities is limited unless the child grows in the ability to read music and to interpret it. It is true that the goal of the elementary school is primarily to help each child enjoy music, not to turn out professional musicians. But it must be remembered that the school is the seed-bed for identifying, nurturing, and developing the potential professional talent. There are, to be sure, more children in the elementary school who will be satisfied with a modicum of ability in performance, notation, harmony, and composition; however, in the school designed to meet the needs of all the children provision must be made for experiences which encourage unusual talents and aptitudes.

*6. To Develop the Child's Voice.* There are children who sing beautifully when they come to school. There are others who have not yet found their singing voices; a few never will. The teacher must know how to help children improve their voices, encourage those who have a little ability, and set up a well-rounded program so that those who cannot sing can participate in other musical experiences with satisfaction. Enthusiasm for learning and singing new songs can be aroused by increasing competency in singing with good tone quality, accurate tone placement, correct phrasing, and good articulation.

However, enthusiasm in singing should not result in shouting. Damage may be done to the child's voice if he is permitted to shout. The singing voice of young children, if properly guided, is pleasing, flute-like, bright, clear, and sweet. Voices should never be strained by singing too loudly or too softly. An open throat is necessary at all times.

### IDENTIFYING THE MUSICALLY GIFTED

Children differ as widely in musicality as they do in other attributes. It is up to the school to provide every child with experiences that will help him realize his potential. This demands the discovery of musical talent as early as possible. Becoming a musician is a long and difficult task. It requires more than aptitude; it requires discipline and hard work. Not only must the child have native ability; he must have encouragement in developing his talent. In identifying the musically talented child the teacher may be guided by the following comparative criteria cited by Kough and DeHaan:[21]

1. Responds more than others to rhythm and melody.
2. Sings well.
3. Puts verve and vigor into his music.
4. Is interested in music; listens to records; puts himself out to be where he can hear music.
5. Enjoys harmonizing with others or singing in groups.
6. Uses music to express his feelings and experiences.
7. Makes up original tunes.
8. Plays one or more musical instruments well.

Equal opportunity is not synonymous with identical experience. Teachers who discover musically talented children in the group sometimes hesitate to give them encouragement and opportunity to perform for fear they are being unfair to the child who lacks talent. Any teacher who is conscientious about trying to help every child realize his potential must make every effort to help the talented child develop his superior talent, not submerge it. More and more the talented child is being encouraged instead of being allowed, or even pressured, to hide his talent and become one of the "average" children

[21] Jack Kough and Robert F. DeHaan, *Teacher's Guidance Handbook*, Part I, "Identifying Children Who Need Help" (Chicago: Science Research Associates, 1955), p. 82.

in the group. It is the responsibility of the teacher not only to discover the gifted child but to organize activities in such a way as to contribute as much as possible to the development of his ability.

## DEVELOPING BASIC COMPETENCIES IN MUSIC

Not all teachers have the requisite skills for teaching music. However, if they are to foster the growth of musical response of children in the elementary grades, they should develop certain competencies through music education courses, independent study, and practice in pre-service and in-service training. It is desirable:

1. To be able to sight-read and sing acceptably, and play an instrument. (In some cases auto-harps and other simple instruments will suffice.)
2. To be able to play the piano well enough to accompany the children in singing simple songs, art songs, community songs, and to play the parts in part music; to be able to play simple selections to which pupils can respond rhythmically.
3. To know how to direct music, with expressive conducting as the long-range goal.
4. To have a working knowledge of vocal and choral technique.
5. To have some musical perception and the ability to judge tone quality, tone production, blend, balance, intonation, and rhythmic response.
6. To be familiar with materials available for use with unchanged, changing, and changed voices. Teachers should have a broad repertory of songs in order to select the right song at the right time.
7. To be able to teach boys and girls in such a way that music becomes a part of their daily lives. "Enthusiasm and interest in music on the part of the teacher are assets to the motivation of boys and girls, but enthusiasm and interest are not enough. The teacher must know music before he can teach it. There is no substitute for a thorough knowledge of music. . . ."[22]
8. To understand the following basic terms: staff, meter, time signatures and accent, piano keyboard, sharps and flats, major and minor scales, chromatic scales, key signatures, intervals, chords, triads, and the seventh chord. Although not all teachers

[22] William Raymond Sur and Charles Francis Schuller, *Music Education for Teen-Agers* (New York: Harper & Brothers, 1958), p. 269.

have these competencies the more of them they can acquire the more effectively they can guide music experiences.

## ORGANIZING MUSICAL ACTIVITIES

One method of organizing a program varied enough to provide for differing interests and broad enough to challenge the capabilities of every student is the spiral method, in which musical concepts are introduced in an early grade and further developed in each succeeding grade.

In the spiral approach the teacher does not wait for the moment when children are "ready" to deal with significant musical concepts. Rather, the concepts are presented in an informal and simple way very early in the child's experience. Instead, for example, of teaching the minor tonality in the later grades, it is introduced early and spread out over a period of years. Thus the children's musical concepts are broadened and extended at each grade level instead of being taught at a specific, predetermined point.

This procedure helps solve the persistent and difficult problems of grade placement, which involves answering questions such as: Which concept will be introduced first? At what grade level should each concept be introduced? When should it recur? How deeply should it be explored or studied? What minimum objectives should be accomplished by the end of each grade? To these questions Mursell gives the following general answer: Concepts should be introduced "whenever any . . . concept has an important and significant function in music with which the children are dealing; whenever a grasp of any . . . concept will lead directly to a more adequate appreciation of music that is being performed or heard."[23] In the spiral approach the content determines the sequence of musical concepts.

This spiral sequence is thought by some educators to facilitate the teaching of music by the classroom teacher. They believe that a teacher with a limited musical background may help children sing a song in a minor mode or demonstrate the lilting effect of % time even if he is unable to explain the minor modality or the % time signature. If music is selected on the basis of the teacher's familarity with it and the intrinsic worth of the music, rather than on the basis

[23] James L. Mursell, "Growth Processes in Music Education," *Basic Concepts in Music Education*, Fifty-Seventh Yearbook, National Society for the Study of Education, Part I (Chicago: University of Chicago Press, 1958), p. 159.

of demonstrating music concepts, classroom teachers might enjoy teaching music more than they now do. Many of them are somewhat fearful about explaining music concepts.

The teacher should use a guide to insure a balancing of experiences for the children: rhythms and dance, singing, instrumental experiences, listening, creative activity, and music reading.

The teacher who uses a textbook series should supplement it with his own compilation of music literature. The availability of many and varied materials and the skill of the teacher will determine the quality of the program. The assistance of the music teacher, music specialist, consultant, or supervisor is highly desirable. The important thing is that music experiences be offered which will provide for wide differences in ability, maturity, and interests, and at the same time help children grow musically.

*Suggested Outline for a Balanced Music Program*

PRIMARY GRADES

1. Rhythms and dance
   a. Creative rhythmic activities
   b. Singing games and simple folk dances
2. Singing
   a. Singing songs
   b. Voice improvement
   c. Choir experience
   d. Assembly singing
3. Instrumental experiences
   a. Rhythm and melody instruments
   b. Class piano
4. Listening
   a. Enjoyment
   b. Developing appreciation

5. Creative activity
   a. Rhythmic interpretation
   b. Creating songs
6. Introduction to music reading
   a. Music-reading readiness
   b. Reading music

INTERMEDIATE GRADES

1. Rhythms and dance
   a. Creative rhythms
   b. Dances
2. Singing
   a. Voice improvement
   b. Art songs
   c. Choir experience
   d. Assembly singing
3. Instrumental experiences
   a. Instrumental classes
   b. Small ensembles
   c. Orchestra or band
4. Listening
   a. Enjoyment
   b. Developing musicality
   c. Concert preparation
5. Creative activity
   a. Composing songs
   b. Performance
6. Music reading

Such an outline is an empty shell until the teacher translates it into musical experiences that have vitality and meaning to boys and girls. A balanced program requires that the children take part in rhythms and dance, singing, instrumental experiences, listening for appreciation, and creating music. Guiding children's rhythmic experiences was discussed at length in the previous section so it will not be re-examined at this point.

## DEVELOPING EXPERIENCES IN MUSIC — SINGING

*Songs Children Like.* Children are eager to sing if the approach is right. If the teacher has a rich musical background, a fine voice, and skill in presenting music the children are indeed fortunate. However, if his knowledge is somewhat meager, his voice ordinary, and his skills not too well developed he can still explore the world of song literature and share songs with the children: folk songs, carols, patriotic songs, experience songs, songs of holidays, seasonal songs, work songs, and rounds.

Children enjoy *folk songs*[24] that are simple but tuneful, repetitive but varied, and related to their interests.

| | |
|---|---|
| Down in the Valley | Skip to My Lou |
| Polly | Rosy Boy, Posy Boy |
| Froggy Went A-Courtin' | Sir Herbert Went a-Wooing |
| Casey Jones | Country Gardens |
| Old Paint | The Sante Fe Trail |
| Home on the Range | Willy, Willy, Will |
| Billy Magee Magaw | The Cowboy |
| The Spinning Mice | Palomita |
| The Woman and the Peddler | John Peel |
| The Hunter | The Raggle-Taggle Gypsies |
| Ah, Lovely Meadows | |
| Pop Goes the Weasel | SEA CHANTIES |
| John Brown Had a Little Indian | Cape Cod Shanty |
| Bluetail Fly | Blow, Boys, Blow |
| Jennie Crack Corn | Rio Grande |
| Hi Betty Martin | Blow the Man Down |
| Old Chisholm Trail | One More Day |

[24] The teacher should be careful not to include folk songs and religious songs which might be offensive to certain races and faiths. Knowledge of the community is important.

| | |
|---|---|
| Boll Weevil | Roll the Cotton Down |
| Betsey from Pike | High Barbaree |
| Way Down Yonder in the Paw-Paw Patch | Sailing, Sailing |

*Christmas carols*, like folk songs, know no age. Young and old alike look forward to the season when Christmas carols are sung.

| | |
|---|---|
| Silent Night | The Wassail Song |
| Adeste Fideles | I Wonder as I Wander |
| Deck the Halls | The Cherry Tree Carol |
| Bring a Torch, Jennette Isabella | The Angel's Message |
| Cradle Hymn | Bring in the Boar's Head |
| We Wish You a Merry Christmas | Christmas Again |
| | O Tannenbaum |
| God Rest You Merry, Gentlemen | The First Noel |
| | Good King Wenceslas |

Children are eager to sing good *patriotic songs*. They sing with gusto those that have a rollicking, rousing melody and a martial rhythm. Even the youngest like to sing the songs included in this list. The older children, too, join in with enthusiasm.

| | |
|---|---|
| The Star-Spangled Banner | Hail Columbia |
| America the Beautiful | Battle Hymn of the Republic |
| America | Dixie |
| Columbia, the Gem of the Ocean | Pledge to the Flag |
| | There are Many Flags in Many Lands |
| Yankee Doodle | |
| God Bless America | The Marine Hymn |

Children enjoy singing of the experiences in which they engage every day — the things they do at home, at school, and at play. *Experience songs* include the following:

| | |
|---|---|
| I Like to Go Shopping with Mother | Jumping Rope |
| | Playing Marbles |
| Games to Play | The Parade |
| Keeping Time | Telling Time |
| Chasing the Wind | Safety First |
| With Our Sleds | Playing in the Sun |
| At the Fair | Swing Song |
| It's Snowing | Away Now Joyful Riding |

Elementary children like to sing *holiday songs*. Among the holidays they observe, with song, dance, and food are Christmas, Thanksgiving, Halloween, Valentine's Day, and Easter. Birthdays are important, too, and other days such as Columbus Day, Veterans' Day, Washington's and Lincoln's birthdays. Children in the primary grades are not as interested in birthdays of famous men as are the intermediate children, who study the lives of these men in the social studies.

| | |
|---|---|
| Harvest Hymn | This Is the Night of Hallow- |
| Swing the Shining Sickle | een |
| Come, Ye Thankful People, | The Witches |
| Come | A Valentine for Mother |
| We Gather Together | Valentines |
| Easter Eggs | Not a Copper Cent Is Mine |
| Easter Parade | Who Will Be My Valen- |
| Easter Time | tine? |
| Happy Birthday | He's (Five) Years Old To- |
| Halloween | day |

*Rounds* not only serve to introduce children to part singing but provide a musical experience that has value in itself. Even the youngest children enjoy singing rounds if the teacher or another adult is able to carry one part while a good singer in the group can take over the leadership of the second part. Popular in the foreign-language program is "Frère Jacques." Other perennial favorites are:

| | |
|---|---|
| Three Blind Mice | Row Your Boat |
| Scotland's Burning | Wise Ben Franklin |
| Little Tommy Tinker | All Through the Night |
| Good Night, Ladies | |

*Selecting Songs.* Some songs sing themselves; others never "catch on." Certain songs are enjoyed by children and adults almost universally; others may be favorites of specific age or grade groups. Songs that children love to sing, that are easily learned, and that remain favorites through the years have definite characteristics:

1. A song must have musical quality. It should have a melody that is appealing and that is easy to sing without being trite.

2. The song should have a rhythmic quality that calls for response. It should have repetition of both rhythmical and melodic patterns as well as phrases that make it easy to learn and a pleasure to sing.

3. The text should be close to the child's experience. If it is not

so related in some way, unless it is a nonsense rhyme he may show little interest in singing it, much less learning it.

4. The range in which a song is written should be one that children can sing without undue strain. At the same time, it should not be too limited. Children vary in their ability to sing in a high or low range. The teacher should find the optimum range for the group. Some keys appeal to children more than others. Sometimes transposing a song from the key of G or F to E flat makes a remarkable difference in learning it.

5. The song should possess unity; words and music should go together. Unless they do, children are not likely to enjoy singing the song. A song should be simple but interesting; short but complete; repetitious but not monotonous. It should, in short, be unified, and exciting to sing.

Blyler[25] investigated the song choices of 9007 elementary school children in Illinois. She found that (1) children generally seemed to prefer a balance between folk and composed songs; (2) words played a major role in determining their preferences; (3) popular songs and religious songs predominated in the lists of preferred songs the children had learned outside of school.

*Teaching a Song.* Children should be provided with models that reveal beautiful tone, correct intonation, accurate phrasing, good enunciation, and vital interpretation.

Children learn their first songs by imitation (rote) and later by reading them. However, even after they have learned to read they enjoy singing certain songs by rote. The teacher should have a large store of rote songs to introduce to the children for variety throughout the elementary grades. For the teacher who cannot sing, there are commercial records that accompany basal music series. Tape recordings may be made by the music supervisor or talented parents in the community. The teacher can encourage the children to sing on pitch by using the pitch pipe, the song bells, the phonograph, the auto-harp, the guitar, or the piano as an aid.

The teacher must know the song he is teaching so well that he is not concerned with the mechanics or memory. He must sing it so expressively that the children want to learn it, and will sing with good quality and interpret the mood. Singing the whole song for the

[25] Dorothea M. Blyler, "The Song Choices of Children in Elementary Grades," doctoral thesis, University of Illinois, 1957.

children, teaching them to "wait for your turn," varying the procedure in presenting the song — all serve to assure interest in learning
yet another song in the wide world of music. The teacher should
avoid teaching the children to *say* the words. Songs are meant to
be sung. When children have to repeat the words after the teacher
and discuss them at length before being allowed to sing, they are
predisposed to dislike the song, the music period, and very often
the music teacher. Singing is for enjoyment; it must be a joyous experience if it is to have lasting value. The teacher who makes singing
both a challenge and a joy is rewarded by a "singing class." Helping
children discover their voices, use them effectively, and sing spontaneously is the teacher's responsibility.

## DEVELOPING EXPERIENCES IN MUSIC — INSTRUMENTAL

The chief value of rhythm instruments in the primary grades is
most certainly not the performance for the public. Too frequently
the exploitation of a group of young children colorfully costumed
and presented formally in the "opening selection" of a music program
is considered the object of having a rhythm band. In such instances
the program emphasizes not the creativity of children in selecting
the music to be played, working out the instrumentation, and playing
for their own enjoyment, but rather a stereotyped performance in
which children are assigned specific instruments and taught to respond in a formalized manner. This kind of automation has no place
in a creative program. There are, however, possibilities for creativity
in the use of the rhythm instruments if the children are free to experiment, learn to listen for musical characteristics of each instrument, and try to determine the instrumentation best suited to a
particular composition. To see young children engage in such a
creative expression is as stimulating as the mechanical performance of
the formal rhythm band is stultifying.

Children can participate in creative experiences with instruments
without chaos. They should be allowed to explore the musical
quality of each instrument. When they are encouraged to arrange
their own instrumentation, when they are permitted to listen to
orchestra arrangements, when they realize that continuous playing
of all instruments simultaneously fails to give the listener the variety
that a good musical composition demands, the experience with
rhythm instruments has a place in the program. Not only percussion

instruments but bells, marimba, water glasses, song flutes, tonettes, flutophones, and symphonettes give primary children satisfactory musical experiences. They enjoy not only the music the instruments make but the group participation.

Where children are permitted to join the violin class or the piano class in addition to participating in group experiences with the less complex rhythm instruments, the opportunities for creative expression are limited only by the child's talent.

The instrumental program in the elementary school should offer opportunities for experiences with rhythm instruments, pre-band instruments, chording instruments, and class instruction in strings, piano, band, and orchestra. The following outline of activities is suggested by the Music Educators National Conference:[26]

### Preschool, Kindergarten, First Grade

Learning to use rhythm instruments — triangle, drum, and simple melody instruments such as tone bells, marimba, and others.

### Grades Two and Three

Continuing use of rhythm instruments, adding simple melody instruments such as melody bells, xylophone, psaltery, and others.

### Grades Four and Five

Class instruction in piano.

Rhythm instruments and simple melody instruments like marimba, song bells, and auto-harp.

Exploratory instruments such as flutophone, tonette, song flute, and recorder.

Class instruction on orchestral and band instruments.

### Grade Six

Class instruction in piano.

Rhythm instruments and simple melody instruments like marimba, song bells, auto-harp.

Class instruction on orchestral and band instruments.

Large and small ensemble experience.

*The Responsibility of the Classroom Teacher in the Instrumental Program.* Much of the responsibility as well as the credit for discovering musical aptitude and interest should go to the classroom teacher. It is he, in many cases, who first introduces children to instrumental activity, helps recruit pupils for instrumental lessons,

[26] Adapted from *Outline of a Program for Music Education,* revised (Chicago: Music Educators National Conference, NEA, 1951), unnumbered pamphlet.

and keeps the instrumental teacher informed of interests, aptitudes, achievements, and performance skills of children. The ability to arouse and maintain interest in music in all phases provides the foundation for an adequate musical experience in the elementary school.

Specifically, the classroom teacher

Provides a music center for experimentation and exploration of musical instruments.

Guides experiences with rhythm instruments, water glasses, xylophones, and song bells.

Teaches simple wind instruments of the pre-band and orchestral type.

Encourages children to play harmonic instruments for accompaniment of singing.

Helps children with simple keyboard experiences.

Cooperates with the special music and/or instrumental teacher.

Sees that children in the musical organizations get to band and orchestra classes, rehearsals, and practice periods.

Unfortunately children in some primary grades are limited in their instrumental experiences to rhythm instruments. In defining the role of rhythm instruments in the school program Andrews and Cockerille state: "The desirable rhythmic experiences emerge from the child's initiative and imagination as a part of his response to music, not from a mass attack on percussion by small children behaving like automatons."[27]

*The Rhythm Band.* Because many kindergarten and primary children like to experiment with band instruments and are limited to the rhythm band this activity can be continued through the primary grades. As the children mature they become increasingly adept at "orchestration." However, some of them like to follow the orchestration of the arrangers if each individual is given a book to use at his desk or stand and actually play in a band. A suggested seating arrangement of a band for thirty children might be:

| Left Stage | Center Stage | Right Stage |
|---|---|---|
| 4 triangles | 1 tom-tom | 2 pairs of cymbals |
| 6 rhythm sticks | 1 snare drum | 4 sand blocks |
| | 1 bass drum | 1 tone block |
| | 2 tambourines | 1 piano |
| | 4 bells | |
| | 4 marachas | |

[27] Frances M. Andrews and Clara E. Cockerille, *Your School Music Program* (Englewood Cliffs, N.J.: Prentice-Hall, Inc., 1958), p. 73.

Instruments such as melody flutes, fifes, and recorders can be added to the rhythm band and can not only help children enjoy making music together but motivate sight reading. Children who have no opportunity to play in other instrumental groups find being a member of a rhythm band enjoyable; however, more and more schools are providing a broad instrumental program in the elementary grades.

## LISTENING TO MUSIC

To listen with enjoyment and satisfaction is as much a creative experience as singing or dancing, playing or composing. The means are different but the end is the same — response to music in a satisfying way. Children can learn to look forward to listening periods if they are made vital by the teacher. In this day of hi-fi, radio, television, records, and tapes, what one listens to, and how, is determined to a great degree by the child's opportunities for listening in his formative and elementary school years. As he learns to recognize design in music, unity within a composition, recurring themes, and developmental sections of the music of the masters, he begins to understand and to appreciate musical form and tonality. This does not come all at once. Nor can it be forced. It happens through association, as with a friend. Gradually the child will come to know the delicate lacy design that is Mozart, the sensitive blending of color that characterizes Chopin, the cymbals and clamor of Wagner, and the delicate tone color of Debussy. He will come to realize the interrelationships of music with the culture of its period. He will come to understand the meaning of style, interpretation, and performance, not from reading about them but from experience.

How the teacher organizes and develops listening experiences depends on his knowledge of musical resources, the facilities at hand, and his ability to interest children in a broad music program. A wealth of recordings, radio and television programs, concerts at school and in the community, recitals in the class or school, and performances at the school by talented parents is generally available.

To teach the child that listening is an art requiring knowledge to heighten the emotional response is the challenge the teacher faces. He has as aids his own enthusiasm, knowledge, and ingenuity. "Listening has become more and more an active thing, a collaboration with the composer instead of a passive unthinking reception of whatever sounds strike the ear."[28]

## CREATING MUSIC

Re-creating music is the process of taking someone else's composition and making it one's own through responding to the mood and emotion that the composer felt. This may be done through interpretation or by arranging and adapting the composition to satisfy his own creative urge. In the resulting interpretation or effect the player or singer relives the emotional experience of the composer.

Creating music, on the other hand, is the act of writing down or having the teacher write down the notes in the songs one hears in his imagination. The creative child frequently composes his own music, using the elements of sound, melody, and rhythm he hears and in his own unique way combines into tonal and harmonic patterns. He brings to it all his musical knowledge and background together with his dreams and experiences. This is not the province of all children. However, those who have such a gift should be encouraged, guided, and helped to analyze, criticize, and evaluate their contributions.

Sometimes a whole class will want to compose a song. Although there is no such thing as a group creation in the realm of true artistic expression, there is value in the experience of participation with a group in bringing together elements of music and weaving them into a design that belongs to a particular group and offers them rich satisfaction. The composition may be performed before an audience in a culminating activity or program for parents. The following is an account of a group composition:

### A Third Grade Creates a Spring Song
One windy day in March Mrs. Cummins and a group of third-graders were singing merrily when in blew a gust of wind and scattered the sheafs of paper across the room. The children stopped and listened to the sound of the wind. In the silence that followed, one of the girls said, "Let's make up a song about the wind and March and spring." "Yes, let's," chorused several other voices, and they were on their way. They began to hum a melody and the

[28] Kitty Barne, *Listening to the Orchestra* (Indianapolis: The Bobbs-Merrill Company, 1946), p. 1.

teacher took the notation down in numbers of the scale. They sang in a waltz rhythm for, as they said, "We want a song you can dance to." Instead of having a phrase composed by an individual child, everyone sang together and the teacher wrote the melody as she heard it. They made up words after the melody was written. These, too, were put on the chalkboard and modifications in the melody occurred as there was need of fitting the words to the melody. They wanted the song written in the key of F because they were learning to play bells and they were in that key. "There are so many possibilities for the song with bell acccompaniment. It makes the song come alive." When they finished, this is what they had written:

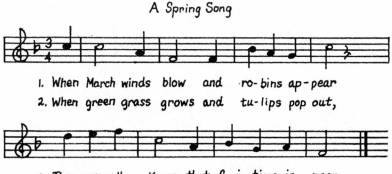

Rarely does a group create a composition for posterity. It is the purpose for which the song is created and the enjoyment the children have in composing and singing it that determines its value. The value of composing the song illustrated lay in the experience of composition, singing it for their own group, and later performing it at the spring music program for parents, to the accompaniment of the bell chorus.

## MUSICAL ORGANIZATIONS

*Choirs and Instrumental Groups.* In order to provide for the musical talent of every child it is customary to offer children with exceptional ability in music an opportunity to become members of a beginning or "feeder" choral or instrumental group in the primary grades. This plan depends upon the cooperation, enthusiasm, and energy of the music teacher, the administrators, and the classroom teachers, and the interest in the community in broad musical experiences.

In some schools full-time choral and instrumental directors take charge of such a program. In others a part-time instructor in music is assigned to both choral and instrumental activities; in still other schools the teacher with ability and interest in music helps organize and direct choral and/or instrumental ensembles. In return, he is relieved of classes in certain areas and other teachers carry out such responsibilities while he directs the musical organizations. In some schools the music teacher arrives an hour early in the morning or remains an hour after school to provide what he considers essential experiences in musical organizations. In other schools there are assembly sings or noon musical recreation activity. Whatever the program, the cooperative action of the entire staff, the administration, and the community is required. Every teacher has a share in the success of the program. Every teacher can foster and nourish creativity in children. In audience situations that frequently are the local outcome of such organizational efforts the product should be worthy of the time and effort expended by the director, the leaders, the children, and the parents. The child, as an individual and as a part of the group, has an opportunity to communicate to the audience the effectiveness of the music program in terms of his own progress.

### EVALUATING MUSICAL EXPERIENCES

Evaluation must be in terms of the objectives of the program. Where enjoyment is the chief objective, the evaluation will be based on the extent to which children participate joyously in musical expression. Where enjoyment is only one factor and musicality is also valued, growth in skills, appreciation, knowledge, and understanding of the elements that make up musical experiences will also be measured.

Most teachers manage to combine in their teaching a love of music with a knowledge of music. In general, by the time a child is ready for the intermediate grades he is able to express himself in song, to respond to basic rhythm and movement, to listen appreciatively to music, to participate in group composing of songs, to play simple rhythmic and melodic instruments, and to enjoy the growing body of musical literature.

By the time he is ready for junior high the child should not only enjoy music experiences but be able to read music, sing in two- and three-part songs, play an instrument of his choice, create rhythmic patterns, compose in a group, and listen with understanding to a wide variety of music that has lasted through the ages.

In determining how effective the music program is, evaluation must be carried on as a continuous process by all the staff, by every child, and by every teacher. The degree to which children express themselves creatively in music is in the final analysis the criterion for the success of a given program. The extent to which they improve in tone quality, intonation, shading, correct tempo, careful phrasing, and appropriate style — in short, the extent to which they advance toward musicality — gives evidence of program adequacy.

A good music program has both depth and breadth. To the degree that it recognizes the functions of music in the development of the children it achieves its objectives. Among the questions that the school staff should ask regarding the effectiveness of the program are the following:

Does the music program contribute to the development of aesthetically sensitive individuals? At any age the child is capable of responding to beauty and is able to experience this kind of response through understanding and enjoying music.

Does the music program develop basic skills and appreciation? If the music program is shallow, if it is little more than a poor imitation of a community sing with little attention to the improvement of basic skills, little musical growth can result. Without the understandings, skills, attitudes, and appreciation that are the outgrowths of a well-balanced music program, the child cannot realize the ultimate values of music.

Are the music materials of high quality and of sufficient variety to stimulate response? Realizing the child's need for beauty and his willingness to respond to it, the teacher must select materials of intrinsic musical worth. It is the teacher's responsibility to know a wealth of material in order to select from this abundance music that will enrich the child's experience. It is the teacher's responsibility to guide, not follow, the children's tastes in music.

Does the music program stimulate creativity? Creative experiences should be an integral part of the music program. Through singing, listening, expressing bodily movement, and reading music, the child should develop in his ability to respond creatively to sound. As his ability grows, so does his sensitivity to music and its values.

Is the teacher well qualified? A broad knowledge of music, an understanding of children, an appreciation of the creative process in the development of the child are essential in guiding effectively children's experiences with music.

Does the program show evidence of careful planning on the part of those responsible?

It is by no means enough for the teacher to fill the music period with favorite songs selected by the children. A growing musicality and appreciation of music is most effectively developed through a carefully planned program which is the result of cooperative effort.

## Music of the Future

Music in the life of the child develops into music in the life of the adult. In view of present trends it is predicted that music will become even more important in this changing world.

Current trends indicate:

1. Experimentation with new forms of melody, rhythm, harmony, and instrumentation mirroring the dynamic impact of new forms of energy and new mechanical inventions upon life now and in the future.
2. Greater emphasis on the national character of music, accompanied by a wider international audience, leading to greater understanding between peoples of all nations.
3. The ever-growing audience potential, through continued advance in means of transportation, communication, and musical reproduction.
4. The expansion of music education, not only to assist the musically gifted to reach their highest development, but also to enable every one of us to share in the glorious adventure of the music of the future.[29]

[29] Harriet Buxton Barbour and Warren S. Freeman, *A Story of Music* (Evanston, Ill.: Summy-Birchard Publishing Company, rev. ed., 1958), p. 287.

That music is affecting in a greater degree the daily life of boys and girls in our schools is evidenced by the following: "In an Indiana high school, members of the school orchestra, as was their custom, brought their lunch to the noon orchestra rehearsal. The musical future of America is in safe hands when you see teen-agers put down a sandwich to pick up a fiddle bow. Music has that sort of hold on many youngsters. It is impressing them with the necessity for hard work and the need for working together to get satisfying results."[30]

## *Conclusion*

Children will have no richer experiences and opportunities in school than their teachers provide. Teachers must understand the objectives of music in the school, identify the children who are highly talented, provide a balanced program of activities that takes into consideration the needs of all. They must have and use enough knowledge of music, children, and materials to offer carefully selected songs, singing games, rhythms and dances, instruments to play, music for listening, and the technical skills essential to and in harmony with the needs and abilities of each child.

The teacher must have an understanding of the child's voice, the curriculum, and methods of teaching music in such a way that no child is satisfied unless the performance is worthy of his best efforts. The teacher should instill in the student the craftsman's joy in performance and appreciation of music. He should help the child find such joy in music that he will turn naturally to it for self-expression, for communication, for physical activity, and for group association.

Music, perhaps more than any other activity, provides each day with vital means of self-expression, self-evaluation, self-realization, and of rich, worth-while relationships in group activity. "Through music, as through great literature, we walk the heights of aesthetic joys, we travel in imagination to distant lands."[31]

[30] Sur and Schuller, *op. cit.*, p. 4.
[31] Earluth Epting, "The Place of Music in Our Lives," *Music for Children's Living*, Bulletin No. 96 (Washington, D.C.: Association for Childhood Education International, 1955), p. 4.

## ACTIVITIES AND QUESTIONS

1. Observe a music class at the grade level in which you are interested. Which phases of the music experiences suggested in the chapter did you see?
2. Examine several series of basal music textbooks and the accompanying manuals. Evaluate them in terms of a well-balanced program.
3. Observe a rhythm band in a kindergarten or first grade. What was the teacher's concept of the role of rhythm instruments as demonstrated by the lesson you observed?

## BIBLIOGRAPHY

Andrews, Frances M., and Cockerille, Clara E. *Your School Music Program.* Englewood Cliffs, N.J.: Prentice-Hall, Inc., 1958.

Association for Childhood Education International. *Music for Children's Living.* Bulletin No. 96. Washington, D.C.: The Association, 1955.

Bailey, Eunice. *Discovering Music with Young Children.* New York: Philosophical Library, 1958.

Barbour, Harriet Buxton, and Freeman, Warren S. *A Story of Music.* Evanston, Ill.: Summy-Birchard Publishing Company, rev. ed., 1958.

Carabo-Cone, M. C., and Royt, B. *How to Help Children Learn Music.* New York: Harper & Brothers, 1955.

Dykema, Peter W., and Cundiff, Hannah M. *School Music Handbook.* Evanston, Ill.: C. C. Birchard and Company, new ed., 1955.

Elliott, Raymond. *Teaching Music.* Columbus, Ohio: Charles E. Merrill Books, 1960.

Fox, Lillian Mohr, and Hopkins, L. Thomas. *Creative School Music.* New York: Silver Burdett Company, 1936.

Henry, Nelson B. (ed.). *Basic Concepts in Music Education.* Fifty-seventh Yearbook, National Society for the Study of Education, Part I. Chicago: University of Chicago Press, 1958.

Hosmer, Helen M. *Singing in the Schools.* Music Educators National Conference. A monograph for the Music in American Life Commission on Standards of Literature and Performance by the Committee on Literature and Interpretation of Music for Choral Organizations. Washington, D.C.: National Education Association, 1958.

Kaplan, Max (chairman). *Music in a Changing World.* Music Educators National Conference, Part II of a report for the Music in American

Life Commission on Music in the Community. Washington, D.C.: National Education Association, 1958.

Landeck, Beatrice (chairman). *Music for Fours and Fives.* Music Educators National Conference. A report prepared for the Music in American Life Commission on Music in Preschool, Kindergarten and Elementary School by the Committee on Music in Nursery and Kindergarten. Washington, D.C.: National Education Association, 1958.

Machlis, J. *The Enjoyment of Music.* New York: W. W. Norton and Company, shorter ed., 1957.

Morgan, Russell Van Dyke, and Morgan, Helen N. *Music Education in Action.* Chicago: Neil A. Kjos Music Company, Publishers, rev. ed., 1960.

Mukerji, Rose. "Music, Dance and Fine Arts," *Childhood Education,* 35:350, April 1959.

Mursell, James L. *Music and the Classroom Teacher.* New York: Silver Burdett Company, 1956.

Myers, Louise Kifer. *Teaching Children Music in the Elementary School.* Englewood Cliffs, N.J.: Prentice-Hall, Inc., 1956.

Parks, Grant. *Music for Elementary Teachers.* New York: Appleton-Century-Crofts, Inc., rev. ed., 1960.

Pierce, Anne E. *Teaching Music in the Elementary School.* New York: Henry Holt and Company, 1959.

Ray, Florence. *Singing Days of Childhood; Songs, Poems, Finger Plays and Rhythms for the Young Child.* Minneapolis: T. S. Denison and Company, 1958.

Sheehy, Emma Dickson. *There's Music in Children.* New York: Henry Holt and Company, rev. ed., 1952.

Sur, William R., and Schuller, Charles F. *Music Education for Teen-Agers.* New York: Harper & Brothers, 1958.

ANTHOLOGIES AND BASAL SERIES

*The American Singer.* New York: American Book Company.

Association for Childhood Education International. *Songs Children Like.* Washington, D.C.: The Association, 1954.

*A Singing School.* Evanston, Ill.: Summy-Birchard Publishing Company.

Landeck, Beatrice. *Songs to Grow On.* New York: William Sloane Associates, 1952.

Landeck, Beatrice. *More Songs to Grow On.* New York: Edward B. Marks Music Corporation, 1954.

*Music for Living.* Morristown, N.J.: Silver Burdett Company.

*Our Singing World.* Boston: Ginn and Company.

*Together We Sing.* Chicago: Follett Publishing Company.

Anderson, LeRoy. *LeRoy Anderson Conducts His Own Composition.* Decca Album D–810.

Bartók, Béla. *Piano Music for Children.* New York: Boosey and Hawkes, Vol. 1 and 2, rev. ed., 1946.

Bartók, Béla. *The Voice of the Arts.* Vox Album 625.

Faith, Percy. *Festival.* Columbia Records No. 39708.

Johnson, Hazel. *Music for Rhythms,* Volume I (album). New York City: 128 13th St.

Luther, Frank. *Children's Corner.* Decca Album A–414.

Marias, Josef. *Songs of the African Veldt.* Decca Album A–471, 113, 302.

Miller, Freda. *Music for Rhythms and Dance,* Album 4. New York: 8 Tudor City Place.

Pitts, L. B., *et al. Singing in Harmony.* Boston: Ginn and Company, Album 6.

Pitts, L. B., *et al. Singing Together.* Boston: Ginn and Company, Album 5.

Trapp, Paul, and Kleinsinger, George. *Tubby the Tuba.* Decca Records CU–106.

Waberg. *Dance Along.* Folkway Records.

Black Mountain Records, 4247 Walnut St., Long Beach Calif.

Children's Record Guild, 27 Thompson St., New York 13, N.Y.

Folkways Record and Service Corporation, 117 W. 46th St., New York 19, N.Y.

Kismet Record Company (folk dance records, international releases), 227 E. 14th Street, New York, N.Y.

The Methodist Radio and Film Commission: The World of Fun Series of Recreational Recordings produced by Larry Eusenberg; recording by RCA Victor. Audio-Visual Department of Local Church General Board of Education, The Methodist Church.

Willis Music Company, Cincinnati, Ohio. All music of all companies.

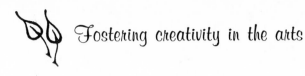 

# Art

> . . . each for the joy of working,
> And each, in his separate star,
> Shall draw the Thing as he sees it
> For the God of Things as They are.
>
> RUDYARD KIPLING

The healthy, happy, uninhibited child expresses himself in all forms of artistic endeavor. He sings, dances, draws, paints, models, builds, and dramatizes spontaneously and without timidity. He splashes on walls as enthusiastically as he splashes on paper. Unless he has been scolded for painting or scribbling on walls he eagerly takes every opportunity to fill the space with riotous color. To some adults it is creative expression; to the child it is playing with paints. If the child receives satisfaction from expressing himself in the graphic arts, if the environment is one in which he finds stimulation, guidance, and encouragement, art is likely to become a satisfactory outlet for a lifetime.

Art is not alone for the gifted; art is for everyone. It appeals to the gifted, the average, and the slow learner. It should be made available in the school because (1) it helps children develop in creative expression; (2) it helps children acquire artistic skills; (3) it helps children gain understanding of their environment as they depict their experiences; (4) it helps children develop taste through contact

with a variety of media and techniques; (5) it helps in the development of intellectual discipline; (6) it provides initial experiences for
future avocational interests.

## The Role of the Teacher

To develop creative power requires an environment in which
creativity can flourish. Art cannot be produced without freedom
to experiment, to manipulate, to experience, and to express. Neither
can it flourish without guidance which stems from (1) knowledge
of stages of development in art, (2) effective methods of teaching,
(3) acquaintance with art media, (4) ability to awaken art appreciation, and (5) insight in evaluation.

The adult who would guide children in the creative process must
know when to stimulate and when to withdraw; when to encourage
and when to analyze; when to praise and when to criticize; when to
suggest the use of new media or new techniques and when to withhold the suggestions. The teacher who senses his responsibility must
keep a fine balance between motivation and evaluation. He must give
the child freedom to express, but not license. "When children are left
to their own devices and lack stimulus and guidance from a teacher,
the results are often deplorable."[32]

### DEVELOPMENTAL STAGES IN ART

Johnny's teacher read a story about a beautiful blue pony, and
Johnny was inspired to paint a picture of it. When he took it home
he held it carefully in his hands as he rushed over to his mother and
said breathlessly, "Here's my picture. I made it for you." His mother
looked at the vague lines and vivid color and said in a puzzled manner,
"What on earth is *that?* What's it supposed to be?" Johnny was
close to tears. The beautiful blue pony was left lying on the table.

If adults fail to understand the various stages through which art
expression develops, they unknowingly discourage children by judging products according to adult standards and adult techniques. An

---

[32] Monica Haley, "Contradictions in Art Educational Theory and Practice,"
*Art Education,* June 1956, p. 6.

understanding of the evolution of the child's art will help the parent or teacher appreciate the product in terms of the maturity of the child's expression and experience. The age at which the child goes through each stage varies with the individual. Every child is unique; every child has unique experiences; every child expresses himself in his own style. But every child goes through the same stages prior to adolescence: the manipulative stage, in which he manipulates materials in an exploratory and random fashion; the symbolic stage, in which he develops a series of distinct symbols or marks which are identified with certain objects in his experience and later related to his environment; and finally the stage in which the symbol is analyzed. The latter is sometimes referred to as the representational stage. It is at this stage that children become dissatisfied and highly critical of their efforts. They may discontinue their interest in art unless the teacher helps them develop the techniques they need to express their ideas in ways commensurate with their high standards.

*The Manipulative Stage: In Search of a Symbol.* The first stage, from infancy to kindergarten or first grade, is sometimes termed the scribble stage. Parents find children less than a year old reaching for a pencil or crayon and making a few tentative scratches. This is the beginning of what may be a promising artistic career. Random manipulation becomes controlled manipulation and finally named manipulation. Children who have had no preschool experience may still be in the stage of random manipulation or scribbling when they enter kindergarten. Other kindergarten children have advanced into the symbolic and even the representational stage. It is important that the teacher accept the child at whatever stage of development he is in and help him move on to the next. Children never entirely leave the manipulative stage; however, most normal children are in the symbolic stage in the primary grades.

*The Symbolic Stage: The Symbol Is Found.* In this stage (approximately first to third grades) the child finds the symbol he has been searching for. In the process of finding it, however, he experiments with variations of the form, shape, or marks he makes. Teachers of young children who are in this stage of art development can identify the work by the symbol. They do not need the name to know that the particular circular or elongated symbol is Mark's, Jim's, or Jane's. Some children produce hundreds of marks or shapes having clear-cut resemblance and distinctive character. The kindergartener frequently finds his symbol and is ready to identify it. It may be a man, an animal, a flower, furniture, or people; it may be a tree, a bird, or a kite. Whatever it is, he works hard at it. Many kindergarten children, and certainly most second-graders, are able to make effective use of two or more symbols in their art products.

After a time of experimenting with the symbol or symbols children begin to think of using them in a composition. They put a border around the edge of the painting or drawing to define the limits of the environment — the room, the playground, the house they are drawing. Later they make use of a base line showing the ground as contrasted with the sky. At first they draw the sky across the top of the paper, leaving a bare portion in the center, and add the earth to the bottom of the paper. The sun with its various points or rays becomes important. Some kindergarten children get the concept of the sky as a solid mass of blue touching the earth. Others do not develop this concept until they are in the intermediate grades. Kindergarten children do not always paint the sky blue and the grass green. They may paint a red sky, purple people, and black grass. It is all the same to them. Second-graders, on the other hand, are very realistic in their painting; for them the sky *must* be blue and the grass green.

Neither is the young child inhibited by lack of technical knowledge in expressing his ideas. He can combine outdoors-indoors in the same composition without the slightest hesitancy or self-consciousness. It is as he approaches the representational stage that he becomes realistic, fearful, and cautious about doing it "just right."

*The Representational Stage: The Symbol Is Analyzed.* Since all artistic expression is a reflection of the personality, one may expect growth as children develop from childhood into preadolescence. The preadolescent (approximately third to sixth grades) is a changed child. He is not the eager, carefree adventurer who "tries anything once." He is more conservative and studied in his response. He gives greater attention to detail, shading, textural effects, realism in depicting objects, and color. He makes use of perspective, shaded color, and overlapping of objects to give depth to his picture. These techniques should be taught to him as he evidences readiness and indicates need.

Interest in design, texture, form, and portraiture characterizes the intermediate grade child. He expresses what he sees more than what he feels. The advanced preadolescent demands sympathetic and skillful teaching from the art teacher. However, not many pupils reach this stage in the elementary grades.

## GUIDING CHILDREN'S ART EXPERIENCES

"Art, like any other subject, of course, contains a certain content and requires of the teacher some specific knowledge and skills. A knowledge of pictorial composition and of other forms of design, an acquaintance with some professional art production, and some ability to use such media as paint, wood, or clay are required."[33] Many teachers have an erroneous concept of creative art and fail to give guidance. It is not enough to provide a permissive environment. The teacher must motivate, define goals, and select media and tools of expression. To do less is to shirk one's responsibility.

*Motivation.* Motivation in art consists in providing stimulating experiences that lend themselves to expression. Motivation must be developed in harmony with interest. With the youngest children, supplying materials, time, and encouragement is enough. However, before long children will be interested in a definite plan for their creative expression. They will make pictures in connection with a center of interest. Even when there is no suggestion made by the teacher, an interest in transportation or pioneer life or Alaska, for example, brings with it creative art that reflects the current interest.

If children lack experiences, if they lack ideas, these must be supplied. If their minds are blocked and "move around in stereotypes, their frame of reference must be extended."[34] The teacher can, for example, help a child who paints boats every day, not by telling him to paint something else, but by broadening his experiences and his understandings. Asking questions such as "Where does the boat travel? What kind of boat is it? Where does it anchor?" he makes the child extend himself until he sees art as a part of himself and his relationship to his environment.

[33] Charles D. Gaitskell, *Children and Their Art* (New York: Harcourt, Brace and Company, 1958), p. 37.
[34] Viktor Lowenfeld, "Do Children Communicate Through Art?" *Everyday Art*, 36:4, Spring 1957.

*Suggestions for Motivating Art Experiences.* Not only current experiences but more remote events that the child remembers because of emotional response, tragic or humorous, motivate children to express themselves in art. Here are some topics that will start children remembering:

The Day I Got Lost

The Day Tuppy Couldn't Climb Down from the Tree

The Day I Fell Out of the Car

The Day Our House Caught Fire

The Day I Fell in the Haystack

Our Ball Team Won the Tournament

Our Puppet Show

Snowed in at School

At the Circus

What I Got for Christmas

At the Farm

My Ride in an Airplane

My Trip to England

Older children enjoy making pictures that use the same subject matter in different situations, such as Before and After:

We Decorated the Christmas Tree

I Lost Fifteen Pounds

My Hair Was Cut

I Got a New Coat

We Moved to Our New House

We Landscaped the Yard

We Painted the House

The First Snowfall

I Had the Measles

I Had the Mumps

The Big Rainstorm

The Tornado

Both young and older children like to search within themselves and express feelings:

I'm Angry About the Game

I'm Happy Because I'm Taking a Trip

I'm Laughing About a Joke

I'm Tired from Working Hard

I'm Through with My Homework

I'm Scowling Because I'm Concentrating

I'm Scared and Whistling in the Dark

I'm Scared and Listening to the Sounds Around Me

*Defining Goals.* Children learn at an early age to define goals for themselves. They want something specific toward which to work. Generally the teacher has only to suggest that clay, painting, or sculpture may be produced in connection with a center of interest or theme and the children are on their way.

Most children, that is. The teacher must be prepared to help the child who has a limited experiential background, little interest, and meager talent. To help such a child requires understanding of his interests, experiences, and abilities. Not all children are self-starters. Some of them have to be primed.

*Teaching.*  Teaching art means helping the child express what he has decided to say in terms of the product he wishes to create, assisting him in techniques and the use of tools and materials, and making suggestions about the composition or design on the basis of the child's desire and need for help. Since the creative act is the child's own, the teacher may help by providing the tools and the materials, and sometimes the ideas, but the child must use the tools, ideas, and media in his own way to compose or create something that is his alone. The dilemma facing the teacher is this: Should I give him help or let him sit there struggling all period trying to think of something to do? Gaitskell warns that "Only a personal knowledge of every member of the class, together with his own good judgment, can tell him when help must be forthcoming. To step in too soon will take away a child's initiative; to be too late will leave the child frustrated in his creative efforts."[35] The child must be ready for teaching and sense the need for it.

*Selecting the Media and Tools of Expression.*  Children vary in their interest in and ability to use media — paint, clay, paper, and other art materials. For this reason it is essential that they be provided with many materials and tools as early as possible so they may all be challenged. Children who are given a choice of art materials express themselves more creatively, think independently, and learn to evaluate their work more objectively.

This is true, too, of the tools for expression. Even kindergarten children like to use a variety of tools in working with paints, for example — easel brushes, water-color brushes, fingers, elbows, and arms. The artist, like the scientist, is ever ready to try a new tool, to seek a new way to express his ideas. He may develop a liking for a particular medium or tool of expression, but he continues to try new palettes, new brushes, and new techniques.

*Arranging the Classroom for Art.*  The experienced teacher realizes how important it is to have the materials, the space, and the

---

[35] Gaitskell, *op. cit.,* p. 46.

time organized to insure a successful art environment. He must make adequate preparation to see that enough materials are available, that they are accessible and usable, and that children know where to get them and where to put them when they are finished.

Enough space is essential. If table surfaces, work boards, and drawing boards are limited, children can color on the floor. There must be room to put the unfinished work, room for things that are not dry, for clay work, and for finger paintings that are waiting to be pressed. Display boards and shelves are needed for two- and three-dimensional products.

The teacher who considers the physical as well as the emotional aspects of the environment will provide space for storing bulky supplies and equipment; putting out supplies for current needs; working quietly as in coloring and painting, or vigorously as in sawing or hammering; drying partially completed work; storing work; displaying art products.

*Supplies and Equipment.* No matter what special subjects are contemplated in art, the following list of general tools and supplies should be basic to nearly any program.

| | |
|---|---|
| 1. brushes | painting, flat, hog bristle, one inch to one-quarter-inch-wide painting, pointed, sable, large (size 6 or 7) |
| 2. chalk | soft, 10 or 12 colors, black, white |
| 3. crayons | wax, soft, 10 or 12 colors, black, white |
| 4. drawing boards | about 18″ × 24″, soft plywood at least "BC" grade (i.e., clear of knots on at least one side) |
| 5. erasers | Artgum type |
| 6. inks | ordinary blue-black fountain pen black India, 2-oz. bottles |
| 7. paint | poster, liquid in pints or powder in pounds (white, black, yellow, blue, green, red, as basic; magenta, purple, turquoise as luxuries; probably twice the quantity of black, white, and yellow as of other colors chosen) water colors in boxes of 8 colors (sometimes useful but not entirely necessary . . .) |
| 8. paper | roll of kraft (i.e., brown wrapping), about 36″ wide, or "project roll," 36″ wide Manila, 18″ × 24″, cream and gray |

colored construction, 12″ × 18″ (red, yellow, blue, light green, dark green, gray, and perhaps some in-between colors like blue-green, red-orange; some 40 colors are obtainable) newsprint, natural, 18″ × 24″

9. paint tins     muffin tins, with at least 6 depressions
10. paste     school, in quarts
11. pencils     black, drawing, soft, about 5B
12. work boards     plywood (3 ply) 18″ × 24″ (old drawing boards are suitable)

Miscellaneous supplies and equipment such as scissors, thumbtacks, and paper cutter (18 inch cut minimum) are not listed since they are part of general equipment for other subjects.

In order that the supplies may be handled efficiently and the work proceed in an orderly fashion, the following supplementary furniture is needed:

1. A storage cupboard with some adjustable shelves, the latter at least 8 inches wide for small items and other shelves at least 18 inches wide for larger items. The outside dimensions of the cupboard will, of course, be determined by the floor and wall space available.
2. Two tables, preferably at least 5 feet long and 30 inches wide, one to be used largely by the teacher in arranging and displaying supplies and the other for children's group work.
3. A sink, or a stand for pails of water. . . .
4. A drying shelf or battery of shelves near a radiator or other source of heat. The shelf should be about 12 inches wide and as long as space permits.[36]

## ART MEDIA AND TECHNIQUES

A good art program includes drawing and painting, working with paper, sculpture and modeling, printing, stenciling, working with colored chalk. Group activities include making murals and puppets, and designing stage scenery and costumes.

*Drawing and Painting.* Teachers themselves should be familiar with the tools and techniques used.

*Wax crayons*
Encourage children to experiment with crayons.

[36] *Ibid.,* pp. 108, 109.

Manila drawing paper is more satisfying than newsprint for crayon work.

Crayons are more effective if they are pressed hard on the paper to give a rich, dark color.

Children like to work out scratchboard designs in which they apply wax crayon over glossy paper, repeating the colors. Then they apply a dark layer over the crayoned area very thickly. Older children enjoy using India ink. They may reverse the point of the pen in the holder and scratch a design on the picture.

### Paint

*Tempera.* 18 ″ × 36″, or 12″ × 18″ newsprint works well with this medium. Brushes should be large with long handles. They may be round or flat and should be about 10″ in length. After use they should be washed in cold water and stored in jars with the bristles up. For sponge painting with tempera, use a small square of rubber sponge. Dip in dishes of tempera paint.

*Finger paint.* Finger paint may be purchased ready for use or prepared by mixing tempera paint with school paste. A small amount of powdered paste may be stirred into the mixture to make it smooth and easier to handle. Glazed paper is required. A spoonful or two of the paint should be placed on well-dampened paper. Finger painting to music results in beautifully designed pictures. Rhythm is improved in line and color areas as the child listens to music. The result is a picture of lovely pastel curves.

### Water colors

Beginners should be encouraged to use pure, not mixed, colors. Water color is clear and transparent and lends itself to designs that are entirely different from those developed by tempera paint. Children should experiment later with mixing color. Mixing a standard color with its complement, adding black to a color, or adding gray by mixing black and white provides surprises. Color wheels are helpful in mixing colors.

### Chalk

Chalk is effectively used on 12″ × 18″ Manila or newsprint. Pastels may be purchased in sets of twelve or twenty-four colors. Both the end and side of the chalk may be used.

Dampening the paper before using colored chalk makes colors richer.

Dampening the chalk makes it easier to apply.

Few children in the elementary grades are ready for formal instruction in design. However, the teacher should not only provide a variety of materials but introduce techniques such as dry brush, wash, stipple, and others to achieve textural effects. The child should begin to understand the requirements of a good composition: unity, variety, and individuality.

*Working with Paper.*  Paper and its derivatives are becoming increasingly important as art media.

### Tearing
Pictures may be created by tearing paper and mounting it on a background.

Variety may be achieved by using different textiles, string, and thin wood in addition to the torn paper.

Variety may also be achieved by putting color against color, texture against texture, mat against glazed finish, transparent papers overlapped against the regular paper of varying hues.

### Three-dimensional
Some ways to achieve a three-dimensional effect in paper are folding and bending, bending, frilling, pleating, stretching, scoring, and twisting.

If the children exhaust their own ideas the teacher should demonstrate some ways in which they can work in paper. However, achievement which comes as a result of personal conquest in this medium is more conducive to development in the child.

### Free-standing forms
Children enjoy activities that involve the use of paper and cardboard to produce free-standing three-dimensional objects. Cardboard containers in various sizes and shapes, cardboard tubes of different lengths and diameters, a few empty spools plus some paint, brushes, and paste become animals, toys, buildings, and people.

### Rolled paper forms
The child enjoys making animals of rolled paper. He may use old newspaper, form it into the shape he wishes, and develop the underlying structure. Arms, head, legs, and body can be made from rolled newspapers. (The basic structure — the body — is tied at several points with string.) Once the main structure is completed the entire object is carefully wrapped with one-inch-wide strips of newspapers until it is completely covered. Before it is dry such details as ears, eyes, tail, etc., can

be added. When dry it may be painted, and if the creation warrants it it may be shellacked or varnished.

The teacher must be on hand to suggest and demonstrate and guide the child in his venture with this type of expression. He must be encouraged to develop skills and work at his own rate and in his own style. It takes time, patience, experience, effort, and guidance to master this activity.

*Cut paper*

All children enjoy cutting paper.

Scissored shapes, such as birds, animals, flowers, fish, may be crushed, curled, snipped, tucked, or pleated to create unusual effects.

The paper may be pulled between thumb and scissors, curled around a pencil, or pulled between thumb and fingers.

*Papier-mâché*

Papier-mâché is centuries old.

To prepare it, newsprint is torn into small bits. The torn paper is left to soak overnight and the next day is boiled for at least two hours. The excess water is drained off and the remaining pulp is wrung dry in a cotton cloth. About a cup of school paste or wheat flour is well mixed with about five cups of pulp. It is now ready for modeling purposes.

*Dampened paper*

Strips of paper dampened with school paste are laid over a mold or form and pressed in place. When dry the paper strips form a hard shell which is removed from the underlying form and may be finished with paint and shellac.

Bowls, tunnels, mountains, igloos, masks can be made this way.

*Collages or mobiles*

Forms in space are popular with children of all ages.

They may be hung from the ceiling or used as Christmas tree ornaments.

Creating collages or mobiles should be approached with the "Try it and see what happens" attitude.

Toni Hughes[37] suggests forms in paper that may be evolved by multiple folding or pleating; cutting strips of paper and joining them in different ways; using one continuous cut, e.g., a spiral from a sheet of construction paper; cutting away parts of the paper. Forms may be developed also by cutting slots in two or more pieces of paper and pushing the pieces together.

---

[37] Toni Hughes, *How to Make Shapes in Space* (New York: E. P. Dutton and Company, 1955).

Children can create designs that are unique, attractive, and satisfying.

*Sculpture and Modeling.* Children enjoy the process as much as they do the finished product.

*Sculpture in wood*

Sculpture is a process in which a portion of the material is removed to form the product.

Only older children will be able to carve in wood.

A set of wood-carving tools and an oilstone are needed.

Because most of the tools for working with wood are dangerous, caution must be observed in their use.

Pride in craftsmanship should be stressed.

Adequate facilities, materials, tools, and guidance are essential.

*Sculpture in soap*

Young children get much satisfaction from carving in soap.

Spoons may be substituted for knives.

Soap carving provides experience with a medium that is inexpensive, is easy to work with, and gives quick results.

*Sculpture in plaster of Paris*

Small cardboard containers make suitable molds.

Plaster is mixed in small quantities by adding water and stirring it with a spoon until the mixture is the consistency of thick cream. Adding a teaspoonful of salt to two cups of plaster retards the drying.

After it is mixed it must be poured quickly into the prepared mold to dry and harden. When it is dry, the cardboard is easily peeled off. The plaster may now be carved. To create an antique finish, it may be soaked in linseed oil, dusted with umber, and then brushed off.

*Modeling with clay*

For the youngest children the teacher must prepare the clay.

Older children can follow directions in preparing their own clay.

Clay that hardens and can be fired gives the most satisfaction. Commercial clay, wrapped in cellophane to keep moist, is the easiest to handle.

Younger children are usually content to manipulate the clay.

Older children want help in making a product that is a more exact replica of the objects they are modeling.

The teacher should demonstrate the two methods of modeling: pulling out from a central mass, and shaping and welding in which prepared pieces such as legs and arms are scored and treated with slip. He should also demonstrate the use of tools. The teacher must provide space for storing products so they are not broken.

*Printing and Stenciling.* Printing is a process in which a paint or dye is spread upon a prepared surface which in turn is pressed upon another surface.

*Block printing*
   The child should work first with linoleum.
   Linoleum blocks offer experiences in the art through various types of cuts, selection of different papers, use of more than one color on a block, the placing of units on cloth, and for older pupils the use of more than one block to form a pattern.
   The child should work out his own design. He can experiment with ways of chopping and slicing out pieces of linoleum.
   When a satisfactory cut is made an impression will be tried.
   When printing on paper, dampen the paper slightly, coat the linoleum evenly with ink, press firmly and evenly.
   When printing on cloth, the cloth should be spread over felt or newspapers.
   Each time the block is used it should be freshly and evenly inked.
*Vegetable printing*
   Even the young child enjoys printing with a potato, carrot, or celery. The piece should be large enough for the child to hold securely and should be cut flat on one side or end.
   The child dips the flat side of the vegetable into water color, tempera, or colored ink and dabs it on a sheet of newsprint. He soon develops a rhythmic sequence of units. He may also use fruit rinds or sponges in printing.
   A design may be cut into the potato.
   The design is painted over and printed on the material in any order desired. Over-all patterns are very effective. Two colors may be alternated.
*Other materials*
   Wood, pencils, corks, spools, sticks, and other objects may be used instead of a vegetable.
*Stenciling*
   Stenciling requires greater skill and is more satisfactory with the intermediate child.
   Holes are cut in the stencil in the desired pattern. Paint is then applied to the surface through the pattern. Only where holes have been cut will the paint appear on the under surface.
   Equipment must be kept clean to avoid smearing.

Designs should be original and created directly on the stencil
paper in the initial experiences.

Time must be allowed to complete the process.

Originality is expressed in the design, use of color, and in combining two or more stencils on the same surface.

In working with children in all art experiences the teacher must
keep in mind that "Art ceases to be art . . . if any form or technique
no matter how good, is imposed from without . . . if it fails to grow
out of the child's own expression and feeling of need as they lead on
to higher levels of appreciation and control."[38]

## DEVELOPING CHILDREN'S ART APPRECIATION

In guiding a child's art experiences the teacher is seeking to combine three strands in his design for living: one strand is self-expression; the second strand is participation with others in creative activities such as designing scenery and costumes, making murals, and so
forth; the third strand is appreciation of the world's heritage in art.

Teachers should remember that the individual brings meaning to
the painting, the sculpture, the architectural design. They must not
be discouraged if boys and girls show little interest in studying the
works of the "Old Masters." ". . . The meanings of pictures are not
in the pictures, but rather in what we bring to them. . . . If the
picture is well within our previous experience it means something.
What it means depends on the kind of our experience."[39]

Gombrich, in this connection, states, "Nothing, perhaps, is more
important than just this: that to enjoy these works we must have a
fresh mind, one which is ready to catch every hint and to respond
to every hidden harmony; a mind, most of all, not cluttered up with
long high-sounding words and ready-made phrases."[40]

In addition, the picture itself must be of good quality of reproduction. Too often children are given miniatures so poorly printed
that they can gain no concept of the picture.

In order to bring meaning to the work of art and develop an in-

[38] Margaret Mathias, *The Beginnings of Art in the Public Schools* (New
York: Charles Scribner's Sons, 1924), p. ix.

[39] Paul R. Wendt, "The Language of Pictures," in S. I. Hayakawa (ed.),
*Our Language and Our World* (New York: Harper & Brothers, 1959), pp.
253, 255.

[40] Ernest H. Gombrich, *The Story of Art* (New York: Phaidon Publishers,
1957), p. 17.

creasing sensitivity to and appreciation for art, it is necessary to understand something of the time in which the artist lived and worked. Griswold points out that "To understand Bach or Leonardo or Shakespeare, to receive the full benefit of their revelations of the ideal, we must rise to their level. We must know at last some of the things they knew, think some of their thoughts, feel some of their feelings, even though we cannot express ourselves in forms so sublime."[41] We must be willing to put forth an effort to understand.

Children who are fortunate enough to live in a home where perception of beauty is a daily experience, to learn in a classroom in which beauty is part of the environment, and to be encouraged by a creative and enthusiastic teacher who himself is a patron of the arts are well on the way to a deep appreciation of art. In the final analysis, "what a person is — emotionally, intellectually and socially — will determine his ability to appreciate art . . . art appreciation, in fact, appears to be the result of a lifetime of education. As for appreciation, this can only undoubtedly be developed by teaching."[42]

*Suggestions for Developing Art Appreciation.* Attempting to force appreciation down the throats of children through a stereotyped formal program does not result in appreciation. However, to ignore beauty is to neglect one of the basic needs of children.

Many teachers help children develop appreciation as an integral part of creative expression. In this approach the teacher utilizes every opportunity to awaken appreciation, not only of drawing and painting, but also of sculpture, pottery, and other three-dimensional work. As he experiments with an art medium, the child becomes conscious of the problems, needs, and goals inherent in his creative activity. As he learns what to look for in the work of another individual who also has created in that medium, his understanding and insight increase and his taste improves.

In guiding experiences in art the teacher not only must be familiar with the media but must make available the art objects themselves and use visual aids extensively to broaden the children's actual acquaintance with the work of others. Whatever area of art the children are exploring — painting, drawing, textiles, pottery — the

[41] A. Whitney Griswold, "The Fine Arts and the Universities," *The Atlantic,* 205:55, June 1959.
[42] Herbert Read, *Education Through Art* (New York: Pantheon Books, Inc., 1945), p. 206.

teacher will provide appropriate objects for comparison, study, reference, and enjoyment.

In order to understand a work of art, one must understand the artist's life and the country in which he lived. Visual aids help children to become familiar with many aspects of historical and contemporary art. Useful visual aids are reproductions, films, film strips, slides, actual works or objects of art in two or three dimensions.

Trips to museums and art galleries stimulate interest in art. In areas where such experience is impossible the teacher may make use of extension services, in which art is brought to children. Often organizations can obtain the loan of famous collections and share them with the school. These may be hung in school corridors and offices as well as in the classrooms.

Many schools set aside certain funds for purchasing fine works of art. It does not take long to build up a presentable art exhibition if teachers are themselves art enthusiasts. Or a school may make use of a rotating library system in which pictures and other art objects are loaned from a permanent collection to schools for a specified period of time. The teacher who is truly concerned with helping boys and girls grow in their art expression and appreciation will try to create an environment in which the advice of Goethe is followed: "Every day look at a beautiful picture, read a beautiful poem, listen to beautiful music."

## Evaluation of Pupil Progress in Art

"Every work of art seems to have a quality of inner consistency; one feels that its forms, lines, colors, textures, and spaces are related by the very fact that they were done by one person; this quality gives them a cohesiveness, a belonging together, that is called style. . . . In attempting to evaluate an individual's work in art three basic principles should be remembered: *balance* (a sense of equilibrium and logical distribution), *continuity* (a rhythmic relationship uniting the various parts of the work of art), and *emphasis* (a reconciling of differences which make for variety and interest through varying the degrees of emphasis."[43]

[43] Daniel M. Mendelowitz, *Children Are Artists* (Stanford: Stanford University Press, 1954), p. 99.

*What the Child Wants to Know.* Even young children enjoy experimenting with balance, rhythm, and emphasis. They like to know that they are making progress in their efforts to express themselves in art. Growth is evaluated on the basis of the objectives of the school. Since art is highly personal, the child would like answers to the following questions, although he might not use these words: Is what I am expressing in art really my own? Does my arrangement of the picture show my personal taste preferences in color, line, shape, design, and technique? If a dozen other children painted the same subject, how could you tell which was mine? How can I intensify this personal quality?

*What the Teacher Wants to Know.* The teacher is primarily concerned with questions of this type:

> To what extent does the pupil express himself creatively in art media?
> To what extent does he express himself emotionally and intellectually in a form in keeping with his stage of artistic development?
> To what extent has he developed a personal style?
> To what extent does his art show ability to use each element of design: line, color, texture, mass and space, light and shade?
> Does he achieve unity and variety in his design?
> Does he seem to be developing technical skills?
> Does he appear to be developing in appreciation of art?
> Does he react favorably to firsthand experiences with art objects at museums and galleries and to audio-visual experiences?
> Is he developing taste in his daily experiences?
> Does he find increased satisfaction in using a variety of materials, techniques, and media of expression in art?
> Does he set realistic goals and strive to reach them?

*What the School Wants to Know About the Child.* Any attempt to evaluate the child's progress in art requires that the teacher himself be familiar with art, with the children he teaches, and with the objectives of the art program. He must remember that his appraisal will influence the child's talent, and the value the next teacher attaches to his art experience. "Any evaluation of an individual's future promise in art . . . would have to be based not only on test data, but on a summarization of his experiences in various art activities; and appraisal of his sketches, paintings or other art products; and observation of his interests and motivation."[44]

For the school's permanent records the teacher must keep on file a complete written report of each pupil indicating his progress in each curriculum area. It is well to keep samples of the child's work in art so as to have something concrete to refer to in case of questions about his ability in this area.

*What the School Wants to Know About the Teacher.* Evaluation is not only for the pupil; evaluation is for the teacher also. He needs to be aware of the pupil's strengths and weaknesses so that he can help him set and reach realistic goals. He needs, too, to be aware of his own strengths and weaknesses. Success in teaching art and professional growth go together. The following check list should be useful to the teacher in appraising his own skill, knowledge, and attitudes toward guiding art experiences. Administrators, too, may use it to determine the adequacy of art teaching in the school.

Am I familiar with the characteristics of the art program?

Do I know the historical and traditional aspects of art?

Do I understand the objectives of art education in the school today?

Do I know how to motivate, help children set goals, select media and tools for art experiences?

Am I acquainted with the principles of design? Can I help children apply principles of design, composition, and color in their art?

Do I provide a variety of media and tools?

Do I know how to create a physical, social, emotional, and intellectual environment in which creative art can flourish?

Am I aware of the developmental stages and modes of expression in children's art?

Do I know how to suggest subjects for art expression?

Are my skills and techniques sufficiently developed so I can give help when and where it is needed?

Am I familiar with the techniques used in drawing, painting, paper work, sculpture, modeling, printing, and stenciling?

Do I enjoy art to the point that children catch my enthusiasm and develop greater interest in art?

[44] T. L. Torgerson and G. S. Adams, *Measurement and Evaluation for the Elementary School Teacher* (New York: The Dryden Press, 1954), p. 370.

Am I willing to make available to them many sources for developing appreciation of good art?

Am I developing effective techniques for evaluating children's art and art appreciation?

Am I improving my own background of knowledge about art, art education, and art appreciation?

Am I making full use of resources in the community, such as museums, art galleries, exhibits, libraries, and local artists?

"The farmer cannot make the germ develop and sprout from the seed; he can only supply the nurturing conditions which will permit the seed to develop its own potentiality. So it is with creativity."[45]

The teacher, like the farmer, can only create an environment and provide the conditions that will encourage each child to develop his potential in all the creative arts. Whichever art or arts the child finds the most satisfying in expressing himself depends upon many factors. The teacher should be so well informed and experience so much obvious joy in expression in the arts that he will be a source of encouragement to children no matter which area they choose for self-expression. He should kindle the flame that releases the creative spark in each child, to guide and develop the activities to the end that "growth, not trees" becomes the prime objective of the art program. He should provide the right materials and select the right tools with which to create. "Half of the teacher's work is to stand by and kindle the child's confidence; the other half is always to be prepared to present the right material and the right stimuli at the right time."[46]

## ACTIVITIES AND QUESTIONS

1. Collect a series of drawings and paintings from a kindergarten and first grade that illustrates the manipulative stage. Collect drawings and paintings that illustrate the child in search of a symbol and the pictures showing that "the symbol is found."

[45] Carl R. Rogers, "Toward a Theory of Creativity," in S. I. Hayakawa (ed.), *Our Language and Our World* (New York: Harper & Brothers, 1959), p. 172.
[46] Carl Reed, *Early Adolescent Art Education* (Peoria, Ill.: Charles A. Bennett Company, 1957), p. 57.

2. Collect pictures from first grade to third grade to show the development of the symbolic stage. Collect pictures from the intermediate grades to show development of the stages from manipulative to representational.

3. What skills, understandings, attitudes, and specific knowledge must classroom teachers have in order to be successful in guiding children's art experiences?

4. How would you go about developing art appreciation with a group of primary children? Intermediate children?

5. Observe a classroom teacher teaching art. Observe a specialist teaching a comparable group of children. Evaluate the results in terms of the values of art education.

# BIBLIOGRAPHY

Alschuler, Rose, and Hattwick, LaBerta W. *Painting and Personality: A Study of Young Children.* Chicago: University of Chicago Press, 1947, 2 vols.

Association for Childhood Education International. *Creating Materials for Work and Play.* Bulletin No. 5. Washington: The Association, 1957.

Barkan, Manuel. *Through Art to Creativity.* Boston: Allyn and Bacon, Inc., 1960.

Bergson, Henri. *The Creative Mind.* New York: Wisdom Library, 1946.

Cole, Natalie. *The Arts in the Classroom.* New York: The John Day Company, 1940.

Conant, Howard, and Randall, Arne. *Art in Education.* Peoria, Ill.: Charles A. Bennett Company, Inc., 1959.

Cox, Doris, and Weisman, Barbara. *Creative Hands.* New York: John Wiley and Sons, 2nd ed., 1955.

D'Amico, Victor. *Creative Teaching in Art.* New York: International Textbook Company, rev. ed., 1953.

Deimel, George C. "Art Promotes Creativity in the Self-Contained Classroom," Special Art Section, *The Instructor,* 68:39–47, April 1959.

Dewey, John. *Art As Experience.* New York: Minton, Balch and Company, 1934.

Erdt, Margaret H. *Teaching Art in the Elementary School.* New York: Rinehart and Company, 1954.

Gaitskell, Charles D. *Children and Their Art.* New York: Harcourt, Brace and Company, 1958.

Gaitskell, Charles D., and Gaitskell, Margaret. *Art Education in the Kindergarten.* Peoria, Ill.: Charles A. Bennett Company, 1952.

Gardner, Helen. *Art Through the Ages.* New York: Harcourt, Brace and Company, 4th ed., 1959.

Harrison, Elizabeth. *Self-Expression Through Art.* Toronto: W. J. Gage and Company, 1951.

Haupt, Dorothy, and Osborn, Keith. *Creative Activities.* Detroit: The Merrill-Palmer School, 1958.

Jefferson, Blanche. *Teaching Art to Children.* Boston: Allyn and Bacon, Inc., 1959.

Johnson, Ivan E. (ed.). "Special Art Section," *The Instructor*, 67:45–60, April 1958.

Johnson, Lois V. "Music Has Design." (Finger Painting to Music.) *Grade Teacher*, 76:58, 59, January 1959.

Kagan, Pauline Wright. *From Adventure to Experience Through Art.* San Francisco: Howard Chandler, 1959.

Lindstrom, Miriam. *Children's Art.* Berkeley: University of California Press, 1958.

Logan, Frederick M. *Growth of Art in American Schools.* New York: Harper & Brothers, 1955.

Lowenfeld, Viktor. *Creative and Mental Growth.* New York: The Macmillan Company, rev. ed., 1956.

Lowenfeld, Viktor. "Creativity and Art Education," *School Arts*, 59:5–15, October 1959.

Lowenfeld, Viktor. *The Nature of Creative Activity.* New York: Harcourt, Brace and Company, 1939.

Lowenfeld, Viktor. *Your Child and His Art.* New York: The Macmillan Company, 1954.

Mathias, Margaret. *The Beginning of Art in the Public Schools.* New York: Charles Scribner's Sons, 1924.

Mayer, Ralph. *Artists' Handbook of Materials and Techniques.* New York: The Viking Press, 1957.

Mendelowitz, Daniel. *Children Are Artists.* Stanford: Stanford University Press, 1954.

National Art Association. *Research in Art Education.* Ninth Yearbook. Washington, D.C.: The Association, 1959.

Paine, Irma. *Art Aids for Elementary Teaching.* Minneapolis: Burgess Publishing Company, rev. ed., 1953.

Read, Herbert. *Education Through Art.* New York: Pantheon Books, Inc., 2nd ed., 1949.

Santayana, George. *The Sense of Beauty*. New York: Dover Publications, Inc., 1955.

Scott, Robert G. *Design Fundamentals*. New York: McGraw-Hill Book Company, 1951.

Shahn, Ben. *The Shape of Content*. Cambridge: Harvard University Press, 1957.

Sieberling, Frank. *Looking into Art*. New York: Henry Holt and Company, 1959.

Ziegfield, Edwin (ed.). *Creative Teaching in the Visual Arts*. Symposium on Education Through Art. Paris: UNESCO, 1953.

# 12
Whatever promotes physical health, promotes the development of a strong mind and a well-balanced character.

ELLEN G. WHITE

# Guiding health, safety, and physical education

It is difficult for any single profession, organization, program, or family working alone to assume sole responsibility for all aspects of a child's health, safety, and physical and recreational education. Interest in the total well-being of the child has grown to such proportions that the cooperative efforts of many professions, agencies, technical skills, and community organizations are utilized.

When health is defined simply as freedom from disease, little attention is given to its positive aspects. However, when health is viewed as the means by which a person lives fully, a new and broader meaning of health education is possible. Hoyman[1] gives a description of personal health which establishes three main divisions: physical fitness, motor fitness, and mental and emotional fitness. Optimal fitness of any individual depends upon several factors: heredity, which determines the basic elements of personal make-up; environment, which includes nutrition, community influences, housing; and behavior, which is the result of education.[2]

More than ever before it is essential to improve the health of our citizens. As rapidly as research makes known findings that will contribute to improved health the knowledge should be applied. Herein lies the role — and the challenge — of health education.

Health education is the channel through which the fruits of research reach the public. Finding ways to strengthen health education in all forms and at all levels is necessary "so that instead of falling behind in the race between knowledge and application, we can progressively narrow the gap. . . ."[3]

Ottman suggests several ways to vitalize the elementary school health program:

1. Health education should be made an integral part of the curriculum, with a planned sequence which will afford adequate health instruction and permit repetition only when it is purposeful.

2. Teachers should recognize the importance of health and through their own interest and concern should motivate students to improve their health attitudes and behavior.

3. Teachers responsible for health instruction should have adequate pre-service training and in-service training to keep abreast of new knowledge in the field.

4. A uniform plan of meaningful health services which are directly related to the educational program of the school should be developed and implemented.

5. Health councils or health committees should be established which are made up of health-minded individuals, both professional and lay.

[1] H. S. Hoyman, *Functional Health Teaching* (Goshen, Ind.: McConnell Map Company, 2nd ed., 1950), p. 18.
[2] Margaret M. Duncan and Ralph H. Johnson, *Introduction to Physical Education and Health Education* (Englewood Cliffs, N.J.: Prentice-Hall, Inc., 1954), pp. 241–242.
[3] John E. Fogarty, "Research and Health Education," *Today's Health*, 34:54, November 1956.

6. Our belief in the significance of health in the life of the individual and strength of our nation should be reaffirmed and translated into action.[4]

Health service should be closely allied with health instruction. The school lunchroom, for example, offers an invaluable aid to the study of nutrition. Observation of some classrooms in which health education is an integral part of the curriculum indicates the teachers' awareness of such important factors in health as body-building foods, dental care, knowledge of nutrition, and personal responsibility for one's health.

## The Health Program in the Elementary School

The modern school health program embraces three major areas: *health education, health services,* and *healthful school living.* Though these are usually discussed separately, they are actually interdependent.

Nurturing health and physical development is the responsibility of the home and the community as well as the school. What the school attempts to do is to bring about more wholesome living conditions and more intelligent health behavior on the part of children and parents by making use of what is known about health, needs of children, and the way children grow and learn. This can be accomplished through a specifically planned program of health education which includes all the activities sponsored by the school that are concerned with the health instruction, health protection, and health guidance of the child. It reaches out to encompass physical education and recreation; it includes activities ranging from eating to resting and from playing ball to swimming.

Increasing emphasis on health and physical fitness in our society has resulted in an expanded program which considers the development of concepts and habits of healthful living as significant as the development of motor skills, creativity in movement, and efficiency in the use of the body.

[4] Adapted from Sidney R. Ottman, "A Plea for Health Education in Our Schools," *Phi Delta Kappan,* 41:80, November 1959.

## HEALTH EDUCATION THROUGH INSTRUCTION

When children enter school they differ in health habits and attitudes toward health. The school cannot assume that all children have been taught in the home to care for their health needs. They must be taught basic health concepts and provided with activities which help them practice what they learn.

*Definition.* Health education is that phase of the school program which is organized specifically for educating the child for healthful living. It is integrated with other phases of the program, is related to physical education, and is closely associated with health services of the school. However, it differs from these in being particularly concerned with the teaching of basic concepts of health.

*Objectives of Health Education.* Health education has as its aim the improvement of the health behavior of the individual, achievement of optimum health, formation of desirable health habits, and fostering of positive attitudes toward health.

In order to achieve this aim the program must provide for medical and health examinations, daily health inspections, health records, a school lunch program, immunization, and other routine services essential to developing optimum health. Optimum health includes mental as well as physical health. The influence of the mind on the body, as well as of the body on the mind, is significant. Teachers must help children learn to achieve positive attitudes toward themselves and others in order to be happier and more relaxed in school and at home. Avoidance of undue tension, anger, fear; protection from overstimulation and overfatigue — these are the teacher's responsibility.

Not only must the teacher create a favorable environment in the classroom but he must also teach and help children develop specific basic health concepts. Among these are "the basic four" food groups,[5] immunization, health, sickness, rest, exercise, diet, nutrition, elimination, snacks, bacteria, germs, disease, tooth decay, dental hygiene, virus, vitamins, calories, etc. They must learn the facts related to the subject matter of health — knowledge of personal

---

[5] The four basic groups of food are the milk group, the meat group, the vegetable and fruit group, and the bread and cereal group.

hygiene in terms of working, playing, eating, and resting. They must learn to assist the teacher in controlling environmental conditions that influence personal health — heating, ventilation, lighting, sanitation, seating facilities, and other physical factors. Above all, they must learn respect for the human body. This comes from an understanding of human anatomy and physiology and the related science fields. To the extent that the pupils translate this knowledge into action in everyday living, health education achieves its aim.

Another objective in health education is the development of good health habits. Children may know why they should wash their hands before the midmorning snack or the noon lunch. However, the teacher must help them practice what they know. With the young child it is necessary to check carefully on such habits. Many a time the teacher will need to say, "I see Jimmie is all ready for his crackers. He washed his hands." Children should be taught, too, their responsibility in case of an accident or sudden illness.

Other health practices which should become habitual include covering the mouth when sneezing, staying home when ill, resting after vigorous play, going to bed early, and brushing the teeth after meals. The young child should take increasing responsibility for his health habits as he progresses through the elementary school. From a focus on self he reaches out to consider others in the home, the school, and the community. Ultimately his concern should be with the health of the wider community — the world.

One of the most challenging phases of the health education program centers around the development of positive attitudes toward health. Many adults suffer from illness and disease that could have been prevented if they had had a positive attitude toward healthful living. Delay in medical examinations, home cures, makeshift remedies, and superstitions still impede progress toward optimum health for all. Children must recognize the need to (1) improve their health and appearance through hygienic care; (2) prevent, detect, and correct physical defects through adequate medical and dental care; (3) help control and prevent communicable diseases; (4) develop and maintain health essential for occupational and recreational purposes; (5) select proper food in appropriate amounts; (6) face daily problems and unexpected emergencies with equanimity in order to maintain mental and emotional health; and (7) develop the desire to be healthy to the extent that they will do something concrete to achieve that end.

For many years wise educators have been urging a greater emphasis on health education. As early as 1903, White stated, "Children should be early taught, in simple, easy lessons, the rudiments of physiology and hygiene. The work should be begun by the mother in the home, and should be carefully carried forward in the school. As the pupils advance in years, instruction . . . should be continued. . . . They should understand the importance of guarding against every disease by preserving the vigor of every organ, and should be taught how to deal with common diseases and accidents. Every school should give instruction in both physiology and hygiene, and in so far as possible, should be provided with facilities for illustrating the structure, use, and care of the body."[6]

In order to achieve these objectives the school must select, organize, and guide learning experiences that are designed to result in maximum health for all the children.

## Organizing the Program

Today there is no question about the value of health education in the school program; there is, however, considerable variety in the way it is organized. "Practice ranges from 'free' play and a morning 'clean-hands check up' to the well organized and supervised health, physical education and recreation programs of schools in all sections of the country."[7] The well-organized program makes health instruction an integral part of the curriculum. It gives proportionate emphasis to incidental teaching, to integration with other curriculum areas, and to direct teaching.

*Incidental Teaching.* In the kindergarten and primary grades particularly, the classroom teacher is in a strategic position to help children live more healthfully throughout the day. He uses the interests and concerns of the children to develop their understandings of basic health concepts and to shape favorable attitudes toward health. Through concrete experiences such as morning inspection, preparation for midmorning lunch and lunch period, medical and dental examinations, immunizations, and outdoor play children practice what they learn about healthful living.

[6] Ellen G. White, *Education* (Mountain View, Calif.: Pacific Press Publishing Association, 1903), p. 196.

[7] Virgil Herrick, John Goodlad, Frank Estvan, and Paul Eberman, *The Elementary School* (Englewood Cliffs, N.J.: Prentice-Hall, Inc., 1956), p. 267.

*Integration with Other Curriculum Areas.* In some schools health education is integrated with science; in others it is a part of social studies. In still others it is alternated with physical education. Combined with social studies it emphasizes problems related to the social aspects of health. Combined with science it deals with such topics as immunization, disease, nutrition, and human anatomy. When alternated with physical education it may be relegated to rainy days. In some schools health education is taught only on days the children are unable to go outdoors for physical education or when the gymnasium is in use for purposes other than physical education. Obviously, this is inadequate.

*Direct Teaching.* In many schools health education is scheduled as a regular subject with definite objectives and plans for selecting content, instructional materials, and evaluation procedures.

## Key Concepts in Health Education

In general, health education in the elementary school centers around the development of concepts, attitudes, and habits related to (1) nutrition, (2) personal hygiene, (3) rest and relaxation, (4) sanitation, (5) clothing, (6) communicable diseases.

*Nutrition.* Nutrition has become an important area of study in the health program of the elementary school. However, knowledge about nutrition is not enough. Children need to translate knowledge into action. They must learn to select balanced meals, consciously including foods from the essential groups, and regulate the amount of food. The following concepts are merely suggestive. They are not all-inclusive and they must be developed in relation to meaningful experiences.

1. A good breakfast consists of fruit or juice, egg and/or meat, cereal and/or bread, butter or margarine, milk or milk drink.

2. A good lunch or dinner includes protein (milk, meat, poultry, fish, cheese), vegetables, cereal (bread), and fruit.

3. Good posture, good bone development, and good muscular development are evidences of good nutrition.

4. The healthy condition of the hair, skin, eyes, and teeth depends on proper food.

5. There is a relationship between poor nutrition and the common cold.

6. Rickets, pellagra, scurvy, beriberi, and night blindness are deficiency diseases.

7. The "basic four" foods are essential to a balanced diet.

8. Raw vegetables should be thoroughly washed.

Frequently parents send children off to school without a suitable breakfast. For such children the school lunch program is a boon. In one school a teacher developed a unit on nutrition in an effort to help children realize the importance of a good breakfast for health and for improved learning at school. Midmorning fatigue decreased in direct proportion to the decrease of "breakfast skippers." At the beginning of the unit seventeen children were habitual breakfast skippers. At the close of the unit the number had decreased to three.

### *Personal Hygiene.*

1. Teeth must receive proper care — visits to the dentist, daily brushing, refraining from excessive use of sweets or using teeth to bite hard objects.

2. Good grooming requires cleanliness at all times.

3. Ears should be properly cared for. They should be washed thoroughly and carefully. Drafts and strong winds should be avoided. Things should be kept out of ears. Any sign of ear trouble should be reported to the nurse.

4. Handkerchiefs or tissues are necessary for good personal hygiene.

5. All foreign objects must be kept away from ears, nose, and mouth.

6. Waiting at least one hour after eating before going swimming is vital.

7. Developing proper dietary habits and using enough water and a mild soap contribute to a better complexion.

8. Squeezing blackheads or pimples tends to spread infection.

### *Rest, Sleep, and Relaxation.*

1. Individuals vary in the amount of sleep they require.

2. Most children under eleven years of age need ten to twelve hours of sleep.

3. Relaxing a few minutes periodically is of greater value than taking a long nap when one is overtired.

4. Work, study, and recreation should be balanced; they should be planned so as not to interfere with getting the required amount of sleep.

5. Wearing loose, proper weight clothing, and bathing before retiring are conducive to relaxation.

6. Additional sleep and rest are required during convalescence following an illness.

7. Overfatigue leads to loss of efficiency in work.

*Sanitation.*

1. Pasteurization and adequate regulation of sources of milk supply are community responsibilities.

2. Sanitation is a civic responsibility as well as a personal one.

3. Sanitary drinking facilities are essential to community health and safety.

4. Drinking fountains must be used carefully in order to insure safety.

5. Hands should be washed thoroughly after toileting.

6. Community health laws should be obeyed.

7. Participation in community health and clean-up campaigns is a mark of good citizenship.

8. Encephalitis may be caused by unsanitary conditions in the community.

9. Insect control is essential to health of a community.

10. A safe, adequate water supply is both an individual and a community responsibility.

*Clothing.*

1. Clothing should be selected in terms of weather. Raincoats and rubbers are needed in rainy weather.

2. Clothing must be cared for in order to look well at all times and to give the wearer the proper value for his investment.

3. White or light-colored materials reflect the sun's rays, whereas black or dark clothes absorb them.

4. Hats, coats, sweaters, and other outer wearing apparel should be carefully hung up.

5. Cottons and linens permit air to pass through and perspiration to evaporate; furs and woolens retain warmth.

*Communicable Diseases.*

1. Communicable diseases may be spread through coughing, sneezing, and discharges from the nose and throat; personal contact with an infected person; contaminated water; contaminated food; unclean milk; flies and mosquitoes; rats, stray dogs and cats.

2. Communicable diseases may be prevented by refraining from

contact with persons having colds or sore throats; isolation; reporting illness to parents, teacher, or nurse.

3. There is a relationship between prevention of communicable disease and good health habits such as keeping the body and clothing clean; washing hands before eating, after toileting, and when dirty; keeping hands away from mouth, eyes, and skin irritations; personal ownership and use of toilet articles; using handkerchief or cleansing tissues when needed.

4. Wearing clothing suitable for weather reduces the danger of communicable disease. Removing wet clothing and shoes as quickly as possible is essential in avoiding colds.

5. There is a relationship between sanitation and communicable disease.

6. Most communicable diseases are preventable or reducible through individual, home, school, and community cooperation. Simple principles of bacteriological cleanliness are needed.

7. Newly discovered drugs are useful if prescribed by a physician in the control of communicable diseases.

## HEALTH ACTIVITIES

*In the Kindergarten and Primary Grades.* How the teacher organizes the learning activities is dependent upon the curriculum design of the school in which he teaches. Selecting and organizing problems of concern in the home, the school, or the community makes health education vital to the child. Among the problems which are commonly explored are the following:

Nutrition: Learning to eat proper food; learning to enjoy new foods; realizing the importance of eating at regular intervals.

Personal hygiene: Knowing the importance of keeping the body clean; knowing the reason for washing hands before eating; washing food before eating; eating one's own food and not transferring food from one plate to another.

Rest and relaxation: Learning to relax at rest periods; alternating periods of vigorous play with rest; using correct posture to reduce fatigue.

Sanitation: Washing hands after toileting; protecting others when coughing by covering the mouth and nose.

Clothing: Wearing clothing appropriate for the weather; taking off wraps during school; caring for boots, raincoats, mittens, and caps so they are readily available when needed.

Communicable diseases: Recognizing the symptoms of illness; learning the importance of reporting illness to teacher or nurse if ill at school; learning the importance of a checkup by doctor or nurse before returning to school after illness; learning to trust and depend upon the nurse, dentist, doctor; getting periodic checkups before serious illness threatens.

Posture: Selecting chairs of suitable size; sitting and standing erect; walking without scuffing the feet; taking corrective exercises if needed.

These topics can be organized around problems such as "What Is My Responsibility for Health of Others and Myself?" "How Can I Care for Teeth, Eyes, Ears?" "How Do We Grow?" "Nutrition — What Does It Mean?"

How a prospective teacher organized a unit on nutrition is illustrated below. Children can learn from a nutrition unit much information that will clarify their thinking and help establish positive attitudes and habits. The chief value of the unit outlined below lies in its motivation of children to explore the reasons for eating a good breakfast, experiment with foods that offer nutritious elements, assume responsibility for choosing foods wisely, and involve parents in the problem of nutrition. It provides opportunity for exploration, experimentation, generalization, and testing of conclusions. Teacher-pupil planning is an integral part of the study as the teacher and the pupils cooperatively find the answers to problems that are of universal concern. As in the case of every group study or unit, the plan of activity suggested below can be varied according to the experiential background and abilities of a given group, the resources and facilities available, and the skill of the teacher in guiding this type of study.

*Nutrition Unit*[8]

I. Title: Choosing a Good Breakfast
II. Level: Primary
III. Length: The amount of time spent on this unit will depend on the class involved and their needs. It should not be drawn out too long because of the limited interest span of the primary child; nor should it be discontinued before adequate understandings have been established. One to two

[8] Prepared by Jane G. Purdie, Evansville College, Evansville, Ind., 1960.

weeks should be sufficient, depending on the children's interests and needs.

IV. Objectives
  A. Teacher's
    1. To develop a recognition of the importance of a good breakfast.
    2. To create favorable attitudes toward:
      a. eating at breakfast time.
      b. the proper breakfast foods
         (fruit, cereal, bread, eggs, meat, and milk).
    3. To develop cooperation between the school and the home in relation to the food and health program.
  B. Pupil's
    1. To learn:
      a. why a good breakfast is important.
      b. what foods are in a good breakfast.
    2. To develop the attitude that eating is a pleasure.

Beyond these, the teacher should strive to accomplish the general objectives of education such as cooperation, tolerance, and other social understandings. This unit might well be integrated with other areas of the curriculum.

V. Building an adequate background
  A. Find out what pupils eat for breakfast.
    1. Have each child illustrate the food he had for breakfast that morning by means of a self-chosen art medium.
    2. Have an informal discussion about breakfast habits.
    3. Send a letter or simple questionnaire to the child's home:

Dear Parent:
  You can help me so much to make our school work of increased value to the children in my group. I wish it were possible to call upon each home rather than to send a note. Since this is not possible at this time, I wonder if you will be kind enough to help me by answering two questions? You can do so right on this note.
  1. Does ............................................... enjoy eating breakfast?
  2. What does $\frac{he}{she}$ usually eat for breakfast?
Thank you kindly for your assistance.
      Signed .........................................................................

B. Study the returned questionnaires for guidance in developing the unit. If one finds that many of the children skip breakfast, the importance of the meal should be stressed.

C. Analyze the classroom situation with respect to the children's family background of habits, income level, and occupations. These definitely influence nutritional habits.

D. Collect materials relating to breakfast and study them so that knowledge is adequate. Ask the children to bring materials to school.

VI. Unit initiation

A. Motivate the unit by using a classroom incident or simply by arranging the environment through the use of books, pictures, and pamphlets displayed in an attractive manner. Allow the pupils to examine and explore the materials.

B. Initiate the unit by introducing a chart depicting a good breakfast.

One might say: "Suppose that it is your birthday and your mother is willing to fix anything you want for breakfast. What things would you choose?" One should then allow ample time for all who wish to describe the breakfast they would choose. Call attention to the chart. Let the children see if they can name the foods pictured. "Why do you suppose the foods are shown in four groups? Yes, because a *good* breakfast generally includes something from each group. Who would like to come up and show us his favorite breakfast?"

VII. Problems

A. After initiating the unit one might follow with this activity: The teacher begins by reading a poem about food. Then he gives the pupils a chance to tell about their own "most favorite" foods for breakfast. Why do they like a certain food? Do they like its taste? The way it smells when it is being cooked? Its color? Its crunchiness or smoothness? This discussion can do much to develop favorable attitudes toward breakfast.

B. Lead the children to make a group decision to try, if possible, to eat a breakfast the next morning that will include fruit, cereal, and milk. When they report the next day, let them tell what they had in each category. The pupils should discuss the value of the breakfasts chosen.

C. Food models can be presented to the class and good breakfasts selected. The cut-outs should be left out and the children encouraged to work with them during free time. Children can also collect pictures from magazines or draw them.

D. Have children make up riddles about the foods on the chart or about their own favorite foods.

E. Have children make booklets about foods from pictures cut out of magazines or of their own creation.

F. Hold a "tasting party" to encourage children to try new foods.

VIII. Culminating activities

A. Have a breakfast party at school; serve a simple breakfast. This can be done by means of classroom and home participation. Perhaps the homeroom mothers will help. Each child would be responsible for a certain item. This would involve teacher-pupil planning.

B. A group letter such as the following might be composed, written, and illustrated by the children.

Dear Mother,

Our class is planning to have a breakfast party in our room. We have learned that a good breakfast is important. For a good breakfast, we should have fruit, cereal, milk, bread and butter. I have drawn the foods I should eat for breakfast every morning. Please help me remember to get plenty of sleep and rest, to play outdoors in the sunshine, to eat the right food, and to start each day with a good breakfast.

Love,

The child's illustrations should be attached or made on the same page.

IX. Vocabulary

| breakfast | meat |
|-----------|------|
| cereal | eggs |
| fruit | toast |
| milk | grapefruit |
| favorite | waffles |
| best | food |
| juice | oranges |

The words above as well as others that come up during the unit should be included.

X. Evaluation

A. The main form of evaluation should consist of observation of the pupils, their reactions and contributions, throughout the unit.

B. Give a picture test having the children choose from illustrations what should compose a good breakfast.

C. Send a letter to the mothers similar to the one sent before starting the unit. This time ask:

1. Does ............................................... now enjoy eating breakfast?

2. What has ${}^{\text{he}}_{\text{she}}$ been eating for breakfast this past week?

3. What part of .......................................'s breakfast does he like best?

XI. Integration

A. Communication skills
1. Reading for information to solve problems.
2. Giving oral and written reports on assigned topics.
3. Spelling words that are used in the unit.

B. Art experiences
1. Painting.
2. Drawing.
3. Modeling.
4. Pasting.
5. Cutting.
6. Lettering.
7. Poster work.

C. Social studies
1. Locate on a map places breakfast foods come from.
2. Visit a plant (dairy, cereal plant, etc.).
3. View a movie about foods.

D. Arithmetic
1. Determine the cost of foods for a well-balanced meal.
2. Learn terms such as dozen, pound, etc., in connection with the classroom breakfast.
3. Work out story problems relating to the unit.

E. Music
Learn songs about health, especially breakfast.

XII. Instructional resources
Collect in advance as well as throughout the unit:
1. Library books.
2. Posters and pictures.
3. Pamphlets.
4. Movies.
5. Magazine and newspaper articles and pictures.
6. Texts.

TEACHER'S BIBLIOGRAPHY

Bogart, L. J. *Nutrition and Physical Fitness.* Philadelphia: W. B. Saunders Company, 6th ed., 1956.

Cole, E. C., Cole E., and Appleyard, L. *Living Today.* Wichita, Kan.: McCormick Mathers Publishing Company, 1957.

LeFevre, John R., and Boydston, N. D. *Annotated Guide to Free and Inexpensive Health Instruction Materials.* Carbondale: Southern Illinois University Press, 1959.

McCollum, E. V. *History of Nutrition.* Boston: Houghton Mifflin Company, 1957.

Shacter, Helen, and Bauer, W. W. *You and Others.* Chicago: Scott, Foresman and Company, 1957.

Sherman, H. C., and Landford, C. S. *Essentials of Nutrition.* New York: The Macmillan Company, 2nd ed., 1950.

Smiley, D. F., and Gould, A. G. *Your Health.* New York: The Macmillan Company, 4th ed., 1954.

CHILDREN'S BIBLIOGRAPHY

Barr, Jene. *Mike the Milkman.* Chicago: Albert Whitman and Company, 1958.

Black, Irma S. *This Is the Bread That Betsy Ate.* Eau Claire, Wis.: E. M. Hale and Company, 1957.

Brown, M. W., and Hurd, E. T. *Two Little Gardeners.* New York: Simon and Schuster, Inc., 1954.

Floethe, L. and R. *The Farmer and His Cows.* New York: Charles Scribner's Sons, 1957.

Krauss, Ruth. *The Growing Story.* Eau Claire, Wis.: E. M. Hale and Company, 1955.

Petersham, Maud and Miska. *The Story of Food from the Fields.* Chicago: Rand McNally and Company, 1950.

Russell, Betty. *Big Store Funny Door.* Chicago: Albert Whitman and Company, 1955.

Scott, William R. *The Apple That Jack Ate.* Eau Claire, Wis.: E. M. Hale and Company, 1957.

Tensen, Ruth M. *In the City.* Chicago: The Reilly and Lee Company, 1951.

*Learning Activities in the Intermediate Grades.* Many of the topics of interest to young children persist as problems of concern through the elementary school. Intermediate children, however, explore them in greater depth and add new topics in harmony with their maturity. Organizing the learning experiences around centers enables teachers to plan effectively with their particular groups. Whether the study is devoted strictly to health or correlated with social studies or science, the unit organization is widely used. Among problems explored are: How can we prepare nutritious meals? How can we get a balance of rest and activity? How can we prevent accidents? How is our body structured and what are the functions of various organs? What qualities should a healthy person possess?

Examination of topics in health education texts and curriculum guides reveals that the learning experiences of young children in the kindergarten, primary, and intermediate grades are primarily selected from and related to the problems of everyday living.

Health education should permeate the total program. Children should not only learn the basic concepts about health in the health class but form good health habits and positive attitudes toward health. The selection and organization of learning experiences is dependent upon the type of curriculum organization, the role of health education in the program, and the skill of the teacher.

*Instructional Materials in Health.* Materials for health instruction are more plentiful and better prepared than ever before. Printed materials include textbooks, pamphlets, magazines, newspapers, and government bulletins. Audio-visual materials include movies, film strips, slides, television and radio programs, transcriptions, tapes, posters, charts, graphs, models, exhibits, pictures, and drawings. Community resources afford an excellent source of varied materials, some of them in the immediate environment. Valuable lessons are gained from persons in the community as they solve health problems. Firsthand observation, interviews, surveys, trips, experiments, investigations all have an important place.

Children can participate in the location of materials and resources and in making arrangements for their use. The teacher, however, remains the key person in locating and exploring community and other instructional resources. "He must consistently explore the field. . . . The teacher with the best source material is the one who makes his own collection rather than relying on a ready-made list that is unrelated to his situation."[9]

[9] Helen N. Smith and Mary E. Wolverton, *Health Education in the Elementary School* (New York: The Ronald Press Company, 1959), p. 82.

HEALTH EDUCATION THROUGH HEALTH SERVICES

Through the years many changes have taken place in the provision of health services for children in the elementary school. Emphasis has shifted from the initial objectives of control of contagious diseases to a broader concept. Concern with the control of contagion resulted in the introduction of public health nursing in schools. The program was then expanded through the introduction of periodic medical examinations and follow-up procedures for the correction of obvious physical defects.[10] Once interest in the health problems of children was aroused, development spread in a number of directions, including the school lunch program, free clinics, dental and health examinations, and other services.

"Today, greater emphasis is placed on more adequate, though possibly less frequent, medical examinations by the family physician or the school physician. Teacher-nurse conferences on suspected health problems and special examinations by the school doctor are being used to see that children most urgently in need of care receive it."[11]

The typical health service program, developed during the past twenty years and particularly through the past decade, has centered on several definable items: examination by the physician; observation by the classroom teacher; screening procedures by the technologist to appraise vision, hearing, and posture; health history. Emergency care procedures, provisions for the prevention and control of communicable disease, services for the physical education program and for the physically handicapped are all a part of the well-organized health service in today's schools.

Emphasis is on health rather than disease, though if a disease is suspected, referral is made through the family to the child's physician for proper care. During the child's years at school periodic health examinations are recommended. Considered of primary importance are those at the entrance to school in kindergarten or first grade, at or near puberty, and early in adolescence. If observation indicates the need for a physician's evaluation, the child is referred without waiting for the scheduled periodic examination.

[10] George Rosen, "A Healthier World," in Eli Ginzberg (ed.), *The Nation's Children: The Family and Social Change*, White House Conference (New York: Columbia University Press, 1960), p. 152.

[11] *Ibid.*, p. 153.

A well-planned program provides opportunity for the teacher to capitalize on the educational values inherent in health services. For example, before the dental examination the teacher may use role playing to orient the children to the procedure so they are not disturbed by the experience. One kindergarten teacher who did not prepare the children for this experience was alarmed to discover that one of them had left the group on the way to the nurse's office where the examinations were given and had run home. Many teachers introduce a unit on dental hygiene in connection with the dental examination. It can include correct ways of brushing the teeth, understanding the role of the dentist, the need for regularity in visiting the dentist, the proper care of six-year molars, and the contribution of proper food to the development of healthy teeth.

The immunization program, too, provides opportunity for vitalizing health education in the classroom. Units organized around the prevention and control of disease and emphasizing good health practices are helpful in making dramatic some of the important health concepts. Audio-visual aids, films, and film strips give added support to the concepts related to keeping healthy and refraining from behavior which contributes to the spread of colds and other communicable diseases.

The procedures established by the school to take care of emergencies provide opportunity for health instruction. In a well-operated health program, plans are outlined for emergency treatment of accidents or sudden illness occurring at or near the school premises. The name of the family physician is recorded on the health record, together with the telephone numbers of the family and the physician. Specific instructions for handling an ill or injured child are worked out cooperatively by the school staff, the local health officer, and the practicing physicians. These are understood by the entire staff. The school nurse has the primary responsibility for administering first aid and contacting the home and the physician. A thorough understanding of procedure to be followed in case of an emergency is an educational responsibility of the teacher, principal, and nurse. Many accidents will be avoided if teachers and children learn the basic rules of safety, have a regard for other individuals, and apply the safety rules. In a specific accident case where the child falls off the jungle gym because he has been showing off and ignoring the regulations the teacher may use the accident to initiate a careful study of safety procedures on the playground. The nurse is usually glad to co-operate in such a study. In many schools at the beginning of the year safety units are developed to help children become aware of the need for caution and for obedience to regulations.

Well-organized health services are becoming an integral part of the curriculum. They are essential for the protection and improvement of health of children in the elementary school. They afford the classroom teacher an opportunity for getting to know pupils better, for demonstrating interest in individual children, and for individualizing his teaching as he participates in daily activities related to this phase of the health program: observing pupils for discovery of health deviations and defects; studying records of absenteeism and accidents to perceive health implications; participating in health appraisal activities; assuming responsibility for simple first-aid measures; cooperating with the school nurse and doctor in helping children with health problems; and working with parents and community agencies to obtain the best possible benefits from school health services.[12] The specific tasks will vary with the school. The opportunities for relating health services and health instruction are limited only by the teacher's time and ingenuity and the curriculum plan under which he works.

While it is evident that schools are moving forward, there are several obstacles still to be surmounted before the goal of a fully effective school health service becomes a reality. Rosen[13] cites these obstacles as (1) the division of responsibility that exists in many communities between educational and health authorities in the administration of health services for children of school age; (2) the frequently vague and restricted role of the school physician, who screens and diagnoses but does not treat, and his relations to the family doctor if there is one; and (3) the influence of economic, social, and cultural factors in facilitating cooperation among family, teacher, doctor, and nurse in giving the child the help he needs. ". . . As long as the care of the 'total' child is divided among several agencies and a variety of personnel, often inadequate in some respects, one cannot expect the full benefits of school health work."[14]

[12] A clear definition of the classroom teacher's role in school health services can be found in C. L. Anderson, *School Health Practice* (St. Louis: C. V. Mosby Company, 1956).

[13] *Op. cit.*, p. 153.

[14] *Ibid.*

Cooperation is the keynote. Only as school, home, and community cooperate can a balanced program of health education and health service be developed. Schools alone cannot see that all the desirable objectives of individual and community health are attained. Parents have the primary responsibility for the health of their children. Doctors, dentists, nurses, health educators, health officers, social and welfare workers, and their official organizations all have responsibility for health activities in the community. Every school personnel roster should include medically trained people to take the burden off the teachers for health inspection. The teacher observes the children, the school nurse inspects them. "The teacher's role in health observation is not difficult since he is never concerned with diagnosis. His responsibility relates only to the detection of possible deviations from health and not to the nature of the condition."[15] When there is no school nurse or physician available, the teacher, with the approval of the principal, should inform the parents of his observation and allow them in conjunction with the principal to determine the action to be taken.

In spite of the inadequacies and defects which still exist in the health services program an optimistic note was sounded as the states made recommendations for improvement at the 1960 White House Conference on Children and Youth.

To improve school health services the States recommend:
Evaluation of existing programs of school health services.
A restatement of school health policies to make the best use of existing resources.
Integration of the school health program into a coordinated community health program.[16]

Many states recommend an expanded school health program including:

Improved instruction in health and physical education; more health teaching and counseling.

[15] Donald A. Dukelow and Fred V. Hein (eds.), *Health Appraisal of School Children,* a report of the Joint Committee on Health Problems in Education of the National Education Association and the American Medical Association (Washington, D.C.: NEA, 2nd ed., 1957), p. 16.
[16] *The States Report on Children and Youth,* 1960 White House Conference (Washington, D.C.: Golden Anniversary White House Conference on Children and Youth, Inc., 1960), p. 178.

Increased federal appropriations for the school-lunch program.

More effective followup of defects found on examination, especially visual and auditory defects; speech therapy if needed.

An increased number of physical examinations of school children, preferably annually.

Expanded safety and accident prevention programs in the schools.[17]

## EVALUATION

How can the teacher determine the extent to which the objectives in health education are being achieved? Evaluation must be in terms of specific objectives. Whether the child is achieving optimum health can be appraised on the basis of his health history and behavior. The team approach is frequently used in order to pool the information of the physician, dentist, and nurse in addition to the observation of the teacher. Standardized tests and teacher-made tests plus teacher observation are useful in determining growth in health understanding.

Personal health habits may be appraised individually. The child records on a chart his own progress in health habits which are not observable by the teacher, such as going to bed at a regular time, brushing teeth after meals, eating balanced meals at home or in the cafeteria, taking baths, and washing the hair.

Attitudes are not as easy to evaluate as health knowledge or habits. However, attitude tests, observation, self-rating scales, interviews, role playing, playground conversation, and dramatizations will be found helpful, as will anecdotal records of the child's health behavior, with periodic analysis of the data. With these methods the teacher should be able to determine the changes in attitudes — favorable or unfavorable — which have occurred as a result of health teaching.

The health program as a whole should be evaluated. Units of work, instructional materials, and community resources, too, should be appraised in terms of the broad health objectives. Among the questions that should be answered are these: Are the children interested in improving their health? Are the children seeking increased knowledge and methods of maintaining and improving health? Do the children have good health habits? Are the children applying their knowledge of health and safety to such an extent that there are

[17] *Ibid.*, p. 179.

fewer absences for illness and accidents? Are they selecting better lunches at the cafeteria?

Strang and Smiley suggest that by the time the child leaves the public school he should have learned:

1. To keep himself healthy and clean.
2. To protect others from colds and other communicable diseases.
3. To render first aid in case of illness or accident.
4. To be able to care for the sick, prepare wholesome food for the family, and take care of infants and small children.
5. To obtain the best medical and dental care that he can.
6. To value social health measures, including health insurance and hospital service plans.
7. To appreciate the history of health progress and to keep in touch with new discoveries that are being made.[18]

HEALTH EDUCATION THROUGH HEALTHFUL SCHOOL LIVING

*Arranging the Physical Environment.* Healthful school living requires a healthful physical environment: plenty of play space, with a safe surface and apparatus; protection from traffic, industrial activity, overcrowding in classes, and fire and safety hazards; adequate water supply, sewage facilities, and waste-disposal services; and proper heating, ventilation, and other custodial services. Satisfactory school buildings are important not alone for the contribution they make to the child's comfort but for the contribution they make to his health. Teachers, too, benefit from a safe, clean, comfortable, attractive, pleasant, and satisfying physical environment.

Children can more readily be taught to take pride in keeping the classroom clean, orderly, and attractive if the school itself offers a wholesome environment. Taking care of physical factors such as adjusting heating, lighting, and ventilation is becoming less a problem as modern school buildings install up-to-date facilities.

*Creating the Emotional Climate.* The most important and the most constant environmental factor in the school is the teacher. How he relates to the children, the other teachers, the administration, the parents, the health personnel, and the many representatives of civic interests and activities influences the mental health in the school and particularly in the class for which he is responsible.

---

[18] Ruth M. Strang and Dean F. Smiley, *The Role of the Teacher in Health Education* (New York: The Macmillan Company, 1941), p. 93.

The teacher who is emotionally well balanced, who is at ease in his position, and who is secure in the knowledge that he is creating an environment in which children can develop their maximum potential will contribute much toward healthful, happy living in the classroom. He will make provisions for emergencies that might upset and disturb children. Every teacher should be able to provide prompt and effective leadership in such emergencies as fire, tornado, earthquake, or air raid. If children are thoroughly instructed as to procedures, if they have practiced the procedures often, if the teacher is calm, the children will rise to the occasion.

For a number of weeks, a group of twenty-five kindergarten children had been rehearsing what to do in case of an air raid or storm. They had readily followed the directions to go to the shelter in an orderly manner. On the day the hurricane descended upon the school the children calmly went to the shelter, where one of them went to sleep and slept until it was time to go home. The principal remarked upon seeing the sleeping child, "It's the teacher who created the calm in the face of the storm that made it possible for this to happen."

The teacher who wants healthy, happy children in his classroom will plan a program in which activity is balanced by rest; group action is balanced by individual expression; and there is time to apply what has been learned in health education. Such an environment is created rather than arranged.

## THE ROLE OF THE TEACHER

The adequately prepared teacher should be a healthy, well-adjusted individual with accurate, up-to-date knowledge about health, the principles of healthful living, and characteristics of child growth and development. He should know what is involved in a good school health program and should be ready to assume the responsibility for the health of the boys and girls in his classroom.

Among the experiences that will help the prospective teacher to assume his role in the health program are the following:

Working with boys and girls at different age levels better to understand growth and developmental characteristics of children.

Understanding the impact of the physical, social, and emotional environment upon children's health.

Becoming acquainted with techniques of working with parents and specialized health personnel.

Learning to plan and direct health education for various educational levels.

Becoming familiar with the multiple aspects of school health programs and the cooperative efforts which specialists and community agencies make.

Taking advantage of every opportunity to participate in school health activities during the pre-service years and later in in-service health education experiences.

These suggestions are illustrative of the recommendations of the Joint Committee on Health Problems in Education of the National Education Association and the American Medical Association.[19]

## Safety Education

"Accidents are the leading cause of death in children 5 to 14 years of age in 13 countries of the Western Hemisphere. If trends of the past two decades continue, we shall find within 20 years that in many nations of the Americas accidents will constitute the leading cause of death for all age groups 1 to 15 years."[20]

Education is an elementary step in prevention of accidents. In all fields, education progresses as distribution of information is fortified by experience. The prevention of childhood accidents is of concern to many agencies including governmental agencies, traffic departments, departments of education, health, social security, and labor. There is a need for closer coordination between agencies engaged in this common effort of education.

The school and the teacher have important roles in safety education. Because hazards to children are not entirely eradicable, efforts must be directed not only toward reducing fatal accidents but toward amelioration of the effects.

Specific hazards must be identified and prevented on an individual

[19] Joint Committee on Health Problems in Education of the National Education Association and the American Medical Association, *Suggested School Health Policies* (Washington, D.C.: NEA, 3rd ed., 1956), p. 36.

[20] James L. Goddard, "Accident Prevention in Childhood," U.S. Department of Health, Education and Welfare, *Public Health Reports*, 74:523, June 1955.

basis, but findings from research should be used to reduce the possibilities of certain types of injuries and deaths. In the past these have been related usually to environmental factors or agent factors immediately associated with accidents. The "agent" in childhood accidents can be almost anything. It is desirable to study causative factors systematically and specifically if even limited progress is to be made. The motor vehicle is cited as an accident agent readily identified and isolated for study.

To understand the child's susceptibility to accidents it is essential to know as much as possible about his growth and development, about the relationships between his mental and physical condition, and about his educational background and progress.

The "environment" of the child may be small as the crib or as large as the community, depending upon the child's age. Geography, climate, sociology, economics, even history and politics play a part in molding the environment and in creating the relationships between that environment and accidents.

To be considered in all accidents are the individual and the environment; their respective susceptibility and potential; habits, attitudes, and pattern of behavior; specific events, changes, or irregularities in the pattern; and the built-in protective factors which may affect or avert the action that sets off an accident. "Accident susceptibility" is more pronounced in some children than others. This factor is conditioned by training, experience, and judgment. Also, some special factors — illness, emotional upsets, and the like — may be expected to disturb children even more than they do adults.

The basic attitudes toward accident prevention are learned in childhood. Parents are responsible for protecting the child against accidents of all types. However, when he enters school, he becomes more independent and may not be able to cope with the sudden extension of his sphere of experience. At school he begins to play on the playground and use recreational facilities. He may enroll in the swimming classes. He uses tools and other mechanical devices. He crosses streets. In order to live safely at home, at school, and outside of school he must have been taught in his preschool years the techniques of self-preservation and accident prevention. He must have learned how to cope with moving traffic, vehicles, fire, sharp instruments, and other hazards.

Unfortunately, many children have not learned these basic techniques of safe living before they enter school. For this reason the school must teach them.

*Education for Safe Living.* An education program organized with safe living as its goal provides an environment in which wholesome human values are promoted.

> Legal and ethical aspects of the school's responsibility for the children enrolled in the school are known and carried out. The responsibility for the welfare and care of the children rests primarily with the administrator of the school. He must instruct the staff so they become familiar with the legal provisions which govern the operation of the school and the welfare of the children within the school.
>
> The staff shows concern for safety provisions. The responsibility for making the school a safe place to live rests primarily with the principal, who enlists the aid of the staff in removing obstacles that threaten pupil safety, plans fire precautions in harmony with city and state ordinances, supplies safe athletic and play equipment, and provides supervision at street intersections.[21]

The teachers plan specifically for children to develop a spirit of consideration for one another. There is a willingness to participate in agreements about safe and desirable behavior in the halls, at the drinking fountain, on the stairs, on the playground. Children are made conscious of the importance of good behavior.

*Developing Understanding and Skills in the Safety Program.* Concern for one's own safety and the well-being of others takes time to develop. It must be taught, sometimes by direct experience, sometimes by discussion and observation. There are things a child learns for himself, things he learns from others. He must be helped to understand the reason for safe behavior and constantly guided so that such behavior becomes habitual.

Long before the child enters school he should be taught to cross the streets carefully, to look both ways, to walk, not run, as he crosses the street, to keep his eyes open on the playground. When he enters school he should be taken on a tour of the building. He should know where his room is in relation to the entrance and exits. He should be shown where the emergency alarm signals are. He should be

[21] Adapted from William C. Reavis *et al., Administering the Elementary School* (Englewood Cliffs, N.J.: Prentice-Hall, Inc., 1953), pp. 344–345.

taught the procedure for entering and leaving the building. He should be taught to walk in the halls, how to go up and down stairs, how to get to the nurse's office, to the rest room, and how to find his way back to his room. He should be taught how to follow the instructions of the safety patrol in crossing the street to and from school. He should be instructed on how to get to the car waiting for him at the close of school. He should be taught to line up carefully for the school bus, or to call a taxi and to give correct instructions to the driver. These things he will learn from parent, teacher, principal, patrol boys, older children. The important thing is that the teacher check to see that he understands what he is to do and then has an opportunity to practice it.

Teachers who are concerned with safe living will provide many opportunities for children to become familiar with safety practices in the school and encourage them to apply their safety learnings outside the classroom.

*Key Concepts in Safety Education.* The importance of safety education cannot be overestimated. Among important safety concepts to be developed are the following:

1. Safety requires the individual to be able to give information: name, address, telephone number, and name of family's baby-sitter.
2. Talking to or riding with strangers is hazardous.
3. Streets and highways are for traffic — not for play.
4. Traffic signs must be obeyed.
5. Look both ways, crossing the street at corners to prevent accidents.
6. Riding a bicycle requires obedience to city's traffic regulations.
7. If an accident occurs, get help quickly; do not panic; try to recognize type of injury.
8. Knowledge of first-aid measures for nosebleed, hiccough, cuts, burns, bruises is important.
9. Safety rules must be observed in school buildings, halls, stairways, restrooms, gymnasium, playground, auditorium, classrooms, lunchrooms, and drinking fountains.
10. Safety rules are especially essential during fire drills and dismissal.
11. Keep to the right when walking up the stairs.

12. Pencils, scissors, rulers, tools, glass objects, and construction and science materials must be used with care.

13. Swimming in unguarded pools is dangerous; so is swimming alone.

14. Sunburn may have serious consequences.

*Organizing a Unit on Traffic Safety.*  One of the finest opportunities for translating safety concepts into action in the elementary school may occur during the first semester of the kindergarten or first grade. The following unit illustrates how children can be taught good safety habits through experiences which are meaningful to them. Through such a unit the child not only learns about safety in the home, the school, and on the street; he experiences it as he translates rules and regulations into action in everyday living. As he is taught the reasons for specific regulations he sees the need for cooperation in planning, carrying out, and evaluating safety rules and practices. Through individual and group effort he learns to cope with the hazards in his environment.

### *Traffic Safety Unit*[22]

Objectives

1. To develop a sense of responsibility on the part of each child for his safety and the safety of others in going to and from school.
2. To develop an understanding and recognition of situations involving safety hazards.
3. To learn safety habits in crossing the streets.
4. To recognize the colors of the traffic light and to understand their significance to the pedestrian and driver.
5. To learn the significance and meaning of safety aids such as yellow crosswalks, stop signs, speed signs, school signs, curbing, etc.
6. To learn the safest route to school and use it.
7. To learn essential information concerning traffic regulations.
8. To understand and appreciate the services of the traffic light, the policeman, the school patrol boys, and other agents that are helpful in crossing the streets.

[22] Adapted from David L. McCooe, Jr., "Planning for a Unit on Traffic Safety," *The Physical Educator,* 14:61, May 1957.

9. To inform the parents of the traffic safety activity.

Activities

1. Preparation for the Safety Tour.
   a. Discuss the role of patrol boys and the policeman as community and school helpers.
   b. Discuss the contributions of other persons or devices that help us cross streets safely.
   c. Formulate safe rules for crossing streets (step to curb; look both ways, watch the light, policeman or patrol boy to learn what to do; walk, never run, across the street).
   d. Plan an excursion around the school area which will assist in learning safe street crossing.
   e. Formulate questions to be solved during the tour.
   f. View film "Safely to and from School."
   g. Arrange bulletin board with safety materials from varied sources.
   h. Dramatize safe crossing of streets.
   i. Dictate a letter to parents concerning the Traffic Safety Tour.

2. Taking the Safety Tour.
   a. Invite patrol boys to accompany the class during the tour.
   b. Arrange for police officer to meet the group and help them cross streets safely.
   c. Point out safety devices on curb (crosswalks, traffic lights, curbs, street signs, etc.).
   d. Cross a few intersections during tour pointing out dangers of alleyways, crossing in middle of block, color of lights (traffic).

3. Follow-up and culminating activities.
   a. Answer the questions formulated in the preparation session.
   b. Discuss what was learned during the Safety Tour.
   c. List the things we learned during our tour.
   d. Make pictures in which we express our ideas about the tour.
   e. Make a big book "Our Trip" using the pictures and writing appropriate captions with the teacher's help.
   f. Invite the parents to a program about our safety trip.
   g. Dramatize the way we cross the streets.
   h. Tell about the exhibit on the bulletin board.

4. Evaluation.
   a. Test the knowledge children have gained about crossing the streets safely by observing their behavior as they come to and from school.

      b. Have children discuss safety practices they learned during the study.

  5. References.

    a McCooe, D. L., "Making a Construction Paper Traffic Light for Bulletin Board" (New Albany, Ind.: New Albany City School, n.d.).

    b. *Teaching Safety Can Be Fun* (Cleveland, Ohio: School Safety Light Corporation, n.d.).

    c. "Letter to Parents Regarding the Traffic Safety Tour," New Albany City Schools.

    d. "Safety to and from School," Young America Films, Inc., New York.

*Evaluating Safety Education in the Schools.* An elementary school which is providing desirable experiences in safety education should be able to point to definite accomplishments in seven specific areas, according to the Elementary School Section, School and College Conference, National Safety Council:

  1. Schools with desirable programs provide safety instruction to meet the needs of the pupils. The needs may be determined by:
    a. an analysis of the temporary and permanent hazards of the pupils' environment
    b. an analysis of the hazards associated with the pupils' activities
    c. an analysis of the hazards associated with the seasons and with such special days as Christmas, Halloween, the Fourth of July
    d. an analysis of the records collected through the standard student accident reporting system
    e. a consideration of individual pupils' abilities, limitations and problems

  2. Schools with desirable programs provide for the active participation of pupils in caring for their own safety. For example:
    a. provision for pupil safety organizations, such as junior safety councils, school safety patrols, student safety committees, school building patrols, monitors and bicycle clubs
    b. provision for pupil information and evaluation of rules for action
    c. provision for inspection by pupils

  3. Schools with desirable programs utilize instructional aids for a well-rounded program of school, recreation, traffic, fire, seasonal, civil defense and home safety. Such aids could include:
    a. text materials: books, lesson units, work sheets

    b. audio-visual aids: motion pictures, film strips, glass slides, posters, models

    c. pupil-made materials

4. Schools with desirable programs provide realistic opportunities for supervised practice in meeting hazards. For example:

    a. in crossing streets and railroad tracks

    b. in using school equipment, such as pencils, scissors, saws, stoves, slides, swings

    c. in using transportation systems

    d. in emergency drills

    e. in performing science experiments

    f. in physical education and recreation activities

5. Schools with desirable programs keep safety in the forefront of the consciousness of pupils, parents and teachers. Among the tools to accomplish this are:

    a. exhibits and bulletin boards

    b. slides or drawings of accident statistics

    c. posters and other art work

    d. assemblies, radio broadcasts and television shows

    e. school and community newspapers

    f. maps showing prevalent accident locations and safe routes for walking

    g. home and community inspections

6. Schools with desirable programs cooperate with other community agencies. Opportunities for such cooperation are:

    a. conducting an active safety program among school patrons

    b. aiding in the preparations of the community's report for the Annual Inventory of Traffic Safety Activities, the American Automobile Association Pedestrian Program, the Inter-Chamber Fire Waste Contest of the Chamber of Commerce

    c. cooperating in communities' safety activities, such as Fire Prevention Week, Clean-up Week

    d. supplying a safety speaker for a community enterprise

7. Schools with desirable programs take the steps necessary to:

    a. establish and maintain school plant, equipment, transportation facilities in safe condition

    b. provide in-service education for the school faculty and other personnel, including opportunities for serving on safety committees, helping to write teachers' guides or courses of study and attending safety conferences.[23]

[23] "Desirable Experiences in Elementary Safety Education," reprinted from *Safety Education*, March 1959 (Chicago: National Safety Council).

## Physical Development

To swim through the cool waters of a lake, or ride the waves of a high surf, or plunge into a pool, or execute a swan dive gives a wonderful feeling of exhilaration. To equip the child with a well-developed, well-coordinated, functional, durable, and disciplined body with which to enjoy life and be of service to the world is the compelling task of the physical education program. "A child who likes to move and has been taught how to use his body effectively usually becomes an active adult who seeks active recreation."[24]

The need for a good physical education program, which provides for physical, neuromuscular, recreational, social, and emotional development through appropriate activities at every educational level has never been greater. The need for a clear statement of purpose on physical activity has increased steadily as teachers have recognized the significance of physical development in the child's total development.

Activity is a basic human need. For children it ranks in importance with food and sleep. To run, jump, climb, bat, and throw, to bend, twist, stretch, and roll, to swim, sway, fly, to walk, hop, skip, and slide is essential to their normal growth.

Physical education has been defined as "a way of education through physical activities which are selected and carried on with full regard to values in human growth, development and behavior."[25] Any definition of physical education should include recognition of its basic purpose in providing sound health, physical development, and skill in physical activities.

*Objectives of Physical Education.* A program is good if children make progress toward the defined objectives. Unlike the traditional physical culture program, which emphasized *only* physical training and gymnastics, physical education activities today are selected in terms of the cultural needs of the child:

[24] Gertrude Krauss Shaffer, "Why the American Children Are Physically Unfit," *The Physical Educator*, 17:60, May 1960.

[25] W. K. Streit and Simon A. McNeely, "A Platform for Physical Education," *Journal of Health, Physical Education and Recreation*, 21:136, March 1950.

1. To promote physical growth, development, and maintenance through activities that develop strength, vigor, vitality, skills, and coordinations leading to ability to do the day's work without undue fatigue and to have additional energy for out-of-work personal and social accomplishment.
2. To contribute to the development of social competencies in the areas of relationships with others, cooperation, competition, tolerance, ethical character, and recognition of fundamental worth of each individual.
3. To promote emotional development through contributions toward individual adjustment, emotional self-mastery, adjustment to others, relaxation, satisfying self-expression, confidence, poise, and freedom from excessive self-confidence.
4. To provide healthful and integrating recreation for the present as well as to lay bases for wholesome, life-balancing recreation in the future.
5. To promote healthful living through contributions to health habits, attitudes, ideals, and information that leads toward elimination of unnecessary strains, drains, and illnesses, and that enables one to protect oneself and others during times of lowered vitality or illness.
6. To help each pupil establish appropriate balances between work, play, exercise, recreation, and relaxation in daily living.[26]

All of these objectives are important. However, it should be observed that there is a growing emphasis on two of them. The first is muscular development, for which physical education has a specific responsibility. "Since the American children are growing to greater stature and maturing younger than ever in recorded history, the need for vigorous body building exercises to help muscular development keep pace with the organic and skeletal growth is most acute at the elementary and junior high school levels."[27] It is believed by some that most children who have had a permissive games program and those who have had no physical education program during the prepubertal and adolescent periods of rapid development fall below clinical standards for minimum muscular fitness and become even more substandard with the passage of time.

The second objective which should be particularly emphasized

[26] Clyde Knapp and E. Patricia Hagman, *Teaching Methods for Physical Education* (New York: McGraw-Hill Book Company, 1953), pp. 69–70.

[27] Shaffer, *op. cit.*, p. 60.

is social and emotional development. To the child in the elementary school physical prowess is extremely important. The child who lacks skill in games and other physical activity very often develops an inferiority complex because he loses status with the group. If he stands around on the playground while the others participate in the ball game, the stunts, or the race, he finds it difficult to overcome the handicap even when he returns to the classroom. Thus it is important that the physical education program be varied enough to give *all* children opportunity for achieving success in some area of endeavor.

THE PHYSICAL EDUCATION PROGRAM IN THE ELEMENTARY SCHOOL

All aspects of the program should be planned in terms of the needs, characteristics, abilities, and interests of the children at various ages and should take into consideration individual differences.

Some children gain most from a vigorous program; others need restricted activities. The wise teacher provides both types. He selects activities according to the groups to be taught, with development of motor coordination, agility, strength, endurance, and bodily poise in mind.

The well-balanced program includes direct teaching, opportunity for practice, co-curricular activities, and adequately organized, carefully supervised, and well-regulated intramural and extramural competition. "A well-planned program . . . includes a progressive development of rhythmic, group, individual, and team activities involving a variety of motor skills, social relationships, and recreational experiences."[28]

Miller and Whitcomb[29] recommend that balance be provided not alone in terms of variety of activities throughout the year but through seasonal, weekly, and daily programs. Some activities take place outside on the playfields; others should be included daily; others are seasonal or offered intermittently through the year.

*Physical Education Activities.*[30] There are certain basic skills of locomotion, body control and object control upon which the devel-

[28] Duncan and Johnson, *op. cit.*, pp. 253–254.
[29] Arthur G. Miller and Virginia Whitcomb, *Physical Education in the Elementary School Curriculum* (Englewood Cliffs, N.J.: Prentice-Hall, Inc., 1957), p. 30.
[30] Adapted from Duncan and Johnson, *op. cit.*, pp. 256–257.

opment of more complex skills in rhythm, games, sports, gymnastics, and other activities depend:

### Fundamental Skills

| LOCOMOTOR SKILLS | BODY CONTROL | OBJECT CONTROL |
|---|---|---|
| Walking | Balancing | Handling |
| Running | Climbing | Rolling |
| Hopping | Hanging | Tossing |
| Jumping | Swinging | Bouncing |
| Leaping | Dodging | Throwing |
| Sliding | Pulling | Catching |
| Skipping | Pushing | Striking |
| Galloping | Resisting | Kicking |
| Whirling | Relaxing | Batting |

### Rhythmical Activities

| FUNDAMENTAL SKILLS | RHYTHMIC SKILLS | DANCE FORMS |
|---|---|---|
| Locomotor movements | Interpretative movements | Free rhythms |
| Body control | Steps and patterns | Traditional dances |
| Rhythmic response | Composition | Modern dance |

### Games, Sports, Gymnastics

| GAMES | SPORTS | GYMNASTICS |
|---|---|---|
| Goal and group | Aquatic | Apparatus |
| Simple or modified team | Individual and couple | Corrective |
| Relays | Team | Conditioning |
| Stunts and self-testing | Track and field | Tumbling |

A suggested sequence in the progressive development of physical education activities is as follows:

### Fundamental Activities

| PRIMARY | INTERMEDIATE |
|---|---|
| 1. Fundamental skills involving simple coordination in various activities. | 1. Fundamental skills requiring increasingly difficult coordination and control. |
| 2. Combinations of fundamental skills used in games and rhythmical activities. | 2. Combined skills of locomotion, body control, and object handling in games and rhythms. |

### Rhythmical Activities

1. Emphasis on fundamental skills in rhythm and dances.

2. Dramatic and interpretative dance movements.

1. Folk, square, and social dances of increasing difficulty.

2. Combinations of movement requiring increasing skill.

### Games, Sports, Gymnastics

1. Circle, group, and tag games and simple contests, involving fundamental activities. Use simple rules and equipment.

2. Marching, stunts, tumbling, apparatus play on jungle gym, balance beams, and boxes.

1. Games and contests requiring skill. Modified team games involving increasing skill.

2. Stunts and selected tumbling activities. Simple trampoline stunts.

### Recreation

1. Supervised play activities.
2. Camping and outdoor education.

1. Supervised recreation.
2. Camping and outdoor education.

### Competition

1. Intramural competition in selected team games and individual sports.

## Scope of the Program

It is essential that the physical education program include many different types of activities.

*Free play.* Kindergarten and primary children profit more from free play — in the gymnasium or outdoors — than do the older children. They make use of play equipment, but they also show ingenuity in organizing and carrying on their own games and activities. Seasonal games, jumping rope, hopscotch, marbles, and jacks continue to be important to them. Many children organize games they learn in the physical education period and play them outdoors. They select their own leader, adapt the rules to suit themselves, and make a real effort to be fair.

Free play has its place, but it is not to be confused with direct teaching. It does, however, require the guidance and direction of the teacher. He should be present if he is to fulfill his obligation to teach — not turn youngsters loose on the playground or in the gym.

*Fundamental Skills.* Children of the kindergarten and primary grades are primarily concerned with developing motor skills. Although they have spent five years or so gaining some control over their bodies — they have learned to walk, and perhaps to skip — they can still profit from activities such as walking on all fours like slow-moving horses with heavy loads, taking giant steps like elephants, or dancing on tiptoe like brownies, elves, and fairies. Galloping, skipping, hopping, side-stepping, and balancing all help them gain greater control and poise.

Outdoor and indoor play on the jungle gym, castle tower, bar, teeter-totter, slide, swing, and walking frame contribute to physical development. Many schools are working out plans for swimming programs either at school or in a community center. With adequate supervision and discipline the opportunity to learn to swim at school has merit.

Intermediate grade children continue the activities they engaged in as primary children. The goal remains the same but the skill increases. The child is not satisfied to be a dilettante. He wants to be an expert as he throws a ball. He imitates the big league players as he flexes his muscles, goes into the wind-up, and pitches. He is more adept at doing stunts on the apparatus, plays games that call for additional skills, and works consciously to be good at an activity. He enjoys dodge ball, horseshoes, and soccer.

Girls, too, enjoy these games and stunts although many of them show a preference for rhythms and dance. They learn to move with ease and grace. Before school and before gym class they work out new patterns of movement.

*Rhythmic Activities.* Creative response to music or rhythm is a significant part of the elementary education program. Each child has the urge to express himself creatively in rhythm, song, or the arts. In the chapter on the creative arts, the role of rhythmic·expression was explored at length. In relation to the physical education program it might be pointed out that basic rhythms require the use of the large muscles; the ideas should come from the children, and they should create their own movements. The teacher guides but does not direct. The children create; they do not imitate. They learn to use their bodies as media of expression, moving subtly and delicately or with precision and intensity as the mood demands.

*Mimetics.* Mimetics provide both exercise and opportunity for self-expression through imitating the actions of animals and people. Teachers and children who are creative can think of numerous ways of interpreting through movement. Some favorites of children are:

1. Chicken walk. The child stands with feet together. He squats low, spreads his knees apart, puts his arms outside his thighs, and clasps his hands tightly in front of his legs below the knees. He walks about on the balls of his feet in a squat position. Clasping his hands in front of the knees permits only very short steps.
2. Rocking chair. The child sits on the floor and grasps his ankles. He rocks forward and backward.

*Group Games.* This category of games is sometimes described as games of low organization, or just games. It refers to games in which a minimum of organization is needed but which allow active participation for the group. Running and tag games; simple ball games such as circle ball, wonder ball, hot potatoes, and dodge ball; relays; and circle games for indoor activity are included in this category.

For children in the lower grades running and tag games form a large share of the program. Miller and Whitcomb suggest in connection with running and tag games that the following teaching techniques and safety precautions be observed:

1. Children should tag easily without pushing or holding others or their clothing.
2. Goals and safety zones should be well marked and large enough to accommodate all children entitled to use them.
3. Goals and safety zones should be specified areas of ground or floor rather than a tree, fence, or wall in order to avoid collisions. Goals should be at least four feet away from walls or fences.
4. Children should follow a specific line of direction when running or being chased.
5. The playing time should be limited so children stop before they are exhausted.
6. When games are played indoors they should be modified to meet the restrictions of limited space.

7. Children should respond immediately to the signal *stop* whether given by whistle or word of mouth.[31]

An example of a popular primary tag game is *Duck, Duck, Goose*:[32]

> Number of players: 8–20
> Equipment: none
> Formation: single circle, all children seated
> Directions: "It" walks around the outside of the circle and pats each child on the head saying "Duck" to each. When "It" pats a child's head and says "Goose" that child gets up and chases "It" once around the circle and back to the chaser's place. If "It" is tagged, the chaser becomes "It" and the old "It" goes into the duck pond (center), where he stays until someone else is tagged. If not tagged, "It" gets another turn.

*Simple Ball Activities.* Dodge ball, circle chase, three deep, and similar games are easy to play, have simple rules, and can be adapted to varying numbers of players. They provide wholesome exercise, fun, and opportunities to teach cooperation and competition. In addition they develop muscular coordination, strength, agility, and skills of catching and throwing which are used in more complex games. Teachers should know games well enough to be able to organize and direct them with a minimum amount of explanation limited to key points. Standards set should be observed.

A popular example of this type of game is *kick ball*:

> Grade level: 3–6
> Number of players: 5–10 per team
> Equipment: 1 playground soccer ball, 4 bases
> Directions: One team is at bat, other team in field (catcher, pitcher, three basemen, fielders). Pitcher rolls the ball to "batter," who kicks ball and runs to first base. Runner may take as many bases, in order, as he safely can or remain at first and be advanced by next kicker. He scores a run when he has successfully tagged all three bases and returned to home plate without being put out. Three outs and teams change sides.

*Relays.* For relays it is essential to establish a starting line and, about thirty or forty feet from it, a turning line. The class is

[31] Adapted from Miller and Whitcomb, *op. cit.*, p. 62.
[32] *Ibid.*

divided into teams of eight or ten pupils, arranged in single file, one behind the other, in back of the starting line. Upon completion of whatever stunt or type of movement is being done, the first pupil touches off the next pupil in line until the whole team has participated.

In *one-leg relay* the first player in line raises one leg behind his body and grasps it with both hands. Holding this leg he hops to the turning line. Here he raises the other foot, grasps it with both hands, hops back, and touches off the second player and the game continues.

In *circle-post relay* one person is stationed directly opposite each team on the turning line to serve as the "post." At the signal the first person in line runs to the "post," completely circles it once without touching it, and then returns to touch off the second player in line, etc.

In addition to running, relays can be played kicking, throwing, passing, and dribbling. Good teaching makes it possible for all to participate at one time. It is possible to have a half-dozen teams going at one time. Teams should be arranged so there is equal ability in the groups.

*Circle Games.* Indoor games such as Here We Go Round the Mulberry Bush, Did You Ever See a Lassie?, The Farmer in the Dell, and other circle games are used when children remain indoors. Teachers who omit these games in the program find children learn them from others and choose them at "favorite activities day" or play them at recess or before and after school.

The teacher should enrich the child's experience in traditional folk games such as Jolly Is the Miller, The Thread That Follows the Needle, and Pop Goes the Weasel. As the child matures he is ready for games that require increased organization. The third grade seems to be the transition stage for children in physical education. They are eager for team sports but usually have not the skills to cope with teamwork, team play, and the competition involved. Simple team games are the answer for this level. These can continue into the intermediate grades as supplementary activity. If they are used in connection with and supplementary to the team sports they serve the needs of the child who although not quite ready for team sports is eager to achieve some measure of success in games as well as to appreciate the achievements of others. Maturity rather than age should be the guide which determines activities.

*Team Sports.* Team sports include large group games such as softball, touch football, basketball, soccer, and volleyball. Team games have long been a source of contention in the physical education program. The belief that they are too competitive, that they are too strenuous, and that they detract from the social values of the program has minimized their use. On the other hand, those in favor of competitive sports point out that they provide motivation for physical development, give the shy child a chance to be a star, encourage group loyalty, and provide wholesome emotional outlets. The middle-of-the-road point of view, which sees value in introducing team games gradually and dividing the classes for boys and girls, making use of the motive of harmless competition, is quite widely accepted. If the physical education program has as its focal point the needs of the boys and girls, the determining factor in the selection of activities will be the welfare, not the exploitation, of the children.

This point of view is well expressed by the report of the National Conference on Physical Education for Children of Elementary School Age. If careful consideration is given to all phases of the problem it is considered by many thinking people that competitive sports must be based on what is best for the growth and development of children — not the desire of sports enthusiasts, fond parents, or overenthusiastic teachers.

There are great differences among children of the same chronological age. In those who are growing rapidly, growth demands a great deal of energy. Emotional pressures and tensions may drive a child beyond the stage of healthful participation. Bone ossification and development are incomplete. The heart may be under too great a strain. The stress and emotional tensions that accompany many of the competitive sports are too much for the child.

In consideration of these factors, the kinds of participation indicated below are recommended as best meeting the physical activity needs of elementary school children.

1. First, as a foundation, all children should have broad, varied, and graded physical education under competent instruction through all grades. In many activities in this program, the competitive element is an important factor. The element of competition provides enjoyment and, under good leadership, leads to desirable social and emotional as well as physical growth.

2. Based upon a sound, comprehensive instructional program in

grades five through eight, children should have opportunity to play in supervised intramural games and contests with others who are of corresponding maturity and ability within their own school. In grades below the fifth grade, the competitive elements found in the usual activities will satisfy the needs of the children.

3. . . . Play or sports day programs may be planned with emphasis on constructive social, emotional, and health outcomes. Teams may be formed of participants coming from more than a single school or agency, thus making playing together important.

Tackle football and boxing should not be included because of common agreement among educational and medical authorities that these activities are undesirable for children of elementary school age.

Schools should plan with parents and community agencies to insure the kind of program outlined above as part of the educational experiences of every child.

It should be kept in mind that the child is important in this setting and not the teacher, parent, school, or agency.[33]

*Apparatus Activities.* The teacher can instruct children in the use of apparatus through comments, observing other children, and on occasion participating in the activities himself. Teacher encouragement is effective in getting children to play.

Playground or apparatus equipment is extremely important. Particularly in the primary grades the classroom teacher should supervise apparatus activities, not only as the child exercises free choice in them but in order to teach him various stunts: pull-up or chinning, monkey swing, ladder walk, and others.

Like stunts and tumbling, apparatus activities have value because they emphasize the development of muscles needed in good posture — arm, shoulder, chest, and back muscles — as well as thigh and leg muscles. Children are challenged to play on apparatus because it gives them an opportunity to be daring. It is highly essential to establish safety rules to insure safe play as well as fun:

1. Using mats at take-off and receiving points.
2. Using apparatus only under supervision.
3. Using only approved activities.
4. Using apparatus only when the child is physically fit.

[33] National Conference on Physical Education for Children of Elementary School Age, *Physical Education for Children of Elementary School Age* (Chicago: The Athletic Institute, 1951), p. 22.

## NURTURING PHYSICAL DEVELOPMENT

All aspects of the child's growth and development are interrelated. In recognition of this generalization the curriculum of the modern elementary school provides for health, safety, and physical education. A well-balanced health program consists of health instruction, health services, and a healthful school environment.

Safety education aims to establish habitual patterns of safe behavior. Safety must be taught; it cannot be left to chance. It is often taught through direct experience, and at other times through vicarious experiences.

The goal of physical education is to equip the child with a well-developed, well-coordinated, disciplined body. Because physical prowess and achievement become increasingly important to the child as he progresses through the elementary school, the physical education program should be broad enough to give him an opportunity to achieve in some area. In order to accomplish this the teacher must have a knowledge of the characteristics, needs, and changing interests of the elementary school child and organize the learning experiences on the basis of such knowledge.

*A healthful school environment does much to foster desirable health practices.*

*The school nurse plays an important part in the life of the elementary school child.*

*A cooperative approach to school health problems offers maximum protection to boys and girls.*

*The school cafeteria can be a laboratory for learning about nutrition.*

*The young child must be taught to cope with traffic problems and hazards.*

The primary child is concerned with developing individual prowess, while the intermediate child is more interested in team games.

A good physical education program helps to develop muscular coordination and self-confidence.

5. Taking turns and keeping away from the playing area.

6. Stationing spotters at each piece of equipment.

*Conditioning Activities.* Stunts, pyramids, and apparatus provide an excellent form of conditioning and satisfying experiences in body coordination. Running and jumping activities increase the power of endurance. Trunk bending, twisting, push-ups, and chinning develop arm, leg, shoulder, and abdominal muscles. Stunts are enjoyed by primary children if adapted to their physical needs and maturity. Outdoor play on apparatus, simple tumbling, and individual stunts with little or no apparatus are recommended. The intermediate group is able to perform feats requiring more skill. Pyramid building, individual and couple stunts, and stunt and partner relays are enjoyed at this level. Track and field events and stunt relays become increasingly enjoyable as the children progress through the elementary school. Activities on apparatus provide an excellent opportunity for developing specific groups of muscles which help to improve posture.

*Corrective Activities.* Postural defects which are remediable in the elementary grades become extremely difficult to remedy in the secondary school. Here the policy should be prevention rather than cure. Good posture should become habitual and stressed not alone in the physical education period but throughout the day. The child with good posture is not subject to strains which result from improper posture. Some tips for good posture for both teachers and pupils are as follows:

1. When standing or walking, toe straight ahead and take most of your weight on heels.

2. Try to form a crease across the upper abdomen by holding the chest up and forward and elevating the front of the pelvis.

3. Avoid high heels as much as possible.

4. Sit with the buttocks "tucked under" so that the hollow of the low back is eradicated.

5. When possible, elevate the knees higher than the hips while sitting. This is especially important when driving (driver's seat forward) or riding as a passenger in an automobile.[34]

Sitting, standing, walking, and thinking "tall" contribute to the development of good posture. Diagrams and pictures are helpful, but

[34] "Postural Instructions," Welborn Clinic, Evansville, Ind., n.d.

the example of a teacher who has learned good posture is the most effective way of teaching the child.

To insure a successful physical education program the teacher must provide a balance among motor skills, rhythms, dances, games, team sports, and conditioning activities. He must also bear in mind the need of balancing indoor and outdoor activities, and the relative importance of large group, small group, and individual activities.

For example, in a weekly program the teacher might alternate large-group and small-group games for primary grades Monday, Tuesday, Wednesday, and Thursday and have circle games on Friday. For the intermediate grades he might alternate group games, conditioning activities, and team sports.

## WHAT ABOUT RAINY DAYS?

Rainy days are a test of the teacher's patience, self-control, and ingenuity. Children react to weather — warm, humid, windy, and rainy; so do teachers. Children can get outdoors for recess on windy days, warm days, or cold days. But on rainy days they have to stay in. Even where there is a special physical education teacher in the school, the classroom teacher has responsibility for the indoor play or recess period. To be ready with a number of interesting and varied activities which offer children release from tensions and opportunity for creative use of their physical skills is one way to make the day endurable and even enjoyable.

*Selecting Activities for Rainy Days.* Activities should meet the following criteria: They should (1) interest the children, (2) afford opportunity to develop skills, (3) include at least a minimum of physical activity, (4) fit in with the space limitations of the classroom, and (5) pose no safety hazards. Where space permits, circle games may be used; in the crowded classroom the children remain beside their tables or desks. These classes should be organized; standards should be formulated, and activities should be informal but orderly. Children dislike chaos. They enjoy themselves more if order, not confusion, reigns. Teachers have used the following games[35] with success in all kinds of weather — sunny and dreary. However, they are especially recommended for rainy days.

[35] Ruth Evans, Thelma I. Bacon, Mary E. Bacon, and Joie L. Stapleton, *Physical Education for Elementary Schools* (New York: McGraw-Hill Book Company, 1958), pp. 239–244.

Classroom Activities

A. Malaga Grapes
   1. Equipment: a cane or a baton
   2. Number of players: any number
   3. Directions: Children sit in their chairs while one at a time comes to the front of the room to take a turn at repeating, *exactly*, as the leader said it, the jingle "Malaga grapes, Malaga grapes, the best we have in the market." The leader starts the game by reciting the jingle while beating time with the cane. As he recites it he does something special which he tries to keep the player from noticing but which the player must repeat when he recites; the catch may be that the leader unobtrusively clears his throat at some point in reciting the jingle. Another catch might be that he changes his cane from one hand to the other or performs some simple movement.

B. Circle Passes
   1. Equipment: several small objects to be passed
   2. Number of players: any number
   3. Directions: The children should stand in a large circle, all facing the center. The captain is given two small objects. He starts the first of these around the circle, and each child receives it and passes it to the next. As soon as one object is on the way, the captain starts the second one. The idea is to see if the second object will overtake the first.

C. Lion Hunt
   1. Equipment: none
   2. Number of players: any number
   3. Directions: Children are seated in a group. The teacher or leader stands facing the group. The leader starts to recite the following story. The children repeat each statement made by the leader and imitate her motions.

   "Let's go on a lion hunt." Children repeat.
   "Come on." Starting with hands on their knees, children slap their knees with alternate hands to simulate walking.
   "Wonder where the lions are." They continue the same motion.
   "Here's a hill; let's go up." Lifting their hands higher, they slap more slowly.
   "Here's the top; let's go down." They slap faster, as though running.
   "Here's a brook; let's jump it." They slap fast and end with a big slap.

"It's dark here." They slap slowly.

"I'm scared." They slap slowly.

"See any lions?" Hands above their eyes, they look left and right.

"There's one." No motion.

"Let's go home." They reverse all the motions from the beginning.

D. Musical Chairs

1. Equipment: chairs for all but one player

2. Number of players: as many as space will accommodate

3. Directions: As the music starts, the children start marching around the chairs. When the music stops, all try to secure chairs. The child without a chair is eliminated from the game. One chair is taken away, and the game is repeated. Game continues until there is but one chair left and two children to play. If this game is played in a classroom with permanently fixed furniture, a book may be placed on each chair that would ordinarily be taken away. (The game may be played using a large ball which is passed around the circle and when the music stops, the person who has the ball in his possession is eliminated from the game. This continues until there are only two children left. The one holding the ball when the music stops is the loser.)

E. Human Ticktacktoe

1. Equipment: nine chairs arranged three in a row

2. Number of players: any number of observers, two directors

3. Directions: Boys and girls form opposing teams. One boy and one girl are selected to direct the game. First the girl, then the boy, seats a member of his team according to the rules of the pencil-and-paper version of ticktacktoe. A win scores 1 point. The number of games to be played should be agreed upon before play is started.

F. Bowling in the Aisles

1. Equipment: several sets of bowling pins. (Class-made pins serve nicely. These may be regular blackboard erasers or cardboard cylinders such as come in rolls of paper towels.) Three balls for each set of pins.

2. Number of players: any number, divided into teams of even size

3. Directions: With each aisle in the classroom serving as a bowling alley, the pins are set up in the front of the room, with 8 inches between the pins and between the rows of pins. A starting line is drawn across each aisle at the back of the

room. Each child takes his turn at bowling, scoring the game as much like regular bowling as possible. . . .

## Additional Activities

| GYM ACTIVITIES | GAMES |
|---|---|
| Shuffleboard | Jolly Is the Miller |
| Ball bouncing | A-Hunting We Will Go |
| Rope jumping | Looby Loo |
| Deck tennis | I Wish I Had a Windmill |
| | Rig-a-Jig-Jig |

### Jolly Is the Miller

Jolly is the miller boy who lives by the mill,
The wheel goes round with a right good will,
One hand in the hopper and the other in the sack,
The right steps forward and the left steps back.

Directions: Couples walk around the circle until they come to the words "The right steps forward." Then the extra dancer steps into the circle and chooses a partner, while the extra person goes to the center for the next game. Couples follow the directions of the song, with the girls stepping forward and the boys stepping back to get a new partner.

### A-Hunting We Will Go

Oh, a-hunting we will go, a-hunting we will go.
We'll catch a fox and put him in a box and then
　　we'll let him go.
Tra, lalalalalala,
Tra, la, la, la, la, la,
Tra, la, la, la, la, la, la, la, la, la,
Tra, la, la, la, la, la.

Directions: Children stand in long sets of four couples, partners stand side by side, and all face the head set.

Verse: The first couple in each set cross hands, skip down the center of the set and return; the others keep time clapping hands lightly as they sing.

Chorus: All cross hands and skip, following the head couple who turn to the left and skip to the head of the set. When they arrive there the head couple forms an arch with their arms under which the others skip, and return to their original places. The second couple becomes the head couple, and the couple which was the head now becomes the foot of the set. The game is repeated until each couple has had a turn at being the head couple.

### Looby Loo

Chorus:

> Here we go Looby Loo, here we go Looby Light,
> Here we go Looby Loo, all on a Saturday night.

Verse:

1. I put my right hand in, I take my right hand out,
   I give my right hand a shake, shake, shake, and turn myself about.
2. I put my left hand in, I take my left hand out,
   I give my left hand a shake, shake, shake, and turn myself about.
3. I put my right foot in, I take my right foot out.
   I give my right foot a shake, shake, shake, and turn myself about.
4. I put my left foot in, I take my left foot out,
   I give my left foot a shake, shake, shake, and turn myself about.
5. I put my head in, I take my head out,
   I give my head a shake, shake, shake, and turn myself about.
6. I put my whole self in, I take my whole self out,
   I give my whole self a shake, shake, shake, and turn myself about.

Directions: The children form a single circle, joining hands, and walk or skip around the circle during each chorus. During the verses they stand in a circle and dramatize the actions suggested by the words.

### I Wish I Had a Windmill

1. I wish I had a windmill, a windmill, a windmill,
   I wish I had a windmill, I know what I'd have it do.
2. I'd have it draw the water, the water, the water,
   I'd have it draw the water up from the river below.
3. I'd have it make a duck pond, a duck pond, a duck pond,
   I'd have it make a duck pond so ducks and geese could swim.
4. The ducks will make their wings flap, their wings flap, their wings flap,
   The ducks will make their wings flap, then they will say, "quack, quack."
5. The geese will stretch their necks out, their necks out, their necks out,
   The geese will stretch their necks out, then they will say, "s-s-s-s."

Walk for verse 1, duck walk for verse 4, arms folded and heads stretched forward for verse 5 pantomiming geese.

1. Form a circle taking hold of hands for first verse, singing the words.

2. Join hands with partners and move arms like windmills.
3. Walk around in small groups to represent duck ponds.
4. Walk like ducks.
5. Fold arms and stretch heads forward like geese.

### Rig-a-Jig-Jig

As I was walking down the street,
Heigh-o, heigh-o, heigh-o, heigh-o,
A pretty girl I chanced to meet,
Heigh-o, heigh-o, heigh-o.

Rig-a-jig-jig and away we go,
Away we go, away we go.
Rig-a-jig-jig and away we go,
Heigh-o, heigh-o, heigh-o.

Directions: Children stand in a circle facing counterclockwise. A child is in the center. On the verse all the children walk around the circle singing. When they sing "A pretty girl I chanced to meet," the child in the center selects one of the children in the circle, who joins him in the center. During the chorus all the children skip around the circle. When the verse is repeated, each of the two children in the center chooses a new partner. The game is continued until all have partners in the center circle.

Another method of taking care of rainy-day problems is to organize a talent show. Children can build up standards for performance if they recognize that one prepares for a performance and does the best he can. Children play musical instruments, dance, recite, give chalk talks, dramatize stories, or play charades. Standards of selection of materials for presentation must be considered.

If the teacher helps the children select interesting things to do, provides for activities which develop skill, require physical activity, present no safety hazards, and are adapted to the limitations of the classroom space, rainy-day problems can be minimized. Here again a great deal depends on the teacher's attitude, skill, and interest.

## TEACHING A NEW ACTIVITY

Opinions vary as to the most effective ways of teaching physical education. However, there are certain guiding principles that can be applied successfully. Among these are motivation, demonstration, explanation, participation, and evaluation. How the teacher will apply these principles to the lesson will depend upon the group, the particular activity, his own skill, the space, and the equipment used.

## In the Primary Grades

1. Motivate the activity through the use of audio-visual aids or discussion.

2. Demonstrate the new activity or have a proficient girl or boy perform.

3. Give a brief explanation of the activity if it seems necessary in addition to the demonstration.

4. Have the class organized so they can practice the activity. This may be accomplished through groups or, if facilities allow, the entire class may participate.

5. Provide time for the children to practice; check each child to see if he is succeeding.

6. Encourage the children to discover their own progress.

7. Set a specific goal for each activity. Check to see that the child knows exactly what he is trying to accomplish.

8. Plan for a progression of difficulty in the activities to demand further concentration and skill.

9. Allow time for evaluation at the end of the period.

## In the Intermediate Grades

1. Define the purpose of the activity to be practiced and relate it to what is going on in the physical education period.

2. Have the class well organized with leaders who can direct their groups in the activities.

3. Demonstrate the skill when presenting a new activity or have a child who is skilled demonstrate it.

4. Allow time to practice each new activity; analyze class and/or individual difficulties.

5. Use group leaders to assist in teaching the skill.

6. Use the rotating group whenever possible. Select several types of activities and assign one group to each activity with the leader in charge. At the end of the practice period give a signal to change to another activity.

7. Encourage proficient students to demonstrate to the class. Encourage creative expression of ideas.

8. After sufficient practice time, arrange a schedule of testing.

9. Permit children to record their scores on individual or group score cards.

10. Rotate the groups.[36]

[36] Adapted from Charles Nagel, *Methods Guidebook in Physical Education and Recreation* (Palo Alto, Calif.: The National Press, 1956), p. 60.

## Supplies and Equipment

In general, the problem of supplies and equipment is one that concerns the administration, not the teacher. The term "supplies" is used to denote movable, expendable types of play paraphernalia that are the essential instructional materials in physical education. Without adequate supplies the teacher is as handicapped in developing a good physical education program as he would be in developing a good reading program without books and supplementary materials. Supplies should be purchased with a view to the needs of the children, the physical education facilities, and the budget. Schools vary in the plan for providing supplies and equipment. In some schools they are purchased for and assigned to each classroom teacher, whose responsibility it is to care for them. In other schools they are purchased for general use and are kept in a central place. In still other schools the physical education teacher is responsible for all equipment to be used in the physical education program and delegates pupils to share in this responsibility.

The term "equipment" is used to denote permanent materials such as basketball backguards, climbing ropes, jump standards, playground apparatus, piano, and record players. La Salle[37] suggests the following supplies as essential: basketballs, beanbags, bowling pins, mats, nets or ropes, rubber balls, soccer balls, and for intermediate grades bases or small rubber mats, batons, softball bats, junior footballs, soft balls, and volleyballs. Additional supplies may be purchased on the request of the classroom teacher, the physical education teacher, or the supervisor as the school budget permits.

## The Role of the Teacher

In the kindergarten and primary grades, the classroom teacher is often responsible for teaching physical education. He may receive help from a supervisor in physical education, intermediate physical education instructors, or, in some cases, the coach. Beginning with the fourth grade, frequently the physical education classes are taught by the regular physical education teacher. It is recommended that at least thirty minutes daily be allocated to physical education

[37] Dorothy La Salle, *Guidance of Children Through Physical Education* (New York: The Ronald Press Company, 2nd ed., 1957), pp. 132–133.

under the direction of either the specialists, the classroom teacher, or the teacher assisted by the specialist.

The role of the teacher is that of guide, not dictator or innocuous, protective benefactor. He must develop in children the capacity to determine their purposes, to direct their planning and activity toward the realization of defined goals, and to profit from their failures as well as their successes through self-evaluation. His function is to guide children from immature behavior to successful participation in activities that have meaning and value for them, creating an atmosphere and situations in which they can develop sound habits and positive attitudes toward physical development, and utilizing methods that contribute increasingly to progress toward the objectives of the physical education program.

When the classroom teacher is aided by the physical education teacher, specialist, and/or supervisor, the program is most effective if there is a mutual understanding of the objectives to be accomplished, the values to be emphasized, the evaluative devices to be used, and the end product to be achieved in terms of children's behavior.

Many physical education experiences enrich other learning activities. Since the teacher is the chief agent in integrating learning activities, he can help children to see how physical education aids both mental and physical health.

## INTEGRATION OF PHYSICAL EDUCATION IN THE CURRICULUM

In the integrated curriculum artificial boundaries of subject matter are eliminated and experiences are organized around significant problems. Physical education is an integral part of the curriculum when teachers and administrators consider it in the light of its significance in the life of the individual — not as an isolated activity.

Unfortunately, many physical education specialists place the emphasis on the skill, on teaching the physical education activities to children, rather than on the end result — the development of each child. On the other hand, there are those who see the values in integrating the program. Miller and Whitcomb give this sound advice on integration: "Physical education should include activities that develop the child according to the objectives of physical education, and also according to what he is experiencing in his total school living and learning. It should not be so completely integrated that it loses its identity. As in every area there are fundamental skills that are best learned as isolated techniques identified solely with physical education. Therefore, the possibilities for integration of physical education activities with classroom learning experiences would be considered part of, not the total physical education program for elementary school children."[38]

Stuart gives thumb-nail sketches illustrating ways of integrating physical education with five curriculum areas:

> *Language Arts.* A sixth-grade class developed a card file of physical education activities. Following each activity, a child wrote a description, another listed the equipment and space needed, and a third gave the evaluation. A creative activity was named for the child who originated it.
>
> *Music.* A class of fifth-graders studying the Western Movement learned some folk and square dances; then created one to the music "I've Been Working on the Railroad."
>
> *Social Studies.* A third-grade class studying Indians made tom-toms and created an original dance which they accompanied with the tom-toms. They learned to play an Indian game with the help of the physical education teacher.
>
> *Arithmetic.* Using a yarn ball a group of second-graders practiced the game Sky Ball in the classroom and learned to keep score. Then they proceeded to the gymnasium where the children kept score, thus getting additional number practice.
>
> *Health and Safety.* A third-grader who refused to heed the safety rule prohibiting a child to run and slide into base cut his arm one day as he was ignoring the rule. The teacher administered first aid and explained her reasons for each application.[39]

Cowell and Hazelton[40] in illustrating correlation cite an example of a group of fifth-graders studying a unit on life in the various United Nations. The music and physical education teachers cooperated in planning corresponding folk songs and dances as a part of the culminating activity of this unit. The areas they suggest as

[38] Miller and Whitcomb, *op. cit.*, p. 236.

[39] Frances R. Stuart, "A Physical Education Program," *The Instructor*, 69:17, April 1960.

[40] Charles C. Cowell and Hazel W. Hazelton, *Curriculum Designs in Physical Education* (Englewood Cliffs, N.J.: Prentice-Hall, Inc., 1955), p. 97.

lending themselves most effectively to integration with physical education are language arts, arithmetic, and social studies.

Torpey makes specific suggestions for correlation with these areas:

### Correlation with Language Arts

Selecting games which give children opportunity to speak and listen

Answering questions and giving directions

Writing the rules of games or descriptions of an activity

### Correlation with Arithmetic

Addition — adding scores in bowling or shuffle board

Measurement — heights, weights, etc.
measuring diameters of circles, using fractions on a stop watch

Understanding a set — in square dancing — 2 people times 4 couples equals 8 in a set

Estimating — judging distances

### Correlation with Social Studies

Learning dances typical of countries being studied

Sports activities such as lacrosse when studying an Indian unit, volley ball, soccer, tennis when studying Europe. . . .

Correlation is a continuous part of a sound program and should be planned accordingly. The effort involved may seem considerable but the result will provide for greater understanding and better teaching.[41]

An excellent example of correlation with creative art activities is provided below. The example also illustrates the way in which a physical education teacher works with the classroom teacher in guiding learning experiences.

### Mrs. Retzlaff's Third Grade

Mrs. Retzlaff is a warm and sensitive person. She is inquisitive and adventurous; she seeks to create ever-expanding experiences for herself and her children. Knowing how important it is for children to create and express ideas, she enlivens the experiences of her children to develop the background out of which they can create ideas. Continuous and varied activities in the arts are the means through which she helps them develop and express their ideas.

[41] James Torpey, "Correlation in the Elementary School," *The Physical Educator*, 14:10, October 1957.

Mrs. Retzlaff's school is located in a prosperous surburban community adjoining a large city. Virtually all of the children come from comfortable professional and business homes. The school building itself is modern. Most of the classrooms are spacious and well equipped.

Mrs. Retzlaff's room is large and bright. There is good storage space and running water. The furniture consists of comfortable tables, which are large enough for four children. They all have regular chairs. From time to time the furniture is moved around, sometimes to facilitate a particular activity, and sometimes merely to create a bit of variety. Mrs. Retzlaff has twenty-five children in her class.

Mrs. Retzlaff's class was studying "Things that Live" — birds, animals, and fish. They had borrowed a collection of books from the school library. Each child selected something special to investigate, and they were reading independently and writing reports of all the information they were collecting.

The art consultant had already been in to talk over with Mrs. Retzlaff and the children the things they were studying about, and some ideas they had for possible things to do in art. In addition to planning with the art consultant, Mrs. Retzlaff had also talked with the music and physical education teachers. They also had some ideas to suggest. Mrs. Retzlaff arranged with the physical education teacher for the children to come to the gymnasium this afternoon to do some work there.

PHYSICAL EDUCATION TEACHER: I know you have been studying and reading a lot about birds. Who can tell me about some different kinds of birds?

JOHN: Some fly, but some don't fly.

PHYSICAL EDUCATION TEACHER: That's right. What about some of the birds that don't fly?

KIM: Penguins and chickens.

PHYSICAL EDUCATION TEACHER: Does a chicken ever fly?

MELANIE: Yes. It just goes up, and it comes down again.

PHYSICAL EDUCATION TEACHER: You mean it doesn't fly very far?

MELANIE: Yes.

PHYSICAL EDUCATION TEACHER: What other birds have you read about?

MARTHA: Thrushes.

KIM: Sea gulls.

PHYSICAL EDUCATION TEACHER: Does a sea gull do a lot of flapping or gliding?

KIM: Gliding.

PHYSICAL EDUCATION TEACHER: I'm going to play some music for you. It's very short, and you'll have to listen very carefully. (*She plays a brief soaring, swinging passage.*) Do you think you can glide to that music? Let's try it just with your arms.

The physical education teacher talked with them further about other birds, and she played more music. They moved their bodies to the rhythm and feeling of the birds, and the music.

PHYSICAL EDUCATION TEACHER: You've been very good birds today and I thought you would enjoy flying on the trampoline.

CHILDREN: (*Cheers*)

PHYSICAL EDUCATION TEACHER: I thought you'd like that. Let's all go over to the trampoline and stand around the edge, so you can take turns flying.

They spent about half an hour in the gymnasium, and after they had all had a turn on the trampoline, Mrs. Retzlaff and her group returned to their classroom.

MRS. RETZLAFF: That was fun in the gym and you were all very good birds. Now do you remember we began talking yesterday about some things we might like to do in art?

CHILDREN: Yes.

MRS. RETZLAFF: I know you enjoyed the bird dances we did in the gym, and I wonder. Did that give you any ideas for something we might do in art? How did that music make you feel?

KAREN: Nice.

MRS. RETZLAFF: What did the gliding music make you want to do?

JOHN: Kind of float.

MRS. RETZLAFF: It did, didn't it? It had such a nice rhythm, and it was so smooth. Was all the music like that?

CHUCK: No. Some was jumpy.

MRS. RETZLAFF: That's right, Chuck. Some of the music was sharp and jumpy. When you danced, you moved very well to the jumpy rhythm. Chuck, does that give you any idea for something you might do in art?

CHUCK: Well —

MRS. RETZLAFF: Would you like to hear some of that music again? I have the records here, and we can play them on our player.

CHILDREN: Yes.

MRS. RETZLAFF: (*She played short parts of several records with gliding, jumping, and swaying passages.*) Listen to the different kinds of music — gliding, jumping, swaying — and let's beat the rhythm on our tables.

When you beat and sway, it's almost as if you were making a design.

NANCY:  Couldn't we kinda paint like that?

MRS. RETZLAFF:  I think you could. What would you try to paint?

KIM:  Well, we could make lines and spots.

MRS. RETZLAFF:  You could make different kinds of lines. You could make gliding lines and swaying ones, just like the rhythm in the music. What colors do you think you might use?

MELANIE:  Different ones.

DAVID:  Bright colors.

MRS. RETZLAFF:  You could combine some bright colors with darker ones. You could make a design like the rhythm you beat on the tables. Would you like to try that today?

CHILDREN:  Yes.

MRS. RETZLAFF:  All right. We can put our smocks on, and get our paints and brushes. Mike, will you get the paper? I'll play the records again. Let's try the one with the gliding music first.

The paints were in jars on the sink counter in their room. They took turns ladling the colors into shallow mixing pans, collected their water jars and brushes, and returned to their tables. Mike distributed sheets of 12″ by 18″ manila paper to each table, and they were ready to begin.

MRS. RETZLAFF:  I'll play the record now, so you can listen to it while you paint. Listen to the glide and sway of the music, and paint what the rhythm tells you to.

They listened to the soaring glide of the music and began to paint. Many of their pictures conveyed the sweep and the mood of the passage. Mrs. Retzlaff played the record a second time, and they worked rapidly.

MRS. RETZLAFF:  You are moving to the music, just as you did in the gym. This time you're dancing on the paper.

CHILDREN:  (*Laughter*)

MRS. RETZLAFF:  Let's look at some of your pictures. Kim, show us yours. How do you like it?

MARTHA:  His glides nice. The spots are like we beat on the table.

MRS. RETZLAFF:  That's a good idea. It does look as if Kim combined the music and the beating on the table. All of you have done real well. Do you want to try another one?

CHILDREN: Yes.

MRS. RETZLAFF: Now I'll play some music that jumps. It hops, just like a bird.

Mrs. Retzlaff played another record, and the children painted again. When they had finished, they talked about some of these pictures, and then they did one more. Altogether, they spent about forty minutes in talking, listening, painting, discussing, and cleaning up. . . .

The work they thus concluded was more than painting to the accompaniment of music. Through this activity, they brought to a climax the total experience of dancing in the gymnasium and listening to the music. The rhythm was in their bodies, and they transformed it into color and pattern on their papers.[42]

*The Role of the Physical Education Teacher in Integration.* In integration learning experiences are organized around a central core. By focusing upon the persistent problems of living, physical education, recreation, health, and personal-social relations are integrated with the other curriculum areas. Such an organization draws upon many subject areas, including physical education, in the solution of problems. The physical education teacher cooperates with other teachers in planning and developing the unit by serving as a resource person. He aids the core teacher or at times works directly with the pupils.

Physical education specialists contribute to the process of integrating the school program to the extent that they accept membership and involvement on school health councils and curriculum and evaluation committees, cooperate in the development of resource units, and participate when invited in a specific unit of study.

OUTDOOR EDUCATION AND RECREATION

An important phase of the physical education program is what for want of a better name is termed "outdoor education." In parks, school yards, and vacant lots elementary children and their teachers explore the mysteries of nature. Classrooms may be empty a week while the entire group is off at a camp. In some schools instruction is offered in archery, bait casting, and skating in addition to the more conventional athletic sports.

[42] Manuel Barkan, *Through Art to Creativity* (Boston: Allyn and Bacon, Inc., 1960), pp. 180–185.

Smith defines outdoor education as consisting of "those direct learning experiences that involve enjoying, interpreting, and wisely using the natural environment in achieving, at least in part, the objectives of education."[43] The unique feature of education in an outdoor setting is the direct approach to learning, the exploration and adventure that result from making the maximum use of physical environment as a laboratory for learning.

Among the chief values of outdoor education in the elementary school are the following:

1. Outdoor education takes into consideration the basic principle that learning is best if it proceeds through direct experience — beginning with concrete activities.

2. Outdoor education encourages creative teaching by affording an opportunity for good teacher-pupil rapport, increased teacher-pupil planning, and escape from stereotyped activity of the classroom.

3. Outdoor education lends itself to achieving certain objectives of the curriculum.

4. Outdoor education affords many children firsthand contact with the physical universe that might otherwise be denied them.

Among the activities included are camping, field trips, cook-outs, construction of shelters, building trails, developing nature trails, planting trees and shrubs.

*A Sample Elementary School Camp Program*[44]

| DAY | TEAMSTERS | CRUISERS | LUMBERJACKS |
|---|---|---|---|
| Monday | Planning | Planning | Planning |
| | Hike around Lake | Hike to Abandoned Farm | Camp Cruise |
| | Cook-Out | Crafts | Tapping Trees |
| | Paul Bunyan Stories | | Square Dance |
| Tuesday | | | |
| | Blacksmith's Shop | Logging | Treasure Hunt |
| | Scavenger Hunt | Make Ice Cream | Plant Trees |
| | Sock Hop | Cook-Out | Fishing |

[43] Julian W. Smith, *Outdoor Education* (Washington, D.C.: American Association for Health, Physical Education and Recreation, NEA, 1956), p. 6.
[44] *Ibid.*, p. 26.

| Wednesday | Boiling Sap | Hike Around | Fire Building |
| | Crafts | the Lake | Compass Hike |
| | Square Dance | Fishing | Crafts |
| | | Square Dance | |
| Thursday | Breakfast | Compass Hike | Cook-Out |
| | Cook-Out | Plan for | Boating |
| | Compass Hike | Council Fire | Council Fire |
| | Council Fire | Council Fire | |
| Friday | Evaluation | Evaluation | Evaluation |
| | Clean Up and | Clean Up and | Clean Up and |
| | Pack | Pack | Pack |
| | Go Home | Go Home | Go Home |

Schools that are unable to provide camp experiences for children can make use of community resources such as museums, zoos, wildlife sanctuaries, and botanical gardens. Schools which offer the benefits of outdoor education find that the children become aware of things going on around them that they never really saw and heard before. They develop a greater sensitivity to the world in which they live than is possible through reading. They may find a life-long interest that will benefit them physically, mentally, emotionally, and aesthetically. "There is a great difference between sensing something and perceiving it. Many persons go through life without hearing the songs of birds, because no one ever directed their attention to them when they were young."[45] The child who becomes aware of the world of nature increases his capacity for enjoyment as well as his ability to meet more effectively the tensions, frustrations, and demands of everyday living.

## EVALUATION

Successful appraisal of progress in physical education calls for a team approach. It requires the combined efforts of the classroom teacher, physical education teacher, supervisor, and pupils to answer the questions related to adequacy in motor skills, physical fitness, and personal satisfaction in the development of recreational interests

[45] *Ibid.*, p. 11.

and skills. Tests and measurements are available which measure such factors of physical development as strength, endurance, body mechanics, motor ability, and special abilities and achievement in sports as well as knowledge of rules, techniques of performance, strategy in sports, and the development of sports.

The teacher should evaluate himself in terms of his ability to provide a balanced program of skills, games, team sports, dance activities, and self-testing activities.

*Evaluation of Children's Progress.* In evaluating growth in the individual and the group in the physical education program the teacher may use criteria like the following:

1. Does the child understand his own body structure, accept its strengths and limitations, and learn to use it with confidence?

2. Does the child explore the possibilities of movement and make an earnest effort to define and solve his individual problems of endurance, strength, and coordination?

3. Does the child gain satisfaction in expressing himself through movement?

4. Does the child gain in skill to move forward toward goals he can achieve?

5. Do the children and teacher work together to solve many kinds of group problems involving skill activities, leisure time and others?

6. Do the children have a voice in selecting, organizing, and evaluating activities?

7. Do the children work together cooperatively and accept all members courteously and generously?

8. Do the children use creative ways of developing or modifying games as needed?

9. Do the children accept official verdicts relating to rules with good grace?

10. Do the children look on physical education activities as vital for healthy, balanced living?

*Evaluation of the Physical Education Program*

1. Do I schedule at least 30 minutes each day for an instructional period in physical education (exclusive of rest and recess periods)?

2. Do I plan a staggered schedule?

3. Do I plan programs in advance?

4. Do I sense the importance of including a balance of activities

in the areas of: rhythms (2 days each week — primary; 1 day each week — intermediate); mimetics, circle games, and story plays — primary; group games, relay, conditioning activities, apparatus activities, and team games — intermediate.

5. Does the school supply suitable equipment for all age levels?

6. Does the school provide an adequate amount of equipment?

7. Does the school arrange for a central storage place for all equipment?

8. Does the school arrange schedules so that the gymnasium may be used by *all* elementary grades?

9. Does the school make play areas and gymnasium free from hazards?

10. Do I encourage the squad method of organization for intermediate grades?[46]

The evaluation in which the community participates comes through carefully planned programs in which children demonstrate growth in the various phases of physical education. Elaborate programs are no longer in vogue. Emphasis is on presenting to the parents a sample of everyday experiences.

Evaluation should always be in terms of the defined objectives if it is to have value. As has been shown, the objectives involve more than the development of physical prowess; they include physical, social, emotional, and intellectual development.

Of primary importance is the physical objective, which includes physical fitness, growth and development, and skills.

The social-emotional objective is significant in helping children achieve emotional stability, social skills and habits of cooperation, friendly competition, leadership, and followership. Fair play and sportsmanship are also important concepts to be developed in connection with the social-emotional objective. Through the outdoor phase of the program aesthetic development, emotional stability, and healthy living are fostered. The opportunity to release emotional tensions through legitimate activity is an important value of this phase of the program.

Intellectual development is an important objective, though it has been somewhat neglected in the emphasis on physical, social, and emotional development. The knowledges and appreciations children gain through physical education should not be underestimated. The

[46] "Ten Timely Tips for the Elementary Physical Educational Program," *The Physical Educator*, 15:9, March 1958.

more an individual understands a sport — its terminology, rules, and scoring strategy — the more he appreciates it and the more he can enjoy it as a participator or as a spectator.

## Conclusion

The health and physical education program in the schools has as its major objective the optimum development of each individual. Nowhere else in the curriculum is the opportunity greater to focus on the physical needs of children. Health education and physical education are closely related. Physical and emotional health is improved by a well-conducted health program which includes health education through instruction, health services, and healthful living in and out of the classroom.

Effective health education contributes to an understanding of and appreciation for sound nutritional practices, medical care, personal hygiene, wholesome home and family living, mental and emotional health, and safety. Health education should develop concepts of personal, community, and national health and an awareness of the broad responsibilities for health of others.

Health and safety education, physical education, outdoor education, and recreation contribute to effective living. Specific contributions of recreational activities are those related to improved physical and mental health, character development, and social adjustment. The individual who enjoys good health and has a satisfying recreational life is predisposed toward being a well-balanced, law-abiding citizen. Recreation brings relief from tensions, rest from the workaday world, and the inspiration of the creative experience.

The physical education program is committed to fostering physical fitness which encompasses the total person, not just the physical self. Through carefully organized activities which develop motor skills, body efficiency, and creativity in movement, the child gains control over movement, develops a stronger body, and finds confidence and satisfaction in recreational activities. He participates in games, stunts, and conditioning and rhythmic activities which are designed to improve his physical and mental health and give him a healthier body, a sound mind, and a positive outlook on life.

The responsibility for a good physical development program rests with the home, the school, and the community. Programs for physical fitness should begin in the home. The school provides health services and instruction and activities for development. The community provides recreational and health facilities to supplement those provided by the home and school. Increased and continual cooperation should be encouraged between home, school, and community in achieving improved physical education and recreational programs.

## ACTIVITIES AND QUESTIONS

1. What state requirements for health and physical education in the schools does your state have? Observe an elementary school to see to what extent it attempts to comply with the requirements.

2. Examine your state course of study for health education and physical education. How does it compare with the courses of two other states?

3. Organize a health or physical education unit and develop it with a group of children in the classroom. Evaluate the children's learning.

4. Observe in a classroom and try to pick out the healthiest child and the one who appears to be the least healthy. Obtain records and information from the school and compare the records with your observations.

5. Observe health and physical education activities at the level you hope to teach. Keep a record of your observations and evaluate the effectiveness of the program in terms of criteria suggested in this chapter.

6. Begin making a file of games and other physical education activities you observe and run across in your reading. Work out a plan to organize the material in such a way that the directions for equipment, position, and playing are clear and can easily be used. Select the games and activities in terms of the age level in which you are most interested.

7. Select one of the rainy-weather games listed and teach it to a group.

8. Discuss the role of the classroom teacher in the physical education and health program.

9. What was your reaction to health education as an elementary pupil? To the physical education program?

10. Examine some books of games and physical education activities and evaluate them in terms of the objectives of the physical education program.

# BIBLIOGRAPHY

American Association for Health, Physical Education and Recreation, N.E.A. *Children in Focus.* Washington, D.C.: The Association, 1954.

American Association for Health, Physical Education and Recreation, N.E.A. *Fit to Teach: Yearbook on Teacher Health.* Washington, D.C.: The Association, 1957.

American Automobile Association. *Policies and Practices for School Safety Patrols.* Washington, D.C.: The Association, 1958.

American Medical Association. *Physicians and Schools.* Chicago: The Association, 1958.

Andrews, Gladys. *Creative Rhythmic Movement for Children.* Englewood Cliffs, N.J.: Prentice-Hall, Inc., 1954.

Andrews, Gladys, *et al. Physical Education for Today's Boys and Girls.* Boston: Allyn and Bacon, Inc., 1960.

Bucher, Charles A., and Reade, Evelyn. *Physical Education in the Modern Elementary School.* New York: The Macmillan Company, 1958.

Byrd, Oliver E. (ed.). *Health Yearbook, 1957.* Stanford: Stanford University Press, 1958.

Callahan, Dorothy, and Payne, Alma Smith. *The Great Nutrition Puzzle.* New York: Charles Scribner's Sons, 1956.

Chatwin, Nora. *Physical Education for Primary Grades.* Toronto: The House of Grant, 1958.

Davies, Evelyn A. *The Elementary School Child and His Posture Patterns.* New York: Appleton-Century-Crofts, Inc., 1958.

Davis, Elwood C., and Wallace, Earl. *Toward Better Teaching in Physical Education.* Englewood Cliffs, N. J.: Prentice-Hall, Inc., 1961.

Diehl, Harold. *Textbook of Healthful Living.* New York: McGraw-Hill Book Company, 6th ed., 1960.

Diehl, Harold, and Sheehy, Anita Laton. *Health and Safety for You.* New York: McGraw-Hill Book Company, 1954.

Donaldson, George W., and Donaldson, Louise E. *Outdoor Education: A Bibliography.* Washington, D.C.: American Association for Health, Physical Education and Recreation, NEA, 1958.

Dukelow, Donald A., and Hein, Fred V. (eds.). *Health Appraisal of School Children.* Washington, D.C.: Joint Committee on Health Problems in Education, NEA, 2nd ed., 1957.

Etheredge, Maude L. *Health Facts for College Students: A Textbook of Individual and Community Health.* Philadelphia: W. B. Saunders Company, 7th ed., 1958.

Evans, Ruth, Bacon, Thelma I., Bacon, Mary E., and Stapleton, Joie L. *Physical Education for Elementary Schools*. New York: McGraw-Hill Book Company, 1958.

Floris, A. E., and Stafford, G. T. *Safety Education*. New York: McGraw-Hill Book Company, 1956.

Goodrich, Lois. *Decentralized Camping*. New York: Association Press, 1959.

Grout, Ruth. *Health Teaching in Schools*. Philadelphia: W. B. Saunders Company, 3rd ed., 1958.

Haag, Jessie. *School Health Program*. New York: Henry Holt and Company, 1958.

Halsey, Elizabeth, and Porter, Lorena R. *Physical Education for Children: A Developmental Approach*. New York: Henry Holt and Company, 1958.

Harnett, Arthur L., and Shaw, John H. *Effective Health Education*. New York: Appleton-Century-Crofts, Inc., 1959.

Hubbard, Alfred, and Weiss, Raymond. *Completed Research in Health, Physical Education and Recreation*. Vol. I. Washington, D.C.: American Association for Health, Physical Education and Recreation, NEA, 1959.

Humphrey, James H. *Elementary School Physical Education: With Emphasis upon Its Integration in Other Curriculum Areas*. New York: Harper & Brothers, 1958.

Humphrey, James, Jones, Edwina, and Haverstick, Martha J. (eds.). *Readings in Physical Education for the Elementary School*. Palo Alto, Calif.: The National Press, 1958.

Hunsicker, Paul A. *AAHPER Youth Fitness Manual*. Washington, D.C.: American Association for Health, Physical Education and Recreation, NEA, 1958.

Hunt, Sarah E., and Cain, Ethel. *Games the World Around*. New York: A. S. Barnes and Company, 1949.

Indiana Department of Public Instruction. *High School Physical Education Course of Study*. Bulletin No. 222. Indianapolis: State Department of Education, 1958.

Indiana Department of Public Instruction and State Board of Health. *Outdoor Education Through School Camping*. Indianapolis: The Department, 1958.

Irwin, Leslie W., Humphrey, James H., and Johnson, Warren R. *Methods and Materials in School Health Education*. St. Louis: C. V. Mosby Company, 1956.

Johns, Edward B., Sutton, Willard, and Webster, Lloyd E. *Health for Effective Living: A Basic Health Education Text for College Students*. New York: McGraw-Hill Book Company, 2nd ed., 1958.

Kozman, Hilda, Cassidy, Rosalind, and Jackson, Chester O. *Methods in Physical Education*. Philadelphia: W. B. Saunders Company, 3rd ed., 1958.

Kraus, Richard. *Play Activities for Boys and Girls*. New York: McGraw-Hill Book Company, 1957.

La Salle, Dorothy. *Guidance of Children Through Physical Education*. New York: The Ronald Press Company, 2nd ed., 1957.

Latchaw, Marjorie. *A Pocket Guide of Games and Rhythms for the Elementary School*. Englewood Cliffs, N.J.: Prentice-Hall, Inc., 1956.

Le Fevre, John R., and Boydston, N. D. *Annotated Guide to Free and Inexpensive Health Instructions and Materials*. Carbondale: Southern Illinois University Press, 1959.

Matthews, Donald K. *Measurement in Physical Education*. Philadelphia: W. B. Saunders Company, 1958.

McCloy, Charles Harold, and Young, Norma Dorothy. *Tests and Measurements in Health and Physical Education*. New York: Appleton-Century-Crofts, Inc., 3rd ed., 1954.

Miller, Arthur G., and Whitcomb, Virginia. *Physical Education in the Elementary School Curriculum*. Englewood Cliffs, N.J.: Prentice-Hall, Inc., 1957.

Mooney, Gertrude X. *Mexican Folk Dances for American Schools*. Coral Gables, Fla.: University of Miami Press, 1958.

Nagel, Charles. *Methods Guidebook in Physical Education and Recreation*. Palo Alto, Calif.: The National Press, 1956.

National Commission on Safety Education. *Unit Guides for You: Safety in the Intermediate Grades*. Washington, D.C.: NEA, 1958.

National Commission on Safety Education. *Unit Guides for You: Safety in the Primary Grades*. Washington, D.C.: NEA, 1958.

Rash, J. Keogh. *Health Education Curriculum Development*. Bloomington: Indiana University, 1958.

Schneider, Elsa. *Physical Education in Urban Elementary Schools*. Washington, D.C.: Government Printing Office, 1959.

Schneider, Robert E. *Methods and Materials of Health Education*. Philadelphia: W. B. Saunders Company, 1958.

Scott, Harry A., and West-Keamper, Richard B. *From Program to Facilities in Physical Education*. New York: Harper & Brothers, 1958.

Shaw, John H., Sprague, Glenn, and Palmer, James. *The Instructor Kit on the Human Body*. Dansville, N.Y.: F. A. Owen Publishing Company, 1958.

Smith, Helen Norman, and Wolverton, Mary E. *Health Education in the Elementary School*. New York: The Ronald Press Company, 1959.

Vannier, Mary Ellen, and Foster, Mildred. *Teaching Physical Education in Elementary Schools*. Philadelphia: W. B. Saunders Company, 1958.

Voltmer, Edward, and Esslinger, Arthur E. *The Organization and Administration of Physical Education.* New York: Appleton-Century-Crofts, Inc., 3rd ed., 1958.

*What Every Teacher Should Know About the Physical Condition of Her Pupils.* Washington, D.C.: U.S. Office of Health, Education and Welfare, 1955.

White, Betty. *Betty White's Latin-American Dance Book.* New York: David McKay Company, 1958.

White, Ellen G. *Education.* Mountain View, Calif.: Pacific Press Publishing Association, 1903.

Willgoose, Carl E. *Health Education in the Elementary School.* Philadelphia: W. B. Saunders Company, 1959.

Williams, Jesse F. *Principles of Physical Education.* Philadelphia: W. B. Saunders Company, 7th ed., 1959.

Zim, Herbert S. *Your Food and You.* New York: William Morrow and Company, 1957.

# 13

If you can't hear what others are saying, or can't understand it, or if they can't hear or understand you, there can't be any dialogue. . . .

ROBERT M. HUTCHINS

# Introducing
## foreign languages

¿Habla usted español? Parlez-vous français? Sprechen Sie Deutsch? In a rapidly shrinking world the necessity of acquiring a better understanding of other peoples; the need for improved skills in the social, economic, and political phases of living; the tremendous amount of information acquired through mass communication media have contributed to the clamor of public demand to teach a second language in the elementary schools.

The teaching of foreign languages in the elementary public schools is not new. At the end of the nineteenth century and the beginning of the twentieth, communities in this country that were predominantly German were influential in having German taught in elementary schools. In Cincinnati, Milwaukee, St. Louis, Evansville, and Buffalo German was taught. As communities became more Americanized and those interested in perpetuating the German language and culture decreased in number, there was less demand for the study of the language and finally it disappeared. French was offered in the elementary schools in San Francisco and in several New England cities; Spanish was taught in some rural schools of New Mexico, and in Corpus Christi, Texas, from 1889 to 1919. At the turn of the century both French and German were taught in the eighth grade of New York City's elementary schools.

The foreign-language idea waned. During World War I instruction was discontinued. However, the idea did not die out; it merely lay dormant. The oldest program now in operation is the one in Cleveland, started in 1921, in which French is taught to superior students in Grades 1 through 6. However, the present interest in foreign-language study in the elementary grades had its real beginning in 1943 when the elementary schools of Los Angeles introduced Spanish. By the autumn of 1953 the movement had 300 school districts and 300,000 pupils involved. The figures doubled and the geographical spread increased so that by 1955, 43 out of the 48 states reported foreign-language programs in the elementary schools.[1] The national picture today is reflected in the following digest of samplings taken from the larger school districts.

In New York City elementary instruction in foreign languages in Grades 4 through 6 is offered for gifted children only and in a limited number of classes. Studies by the Board of Education through experimental programs indicated that the system was not ready to undertake widespread instruction and not enough children evidenced readiness for it.

In Newark, New Jersey, French, Spanish, Italian, German, and Hebrew are taught at the ninth grade. No instruction is offered in foreign languages in the elementary grades.

In Boston, Massachusetts, an experimental program in which French is offered in Grades 4 through 12 is under way for those with "demonstrated ability."

---

[1] Kenneth Mildenberger, *Status of Foreign Language Study in the American Elementary Schools*, U.S. Department of Health, Education and Welfare, Committee on Foreign Language Teaching (Washington, D.C.: Government Printing Office, 1956).

In Philadelphia, Pennsylvania, television programs in French and Russian are offered at the elementary level. Most foreign-language teaching is postponed until the secondary school.

In Detroit, Michigan, some 10,000 pupils are receiving instruction in Grades 2 through 6. Instruction is limited to those of average ability or above. French, German, and Spanish are available through special teachers, television, and radio.

In Chicago, Illinois, plans are under way to begin instruction in the kindergarten so there will be continuity in the program from the elementary school through high school. At the present time (1960) 162 schools are involved in foreign languages from the kindergarten through the eighth grade. French, Italian, Spanish, and Russian are taught.

In St. Louis, Missouri, gifted children in Grades 5 through 8 are taught French. Teachers are interested in expanding the program to include average children with special aptitude and interest in languages.

In Houston, Texas, French, German, or Spanish are taught to more than 6000 elementary pupils in Grades 3 through 7.

In Denver, Colorado, more than 3000 pupils in 87 elementary schools are studying Spanish or French, mostly in the fifth and sixth grades. French is taught from first through sixth grade in one school, and Spanish is taught in Grades 4 through 6 in two other schools.

In Sacramento, California, Grades 7 through 12 are favored for teaching foreign languages; however, many elementary schools are introducing foreign languages in Grades 4 and 5.

In Los Angeles, California, Spanish is emphasized because of geographical and historical background. Spanish is taught in all grades in the elementary school. In the secondary school a wide variety of languages is offered.[2]

This cursory examination indicates an emphasis on European languages. The broadening global commitments of the United States since the Second World War have necessitated the training of linguists in the languages of Asia, Africa, and the Pacific islands. These have been largely ignored by educational institutions.

Yet today Asia alone contains as many people as the entire world contained half a century ago. In the rapidly shrinking world where boundaries that were once recognized as barriers are fast disappear-

[2] Gene Currivan, "Languages Gain in Lower Grades," *The New York Times*, March 20, 1960, Sec. I, p. 69.

ing, it becomes essential that the study of foreign languages in the elementary school be considered more than a fad, an extra, or a frill subject. We must realize that changes in the curriculum have to be made in terms of the world that children will live in, not the culture of the past several years.

## Point of View

Widely evident today is the increasing interest in teaching foreign languages in the elementary school. There is a growing belief that a primary purpose of education is to help individuals live with other peoples in a world become smaller and more interdependent, and with a more mobile population. There is a greater need for improved cooperation, mutual understanding and respect, and positive human relations.

The school has a responsibility for teaching its youth to understand and respect the culture, attitudes, and feelings of foreign peoples. Development of skill in communication is an important step in this direction. In the elementary school curriculum the integration of learning experiences that include both a knowledge of a foreign culture and a study of the language might well contribute to improved international good will.

Advocates of such a program would "require the introduction of a modern language in the elementary school and its continuation for from six to ten years — through high school and college. Every youngster of average intelligence would thus be assured of a reading, writing, and speaking knowledge of at least one foreign language by the time he is graduated from high school. . . . There is nothing visionary about such an objective when one considers that many smaller and less prosperous nations succeed in equipping their young people with not one but several languages."[3]

Proponents of the foreign-language program are convinced that

1. Only by an early start can language mastery be assured.
2. Preadolescents can learn a foreign language without self-consciousness. They are free of the inhibitions of the adult learner.

[3] Jacob Ornstein, "The Crisis in Language Training," *Education Digest*, 25:26, 27, May 1960.

3. The early start instills respect for other people and fosters tolerance.

4. Appreciably more children will be eager to study a foreign language later on.

5. The student who began early will be much farther along in high school and college.[4]

There are problems to be considered in introducing a foreign-language program in the elementary schools:

1. Which language or languages should be offered?
2. What approach should be used?
3. What guiding principles may be utilized?
4. What instructional procedures and materials are effective?
5. How shall sequence and continuity be provided?
6. When should the foreign language be introduced?
7. How shall time be provided for teaching the language?
8. Who shall learn foreign languages?
9. Who should teach the languages?
10. What is the role of the parent in the foreign-language program?
11. How shall the program be evaluated?

## Determining Which Language to Offer

One of the most perplexing problems is what language or languages should be offered in the elementary school. The selection may be made on the basis of (1) the staff, the curriculum, the community resources, (2) a survey of the community and its need for skill in a particular language, (3) languages most used in international affairs, (4) ease of learning the language.

The abilities and skills of the teacher are particularly important in determining the language to be taught. Unless a school can provide a teacher who by birth or training speaks the language "like a native" the child will not gain in the ability to speak. If he learns to speak in an unidiomatic, mispronounced version of the language, he will never be an effective ambassador of good will. In such a situation, the program should be delayed until someone with skills in the lan-

---

[4] Theodore Huebener, *How to Teach Foreign Languages Effectively* (New York: New York University Press, 1959), pp. 167–168.

guage is available. In the meantime, children may gain some measure of acquaintance with the culture of the country, listen to recordings of its music, and have other incidental experiences. These, however, are no substitute for learning to speak and understand another language.

A second consideration in selection is the community. In certain communities French is the native language for the majority of the population (in Louisiana, for example, and some Canadian border regions). Spanish, on the other hand, is spoken in many of our southwestern communities, where it is natural that Spanish be given a prominent place in the schools. German is spoken by large numbers of residents in some cities, including Milwaukee, Cincinnati, Cleveland, Indianapolis, and Baltimore. The cultural heritage of these people has been kept alive in large part by the introduction of the German language into the school system.

Russian is winning a significant place in the college and university curriculum on the basis of the importance of Russia as a world power. In view of the fact that a majority of the peoples of the world speak languages other than French, Spanish, and German — the most commonly selected languages in the elementary curriculum — the question arises: Are we selecting the right languages?

The third consideration is that of the language most used in international affairs. Many international conferences are conducted in English and French. "Of the other official languages of the United Nations — Spanish, Russian, and Chinese — Spanish is spoken by the smallest number of people (120 million) but it has real international importance by virtue of its broad geographical distribution."[5]

The 85th Congress passed the National Defense Education Act, which authorized a total of $887,000,000 to be utilized for a four-year program of development of science, mathematics, and foreign-language training. Under this act six languages for which students are to receive stipends to study, because these are the ones for which there is the most urgent national need, are Arabic, Chinese, Hindi, Japanese, Portuguese, and Russian.[6]

A fourth consideration in selecting the language to be learned is

[5] Theodore Andersson, *The Teaching of Foreign Languages in the Elementary School* (Boston: D. C. Heath and Company, 1953), p. 21.

[6] Marie Fraser, "Modern Language Dilemma," *The Indiana Teacher*, 103:432, May 1959.

ease of learning. Children without previous exposure to a second language, in general, find Spanish and French easier to learn than they do German. "In a survey of languages offered, 322 schools offered French, 461 Spanish, 42 German, 10 Japanese, Slavic or Norwegian."[7] In an analysis of the third year of French in an elementary school, Dunkel and Pillet state that "when both French and German were available eleven pupils who had begun German were allowed to shift to French."[8] The structure of the German language is difficult for the child. Problems of word order, intonation, and pronunciation appear to many children to be greater in German than in Spanish or French. Motivation, maturity level, language aptitude, skill of the teacher, and methods of teaching and instructional materials, however, influence the ease with which children learn a second language.

## *Approach to be Used*

Another problem relates to the skills to be emphasized and is a matter of the approach used in teaching a foreign language.

*The Culture-Focused Approach.* How the teacher goes about introducing children to a foreign language depends upon the objectives of the program. If the objectives are primarily concerned with cultural values — learning about the life and customs of the peoples — the method of teaching will reflect these purposes. If, on the other hand, the objectives are command of the language, proficiency in reading, and background for further study at a higher level, the method will reflect them.

Hoppock and Miel[9] advocate informal contacts with several languages and cultures to make children aware that people every-

---

[7] Elizabeth Henson, "What About Teaching a Second Language to Elementary Children?" *Childhood Education*, 34:368, April 1958.

[8] Harold B. Dunkel and Roger A. Pillet, "A Third Year of French in the Elementary School," *Elementary School Journal*, 59:265, February 1959.

[9] Modern Language Association of America, *Childhood and Second Language Learning*, Foreign Language Bulletin No. 49 (New York: The Association, 1956), p. 9.

Alice Miel, "Does Foreign Language Belong in the Elementary School?" *Teachers College Record*, 56:139–148, December 1954.

where communicate common experiences by means of different sound symbols. In programs of this type the way of life and the culture of the people who speak the language are emphasized. Children get a picture of the way of life of boys and girls whose language they are trying to learn. They sing the songs and dance the dances, play the games and listen to stories about children who speak other languages. The customs, traditions, mores, and geography of the country may be stressed, and learning the language is incidental — no serious attempt is made to give the child a command of the language.

*The Audio-Lingual Approach.* In this approach four basic communication skills are progressively emphasized: the ability to comprehend, to speak, to read, and finally to write the language. Teaching a foreign language is more effective if the teacher follows the natural pattern for developing the communication skills. The child listens before he speaks, speaks before he reads, and reads before he writes. The wise teacher teaches him *first* to understand the spoken language, *second* to express himself orally in the language, *third* to read the language, and *fourth* to write it.

The children learn the language by hearing and speaking it. In most cases they have two or three years of audio-lingual teaching before they are introduced to reading and writing the language. This is consistent with the way children learn any language. They hear, see, associate objects and actions with sounds, repeat, imitate, and finally speak. They learn the second language as they learn the native tongue.

Not until much later do they get into the complexities of grammar and construction. Not until they have considerable experience in speaking do they begin to read the language. Facility in oral expression is a prerequisite for reading. Writing in the foreign language follows considerable experience in speaking and reading.

"The formation of language habits is the same for foreign language as it is for the native language: practice, correction, practice. It is through stages of recognition, imitation, repetition, variation, and selection."[10]

*The Dual-Emphasis Approach.* A third approach is that in which

[10] Patricia O'Connor and W. F. Twaddell, "Intensive Training for an Oral Approach in Language Teaching," Monograph, *Modern Language Journal,* Part 2, 44:4, February 1960.

the dual aspects of language — skills and culture — are integrated. This approach progressively broadens the child's horizon through the introduction to a new mode of communication and a new culture pattern simultaneously. It combines

1. The acquisition of a set of *skills*, which can become real mastery for professional use when practised long enough. . . . These skills include:
   a. The increasing ability to understand a foreign language when spoken, making possible greater profit and enjoyment in such steadily expanding activities as foreign travel, business abroad, foreign language movies and broadcasts at home and abroad.
   b. The increasing ability to *speak* the foreign language in direct communication with people of another culture, whether for business or pleasure.
   c. The ability to *read* the foreign language with progressively greater ease and enjoyment. . . .
2. A new understanding of *language*, progressively revealing to the pupil the *structure* of language and giving him a new perspective on English.
3. A gradually expanding and deepening knowledge of a foreign country — its geography, history, social organization, literature, and culture — and, as a consequence, a better perspective on American culture.[11]

As the child studies the culture of another people through contacts with individuals of foreign extraction in the local community, through contacts with the objects of culture of the country — the music, the art — and through films and other audio-visual media, he develops an understanding of other people. An effective foreign-language program in the elementary school should be concerned both with the development of a greater understanding and other-culture-mindedness and with the acquisition of linguistic skills. It is highly questionable that emphasis upon the skills alone will contribute toward world-mindedness. "Out of our personal, school, social and community relationships with foreign peoples should come the mutual need, desire and willingness to learn another's language."[12]

[11] William R. Parker, "A Discussion Guide and Work Paper," *The National Interest and Foreign Languages* (Washington, D.C.: Government Printing Office, preliminary ed., April 1954).
[12] Elizabeth E. Thompson and Arthur E. Hamalainen, *Foreign Language Teaching in Elementary Schools* (Washington: Association for Supervision and Curriculum Development, NEA, 1958), p. 23.

Children who are introduced to a second language through the dual-emphasis approach have the benefit of the best aspects of each of the other two approaches. Not only do they learn the skills of communicating in the second language but they learn about the people of the country whose language they are studying. Every child who is privileged to explore another's culture and speak another's language opens a door that leads to greater understanding and enriched appreciation throughout a lifetime.

## Guiding Principles

The teacher must begin where the *child* is, not where *he* is in ability to use the language. He must establish rapport with the class and create a climate in which the learning of the language is purposeful and has meaning. This he can do by capitalizing on the children's innate love of new words, by establishing a "climate of sound," by creating appropriate visual impressions, by translating as much as possible of the second language into actions, by relating foreign language to the other curriculum areas, and by using meaningful evaluation procedures.

*Capitalizing on the Child's Innate Love of New Words.* Young children are intrigued with words. Listen to a preschool child as he makes up new words and uses old words in new combinations. He is interested in the flow of language. He likes to experiment. He is not self-conscious about expressing himself orally. He may not even know what the words mean, but he likes to say them — especially those that run trippingly off the tongue. He is eager to learn new words and uses them regardless of the language in which they are expressed. The teacher capitalizes on this fluency.

*Creating a "Climate of Sound."* Children are quickly oriented to a different environment. In observing American children in a foreign country, it is interesting to note how soon they are at home in a world of strange sounds and experiences. Where adults seem confused and bewildered by the strange sounds, children enjoy them. Consequently, they easily fall into the behavior pattern of the natives and absorb foreign words. They find themselves adapting to the new environment and begin in a short time to communicate in the new language. Children in a bilingual or multilingual environment move from one language to another as the need arises.

A child who is exposed to two or three languages during the ideal period for language beginning, pronounces each with the accent of his teacher. If he hears one language at home, another at school, and a third, perhaps, with a governess in the nursery, he is not aware that he is learning three languages at all. He is aware of the fact that to get what he wants with the governess he must speak one way, and with his teacher he must speak in another way. He does not reason it out at all. There is no French, no German, no English. It is simpler than that. Although the cortico-thalamic speech mechanism serves all three languages and there is no evidence of anatomical separation, nevertheless, there is a curiously effective automatic switch that allows each individual to turn from one language to another.[13]

*Speaking Only in the Foreign Language.* "Ideally, the best way to create the new climate of sound is for a teacher who speaks the second language natively to speak nothing but this language."[14] Carlos Rivera,[15] who describes vividly the technique he uses in the first grade, follows this principle by speaking only Spanish to the children.

One reason many teachers fail to speak in the foreign tongue is that they are, unfortunately, inadequately prepared. They know a few simple phrases and they can teach a specific lesson, but they have only a slight knowledge of the language. The child imitates the teacher's inaccurate Spanish. He commits to memory a few isolated French words that he will forget during the summer. He may take a trip and try out his language hoping to communicate, but how disappointed he is to discover that the natives do not understand him because he is speaking a garbled version of their language. The most effective teacher is one who knows the language and speaks it like a native, or a native who knows not only the language but how to teach children.

[13] Wilder Penfield and Lamar Roberts, *Speech and Brain-Mechanisms* (Princeton: Princeton University Press, 1959), p. 253.

[14] Andersson, *op. cit.*, p. 51.

[15] Carlos Rivera, "The Teaching of Spanish in the First Grade of the El Paso Public Schools," *Hispania*, 36:452–457, November 1952.

It is not always possible to have the services of a teacher whose native language is the one being learned. It is, however, possible to make use of such aids as radio, television, tape, wire, and disk recordings, sound films, and records accompanying basal textbook series. Even here, the climate of sound is largely the problem of the teacher, who should provide a constant example of correct speech in the language being learned.

*Creating Appropriate Visual Impressions.* The teacher should present not only the correct speech sounds in the language but also the gestures, movements, and general behavior that accompany the speaking. The eye is as important in learning the language as the ear. The children observe the teacher closely as he speaks the new language. They watch his mouth, his face, his gestures, his total behavior. Then they try to imitate it. Imitation plays an important role in learning a new language, and the primary child is uninhibited as he absorbs this behavior through observing the speaker.

*Tranlating the Language into Action.* Children are naturally creative. They dramatize every situation possible — stories, greetings, songs, games, native dances. They like, too, to dramatize life in other countries making use of their new-found vocabulary. They like to listen to stories about children in the other lands so that their representations of them will be authentic. They like to watch movies of the life of these children. They become interested through such activities in the culture of the people whose language they are studying.

*Relating Foreign Language to Other Curriculum Areas.* The opportunities for relating foreign languages to the social studies, the language arts, and the creative arts are numberless. In social studies there are many questions to investigate: How do the children of another country live? What are their homes like? What are their schools like? What games do they play? How do they celebrate their holidays? What songs do they sing? What foods do they eat?

In the language arts children are learning to express themselves through speaking. They tell about familiar experiences and everyday activities in English. They may begin to tell about these things and dramatize them in the second language. Learning to speak and understand the language before the written symbols are introduced is a sound approach to the second language.

## Instructional Procedures and Materials

"The human ear is still the best all-around instrument for language learning, and certainly the one most extensively used. The contribution of modern science to the language picture lies largely in the invention of tools and instruments that help supplement the ear."[16]

Language is primarily an oral means of communication. Consequently, the methods and materials used emphasize the audio-lingual approach in the learning experiences. Examples of classes in foreign language reveal this emphasis.

*A Second-Grade French Class.*   The teacher enters the classroom speaking French. The children are eagerly awaiting her arrival.

TEACHER:  Bonjour, mes enfants.
CHILDREN:  Bonjour, madame.
TEACHER:  Bien, bien, mes enfants. Today I will practice questions with you. Each of you will have a turn to reply.
TEACHER:  Bonjour, mes enfants.
CHILDREN:  Bonjour, madame.
TEACHER:  Comment allez-vous?
CHILDREN:  Très bien, merci. Et vous?
TEACHER:  Très bien, merci.
TEACHER:  Bonjour, Marie.
MARIE:  Bonjour, madame.
TEACHER:  Comment vas-tu?
MARIE:  Très bien, merci.
TEACHER:  Comment va ta mère?
MARIE:  Elle va bien, merci.
*(Each child is asked a simple question and is given opportunity to respond.)*
TEACHER:  We will now review counting to ten.
  Un, deux, trois, quatre, cinq, six, sept, huit, neuf, dix.
*(The class responds in unison twice.)*
TEACHER:  Nous chantons.
    Frère Jacques, frère Jacques,
    Dormez-vous, dormez-vous?

[16] Mario Pei, *Language for Everybody* (New York: The Devin-Adair Company, 1956), p. 114.

Sonnez les matines, sonnez les matines,
Din, din, don. Din, din, don.
(*The entire class sings with great enthusiasm.*)
TEACHER: Comment tu t'appelles?
CHILDREN: Je m'appelle Marie, Jean (*and so forth.*) (*Each child answers as the teacher nods to him.*)
TEACHER: Marie, as-tu une sœur?
MARIE: Oui, madame, j'ai une sœur.
TEACHER: Marie, as-tu un frère?
MARIE: Oui, madame, j'ai un frère.
TEACHER: Paul, as-tu une sœur?
PAUL: Non, madame, je n'ai pas de sœur.
TEACHER: Paul, as-tu un frère?
PAUL: Non, madame, je n'ai pas de frère.
(*The teacher asks each child a question.*)

The children ended the lesson by playing the game "Chaud ou Froid." One child was chosen to be "it" and was sent from the room while the rest chose an object. Then the child was called back into the room and the others guided him in his search by saying "Tu as chaud" or "Tu as froid," depending on whether he was near (chaud) or far (froid) from the object selected. Among the objects from which the children chose were: le crayon, le livre, le tableau, l'image, la fenêtre, la porte, le plafond. They were able to identify these words as pencil, book, blackboard, picture, window, door, ceiling.

The teacher always began the class by running the gamut of salutations and questions. She tried to plan for a song, a game, and some conversation practice, as well as for the introduction of new vocabulary.

### A French Lesson with Fourth-Grade Pupils

The teacher began the lesson by greeting the class in French and asking a few simple questions. The class answered these in concert and then several pupils answered individually.

Next, the teacher explained the reason for the vocabulary which appeared on the front board and which was entitled *La Cuisine Française*. She had written the chef of the Restaurant Louis XIV for a bill of fare and for some recipes. The chef had sent these and now the class was making a study of the menu.

As the teacher pointed to each word she pronounced it and the class repeated it in concert. In a number of instances she brought in very interesting cultural references. In connection with *bouilla-baisse* she elicited that this soup was made in Marseille, the largest port in southern France, from which ships sailed to Africa. One pupil was called upon to explain just what *crêpe suzette* was.

Next, various pupils were called on to point out objects in the room and to perform simple actions. A boy went to the door, opened it, closed it, and sat down again. The class showed the teacher their rulers, their pencils, their notebooks, etc. The teacher employed such expressions as *montrez-moi, touchez, où est, donnez-moi*, etc.

The masculine and feminine forms of the definite article were distinguished. The teacher also asked, "From what language does French really come? What kind of Latin did the Roman soldiers speak?" Then she introduced the class to a little elementary etymology, explaining the derivation of *tête* from the Latin *testa* (bean), the humor in back of the word, and the significance of the circumflex accent. She also discussed the relationship of French to English.

The form *j'ai* was then reviewed. A lively exercise in oral composition resulted when the pupils were asked to say something about their family. Many of them contributed, beginning their sentences with *j'ai*. The teacher then used the blackboard to illustrate the use of *a* as the third person of the verb, without, however, using any grammatical nomenclature. She used the model sentence, "Marie a une mère." While paper was being passed out, six pupils were sent to the front board and six to the rear. The teacher dictated three sentences as follows:

"Je m'appelle . . ."

"J'ai un père et une mère."

"Qui a trois livres?"

The sentences on the board were quite correct except for the last word. Evidently the pupils were not yet familiar with the plural. The teacher explained it to them. After going over the board work and commenting on the significance of the apostrophe and the grave accent, the teacher had the class sing a French song.

*Comments.* The teacher's lively manner and her skill in employing a wide variety of exercises made this a very interesting lesson. Precision pronunciation was insisted on, although the teacher did not demand too much in this regard. Grammatical terminology was dispensed with. The children learned forms and constructions as if they were vocabulary.[17]

[17] Huebener, *op. cit.*, pp. 172–173.

*A Fifth-Grade French Class.*[18]   These children come from three schools to the language laboratory for their class in French. They are selected on the basis of IQ tests. However, their teacher is emphatic in the belief that test scores alone are inadequate for screening.

TEACHER:   Bonjour, mes enfants.
CHILDREN:   Bonjour, madame.
TEACHER:   Voici une boîte. Odine, ouvre la boîte et compte les bonbons.
(*Odine opens the box and counts the pieces of candy.*)
TEACHER:   Combien de bonbons y a-t-il?
ODINE:   Il y a seize bonbons.
TEACHER:   Combien de bonbons jaunes y a-t-il?
ODINE:   Il y a six bonbons jaunes.
TEACHER:   Combien de bonbons sont verts?
ODINE:   Trois bonbons sont verts.
TEACHER:   Qui veut un bonbon jaune?
ODINE:   Moi. Je veux un bonbon jaune.
TEACHER:   Qui veut un bonbon vert?
ODINE:   Je veux un bonbon vert.
TEACHER:   Maintenant, ouvrez la bouche, fermez les yeux. Je donne un bonbon à Jean, un bonbon vert à Suzanne, un bonbon noir à Simone. Moi aussi, j'aime les bonbons, j'ouvre la bouche et je mange un bonbon jaune. (*When this review exercise is completed the teacher continues the next part of the lesson.*)

*Songs*

TEACHER:   Aujourd'hui nous apprenons une nouvelle chanson amusante. Ecoutez-moi bien. Cette chanson est aussi une danse. Attention, écoutez les paroles.

Les filles demandent:   Quand allons-nous nous marier?
Nous marier, nous marier?
Quand allons-nous nous marier?
Mon cow-boy adoré.

Les garçons répondent:   On s'mariera dimanche prochain,
Dimanche prochain, dimanche prochain.
On s'mariera dimanche prochain,
Ma petite fille adoreé.

In playing this singing game the girls form a line holding hands. The boys form another line facing the girls. When the girls sing

[18] Observation of fifth-grade French class, St. Louis, Mo., Public Schools. Jeanne H. Brossard, teacher.

they advance and the boys retreat. When the boys sing it is their turn to advance while the girls retreat. The song seemed to embarrass some of the pupils so the teacher said they probably would omit this particular song when there are visitors in the future.

### Conversation

TEACHER: Regardez! Voici une montre. Voici la grande aiguille et la petite aiguille. Nous allons dire l'heure.
TEACHER: Robert, quelle heure est-il?
ROBERT: Il est une heure.
TEACHER: Charles, quelle heure est-il?
CHARLES: Il est deux heures.
TEACHER: Jean, quelle heure est-il?
JEAN: Il est midi.
TEACHER: Jean à quelle heure vas-tu à l'école?
JEAN: Je vais à l'école à huit heures.
TEACHER: A quelle heure bois-tu ton verre de lait, Françoise?
FRANÇOISE: Je bois mon verre de lait à sept heures.
*(Several children are chosen to set the hands of the clock and ask the children in the group the time of day signified by the hands of the clock.)*

The group reviewed the numbers from 1 to 50.

TEACHER: Nous allons compter de un à cinquante. Un, deux, trois, quatre, cinq, six, sept, huit, neuf, dix, onze, douze, treize, quatorze, quinze, seize, dix-sept, dix-huit, dix-neuf, *vingt*, vingt et un, vingt-deux, vingt-trois, vingt-quatre, vingt-cinq, vingt-six, vingt-sept, vingt-huit, vingt-neuf, *trente*, trente et un, trente-deux, trente-trois, trente-quatre, trente-cinq, trente-six, trente-sept, trente-huit, trente-neuf, *quarante*, quarante et un, quarante-deux, quarante-trois, quarante-quatre, quarante-cinq, quarante-six, quarante-sept, quarante-huit, quarante-neuf, *cinquante*. Très bien!

As soon as the group had practiced these numbers they used them in playing number lotto. The teacher had prepared large cards divided into squares, one card for each child. Some of the squares contained numbers of which the children had learned the French names. The teacher had a full set of the numbers on squares of cardboard of the same size as the squares on the large cards. She put them all in a bag and picked one out. The child on whose card the number appeared asked for the square and placed it on the corresponding square on his card. The one who first succeeded in covering all the numbers on his card was the winner. (This can also be played with objects instead of numbers.) The game appeared to be one of the favorites of the children.

The teacher created a situation that aroused pupil interest in finding out something new. She made certain that she had the attention of the group and the materials needed to satisfy the curiosity aroused in the children. She showed appreciation for the efforts of the children and praised them for good work. She tried to involve everyone in the learning process, not just the bright ones. As Miss Brossard expressed it, "I want to draw French out of my pupils. I want them to want to say something badly enough so that they will take the trouble to think out the answer and supplement it with dictionary work and reading on their own. Praise and sometimes extra points (in games) are given if the answer or comment in conversation is very original. I try to create this desire to speak in French by discussing controversial subjects; favorite things to read, to do, to eat; or vacation and week-end activities. I try to give careful thought to my daily lesson plan in order to challenge each pupil and not to overtax a pupil."[19]

MacRae[20] makes some helpful suggestions relative to the effective teaching of Spanish. She suggests that one timesaver is a lesson plan that provides for consistent practice, integrates review and new material, and indicates the next step forward. She has provided daily lesson plans for a full year of Spanish in her program, *Spanish in the Grades*, Book One, Book Two, Teachers' Editions (Boston: Houghton Mifflin Company, 1960, 1961).

DESIGN FOR DAILY LESSON PLAN

The introductory part of the lesson should be a brief conversation that reviews useful phrases: "¿Estamos listos, niños? Vamos a hablar español, clase," instead of "Let's get ready for our Spanish lesson." Quite naturally, then, comes "¿Cómo están ustedes, niños?" and the children make individual responses. It is well to keep using these

[19] Jeanne H. Brossard, teacher in elementary school French, St. Louis, Mo., Public Schools. Mimeographed manuscript discussing the philosophy and method used in teaching French to fifth-graders in St. Louis.
[20] Margit W. MacRae, *Teaching Spanish in the Grades* (Boston: Houghton Mifflin Company, 1957), pp. 208, 209.

phrases at the beginning of each Spanish period as a warm-up and as an opportunity to check responses until they become a part of the active vocabulary and are used spontaneously whenever the situation seems to call for it.

The main part of the lesson should be connected with something that has preceded it. A review game that ties into the new material makes a smooth transition. Games whet the children's interest in the language.

The last part of the lesson should provide a hook or connection for next day's practice as well as enough slowing down in tempo to permit whatever comes next on the day's agenda to begin smoothly. Classroom teachers frequently complain that special teachers of foreign language, music, or art leave the children at such a high pitch at the close of a class period that it takes fifteen minutes to "settle them down."

The planning of a lesson is vital. However, it is important to recognize that the plan must be flexible enough to allow modification. Basic to a successful program is a lesson plan that provides for consistency in practice, integrates the old with the new, indicates the next step to be taken, and makes use of instructional materials that carry the lesson forward.

## INSTRUCTIONAL MATERIALS

Among the modern devices that have wide application in language learning are the record player and the tape or wire recorder. A student cannot have his teacher with him at all times. He can, however, make use of one of these devices for learning a new language. Not only can he hear the language spoken correctly, but he can compare his pronunciation with that of the speaker and determine the extent of progress.

Such tools are concerned primarily with the language sounds. Vocabulary, grammatical forms, and the uses and meanings of words must be left to the ingenuity of the teacher. Audio-visual materials — records, films, tapes, television — and songs, rhymes, stories, and games all play their part in arousing and maintaining interest in the new language. The sense of achievement that comes from "catching on" keeps interest high. Without this growing interest the introduction of a foreign-language program is doomed to failure. With it, success is more nearly assured.

Finding suitable materials presents almost as great a problem as finding qualified teachers. Among the workable teaching aids are pictures, films, and film strips based on the daily life in the country whose language children are studying and on its literary works. The classroom audio aids motivate learning. Supplementary listening and individual recordings contribute toward further development of language skills and understanding. In addition, radio and television, either as supplementary learning experiences or as part of the instructional pattern, are resources to be used.

The use of electronic devices is steadily growing. In many cases the total foreign-language program through the elementary grades is presented via television. Flexibility must be maintained even in such programs and provisions made for individual differences or the program defeats its purpose. Two questions well worth asking about teaching aids are: "Are teaching aids used without loss of the interpersonal relationships so important in the teaching-learning process? Are appropriate provisions made to provide for individual differences?"

> There is still a considerable difference of opinion as to what constitutes a foreign language lab. The equipment is of many types and combinations and it is used in various ways. The germ of the laboratory was the use of phonograph records and films for instructional purposes. It was not, however, until the organization of the courses of the Army Specialized Training Program that one could speak of a laboratory proper. . . .
>
> The chief value of the laboratory is that it trains students to listen, to distinguish differences in sounds, and to imitate a model.
>
> The laboratory now usually consists of mechanical equipment by means of which the student hears and repeats material recorded in the foreign language. He listens through earphones, repeats sentence by sentence through a microphone, and records his voice on a disc or on a tape. Later he plays back his own recording and simultaneously listens to the model. In this way he can make comparisons of his own voice with that of the model. Great reliance has to be placed on the student's ability to criticize his own performance. In some laboratories the teacher circulates, listens to the student's voice, and suggests corrections. In other setups there is a monitoring system which is centrally controlled.[21]

In addition to audio devices, a laboratory is equipped with visual aids, including a motion-picture projector, slide and film-strip pro-

[21] Huebener, *op. cit.*, p. 125.

jector, screen and other mechanical devices which facilitate visual presentation of material. Combination slide and film-strip projectors are available.

A good radio set with FM and short-wave facilities is another integral part of the language laboratory. Television, too, is important.

Mead interjects a word of caution to those who consider the language laboratory the panacea for teaching foreign language effectively: ". . . A word of warning about language laboratories must be inserted by one who actually promoted their establishment. They are rapidly becoming gimmicks, run frequently by individuals whose mastery of spoken foreign language displays singularly little benefit from the use of tape recorders and who seldom have an intelligent interest in the countries whose language are represented on the tapes."[22]

Hirsch points out: "Only a great deal of research and cooperation will make possible the development of effective audio-visual aids. The advances in technology, the study of language by linguists, the experience of language teachers, the result of psychologic research, all these can contribute and should be utilized."[23]

The important factor to consider in the use of materials for improving the teaching of foreign language in the elemenetary school is the teacher's willingness to make use of audio-visual equipment and materials. A survey made by the National Education Association in 1957 showed, for example, that about 50 per cent of the teachers did not feel confident in their ability to use audio-visual materials or equipment.[24] This situation is being improved through opportunity for in-service training. If the teacher is willing to accept new types of equipment as they become available, though at first they may disturb the customary procedure and serve him rather awkwardly as he is learning to use them effectively, he will find that they may become important — even indispensable — tools later.

There is no doubt that the audio-visual aids to teaching a foreign language — especially instruction by radio and television — and the

---

[22] Robert G. Mead, "Notes and News," *Hispania*, 43:98, March 1960.

[23] Ruth Hirsch, *Audio-Visual Aids in Language Teaching*, Monograph Series on Language and Linguistics, Institute of Language and Linguistics (Washington, D.C.: Georgetown University Press, March 1954), p. 52.

[24] National Education Association, *The Status of the American Public School Teacher*, Research Bulletin 35 (Washington, D.C.: NEA, 1957), pp. 30, 57.

effective use of language laboratories can help the skilled teacher do an even better job of teaching. As teachers receive the cooperation of the administration in providing adequate laboratory equipment the introduction of foreign language in the elementary program will become more meaningful and effective.

If teaching machines and language laboratories are to serve a real purpose and facilitate the learning of languages the objectives of the program must be kept uppermost in mind. William Alexander, as president of the Association of Supervision and Curriculum Development, suggested that ". . . If we are smart enough to utilize automation and electronic equipment where it is appropriate in large groups, and where it helps in providing a variety of experiences for different individuals, if we capitalize on these new developments for good ends, then we can free ourselves to work with children and provide genuinely individualized education. But if we somehow forget about the human element, the need in teaching for a warm, friendly child-adult relationship, then these new developments will not be good for education."[25]

## Sequence and Continuity

There are many blueprints for foreign-language programs. Although no "model" course fits the needs of every school system, a plan is called for if progress is to be made. A teacher who worked in an experimental French program with fifth-graders, in which there was no outline for the course, found it difficult to provide for continuity and sequence in learning. To plan the daily program to meet individual needs of the children, adjust to their growing vocabulary, and fill in the weak spots required hours of planning which should have been done before the program started. The teacher left to the pupils the problem of deciding what they wanted to learn, what suggestions they had for the next experiences, and what they most enjoyed. This particular group liked games best; but they felt that if they had had a textbook or a specific outline of graded exercises and activities they could have profited more from

[25] Robert S. Gilchrist, "Promising Practices in Education, II," *Phi Delta Kappan*, 41:272, March 1960.

the first year. "Next fall," remarked this teacher, after a purely experimental year, "I'm going to give a review for a week or two and then test to determine their level for the beginning of the second year. I plan to use an outline and they will have textbooks so they know where they are going and so will I. I will continue, however, with the variety of experiences — games, songs, oral reports, making maps and charts of the provinces, reading French newspapers, and answering questions about the country."

To provide for sequence in the primary grades MacRae suggests a brief list of learning experiences on which her program of teaching Spanish is built:

*Sequence of Learning Experiences*

*Hearing* the new language in meaningful patterns (familiar folk tales, dialogues, riddles, songs, rhymes).

*Imitating* the new sounds by rote (counting, singing, repeating rhymes).

*Speaking* the new language in meaningful situations (dramatizing stories, using dialogues in classroom activities, playing language games, answering riddles).

*Recombining* vocabulary thus acquired in class-originated oral experience stories.

*Recognizing* the written symbols for sounds already completely familiar in spoken situations.

*Reading* in whole patterns (workbooks based on oral vocabulary, oral experience stories recorded by the teachers).

*Continuing* the learning of new words by ear and by context to develop independence in aural discrimination. (Constant repetition of known phrases without the need to listen for new words will retard growth in comprehension and original expression.)[26]

In providing sequence the teacher should take into consideration what is known about the way children learn and the specific skills that children in a particular elementary school are expected to develop. Sequence should be accomplished within the framework of the content planned for a particular level. While allowing for differences among pupils, at the same time plans should be made for moving ahead. Outlines, syllabi, manuals, textbook series, and planned programs of instruction are valuable in aiding the teacher to solve his problem of what and how much of the foreign language to teach

[26] MacRae, *op. cit.*, p. 25.

and when to teach it. The term "sequence" is used by some to refer to the learner's experience rather than to the order of logically organized subject matter at various grade levels.

## CONTINUITY IN LEARNING EXPERIENCES

One of the problems in language teaching has been that of providing continuity. Pupils have been exposed to a language either too early, too late, or too little. If a program of a second or third language is to succeed it must be planned carefully to assure continuity.

Grew offers suggestions for a ten-year course.[27] He maintains that delaying foreign-language study until the third grade allows the child to become completely adjusted to school and ready to give attention to a second language. Grew would divide the language experiences into three stages, Grades 3, 4, 5, and 6; Grades 7, 8, and 9; and Grades 10, 11, and 12.

Andersson[28] recommends a four-step program from kindergarten through the senior high school: kindergarten through third grade, fourth through sixth, seventh through ninth, and tenth through twelfth. The audio-lingual approach is used for the first two stages. In the second and third grades the children keep notebooks in which to paste cutouts or draw objects or scenes they have discussed in class. In the fourth, fifth, and sixth grades the audio-lingual emphasis continues, but children are taught to read and write as well.

In the final analysis the content and activities will be determined by the experiential background of the children, the skill and background of the teacher, the materials available, and the place of foreign languages in the total school curriculum.

Continuity in the development of the foreign-language program has been sought through the use of various means.

*Special Teachers.* In a program handled by a special teacher the language skills may be carefully and sequentially taught, but language teaching is frequently unrelated to the classroom experiences of the children. The classroom teacher, who perhaps has little if any

[27] James H. Grew, "A French Course for the Modern World," *French Review*, 26:210–215, March 1953.
[28] *Op. cit.*, pp. 37, 38.

knowledge of the language studied, is not present during the lesson and the contacts children have with the language are usually limited to the relatively short periods given by the specialist each week. There is little time for the specialist to know the children or plan with the individual teacher in terms of their interests, needs, and experiences. Here continuity is achieved through the sequential development of skills.

*Cooperation of Specialists and Classroom Teachers.* Ideally the cooperative approach affords a more integrated teaching of language. However, the attempt of the classroom teacher to learn the language with the pupils as they observe and listen to the special teacher is not always worth while. A few interested teachers who are eager to learn the language in order to cooperate with the specialist take adult education classes or avail themselves of other opportunities. This program, too, is beset by difficulties: lack of time, lack of harmony between the teachers, and added responsibilities for both of the teachers involved.

*In-Service Programs.* Special teachers or supervisors may teach not only children but also teachers through an in-service program. The audio-lingual approach is generally used. The teachers cooperate in preparing unit material to be used for each elementary grade level. This plan directly involves the teachers in developing the course of study to be used. As they grow in skill they take over the teaching of the language, making use of materials they developed through the workshop. As the clasroom teachers become competent the responsibility of the special teacher or supervisor decreases. Such a program is successful to the extent that the interest, efforts, and language abilities of the classroom teachers are utilized. A serious problem is that each teacher, regardless of the grade level, has had the same basic preparatory program and consequently the possibility for extending the children's language experiences and abilities is limited.

*The Classroom Teacher Competent in Foreign Language.* This teacher makes foreign language an integral part of the curriculum and can readily relate the program to social studies, art, or music. Children, in addition to having a period in which they learn the language, make use of the language in other areas of the curriculum and throughout the day as the opportunity presents itself. The teacher must be skilled in the foreign language to be taught and plan the learning experiences to provide time for the regular *plus* the added enrichment of the language. This method, although highly desirable, poses the problem of an extra load for an already over-worked classroom teacher.[29]

Perhaps the most feasible solution to the problem of providing an adequate program in the elementary school is that of cooperation between classroom teacher and specialist, supervisor, or consultant so that foreign language may become an integral part of the learning experiences of the children in the school and community.

## Time of Introduction of Course

It is generally accepted that an early beginning aids children in using correct pronunciation and intonation. "The ideal starting point in school for language learning, if one is to take advantage of children's natural gifts, is kindergarten or first grade. This intuitive linguistic power, which has been observed by many students of language, apparently declines steadily from infancy to adolescence."[30]

The ability children have to learn language seems something of a mystery. Gatenby contends, however, "It is no mystery at all, but the natural result of children being placed in such conditions that in order to satisfy their many desires they have to learn certain forms of speech. It seems that children learn not *a* language, but language."[31]

MacRae concurs. "It is generally conceded that the younger the child the more easily he learns to interpret and say new words. While this is probably true, there are other factors which need to be considered in choosing the grade in which to start the second language instruction. If the classroom teachers in kindergarten through second grade have excellent accents, and if the children are

[29] Thompson and Hamalainen, *op. cit.*, pp. 28–30.
[30] Andersson, *op. cit.*, p. 31.
[31] E. V. Gatenby, "Popular Fallacies in the Teaching of Foreign Languages," *English Language Teaching*, Autumn 1952, published by the British Council, quoted from *ibid.*, p. 30.

making satisfactory progress in their primary objectives — adjustment to school living and learning to read their own language — Spanish may begin in these earlier grades."[32]

Arguments advanced in favor of introducing a second language in the third or fourth grade are that it gives the child opportunity to study the new language after he has become adjusted to school. He has already begun to speak and write his own language with some skill, and the printed page makes sense to him. More time is available in the daily program since the school day is frequently longer in the third and fourth grades than in the first or second grade.

On the basis of a three-year expriment with French in the elementary school Dunkel and Pillet state that "Our limited data suggest that the third and fourth grades are better than later grades. Among our pupils who are most proficient in French, the greater number began at the fourth grade. This fact suggests that the level of maturity reached by pupils at this grade best fits our type of course."[33]

Kirch[34] concluded, after teaching German in first, third, and sixth grades, that he would begin in Grade 1 if possible, that he would integrate the instruction with social studies, and that he would prepare the regular teacher to handle the foreign language rather than use a specialist. An examination of the literature points to a trend toward beginning in the third grade.

## Providing *Time to Teach the Language*

Another critical question to be considered in planning the foreign-language program is that of time. The school must decide not only when to initiate the program but also how much time to allow for instruction.

In the elementary school the amount of time allotted to initial work in a foreign language can well determine the type of objectives the teacher can set out to achieve. In a survey[35] reported in 1955 it was

[32] MacRae, *op. cit.*, p. 21.
[33] Dunkel and Pillet, *op. cit.*, p. 265.
[34] Max Kirch, "At What Age Elementary School Language Teaching?" *Modern Language Journal*, 40:399–400, November 1956.
[35] Educational Research Service, *Foreign Language Programs in Elementary Grades*, Dir. No. 6 (Washington, D.C.: American Association of School Administrators and Research Division of the NEA, 1955).

found that generally about 60 to 75 minutes a week were devoted to foreign-language teaching in the elementary schools. The most time reported was 175 minutes and the least was 20 minutes a week. Since the survey was made, it is highly possible that there has been an increase, but perhaps not too great an increase. Obviously the teacher who has less than 100 minutes a week to teach a foreign language is limited. Under such conditions it is no great wonder that criticism of the results is frequent.

Kettlekamp states that "the limitation of time under which many foreign language teachers in the elementary school are working may force them to develop methods more efficient than those being employed by their colleagues abroad. However, even with good teaching a reasonable amount of time is needed to achieve reasonable success."[36]

## Selection of Pupils

Should a second language be offered to all or only to a select few? This question has caused concern to administrators, parents, teachers, and children. Various methods for selecting the pupils for foreign-language classes have been the use of IQ test scores, teacher observation, interest inventory, language aptitude tests. The following arguments are advanced in favor of selectivity: (1) The correlation between high IQ and language aptitude is high. (2) It is believed that the better student is able to take a foreign language in his stride. (3) A gifted student will cover the material more rapidly. (4) The shortage of qualified teachers justifies their assignment to gifted pupils. (5) Budgetary restrictions limit the number who may be taught.

On the other hand, there are arguments opposed to the principle of selectivity: (1) There is no absolute correlation between high IQ and language aptitude. Teachers have discovered that some children with average or below IQ have greater aptitude for language than children of high IQ. Such factors as foreign language in the home, interest in language study, and feeling for language patterns contribute to variation in this area. (2) Selectivity is a renouncement

[36] Gilbert C. Kettlekamp, "The Time Factor in Beginning Foreign Language Classes," *Modern Language Journal*, 44:70, February 1960.

of the democratic principle of equal educational opportunity for all. However, equal opportunity does not necessarily mean the same experiences for every child. Certain children may not profit from foreign-language study and should not be forced to take the subject. (3) Learning experiences should include a knowledge of the country, and even the slow pupil can gain from such a broadening experience.

There is not adequate research to justify limiting the teaching of foreign language to children with high academic intelligence. Supervisors of programs of long standing indicate that children who are slow learners in other curriculum areas are sometimes outstanding in learning to speak a foreign language.

Thus the wisdom of restricting foreign-language study to a select group based on academic intelligence alone might well be questioned. On the other hand, to expect every child to participate in a foreign-language program regardless of interest, need, or ability is foolhardy. Experimental programs in which all children of a given grade level were assigned to participate in learning Spanish, clearly evidenced results of boredom and negative behavior such as inattention and fighting. The following year the program was put on a voluntary basis and the children who participated were able to learn more, develop better habits of concentration, study better, and improve in language skills. The children who were not in the Spanish class were permitted to select activities of their choice in the classroom and likewise profited. It is highly doubtful whether the study of foreign languages by *all* pupils in the elementary grades justifies the cost in terms of loss of self-respect and self-confidence.

The opportunity of choosing to participate in the foreign-language classes has been found to be an effective stimulus. Initially those children who because of their inclination and aptitude choose to participate do much better than those who are required to take the subject. Schools must set up their own criteria for offering a second language. They must plan for grouping pupils in such a way that they profit from the experiences provided. They must gear the teaching methods to the needs, abilities, and interests of the children. Foreign-language programs, like other phases of the curriculum, need to take into consideration the requirements of society, needs of the community, abilities and interests of the children, skills and background of the teachers, resources of the community, and instructional materials.

## Teachers of Foreign Languages

Ideally, the one to teach is the classroom teacher skilled in working with boys and girls and skilled in the foreign language selected. He should have (1) a knowledge of the philosophy and objectives of the school; (2) a knowledge of child development; (3) a broad cultural background; and (4) knowledge, skill, and enthusiasm for the language he is to teach as well as knowledge of the culture, civilization, and history of the country or area the study embraces.

However, to be realistic, not all elementary classroom teachers possess the experiential background and skills listed above. Until they do, it will be necessary to make use of language specialists, consultants, and supervisors to work with them. Summer study abroad, tutoring with a specialist, participating in workshops and extension courses help the teacher gain the required background. Once a community sees the need for launching such a program, once the administration is committed, once the classroom teacher knows he has the support of the community and administration and the concrete help of in-service training, the battle is at least half won.

Campbell,[37] surveying foreign-language teaching in large city school systems, found that (1) teachers lack training in oral proficiency, (2) school systems and state departments did not give direction to foreign-language programs, and (3) teachers felt the need of student and teacher exchanges and travel abroad on sabbatical leaves with adequate pay. Cooperation between high schools and colleges was needed to redesign courses and workshops for the self-improvement of language teachers in the elementary schools.

In surveying the needs of parents, teachers, and pupils who participated in occasional and part-time (after-school) elementary Spanish classes, Borst[38] discovered that parents needed materials to help the children.

[37] Walter H. Campbell, "Self-Improvement for Teachers of Foreign Language," *Clearing House*, January 1955, 277–279.

[38] Roma J. Borst, "A Survey of Needs and a Suggested Program for Parents, Teachers and Pupils in Occasional and Part-Time Elementary School Spanish Classes," doctoral dissertation, University of Wisconsin, 1956.

## *The Role of the Parent*

One of the difficulties encountered in learning foreign languages lies in the lack of opportunity for practicing outside the class. Often there is a considerable time lag before the child has an opportunity or need for applying his language skills to a functional situation. It has been suggested in several studies[39] that if the teaching of a foreign language is to be successful there must be reinforcement and support in the home. Sometimes parents participate in the foreign-language program. When the language is taught via television, parents can easily take the course along with the children. Parents may be involved, too, in teaching the foreign language in the school. A study to test the effect of parental reinforcement on the learning of French sought to answer the following questions: Does a child who is taking French do significantly better if his mother or father is studying the language at the same time? Do children whose parents already know the language learn better than children whose parents know little or no French?

Some thirty children in Grades 4A and 5B participated in the experiment. The two groups were taught by the same teacher — a native of France. Identical materials were used in both groups, and the classes were scheduled for the same length of time — two and a half hours per week for twenty weeks. The method used emphasized the audio-lingual approach. Throughout the experiment the mothers of all children in the experimental group were enrolled in a separate French class taught by the same teacher with the materials adapted for adults.

The results indicated that a parent's studying French at the same time the child was did not influence the child's learning of the language. Neither did the parent's previous knowledge of French have any effect on how well his child learned the language. There was no significant difference between the achievement in the two groups in relation to either of the questions.

[39] *Ibid.* Gertrude Hildreth, "Learning a Second Language in the Elementary Grades and High School," *Modern Language Journal*, 63:136–141, March 1959. Lois G. Mardell, "How Parents Can Help Teach Reading," *School and Community*, 45:17–22, November 1958.

One of the problems encountered was the self-conscious attitude of the parents toward learning a foreign language. Another was the competitiveness between child and parent in a number of cases. A third arose from the difference in the teaching materials and the failure to relate the parents' lessons to those of the children.[40]

Parents can help children through encouraging them to practice the new language outside the classroom even if they themselves have no skill in it. Very often the greatest contribution the parent can make is in the area of encouragement, interest, and materials. Cooperation between the parent, the foreign-language teacher, and the library can do much toward providing materials that will stimulate greater interest.[41]

## Evaluating the Program

The evaluation of growth in foreign languages must always be on the basis of the objectives to be achieved. Children should be aware of the basis upon which evaluation is determined. Performance in pronunciation, oral comprehension, fluency in speaking, skill in reading, and ease in taking dictation are among specific skills measured. In addition, some schools attempt to appraise the less objective factors, such as attitude toward the language program and learning about the culture of the people.

The following objectives were used by one school system as a basis for evaluating growth in teaching Spanish in the elementary school.

1. To awaken in children an interest in another language, in the people who speak it, and in the countries where it is spoken.
2. To relate the work in Spanish to the regular grade work in language, social studies, arithmetic, art, music, and physical education, and so to make it an illumination and enrichment of the regular elementary school program.
3. To help children to acquire an acceptable pronunciation of Spanish words and to enunciate clearly; and thus, indirectly, to contribute to a better use of English. . . .
4. To introduce children through play activities, songs, and creative

[40] Philip Lambert, "Should Parents Study Languages Too?" *Elementary School Journal*, 60:124–127, December 1959.
[41] Esther M. Eaton, "Foreign Languages and the Library," *School Life*, 42:12–14, January 1960.

dramatization and dialogues to a simple vocabulary of Spanish words and expressions which are directly related to living in the home, in the community, and in the school.

5. To help children to use these words and expressions in ways that have meaning for them, and

6. To help children acquire language skills of value to them in their general education and to help them to improve their thought processes. . . .[42]

*Criteria for Evaluating a Foreign-Language Program.* Much has been written concerning the characteristics of an effective foreign-language program. The following criteria serve to aid in evaluating its effectiveness:

1. The program should be based on a consideration of both general and specific educational aims. Among the general aims are recognition of the role of foreign language study in personal, intellectual, and spiritual development and in the provision for direct cultural experience. The specific educational aims center around the development of skill in speaking and understanding the language.

2. The program should be preplanned to insure continuity and sequence of instruction through Grade 12, regardless of the starting point.

3. There should be a careful cooperative study of all the problems involved by a committee composed of administration, foreign-language teachers, elementary school teachers, and lay representatives of the community. Such study should involve observation of foreign-language programs at this level which have been judged successful by qualified objective individuals.

4. The program should have the same administrative and community support as the rest of the curriculum and be accepted on that basis by the classroom teachers.

5. It should be offered on a grade-wide or educational level basis.

6. Criteria for selection should be established on the basis of pupil interest, scholastic achievement, and recommendation of the classroom teacher.

7. Instruction should be an integral part of the program and given during the regular school day, in a regular school classroom, inside the regular school building.

[42] Carl F. Hansen, *A Guide for the Teaching of Spanish in the Elementary Schools* (Washington, D.C.: Board of Education, Public Schools of the District of Columbia, 1952), p. v.

8. There should be at least four regularly scheduled instruction periods each week.

9. The selection of the language should be determined on the basis of the foreign-language program in the rest of the school district, and with special reference to foreign-language instruction in the junior high school.

10. The instruction should be integrated with other curriculum areas and coordinated with communication skills.

11. The immediate goal should be to understand cultural meanings and to develop skill in speaking the language. This is accomplished through the dual-emphasis approach.

12. The program should follow the developmental sequence of the foreign-language skills.

13. Evaluation should proceed on the same basis as for art, music, and the communication skills.

14. Instruction should be given by the classroom teacher (when qualified) or by a visiting teacher, by a foreign-language teacher, or by any combination of these.

15. All persons teaching the foreign language at this level should have oral command of the language, understand the elementary school child, have a working knowledge of the instructional methods, keep abreast of developments in techniques and materials.

16. Full advantage should be taken of available and suitable television programs, other audio-visual aids, in-service programs, and other resources.

17. Direction of the program should be assigned to a fully competent and qualified foreign-language teacher who sometimes teaches in the program.[43]

*Evaluating the Foreign-Language Class.* In evaluating the foreign-language class the teacher might ask such questions as:

Did I make use of repetition in teaching the new language? The same word, the same expression, the same phrase must be practiced until it becomes automatic.

Did I make use of variety in presenting and reviewing materials? Did I vary the questions, introduce new activities, use different kinds of illustrative materials, and employ new devices?

Did I make use of imitation? Children imitate readily and acquire sounds of another language if they hear them correctly.

[43] Adapted from Paul M. Glaude, "The Establishment of FLES Programs," *Modern Language Journal,* 44:158–159, April 1960.

Much use can be made of chorus response. Spot checking to see that individual children are pronouncing accurately is a good idea.

Did I use the foreign language primarily, but occasionally break into the vernacular to relieve the tension and frustration that results from exclusive use of the foreign language?

Did I start and maintain a brisk tempo for each lesson, keep the atmosphere cheerful, provide a variety of activities. Did I limit a single type of activity or exercise to ten minutes?

Did I employ activities that allow physical expression? Games, dialogues, and creative dramatization combine the spoken word with the appropriate action.

Did I make use of singing or other musical activities? Did I sing at least one song at every lesson? The children prefer a teacher with a good singing voice to singing with a recording.[44]

## *Conclusion*

Interest in introducing foreign languages in the elementary school is growing rapidly. It is logical that the shrinking world in which we live and the growing interdependence of men should be reflected in the demands for a second language. Children acquire skill in language at an early age if they are exposed to a well-planned program under the guidance of a teacher who is skilled in the language and enthusiastic about teaching it.

It is generally conceded that there is a distinct value in teaching foreign languages to children. Problems, however, must be solved in connection with finding the time in an already crowded curriculum and obtaining qualified teachers. Suggestions for solving these and related problems have been explored but not universally adopted.

Integrating the language learnings with other areas of the curriculum has been suggested. However, unless the school works out a program in which the language stands on its own feet as an area worthy of study, the children are likely to learn little that will remain with them through the years. A regularly scheduled program based on a sequence of learning experiences that provides continuity, balance, and scope is essential if progress is to be made.

Decisions as to which language to offer, when to introduce it, and

44 Adapted from Huebener, *op. cit.*, pp. 169–170.

which methods are most effective must be based on the particular school community — its needs and its resources for making the project a success. No final blueprint can be given; a planned program, however, with due consideration for the philosophy and objectives of the school, is of prime importance.

The early years of language learning are audio-lingual centered. Children learn the language as they do their native tongue through hearing, then speaking; not until they get into the intermediate grades do they make a real effort to read and write it. Grammar is taught in the intermediate grades, not in the primary school.

The ideal language program combines interest in the culture with growing ability in the skills of communicating in the second language. It calls for time in the daily schedule, a teacher who is skilled in speaking and using the instructional aids and devices, and parents who will encourage the children and provide books and resources at home. Scope and sequence must be planned; the teacher must be ingenious in developing the program through vital activities that make the language meaningful to the children. Knowledge plus enthusiasm and careful planning will result in a foreign-language program worthy of the name.

"Teachers can do much to improve themselves through independent work at home. Language recordings can be used for continued training in listening to the language. . . .

"Copies of professional magazines should be provided by boards of education through school libraries to teachers who teach foreign languages. Among the commonly used journals are *Modern Language Journal, French Review, Hispania, German Quarterly, Classical Journal,* and *Classical Outlook.*"[45]

ACTIVITIES AND QUESTIONS

1. Trace the development of the foreign-language program in the United States.
2. Discuss some of the major problems in introducing a foreign-language program in the elementary school.

[45] "Teaching Foreign Languages in Illinois," quoted in *Modern Language Journal,* 43:242, May 1959.

3. Observe a school in which foreign language is being taught at the elementary level. How has it met the major problems?

4. Discuss the approaches to a study of a foreign language in the elementary school. On the basis of your reading and observation which approach would you consider most effective? Why?

5. Evaluate one of the lessons illustrated in the text on the basis of the principles suggested in the chapter. Compare the techniques used by the different teachers in motivating the lesson, providing for individual differences, developing the main part of the lesson, and looking forward to the next lesson.

6. Through role playing present to the class a situation in which the principal of a small elementary school announces at a staff meeting that requests have come from the school board to make definite plans for introducing a foreign-language program the following school year.

7. You have been asked to serve on a committee to study the problems of setting up a language laboratory in an elementary school in which the foreign-language program is to be introduced in the fourth grade. What recommendations will you make in regard to minimum equipment and materials?

8. There are differences of opinion as to the feasibility of offering a foreign-language program to every child in the elementary school. What evidence do you find to support the pros and cons of the argument?

9. Define the roles of the classroom teacher, the foreign-language specialist, the parent, and the administrator in providing an effective foreign-language program.

# BIBLIOGRAPHY

Allen, William H. "Spanish and German by Television," *Modern Language Journal*, 40:139–142, March 1956.

Allerton House Conference on Education. *Foreign Language Teaching in Illinois*. Report of the Foreign Language Study Group. Urbana: University of Illinois, 1957.

Andersson, Theodore. *The Teaching of Foreign Languages in the Elementary School*. Boston: D. C. Heath and Company, 1957.

Andersson, Theodore. "The Teaching of a Second Language in the Elementary Schools: Issues and Implications," *Education*, 75:490–497, April 1955.

Barthold, Allen J. "A Blueprint for Foreign Languages in Our Public Schools," *Modern Language Journal*, 41:72–74, February 1957.

Borst, Roma J. "A Survey of Needs and a Suggested Program for Parents, Teachers, and Pupils in Occasional and Part-Time Elementary School Spanish Classes." Doctoral Dissertation, University of Wisconsin, 1956.

Dunkel, Harold B. "A Few Facts About Foreign Language Study," *Elementary School Journal*, 59:31–35, October 1958.

Dunkel, Harold B., and Pillet, Roger A. "A Third Year of French in the Elementary School," *Elementary School Journal*, 59:264–267, February 1959.

Franzen, Carl G. F. *Foreign Language in the Curriculum*. Bulletin of the School of Education. Bloomington: Division of Research and Field Services, Indiana University, 1958.

Heath, Douglas L. *A Language Laboratory: Handbook and Directory for 1956*. Silver Spring, Md.: Language Training Aids, 1956.

Henson, Elizabeth. "What About Teaching a Second Language to Elementary School Children?" *Childhood Education*, 34:367–371, April 1958.

Hirsch, Ruth. *Audio-Visual Aids in Language Teaching*. Monograph Series on Language and Linguistics, No. 5. Washington, D.C.: Georgetown University Press, March 1954.

Huebener, Theodore. *How to Teach Foreign Languages Effectively*. New York: New York University Press, 1959.

Hughes, Marie M., and Sánchez, George I. *Learning a New Language*. Bulletin 101. Washington, D.C.: Association for Childhood Education International, 1958.

Johnston, Marjorie C. "The Urgency of Accelerating the Teaching of Foreign Languages in the New Key," *Modern Language Journal*, 42:163–168, April 1958.

Johnston, Marjorie C., and Remer, Ilo. "References on Foreign Languages in the Elementary School." Circular No. 495, revised. Washington, D.C.: U.S. Department of Health, Education and Welfare, 1959.

Kirch, Max S. "Specialist or Classroom Teacher for FLES?" *Modern Language Journal*, 42:132–135, March 1958.

Kolbert, Jack. "Foreign Language in the Self-Contained Classroom," *Modern Language Journal*, 42:313–316, November 1958.

Kolbert, Jack, and Goldby, Harry. *A First French Handbook for Teachers in Elementary Schools*. Pittsburgh: University of Pittsburgh Press, 1958.

MacEpin, Gary. "The Cultural Need of Foreign Language Competence," *Modern Language Journal*, 43:211–217, May 1959.

McHugh, Mary C. "Teaching Foreign Language in the Elementary Schools," *Chicago Schools Journal*, 39:77–82, November-December 1957.

MacRae, Margit W. *Teaching Spanish in the Grades*. Boston: Houghton Mifflin Company, 1957.

Marty, Fernand. *Language Laboratory Learning*. Wellesley, Mass.: Audio-Visual Publications, 1960.

Miller, M. H. "Foreign Language Day in North Carolina," *French Review*, 31:557–558, May 1958.

Pargment, Lila. *Beginner's Russian Reader*. New York: Pitman Publishing Corporation, 2nd ed., 1957.

Pei, Mario. *Language for Everybody*. New York: The Devin-Adair Company, 1956.

Previtali, Giovanni. "Foreign Language by Motion Pictures," *Modern Language Journal*, 44:171–177, April 1960.

Rivera, Carlos. "Manual of Materials, Aids, and Techniques for the Teaching of Spanish to English-Speaking Children." El Paso, Texas, Public Schools, n.d.

Sánchez, José. "Audio-Visual Aids," *Modern Language Journal*, 44:136–142, April 1960.

Sánchez, José. "Foreign Language Motion Pictures (An Annotated Bibliography)," *Modern Language Journal*, 44:177–185, April 1960.

Sánchez, José. "Twenty Years of Modern Language Laboratory (An Annotated Bibliography)," *Modern Language Journal*, 43:228–232, May 1959.

Smith, George E. "Foreign Languages in the Elementary Schools," *The Indiana Teacher*, 104:254–258, February 1960.

Van Eenenaam, Evelyn (compiler). "Annotated Bibilography of Modern Language Methodology for 1953, 1954, 1955, 1956," *Modern Language Journal*, 39:27–50, January 1955; 40: 83–104, February 1956; 41:81–103, February 1957; 42:27–43, January 1958; 44:24–43, January 1960.

Wischner, George J., and Schier, Ivan H. "Some Thoughts on Television as an Educational Tool," *American Psychologist*, 10:611–614, October 1955.

Yakobson, Helen B. "The Present Status of Russian Language Teaching," *Modern Language Journal*, 43:237–242, May 1959.

PROGRAMS AND MATERIALS

*French*

Cleveland Public Schools. *Course of Study for French in the Elemenetary Grades*, Part I and Part II, revised. Cleveland: Board of Education, 1958.

Grew, James H. "An Experiment in Oral French in Grade III," *Modern Language Journal*, 42:186–195, April 1958.

Hicks, Georgina L. "Teaching Foreign Language to Children: Observations and Suggestions," *Modern Language Journal*, 43:29–31, January 1959.

*Le Pardis est une Plage*. 16mm. film. Detroit: College of Education, Wayne State University, 1958.

### Spanish

Babcock, Edna E., *et al. Children of the Americas, Spanish Series*, San Francisco: Harr Wagner Publishing Company, 1957, 1958.

Bachemont, Otto G. *Spanish in the Elementary Schools*. Tacoma, Wash.: College of Pudget Sound, 1959.

Berges, George. "Miles City Introduces Foreign Languages in the Elementary Schools," *Montana Education*, 35:15–16, September 1958.

*El Cumpleaños de Pepita*. 16mm. film. Chicago: International Film Bureau, 1957.

Etnire, Elizabeth. "Five Years of Spanish in the Elementary School," *Modern Language Journal*, 42:349–351, November 1958.

Loucks, Robert Edwin. "Teaching Spanish Through Games in the Elementary Schools: An Experimental Study," *Hispania*, 42:246–247, May 1959.

MacRae, Margit W. *Mi cuaderno de español, Spanish in the Grades, Book One, Teachers' Edition*. Boston: Houghton Mifflin Company, 1959.

### German

Alexander, Theodore W. "German for Children: A Program at Texas Technological College," *German Quarterly*, 31:38–41, January 1958.

Ellert, Ernest E. "German in the Elementary Schools — An Analysis of an Existing Program," *German Quarterly*, 31:42–47, January 1958.

Ellert, Ernest, and Ellert, Lois. *German for Elementary School Children: A Teachers' Manual*, revised; *Die Brücke: Ein Lesebuch* and *Ein Arbeitsbuch*. Holland, Mich.: Ernest Ellert, Hope College, 1958, 1959.

Heggen, W. Gregor. "German in the Third and Fourth Grade," *German Quarterly*, 31:298–303, November 1958.

### Russian

Calandra, Alexander, and McClain, Charles J. "Experiment in the Teaching of Russian in the Elementary School," *Modern Language Journal*, 43:183–184, April 1959.

Snyder, C. W. "Experiment in Teaching Russian in Grade Three," *School and Society*, 86:353–354, October 11, 1958.

part four

The Opportunities
We Face

# 14

Justice to the groups now neglected must be sought without sacrificing the quality of education provided for groups that are now favored.

FRANCIS S. CHASE

# Educating the exceptional child

Wherever one teaches, sooner or later he will discover in his classroom a child who because of intellectual or physical deviation has needs so unusual that he requires very special help. Such a child is one we call exceptional. "It has been estimated that there are at least four or five million exceptional children of school age in the nation."[1] About half of these are either mentally gifted, mentally retarded, or socially or emotionally maladjusted. The other half have marked physical defects including crippling or special health

[1] Romaine P. Mackie, "Educational Opportunity for Exceptional Children," *The Grade Teacher*, 77:18, May 1959.

conditions, blindness or partial sight, deafness or impaired hearing, or defective speech.

Much has been done in the twentieth century to meet the needs of these children. But much remains to be done if every child is to realize his birthright of an education that allows him to develop to his highest potentialities. There is evidence to show that "less than one-fourth of the children who need special educational provisions have access to them."[2]

Not too long ago all children were expected to attain the same inflexible standards set by the school, in spite of differences in ability and in physical development. As recognition of the significance of these differences spread, teachers and administrators realized that specialized treatment was called for. Children of exceptional mental or physical development demand education specifically adapted to their needs.

Goodenough defines individualized instruction as "education that begins where the child is and proceeds according to a definite plan that takes account of his potentialities for the future. It permits progress by rapid or by slow stages according to his abilities. It seeks to discover and to develop his talents and to minimize the effect of his deficiencies. . . ."[3]

The rate of the presentation of the material, the type of material, and the method of instruction in the regular classroom fail to meet the needs of exceptional children. Special schools, special classes, special methods, and appropriate organization of the curriculum are essential. Unfortunately, until such time as provisions and facilities are available and qualified teachers can be secured to give the specialized help needed, the burden will fall upon the classroom teacher. It is he who must aid in identifying the ones who can be helped in the regular classroom and those in need of special schools or classes. Communities are becoming conscious of their responsibility for providing educational opportunities for all who can profit from them. New doors are being opened and new avenues of creativity are being provided for the gifted and improved opportunities for the handicapped.

The school should make provision for early identification and

[2] *Ibid.*

[3] Florence L. Goodenough, *Exceptional Children* (New York: Appleton-Century-Crofts, Inc., 1956), pp. 19–20.

prevention, insofar as possible, of disease, accidents, and unfavorable experiences that could cause disability or affect adversely the emotional stability of the individual. It should provide early and complete diagnosis to determine each child's capacities, needs, strengths, and limitations.

Finally, programs for educating the exceptional child should nurture all phases of the child's mental growth, social development, and physical health. How this can most effectively be done is the concern of this chapter.

# The gifted child

> . . . An active mind, if not occupied with useful things, will busy itself with what is useless, curious, and pernicious; and just as the more fertile a field is, the richer the crop of thorns and of thistles that it can produce, so an excellent intelligence becomes filled with fancy notions, if it is not sown with the seeds of wisdom and virtue.
>
> JOHN AMOS COMENIUS

Concern for the gifted is not new. Paralleling the interest in educating the individual with superior gifts has been the tendency to regard him as something less than normal. The belief existed for centuries that genius and mental or emotional abnormality were related. "According to the thought pattern of the age into which he was born, the gifted child has variously been labeled as bewitched, favored of God, the child of the Devil, or simply a genius."[4] That even today there is a popular feeling that to be mentally superior is not without its handicaps is evidenced by the following bit of verse:

> Johnny's healthy; Johnny's clever;
> Johnny's nine, but Johnny never
> Sailed a kite or trailed a lark
> Or caught a catfish in the park.[5]

[4] John Knight, "The Gifted Child," *Educational Quest* (Memphis State University School of Education Quarterly), 2:13, Summer 1958.
[5] Philene Hammer, "Saturday's Child," *Harper's*, 218:77, June 1959.

Among educators there has always been an urge to discover and develop talent to its highest potential. Today's schools are making an even greater effort to identify and provide for the gifted. They are realizing more and more the significant contributions talented individuals are destined to make and the importance of a program which helps them fulfill their destiny.

## Who Are the Gifted?

*Definition.* There is no universally accepted definition of giftedness. In some communities the identification of the gifted is based on the IQ alone. Depending upon the cut-off point, the gifted person is identified as one having an IQ between 115 and 180. From the literature this definition is derived: The term "gifted" refers to those children who possess a superior intellectual potential and functional ability to achieve academically in the top 15 to 20 per cent of the school population, and/or who have talent of a high order and consistently remarkable performance in such special areas as mathematics, science, creative arts, social leadership, physical and mechanical skills, and who have a unique ability to deal with their environment creatively. Depending upon the definition of "gifted children" and upon the criteria used to identify them, the number falling within the group varies. If we use the revised Stanford-Binet scale and assume a total school population of 30,000,000 the upper 1 per cent (those above 170 IQ) of that population equals 300,000 gifted children. If the lower limit is set at 130 IQ, some 1,200,000 children, or 4 per cent, may be classified as gifted. If the "gifted" IQ is lowered to 125, as is the practice in Cleveland, the number of gifted children is 1,900,000, or 6½ per cent.[6] The National Manpower Council and the National Education Association estimate that 400,000 bright children each year are being denied a chance to reach their potential.[7]

Even if the national need for leadership were not acute, the su-

[6] Arch O. Heck, *The Education of Exceptional Children* (New York: McGraw-Hill Book Company, 2nd ed., 1953), p. 90.

[7] *Administration: Procedures and School Practices for the Academically Talented Student* (Washington, D.C.: National Education Association, 1960), p. 15.

perior child would still merit special provision because he *has* the capacity to profit from educational opportunities different from the average. If the schools are to achieve the aim of optimum education of each child, the gifted too must be educated in terms of their special needs and abilities. "Democracy is not to be conceived as an invitation to share a common mediocrity but as a system that allows each to express and live up to the special excellence that is in him."[8]

*Identification.* Research[9] has shown that the gifted are not social misfits, physically retarded, unattractive, and bookwormish. As a matter of fact, the gifted are generally physically attractive and well adjusted socially. They have many hobbies and interests, and are superior to their age-mates in size, strength, and general health as well as in intellectual qualities.

The fifth volume of *Genetic Studies of Genius*[10] corroborates the research begun by Terman and his associates in 1921. There were two unexpected findings reported: (1) mental development of this group seemed at mid-life not yet to have reached its peak; (2) an unexpected degree of distinction had been achieved by the group. "Compared with predictions made in earlier reports, the latest data showed that 'instead of doubling of listings in *American Men of Science* . . . by 1960 [as predicted], the number quadrupled [by 1955]' while the names in *Who's Who* increased sixfold."[11]

As a part of the study, these "mid-life" men and women gave answers to the question "What constitutes success?" which fell for the most part into four categories: "(1) realization of goals and a sense of achievement, (2) a happy marriage and home life, (3) leaving the world a better place, (4) peace of mind and a well-adjusted personality."[12] These goals should give clues to the type of education which gifted children need. The contributions made by this group

---

[8] Rockefeller Brothers Report, *The Pursuit of Excellence — Education and the Future of America*, Panel Report of the Special Studies Project (Garden City, N.Y.: Doubleday and Company, 1958), p. 33.

[9] Lewis M. Terman, *The Discovery and Encouragement of Exceptional Talent*, Test Service Bulletin No. 14, Division of Test Research and Service (Yonkers-on-Hudson, N.Y.: World Book Company, 1954).

[10] Lewis M. Terman and Melita H. Oden, *The Gifted Group at Mid-Life: Thirty-five Years' Follow-up of the Superior Child* (Stanford: Stanford University Press, 1959).

[11] Frank T. Wilson, "Review of *The Gifted Group at Mid-Life: Thirty-five Years' Follow-up*," *Saturday Review*, 42:44, June 20, 1959.

[12] *Ibid.*, p. 45.

should justify identifying and providing for the gifted in every community.

*Characteristics of the Gifted Child.* Vigilance is the key to identification. Parents and teachers should watch for such indications of giftedness in preschool children as

1. Ability to talk better and earlier than other children. The gifted child uses a large vocabulary correctly and employs phrases and entire sentences at an early age. Many gifted children speak by the time they are eight months old and talk in sentences at two.
2. Ability at an early age to tell in sequence a story he has heard.
3. Keen powers of observation and retention of what he has observed.
4. Absorbing interest in books. Later he enjoys atlases, dictionaries, encyclopedias.
5. Early interest in calendars, clocks, thermometers.
6. Ability to concentrate to a greater degree and for a longer period than most children of the same age.
7. Unusual talent in art, music, dramatics, and related art forms.
8. Insight into cause-and-effect relationships while very young.
9. Ability to read before he enrolls in school. Many gifted children read before they are four.
10. Interest in many and varied activities.[13]

DeHaan and Wilson emphasize the need for discovering a wide variety of abilities in addition to intellectual ability in the identification of the gifted. Among these are artistic aptitudes of all types, practical and scientific skills, social leadership, and creative ability. "These aptitudes are not always clearly defined and are often found in a combination of abilities, interests, and social and personality factors."[14]

Next to aptitudes, the factor of interest looms large in significance. Interest is indicated by the activities in which the child prefers to engage when given a free choice. Interests usually grow out of ability and are related to activities in which the child excels as he is

[13] Adapted from Paul Witty, "Gifted Children — Our Greatest Resource," *Nursing Education*, September 1955, pp. 498–500.
[14] Robert DeHaan and Robert Wilson, "Identification of the Gifted," in Nelson B. Henry (ed.), *Education for the Gifted*, Fifty-Seventh Yearbook of the National Society for the Study of Education, Part II (Chicago, University of Chicago Press, 1958), p. 169.

likely to repeat his successes and receive increasingly rich rewards from them. The gifted child usually has many interests, which become more clearly differentiated as he approaches adolescence.

Important, too, in identifying the gifted is the knowledge of the level at which the child is achieving academically. Too frequently gifted children conduct themselves in such a way that they remain undiscovered. They may be bored, lazy, diffident, or afraid of being "different." The line between what a child can accomplish and what he actually achieves is not always clear cut. In a sense measures of aptitude are measures of achievement as well. One of the persistent problems of the teacher is to challenge the child so that he will become increasingly self-motivated and live up to his potential.

Factors such as motivation, personality, and social considerations also give the teacher a clue to outlining and planning learning experiences which challenge and extend a child's abilities.

Not until administrators and teachers working in harmony with parents provide experiences that are meaningful and demand his best efforts can they feel they are discharging their responsibility for educating each child toward his highest level of achievement. The benefit is not only to the individual but also to society, for "it is precisely this group of individuals who, in the long run and as a group . . . by their inventions and discoveries, their creative work in the arts, by their contribution to government and social reform, by their activities in all fields, will in the future help humanity in its groping struggle upward toward a better civilization."[15]

Education of the gifted today includes greater emphasis on early identification, guidance in learning activities, and stimulation of the under-achiever who has potential capacity. These children need to become aware of their special gifts. Strang points out that "They need guidance — not the mechanical type that is predicated on a few standardized tests, but a broad consideration of their individual backgrounds, capacities, goals, ideals, values, and character traits."[16]

All too often identification has been based on the results of an intelligence test alone. This is a means of identifying one type of gifted children — those with high verbal intelligence. However,

[15] Rudolph Pintner, "Superior Ability," *Teachers College Record*, 42:419, February 1941. See also Pintner in *Teachers College Record*, November 1956.
[16] Ruth Strang, "Foreword: Developing the Potentialities of Individuals," *Teachers College Record*, 61:421, May 1960.

there are other gifted children who cannot be identified this way: the writers, the musicians, the artists, the group leaders. Characteristics of exceptional creativity may not be revealed by an intelligence test.

*Characteristics of the Creative Child.* Not all teachers can recognize creativity in children. In a meeting sponsored by the National Science Foundation to consider creativity the following conclusions were reached: "(1) success in the scientific age is not merely a matter of intellect; (2) education in our country is distressingly geared to uncovering the 'bright boy' who can dutifully find the one right answer to a problem; (3) schools ignore the rebellious 'inner directed' child who scores low in IQ tests because they bore him; (4) teachers not only make no effort to nurture the creative rebel, but usually dislike him. More than 70 per cent of the 'most creative,' reported Jacob W. Getzels of the University of Chicago, are never recognized and so never have their talents developed."[17]

Some of the characteristics of the highly creative child, which an intelligence test may never reveal, are the following:

1. He is more sensitive to problems than his less creative peer. He not only is aware of problems; he wants to solve them.

2. He comes up with unusual but effective ideas. He is not conforming; he does not reproduce another's ideas. He is flexible in his approach to a problem; he sees relationships in a unique way, avoids widely accepted points of view, and finds his own solutions.

3. He is interested in a great number of projects, activities, and ideas at any one time. He is brimming over with enthusiasm.

4. He persists at a job in face of frustration, temporary defeat, or distractions. He can concentrate on what he is doing in spite of physical discomfort, distractions, or stimuli.

5. He often prefers individual enterprises to group projects. He is not concerned with conformity to the mores of the group.

6. He may not excel in academic achievement. This may in part be the result of inadequate rewards for his talent, lack of appreciation on the part of his teachers, and the lock-step system of the school curriculum.

An experiment in which a group of "highly intelligent" children and a group of "highly creative" children were compared to each

[17] "Digging the Divergent," *Time*, 42:66, June 29, 1959.

other and to the population from which they were drawn produced some interesting findings:

1. With respect to school achievement, despite the difference of twenty-three points in the *mean* IQ of the two groups they were equally superior in school achievement to the student population as a whole.

2. When asked to rate the children on the degree to which they would like to have them in class, the teachers exhibited a clear-cut preference for the high IQ child. . . .

3. . . . The creative child himself rates high marks, IQ, pep and energy, character, and goal-directedness *lower* than do members of the highly intelligent group, and he rates wide range of interests, emotional stability, and a sense of humor *higher* than do members of the highly intelligent group. . . .

4. The groups show distinct differences in the degree to which they aspire for "success" in adult life. The high IQ child desires to possess those qualities *now* which he believes will lead to success in adult life; the creative child does not seem to use this remote goal as a criterion in the selection of his present aspirations.

5. The relationship between the child's personal aspirations and those qualities which he believes teachers prefer is quite different for the two groups. The high IQ child holds to a self-ideal which is consonant with the one he believes teachers will most readily approve, the self-ideal of the creative child is not only *not* consonant with what he believes to be the teacher approved model but shows a slight *negative* correlation with such a model.

6. In their written responses to six stimulus pictures, the creative students exhibited a degree of imagination and originality unmatched by the high IQ students. Compared to the latter group, the creative students produced stories which seemed to "spring from" the stimulus rather than to be "tied down" by it. Their stories made abundant use of humor, novel situations, and unexpected endings. . . .[18]

The highly creative child may be missed by the usual IQ test, and in spite of his superior achievement he may fail to gain the same personal consideration from teachers that the high-IQ child has. Once teachers accept and value the highly creative child he may be motivated to remove the differential between his personal aspiration

[18] J. W. Getzels and P. W. Jackson, "The Meaning of 'Giftedness' — An Examination of an Expanding Concept," *Phi Delta Kappan*, 40:76, 77, November 1958.

and the aspirations he believes are valued by the teacher and society in general. Removal of such a barrier may well mean the nurturing of talent hitherto lost through a lack of understanding on the part of the teacher and a lack of challenging learning experiences for the creative individual.

*The Potential Scientist.* Increasing dependence upon scientific and technological advancements points up the need for scientists. Educators and scientists, parents and teachers, are concerned with identifying and starting on the road those youngsters who appear to be embryonic scientists. Brandwein has cited some characteristics of the potential scientist that are useful in identification at the elementary school level.

> Three factors are considered as being significant in the development of future scientists: a Genetic Factor, with a primary base in heredity (general intelligence, numerical ability, and verbal ability); a Predisposing Factor, with a primary base in functions which are psychological in nature; an Activating Factor, with a primary base in the opportunities offered in school and in the special skills of the teacher. [He also includes:] (1) a marked willingness to spend time, beyond the ordinary schedule, in a given task. (2) A willingness to withstand discomfort. This includes adjusting to shortened lunch hours, or no lunch hours, working without holidays, etc. It includes withstanding fatigue and strain and working even through a minor illness, such as a cold or a headache. (3) A willingness to face failure. With this comes a realization that patient work may lead to successful termination of the task at hand.[19]

Potentially gifted children in the science area are characterized by high verbal ability, high mathematical ability, and superior response to various aspects of science as revealed on tests. They are characterized, too, by drive, determination to make the best possible use of their ability, and an inquisitive, searching attitude. They show their versatility by an interest in various phases of science.

*The Potential Leader.* "There is probably a positive relationship between intelligence-test results and social leadership."[20] This is

[19] Paul Brandwein, *The Gifted Student as a Future Scientist* (New York: Harcourt, Brace and Company, 1955), pp. xi, 9, 10.
[20] Paul Witty, "Who Are the Gifted?" in Nelson B. Henry (ed.), *Education for the Gifted.* Fifty-Seventh Yearbook of the National Society for the Study of Education, Part II (Chicago: University of Chicago Press, 1958), p. 61.

suggested in genetic studies of children of high IQ. The gifted group are socially adjusted; they play with other children although they spend a great deal of time with hobbies and reading; they hold elective offices more frequently than the other children, although they are not often chosen to be president. The child who is a leader works well with children in various groups. He shows understanding of others and tact in working with them. Frequently he helps them raise their sights and strive for greater accomplishments. Identifying children who have the ability to be leaders — the skill to help a group reach its goals, to improve human relationships within a group, and to achieve distinction by individual and group effort — is important. Such children, if identified early and helped to improve these skills, will be able to take their place in the adult world in positions of leadership in government, international affairs, business and industry, professional organizations, labor organizations, and community groups.

Social leadership has been defined as "certain kinds of behavior that arise from the *social interaction among individuals in groups.* A definition of leadership should include both the characteristics of the individual child, his personality, character, needs, motivations, as well as the characteristics of the group, its goals, needs and membership composition."[21]

Studying groups in operation is an essential part of understanding the factors that contribute to the development of leadership behavior. Equally important is the study of the individual to determine the traits that bear on leadership behavior. The two interact; the two are essential for a complete understanding of individual leadership. The beginning teacher may be puzzled by the child who seems to have excellent leadership skill on the playground, but withdraws from the group when he returns to the classroom.

In a formal organization the degree of leadership the individual can exert will depend to a large measure on the contributions he can make, his preparation to help the group organize and carry out worth-while projects, and his ability to assume responsibility for the official leadership. The more democratic the group, the more the members can influence the decisions made. The more autocratic the group, the more leadership is centralized in the hands of a few. Each

---

[21] John K. Hemphill, *Situational Factors in Leadership* (Columbus, Ohio: Ohio State University, 1949), p. 5.

member of the group is concerned not alone with the group goals and agenda but with his individual goals — the hidden agenda. Schools can help children develop leadership skills. However, they cannot insure their being selected as leaders or even given important roles as sub-leaders in group organizations. Although all leaders exhibit some traits which can be identified, it is clear that leadership is not a single trait or ability but is made up of many personal abilities and traits which bring the leader to the fore, plus consistent performance as a specialist in human relations and as a task specialist. The leader must understand not only how to work with people but also how to help a group get things done.

In the area of human relations the leader should have sensitivity to the needs and feelings of others and the ability to give and receive affection, release tension, show agreement in a group, and facilitate a feeling of group solidarity. The use of role playing is an excellent device for teaching children to develop this type of leadership behavior.[22]

## *Types of Programs*

The average classroom offers too little challenge to the gifted child. For much of their education the majority of gifted children have to rely on out-of-school experiences — reading, conversing with adults, viewing television, and observing the world around them. "In general the gifted child has mastered the subject matter . . . to a point 40 per cent above his chronological age though he has been held back to a grade location only 14 per cent above the norm for his chronological age."[23]

Methods of dealing with the gifted child can be grouped into four categories.

*Acceleration.* Contrary to popular belief, acceleration of the gifted does not have unfavorable consequences. Studies have shown that gifted children who are emotionally mature profit from being

[22] Robert DeHaan, "Social Leadership," in Nelson B. Henry (ed.), *Education for the Gifted*, Fifty-Seventh Yearbook of the National Society for the Study of Education, Part II (Chicago: University of Chicago Press, 1958), p. 143.

[23] Goodenough, *op. cit.*, pp. 76, 77.

with others with whom they can communicate and share common interests. Acceleration allows the gifted pupil to move at a rate in harmony with his ability and maturity and to complete the educational program in less than the usual time required. Grade skipping, early entrance to kindergarten or college, and progressing through the series of levels of learning experiences in less than the usual time are three common methods of acceleration.

Early entrance to the kindergarten has been advocated as an advantageous method of acceleration. Studies by Worcester[24] and Birch[25] have pointed out that children with IQ's of 130 or above who entered the kindergarten before they were five were successful in later years provided they were superior not only intellectually but socially, emotionally, and physically upon entrance to school and had an interest in reading. One of the writers has kept in touch with children in the program of early entrance to kindergarten and has witnessed its effects on a few children who were mature, accelerated, and had a kindergarten curriculum which was similar to that of the nursery school. In many cases such children would benefit from a regular nursery school experience rather than early admission to kindergarten.

Unfortunately, many schools make no provision for the gifted child. Douglas is an example of the child who is caught in the controversy over acceleration. He enrolled in kindergarten before he was five. "He was one of fifty-nine children who attended the afternoon session. A cursory glance revealed that he was a slim, dark-haired, brown-eyed, shy youngster who seemed to enjoy being with other children. It was not long before the teacher realized that he was reading. He stopped to read all the signs on the bulletin board in the hall and on the street when the class took excursions. He read the books on the library table. When the teacher asked him, "When did you learn to read?" Douglas replied, "I can't remember when I didn't know how to read." Douglas had learned to read at three years of age, while his father was in the army. Each week the father wrote a letter, which Douglas wanted to read by himself."[26]

---

[24] Dean A. Worcester, *The Education of Children of Above-Average Mentality* (Lincoln: University of Nebraska Press, 1956).

[25] Jack W. Birch, "Early Admission for Mentally Advanced Children," *Exceptional Children*, 24:84–87, December 1954.

[26] Lillian M. Logan, *Teaching the Young Child* (Boston: Houghton Mifflin Company, 1960), pp. 57–58.

Douglas had been reading ever since. It was not unusual that he should want to continue this satisfying activity when he attended kindergarten. The fact that he was only four and a half years of age presented no obstacle to him or to his teacher. He was permitted to read to the children, to read for his own enjoyment, and to read to the teacher during free time. No effort was made to teach him to read. He just chose reading activities as freely as other children chose to build with blocks or play in the doll corner. Before the year was over he was reading fourth-grade books.

The following year he entered the first grade with a group of gifted children. He was encouraged to proceed at his own rate and profited from an enriched program. The next semester he moved to another state in which no provision was made for his giftedness. He was placed in the kindergarten because the school law permitted no one to enter first grade unless he was six before the school year began. At this time he was reading fifth-grade material. Because the school made no provision for acceleration he was forced to spend the remainder of the year in kindergarten — bored, frustrated, and unhappy. He suffered not only academically but socially. He had nothing in common with the children and developed a severe dislike for school.

The education of children under the guidance of teachers who understand a child's needs and abilities may well be an advantage over the haphazard experiences provided in some homes. Early identification of the gifted is useless unless giftedness can be fostered.

*The Nongraded Plan.* The nongraded elementary school allows children to advance at their own rate through the learning experiences of the regular school program. When a child has mastered the skills of the primary unit he goes into the fourth grade or the intermediate unit regardless of his chronological age and the fact that he may have spent less than three years in the primary school — or more than three, depending upon his need. The child is promoted on the basis of his maturity in all respects and his ability to take his place successfully with the children in the fourth grade or the intermediate level.

Traditionally, grade skipping was the method commonly used to take care of children who were obviously ahead of their classmates. The practice fell into disrepute for two main reasons: children missed the fundamentals they would later need, and problems of personality adjustment arose.

In the nongraded school the problem of providing the fundamentals is solved by the nature of the program. As for the problem of adjustment, it has been found that chronological age is no indicator of social, emotional, intellectual, or physical maturity.

There is little question now about the advisability of acceleration on an individual basis. The question is which type of acceleration is best for a particular child. Grade skipping and early entrance to formalized kindergartens constitute potentially more serious threats to the child than the progression through the school curriculum according to a levels or nongraded plan in which all the essential experiences are provided.

The follow-up of Terman's gifted students points to evidence that children with an IQ of at least 135 who are accelerated from one to three years are usually more successful in later life than equally bright children who are held in the sequential lock step.[27]

*Separate Classes.* There are many variations of the separate-classes plan. They allow the child to explore the curriculum in depth; to study additional subjects, including foreign languages, advanced science, and mathematics; to join special-interest clubs; to take industrial arts; and to participate in many creative activities. Such classes challenge the child to proceed at his own rate. In a special class children enjoy friendship with others of similar interests and maturity. They are stimulated to put forth their best efforts. The special class provides an effective method of enriching the curriculum, permits a reasonable amount of acceleration, makes possible competition with others of similar intellectual capacities, encourages the friendship of congenial companions whose interests and mental abilities are similar, and challenges the child to do his best.

Certain hazards of special classes must be recognized if they are to be met and solved: jealous reactions of parents and other children, concern that segregated children will become egotistical, and too narrow an acquaintance by the gifted group with the activities of other children. However, in communities where special classes have ex-

[27] Lewis M. Terman and Melita Oden, "Major Issues in the Education of Gifted Children," in Joseph L. French (ed.), *Educating the Gifted* (New York: Henry Holt and Company, 1959), p. 149.

isted for years, the negative factors are outweighed by the positive.

Special full-time classes for the gifted in regular schools are becoming an integral part of the public schools in New York City; Birmingham, Alabama; Berkeley, California; Indianapolis, Indiana; Brockton, Massachusetts; Allentown, Pennsylvania; University City, Missouri; Cleveland, Ohio; and other cities.

Cleveland offers a typical example of the way a community can provide for its gifted in special classes in the regular school. Here the children are selected for the special classes on the basis of a series of group intelligence and achievement tests in Grades 2B, 4B, and 6A. The results of the tests are studied to determine the students to be selected for the Stanford-Binet test. Children having an IQ of 125 and over are considered for placement in "Major Work Classes." Other factors such as emotional maturity, social adaptability, health status, teacher judgment, and parent consent are also considered. Responsibility for the child's transportation to and from school is assumed by the parents. Efforts are made to enroll the child in the nearest Major Work Class center.

Several grades are grouped in one classroom. For example, the primary grades have one classroom, the intermediate another. Placement in the Major Work Classes may occur at any time during the child's elementary school experience. The earlier the placement, the earlier the challenge and the greater the progress.

The curriculum includes the language arts, creative arts, science, social studies, home economics, health and safety, physical education, and industrial arts. The children study French and receive special instruction in arts and intensive work in language and literature, typewriting, creative writing, giving reports, book reviews, and expository writing. They carry out research projects in topics of interest in science, history, biography, travel, fiction, and poetry. They have contacts with other students in the school in regularly scheduled activities such as gymnasium, orchestra, crafts, clubs, and student council.[28]

Among the objectives followed in the Major Work Classes are

1. Increasing the range of knowledge and skills for the students.
2. Developing alertness.

[28] Robert J. Havighurst *et al., A Survey of the Education of Gifted Children,* Supplementary Education Monographs No. 83 (Chicago: University of Chicago Press, 1955), pp. 83–84.

3. Developing initiative and creative power.
4. Developing critical thinking.
5. Developing the power to work independently, to plan, to execute, and to judge.
6. Developing increased ability to share in undertakings.
7. Developing leadership.[29]

These objectives, if followed in the average classroom, will challenge the children with average as well as above average potential. Among the activities that are an integral part of the Major Work Classes are discussion, research, talks, projects of special interests, and reading clubs. Much emphasis is placed on such vital activities as finding information, giving talks, carrying on research, evaluating, experimenting, listening, observing, interviewing, writing and outlining. An important characteristic of the Cleveland program is the emphasis on social growth and adjustment and other developmental needs of the gifted child. Opportunity to engage in creative activities in music, art, and foreign language has long been a part of the Cleveland program and has in no small measure contributed to the later success of the students in these classes.

Indianapolis, too, has a program for meeting the needs of the gifted in special classes. Children are selected on the basis of their intelligence, results of group tests and individual tests administered by the school psychologists, recommendations of teacher and principal, and approval of the parents. The candidate must have an IQ of 130 in order to be considered. Principals send the test results to the supervisor, who determines the feasibility of administering an individual test. Following the study of test results, conferences with the parents, and the recommendation of the school psychologist, the child is enrolled.

Emphasis is on enrichment. The children have the same curriculum as the regular classes, but they delve more deeply into literature, history, science, and social studies than is possible in the average classroom. The regular subject matter is supplemented by teacher-pupil conferences, educational excursions into the community, special research projects, and individualized instruction. Freedom to

[29] Merle R. Sumption *et al.*, "Special Education for the Gifted," *The Education of Exceptional Children*, Forty-Ninth Yearbook of the National Society for the Study of Education, Part II (Chicago: University of Chicago Press, 1950), p. 266.

explore, to experiment, to create in areas of special interest is part of the program. The study of French begins in the fifth grade and the fundamentals of typing are taught in the sixth. Many other special skills are developed by the teacher, pupils, and parents working together. The close relationship developed and maintained with the home is an important phase of the program and a contributing factor in its success.[30]

*Partial Segregation.* Another method of providing for the gifted is known as partial segregation, an example of which can be seen in the Colfax Elementary School in Pittsburgh. Here the gifted pupils spend half the school day in a "workshop" designed to extend worthwhile interests and stimulate academic progress. Children plan, discuss their projects, evaluate, and work together. The study of German, typing, and the extension of various interests through independent research are some of the special opportunities offered. In describing the plan Pregler, the principal of the school, states:

> The mentally superior child is defined as one measuring 130 or more on the Stanford-Binet Test and showing advanced achievement.
>
> In the primary grades all children spend the first half of the morning with their regular classes, at which time they have their social activities, sharing experiences, music, games, safety and character education, and similar things normally done by the entire group. Midway through the morning, the children move into their skill subjects, at which time the mentally superior children leave for their Workshops.
>
> In the upper grades the school is run on the platoon plan. The gifted children leave class when the group goes to the academic teacher and rejoin it for the special subjects, like art, music, and physical education.[31]

*Special Schools.* Grouping of gifted children may take the form of placing them in a special school. The Hunter College Elementary School enrolls gifted children from nursery through the sixth grade. Pupils are admitted on the basis of IQ and achievement scores, an

[30] See "The Gifted Child in the Indianapolis Public Schools" (Indianapolis: Supervisor, Special Education, The Indianapolis Public Schools, n.d.).

[31] Hedwig O. Pregler, in Robert J. Havinghurst *et al.*, *A Survey of the Education of Gifted Children*, Supplementary Educational Monographs No. 83 (Chicago: University of Chicago Press, November 1955), p. 95.

interview with parents, and a visit to the school by the child and parent. An effort is made to keep the numbers of boys and girls in each class equal. Groupings are kept flexible. Children study the language arts, social studies, science, health, the arts and crafts, and physical education. The academic skills required for success in school and daily life, such as the language arts, are treated as tools for problem solving in the curriculum areas. Special teachers are responsible for music, arts and crafts, foreign languages, and physical education. Instruction is related to other class projects.

"An important feature of school life at Hunter is the club period. For one hour each week other school activities cease and interest groups meet for activities in art, cooking, dancing, dramatics, French, poetry, photography, radio workshop, science, hobbies, and music."[32]

Unless the community is large, however, it is impractical to maintain special schools for the gifted. In small communities families are more closely knit and may become seriously disturbed over segregation of the gifted. In larger communities social levels are less likely to intermingle and families are less concerned with comparing the progress of their children to that of children they do not know.

*Enrichment.* Enrichment for the gifted child consists of providing experiences appropriate and adequate in terms of his unique design of development. Enrichment in the regular classroom should offer a broader scope of activities, freedom to follow special interests, opportunity to apply creative ideas in organizing and developing projects, and many experiences in problem solving. Ideally, enrichment can be accomplished when children are enrolled in the regular class through special projects, additional subjects in the curriculum, and dismissal from regular classwork for part of the day to pursue special interests in music, art, languages, advanced science, or mathematics. Differentiated assignments, teacher-pupil compacts, independent research, wide reading, individual and group projects, experimental and creative activity all are forms of enrichment.

The teacher who is creative, who is well grounded in the subject-matter fields, who understands children, and who is able to identify, diagnose, and challenge each child's ability and creativity provides a good education for pupils of *all* ability levels. To properly take care

[32] Havighurst, *op. cit.,* p. 68.

of individual differences in the classroom, however, smaller classes, a larger number and greater variety of materials, a modification of the graded elementary school, and greater opportunities for individualized instruction and varied experiences are necessary.

"The basic challenge is that of knowing how to develop the children, the youth of the land, to their fullest capacities. This requires the intangible skill of learning how to recognize the abilities, the needs of . . . children, particularly learning how to cope with the gifted child and the child who needs special attention. . . ."[33]

Obviously, the establishment of programs for the gifted is in the province of the school administration to a great extent. It is the decision of the administration that affects the size of classes, the organization of the school, the number and variety of instructional materials and equipment, and the opportunities for providing blocks of time for individualized instruction. Where administrators see fit to set up an organizational structure that allows children to proceed at their own rate, participating in multi-track programs or dual-progress plans, the problems of the teacher are minimized and the possibilities for optimum education are greater.

However, within a regularly graded organizational structure the teacher is faced with planning a wide range of experiences. He must make an effort to enrich the program for each child in the framework of the grade structure. Unfortunately, he is frequently so overburdened that his task is well-nigh impossible. Enrichment in the regular classroom does have, however, many advocates. It is comparatively inexpensive to organize, easy for principals to administer, and does not offend parents by singling out the talented child. This plan for providing for the gifted is popular, though admittedly it is not always effective. It is, of course, only as effective as the teacher, time, instructional materials, and physical facilities permit.

## Teaching the Gifted Child in the Regular Classroom

The classroom teacher is one who introduces the gifted child to his educational experience and in most cases will be responsible for

[33] Benjamine Fine, *Saturday Review*, 42:30, February 14, 1959.

his education. He must, therefore, have an understanding of his role in teaching the gifted child and of activities that will increase love of learning, ability to think critically, and motivation.

Teachers who understand the gifted child are sensitive to his needs and modify the program in order to meet them. They realize that good teaching widens differences in children. They are not like the teacher who remarked, "I had a difficult time last year. At the beginning of school in September there were some smart young-sters, some slow ones, and some in between. But when I got through in June the fast ones had slowed down, and the slow ones were a little faster, and the ones in between were still there." Such a teacher ig-nores every principle for working with children.

## GUIDING PRINCIPLES IN TEACHING THE GIFTED

1. The gifted child is first of all a child. While helping him de-velop his special talents, the teacher should also assist the individual to understand many phases of life and to have satisfying interests.

2. Each child has talents to be discovered. Beginning in the kinder-garten the teacher should make a conscious effort to find them.

3. The child's giftedness should be provided for at every educa-tional level in a continuous program. Children should be helped to make the most of the talents and abilities with which they are en-dowed.

4. The gifted child is entitled to a program of instruction that includes competent teachers, progressive administrators, well-trained counselors, and curriculum specialists who work together to help him reach his highest level.

5. The gifted child, together with his parents, should have a part in determining the kind of program he goes into. The school personnel may recommend a program that deviates from what is provided for other children, but the parents must have a voice in deciding whether or not the child will be placed in a modified program.

6. The gifted child should be educated in a setting that does not ignore the needs of the other children.

7. The gifted child requires less drill than the average or slow child; he needs more opportunity for working independently on projects requiring problem solving and independent research.

8. The gifted child needs sympathetic understanding, challenging

learning experiences, and an environment in which high goals, persistent effort, feelings of achievement, and self-acceptance are taken for granted.

## ENRICHMENT ACTIVITIES

It is important that the learning experiences be carried on in a setting that is rich in creative media, stimulating in atmosphere, well supplied with instructional materials, and closely allied with the resources of the community.

Organizing the program around a unit of work or a unit of experience meets the needs of the gifted more effectively than do the traditional methods of separate subjects. It fosters initiative and creativity in the child and allows him to follow his special interests and maintain his level of ability in solving problems related to the unit.

The following are suggested enrichments of the regular program.

*Delving Deeply into the Topic.* Explore in more detail and greater depth social science, reading, arithmetic, science, or spelling.

*Carrying on Handicraft Projects.* Make maps, dioramas, charts, models, costumes, puppets, color slides, transparencies, still or moving pictures in conjunction with a project.

*Participating in Creative Activities.* Write and dramatize original plays or adaptations of stories; write stories for sharing; illustrate stories; make murals and pictures using various art media; participate in music and dance groups for enjoyment or as a part of special programs.

*Planning Special Programs.* Organize, rehearse, and conduct programs for various holidays and occasions.

*Preparing Exhibits.* Display science, historical, regional, community, creative writing, art, or hobby exhibits.

*Joining Clubs.* Become members of class, school, or community clubs and organizations.

*Participating in Debate and Panel Discussions.* Learn the principles of debate and group discussion and put them into practice in language arts, social studies, and science classes. Engage in interscholastic, assembly, or classroom programs.

*Broadcasting.* Participate in broadcasting via school or commercial broadcasting stations in such roles as speaker, actor, soloist, reader, or member of an orchestra or band.

*Carrying on Independent Research.* Pursue independent research on such topics as children in other cultures, weather, astronomy, inventions, industry, animals, etc. Children read, organize material and finally present to the group reports based on independent research. The teacher helps them define, locate, and organize information needed in initial experiences. Later children work on their own with a minimum of direction.

*Giving Demonstrations.* Demonstrate science experiments, models, dances, costumes, or playing an instrument for the class.

*Giving Reports.* Participate in oral and written research reports which critically analyze and evaluate material read for book reviews and research topics.

*Gaining Seminar Experience.* Participate in group seminars and take turns in the roles of leader and participant.

*Carrying Out Projects.* Explore special interests in all subjects of the curriculum. Many times such projects help guide one into profitable channels toward the pursuit of a life profession or avocation.

## A TYPICAL EXAMPLE OF ENRICHMENT

The following example of classroom enrichment has been carried out in the intermediate grades in the pilot elementary schools participating in the Portland, Oregon, Gifted-Child Project.

### A Unit of Work

The subject for study in a sixth grade was the "Inca Civilization." The chairman of one of the committees was a very intelligent boy, talented in art, creative dramatics, creative writing, and leadership. Under his leadership the committee decided to write a play entitled "The Conquering Incas." This was a serious portrayal of life in an ancient Inca Village, which necessitated wide and extensive research. The talents of many children in the class were used to produce the play, under the leadership of the committee members. Artists in the class painted the stage scenery and the fighting equipment of the warriors; murals were painted for backdrops, and water jars were decorated with Inca designs. Three girls, talented in rhythms, presented an Inca tribal dance; chants and songs were written by a boy who for several years had done interesting things in poetry; a girl who has an outstanding singing voice sang the burial chant;

another girl brought records of the Peruvian singer Yma Sumac, which were used as background music. Much originality was shown in planning and making the costumes and scenery for the play.

The culminating activity of a unit study on "Peoples of the Western Hemisphere Outside of the United States" gave evidence of many opportunities provided for superior and talented children. Two classes worked in cooperation to give a "Fiesta" on Pan-American Day. The pupil steering committee met with room mothers and planned a luncheon of Mexican food to be served in the classrooms which were ablaze with the colorful exhibits and art work of the children.

After the luncheon, under the leadership of the pupil chairmen, children gave reports, showed slides which they had made, and presented short, original, dramatic plays. These short plays gave the children an opportunity to use Spanish words and phrases they had had so much fun learning.

The second part of the program was in the gymnasium where the children sang some of the songs and played some of the games of Latin America and Canada. They danced with great gusto the samba, the rumba and the La Raspa.[34]

An examination of programs for the gifted reveals that what is good for the gifted would be good for the average child also. No matter what administrative procedures are designed for launching and carrying out a gifted-child program, the teacher is, of course, most directly responsible for the actual work with the children. He is charged, too, with identifying the gifted child through observation and other evaluative techniques.

If the program is based entirely on enrichment in the classroom, the burden of diversified instruction falls entirely on the teacher. If the program includes a combination of classroom enrichment and special classes, the teacher still has the primary responsibility. No curriculum in existence can remove from him the obligation of teaching, although the use of special schools, special classes, ability grouping, and specialists in certain areas lightens the load considerably.

Working with the gifted has its unique rewards. It is a challenge to help a gifted child reach his potential. When teachers realize that

[34] Dorothy E. Norris, "Programs in the Elementary Schools," in Nelson B. Henry (ed.), *Education for the Gifted*, Fifty-Seventh Yearbook of the National Society for the Study of Education, Part II (Chicago: University of Chicago Press, 1958), pp. 251, 252.

even in a heterogeneous classroom it is possible to schedule the daily activity to make provision for him his needs will be met more adequately.

## A TYPICAL DAILY PLAN

One of the problems the classroom teacher faces is that of integrating the gifted child's activities and experiences with those of the rest of the class. In some activities the gifted child joins the class. He may remain for the entire period or he may be excused as soon as he understands the process and works independently.

The following schedule[35] shows how a teacher might provide enrichment activities in the daily program. It is merely suggestive, for current needs will determine the learning experience.

| CLASS ACTIVITIES AND EXPERIENCES | GIFTED CHILD'S ACTIVITIES AND EXPERIENCES |
|---|---|
| Social Studies (9:00–10:00) | |
| Planning. | Participation in planning. Summarizing, recording class plans, committee personnel, material needed. |
| Work period. | Research (utilizing materials of higher reading level), making a model, preparing and typing a report, dialogue, or script, conducting a science experiment — carried on *independently or with a committee*, but contributing to the total class activity. |
| Evaluation. | Participation in evaluation. (Same as planning, above.) |
| Reading (10:10–11:00) | |
| Silent and/or oral reading, with discussion and related independent work activities. | Participation with the top reading group if his developmental reading needs warrant |
| | AND/OR |
| | Independent reading in area of special interest (science, biography, history, poetry). |

[35] Marian Scheifele,*The Gifted Child in the Regular Classroom* (New York: Bureau of Publications, Teachers College, Columbia University, 1953), pp. 58, 59.

### Physical Education (11:00–11:20)

Games, relays, self-testing activities.

Participation with classmates. Individual instruction in specific game skills, if needed.

### Arithmetic (11:20–12:00)

Thought problems, practice of computation skills.

Individual work at his level to develop or refine skills needed for independent and group projects — computing percentage, measuring area, volume, distance, or time, studying metric system; drill *as needed* in computation skills; supplementary study pertaining to social functions of arithmetic; free time for pursuit of special interests.

### Language Arts (1:00–1:50)

Spelling, oral and written language skills, handwriting.

Individual work at his level to develop or refine skills needed for independent and group projects — compiling his own dictionary, studying techniques of specific kinds of writing (newspaper reporting, dialogue, science experiments); study to attain achievement commensurate with his grade level, if needed; free time for pursuit of special interests.

### Creative Expression (2:10–3:00)

Music, art, rhythms, creative writing.

Developing individual projects in these areas; participating with the class; joining another class or group to pursue special interests.

## *Challenging the Gifted Child in School*

Literally thousands have cheated themselves and society by setting their sights too low, mainly because no one has ever challenged them to aim higher. Once the gifted child is identified, something must be done to challenge him at school. Whether a program of acceleration, special schools, separate classes, or enrichment or a combination of these methods is adopted depends upon the objectives to be attained, needs of the children who are gifted, facilities and materials available, and school resources and personnel that can be utilized.

Currently opinion is in favor of acceleration of mature gifted pupils and special grouping. It is much easier to provide enriched learning experiences in a class made up entirely of gifted pupils than to plan for a wide variety of assignments in a heterogeneous class.

## The Achievement of Gifted Children

"Watching a gifted child in search of knowledge is like watching a moth in search of a bright light on a dark night."[36] His eagerness to achieve is the result of his ability to make the best of his opportunities to learn. He is curious about everything under the sun. He has an insatiable thirst for knowledge that is not easily quenched.

As a group, intellectually gifted pupils have a significantly higher academic achievement than do less able pupils. There are, however, some gifted pupils who on all rungs of the educational ladder are not working up to capacity. This number is comparatively small, and such children require additional encouragement, motivation, guidance, and opportunities. Evidence from growth studies of a group of gifted pupils reveals that "the academic achievement of the gifted child and youth is a function in part of his design for growing, and in part of the learning experiences provided for him. Evidence suggests that under conditions of deprivation, achievement of individuals might not have occurred."[37]

During the elementary years, some gifted children tend to exhibit extreme inconsistencies in their learning pattern. For example, one may show an absorbing interest in a particular skill or narrow field of knowledge. His teachers become upset because he neglects his required assignments for this interest. They want him to get all his lessons, and consider him careless, irresponsible, and contrary.

At another time he may disappoint them by dabbling in many

[36] Warren A. Ketcham, "What Research Says About the Education of Gifted Children," University of Michigan *School of Education Bulletin*, 28:67, February 1957.

[37] Warren Ketcham, "Growth Patterns of Gifted Children," *Merrill-Palmer Quarterly*, 1:196, Spring 1957.

areas of interest without trying to excel in any one. This is a part of growing up, and although parents or teachers may be unhappy about these alternating periods of concentration and exploration the child will in good time fulfill the promise of his potential to a far greater degree than the average or less-than-average child. It must be remembered, also, that if the child were always working at capacity in every area of endeavor the strain might be too severe. Children are often the best determiners of the amount of energy they can expend and still retain optimum health.

The teacher is the key person in providing for individual differences. It is he who must identify the gifted child and help him develop his talents. He must continue to improve his own skills, enrich his knowledge and insights, and develop his own personality to the end that he will be able to challenge each child in the classroom to achieve in harmony with his innate abilities, drive, and needs.

". . . It is still the classroom teacher who must orient the gifted pupil in his first years of school work, accurately identify him, and nurture him intellectually. . . . Her work with him will be basic and useful in all follow-up programs with the child. For this she must temper her understanding of children with a broadened and most extensive background of knowledge and the most insightful use of excellent methods of teaching she can call up for the task."[38]

The reward that brings the teacher the greatest satisfaction is to see individuals develop, to watch a child discover or rekindle the creative spark within him. ". . . The child is the person who will continue what you have begun, who will sit right where you are sitting and witness the things you consider very important, when you are gone. You may take all the measures you like, but the manner in which they are treated will depend on him. Even though you may sign alliances and treaties, it is he who will execute them. He will take his seat in the assembly and will assume control of cities, nations and empires. It is he who will be in charge of your churches, schools, universities, councils, corporations, and institutions. All your work will be judged, praised, or condemned by him. The future and the destiny will be in his hands. . . ."[39]

[38] Frank Yuhas, "The Gifted Child in the Classroom," *Educational Administration and Supervision*, 43:437, November 1957.
[39] Translation of a Christmas card sent out by the Official Children's Agency in Panama, 1944. *Children*, 4:8, January–February 1957.

## ACTIVITIES AND QUESTIONS

1. Define the exceptional child. What forms does exceptionality take?
2. How can giftedness be identified? In younger children particularly?
3. What methods of providing for the education of the gifted are the most feasible for a small school system? A large system? Observe in an elementary school and see what provisions are being made for the education of the gifted.

## BIBLIOGRAPHY

Abraham, Willard. *Common Sense About Gifted Children*. New York: Harper & Brothers, 1958.

Abraham, Willard. *Guide for the Study of Exceptional Children*. Boston: Porter Sargent, Publisher, 1956.

American Association for Gifted Children. *The Gifted Children*, Paul A. Witty (ed.). Boston: D. C. Heath and Company, 1951.

Birch, J. W., and Williams, E. M. *Challenging Gifted Children*. Bloomington, Ill.: Public School Publishing Company, 1955.

Bond, H. M. *Search for Talent*. Cambridge, Mass.: Harvard University Press, 1959.

Brandwein, Paul. *The Gifted Child as a Future Scientist*. New York: Harcourt, Brace and Company, 1955.

Brumbaugh, Florence N. "The Intellectually Gifted," *Special Education for Exceptional Children*. Vol. III. Boston: Porter Sargent, Publisher, 1957.

Brumbaugh, Florence N., and Roshco, Bernard. *Your Gifted Child*. New York: Henry Holt and Company, 1959.

Cruickshank, William M., and Johnson, G. Orville (eds.). *Education of Exceptional Children and Youth*. Englewood Cliffs, N.J.: Prentice-Hall, Inc., 1958.

Cutts, Norma E., and Moseley, Nicholas. *Teaching the Bright and Gifted*. Englewood Cliffs, N.J.: Prentice-Hall, Inc., 1957.

DeHaan, Robert F., and Havighurst, Robert J. *Educating Gifted Children*. Chicago: University of Chicago Press, 1957.

Fisher, J. Sherrick. "Significance of the I.Q.," *Phi Delta Kappan*, 40: 257–260, March 1959.

French, Joseph L. (ed.). *Educating the Gifted*. New York: Henry Holt and Company, 1959.

Getzels, J. W., and Jackson, P. W. "The Meaning of 'Giftedness' — An Examination of an Expanding Concept," *Phi Delta Kappan*, 40:75–78, November 1958.

Greer, Edith S. *The Education of the Able Student*. A Selected Bibliography. Publications Inquiry Unit, Circular No. 525, Washington, D.C.: Government Printing Office, 1958.

Hall, Theodore. *Gifted Children*. Cleveland: The World Publishing Company, 1956.

Havighurst, Robert J., *et al. A Survey of the Education of Gifted Children*. Chicago: University of Chicago Press, 1955.

Hildreth, Gertrude H. *Educating Gifted Children: At Hunter College Elementary School*. New York: Harper & Brothers, 1952.

Hill, George, *et al. Identifying and Educating Our Gifted Children*. Pupil Services Series, No. 1. Athens, Ohio: Center for Educational Service, College of Education, Ohio University, November 1957.

Ketcham, Warren A. "What Research Says About the Education of Gifted Children," University of Michigan *School of Education Bulletin*, 28:65–69, February 1957.

Ketcham, Warren A., and Laffitte, Rondeau G., Jr. "How Well Are They Learning?" *Educational Leadership*, March 1959. (Reprint.)

Knight, John. "The Gifted Child," *Educational Quest* (Memphis State University School of Education Quarterly), 2:13–20, Summer 1958.

Louttit, C. M. *Clinical Psychology of Exceptional Children*. New York: Harper & Brothers, 1957.

National Society for the Study of Education. *Education for the Gifted*. Fifty-Seventh Yearbook, Nelson B. Henry (ed.). Chicago: University of Chicago Press, 1958.

Russell, Donald. "A Functional Approach to the Study of the Gifted Child," *Elementary School Journal*, 58:45–48, October 1956.

Scheifele, Marian. *The Gifted Child in the Regular Classroom*. New York: Bureau of Publications, Teachers College, Columbia University, 1953.

Strang, Ruth. *Helping Your Gifted Child*. New York: E. P. Dutton and Company, 1960.

Strang, Ruth. "The Mental Diet of Gifted Children," *NEA Journal*, 44:265, May 1955.

Terman, Lewis, *et al. Mental and Physical Traits of a Thousand Gifted Children. Genetic Studies of Genius*. Stanford: Stanford University Press, 1926.

Terman, Lewis, and Oden, Melita H. *The Gifted Child Grows Up*. Stanford: Stanford University Press, 1947.

Terman, Lewis, and Oden, Melita H. *The Gifted Group at Mid-Life: Thirty-five Years' Follow-up of the Superior Child*. Stanford: Stanford University Press, 1959.

Witty, Paul. "Gifted Children — Our Greatest Resource," *Nursing Education*, September 1955, pp. 498–500.

Witty, Paul, Conant, James B., and Strang, Ruth. *Creativity of Gifted and Talented Children*. New York: Bureau of Publications, Teachers College, Columbia University, 1959.

Worcester, Dean A. *The Education of Children of Above-Average Mentality*. Lincoln: University of Nebraska Press, 1956.

Yuhas, Frank T. "The Gifted Child in the Classroom," *Educational Administration and Supervision*, 43:429–438, November 1957.

# The mentally retarded child

And when into the commonplace
Some bit of leaven is instilled
To mingle with the mediocre
And lift it quite beyond itself —
This is reward.

JOSEPHINE LESTER

The child who shows no promise may become a contributing member of society or remain what he is — a charge of society. Many times the teacher makes the difference between the two extremes.

If mental status is to improve, treatment must begin early. "The time is short — far shorter than most people realize — for 90 per cent of the growth of the brain has been accomplished by the age of six years. . . . The child who on arriving at school age has already fallen so far behind his classmates as to be classed as mentally defective may show improvement under the kind of therapeutic treatment that is adjusted to his needs, but it is unlikely that the loss will be completely made up. Time is inexorable."[40]

There is some confusion in the terminology used to define the various categories of the mentally retarded. Here the terms "mentally educable retarded," "trainable mentally retarded," and "slow

[40] Goodenough, *op. cit.*, p. 26.

learner" will be used. The mentally educable retarded individual is one who, for temporary or long-standing reasons, functions intellectually below the average of his peer group but whose social adequacy is not in doubt, or, if it is in doubt, he can probably learn to function independently and adequately as a citizen in the community.

The trainable mentally retarded individual, on the other hand, is socially inadequate as a result of an intellectual defect which reflects an incurable impairment of the central nervous system. This condition has existed from birth or shortly thereafter. He will always need supervision and assistance, whereas the educable mentally retarded may require only temporary specialized assistance.

The slow learner is one who requires modification of instruction in the regular grades. He is not mentally handicapped to the extent that he requires a special class and different curriculum; he may remain in the class. The total-care retarded are not the problem of the school.

For educational purposes of planning and administration the mentally retarded are frequently divided into the following categories:[41]

| Classification | IQ Range | Minimum Percentage of Population |
|---|---|---|
| Total-care cases | Below 30–35 | 0.1 |
| Trainable mentally retarded | 30 or 35–50 | 0.2 |
| Educable mentally retarded | 50–75 or 80 | 3.0 |
| Slow learners | 75–90 | 14.0 |

*Early Identification and Diagnosis.* The earlier the child with special needs is detected, the more quickly can plans be made for helping him. Those who have worked with the handicapped know that early detection and treatment bear rich rewards.

Procedure varies in identifying and diagnosing the needs of the mentally retarded. Usually a survey is made to determine how many children of a given age are one to two years below average in grade level. Teachers are asked to make recommendations concerning boys and girls who are having difficulty keeping up with their grade. Records are checked to ascertain adequacy of the child in various areas including academic achievement. Group intelligence tests and,

[41] Adapted from Merle M. Ohlsen (ed.), *Modern Methods in Elementary Education* (New York: Henry Holt and Company, 1959), p. 594.

if needed, individual tests are administered. If necessary, a psychological study is made by an authorized person. A cooperative approach to the problem of identifying, diagnosing, and treating the individual is recommended. Such factors as social-emotional development, physical growth, educational and mental status, home relationships, and advisability of prescribing a special class must be considered.

## Education of the Mentally Retarded Child

*A Cooperative Approach.* "Mental retardation is not an entity — it is a complex of factors. . . . The mentally retarded child has medical problems, psychological problems, educational problems, vocational problems, social problems, and the like, and needs the appropriate specialized professional services for problems in each of these areas."[42]

In the cooperative approach, teachers, parents, physicians, therapists, psychiatrists, neurologists, recreational and social workers, physiologists, internal medicine specialists, and others form a team of experts. Not many retarded children will require the services of all of them, but they should all be available when needed.

*The Need for Special Classes.* The exceptional child must always be considered first from the point of view of normal growth and development. To conserve what is normal as well as to make the most of what is exceptional is the aim of the school. It has been found that the retarded child can profit from learning experiences *if* they are adapted to his needs. The average classroom is not particularly suited to his needs; neither is the average classroom teacher trained to deal with his unique problems. In the ordinary classroom his handicaps are accentuated and he feels inferior to the others in the group. Through the establishment of the special classes some of the unhappy experiences are avoided.

Special classes offer programs specifically designed to meet the needs of the mentally retarded. No seriously mentally retarded child is capable of getting sufficient good from the usual academic program to enable him to cope satisfactorily with the demands of life.

[42] Max L. Hutt and Robert Gwyn Gibby, *The Mentally Retarded Child* (Boston: Allyn and Bacon, Inc., 1958), p. 267.

*The Trainable Mentally Retarded Child.* Trainable mentally retarded children are those whose IQ's range from 30 or 35 to 50 and who show potentiality for growth in such areas as self-care, socialization, and economic usefulness if they are given guidance by a responsible adult. Included in this category are Mongoloid, cretinoid, and brain-injured children.

Even with proper guidance these people may never become self-supporting and independent. They will need sympathetic, intelligent, understanding guidance perhaps for an entire lifetime. The contribution of the school is to improve behavior through training — not to produce adult independence. The program emphasizes personal care activities such as responsibility for eating habits, dressing, cleanliness, toilet training; and household tasks such as setting the table, washing dishes, cleaning house, gardening, shoveling sidewalks, and washing the car. These children learn how to get along with others, to share, take turns, accept responsibility, and observe courteous behavior.

Through such training they can become more worth-while members of the family, the community, or the institutions in which they reside. Many of them can find unskilled employment of some type by the time they reach eighteen. They will continue to need the support and guidance of an adult to help them make wise decisions, but they can learn to become more useful members of society. They require not only a special teacher fully qualified but special facilities. They do not belong in the regular classes.

*The Educable Mentally Retarded Child.* The most important characteristic of this child is that he is educable. Unlike the trainable mentally retarded child, he can become a self-sustaining, productive member of society, capable of caring for his needs and taking full responsibility for a job. Intelligence quotients of this group range from 50 to 75 or 80 on the Stanford-Binet test. There are certain traits which the teacher may look for in identifying those to be tested:

1. Retarded language development.
2. Short memory and attention span.
3. Difficulty in understanding and remembering assignments.
4. Failure to grasp abstract concepts.
5. Limited ability in generalization and seeing commonalities in a situation.

6. Limitations in incidental learning.
7. Inability to work without an undue amount of guidance.
8. Inability to understand cause-and-effect relationships.

Most of these children will learn the basic fundamentals of reading, writing, and arithmetic up to about the fourth-grade level by the time they are sixteen years of age. The crucial factor in dealing with them are "the extent to which the teacher is trained and able to work constructively with them, the extent to which teachers and administrators plan and develop a consistent educational program for them and the ability of teachers and administrators to carry out a comprehensive program of education for them that will fulfill the long-range goals of public school education."[43] Such goals include life functions related to citizenship, communicating, home and family, leisure time, management of materials and money, occupational adequacy, physical and mental health, safety, social adjustment, and travel.[44]

It is generally agreed that the content of instruction should be presented at a rate approximately one-fourth slower than for the average child. In addition both repetition and reinforcement of the materials should be considerably more intensive.

At the primary level the major objective is to prepare the children to profit from their subsequent school experiences. The program is designed to teach them first the social skills. Each child is observed carefully to determine when he is ready for academic work. The primary program emphasizes (1) character training, (2) social learnings, (3) communication skills, (4) play activities, and (5) creative activities.

The intermediate level emphasizes academic work as well as skills in the areas of music, art, and literature. Here the children are old enough to learn, and developed enough physically to have greater muscular control and coordination. They are successful in writing and drawing. Their attention span is greater and their interests are more mature. Training in group living and social skills continues. Children work on their own level and proceed at their own pace. The teacher provides a variety of individual activities and change of

[43] Herbert Goldstein and Dorothy M. Siegle, *The Illinois Plan for Special Education of Exceptional Children:* A Curriculum Guide for Teachers of the Educable Mentally Handicapped, Curricular Series B–3, No. 12 (Chicago: Illinois Council for Mentally Retarded Children, 1958), p. 18.
[44] *Ibid.,* p. 19.

pace in group activities to arouse and maintain interest. Intermediate children are capable of more sustained interest and longer work periods. More cooperative projects may be introduced at this level. Children are taken on excursions into the community. They are taught to use transportation facilities, to handle money, make change, and become more independent.

Intellectual growth in the mentally retarded child is slower than normal. Current research indicates that the learning process of the retarded child differs qualitatively as well as quantitatively from the normal.

The average classroom teacher cannot be expected to accept children whose IQ falls below 55–60. In the face of large enrollments, inadequate facilities, and lack of time to create needed materials for such children in the regular classroom, other provisions must be made. In some schools the children are allowed to enter and remain until the situation becomes intolerable and then they are excluded. This creates a more severe hardship than exclusion before the child has entered the classroom.

*Some Differences Between the Educable and Trainable Classes.* Although the broad goals to be achieved with these two groups are similar, the final expectations are reflected in the expected degree of independence in adult living, as is evident in classroom practices.

1. Educable children, although they still need individual attention and help, are expected to progress faster toward self-responsibility. Children in the educable class are more quickly advanced to choice of activity, independence in the activity, and self-dependence.

2. Educable children are expected to learn academic subjects more efficiently. Since they have a longer attention span than trainable children, greater curiosity, and increased comprehension, academic learning is more meaningful and useful to them.

3. Educable children are .expected sooner to achieve a group feeling for observing the rules. It takes trainable children much longer to develop this, and some never achieve it.

4. Educable children, more than trainables, understand some simple principles of cause-and-effect relationships. Learning to anticipate results and accept responsibility for the consequences of one's behavior is more difficult for trainable children to achieve. They need closer supervision and more detailed, specific, and extended training because of their limited ability to foresee what will

happen. On the other hand, educable children are expected to accept a reasonable amount of responsibility for their behavior.[45]

*The Mentally Retarded in the Regular Classroom.* While the special class provides an ideal environment for the mentally retarded child, it is not always possible to make such an arrangement. The teacher in the regular classroom is faced with simultaneously providing for his needs and for the needs of the other children. It has been found that in an average class of thirty to forty youngsters, one to four are likely to be retarded to the extent of having special needs.

The retarded child has the basic needs of all children in addition to specific needs of his own. Thus he should be dealt with as a child before provisions are made for his handicap.

The teacher must make use of all possible aids to determine the needs of each child. He must observe the personality, behavior, and learning characteristics of each. Even where special classes are available the mentally retarded child may be enrolled in a regular class before he is transferred to the special class.

The deviating child should be identified through medical and psychological tests to discover the factors contributing to his behavior. The teacher should have access to the cumulative record file and the assistance of counselors. Audio-visual aids and concrete teaching materials and procedures are essential. Learning experiences should be organized around centers of vital interest and should provide for manipulative and creative activities.

Mentally retarded children profit from imitative techniques. They grasp what they see better than what they have to imagine. The teacher should explain clearly what it is he wants them to do. He must help them understand the assignment by explaining, supplementing, and reinforcing. The teaching must be largely individualized, developmental in method, and remedial in nature.

*The Slow Learner.* Nation-wide, some 20 per cent of the school population are classified as slow learners. The slow learner has been defined as a child whose intelligence quotient falls between 75 and 90 in the standard Stanford-Binet test. The slow learner can usually be educated in the regular classroom if the teacher modifies the program

[45] Harriet E. Blodgett and Grace J. Warfield, *Understanding Mentally Retarded Children* (New York: Appleton-Century-Crofts, Inc., 1959), pp. 85–86.

to allow him time to master the subject matter, provides concrete materials that facilitate learning, and provides extra help with problems which are difficult for him. Modifying the curriculum, supervising the activities, and giving additional guidance will help this child succeed. The slow learner can learn, but he needs more time to accomplish what the average child accomplishes. The teacher should discover the rate at which he learns and give him assignments that he can master. All children learn from experience, but some need a greater number and variety of experiences than their classmates.

Projects and activities for the slow learner should be simpler, and modified to meet their specific, individual needs. Materials should be closely related to their environmental and experiential background. Explanations must be clear and brief. Presentations should be concrete and, when possible, illustrated. Applications and generalizations should be simple. Individualization is important in helping the slow-learning child.

Mahoney suggests a few simple rules for facilitating the teaching-learning of the slow learner in the regular class:

> 1. Repeat often. The mentally retarded child learns primarily through habit formation, and to form habits patient repetition is necessary.
> 2. Allow plenty of time to complete a task. . . .
> 3. Help him only when he needs help. Encourage him to do as much as he can for himself.
> 4. Assign work units that are comparatively brief and within his capacity.
> 5. Show him how to do a thing rather than just giving him oral directions.
> 6. Arouse his interest so that he feels the need of knowing. . . .
> 7. Help him to relax — to forget frustrations and tensions. Help him to find joy and happiness in what he is doing.
> 8. Never forget to reward his honest efforts by a smile, a pat, or some other encouraging acknowledgement.[46]

Valuable as these suggestions are, they do not focus on the teaching of a specific subject such as reading. Many teachers of retarded children report that the reading program is really the most difficult part of their teaching. It is time-consuming and complicated to

---

[46] Agnes Mahoney, "The Slow Learner," *NEA Journal*, 47:621, December 1958.

handle.[47] Since the teaching of reading to the slow-learning child is difficult, some suggestions for facilitating the process are given:

1. Delay reading until the child shows evidence of being ready regardless of his chronological age.

2. Expect less of him than of the average child. Remember, his IQ may be around 70.

3. Select material on the basis of interest, ability, and need. Provide a large variety of easy books.

4. Use individualized instruction whenever possible.

5. Plan short but frequent periods of instruction.

6. Experiment with various techniques for improving word recognition — phonetics, ear-training activities, word-building games, and so forth.

7. Give special attention to mechanics of eye movements, line-by-line sequence, use of markers, and so forth.

8. Praise the child for each successful attempt to read. The factor of success in reading is most important in maintaining interest for the slow learner or the mentally retarded.

In working with the slow learner the teacher must keep in mind that the pace is slow. ". . . There are cases in which to lose time is to gain time, and by training the child in attention, in observation, the use of the senses, progress is far more surely made than by cramming him prematurely with food that he cannot assimilate — a process painful alike to teacher and pupil."[48]

## The Teacher of the Mentally Retarded

The mentally retarded child needs many things. He needs vocational training; he needs basic academic skills; he needs to develop motor and perceptual skills; and he needs, as do other children, security, affection, and a variety of learning experiences that will help him weave the design for development that is his alone. He needs, above all, a teacher who not only accepts him but possesses the

---

[47] Blodgett and Warfield, op. cit., p. 83.

[48] Alice Decoeudres, The Education of Mentally Defective Children, translated from the second French edition by Ernest F. Row (Boston: D. C. Heath and Company, 1928), p. 214.

knowledge and skill to help him. "Certain personal and professional qualifications are required for teaching mentally retarded children in school, interpreting them to parents and the community, and helping them to find their place in a society that does not always understand and accept them."[49]

In a recent study the distinctive competencies necessary were grouped under four broad headings:

1. Understanding the characteristics of the mentally retarded child and his place in society.
2. Developing a functional curriculum through relating the broad personal and social needs of the mentally retarded.
3. Understanding and applying pedagogical procedures based on an understanding of the known learning characteristics of the mentally retarded.
4. Selecting, developing, and using appropriate instructional materials and equipment in teaching mentally retarded children.[50]

The 150 teachers who participated in the study emphasized the following specific competencies:

1. Understanding the retarded child in a general and practical way with special emphasis on understanding social and emotional development and causes of maladjustment.
2. Ability to interpret tests, social work reports, and other diagnostic data.
3. Ability to participate cooperatively with other agencies.
4. Ability to teach the three R's effectively.
5. Socialization through unit teaching and participation in group activities and community-type experiences.[51]

The work of the teacher in guiding the mentally handicapped cannot be overestimated. He plays a significant role in helping the child rise above his handicap by inspiring confidence and by creating the kind of climate in which the handicapped child is free to learn.

---

[49] Romaine P. Mackie *et al., Teachers of Children Who Are Mentally Retarded,* A Report Based on Findings from the Study Qualifications and Preparation of Teachers of Exceptional Children, U.S. Department of Health, Education and Welfare, Bulletin No. 3 (Washington, D.C.: Government Printing Office, 1957), p. 4.
[50] *Ibid.,* p. 6.
[51] Adapted from *ibid.,* p. 63.

# ACTIVITIES AND QUESTIONS

1. Observe in a class for mentally retarded children if there is one nearby. What specific techniques does the teacher employ in working with these children? How do they differ from the techniques used by a teacher of a regular classroom in providing for the slow learner?
2. What are some specific suggestions for teaching reading to slow learners? Did you observe a teacher using any of these?

# BIBLIOGRAPHY

Baker, Harry J. *Introduction to Exceptional Children.* New York: The Macmillan Company, 3rd ed., 1959.

Blodgett, Harriet E., and Warfield, Grace J. *Understanding Mentally Retarded Children.* New York: Appleton-Century-Crofts, Inc., 1959.

Cook, Walter W. "The Gifted and Retarded in Historical Perspective," *Phi Delta Kappan,* 39:249–255, March 1958.

Cruickshank, William M., and Johnson, G. Orville (eds.). *Education of Exceptional Children and Youth.* Englewood Cliffs, N.J.: Prentice-Hall, Inc., 1958.

Davies, Stanley P., and Ecob, Katherine. *The Mentally Retarded Child in Society.* New York: Columbia University Press, 1959.

*Directory for Exceptional Children: Educational and Training Facilities.* Boston: Porter Sargent, Publisher, 3rd ed., 1958.

Goodenough, Florence L. *Exceptional Children.* New York: Appleton-Century-Crofts, Inc., 1956.

Harrison, Sam. "A Review of Research in Speech and Language Development of the Mentally Retarded Child," *American Journal of Mental Deficiency,* 63:236–240, September 1958.

Heiser, Karl F. *Our Backward Children.* New York: W. W. Norton and Company, 1955.

Hutt, Max L., and Gibby, Robert Gwyn. *The Mentally Retarded Child.* Boston: Allyn and Bacon, Inc., 1958.

*The Illinois Plan for Special Education of Exceptional Children.* A Curriculum Guide for Teachers of the Educable Mentally Handicapped. Curricular Series B3, No. 12, 1958. Issued by Vernon L. Nickell, Superintendent of Public Instruction.

Ingram, Christine P. *Education of the Slow-Learning Child.* New York: The Ronald Press Company, rev. ed., 1960.

Johnson, G. Orville, and Blake, Katheryn A. *Learning Performance of Retarded and Normal Children.* Syracuse: Syracuse University Press, 1960.

Kirk, Samuel A., and Johnson, G. Orville. *Educating the Retarded Child.* Boston: Houghton Mifflin Company, 1951.

Krugman, Morris (ed.). *Orthopsychiatry and the School.* New York: American Orthopsychiatric Association, 1958.

"Language Gains of the Retarded," *School Life,* 41:15, September 1958.

Lloyd, Frances. *Educating the Sub-Normal Child.* New York: Philosophical Library, 1953.

Mackie, Romaine P. "Educational Opportunities for Exceptional Children," *The Grade Teacher,* 77:18, 19, 79, May 1959.

Magary, James F., and Eichorn, John R. (eds.). *The Exceptional Child: A Book of Readings.* New York: Holt, Rinehart & Winston, 1960.

Magnifico, L. X. "The Education of the Mentally Retarded: In the Light of the New Emphasis on the Education of the Gifted," *Educational Admininstration and Supervision,* 45:77–83, March 1959.

National Association for Retarded Children. *Basic Library on Mental Retardation.* New York: The Association, n.d.

National Association for Retarded Children. *The Trainable Child in a Community School.* New York: The Association, 1955.

Salvatore, G. Michael. *Counseling and Psychotherapy with the Mentally Retarded.* Glencoe, Ill.: The Free Press, 1957.

Smith, Marion F. *Teaching the Slow Learning Child.* New York: Harper & Brothers, 1954.

*Teachers of Children Who Are Mentally Retarded.* U.S. Department of Health, Education and Welfare, Bulletin No. 3. Washington, D.C.: Government Printing Office, 1956.

Wallin, John E. Wallace. *Education of Mentally Handicapped Children.* New York: Harper & Brothers, 1955.

# The physically handicapped child

Not only of the great-to-be she sent
Ahead, but of each weaker child, endowed
By her strength, each stumbling, awkward one.

ELIAS LIEBERMAN

## The Crippled Child

"Children are crippled when through accident, disease, or abnormal development they have suffered a defect in bone or muscle tissue. They are not usually classified as crippled, however, unless the extent of their disability interferes with their education and training or may later interfere with their choice or competence in a vocation."[52]

Whenever the degree of crippling and the personal-social adjustment warrant it, these children benefit from regular class attendance. However, placement in special classes or schools may be required. In general, the child should be encouraged to participate in the work

[52] John J. Lee and Lee M. Vincent, "Exceptional Children," in Nelson B. Henry (ed.), *Early Childhood Education*, Forty-Sixth Yearbook, National Society for the Study of Education, Part II (Chicago: University of Chicago Press, 1947), p. 324.

and play of normal children whenever it is possible for him to do so. Early identification, diagnosis, and treatment are important in preventing, removing, or minimizing the disabilities.

The more seriously crippled child should be enrolled in special classes and/or schools where special equipment and therapeutic treatment are available. The nature of the techniques and equipment used will depend upon the degree of the handicap and the vocational goals toward which the child is encouraged to aim.

The severely handicapped child belongs in a school which has unique features geared to meet his needs: elevators, numerous and/ or specialized toilet facilities, handrails in corridors, wide halls, full-length mirrors, wheel chairs, specially designed desks, tanks, therapeutic equipment, swimming pools, baths, sunrooms, sleeping rooms, light treatments, special diets, close medical supervision, and transportation to and from school.

In many ways crippled children need an educational program similar to that of the average child. Mentally, socially, and emotionally they are typical school children. The child with only a slight deviation may remain in the regular classroom. Because he is not able to enter into the activities which emphasize physical prowess he is often at a disadvantage in physical and social learnings. The teacher should make a point of including in the program some games and physical activities in which he can engage with satisfaction. For example, the child with crippled legs may be able to achieve satisfaction and status by excelling in games which require skill in using the hands and arms or ears and eyes. For at least a part of each play period the handicapped child should become a participator, not a spectator.

In educating the crippled child it is important to realize that he has the same ambitions, desires, and mental abilities as the child who is not physically handicapped. He may differ only in not being as active physically as the other children. A good program provides appropriate educational opportunities, recognizes the handicap from which the child is suffering, helps him develop initiative and self-reliance, and gives physical, emotional, and educational assistance.

Some simple guidelines a teacher may find helpful in a situation where a crippled child is in the regular classroom are the following:

1. Treat the child like any other youngster. Encourage him when he needs it; praise him when he is deserving.

2. Find ways for him to be useful to others. He needs to offer service before he can comfortably accept the help he needs.

3. Accept the handicap. Show a normal interest in how he does the things he can do and in how he might extend his range of activities.

4. Emphasize the right to be different, not alone for this child but for each child in the class.[53]

The number of crippled children who can effectively be taught in regular classes will increase as classroom teachers extend their knowledge of the needs of handicapped children and administrators provide facilities for them. There is growing evidence that more people than ever before look upon a handicapped person as a normal individual with a handicap and focus attention on his abilities rather than his disabilities. They are more concerned with what he can do than with what he cannot do.

## *The Blind Child*

The number of blind children enrolled in school is decreasing as medical science makes advances in the control of retrolental fibroplasia. Today there are over 17,000 blind children below the age of twenty in our country.[54] The needs of these children must be met if they are to become contributing members of society. The notion that all the blind can do is weave rugs, make baskets, and cane chairs is fortunately outmoded. The trend is to provide educational opportunities similar to those of physically normal children. Emphasis is upon early identification and providing an education that will aid them in living as normal a life as possible.[55]

The child blind from birth or an early age is seriously handicapped. He can lead a full life only if he develops to a high degree the

[53] Adapted from Frances A. Mullen, "The Crippled," *NEA Journal*, 47:617, December 1958.

[54] White House Conference on Children and Youth, *Children in a Changing World*, (Washington, D.C.: Golden Anniversary White House Conference on Children and Youth, 1960), p. 38.

[55] According to Dean, the Emotional Factors Inventory results suggest that the "blind are not paranoid or depressed as a group; a finding at variance with previous assumptions." Sidney I. Dean, "Testing and Personality Factors of the Blind," *Journal of Consulting Psychology*, 21:171–177, April 1957.

abilities he does possess. He needs to be helped to do things for himself, and to alleviate fears that arise from not being able to see.

The local community has a responsibility for educating blind children, which means identifying the blind, establishing a center, transporting the pupils, equipping the classroom, developing good relationships between the special teacher and the regular classroom teacher, furnishing an adequate number of books and other instructional materials, and selecting a capable teaching staff. Because normal children receive so many of their sensory impressions through the eyes, blindness is perhaps the greatest handicap among exceptional children.

Abel calls attention to variations of patterns in the education of blind children in this country: First is the residential school, which is state supported, privately supported, and/or supported through state-paid tuition and private funds. It is characterized by a functional physical plant, active home-school relations, articulation with the regular public school, and professional sociological and psychological personnel.

Second is the special class for blind with sighted children in the public school, established on the premise that unless the program achieves participation of blind with sighted children it defeats its purpose. More blind children are being accepted in science classes, physical education programs, and most of the other subjects that meet their individual needs.

Third is the consultative or itinerant teacher plan, developing mainly in rural areas. The itinerant teacher makes his services available to various schools in a larger community or state where an occasional blind child is enrolled in a regular public school. With his help the blind child is able to attend school in his own or a nearby community. In this pattern the blind child is able to function with much less dependence on a special teacher. The itinerant teacher concentrates mainly on counseling or teaching specific skills.[56]

The kind of specialized education blind children need usually involves learning to read Braille and learning to use resources other than sight for moving from place to place. Physical orientation is an important part of the training.

---

[56] George L. Abel, "New Frontiers in the Education of the Young Blind Child," in Vincent J. Glennon (ed.), *Frontiers of Elementary Education*, I (Syracuse: Syracuse University Press, 1954), pp. 72–76.

"Much progress has been made in the education of the blind. . . . However, the very fact that the Braille system seemed to provide blind children with an effective reference for their education, as well as necessary writing of details in their daily living, may have retarded recognition for the need of more recorded materials which are available today in most programs."[57]

## *The Child with Partial Vision*

A partially seeing child may be defined as "one whose visual acuity is 20/70 or less in the better eye after the best medical and optical correction and who can still use sight as his chief channel of learning. Any child suffering from disease of the eye or disease of the body that seriously affects vision and who, in the opinion of the specialist and the teacher, would benefit from special education facilities may also be classified as partially seeing."[58] In addition, some children may need the special services on a temporary basis.

Although the child with partial vision is not nearly as handicapped as the blind child, he, too, has problems. He is deprived of many sources of stimulation for development, and his participation in play and recreational activities is limited. For this reason he should be identified early so that every effort can be made to preserve the eyesight he does possess. Sight-saving classes are frequently organized to prevent the further loss of vision. Children who also need special attention are those with serious, progressive eye difficulties and those suffering from diseases of the eye or diseases of the body that seriously affect vision. Temporarily included in the sight-saving classes may be children who have had eye operations and need eye readaptations or psychological adjustment, and those who have strabismus or other muscle anomalies that necessitate re-education of the deviating eye, especially when negative psychological reactions are evident.

In working with partial-visioned children the objective is the

[57] *Ibid.*, p. 76.
[58] Romaine P. Mackie *et al.*, *Teachers of Children Who Are Partially Seeing*, U.S. Department of Health, Education and Welfare, Bulletin No. 4 (Washington, D.C.: Government Printing Office, 1956), p. 5.

prevention of blindness. All materials selected, classrooms used, and work required will be determined on the basis of the effect they have upon the sight of the children. These children can see. They use their eyes and they read from books. They do not learn through their fingers.

Children are generally identified for the program cooperatively through (1) examination of preschool children at summer round-up, (2) annual examination by the nurse of the elementary school, (3) examination of a child who comes in after the regular check has been made, or who manifests signs of deviation in sight, (4) examination of a child whom the regular classroom teacher refers as a candidate for the sight-saving class, and (5) alerting the teachers in the classroom to signs of defective vision. As soon as the condition of their eyes permits, these children return to their regular classroom.

The National Society for the Prevention of Blindness recommends an annual vision test using the Snellen chart at twenty feet. Children are referred if (1) they fail the vision test or (2) they have signs or symptoms suggesting eye disorder (redness, styes, squinting, headaches, difficulty in reading, or similar symptoms).[59] "It is felt that this method will find not only nearsightedness but significant amounts of farsightedness, astigmatism, muscle imbalance, or any other defects of importance. If an eye condition does not impair vision or cause symptoms, the child need not be referred for treatment."[60]

A perfect screening test is one that finds every child who needs special help and refers no one unnecessarily. Such a test has not yet been discovered and probably never will be. Certain features of a good test are characteristic, however: it is quick, inexpensive, easy to administer for the examiner, and acceptable to the child. Ideally, it should be administered by the school nurse after the children have been prepared for it. Frequently the teacher or nurse orients the children and instructs them in the procedure.

The educational needs of the partially seeing can be met in a number of ways depending upon the individual child, the facilities provided by the local school system, and the community resources:

---

[59] A pamphlet describing procedures may be obtained by writing to the Society at 1790 Broadway, New York 19, N.Y., and requesting Publication 180.

[60] Edward U. Murphy and Evannah Thyng, "School Vision Screening," *Journal of the Indiana State Medical Association*, 10:1346, October 1957. (Reprint.)

(1) Children are enrolled in a special room where the teacher plans their work, scheduling part of it in the regular class.

(2) Children are enrolled in regular classes and report to a special resource room for the help they need from a special teacher.

(3) The itinerant teacher works with partially seeing children and their regular teachers. He may provide needed equipment, counseling and guidance, and tutoring in special areas where children indicate a need.[61]

Whatever plan is used, it is essential that the program be an integral part of the regular school curriculum. Special services and materials which are needed to help the child in reaching his optimum potentialities should be provided. The trend is toward educating these children in regular public schools so that partially seeing and normally seeing children can work and play together.

When partially sighted children are in the regular class the teacher should help them as much as possible by placing them where they can see the board work, by giving them individualized attention, by checking with parents and school nurse to see that they have needed medical attention and are fitted with proper glasses, and by preparing special materials for academic work, with large type to avoid undue strain. In addition, the teacher should encourage the child to look away from his work periodically in order to rest his eyes. He must provide, too, for relaxation of his body.

The teacher has another responsibility: to help the child "find himself," discover his talents. The thick glasses he wears, the clumsy and awkward movements in play, may make him unattractive to other children. Unless the teacher accepts and values him he may become an isolate. Unless he discovers his special abilities he may be "lost."

Martin was such a child. When he enrolled in kindergarten he presented a sorry picture. Unattractive in appearance, having the sight of only one eye, cluttered in his speech, handicapped in his ability to walk, completely dependent upon his mother, he stood out from the group — but in a way that evoked undesirable responses in the other children. Either they shunned him or made fun of his hopeless attempts to speak. The teacher realized that something must be done.

Fortunately, Martin had a sense of artistry that made itself felt

[61] Mackie, *Teachers of Children Who Are Partially Seeing*, p. 5.

in the creative dramatics activities. Even when he was not chosen to participate, he would get up and mimic those chosen. He had original ideas about playing the characters in the nursery rhymes. He could think of more ways of portraying the king in "Sing a Song of Sixpence" or "Old King Cole" than anyone else. He *became* the character. Before long the children began to choose him because of his originality and spontaneity. He became the child most sought after when they dramatized, pantomined, or played stories. And when he played a part everyone forgot that he was not handsome in appearance, fluent in speech, or graceful in movement. They forgot because temporarily he *was* handsome, fluent, and graceful. They forgot because a teacher remembered the importance of understanding the child's social and emotional problems stemming from his visual impairment. The teacher remembered, too, the importance of providing a classroom atmosphere in which each child is valued, which is conducive to good mental health and helping shy pupils become well adjusted.

One teacher summed up several important competencies which teachers of partially seeing children should possess: "Treat the handicap matter-of-factly. Help the child to understand it. Teach the importance of general good health and encourage him to function to the height of his abilities. Train the ear, the heart, and the spirit so that even the impaired eye will have a 'twinkle.' "[62]

## The Child with Defective Hearing

The development of speech is normally dependent upon auditory impressions. Impaired hearing involves, potentially or actually, some degree of distortion of auditory perception. The normal child who enters school has developed speech skills, has an extensive vocabulary, and is eager to learn and to discuss what he learns in the language he has acquired up to this point.

The deaf child has no such advantages. He cannot imitate the voices of others. He has to imitate the movements of the speaker's

[62] *Ibid.*

face, throat, tongue, lips through seeing or feeling. His eyes have to do, alone, the work of the eyes and ears of the hearing child. From the point of view of instruction, no other group, perhaps, presents so complex and difficult a problem.

It has been estimated that "the number of severely handicapped hard-of-hearing needing the special class is almost as great as the partially seeing, since the number of the totally deaf is approximately equal to the blind."[63]

Children with defective hearing fall into three classes: the deaf, the deafened, and the hard of hearing. The deaf suffer the greatest handicap because they lost all perceptual hearing *before* they had an opportunity to acquire normal speech. The deafened lost their hearing *after* they acquired speech. The hard of hearing have partial hearing.

The deaf child, because he has no concept of sound, has special needs. Every child has problems of adjusting to the world, the neighborhood, the community, and the family. The deaf child has these adjustments to make plus many more. Because he has no concept of sound, he must have special training. The deafened, too, must have special training or they will lose the concept of sound. The hard of hearing have the problem of conserving the residual hearing they possess.

Ideally, every school child should have a hearing test each year. It is essential that loss of hearing be discovered early and that treatment be made available to reduce the functional hearing losses. An accurate diagnosis must be made in order to determine the extent of the child's hearing loss and the treatment required. The child with impaired hearing needs a balance of parental love and affection, and an opportunity for developing self-confidence and independence.

Special schools are required to meet the needs of the deaf and deafened. State schools, and some city schools, have programs for educating deaf children and their parents based on the principles (1) that the child be the focal point in the program, (2) that equality of opportunity be provided, (3) that children be educated for living in a society of hearing individuals, and (4) that prevention be the core of the program. Prevention can be facilitated by educating

---

[63] Harry Baker, *Introduction to Exceptional Children* (New York: The Macmillan Company, rev. ed., 1953), p. 98.

parents concerning the dangers of children's diseases and their own responsibility for their prevention; by having schools maintain a regular system of physical examination to detect hearing loss; by urging state and local communities to supervise and develop classes and schools for the deaf; by enacting legislation that makes possible the maintenance and extension of state support; by compulsory education of the deaf; and by an increased measure of support as the needs increase. Prevention should be the core of the program.

The teacher who is interested in working with children of this type should become familiar with facilities and methods used in special classes. He must not underestimate the importance of the child's interests or needs as he plans learning activities. The child must be challenged, his experiences must be broadened, and his communication skills must be made more effective. The average classroom teacher lacks the training needed to help the child in special skills, but he can refer the child to the proper specialists. It is his responsibility to insist upon an ear examination and other services.

The teacher of the special classes must always be on the alert to learn about the advances in the field. Dr. R. W. Guelke and Dr. R. M. J. Huyssen at the University of Capetown, South Africa, have developed and are testing a machine that permits the deaf to hear with their fingers. The objective is twofold: to teach the deaf how to read lips faster, and to help them master correct pronunciation so that their speech will sound more normal.

The machine operates in this manner: Different sounds — vowels, consonants, diphthongs, words — are fed into a microphone. They are translated by electricity into mechanical vibrations which a person can hear by resting his fingers on a series of quivering reeds. Different sounds have different frequencies. The different frequencies are fed to different parts of the finger because the touch nerves of the skin respond differently.

Many sounds, especially vowels and diphthongs, can be distinguished without any training whatever. The tests revealed, however, that it is hard to recognize consonants because the fingers do not decode their sounds as well as the ears do.

It is believed that with longer training and improved equipment a person who is totally deaf should be able to hear consonants clearly with his fingers. Then an instructor could use the device while giving lip-reading instruction and so make it possible for a deaf person to learn to communicate faster and better with the people around him.

A recent study focusing on the competencies required for teachers in this area revealed that teachers of hard-of-hearing children

1. Should be primarily specialists in teaching communication skills, particularly the skills of speechreading (lipreading), auditory comprehension, and speech and language development.
2. Should have a sound background in medical, physiological, psychological, and physical science with reference to the problems of communication (especially hearing).
3. Are more concerned with general programming and broad curriculum than with specific curriculums. (Although the teacher feels a responsibility for the child's total education, certain specific educational experiences may be the responsibility of other teachers.)
4. Are less concerned with the importance of equipment, materials, and tests than with the importance of competencies involved in understanding the child.
5. Must be able to cope effectively with the multifaced problems of counseling and guiding the child, and cooperating with his parents and other professional persons on whom the child's education rests.
6. Must be able to work as a close team with other professions and agencies concerned with the hard of hearing child.
7. Do not feel that it is necessary to be highly competent in other areas of exceptionality.
8. Need a greater degree of certain personal characteristics for teaching hard-of-hearing children than for teaching "normal" children.
9. Consider supervised student teaching in lipreading, speech development, and voice improvement to be of most importance.
10. Should spend approximately 210 to 260 clock hours in supervised practice for an "ideal" preparation.
11. Should have at least one year of classroom teaching experience with "normal" children for an "ideal" preparation.
12. Will be most likely to succeed if the program of professional preparation includes one year of graduate study in the specialized field and teaching experience with "normal" children.[64]

64 Romaine P. Mackie and Don A. Harrington, *Teachers of Children Who Are Hard of Hearing* (Washington, D.C.: Government Printing Office, 1959), pp. 48, 49.

*The Hard-of-Hearing Child in the Regular Classroom.* The class-room teacher must always be on the alert for hearing defects. Berry cites signs of defective hearing that the teacher should not ignore: "earache complaints, running ears, stupid expression, imperfect speech, poor spelling, frequent asking that questions be repeated, one side of head turned toward the speaker, and a way of looking at the speaker with a peculiar intentness."[65]

Children learn by seeing, feeling, and hearing. Schools have long tried to help the child with poor vision. Most schools today are trying to find and help the child who has impaired hearing. If the school system provides regular hearing tests such a child will be discovered. If not, the teacher must watch for signs that will indicate that he is not hearing clearly. The child who is uninterested in the lessons, who consistently makes mistakes that indicate the question was not understood in answering questions, and who has a tendency to withdraw, may be suffering from a hearing loss. A hearing test should be arranged. Keaster suggests that the teacher consider the following points:

(1) The child should be seated as near as possible to the place where the teacher is likely to be standing the majority of the time during instruction periods.

(2) The child should be allowed to move freely about the room in order to hear what is going on.

(3) The teacher must make a little extra effort to be certain that the child hears what is being said, both by herself and by other children in the class.

(4) Some time should be found to explain the problem of the hard of hearing child to the rest of the class. If the child is old enough he may be helped to explain it to the class himself.

(5) The child must be included in all of the extra-curricular activities participated in by his classmates. In other words, some attention must be given to being certain that he belongs to the group and is at all times an integral part of it.[66]

[65] Charles Scott Berry, *How the Teacher May Help the Exceptional Child* (Columbus, Ohio: Ohio State University, Bureau of Special Education, 1951), p. 8.

[66] Jacqueline Keaster, "Children with Impaired Hearing," in Wendell Johnson (ed.), *Speech Problems of Children* (New York: Grune and Stratton, Inc., 1950), p. 253.

## ACTIVITIES AND QUESTIONS

1. What principles should be observed in working with the physically handicapped child in the regular classroom?
2. Observe in a special class for physically handicapped children and compare the teaching methods used with those that are used for a handicapped child in the regular classroom. What modifications did the teacher of the regular classroom make to provide for the handicapped children?
3. Find out what the certification requirements are for teachers of exceptional children in your state.

## BIBLIOGRAPHY

*Crippled Children in School.* U.S. Office of Education, Bulletin No. 5. Washington, D.C.: Government Printing Office, 1948.

Cruickshank, William M., and Johnson, G. Orville (eds.). *Education of Exceptional Children and Youth.* Englewood Cliffs, N.J.: Prentice-Hall, Inc., 1958.

Cutsforth, Margery, *et al.* "Blind Youngsters in Nursery School and Kindergartens: Part I, The Preschool Blind Child at Home; Part II, Panel Discussion, The Blind Child as a Member of a Nursery School or Kindergarten," *Exceptional Children,* 24:58–66, October 1957.

Davis, Hallowell. *Hearing and Deafness: A Layman's Guide.* New York: Rinehart and Company, 1947.

Fornay, Katherine. *Up and Away: The Education of Handicapped but Exceptional Children.* New York: Exposition Press, 1957.

Frampton, M. E. *Special Education for the Exceptional Child.* Boston: Porter Sargent, Publisher, 1955.

Garrison, Karl G., and Force, Dewey A. *The Psychology of Exceptional Children.* New York: The Ronald Press Company, 3rd ed., 1959.

Graham, J. P. "When You Build Don't Forget the Handicapped," *Illinois School Board Journal,* 24:7–10, September–October 1957.

Irwin, Ruth Becky. *Speech and Hearing Therapy.* Englewood Cliffs, N.J.: Prentice-Hall, Inc., 1953.

Johnson, Wendell. *Children with Speech and Hearing Impairment.* U.S. Department of Health, Education and Welfare, Bulletin No. 5. Washington, D.C.: Government Printing Office, 1959.

Kvaraceus, William C. "Selected References from the Literature on Exceptional Children," *Elementary School Journal,* 60:343–348, March 1960.

Lassman, Grace Harris. *Language for the Preschool Deaf Child.* New York: Grune and Stratton, Inc., 1950.

Magnifico, L. X. *Education for the Exceptional Child.* New York: Longmans, Green and Company, 1958.

Morris, Miriam, Spaulding, Patricia, and Brodie, Fern. *Blindness in Children.* Chicago: University of Chicago Press, 1957.

Murphy, Edward U., and Thyng, Evannah. "School Vision Screening," *Journal of the Indiana State Medical Association,* 10:1345–1347, October 1957.

Newby, Hayes A. *Audiology, Principles and Practices.* New York: Appleton-Century-Crofts, Inc., 1958.

*Some Problems in the Education of Handicapped Children.* Bulletin No. 17. Washington, D.C.: U.S. Office of Education, Federal Security Agency, 1951.

*Teachers of Children Who Are Partially Seeing.* U.S. Department of Health, Education and Welfare, Bulletin No. 4. Washington, D.C.: Government Printing Office, 1956.

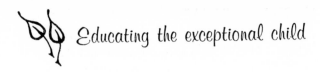 

# The speech-defective child

The ability to speak clearly and understandably is basic to living useful, happy lives in our society.

JAYNE SHOVER

The pattern of the child's speech is established before he enrolls in school. In most instances he speaks adequately for his level of maturity. Various authors give widely differing percentages of the elementary school children who are handicapped in their oral communication because of speech disorders. Some have called handicapped only those who need the services of a trained speech therapist; others have included all who speak in such a way as to be noticeably "different" from their associates. The most conservative of them estimate that nationally at least 5 per cent must have speech correction if they are not to suffer serious drawbacks in life. If the mild speech problems are included, the estimates run as high as 25 per cent.

## The Role of the Teacher

First of all, the teacher must understand that the child who has difficulty in his speech usually differs from the rest of the children in no other respect. The same range of intelligence, the same likes and dislikes will be found in those who speak easily and those who have problems in speaking. Differences in personality are usually the result not of any basic differences in the children but the frustrations and misunderstandings brought about by their speech problems. When there is a speech disorder the parents, and later the playmates and the teachers, too often look on the child as something apart and peculiar and treat him accordingly. He may be ignored, punished, teased, or coddled and he reacts accordingly. If the problems he faces in his communication difficulties could be understood there would be fewer extreme differences in his behavior pattern.

The teacher should understand also that the children with common types of difficulty have usually developed them in more or less the same ways and for the same reasons. Those who have hesitant speech have not learned to progress easily from one sound or word to the next. The hard of hearing do not hear the sounds made by others. Those with faulty articulation have not learned to make the sounds. Those with physical disabilities have had to adjust their speech to their handicaps in attempting to reproduce the sounds they hear and understand.

Finally, the teacher should recognize that there is no "method" that will cure speech problems. Drills, games, speech exercises are all good. But they are not the whole answer. Cooperation with the parents, speech therapists if they are involved in the correction, and the child himself is essential to make sure that both the goal and the methods for reaching the goal are mutually understood. The teacher must know the child and his parents in order to find the causes for the problem and to get their help in solving it.

## Types of Speech Disorders

*The Child Who Does Not Speak Plainly.* Speech is a complex skill. A child must learn to make the forty-two sounds of the American language through hearing and imitating the speech around him. In addition, he must learn to combine them into meaningful words arranged in an acceptable order. Many children who do not speak plainly can produce each sound separately but have never gained the necessary skill to combine them into meaningful speech. Certain sounds are omitted, others may be substituted, some are distorted, or additional sounds may be added. In the very young child this all passes as a normal part of his learning to speak. As he grows older, more is expected of him. When his pattern becomes too different from that of his playmates they usually tease him, or show their disapproval by ignoring or ridiculing him. Parents frequently believe they can improve the situation by shaming the child into speaking correctly. The result is usually withdrawal from all possible speech situations. Occasionally, however, the child finds the attention desirable. He is "noticed" and likes it.

The classroom teacher can do much to alleviate problems with articulation. In the primary grades a child may still be in the process of learning some of the sounds. Roe and Milisen[67] tested nearly 2000 children in Grades 1 through 6 and found a significant difference in the number of errors made in the first three grades. They interpreted this to mean that maturation played an important part in the elimination of many of the errors. It would seem, then, that the classroom teacher, through intelligently planning speech games and drills, can do much to aid many of the children in acquiring acceptable articulation, allowing the speech therapist to work with the more serious problems.

Traditionally, the child who has difficulty in producing a sound is taught to say it first in isolation, then combined with vowels in initial, medial, and final positions. Next he is drilled on the sound in difficult blends. Finally he is asked to use it in words and sentences. All too often it is at this last stage that he fails. He becomes too eager to communicate and reverts to his old patterns.

Shames[68] reports on an experiment in which he endeavored to bridge the gap between deliberate and automatic sound production. In normal development of speech the babbling phase is followed by the jargon phase, in which the child practices sounds at various rates, inflections, rhythms, and in various combinations. Shames believed that this developmental sequence should parallel the learning sequence in articulation therapy. He devised a type of nonsense jargon

[67] V. Roe and R. Milisen, "The Effect of Visual, Auditory, and Combined Visual-Auditory Stimulation upon the Speech Responses of Defective Speaking Children," *Journal of Speech and Hearing Disorders*, 7:37–50, February 1942.

[68] George H. Shames, "Use of the Nonsense-Syllable in Articulation Therapy," *Journal of Speech and Hearing Disorders*, 22:261–263, June 1957.

composed of the sounds being learned. This drill followed the learning of the sound in isolation and in combinations to close the gap between practice and automaticity. "With repeated practice, there seems to be a long term carry-over into automatic, typical talking. These reports have also indicated the ease with which such a procedure can be used. It does not necessitate a book, or materials, or even another person. It can be done alone, applied to singing and self-talking, and seems adaptable to motivational games for children. It seems that this technique of structured jargon can build up the automaticity of correct sound production and enable the use of new sounds in talking to be a rewarding experience that will become reinforced with continued usage."[69]

In addition to speech games and the structured jargon suggested above many teachers use stories with particular sounds marked for drill. These may be stories written by the child or teacher with specific sounds in mind, or they may be stories from the library with the sounds marked for particular attention. An example of a story written for such drill is shown below:

### *Sally, Sue, and the Fireflies*[70]

*The "s" sound*

Once upon a time there were two little girls whose names were Sally and Sue. Sally and Sue loved animals. They had a little puppy whose name was Snoopy. One summer day while Sally, Sue and Snoopy were staying at Grandmother's farm a very strange thing happened.

*The "r" sound*

Sally and Sue rushed up to Grandmother and said "Grandmother, may we go out and play? The sun is going down and we want to run out right now and see the fireflies!"

*The "g" sound*

"Go on out and play," laughed Grandmother. "But don't go into the great big woods for you might get lost and Grandmother wouldn't be able to find you in the great big dark woods."

[69] *Ibid.*, pp. 262–263.
[70] Janet Brashier, original story prepared as class assignment for Speech 131, Evansville College, Evansville, Ind., June 1960.

*The "k" sound*

"Come on, let's go," Sally *c*alled to Sue, "before the fireflies *c*an fly away!"

"I thin*k* I'll *c*all Snoopy to go with us," said Sue. "He li*k*es to watch the fireflies, too."

*The "n" sound*

Whe*n* Sally, Sue, a*n*d S*n*oopy ra*n* out the back door to see the fireflies glowing i*n* the dark, they *n*oticed that the *n*ight was *n*early there. The su*n* was dow*n* and the moo*n* was hidde*n* by black clouds and *n*o fireflies were to be see*n*.

*The "t" sound*

"This is *t*errible," Sally said *t*earfully to Sue and Snoopy. "*T*o-nigh*t* the fireflies mus*t* have gone *t*o bed early."

*The "d" sound*

"*D*on't worry, said Sue. "I *d*on't believe that they went to be*d* early. I think they are *d*oing this to tease us. *D*o you know what we can *d*o to find them? Let's hunt for them in the woo*d*s!"

*The "sh" sound*

"*Sh*!" whispered Sally. "We *sh*ouldn't go into the woods. Grand-mother warned us not to. We might get lost and *sh*e couldn't find us."

"I wi*sh* we could, because I want to find the fireflies," whined Sue.

*The "ch" sound*

"All right, whi*ch* way should we go?" asked Sally as Sue tried to *ch*oke back her tears. "*Ch*eer up, Sue, we'll find them."

*The "zh" sound*

"Well," said Sue, " I u*s*ually wouldn't go. But we'll pretend we are on a trea*s*ure hunt."

*The "z" sound*

The two girl*s* and Snoopy started looking for their treasure and before they realized it Grandmother'*s* house was completely out of sight.

*The "th" sound* (voiced)

"*Th*is woods is bigger *th*an I thought it was," whispered Sally. "All of *th*e trees look as if *th*ey have arms reaching out." *Th*e trees stood silently as *th*e two little girls and *th*eir dog walked through *th*em.

*The "th" sound* (voiceless)

"I *th*ink we should go back," Sally said. "Can you see the pa*th*?"

*The "hw" sound*

"Don't say things like that," cried Sue, "because *wh*en you *wh*isper about the trees, it scares me. I don't know *wh*ich way the path is, do you?"

*The "w" sound*

"*W*ell, *w*e *w*ill never find the fireflies if you get scared," Sally said *w*istfully.

*The "l" sound*

*L*itt*l*e by *l*itt*l*e the two gir*l*s and Snoopy *l*eft Grandmother's house far behind and s*l*owly found their way deeper and deeper into the *l*onely woods.

*The "f" sound*

Grandmother had *f*inished doing the dinner dishes and *f*ound herself wondering and worrying about her two *f*avorite grandchildren. She went to the *f*ront door and looked out the window. She went to the back door to look *f*ar out into the woods. She still could not *f*ind her two *f*avorite grandchildren because it was so very dark.

*The "v" sound*

"Ha*v*e they gone into the woods? If they are ro*v*ing around in that big dark woods, I'll ne*v*er be able to find them," thought Grandmother.

*The "ng" sound*

"Why don't we si*ng* a so*ng* so that we won't be so scared while we are walki*ng* alo*ng*," said Sally. "Perhaps the fireflies will hear our singi*ng* and we will find them."

*The "p" sound*

"Let's sing, '*P*ut a *P*enny in Your *P*ocket,'" said Sue *p*layfully. "We can *p*retend we are *p*irates hunting for that *p*ot of gold."

*The "m" sound*

Sally and Sue began to sing loudly as they *m*oved deeper into the woods. The *m*oon was still hidden a*m*ong the trees, not a creature was *m*oving, and the fireflies were nowhere to be seen.

*The "b" sound*

A*b*out that time Snoopy stum*b*led and fell. He was ru*b*bing his paw with his nose. "Poor Snoopy," cried Sally, "his little *b*rown paw has *b*een stu*bb*ed." She picked him up in her arms and carried him as *b*oth of the girls *b*egan to walk again.

*The "y" sound*

"*Y*ou *u*sed to be able to run and play in the dark, Snoopy, when *y*ou were *y*ounger," Sue said. "*Y*ou must be as tired as I am."

(The consonant sounds have been drilled up to this point. In the rest of the story have the children indicate the sounds on which they need further practice.)

"I agree," said Sally. "Oh, do you see what I see?" Sally saw what Snoopy had stumbled over. It was an old tree stump.

"Look," cried Sue, "there are little bugs that look like fireflies going into that stump." The two girls and Snoopy slipped up to the stump to see what was going on. Inside they could hear a tiny voice giving orders.

"It is for your sake that the King of the Fireflies has sent me to you. As you realize, it is your purpose on earth to aid the people here. For the past eight days you have done nothing to achieve this aim. You know full well you are required to help the earth people and light their way for them. You have not done your duty, so the King of the Fireflies has decreed that never again will you be sent as emissaries to light the way."

All of the little fireflies were so upset that their lights had been taken away from them that they said frantically to each other, "What shall we do?" They demanded their rights as fireflies. When the two little girls heard the terrible fate of the fireflies it only made them sadder. They sat down on the grass by the old tree stump and began to cry.

The fireflies heard their crying and buzzed out of the stump to see what was wrong. One little firefly darted up to Sally and said, "Calm down and tell us what is troubling you."

"We want our Grandmother," sobbed Sally as tears fell down her cheeks. "We left our Grandmother's house a long time ago and she doesn't allow us to go into the woods. Now we are lost and all of the trees look alike to us. We haven't had our supper and we're hungry."

The fireflies huddled together to try to find the solution. "I wonder if we could find their Grandmother's farm without our lights?" said one little firefly.

"There wouldn't be much loss in trying," said another.

"Let's do it!" they all shouted.

The fireflies buzzed back to the children. "We know this forest. Just follow us!"

"OK," sniffled Sally and Sue. "It's sooooooo dark though, and you don't have any lights."

"You don't have to worry about that," said the fireflies. "Just walk along with us and bring Snoopy, too."

So the little brave fireflies put out their wings and took the children along the crooked path out of the dark, dark woods.

The children clapped with joy to have the fireflies helping them and they sang "Friend, Ahoy!"

Snoopy sniffed along the ground happily as the fireflies led them out of the woods. "We should be about south, now," said one of the fireflies. Suddenly they found themselves at the edge of the forest and there was Grandmother's farm.

Instantly thousands of tiny lights appeared in the dark, dark night.

"I can't believe my eyes," said one little fellow. "Why, we have our lights back again. How happy I am!"

"Yes, and I know why," said Sally. "You helped us find Grandmother's farm. We were lost and you found the way for us!"

*The Child Who Is Slow in Learning to Speak.* If a child is slow in developing physically he may be slow in learning to talk. It does no good to try to force him. Usually by the time he is in school he has made an attempt to talk. Among the common factors in delayed speech development are the following:

1. Mental subnormality.
2. Illness and physical impairment, such as brain damage or paralysis.
3. Lack of sufficient speech stimulation, as in homes where no one coos or babbles to the baby, or where the members of the family talk very little among themselves.
4. Impaired hearing.
5. Inadequate or disturbing or inconsistent rewards — even a certain amount of misplaced punishment — for the child's early attempts at speech.

6. A pattern of rewards and in general a relationship of such a nature that he gets along so well without speaking that he lacks sufficient motivation for attempting to learn to speak.

7. Intense shock, fright, or shame, experienced over a sustained period or on one or more crucial occasions.[71]

*The Child with the Cleft Palate or Lip.* Many states today provide free clinical care for the child who has a cleft palate or lip if the family cannot afford it. As a result, few children enroll in school who have not had surgical repair when it is possible. Unfortunately, many times the speech cannot become normal, in which case there is little the classroom teacher can do as far as speech is concerned. He can, however, help the child adjust to his problem and help the other children to understand it so that he is accepted by the group and is not so sensitive to his condition.

*The Child with Cerebral Palsy.* Again, this is a physical impairment with which the classroom teacher can do little. Often the brain injury is so extensive that one or more of the functions involved in speech cannot be performed. When the speech impairment is slight, the child can communicate with little difficulty. If it is great, however, he should be under the guidance of a trained speech therapist. The teacher can help him adjust to the group, accept his limitations, and learn to make the best use of the abilities he has.

*The Child with a Voice Disorder.* Only about 10 per cent of the children with speech disorders have voice disorders. Children whose voices are different from those of their playmates need help. Frequently a voice that is too loud, too soft, too harsh, or irritating indicates a personality problem. Occasionally it is an indication of an organic disorder. Voice disorders are usually classified as those of pitch (too high or too low), loudness (too soft or too loud), and quality (harsh, strident, nasal, hoarse). The child with a voice disorder should always be checked by a physician before any remedial help is given to make sure that speech training will not aggravate the situation and that there is a reasonable hope of improvement.

*The Child with Hesitant Speech.* All children as they learn to speak hesitate, repeat, and start over. This is the natural process.

[71] Wendell Johnson, *Children with Speech and Hearing Impairment*, U.S. Department of Health, Education and Welfare, Bulletin No. 5 (Washington, D.C.: Government Printing Office, 1959), p. 11.

Even adults have many periods of non-fluency. Observe the number of people with the "uh — uh" habit, a common form of hesitant speech — so common, in fact, that little notice is taken of it. The preschool child is learning new sounds, new combinations, new words, new meanings for the old words. No wonder he hesitates. Many times during this hesitancy the adult does not wait. He either turns from the child without waiting for the completion of the word or sentence or tells him to "hurry up." The child may fill in the gaps with repetition of the last sound or a prolongation of it. This is so natural that, as Henrikson says, ". . . The speech of the preschool child contains, on the average, repetition and hesitation on one out of every four words."[72] Unless an adult makes an issue of it, the child usually ignores it. When the adult becomes concerned, labels the normal hesitancies "stuttering," and proceeds to treat the child as though he were something special, the trouble usually begins. Many theories of stuttering are held today. Perhaps the most common is that stuttering is caused in some such way as just described. Another theory has it that stuttering grows out of organic problems. Regardless of the cause, there are some things that the classroom teacher can do. He must, first of all, get the other children, and himself, to accept the stutterer as a person who has a problem — different from some of theirs, but it is the problem and not the person that is different. The teacher should not try to become a therapist and "treat" the stutterer. Rather, he should provide a classroom environment that is free from tensions. He should help the child see how much like the other children he is and how all have areas in which they differ. He should help the child evaluate and accept his differences.

*The Child with the Foreign-Language Background.* The child whose parents converse entirely in a foreign language has a handicap when he enters school. In some cities of the United States there are sections where Italian, Swedish, Spanish, or a number of other languages are spoken exclusively. Many of the children have had little contact with English before enrolling in school. The speech problem is a part of the total economic and social picture of the community.

[72] Ernest Henrikson, "Children with Hesitant Speech," in Wendell Johnson (ed.), *Speech Problems of Children* (New York: Grune and Stratton, Inc., 1950), p. 204.

The teacher must help the child who has a foreign-language background to have pride in his heritage, point out to the other pupils the contributions that have been made by various nationalities, and bring them together in the development of an attitude that will make them better Americans. The teacher should understand the language differences. Many of our sounds are not made in the foreign language or are articulated differently. The stress is often different, the melody pattern varies, and the sentence structure and idioms are not the same.

## *The Speech-Impaired in the Classroom*

Because most children speak easily, good speech is taken as a matter of course. Some teachers are concerned with the problem of the impairment of speech and its relation to the class as a whole, but too often the child with the impairment is neglected. It is true that the parent has a definite responsibility for providing for the child's speech needs, but after the child enters school the school has a more pronounced effect upon his speech than the home.

What can the parent expect from the school for the child who has impaired speech? First of all, he should expect the school to do nothing to make the impairment worse. Every teacher should know what not to do as well as how to help the child improve. The child must not be made to feel inferior because of his handicap. He should not be singled out for correction as an "example" for the others. Students quickly pick up the attitude of the teacher. If he is considerate, understanding, and helpful the children will tend to follow his example. If he is critical, disapproving, and demanding they will tend to pick on the child to relieve their own feelings of insecurity.

The child, then, should not be forced to try to speak better than he is able. His best speech should be required of him, but he should not have to meet the standards of those whose speech is normal. He should not be rewarded for his defect by being let out of assignments. When he *cannot* do the oral work, written assignments may be substituted. He should always be encouraged, though, to make every effort possible to do what oral work he can. His grades should not depend on the oral recitations.

Good teachers have classrooms with a relaxed atmosphere. There is a bond of common trust and respect. The child is challenged and he responds. It is in such a room that he tries to do his best. He recognizes that his defect has not in any way caused him to lose the respect of the teacher or the students. They accept him for himself. He is encouraged to excel in the things that he can do. He learns to face his problems objectively, to evaluate his assets and accept his liabilities. He is given encouragement to "talk out" his speech problems.

Because of the prevalence of speech impairment in the classroom a number of states require all elementary teachers to study speech correction before they receive state certification. This is highly desirable. Where no state ruling is in effect many schools require or strongly advise the student teacher to include such a course in his college curriculum. The elementary classroom teacher is not a speech therapist, but he should have sufficient knowledge of speech correction to help every student in his classes become more at ease in a speech situation.

## ACTIVITIES AND QUESTIONS

1. Visit a public school speech correctionist and find out what his suggestions would be for cooperation between the classroom teacher and the speech therapist.
2. Make a list of the articulatory errors that you observed in an elementary classroom.
3. Make a notebook of speech drills for the various consonant and vowel sounds that you can use later in your own teaching.
4. Discuss with a classroom teacher the provisions that are made in his school for meeting children's articulatory problems.

## BIBLIOGRAPHY

Ainsworth, Stanley. *Galloping Sounds*. Magnolia, Mass.: Expression Company, n.d.

Akin, Johnnye. *And So We Speak: Voice and Articulation.* Englewood Cliffs, N.J.: Prentice-Hall, Inc., 1958.

Backus, Ollie, and Beasley, Jane E. *Speech Therapy with Children.* Boston: Houghton Mifflin Company, 1951.

Barrows, Sarah T., and Pierce, Anna E. *The Voice: How to Use It.* Magnolia, Mass.: Expression Company, n.d.

Berry, Mildred F., and Eisenson, Jon. *Speech Disorders: Principles and Practices of Therapy.* New York: Appleton-Century-Crofts, Inc., 1956.

Brodnitz, Friedrich S. *Keep Your Voice Healthy.* New York: Harper & Brothers, 1953.

Bryngleson, Bryng, *et al. Know Yourself: A Workbook for Those Who Stutter.* Minneapolis, Minn.: Burgess Publishing Company, 1958.

Cypreansen, Lucile, *et al. Speech Development.* New York: The Ronald Press Company, 1959.

Eisenson, Jon. *Stuttering: A Symposium.* New York: Harper & Brothers, 1958.

Johnson, Wendell, *et al. Speech Handicapped School Children.* New York: Harper & Brothers, rev. ed., 1956.

Johnson, Wendell, *et al. The Onset of Stuttering.* Minneapolis: University of Minnesota, 1959.

McCausland, Miller and Okie. *Speech Through Pictures.* Magnolia, Mass.: Expression Company, n.d.

Mikalson, Elaine. "Listen and Learn," two albums of speech correction records. Los Angeles: Children's Music Center, n.d.

Nemoy, Elizabeth McGinley. *Speech Correction Through Story-Telling Units.* Magnolia, Mass.: Expression Company, n.d.

Nemoy, Elizabeth, and Davis, Serena. *Correction of Defective Consonant Sounds.* Magnolia, Mass.: Expression Company, n.d.

Nichols, Ralph G., and Stephans, Leonard A. *Are You Listening?* New York: McGraw-Hill Book Company, 1957.

Paratore, Angela. *English Dialogues for Foreign Students.* New York: Rinehart and Company, 1956.

Paratore, Angela. *English Exercises: English as a Foreign Language.* New York: Rinehart and Company, 1958.

Philbrick, F. A. *Understanding English.* New York: The Macmillan Company, 1942.

Prator, Clifford H. *Manual of American English Pronunciation.* New York: Rinehart and Company, 1957. (Accent Inventory and two long-playing records available with the *Manual.*)

Rubenstein, Ben O. "Some Comments About Stuttering for Teachers," *Educational Administration and Supervision,* 45:162–168, May 1959.

Rutherford, Bernice. *Give Them a Chance to Talk.* Minneapolis, Minn.:

Burgess Publishing Company, 1956.

Schoolfield, Lucille D. *Better Speech and Better Reading*. Magnolia, Mass.: Expression Company, n.d.

Schreiber, Flora Rheta. *Your Child's Speech*. New York: G. P. Putnam's Sons, 1956.

Scott, Louise Binder. "Talking Time Filmstrips," St. Louis: Webster Publishing Company, 1955. (Two series, eight full-color film strips each for primary and intermediate speech correction.)

Scott, Louise Binder, and Thompson, J. J. *Speech Ways*. St. Louis: Webster Publishing Company, 1955. (Speech guidance handbook for middle grade teachers.)

Scott, Louise Binder, and Thompson, J. J. *Talking Time*. St. Louis: Webster Publishing Company, 1951. (Speech correction handbook for primary teachers.)

Stoddard, Clara B. *Sounds for Little Folks*. Magnolia, Mass.: Expression Company, n.d.

Van Riper, Charles. *Teaching Your Child to Talk*. New York: Harper & Brothers, 1950.

Walsh, Gertrude. *Sing Your Way to Better Speech*. New York: E. P. Dutton and Company, new rev. ed., 1947.

Wood, Alice L. *The Jingle Book for Speech Improvement and Speech Correction*. New York: E. P. Dutton and Company, rev. ed., 1946.

Wood, Alice L. *Sound Games: Speech Correction for Your Very Young*. New York: E. P. Dutton and Company, 1948.

Zedler, Empress Young. *Listening for Speech Sounds*. New York: Harper & Brothers, 1955.

# The child with emotional problems

> Only when their emotional needs are met can children learn.
>
> KATHERINE D'EVELYN

The most critical years in the emotional development of the child are the first six; the importance of parent-child relationships based on love, and teacher-child relationships based on affectionate understanding, cannot be overemphasized. "Giving love," says Leon J. Saul, specialist in preventive psychiatry, "means giving security, affection, respect for the child's personality and understanding of his point of view and feelings."[73]

Coupled with love, understanding, and acceptance should be good models in the attitudes and behavior of the adults who are guiding the child's development. In addition, the adults (parents, teachers, and others) should be cognizant of the dangers of neglecting a child's early needs and of setting poor examples for him — examples which often create the hostility that results in much of the conflict, violence, and crime in our society.

"Some tensions are inevitable in the ordinary give-and-take of life;

[73] Dorothy Barclay, "Rearing a Child of Good Will," *The New York Times Magazine*, February 21, 1960, Sec. 6, p. 52.

most adults have learned to contend with them. To children, however, the tensions of everyday living often present emotional threats with which they are unable to cope. But cope they must — in the school room, on the playground, at home — and learn to face the problems of right and wrong, of good sportsmanship, of sharing with others without being unduly disturbed."[74]

Too often the teacher fails to understand that basic to emotional disturbance is a persistent anxiety or fear that gnaws at the unhappy child. ". . . It is characteristic of maladjusted children that they are insecure and unhappy, and that they fail in their personal relationships. Receiving is difficult for them as well as giving, and they seem unable to respond to simple measures of love, comfort and reassurance. At the same time they are not readily capable of improvement by ordinary discipline."[75]

As teachers study children they discover that some of them have emotional needs that cannot readily be met. "Studies show that about 10 per cent of the children in each school fall in this category. For example, in a class of thirty, there will be approximately three children who show behavior deviant enough to cause real concern to the teacher. . . . In some classes you will find fewer disturbed children and in others more, but the average runs as stated above."[76]

## *The Role of the Teacher*

Behavior that disturbs one teacher may not concern another. In general, teachers are unhappy about such overt behavior as quarreling, fighting, destructiveness, stealing, excessive timidity, school phobia, truancy, temper tantrums, jealousy, and hyperactivity. However, the ways they react to this symptomatic behavior differ. The teacher's responsibility consists of (1) understanding the background of behavior, (2) identifying symptoms early, (3) helping the disturbed child, (4) enlisting the aid of experts in dealing with

[74] Dorothy T. Spoerl (ed.), *Tensions Our Children Live With: Stories for Discussion* (Boston: Beacon Press, 1959), p. i.

[75] *Report of the Committee on Maladjusted Children* (London: Her Majesty's Stationery Office, 1955), p. 22.

[76] Katherine E. D'Evelyn, *Meeting Children's Emotional Needs* (Englewood Cliffs, N.J.: Prentice-Hall, Inc., 1957), p. 40.

difficult problems, and (5) creating and maintaining a classroom environment which nurtures mental health.

*Understanding the Background of Behavior.* "The teacher who understands the basic emotional drives that underlie all behavior and appreciates the ways in which these drives are manifested at various stages of development is in a much better position to help the student achieve adjustment. Where discipline and . . . teaching are examined from the point of view of their effect upon adjustment and emotional help, the more successful the teacher is in discovering the causes of unsatisfactory behavior . . . , the more likely he will be to get at the emotional problems which the student must be helped to solve."[77]

*Identifying Symptoms of Emotional Problems Early.* Research has shown that early detection of emotional problems is essential. When the child enters kindergarten or first grade the teacher has an excellent opportunity to observe his behavior. If the teacher is to be helpful to children who are having problems he must be careful not to exaggerate the importance of minor deviations. Rivlin cites three characteristics that appear to be telling the teacher that the child's needs are not being adequately met: (1) the child's responses are disproportionate to the situation, (2) there is a degree of permanence in the child's responses to a situation, and (3) the child's reactions are out of touch with reality.[78]

*Helping the Disturbed Child.* Many minor problems can be helped directly by the teacher *if* he has the interest, the insight, and the time. "Much that we regard as problem behavior is a matter of habit formation without deep-rooted emotional causation. Shyness and timidity, for example, may be symptomatic of a child's withdrawal from a group in which he feels he cannot compete successfully. On the other hand, there may be nothing more involved than habits of behavior.[79]

A sympathetic and understanding kindergarten teacher may by

[77] Harry N. Rivlin, "The Role of Mental Health in Education," in Nelson B. Henry (ed.), *Mental Health in Modern Education,* Fifty-Fourth Yearbook of the National Society for the Study of Education, Part II (Chicago: University of Chicago Press, 1955), p. 21.

[78] *Ibid.,* p. 23.

[79] *Ibid.,* p. 25.

cheerful encouragement help the child adjust to others and enjoy doing it. Similarly, a competent intermediate teacher can help a child overcome his shyness in getting along with others by providing opportunities for informal social contacts.

*Enlisting the Aid of Experts.* Enlisting the aid of others in dealing with deep-rooted problems is the mark of a competent teacher. Problems that are beyond the skill and ability of the classroom teacher must be referred to the proper agency: guidance counselor, psychologist, psychiatrist, school therapist, or guidance clinic. In the case of a seriously disturbed child there is no effective substitute for the child guidance clinic, in which the combined efforts of the specialists on the clinical staff are utilized.

*Creating and Maintaining a Classroom Environment Which Nurtures Mental Health.* The teacher's job is to create a classroom environment conducive to good mental health, not to administer therapy. The teacher with insight into mental and emotional health creates an emotional climate which supports the child — a classroom atmosphere of friendliness and genuine concern where each child is accepted and liked as he is, not because of or in spite of his special abilities or limitations.

## Types of Emotional Problems

*The Aggressive Child.* The excessively aggressive child is a source of difficulty for the teacher and the group. Aggression shows itself in many forms of behavior from name calling to harming other children. The aggressive child often is destructive. At any age he needs help. He is full of fight and bluster. He feels that life is unfair and shakes his fist at what he considers a fickle world. He is angry and fearful, and fighting for what he considers his rights. He strikes out at whoever is nearby. He does not realize that he is not accepted because of his undesirable behavior. This child presents a problem both in the classroom and on the playground. He must be helped to gain a feeling of security before he can react with more positive behavior.

The teacher is responsible for finding the cause of his behavior and helping him develop qualities that make it possible for him to conceive a better self-image. The teacher must help him realize that he has strengths as well as weaknesses. With the knowledge that the teacher likes him, even though he does not approve of the aggressive behavior, he may gradually modify his behavior and become a contributing member of the group.

Some aggressive children have to be re-educated. Those who come from neighborhoods where pushing, fighting, grabbing, shoving, and quarreling are accepted have to substitute behavior that helps the class live happily together. This change requires a patient teacher and group experiences in which each child respects the rights of others and assumes personal responsibility for contributing to a happy environment. The teacher should look for the cause of deviant behavior, not merely treat the symptom. He must be firm yet kind; he must set limits and yet help the child to see that he wants to help him; he must accept the child while rejecting the undesirable behavior. He must not be afraid to say, "We don't kick the other fellow. We don't allow fighting in our school." Conferences with the child, the parent, and the previous teacher may reveal why the child is angry, hurt, or scared. Warm, friendly relationships help him identify with an adult in whom he has confidence. What he needs is (1) help in controlling his aggressive behavior through defined, firm limits, (2) treatment of his behavior, and (3) positive meaningful experiences with adults who are kind but firm.

In spite of all that the teacher and group may do to establish a good classroom environment there will still be the child who transgresses. It is not enough to stop his aggressive behavior. He needs help. He is trying to tell the teacher and the world that all is not well. The teacher has to help him find out how he felt and why he perceived his behavior as appropriate.

Among the methods teachers use in the procedure are role playing, class discussion on causes of behavior, and individual counseling. If these techniques are ineffectual the teacher should feel free to call on other agencies within or without the school. Some teachers are fearful of admitting that they are in a quandary about a certain child and allow him to continue to disrupt the class. This is not fair to the other children, who have a right to a good learning situation, nor to the child at fault, who has a right to be helped.

Self-discipline is a part of an environment in which mental health of *all* children is nurtured. It permeates the total classroom situation. "It is not synonymous with taking action in an emergency. It needs to be built upon the recognition of the urge of children to develop, recognition of the uniqueness of the child and his needs for self-evaluation and self-control."[80]

*The Child Who Steals.* Stealing is a common symptom observed in certain disturbed children and should be curbed because it can lead to dire consequences. The teacher aims at finding the reasons for the child's conduct, trying to understand how he feels about himself and others, finding ways to help him achieve status with his peers in other ways than buying friendship and gain greater satisfaction from his achievements.

Children who steal have varied reasons. Sometimes they seek attention. They do not know how to gain friends so they often steal to bring gifts and treats to other children. Sometimes they steal because they are hungry, sometimes because they want excitement. Some need is unfulfilled.

*The Withdrawn Child.* The timid child may not present as formidable a problem to the average teacher as does the aggressive child. However, the seriously withdrawn child, like the aggressive child, may carry a deeply rooted burden of anger and resentment toward others. Such anger may stem from his own feelings of inadequacy. He may believe that he is unacceptable to others and since he is afraid to be overtly angry he keeps his attitude hidden. He exhibits a desire for flight rather than fight. To the observer, parent, or teacher, he appears quiet, amenable, and very, very good.

Again the teacher should look for the cause, in home or school, of inter-personal relationships which are not satisfactory to the child. The "silent ones" can often best be helped by creating situations in which they begin to form friendships with others of like temperament.

Sometimes parents criticize the timid child because he does not stand up for his rights, or because he will not talk in the presence of others. Often they shove when they should merely stand by. Later they may step back, but never far enough to be out of sight. The child needs many experiences in trying his wings. He needs the

[80] Ira J. Gordon, *Children's View of Themselves* (Washington, D.C.: Association for Childhood Education International, 1959), p. 33.

support of parents and teachers to "come out of his shell." As he ventures toward greater independence, the supporting hand of the teacher can help him accept challenges for what they are — experiences to be approached with confidence, not fear.

*The Child Who Is Afraid of School.* Children who have an acute fear of school are said to be suffering from school phobia.[81] Kindergarten teachers in particular have to deal with this problem. Many times the mother-child relationship is so complex and emotional that the teacher is at a loss to know how to handle the situation. It may be the result of the mother's unhappy marriage. She has clung to the child in an effort to ignore the relationship with her husband. The child is caught in the middle. If he enjoys school, the mother may feel he is rejecting her in favor of the teacher. The mother may keep the child at home so she can continue to be the center of attraction. In this case it is the mother who needs help. If she can see that keeping the child at home is handicapping him educationally, she may take a different attitude. On the other hand, she may ignore the problem and not face it until the attendance counselor takes it in hand.

It is not always possible for the teacher to help a child who is afraid of school. It is even more difficult to help the mother. Special guidance services, if available, may facilitate the child's adjustment to school. Mothers must learn to let go with the heart as well as with the hand.

A strict or complaining teacher, a seriously disturbed teacher, a disorderly class, low achievement in school subjects, real or imagined problems associated with toileting, reciting in front of the class, and fear of outdoor play — these are some of the factors in addition to problems centered in parent-child relationships, which contribute to school phobia.

*Truancy.* Truancy consists of a habitual pattern of staying away from school without apparent legitimate reason. Truancy can be a signal that the child is suffering from serious emotional conflict. It can mean that the situation at school is so intolerable that it brings the child nothing but frustration, fear, failure, and ridicule from his classmates.

[81] See "School Phobia," *Time,* 76:99, October 17, 1960.

It is the responsibility of the school to determine the cause for the truancy. Once the reason or reasons are found the program must be adjusted to meet the child's needs, or the child must be helped to adjust to the program. In most cases it is possible to gear the educational program to the child's developmental needs and abilities. If the child is emotionally disturbed, however, the school must refer his case to the proper individuals. Schools may contribute to delinquency and truancy by failing to assume their responsibility to truant pupils.

The teacher has a real contribution to make here. It is he who can read the danger signals if he will. The child who is a social misfit, who does not find satisfaction in school experiences, who fails consistently to win friends, to get his assignments, to get along with others on the playground or in the classroom, or who allies himself with troublemakers is signaling the teacher that he is in distress.

Children in this category give legitimate excuses for frequent absences at the outset. Minor ailments, visiting relatives, failure of the mother to get them off to school, and similar reasons are given for absenteeism. The teacher should call such a child to the attention of the attendance counselor, the school psychologist or the social worker. He should have a conference with the parents if possible to help them take an improved attitude toward school.

There are times when the teacher cannot help the child to *want* to come to school. Perhaps the home is creating the problem. The child comes to school too weary and frustrated to make an effort to participate in school experiences with any degree of satisfaction. In such a case the teacher may try to change the situation, change the child's attitude toward his environment, or refer the case.

*Temper Tantrums.* Teachers of young children are often faced with the child who suddenly, without any apparent provocation, reverts to infantile behavior and announces his needs by crying, screaming, and kicking. The child who throws himself on the floor, kicks with his feet, hammers with his fist, shouts at the top of his lungs is exhibiting what he believes to be intelligent behavior. For the moment one cannot reason with such a child. He is suffering from an acute, if temporary, emotional explosion. He is blind, deaf, and insensible to the world around him. Words are useless. Action is imperative. He must be restrained firmly and in as matter-of-fact a manner as the teacher can muster under the circumstances. He cannot be permitted to harm himself or others. Some children show such strength during a temper tantrum that the principal may have to be called upon to help restrain them.

The older pupil is more prone to strike out at others. Teachers of older children who attempt to restrain them are frequently rewarded with black and blue shins. Sending to the office to get the assistance of the principal is usually advisable. If the child exhibits this behavior frequently he must be helped by either the school psychologist or the school counselor. It may be necessary to exclude him from school until such time as treatment can be provided for his emotional disturbance.

*The Hyperactive Child.* The term "nervous" is often used to describe the jittery, overly active child. Such a child is showing through his nervous behavior that something is wrong. Tics, facial twitches, tenseness, anxiety, random bodily movements, and scraping the feet, tell the teacher that physical or psychological needs are not being met.

To find the reason for the behavior is important. A thorough physical examination may reveal the source of the problem. Illness, fatigue, poor nutrition, vitamin deficiency, eyestrain, or hearing defects may contribute to the nervous behavior. The teacher should make every effort to relieve strain and tension in the classroom and to ease pressures that may be contributing factors. Conferences with parents, school physician, and psychologist are helpful in determining causes and prescribing treatment. The cause may lie in home conditions. If so, establishing good relationships with the family is a prerequisite to success in alleviating the problem.

*Jealousy.* "A child who feels accepted and who becomes an active participant in a good school program is helped to overcome his feelings of jealousy, of not being wanted, or of not getting his share of adult and peer recognition."[82]

Jealousy is the fear of losing something that is valued. Children may be jealous of the new baby brother or sister. They may be jealous of the attention the teacher gives other children. They may be jealous of their own brothers and sisters, or of another child in the room who is "taking my friend away from me."

[82] D'Evelyn, *op. cit.,* p. 131.

## Guides for Helping the
## Disturbed Child in the Classroom

Every situation requires its own analysis, every problem its own solution. General prescriptions for handling the child with emotional problems in the classroom will have limited application for individual cases. However, there are guides for making decisions about what to do.

The teacher is a teacher, not a therapist. It is true that until the child's emotional needs are met he is unable to learn. It is therefore the responsibility of the teacher to help the child cope with his problems while he is at school. When the emotional disturbances become entangled with classroom and learning situations, it is the teacher's job to *try* to disentangle them.

The problem should be referred if it is too much for the teacher. Psychiatrists, social workers, and psychologists are clinicians. They are not expected to teach classes; neither is the teacher expected to take over their jobs. He does, of course, cooperate with appropriate agencies by giving the information required to diagnose and treat the case *outside* of the school. He does cooperate in the treatment of the problem by providing an environment in which the child can feel accepted and can gain status in some area of achievement. Therapy is for the experts.

The teacher must recognize that the problem is very real to the child. Whatever is troubling him is as serious a disturbance as if he had poor eyesight or a similar physical handicap. It does not help to insist that he get his work done, that he behave, or that he is being just plain ornery. He needs help, not censure. Scolding him will not help; on the contrary, because of his intense feelings, hostility, self-pity, or rationalization it may actually do harm. How a child feels may be more important than what he does or how he does it. Teachers should make an effort to understand "the language of behavior — how the situation looks to the child and what his behavior means to him. Teachers should learn to listen more and talk less."[83]

[83] Ruth Strang, "Many-Sided Aspects of Mental Health," in Nelson B. Henry (ed.), *Mental Health in Modern Education,* Fifty-Fourth Yearbook of the National Society for the Study of Education, Part II (Chicago: University of Chicago Press, 1955), p. 37.

The child's hostility is not directed at the teacher personally. He is unhappy with everyone and everything that is in his path. It is not the teacher who is at the root of his problem, nor is he exhibiting negative behavior to punish the teacher. The latter, however, may be symbolic of all the grownups who take the joy out of living by "bossing him around." On the other hand, he may get satisfaction out of being unruly to win favor with his peers.

Some disturbed children need the help of specialists. They do not benefit from the average classroom experiences. They need special classes or special schools. Some of them may need therapy to help them gain a new self-image. Others can be helped in a group situation in the classroom if their differences can be provided for in a flexible schedule. Some children require temporary isolation from the group. Others get along better if they are required to stay home on rainy days or on days when they obviously will have difficulty. What is right for a particular disturbed child depends on a knowledge of that child based on reliable evidence of competent individuals.

The teacher who notices a troubled child in his classroom turns to the supervisor or to the guidance counselor for help. Together they discuss the child, consulting his cumulative record, which contains information about his health, achievement, family, and social adjustment. They may call in other specialists in the school, including the nurse, the speech therapist, or the reading specialist. They may plan a parent conference or ask the visiting teacher to make a home visit.

Suppose the teacher considers the problem, "Why is a boy as bright as Pete not achieving up to his potential in my class?" Information needed to diagnose this problem might answer the following questions:

Does Pete actually have the ability to do the work I assign?
Does he have the necessary previously learned skills to achieve at this level?
Does he have any specific learning problems, such as a reading disability?
What does his health history tell me about him?
Has he missed school frequently in the past because of illness?
Is he in good health now?
Has he any vision, hearing, coordination, or speech problems?
Has his family moved frequently?
Is he happy at home and school?

How do his parents feel about him?

What expectations have they of him as a person and as a student?

To obtain the information the teacher will make use of the cumulative record, the specialists who work individually with him, and his parents.

In the team approach, the teacher, administration, and specialists share the responsibility for getting the information and using it to help the child solve his problem. The school psychologist and/or the school psychiatrist are called on to review and study the data. As the psychiatrist becomes a member of the team in sharing information he presents and interprets the facts *he* has gained. The team approach enables the school more adequately to meet the problems of its children.[84]

The following are types of socially maladjusted or emotionally disturbed children who might profit from a special education program:

1. A child who, because of his serious emotional problem cannot be helped adequately by his regular teacher, but needs the assistance of a specially qualified instructor who can give him individual attention and assistance, preferably in a small class.
2. A child whose behavior is a destructive influence on other children, and who requires disproportionate attention, thus depriving the other children of their educational opportunities.
3. A child whose home is so disorganized and otherwise inadequate that he requires a change from the home environment in order to have constructive learning and living experiences under a teacher who is prepared to take on some educational responsibility which might otherwise be considered the function of the home.
4. The child who is severely disturbed and unresponsive to wholesome educational opportunities and ordinary psychotherapy; and who needs residential treatment which provides: (a) regulated living experience derived from an understanding of the psychic needs of the child; (b) therapeutic education and tutoring in which methods and materials are contrived to counteract and re-educate distortions of perception, idiosyncratic thinking processes and inappropriate emotional responses to learning situations; and (c) deeper psychotherapy.[85]

[84] Ruth Fedder, "Teacher and Psychiatrist Work Together," *Teachers College Record*, 61:343–347, March 1960.

[85] Romaine P. Mackie *et al.*, *Teachers of Children Who Are Socially and Emotionally Maladjusted*, Bulletin No. 11 (Washington, D.C.: Government Printing Office, 1957), p. 9.

# ACTIVITIES AND QUESTIONS

1. Observe in an elementary grade of your choice and see if any of the children have problems of emotional adjustment. How would you describe the problems? What did the teacher do to help the child?
2. What guiding principles would you suggest to a beginning teacher concerning the diagnosis and treatment of emotional problems in the classroom?

# BIBLIOGRAPHY

Axline, Virginia. *Play Therapy.* Boston: Houghton Mifflin Company, 1947.

Cutts, Norma E., and Moseley, Nicholas. *Teaching the Disorderly Pupil.* New York: Longmans, Green and Company, 1957.

D'Evelyn, Katherine. *Meeting Children's Emotional Needs.* Englewood Cliffs, N.J.: Prentice-Hall, Inc., 1955.

Hymes, James L., Jr. *Behavior and Misbehavior.* Englewood Cliffs, N.J.: Prentice-Hall, Inc., 1955.

Josselyn, Irene. *The Happy Child: A Psychoanalytic Guide to Emotional and Social Growth.* New York: Random House, 1955.

Lee, J. Murray, and Lee, Dorris May. *The Child and His Development.* New York: Appleton-Century-Crofts, Inc., 1958.

Lippman, Hyman S. *Treatment of the Child in Emotional Conflict.* New York: McGraw-Hill Book Company, 1956.

Mackie, Romaine P., *et al. Teachers of Children Who Are Socially and Emotionally Maladjusted.* Bulletin No. 11. Washington, D.C.: Government Printing Office, 1957.

Millard, Cecil V., and Rothney, John. *The Elementary School Child: A Book of Cases.* New York: The Dryden Press, 1957.

Moak, Helen. *The Troubled Child.* New York: Henry Holt and Company, 1958.

Mohr, George J., and Despres, Marian. *The Stormy Decade: Adolescence.* New York: Random House, 1958.

Moustakas, Clark E. *Children in Play Therapy: A Key to Understanding Normal and Disturbed Emotions.* New York: McGraw-Hill Book Company, 1953.

Moustakas, Clark E. *The Teacher and the Child.* New York: McGraw-Hill Book Company, 1956.

National Society for the Study of Education. *Mental Health in Modern Education.* Fifty-Fourth Yearbook, Part II, Nelson B. Henry (ed.). Chicago: University of Chicago Press, 1955.

Patterson, C. H. *Counselling the Emotionally Disturbed.* New York: Harper & Brothers, 1958.

Prescott, Daniel A. *The Child in the Educative Process.* New York: McGraw-Hill Book Company, 1957.

Redl, Fritz, and Weinman, David. *The Aggressive Child.* Glencoe, Ill.: The Free Press, 1957.

Redl, Fritz, and Weinman, David. *Controls from Within.* Glencoe, Ill.: The Free Press, 1952.

Rogers, Dorothy. *Mental Hygiene in Elementary Education.* Boston: Houghton Mifflin Company, 1957.

Schwarz, Berthold, and Ruggieri, Bartholomew A. *Parent-Teacher Tensions.* Philadelphia: J. B. Lippincott Company, 1958.

Selye, Hans. *The Stress of Life.* New York: McGraw-Hill Book Company, 1956.

Soaper, Daniel. "Importance of Children's Feelings," *How Do Your Children Grow?* Washington, D.C.: Association for Childhood Education International, 1959.

Strang, Ruth. *An Introduction to Child Study.* New York: The Macmillan Company, 1959.

White, Verna. *Studying the Individual Pupil.* New York: Harper & Brothers, 1958.

Ziman, Edmund. *Jealousy in Children.* New York: A. A. Wynn, Inc., 1949.

# Concluding Statement

In a democratic society all children are entitled to an education appropriate to their needs and abilities. This includes the gifted as well as the mentally retarded, the physically handicapped and the speech defectives, and the children who suffer from emotional and social maladjustments.

Responsibility for the education of the mentally retarded and physically handicapped has been taken more seriously than responsibility for the education of the gifted child. What is needed at this point is increased encouragement for the child who is able and willing to go forward to more advanced, demanding, and creative types of learning. To neglect this part of our responsibility in the view that it is undemocratic to provide for giftedness but democratic to provide for retarded and handicapped children is as shortsighted as it is fallacious. The goal of American education is to help every individual achieve his optimum development, whatever that optimum may be. Equal opportunity for all is not synonymous with identical education for all.

A healthy society needs the contributions each individual is endowed by innate capacity and training to make. Our world is becoming so complex and so demanding that the resources and contributions of every individual must be evoked in order to cope with it. Educating the exceptional children in our society thus offers teachers a great challenge and opportunity.

"We can then insist, as we must, that democracy is not to be conceived as an invitation to share a common mediocrity but as a system that allows each to express and live up to the special excellence that is in him. We can then demand the best of our most gifted, most talented and most spirited youngsters. And we can dedicate ourselves to the cultivation of distinction, and a sense of quality."[86]

## SPECIALIZED AGENCIES

Alexander Graham Bell Association for the Deaf, 1537 35th Street, NW, Washington 7, D.C.

American Association for Gifted Children, Inc., 15 Gramercy Park, New York 3, N.Y.

American Association on Mental Deficiency, P.O. Box 96, Willimantic, Conn.

American Foundation for the Blind, 15 W. 16th Street, New York 11, N.Y.

American Hearing Society, 1800 H Street, NW, Washington 25, D.C.

American Heart Association, 44 E. 23rd Street, New York 10, N.Y.

American Speech and Hearing Association, 1001 Connecticut Avenue, Washington, D.C.

Boy Scouts of America, New Brunswick, N.J.

[86] *The Pursuit of Excellence: Education and the Future of America*, Panel Report V (Garden City, N.Y.: Doubleday and Company, 1958), p. 33.

Convention of American Instructors of the Deaf, c/o Gallaudet College, Washington, D.C.

Council for Exceptional Children, 1201 16th Street, NW, Washington, D.C.

Girl Scouts of the U.S.A., 830 Third Avenue, New York 22, N.Y.

League for Emotionally Disturbed Children, 10 W. 65th Street, New York, N.Y.

Muscular Dystrophy Association of America, 39 Broadway, New York 6, N.Y.

National Association for Gifted Children, 409 Clinton Springs Avenue, Cincinnati, Ohio.

National Association for Retarded Children, Inc., 99 University Place, New York 3, N.Y.

National Epilepsy League, Room 1916, 130 N. Wells, Chicago 6, Ill.

The National Foundation, 800 Second Avenue, New York 17, N.Y.

National Society for Crippled Children and Adults, Inc., 11 S. LaSalle Street, Chicago 51, Ill.

National Society for the Prevention of Blindness, 1790 Broadway, New York 19, N.Y.

National Tuberculosis Association, 1790 Broadway, New York 19, N.Y.

United Cerebral Palsy Association, Inc., 369 Lexington Avenue, New York 17, N.Y.

# 15

A relationship between adults must be created in which two people are able to talk to each other; two people are able to appreciate each other; two people like each other; two people are able to learn from each other. Until this happens there can be no real teamwork for the benefit of the child.

JAMES L. HYMES

# Working with parents

Working with parents for the benefit of the child is not a new concept. As early as 1903, White was emphasizing the importance of an improved relationship between elementary teachers and parents. "The parents' intimate knowledge of both the character of the children and of their physical peculiarities or infirmities, if imparted to the teacher, would be an assistance to him. It is to be regretted that so many fail of realizing this. . . . Since parents so rarely acquaint themselves with the teacher, it is more important that the teacher should seek the acquaintance of parents. He should visit the homes of his pupils, and gain a knowledge of the influence and surroundings among which they live. By coming personally in touch with their homes and lives, he may strengthen the ties that bind him to his pupils, and may learn how to deal successfully with their different dispositions and temperaments."[1]

Today, elementary schools accept the responsibility of building wholesome relationships with parents. Rose states clearly: "More and more, school leadership is emphasizing the importance of developing a closer understanding and a more active partnership between home and school."[2]

With record enrollments engulfing the schools, with new buildings to be erected to house the multitude of children, with additional teachers to be found to teach them, with increased costs and higher budgets, and with critics using education as a whipping boy, teachers have a dual challenge in working with parents, not only to improve the quality of education for their children, but to interpret the school program to them.

## Building Wholesome Relationships with Parents

Throughout the elementary school the teacher has a key role in the establishment and improvement of home-school relations. The parents of the young child are keenly interested and cooperation is at a high level when the child enrolls in kindergarten or the primary grades. It is the kindergarten or first-grade teacher who lays the groundwork for parent-school relations. In many schools the kindergarten teacher is free a part of the school day to have conferences with parents.

It is the responsibility of the teacher to make every possible effort to interpret the school to the parents through maintaining a friendly attitude and informing them of educational opportunities for their children and the type of learning experiences the school provides. The teacher must become competent in parent-teacher communica-

[1] Ellen G. White, *Education* (Mountain View, Calif.: Pacific Press, 1903), p. 284.
[2] Clayton E. Rose, "Person to Person," *NEA Journal*, 49:20, February 1960.

tion, essential skills in leadership and group participation, and parent education.

## *Parent-Teacher Communication*

Involved in parent-teacher communication is sharing what each knows about the child and willingness to cooperate for the child's best interest. The teacher's sphere of responsibility includes (1) interpreting the school program to parents, (2) reporting to parents, (3) encouraging parent participation in the school program, (4) seeking the help of parents in planning and developing learning experiences, and (5) helping establish sound promotion policies.

### INTERPRETING THE PROGRAM

Not only when the child enrolls in the school or at open house during American Education Week does the teacher interpret the program to parents. As a matter of fact, the teacher interprets the program through day-by-day contacts with the pupils, scheduled visits, parent-teacher conferences, handbooks, preschool roundups, mothers' clubs, workshops, parent-teacher meetings, telephone conversations, chance meetings at the market or social functions, and on the street. In meetings with individual parents or in a group he has an opportunity to (1) explain the curriculum, (2) secure information from parents in regard to the child, (3) enlist parental cooperation and interest in the school program, and (4) give practical suggestions for helping the child in his educational experiences.

Various types of activities may be planned to help parents understand the curriculum. A few which have been found effective are as follows:

1. An arts and crafts workshop in which parents use clay, papier-mâché, finger paint, colored chalk or easel paint just as children do.
2. Field trips to such places of interest as the harbor, zoo, farm, or library taken by children and parents. . . .
3. An exhibit of suitable books, records, or play materials which

answers parents' questions about what to buy for children . . . to stimulate worth-while interests.

4. A music workshop in which parents create songs and use rhythmic and melodic instruments to accompany singing.

5. A work session in which parents make equipment or materials for children's use at school.

6. Study and discussion groups to evaluate radio and television programs, comic books or such topics. . . .

7. Open House . . . for parents to become acquainted with the room, equipment, materials, and types of activities.

8. Social affairs in which parents share such experiences as a Thanksgiving Party in which children serve food they prepare, or a day to "See Us Play" when children show the physical development activities, games and uses of material outdoors that contribute to all-round growth of the child. . . .

9. Individual conferences — scheduled, snatched, telephoned, at the market — offer unlimited opportunities to teachers and parents. . . . The teacher's anecdotal observations, records of participation in activities, evidence of special interests, and samples of child's use of materials are shared with parents in these conferences.

10. Invitation to tea and discussion for mothers of entering children planned by previous year's Mothers' Group.[3]

Classroom visits are effective in helping the parents understand the program. Children in the primary grades are particularly eager to have parents visit school. As youngsters mature they are not always as anxious for the parents to visit. However, when parents do come, the teacher and children should make them feel welcome, and the program which is scheduled should be followed to give them a true picture of the learning experiences going on in the school. If it is convenient, the teacher should be available for answering the parents' questions *after* the children have been dismissed. Brochures are frequenetly provided to tell the parents what is expected of them during such a visit. Such brochures give information about length of time of visit, the procedure to be followed during the visit itself, suggested questions to ask the teacher after the visit, invitations for a scheduled conference with the teacher, and an invitation to return.

[3] Sybil Richardson *et al.*, "How Good School-Home-Community Relations Aid the Kindergarten Program," *California Journal of Elementary Education*, 24:51–52, August 1955.

## REPORTING TO PARENTS

Reporting to parents is a part of the broader program of communication.

*The Report Card.*  Traditionally the report card, sent home periodically to inform parents of their child's progress in school, has been the chief method of reporting. Many schools use this form of communicating progress two to six times a year.[4]

The form and appearance of current report forms differ from those used in earlier days. The colorless, single-page report' card which merely listed numerical or letter grades and number of days present, absent, and tardy had space for the parent's signature. It has largely been replaced by a colorful, illustrated four- or six-page booklet which contains a message for the parents, a note explaining the program, the record of academic achievement, data concerning the child's total development, teacher's comment, and a space for the parent's reply. Frequently there is space for the parent to request a parent-teacher conference if desired.

Report forms often are developed cooperatively by teachers, administrators, and parents. They are more adequate in achieving improved communication with parents if they are supplemented by a conference in which the teacher and parent can sit down and discuss the meaning of the evaluation checks. Such a procedure allows the teacher and parent to discuss the progress made not only in academic fields but also in personal and social growth, attitudes, and work habits.

*Letters to Parents.*  Some systems prefer writing letters to parents to sending regular report cards. The assumption is that the letter has the advantage of flexibility. Usually there are a few general categories under which the teacher writes a statement: (1) physical development, (2) social development, (3) emotional development, (4) intellectual development, and (5) creative expression. Other letter forms use two headings: (1) academic achievement and (2) attitudes and behavior. Whatever form the letter takes, the teacher

[4] Gertrude L. Lewis, *Reporting Pupil Progress to Parents*, Brief 34, U.S. Department of Health, Education and Welfare (Washington, D.C.: Government Printing Office, 1957).

must concern himself with giving information about the child's attitudes, habits, skills, development, and achievement.

Letters to parents should be characterized by originality, tact, spontaneity, and friendly interest. In order to avoid the stereotyped letter which has little meaning for the parents the teacher should (1) visualize each child as he writes, (2) begin by writing the most encouraging news about the child, (3) solicit the parents' help if there is a problem, (4) deal with specific aspects of development, (5) avoid jargon, (6) compare the child's progress with previous progress, (7) speak of his achievement in terms of his ability to cope with school work, (8) suggest possible reasons for lack of progress (ill health, frequent absence, poor eyesight, lack of application), (9) invite the parent to a conference, and (10) close on an optimistic note.

*The Parent-Teacher Conference.* The parent-teacher conference, which has long been effective at the preschool level, is now being used in the elementary school in place of or in combination with the report card or letter to parents. Many parents are highly enthusiastic about this method of reporting progress.

Parents differ in their ability to motivate children to their best efforts. Often teachers can help them better to understand and appreciate a child's potential and talents. They can help parents recognize their responsibility in stimulating interest in learning and fostering a sense of curiosity. The result is a greater mutual respect and understanding of goals. When the school and home work as partners in the educational process the interests of both are more effectively met.

The teacher can discuss the work samples of the child, the standardized tests, achievement, behavior inventories, aptitude tests, anecdotal records, and other evidence of the child's progress. Adequacy can then be determined on the basis of what the teacher knows about the child, what the child knows about himself, and what the parent can contribute to a better understanding of the child. The teacher who can put the parent at ease, who is genuinely interested in the child's welfare, and who understands conference techniques can be succesful in this type of communication.

In the survey[5] conducted by the National Education Association,

[5] "Teachers View Public Relations," *NEA Research Bulletin,* 37:35, April 1959.

parent-teacher conferences were designated by the highest number of teachers as the most effective means of working with parents. Although "99 per cent believe conferences with parents contribute to better relations only about 40 per cent use them."[6] This discrepancy is explained in part by the fact that certain conditions are essential if the conference is to be successful.

The teacher-parent conference or the teacher-parent-child conference requires a great deal of tact, understanding, insight, and skill in conference techniques. Not every teacher is endowed by nature and equipped by training to use it. However, if the conference is scheduled as a part of the teaching-learning day and time is allowed for putting into practice principles of good human relationships, considerable success can be achieved. The following suggestions will be helpful:

1. Prepare carefully in advance.
2. Insure privacy and freedom from interruptions.
3. Have an informal setting.
4. Plan a scheduled time limit.
5. Begin on a positive note.
6. Listen with interest, sympathy, and understanding.
7. Establish a friendly feeling with the parent, or parent and child as the case may be.
8. Encourage the parent to talk.
9. Develop an attitude of mutual need and cooperation.
10. Let suggestions come from the parent.
11. Build on the parent's suggestions whenever possible.
12. Delay making definite suggestions.
13. Have some of the child's work at hand to talk over.
14. Make future plans cooperatively.
15. End the conference on a friendly note.
16. Make arrangements for a future conference when necessary.
17. Make notes after the parent leaves.[7]

Three don'ts are useful to remember: don't feel superior, don't pry, and don't do all the talking. A great deal can be learned from the parent. Remember that cooperation is the key to success in parent-teacher relationships.

[6] *Ibid.*

[7] For a more extensive description of this type of conference see Katherine E. D'Evelyn, *Individual Parent-Teacher Conferences: A Manual for Teachers of Young Children* (New York: Bureau of Publications, Teachers College, Columbia University, 1952), pp. 95–97.

# WAYS OF COMMUNICATING WITH PARENTS

**Incidental visit**

**Home visit**

**Group conference**

**Scheduled visit with follow-up**

**Open house**

**Progress report card**

Reprinted by permission of the Association for Childhood Education International. From *Childhood Education*, March 1959, "Ways of Communicating with Parents," by Nadeen Waggener, Vol. 35, No. 7, p. 302.

Working with parents is not the province of the teacher alone; the administration is involved as well. If such means of communication as school visits, home visits, and teacher-parent or teacher-parent-child conferences are employed, the teacher must be free to make the conference period serve a useful end. Parents should be informed in advance of the purpose of the conference.

*A Combination of Methods.* Some schools have found through experimentation that using a combination of the three methods cited is most effective. They begin with an interview with the parent near the beginning of the school year. Parent and teacher discuss information pertinent to giving the child more effective guidance both at school and in the home. About the middle of the year the teacher makes an evaluation report, in a letter, on a report form, or at a parent-teacher-child conference. The various aspects of growth are appraised in terms of the progress the child has made up to that point. The third evaluation comes at the end of the year on a standard report card. Here emphasis is on all phases of the child's progress, again on the basis of growth in relation to abilities. Many schools require the teacher to notify the parent of lack of progress or failure before the last grading period.

The problem of reporting is a complex one and requires the best thinking of the administrator as well as the staff. It should be subject to constant evaluation and should be explained thoroughly to parents to assure maximum cooperation. This means of working with parents is fraught with fewer difficulties if there is an open line of communication between home and school. Reporting involves the total study of the child's behavior.

*Improving Reporting Techniques.* Parents, teachers, administrators, and the child alike are concerned with finding a means of reporting that helps the child understand himself and increase his desire to develop mentally, socially, and physically. To improve this method of working with parents requires a cooperative effort to determine which method or combination of methods best meets the needs of a particular community and a particular school. In general, parents are interested in obtaining information which answers questions like the following:

1. How does my child compare in academic achievement with the others of his class?

2. Considering his ability and potential, is he working up to his level?
3. What specific strengths and weaknesses does he evidence in his class work?
4. How is he progressing in social development — citizenship, conduct, and attitudes?
5. How is he progressing in study skills and work habits?
6. What can I do to help him improve in his school work, behavior, attitudes, and study habits?

## ENCOURAGING PARENT PARTICIPATION IN THE SCHOOL

The day is past when parents are considered outsiders. They have come into the school in workshops, councils, and committees. Parent participation is becoming an integral part of helping communities improve school programs throughout the country. In addition to the more traditional means of participation — parent-teacher conferences, parent education groups, cooperatively developed reports — many schools welcome parents in workshops and in curriculum planning.

*Workshops for Parents.* Workshops provide parents and teachers an opportunity to consider together problems of mutual concern in a flexible, informal, give-and-take atmosphere. The success of a workshop depends upon skill in group processes. It requires leaders who fulfill the functions of good leadership by preparing introductory activities designed to motivate interest and develop an awareness of problems, organizing the program with consideration for individual differences of participants, developing techniques of democratic group planning and discussion, and assisting parents to set up "developmental" activities to carry out their objectives. Workshops are experiences in democratic learning for parents and teachers alike. Some of the most successful workshops have centered on problems of child behavior, child guidance, understanding the elementary school curriculum, and developing materials. In some schools primary teachers and supervisors meet with parents to develop materials and equipment for use in the classroom. Through such cooperative action the teacher not only receives help in preparing materials but acquaints parents with the types and purposes of the materials and encourages them to use similar materials with the children in experiences outside the school.

*Parent Participation in Curriculum Improvement.* "The schools belong to the general public; citizens should have much to say about the curriculum. On the other hand, professional educators have received special training for this work and should be expected to know more about it than anyone else."[8]

On what basis can parents participate in curriculum development programs? Krug suggests that "When agreement on purposes is reached, lay people should defer to professional judgment on specific techniques used in carrying out the purposes. Four of the major jobs of curriculum planning — setting up the all-school programs, outlining the broad fields of instruction, providing aids for teachers, and teaching — are therefore generally more the responsibilities of professional educators."[9]

In 1946 the Association for Supervision and Curriculum Development publication, *Laymen Help Plan the Curriculum*,[10] gave national help and direction to such procedures. Strong professional guidance together with enthusiastic lay participation is important in curriculum improvement. Typical of lay discussion guides at the state level are *What Is the Job of Public Education?*[11] and the *Illinois Curriculum Program Consensus Study*.[12]

The purpose of such guides is to help parents and educators come to an agreement about what they should be doing cooperatively in the development of a better school program, to decide what things they want to start working on in order to improve the curriculum, and to work out a feasible plan whereby teachers may work together most effectively with parents.

Some of the ways in which these objectives are being accomplished are panel discussions, demonstration meetings, debates, symposiums,

[8] Edward A. Krug, *Curriculum Planning* (New York: Harper & Brothers, 1950), p. 16.

[9] *Ibid.*

[10] Association for Supervision and Curriculum Development, *Laymen Help Plan the Curriculum* (Washington, D.C.: The Association, 1946).

[11] Wisconsin Cooperative Educational Planning Program, *What Is the Job of Public Education?* Bulletin No. 2 (Madison: State Department of Education, n.d.).

[12] Illinois State Department of Education, *Illinois Curriculum Program Consensus Study*, No. 8, Inventory A, B, and C (Springfield: Superintendent of Public Instruction, State of Illinois, June 1952).

open forums, lectures, meetings using audio-visual aids, role-playing situations, and parent-teacher discussion groups.

## PARENTS AS RESOURCE PEOPLE

Parent participation in the learning experiences of children is becoming an increasingly valuable tool in education. Parents are coming into the classroom to teach special subjects, as teacher aides (to relieve the teacher of routine chores), and as consultants in special areas such as science, music, art, literature, foreign languages, and social studies.[13]

An illustration of how a teacher encouraged parents to participate in learning activities is seen in the following example: When Fred brought a homemade telephone to school one morning and boasted that his father had made it, everyone in the class wanted to talk on Fred's telephone. The result was that the teacher invited Fred's father to teach a science lesson to first-graders in which he demonstrated the way sound is transmitted over the wires.

The teacher then checked records for occupations of parents and began telephoning them to ask if they could share their special skills with the class. Parents were cooperative, and soon every area of the curriculum was enriched through parent contributions. Mothers taught children to sing, played instruments for the children, and demonstrated making pictures of flowers from bird feathers. The father who was a policeman taught lessons in safety, a carpenter built a scarecrow for Halloween, and a traveling salesman brought an enormous pumpkin from Michigan to Florida and with the help of his wife carved a jack-o'-lantern which was later made into a pie.[14]

In other schools parents are invited to help the teacher with routines and duties which are not considered teaching functions. These helpers may or may not be hired by the school board. Where there is no provision for supplying the teacher with such assistance, some mothers' groups volunteer their services to help the teacher on several afternoons a week. Of course, this procedure must be sanctioned by the local school system.

[13] For additional ideas on parent participation in the school program see "We Recognize Parents as Resource People," *Childhood Education*, 34: entire issue, March 1958.

[14] Adapted from Leila D. Bain, "I Put Parents to Work," *NEA Journal*, 49:49, January 1960.

Parents are coming into the classroom, too, through a program that is preparing mature women college graduates to meet state certification requirements for teaching. "The American Association of University Women, for instance, long interested in the teacher shortage and including many teachers in its membership, has encouraged its state divisions and local branches to concentrate on this problem. In some communities, surveys of local members available for teaching have been made; in a few, wider surveys to reach all eligible women college graduates have been initiated. In some small communities, no formal training programs were set up but the efforts resulted in arranging individual programs at nearby teacher-training institutions for a few women. But, in many, the AAUW has been successfully recruiting mature women college graudates for programs of this type."[15]

## HELPING ESTABLISH SOUND PROMOTION POLICIES

One of the most sensitive areas in teacher-parent relations is that of promotion. Each year teachers are faced with the problem of promoting or retaining children in the same grade for another year. Often a child has had so much failure and frustration that the teacher is fearful that yet another failure may be more than he can bear.

Decisions on promotion must take into consideration the child's ability to read acceptably for his grade level, the family's reaction to nonpromotion, the pressures of after-school reading sessions with upset and/or unqualified "teachers," the child's frustrations in sensing failure and his own view of his inadequacy. How the child and parents perceive the situation may well influence the teacher's decision to promote or retain the child.

Traditionally schools have adhered to the *fixed standard policy* of promotion, based on the assumption that each child assimilates a predetermined body of knowledge within a given year as a requirement for promotion. It accepts the theory that fear of failure and/or repeating a grade will bring a child "up to standard" and that failure prepares a child for the competition he will meet in the adult world. It is, incidentally, easy to administer.

Such a basis for promotion fails to take into consideration individ-

[15] *An Idea in Action: New Teachers for the Nation's Children*, Pamphlet Two (Washington, D.C.: Government Printing Office, 1956), p. 14.

ual differences in the classroom. That it rewards or punishes a child on the basis of his capacity and results in many cases in a feeling of inadequacy, emotional instability, and a negative attitude toward school makes it unacceptable to most educators.

In an attempt to counteract the shortcomings of the fixed standard basis for promotion, the policy of *continuous promotion,* or social promotion as it is frequently called, came into vogue. This practice is based on the belief that everyone should be promoted each year. It does not, however, make provision for individual differences. It ignores the fact that some children need additional time to learn. Children differ; so does their progress. Promotion on the basis of chronological age also does not take into account the child who needs less time to learn.

A more recent practice known as *guidance promotion* is based on the assumption that continuity of learning and optimum growth are individual matters. It is concerned with the individual, has a long-range plan of appraisal, and considers the fact that children differ and that the acquisition of knowledge should not be the sole criterion for promotion.

Dimond points out that "Under this system pupils are promoted on the basis of careful study and analysis of what seems best for each individual. The system assumes that teachers and administrators know enough about learning, the nature of the individual, and the effects of promotion and retention to make wise judgments for each individual. The system accepts continuous promotion as desirable for most pupils, but reserves the right to modify the policy for any individual pupil."[16]

The continuous progress plan has guidance as its core, recognizes individual differences in children, allows for varying tempi of development, provides larger blocks of time for learning, and is flexible in operation. Sorenson comments, "A continuous-progress plan is less concerned with arbitrary standards, grade lines, beginnings and endings, failures and promotion. It is more concerned with continuity of learning and optimum growth for each child."[17]

Goodlad summarizes the arguments for promotion and nonpromotion. Among the reasons for nonpromotion are the following:

[16] Stanley E. Dimond, "Who Should Fail?" *The Nation's Schools,* 63:64, May 1959.
[17] "Promotion Policies in Our Schools: A Symposium," *NEA Journal,* 49:20, April 1960.

When promotion is assured, pupils are unconcerned about their school work, developing poor work habits and careless attitudes.

Bright children come to resent equal promotion rewards for work that is obviously inferior.

Because of the need for teachers to spend a disproportionate amount of time with slow-learners the presence of these children in the room serves as a hindrance to progress. The range of achievement is widened and group homogeneity reduced.

Achievement levels are enhanced through the repetition of only partially learned material.

Immature children, through grade repetition, are more likely to find suitable play and work companions at the lower grade level.

The promoted slow-learner, unable to do the work of the grade, frustrated and discouraged, develops inferiority feelings which adversely affect his social relationships and personality development.

Some reasons given for promotion are the following:

The possibility of nonpromotion is a threat that constitutes negative motivation. Children learn best under conditions of positive motivation and therefore should be promoted.

Children distribute themselves from poor to excellent on each of the many school endeavors in which they engage, usually with only slight variations from child to child on the continuum. To average these attainments is unrealistic. To determine arbitrary cutting points for passing or failing demands a refinement in judgment that defies human capacities.

The presence of older, repeating children in a classroom decreases group homogeneity.

Learning is enhanced when children move on to new endeavors instead of experiencing the dullness and boredom of repetition.

Grade repetition results in over-ageness which, in turn, produces behavior problems requiring special disciplinary action.

Promotion retains approximately equal chronological age as a common factor and results in improved personal and social relationships.[18]

Establishing a sound promotion program presents the task of trying to steer a safe course between the rocks of routine retentions and the whirlpool of routine social promotions. What is needed is some way of allowing each child to proceed at his own pace and on his own level of ability.

[18] John I. Goodlad, "To Promote or Not to Promote?" *Childhood Education,* 30:212–216, January 1954.

Each set of arguments claims the solution to the problem; each regards the opposite point of view as unworthy of acceptance. A closer look will help the teacher make the wise instead of the expedient decision.

Studies[19] over a period of forty years have shown that, on the whole, pupils who move along with their age groups learn as much as or more than comparable students who are failed.

Saunders, in summarizing an extensive survey of the effects of nonpromotion, pointed out: "It may be concluded that nonpromotion of pupils in elementary schools in order to assure mastery of subject matter does not often accomplish its objective. Children do not appear to learn more by repeating a grade but experience less growth in subject-matter achievement than they do when promoted. Therefore a practice of nonpromotion because a pupil does not learn sufficient subject matter in the course of a school year, or for the purpose of learning subject matter, is not justifiable."[20]

However, social promotion is no real solution to the problem of learning difficulties. It is in some cases merely the lesser of two evils. In individual cases, it has been found that if a child repeats a grade with a different teacher and new experiences are provided he will gain from the opportunity the second time. ". . . Children who repeat a grade are not likely to do better the second time *unless the cause of their previous failure is discovered and remedial work is accomplished.*"[21] In a five-year experimental program carried on cooperatively by the Bayless School District and the School Mental Health Service of the St. Louis County Health Department such remedial work is being carried on. Stringer reports on this program:

1. More learning failures are due to emotional problems than to specific, organically determined learning disabilities. These are remediable if detected early enough and treated appropriately.

2. Parents seem to be the key people. When they are cooperative

[19] John I. Goodlad, "Research and Theory Regarding Promotion and Non-Promotion," *Elementary School Journal*, 53:150–155, November 1952.

[20] Carleton M. Saunders, *Promotion or Failure for the Elementary School Pupil?* (New York: Bureau of Publications, Teachers College, Columbia University, 1941), p. 29. Similar conclusions were reached by William H. Colfield, "A Longitudinal Study of the Effects of Nonpromotion on Educational Achievement in the Elementary School," doctoral dissertation, State University of Iowa, 1954.

[21] "Promotion Policies in Our Schools," *NEA Journal*, 49:16, April 1960.

and willing and able to work with the school in behalf of the child social promotions achieve excellent results.

3. Where parents are unable or unwilling to work with the school, retentions can help a significant proportion of failing children if two criteria are used in selecting children for retention:

a. A pre-retention rate of progress of less than half of normal.

b. A lag amounting to between 1.0 and 1.9 grades except at the first and second grade levels where lags of more than 0.3 and 0.7 have been used.[22]

Dimond suggests the following principles for a guidance promotion policy:

1. *Promotion or failure should be recognized as a means, not an end.* The decision should not be arbitrary, either by a fixed grade level standard or by a fixed age standard. The decision should be a part of the guidance function.

2. *Most students should pass through our schools with a steady progression, but there should be exceptions.* In making these exceptions educators recognize that failing a student is justified as a means to the end of improved learning for that student. . . .

3. *Under a guidance promotion policy, promotion is flexible, based on multiple standards.* All facts about the individual are appraised. Conferences with those involved are held. The possible risks are analyzed.

To one child failure might be damaging, to another it might be a challenge. The decision to fail a child becomes a major professional responsibility akin to the decision of a surgeon to perform an operation.[23]

# Essential Skills in
# Leadership and Participation

In working with parents it is important for the teacher to develop skills useful both in leadership and in group participation. Parents look to the teacher and have a right to expect help in improving their own ability to solve common problems in group situations.

[22] Lorene A. Stringer, "Report on a Retentions Program," *Elementary School Journal*, 60:370–375, April 1960. This article is based on the Report to Bayless Schools, June 1959; issued by the St. Louis County Health Department, Research Report No. 2.

[23] Dimond, *op. cit.*, p. 65.

## THE FUNCTIONS OF GROUP LEADERSHIP

"The overall function of leadership is to lead in many different ways, with many kinds of groups, under a variety of circumstances. The functions of a leader are varied and the possible combinations are many."[24] Certain general functions of leadership involve helping the group

Define its purposes.
Interpret these purposes into practical goals.
Clarify the assignment of responsibilities.
Guide the planning processes.
Suggest the potentialities of available resources.
Keep operations consistent with objectives.
Maintain action and move the discussion along.
Evaluate contributions made and summarize the results achieved.[25]

## UNDERSTANDING THE GROUP AT WORK

An understanding of the factors that affect a group at work is essential if the teacher is to take any role he may be called upon to assume in group participation. As a group leader or as a participant he will be able to use this knowledge to help the group plan more effective procedures. Dimock suggests five factors that affect the work of the group: (1) climate, (2) involvement, (3) interaction, (4) cohesion, and (5) task requirements.[26] These factors cannot be isolated for they are usually interacting. However, for sake of clarification they will be discussed separately.

*Climate.* The physical climate — the place of the meeting — includes size of the room, type of heating, ventilation, and freedom from distractions. The atmosphere is influenced by the type of furniture, brightness and cheerfulness of the room, and the arrangement of the furniture.

The emotional climate is determined by the feelings that pervade

24 Wilbur C. Hallenback, "The Functions of Leadership," *Training Group Leaders*, Leadership Pamphlet No. 8, Adult Education Association (Chicago: The Association, 1956), p. 8.
25 Adapted from *ibid.*
26 Hedley G. Dimock, "The Group at Work," *Adult Leadership*, 5:81, September 1956

the meeting. A climate that is friendly and warm, that accepts people and encourages them to express their ideas freely contributes toward the promotion of harmony and the accomplishment of goals.

"A healthy emotional climate is created and maintained when members concentrate on (1) being receptive to 'ideas' of members, (2) being friendly and considerate, (3) encouraging everyone to feel free to participate in the discussion, (4) easing tensions within the group and mediating personal conflicts, and (5) analyzing ideas rather than giving value judgments. . . ."[27]

*Involvement.* The extent to which members are involved depends upon their interest in the topic to be discussed and their freedom from outside distractions. If the group is friendly, has prestige value, accomplishes worthy goals, meets personal needs and interests of the members, and makes a point of rotating leadership positions and soliciting ideas from the membership, the degree of participation is high.

*Interaction.* The factors that affect the interaction of a group include size of the group, status differences of members, and "problem" members. A study of group interaction will reveal whether a few people are dominating or whether everyone is participating and assuming group functions. As the group increases in size problems of communication increase. Six to ten or twelve has been suggested as the optimum size.

Differences in status may have an adverse effect on interaction. However, the leader can encourage individuals of low status to participate and he can make an effort to analyze each contribution on the basis of its own merit.

"Problem" members may be classified as blockers, special-interest pleaders, withdrawn members, dominators, or overparticipating or underparticipating members.

*Cohesion.* The degree of "group spirit" is closely related to the involvement of members, which in turn is influenced by such factors as mutual interest and/or mutual friendship. Cohesiveness is important in maintaining the group and developing standards of cooperation. As a rule it is developed in much the same way as a healthy emotional climate is created, and the involvement of members is

[27] *Ibid.*

increased. A certain amount of sociability, in coffee breaks, for instance, tends to contribute to cohesion.

*Task Requirements.* The methods used have much to do with the success. The goals should be determined by the group, methods of communication should be clearly established, and evaluation should be a group concern. In discussion of problems some design should be used — for example, (1) defining the problem, (2) suggesting solutions, and (3) reaching decisions.

The *chairman*, in general, is responsible for opening and closing the meeting, helping define and explore the problem, helping to stay within the time limit set by the group, involving all members in the discussion, and clarifying and summarizing ideas put forth by the members.

The *recorder* serves as a co-leader. He keeps a record of what has been discussed. He sifts the contributions and records what is pertinent to the discussion, helps the chairman keep the discussion on the track, asks for clarification of ideas, and summarizes frequently. In essence, he is a co-chairman and shares responsibility, as should all the members. He does not leave this responsibility entirely to the leader.

"Planning group procedures and development in an organized fashion means higher morale and more efficient and effective group meetings."[28]

### Evaluating Successful Leadership in Group Discussion

A leader can develop a great amount of sensitivity to certain signs and symptoms that indicate how well he is carrying out his leadership function of facilitating discussion. If the following criteria are met the discussion leader is succeeding.

............... Members address me no more formally than others in group
............... Members frequently express real feelings
............... Group starts itself at beginning of each meeting
............... Sometimes members openly disagree with me
............... Members address their remarks to each other rather than to me

[28] *Ibid.,* p. 82.

## STRENGTHENING PROFESSIONAL LEADERSHIP

The professional teacher is simultaneously a leader in the community as he keeps parents and other citizens informed of educational developments in his area of special competence; a guide to youth as he helps them understand themselves and their role in society; an experimenter as he approaches problems creatively; and a transmitter of the cultural heritage as he helps students to see relationships essential to an understanding of our world.

The professional teacher possesses unique qualifications: a liberal education that gives him a broad understanding of the world; a knowledge of scientific method that helps him reason intelligently; professional training that enables him to teach effectively; and human-relations skills that assist him in working with people. Becoming a professional teacher is a continuous, rewarding experience in which growth is the chief requisite.

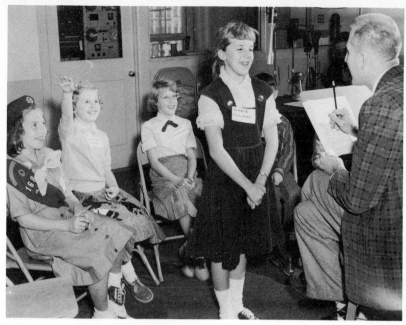

An imaginative teacher plans a
program that stimulates the
child's learning and participation.

Welcoming parents into the
classroom creates a wholesome
environment.

*Superior ability in the class-room is a characteristic of the professional teacher.*

*The teacher can often enlist the parents' aid in challenging the child.*

*Continuous growth distinguishes the professional teacher.*

............... Group has a tendency to want to remain after the time limit has been passed

............... Group makes decisions without depending on me as the final judge

............... Members seem to know what goals they seek

............... Members speak up without asking for my permission

............... Members do not count on me alone to handle "problem" members

............... "Bright ideas" originate with many members of the group

............... Different individuals frequently lead the group's thinking, discussion and procedure

............... Members seem to listen to each other without interrupting

............... Conflicts and disagreements frequently arise, but people try to understand the nature of these and deal with them

............... Members often accept insights and information from other members

............... There is absence of hostility toward me

............... Members draw out and question each other to better understand their contributions[29]

Questions that the group can use to improve their discussion appear in the following check list. The continuum is from *never* to *occasionally* to *frequently*.

1. Do we plan our meetings in relation to our objectives?
   a. Does the *leader* take on this responsibility?
   b. Do the *members* share in this responsibility?
2. Do we plan our meetings in relation to what members expect from them?
   a. Does the *leader* consider member expectations?
   b. Do the *members* cooperate in informing the leader?
3. Do we define or clarify our goals during meetings?
   a. Does the *leader* suggest that this is needed?
   b. Do the *members* ask for definition or clarification of goals?
4. Do we summarize our progress from time to time?
   a. Does the *leader* take the initiative for this?
   b. Do the *members* take the initiative for this?
5. Do we use suitable methods of procedure?

[29] Thomas Gordon, "Improving Your Leadership in Discussion Groups," *The Leader's Digest,* Vol. I (Chicago: Adult Education Association of the U.S.A., 1954), p. 31.

    a. Does the *leader* raise questions about procedure?
    b. Do the *members* take the initiative in this?
6. Do we evaluate the efficiency of our methods of operating?
    a. Does the *leader* take responsibility for suggesting evaluation?
    b. Do the *members* take responsibility for suggesting evaluation?
7. Do we watch our discussion to see if we understand one another?
    a. Does the *leader* assume this responsibility?
    b. Do the *members* share the responsibility?
8. Do we test for agreement to see if we are ready to make decisions?
    a. Does the *leader* assume this responsibility?
    b. Do the *members* assume this responsibility?
9. Do we invent new jobs when we undertake new activities?
    a. Does the *leader* suggest possibilities for new jobs?
    b. Do the *members* suggest possibilities for new jobs?
10. Do we spread responsibilities throughout the group?
    a. Does the *leader* suggest that other persons participate in responsibilities?
    b. Do the *members* volunteer for responsibilities?
11. Do we discuss morale problems such as lack of interest, conflicts, and anxieties in the group?
    a. Does the *leader* help the group face and solve these problems?
    b. Do the *members* raise and try to solve these problems?
12. Do we tackle tense situations such as minority disagreement, violations of rules, no response to requests for volunteers?
    a. Does the *leader* help solve these problems?
    b. Do the *members* help solve these problems?
13. Do we have an atmosphere in which all feel free to express ideas and feelings?
    a. Does the *leader* encourage a climate of free expression?
    b. Do *members* stimulate other members to express themselves?
14. Do members exhibit a feeling of responsibility to restrict their contributions to those which are helpful to the group?
    a. Does the *leader* help keep the group "on the beam"?
    b. Do *members* keep on the alert for wandering?
15. Do we freely communicate our feelings and expectations about his performance to the leader?
    a. Does the *leader* encourage members to discuss his plans and performance?
    b. Do *members* take responsibility for expressing themselves to the leader about his performance?[30]

PROGRAM PLANNING

Teachers are frequently placed on committees for planning programs for the PTA or other professional organizations where they work with parents and colleagues. The ease and success with which they carry on this activity depends not alone upon attitudes toward working with others but also upon skills. The attitude that one is working *with* people, rather than doing things *for* them, together with the necessary skills, will enable the individual to take his part successfully.

When a committee meets for the first time to work on a new project, it is well to orient the members one to another and to the common task which they have been asked to perform. Some biographical information about each member of the committee might prove to be a good starting point, followed by a discussion centering around the questions: What are the ingredients of a good program? What can each member of this committee contribute toward developing a good program? How can we go about planning the program? Once these questions are settled the committee can decide on methods to be used in achieving their objectives.

Knowles' brief table will be helpful:[31]

| Objectives To Be Served | Methods That Can Be Used |
|---|---|
| To build fellowship | Group singing — informal discussion |
| To present information and relate it to members' experience | Film — discussion |
| | Lecture — questions |
| | Informal dramatization — buzz groups |
| | Group interview — group reports |
| To bring out problems and relate them to facts | Workshop — field trip — reports |
| | Exhibit — buzz groups — discussion |

The chart on pages 824–825 suggests useful program methods.

[30] Alvin Zander and Ronald Lippitt, "Measuring Leadership Performance," *Training Group Leaders* (Chicago: Adult Education Association of the U.S.A., 1956), pp. 40–47.
[31] Malcolm S. Knowles, "Your Program Planning Tool Kit," *The Leader's Digest*, Vol. I (Chicago: Adult Education Association of the U.S.A., 1954), p. 67.

Check List of Program Methods

| METHOD | CHIEF CHARACTERISTIC | PATTERN OF PARTICIPATION | SPECIAL USEFULNESS | LIMITATIONS |
|---|---|---|---|---|
| Lecture, film, reading, recitals, etc. | Information-giving. | | Systematic presentation of knowledge. | Little opportunity for audience to participate. |
| Forum | Information giving followed by questions for clarification. | | Audience can obtain the specific information it wants on particular aspects of the subject. | Formality; lack of freedom to interchange ideas. |
| Symposium panel or debate | Presentation of different points of view. | | Different points of view spotlight issues, approaches, angles; stimulate analysis. | Can get off the beam; personality of speakers may overshadow content; vocal speaker or questioner can monopolize program. |

| Method | Use | | Advantage | Limitation |
|---|---|---|---|---|
| Discussion | High degree of group participation. | | Pooling of ideas, experience, and knowledge; arriving at group decisions. | Practical with only a limited number of people. |
| Project, field trip, exhibits, etc. | Investigation of a problem cooperatively. | | Gives first-hand experience. | Requires extra time and energy for planning. |
| Buzz groups | 100% participation by large audiences through small clusters of participants. | | Makes individual discussion, pooling of ideas, possible in large groups. Develops leadership skill in members. | Contributions are not likely to be very deep or well organized. |
| Group interview | Spontaneous giving of opinions and facts by experts in response to questions. | | Brings knowledge from a number of sources to bear on one problem. | Becomes disorganized without careful planning of material to be covered. |

Source: Malcolm S. Knowles, "Your Program Planning Tool Kit," *The Leader's Digest*, Vol. I (Chicago: Adult Education Association of the U.S.A., 1954), p. 69.

## *Parent Education*

Parent education usually involves teaching and guiding parent groups in child development and related problems of family living. Programs are organized on the basis of the needs and interests of parents. Goals, methods, resources, evaluation procedures, and plans for the future are dependent upon the emerging needs of the group.

Teachers of young children, particularly, are frequently called upon to serve as speakers, discussion leaders, consultants. They are also asked to assist with the planning and guidance of the programs. In some schools the programs are organized under the sponsorship of parent-teacher associations. In other schools mothers' clubs assume the responsibility, meeting at specified intervals to study under the direction of the kindergarten teacher. The parents discuss common problems related to behavior and development of their children, frequently following a cooperatively organized course of study and reading material germane to the topic. Individual problems are usually reserved for private conferences and not "aired" at the open meetings.

Many schools plan meetings to acquaint parents with the curriculum, emphasizing provisions made for children's intellectual, emotional, social, and physical growth. A brochure citing school objectives and describing typical learning activities is often distributed at the first meeting. The teacher discusses the objectives to be achieved and the implementation of the objectives through the learning activities.

Parents are frequently invited individually or in groups of five or six to observe children in the classroom. A conference with parents sets the stage for this visit. The observation should be followed by a discussion period and arrangements should be made for individual conferences. The use of films and other audio-visual materials is effective as a basis for group discussion if it is related to the problems of the group.

In a study of the comparative effectiveness of presenting information to parents relative to speech and language development in the preschool child, it was found that facts are better received when presented in a regular classroom lecture than when presented in lecture form on television. "Both television and classroom presentation however, produce a highly significant change in the attitude and beliefs toward the subjects." The difference obtained in favor of the face-to-face lecture method does not rule out the use of television for parent education in this area since there "appears to be no difference between the two methods in terms of the amount of internalization or acceptance of the material."[32]

Television as a medium of significance in parent education is important because a larger number of parents can be reached. Adding a new avenue to parent education, however, does not preclude continuing the use of methods which have been successful in the past and are still successful.

Although most communities have some organizations working in the parent-education area, few offer a coordinated program of services. Ideally, the public schools should coordinate educational programs for parents because they have direct contact, both with the families and with the community organizations. However, only a few state departments of education provide permanent personnel in this area.[33]

In a study of parent education to determine present practices, to ascertain desirable practices, and to recommend appropriate activities for improvement, it was found that schools practice various approved leadership functions, including (1) inviting parents to planned educational experiences, (2) informing parents of major curriculum changes, (3) encouraging special-interest groups, (4) having preschool or kindergarten orientation programs for parents, (5) providing a meeting room for parents participating in study groups, (6) using personal methods such as letters and telephone calls to encourage parents to attend activities, (7) providing counseling for parents whose children have serious school problems, (8) inviting parents to act as chaperons for school functions, and (9) providing parents with printed information on pupil needs and school routines.[34]

[32] Ray R. Battin, "A Study of the Comparative Effectiveness of Two Methods of Presenting to Parents Information Relative to Speech and Language Development in the Preschool Child," doctoral dissertation, University of Florida. Reviewed in *Speech Monographs*, 27:78, June 1960.

[33] Norejane Johnston Hendrickson, "Parent-Education Practices in Ohio's Public Elementary Schools," *Educational Research Bulletin*, 38:30, February 11, 1959. Based on the author's doctoral dissertation on file in the library of Ohio State University, "Parent Education Leadership Functions of Ohio's Tax-Supported Colleges and Universities, and Public Elementary Schools, 1958."

[34] *Ibid.*

On the basis of this study and observation of present practice it is evident that the elementary school does not yet fully accept responsibility for parent education. Although much is done at the nursery and kindergarten level, much remains to be accomplished in the primary and intermediate school. Many schools appear to consider they are meeting their parent-education obligations adequately if individual teachers consult with parents of children in their immediate classrooms. Even where schools are intensely interested in expanding their parent education in this vital area, inadequate budgets, limited staffs, and teachers inadequately prepared for leadership curtail their activities.

Basic to improvement in parent education is the need for the teacher to develop leadership skills in order to work more effectively with a group of lay leaders as an occasional consultant or a leader to train parents in leadership roles.

## Conclusion

Teachers are accepting the challenge of improving the child's educational opportunities through working with parents. They assume responsibility for establishing and maintaining wholesome relationships in communicating with parents, developing skills in group leadership and participation required to improve communication with parents, and assisting in parent education in the school and community.

Through informal contacts with parents and more formal scheduled contacts the relationships between teacher and parent and school and home are strengthened to the end that the child's welfare is improved, educational opportunities are more fully utilized, and the child's potential abilities are realized.

Working with parents brings a new dimension to teaching as the teacher discovers greater satisfactions and develops new insights into the child's background which make his teaching more vital. "Parents in America prize their children. They work for them. They care for them. They want the best for them. A child is treasured, not exploited. This is true for all but an infinitesimal number of children in our country."[35]

[35] James L. Hymes, *Effective Home-School Relations* (Englewood Cliffs, N.J.: Prentice-Hall, Inc., 1953), p. 13.

Everything the teacher does in home-school relations touches on sacred soil. "In this field tread lightly. You are not talking about the weather, but about the parents' children — and about the parents' efforts — and the parents' hope."[36]

# ACTIVITIES AND QUESTIONS

1. Define the competencies the teacher needs in parent-teacher comunication, essential skills of leadership, and parent education.
2. How would you handle the following situations?
   a. A mother insists on remaining in the kindergarten the first day of school because she is afraid the child will cry when she leaves.
   b. An irate mother comes to school to complain about John's report card. He received an unsatisfactory grade in behavior and in reading. John is a third-grade pupil and his mother is known to have made trouble for the teacher last year.
   c. The mother of Mary and Jennie, who are twins, has requested that they be enrolled in the same first grade so they can be together. Mary is apparently overly dependent upon Jennie. There are two other first grades in the building. There is no policy covering this situation.
   d. You are asked by the president of the Parent-Teacher Association to lead a group discussion on a controversial topic at the next PTA study group. Last year an unfortunate incident occurred when one of the teachers led a similar discussion.
3. Organize a panel discussion on the problem: How can we improve our promotion policy in the schools?
4. Work out a role-playing situation in which the teacher applies the principles suggested in this chapter for making a parent-teacher conference successful. Work out a situation in which these principles are flagrantly disregarded. Observe the reactions of the participants and discuss the implications of your observations.
5. In your first grade you have five pupils who have not started reading from books by Thanksgiving. You receive notes from four of the parents asking if they can come to school to find out what is wrong? What can you do to prepare for the conferences?

[36] *Ibid.*, p. 17.

6. Examine a number of report cards from school systems in various parts of the country. How do they differ in the emphasis on academic subjects, social and emotional development, work habits, and attitudes? What explanations do you have for the differences?

7. From your reading, observation, and experience, what type of reporting to parents appears to have the greatest value for the child? The parent? The teacher?

8. Talk with a teacher about the method of reporting to parents used in the school in which he teaches. Talk with a parent in the same school. How do their views compare on the adequacy of the reporting system?

# BIBLIOGRAPHY

Association for Childhood Education International. *Learning About Role-Playing for Children and Teachers.* Margaret Rasmussen, Editor. Washington, D.C.: The Association, 1960.

Association for Childhood Education International. "We Recognize Parents as Resource People," *Childhood Education,* 34: entire issue, March 1958.

Bennett, Mabel C., and Bishop, Katherine V. *Sharing and Showing: Pupils and Teachers Interpret Education Through Parent Group Conferences.* Los Angeles: Education Press, 1952.

Bossard, James H. *The Parent and Child.* Philadelphia: University of Pennsylvania Press, 1953.

Camp, Louie T. "Improving Reporting Techniques," *NEA Journal,* 48:26, December 1959.

Camp, Louie T. "The Parent-Teacher Conference — A Symposium," *NEA Journal,* 48:21–23, December 1959.

Department of Elementary School Principals. *Parent and the School.* Thirty-Sixth Yearbook. Washington, D.C.: The Department, 1957.

D'Evelyn, Katherine. *Individual Parent-Teacher Conferences: A Manual for Teachers of Young Children.* New York: Bureau of Publications, Teachers College, Columbia University, 1952.

Elder, Franklin L. *Explorations in Parent-School Relations.* Austin: University of Texas Press, 1954.

*Evaluating and Reporting Pupil Progress: What Research Says to the Teacher.* Department of Classroom Teachers and American Educational Research Association. Washington, D.C.: National Education Association, 1955.

Frank, Martha. *The Challenge of Children.* New York: William Morrow and Company, 1957.

Goodlad, John I. "To Promote or Not to Promote," *Childhood Education*, 30:212–216, January 1954.

Gronlund, Norman E. *Sociometry in the Classroom.* New York: Harper & Brothers, 1959.

Hutson, Percival W. *The Guidance Function in Education.* New York: Appleton-Century-Crofts, Inc., 1958.

Hymes, James L. *Effective Home-School Relations.* Englewood Cliffs, N.J.: Prentice-Hall Inc., 1953.

Johnston, Edgar, *et al. The Role of the Teacher in Guidance.* Englewood Cliffs, N.J.: Prentice-Hall, Inc., 1959.

Langdon, Grace, and Stout, Irving W. *Teacher-Parent Interviews.* Englewood Cliffs, N.J.: Prentice-Hall, Inc., 1954.

Leonard, V. E., *et al. Counseling with Parents in Early Childhood Education.* New York: The Macmillan Company, 1954.

Read, C. H., and Roberts, D. D. "What Parents Like in the Kindergarten Interpretation Program," *Nation's Schools*, 59:50–52, April 1957.

*Reporting Is Communicating: An Approach to Evaluating and Marking.* Washington, D.C.: Association for Supervision and Curriculum Development, NEA, 1957.

Smith, Norvel L. "Primary Schools and Home-School Relationships," *Educational Administration and Supervision*, 42:129–133, March 1956.

Spears, Harold. "Parent Conferences," in *Curriculum Planning Through In-Service Programs.* Englewood Cliffs, N.J.: Prentice-Hall, Inc., 1957.

Strang, Ruth. "Study-Discussion Program, Preschool Course," *National Parent Teacher*, 53: monthly feature, September 1958 to April 1959.

Warters, Jane. *Techniques of Counseling.* New York: McGraw-Hill Book Company, 1954.

Wertheim, Eleanor S. "A Joint-Interview Technique with Mother and Child," *Children*, 6:23–29, January-February, 1959.

Yeager, W. *School-Community Relations.* New York: Henry Holt and Company, 1954.

# 16

What greater or better gift can we offer the republic than to teach and instruct our youth?

CICERO

# Meeting the challenge

Today's teacher must take the broadest view of his professional responsibility. He is essential in any society. His career becomes increasingly significant as the demand for leaders grows.

The challenge of teaching was never greater, the need for professional teachers never more urgent. The effort to develop public understanding and appreciation of the role of the school in our society is an acknowledged part of every teacher's responsibility. To the extent that the teacher views his opportunity in the same light as other professional people view theirs — the physician for the care of his patients, the lawyer for the counsel of his clients — will large numbers of highly competent men and women be attracted to the teaching profession.

According to Flexner there are six criteria of a profession:

*First,* a profession is essentially intellectual. Tools and manual labor may be employed, but they are incidental and the problems that are encountered are solved through the use of intelligence. . . .

*Second,* a profession is based upon a vast amount of scientific knowledge and requires a great deal of learning on the part of its members. . . .

*Third,* a profession must be essentially practical as opposed to being merely theoretical. It must have some purpose and serve some concrete function in society.

*Fourth,* a profession has a body of knowledge and a number of well-established techniques that can be communicated.

*Fifth,* a profession has a high degree of organization.

*Sixth,* a profession is concerned with the welfare of society.[1]

## Characteristics of the Professional Teacher

The professional teacher is fully prepared and thoroughly competent. He is intellectually capable, possesses skill in teaching, commands a defined body of knowledge, is conscious of his role as a member of the teaching profession, and realizes he must earn status, prestige, and respect as a member of the profession through outstanding service.

The professional teacher pursues teaching as a career. He is eager to see standards raised in requirements for teacher certification and is enthusiastic about improving his knowledge, skills, and competencies. He takes responsibility for continual growth in the profession.

The professional teacher keeps abreast of new developments. He is eager to try new tools and techniques that will improve teaching methods. He does not insulate himself against them. He realizes that the materials and methods of yesterday are as inadequate to present and future needs in education as in science and industry. He realizes, too, that although tools and techniques by themselves cannot solve educational problems, they are essential.

The professional teacher makes use of action research. Corey defines action research as "research undertaken . . . in order that

[1] Abraham Flexner, "Is Social Work a Profession?" *School and Society,* 3:904, June 26, 1915.

[teachers] may improve their practices. The people who actually teach children . . . attempt to solve their practical problems by using the methods of science."[2] They gather evidence to define their problems, draw upon all available experience for hypotheses that give promise of helping alleviate or eliminate the problems, and test these promising procedures as they work with children in the classroom, accumulating evidence of their effectiveness.

The professional teacher recognizes the importance of human relations. He is skilled in working with people, realizing well that in order to interpret the teaching profession to the community he must exemplify the qualities that are desirable in a human being. He is a firm believer in maintaining excellent parent-school relations and welcomes visits from parents at other times than during American Education Week. He believes that communication with parents is essential in understanding the child and his problems and makes a conscious effort in this direction.

The professional teacher is creative. Teaching is an avenue for his creativity. He tries new approaches in guiding children and helping them to express their ideas. He seeks new methods of stimulating them to their highest endeavor.

In describing the creative individual Zirbes states:

(a) He uses his problems as challenges to go beyond his habit tracks and prior experiences

(b) He is open to new ideas and possibilities in an exploratory, tentative but evaluative way

(c) In due time he aspires to try out some new ideas which he has been considering

(e) He demonstrates in his action that he expects to learn by doing, and does not want a "ready made" "know-how" of pattern to which he can conform

(e) He does something with his ideas and "hunches" besides dream or give way to wishful thinking. . . .[3]

Openness to new experiences and ideas, the ability to be spontaneous in handling new ideas, materials, or techniques, and an inner sense of evaluation for deciding when the time is ripe for initiating,

[2] Stephen M. Corey, *Action Research to Improve School Practices* (New York: Bureau of Publications, Teachers College, Columbia University, 1953), p. 141.

[3] Laura Zirbes, *Spurs to Creative Teaching* (New York: G. P. Putnam's Sons, 1959), pp. 9–10.

implementing, and culminating an experience — these characterize the creative teacher.

Pusey summarizes the qualities essential in teaching: "Devotion, knowledge, imagination, quick intelligence, patience, concern for others, awareness of beauty, grasp of principle, attractive personality — these are the great qualities that make creative teachers."[4]

The professional teacher is active in the community. No longer does the teacher isolate himself from the activities and organizations of the community. He realizes that by taking his place in the community he can have a greater impact. He feels a sense of responsibility for the welfare and improvement of the community in which he lives. He is not a "suitcase" teacher who takes off at four o'clock on Friday and returns at eight o'clock on Monday morning. Through activities, projects, and organizations he participates in the life of the community.

The professional teacher is a leader as well as a follower. Leadership can be exerted in many ways; it does not necessarily mean that the teacher must be the president of the PTA. Leadership comes from many sources: (1) the visionary who protests the *status quo*, (2) the writer who puts ideas on paper, (3) the planner who gets things started, (4) the executive who implements ideas with methods. Leadership comes in many forms and may exist in many roles at a given time. The teacher may be a leader in an educational activity, a civic project, and a social enterprise simultaneously. The degree to which he is involved in leadership is dependent upon physical stamina, creativity, and ability to organize his time.

The professional teacher works through organizations. He recognizes that organizations are the agencies through which ideas are realized and goals are achieved. In such critical areas as educational responsibilities, teacher education, personnel relationships, community relationships, and professional economic security the teacher cannot work alone. He must join with others. "Until teachers engage in more out-of-school activities which they express as being professional, they will have little claim to be regarded as members of a profession comparable to those of medicine, law, or the ministry."[5]

[4] Nathan M. Pusey, "The Exploding World of Education," *Fortune*, 52:198, September 1955.

[5] Lawrence W. Drabick, "The Teacher's Day: Analysis of Professional Role Perceptions," *Educational Administration and Supervision*, 45:336, November 1959.

The professional teacher is aware of the functions involved in teaching. The Yale-Fairfield Study of Elementary Teaching attempts to define the twelve major professional functions of the practicing teacher. They must be viewed as parts of a single whole — not in isolation. There is no priority in the way they are listed, for each contributes to the teaching process.

1. Organizing, initiating, directing activities.
2. Informing, explaining, and showing how.
3. Establishing a psychological climate, a wholesomeness in relations, a stimulus for activity that promotes learning.
4. Helping children clarify thoughts, feelings, aims, purposes, beliefs, interests, and attitudes.
5. Unifying groups in achieving the aims of the school.
6. Developing closer school-community relationships.
7. Making diagnoses respecting individual children and trying out these "hunches" in action research.
8. Evaluating individuals and groups, reporting to parents, children, to other teachers within the school, to other schools. . . .
9. Assuming responsibility for upkeep, maintenance, and certain requirements in respect to the elementary classrooms.
10. Assuming responsibilities in the wider setting of the school; assemblies, committee work, helping with such routine chores as lunchroom, mid-morning lunch, and bank collections, duty on the playground, in the hall, and other supervisory duties related to behavior of children in the classroom and in maintaining and preserving school property.
11. Developing materials for the curriculum. Associated with this is the study of form catalogues, putting work on the chalkboard, selecting books and workbooks, planning work on a daily and long-range basis.
12. Professionalizing one's career; functioning successfully as an individual citizen.[6]

The professional teacher looks toward the future. The professional teacher is not content with developing the most promising teaching methods and using the most effective teaching tools currently available. He is not satisfied with the *status quo*. He is

[6] Burton P. Fowler, *Yale-Fairfield Study of Elementary Teaching*, abridged edition of the Report for 1954–1955 (New York: Fund for the Advancement of Education, 1956), pp. 51–53. (Adapted.)

aware that the promising practices of today are the result of the dreams of yesterday and that the dreams of today will become the realities of tomorrow. Looking into the crystal ball and surveying the school of the future, Lee suggests a blueprint for buildings, staff, organization, curriculum, research, in-service programs, and parent education.

*Buildings.* The elementary school of 1985 will be a one-story air-conditioned structure housing 500 to 1000 pupils. Distinctive features will be health and psychological centers, a library unit in conjunction with an individualized instruction room, a cafeteria, a multipurpose room doubling as a gymnasium, conference areas, outdoor play areas with swimming pool facilities, a work laboratory, a language laboratory, a science laboratory, facilities for automatic teaching devices, television, and an audio-visual center.

*Staff.* The staff will include a full-time supervising principal, a school secretary, secretarial aides for classroom teachers, teachers who have masters degrees in areas of specialization, and such consultants as a psychologist, a nurse, a speech correctionist, and art, music, and general elementary supervisors.

*Organization.* Experimentation with various patterns of organization will be characteristic. The plan of permitting a teacher to continue with his class for a two-year period will be common. The lock-step graded system may have disappeared as have split-grades in the past quarter-century.

*Curriculum.* Greater flexibility will characterize the curriculum. Simultaneously, in certain areas greater uniformity will exist as the result of televised teaching. Schools will give greater attention to physical and motor development; school camping will be an integral part of the curriculum.

*Research.* Research will provide the basis for selection of important concepts, better understanding of children's knowledge, and increased integration of subject fields.

Critical thinking, problem solving, and creative thinking will receive greater emphasis. Increased opportunities for creative experience in the arts, music, and literature will result from the wider use of audio-visual materials.

*In-service programs.* More emphasis will be placed on mastery of content through the use of television, and greater availability of professional materials in each school will help strengthen the subject-matter backgrounds of teachers in content areas.

*Parents.* Child-study groups will be organized utilizing television and supplemented by the skills of the kindergarten teacher, who will teach only half a day, devoting the remainder of the day to giving individual tests, conferring with parents, and conducting child-study groups. Consultants will be available to work with parents of children with special problems.[7]

These ideas are far from visionary. Many are already in practice. However, since some 20 per cent of the children in the United States still attend one-room rural schools they are in the "to-be-hoped-for" category. "The rapidity with which they will become common practice depends on the willingness of school systems to intensify their experimentation and research, upon increased support for public education, and upon creative use of the products of technology which appear in the offing."[8]

## *The Role of the Teacher in the Classroom*

The future of the nation will reflect to a significant degree the teacher in the classroom who inspires or frustrates, who motivates or stultifies, who challenges or depresses.

*Organizing the Classroom.* The classroom should be a laboratory for learning. The teacher should plan with the children the most effective way of working so that maximum energy and time can be devoted to teaching-learning and a minimum amount of time will be spent on routine duties. The day-by-day responsibilities of the teacher include planning with pupils, scheduling activities, making assignments, directing learning activities, evaluating progress, and maintaining discipline; distributing materials, caring for equipment, supervising recess periods and lunchroom periods, keeping records, and writing reports. Some of the teaching-learning activities offer the teacher opportunities for creativity and experimentation. Others should be quickly disposed of by so organizing them that they demand the least amount of the teacher's time and energy and release him for his main responsibility — teaching.

[7] Adapted from J. Murray Lee, "Elementary Education: 1985," *Educational Leadership*, 17:475–480, May 1960.
[8] *Ibid.*, p. 480.

*Creative Activities*

Organizing the classroom.

Studying the needs of children and deciding what help and guidance each child needs.

Making decisions about selecting, organizing, developing, and evaluating learning experiences — both short- and long-term decisions.

Making decisions about teaching procedures and instructional materials that are most effective for the various activities.

Individualizing instruction and guiding group activities.

Supervising student activities — both in school and cocurricular.

Informing, explaining, and showing how to perform a process.

Helping children clarify their thinking, feelings, aims, interests, beliefs, and attitudes.

Directing the group processes through an understanding of group dynamics.

Carrying on action research in connection with problems to be solved.

Evaluating progress and reporting to parents.

Working with other faculty members on all-school activities.

Interpreting the school to the community.

Participating in professional and personal enrichment activities.

*Routine Activities*

Keeping records and making reports.

Administering and scoring tests.

Correcting papers.

Distributing and caring for teaching materials.

Preparing teaching materials.

Checking comfort index of the classroom, ventilation, etc.

Supervising playground, halls, and lunchrooms.

Observing the child's health for evidence of impaired sight, defective hearing, infectious diseases, impaired speech.

Collecting money for drives, lunch tickets, book rentals, excursion fees, PTA fees.

Taking care of housekeeping responsibilities.

Signing excuse slips, checking daily attendance.

The typical elementary teacher's week, according to the Yale-Fairfield Study,[9] ranges from 29 hours and 45 minutes to 58 hours and 40 minutes, the average being 39 hours and 30 minutes. A survey conducted by the National Education Association[10] showed that the typical teacher works about 47 hours a week. Among elementary teachers slightly more than half of the time is spent in teaching. The majority of teachers report that their work load is about right. Many of them, however, dislike the routine chores that take their time and energy from the main job — teaching. Progress is being made. Loads are being lightened through the use of teacher aides who take over routine chores.

Redefer[11] found in a study involving 5000 teachers in 24 school systems that these four areas need to be improved to raise teacher morale: (1) relations of board of education and central administration with teaching staff, (2) personnel practices and policies, (3) school equipment and supplies, (4) educational leadership of the school system as a whole and leadership of a particular unit of the system.

*Classroom Control.* Perhaps no aspect of teaching is of greater concern to the teacher than that of discipline. Maintaining classroom control is a part of the total instructional program. When the teacher knows his subject matter, when he is skilled in motivating and guiding pupils, when he understands how children learn and how they develop, and when he knows the fundamentals of group dynamics and how to apply them, teaching is usually good and problems are at a minimum.

Suggestions for classroom control may be helpful:

Maintain a classroom environment in which children are accepted.
Be creative in your teaching.
Vary the program — invite visitors, take field trips, use audio-visual aids and community resources.
Maintain a warm personal realtionship with each child.
Provide for individual differences in the classroom.

[9] Fowler, *op. cit.,* pp. 104–115.
[10] "Teaching Load in 1950," *Research Bulletin,* 29:17–18, February 1951.
[11] Frederick L. Redefer, "Factors That Affect Teacher Morale," *The Nation's Schools,* 63:6–61, February 1959.

Be consistent in your expectations of a child's behavior.

Establish classroom regulations early. Children need to know what they may and may not do.

Help children improve their study habits. Allow for supervised study time in class.

State your questions clearly and check to see that you are understood.

Expect your pupils to state their answers clearly.

Check with the principal to see what types of problems he will help you with.

Keep alert to what is going on in all sections of the room.

Move about the room frequently during a study or work period.

Use a clear, pleasant voice.

Do not talk too much, too fast, too loud, or too often.

Avoid making an issue over minor or trivial offenses.

Avoid making threats you cannot or do not intend to carry out.

Avoid making the group suffer because of the misdemeanor of a single individual.

The responsibility for a good classroom environment is the teacher's, whether he participates democratically with the pupils in planning and carrying out the activities or plans them himself. Democratic control of the classroom involves planning, preplanning, and evaluation. It demands flexibility and understanding of the boys and girls. Children need guidance. They need someone who can lift their sights and motivate them to achieve.

Caswell asserts: ". . . The power to stimulate the pupil to high endeavor, to help him grow, . . . to lead him to develop a sense of inquiry, to create the drive to continue his education, to develop a sense of beauty and appreciation of the world in which he lives — these are qualities which must be cultivated pretty largely by the teacher through a multitude of small actions in day-by-day association with the pupil."[12]

*Knowing the Child.* In recent years emphasis has been placed on "equating teaching with the idea of responsible professionalized citizenship. To achieve such an end it becomes necessary that the teacher know the child and understand the community."[13] Understanding a child involves more than knowing what he does. It means

[12] Hollis L. Caswell, in *Teachers College Record*, 58:74, November 1957.

[13] William E. Drake, *The American School in Transition* (Englewood Cliffs, N.J.: Prentice-Hall, Inc., 1955), p. 587.

knowing why he does it, how he feels about what he is doing, and what his behavior means to him. The adult who studies a child must try to understand himself — why he reacts to the child as he does, why he is annoyed or pleased by the child's behavior, why he feels as he does about the child's reactions to his attitudes and behavior. Studying the child's behavior becomes the basis for more effective guidance.

Ways of studying children range from the simple to the complex:

1. *Observation* — of parents and children together, or of the child alone or in a group of children in everyday situations; free-play and other informal activities offer ideal opportunities to make significant observations.

2. *Observation in controlled experimental situations.* [Here the teacher may structure a situation in order to compare the behavior of the child with that of other children of similar age.]

3. *Compilation of a developmental history and record of family background.* [Through an understanding of the child's previous experiences and family background the teacher can better guide the child's development. Knowledge of such factors as illness during infancy, broken home, unemployment of parent, relationships with family members, etc., helps the teacher in understanding the child at the present time.]

4. *Study of the child's . . . [creative] art products, and his handwork.*

5. *Techniques that elicit information about his feelings and relationships* — incomplete sentences, incomplete stories, pictures and stories to which children are asked to respond, "Three Wishes," and similar projective-type material.

6. *Talks with the child and the parent.* [Here the teacher seeks to get the child's own story to better understand his behavior. The teacher learns about his attitudes toward school, home and family.]

7. *Sociometric techniques.* [The teacher discovers the complex interpupil social relationships through observation, group discussion, casual conversation, and sociometric devices.]

8. *Dramatization and role playing.* [The children act out problems in human relations spontaneously and analyze the enactment with the help of other role players and observers.]

9. *Standardized and teacher-made tests.*

10. *Standardized individual tests.*

11. *Projective techniques.* [Administered by persons having clinical

background and special training. These include such methods as
the Rorschach Test,[14] the Children's Thematic Apperception
Test, and the Draw-A-Man Test.]

12. *Clinical Study.* [This method provides the teacher with health
records from the school. It differs more in degree than in kind
from the study made by a teacher alone. It deals more specifically with underlying causes.]

13. *Medical and neurological examinations.* [These are given by
the school physician, family physician, or a team of health personnel.][15]

Effective guidance is possible if the teacher not only studies the
children but makes use of this knowledge in planning, developing,
and evaluating the instructional program. An intensive study of a
few children provides an understanding of child behavior and development that cannot be gained in a superficial study of many children.
Direct observation in a number of situations will give the teacher
insight into problems that may be of deep concern to the child.

*Studying the Child*

I. Abilities of the child
   A. Physical
      1. Is he well?
      2. Has he any physical impairment of vision, hearing, coor-
         dination, and so forth?
      3. Does he become fatigued easily?
      4. Does he give evidence of nervous tension?
   B. Intellectual
      1. Does he learn readily?
      2. Does his performance compare favorably with that of
         others of his age?
      3. Does he have special abilities in
         a. construction           f. painting
         b. creative dramatics     g. physical activity and play
         c. mathematics            h. reading
         d. modeling               i. science
         e. music                  j. speech

[14] Kennison T. Bosquet and Walter C. Stanley, "Discriminative Powers of
Rorschach Determinant in Children Referred to a Child Guidance Clinic,"
*Journal of Consulting Psychology,* 20:17–21, February 1956.

[15] Ruth Strang, *An Introduction to Child Study* (New York: The Macmillan
Company, 4th ed., 1959), p. 457.

II. Socioeconomic background
   A. From what kind of home does he come?
   B. In what kind of neighborhood does he live?
   C. What kind of significant experiences has he had?
III. Social-emotional development
   A. How does he respond to people, places, and things?
      1. Is he timid, fearful?
      2. Is he unusually aggressive?
      3. Is he normally independent and self-directive?
      4. Is he cooperative?
      5. Is he antagonistic?
   B. How does he respond to his parents?
      1. Is he overly dependent on them?
      2. Is he resistant toward them?

How effectively the teacher carries out his responsibility in the classroom can be determined by self-evaluation.

*A Self-Evaluation Scale for the Teacher*[16]

Circle One

I. Personal qualities
   A. Considerateness (kindliness, courtesy, tact)  5  4  3  2  1
   B. Emotional stability (poise)                   5  4  3  2  1
   C. Resourcefulness (initiative, drive)           5  4  3  2  1
   D. Attractiveness (appearance, dress)            5  4  3  2  1
   E. Intelligence (personal, professional)         5  4  3  2  1
   F. Cooperativeness                               5  4  3  2  1
   G. Adaptability                                  5  4  3  2  1
   H. Reliability                                   5  4  3  2  1
   I. Sense of humor                                5  4  3  2  1
II. Competencies
   A. Creating emotional climate to free children
      to use their intelligence                     5  4  3  2  1
   B. Identifying pupil needs and formulation of
      objectives                                    5  4  3  2  1
   C. Selecting and organizing meaningful ex-
      periences                                     5  4  3  2  1
   D. Directing learning experiences                5  4  3  2  1
   E. Developing concepts                           5  4  3  2  1
   F. Regulating tempo of learning activities       5  4  3  2  1
   G. Providing for individual differences          5  4  3  2  1

[16] Lillian M. Logan, *Teaching the Young Child* (Boston: Houghton Mifflin Company, 1960), p. 76.

|  | Circle One |
|---|---|
| H. Using desirable methods of control | 5  4  3  2  1 |
| I. Providing opportunities for creative use of materials and self-expression in the arts | 5  4  3  2  1 |
| J. Evaluating pupil growth | 5  4  3  2  1 |
| K. Staff planning | 5  4  3  2  1 |

III. Behavior controls
  A. General knowledge

| | |
|---|---|
| 1. Child behavior and development | 5  4  3  2  1 |
| 2. Educational principles and practice | 5  4  3  2  1 |
| 3. Subject matter | 5  4  3  2  1 |
| 4. Cultural background | 5  4  3  2  1 |

  B. General skills

| | |
|---|---|
| 1. Human relations | 5  4  3  2  1 |
| 3. Professional attitude | 5  4  3  2  1 |
| 3. Use of language | 5  4  3  2  1 |

  C. Interests, attitudes, ideals

| | |
|---|---|
| 1. Interest in children | 5  4  3  2  1 |
| 2. Emotional and intellectual acceptance of all children | 5  4  3  2  1 |
| 3. Professional attitude | 5  4  3  2  1 |

  D. Health

| | |
|---|---|
| 1. Physical | 5  4  3  2  1 |
| 2. Mental | 5  4  3  2  1 |
| 3. Emotional | 5  4  3  2  1 |

Highest possible score
Sums of all scores
Average score

The professional teacher is as objective as possible in evaluating his personal qualities, competencies, and behavior controls. He recognizes that there may be room for improvement; he recognizes also strengths he has. The habit of self-appraisal in day-by-day teaching is important.

# The Role of the Teacher in Working with the Staff

Typically, the beginning teacher plays a new role as he becomes a staff member in an organizational hierarchy. He is no longer a student to be guided and protected but is largely now on his own, to be judged by what he knows and by what he does. He must discover the organizational patterns and the attitudes toward new ideas. He needs to know where the power lies — with the principal, the supervisor, the superintendent, or a clique of older teachers.

He should be shrewd enough to recognize the responsibilities he should assume in regard to professional activity in faculty meetings, faculty committees, and parent-teacher associations. He should be able to recognize the functional roles of his colleagues — whether they are constructive, supportive, or disruptive — and to make his contributions on the positive side. He will need to use his innate intelligence, social perception, and common sense in doing the best possible job of teaching and contributing to professional activities in the school.

If teaching is to be a challenging, satisfying experience there must be opportunities for growth or the teacher will lose interest in the job and the work will lose its zest. Action research, curriculum improvement, professional organizations, reading in a chosen field of interest, and community projects offer areas for enrichment. The teacher who combines travel, reading, and hobbies with professional activities is much more likely to become and remain a well-balanced individual. Satisfaction in his work and the ability to get along well with other people characterize the professional teacher.

## INTERPERSONAL RELATIONSHIPS

No matter what grade level or subject one chooses to teach, success is dependent in large measure upon ability to establish and maintain good relations with colleagues, principal, and supervisors. Getting along with others means accepting them as they are, being open-minded about suggestions, giving credit where credit is due, assuming a fair share of responsibility in the total school program, being friendly and fair, avoiding hasty judgments, and avoiding becoming a member of the "gripe clique."

*Accepting People as They Are.* People differ. That is what makes them interesting. A teacher is prepared to accept individual differences in children, to make allowances for behavior. He must do the same with adults. All have their idiosyncrasies and some may be annoying, but there is no point in psychoanalyzing or trying to change them.

*Being Open-Minded About Suggestions.* When one of the staff makes a suggestion, he may be trying to help. The suggestion should be taken in good faith even though it may not be feasible to carry it out. Teachers who have been in the school for a longer period understand the local situation and customs. If help is needed in making up one's mind about suggestions, the principal or supervisor may be called upon. It is well to be willing to learn from others.

*Giving Credit Where Credit Is Due.* No matter how good a job of teaching one does, someone else paved the way. Success is dependent to a great degree upon what the pupil already knows when he comes into the class. What others have taught him influences the impact that can be made upon him, and they should receive the credit for his background. Then, too, if another teacher comes up with an excellent idea and is successful in attracting the attention and favorable comments of the principal and superintendent, congratulations are due him. Sharing in another's achievement may not be as easy as getting acclaim, but it is one hallmark of the mature individual.

*Assuming a Share of the Responsibility.* Unfortunately, some teachers cannot be counted upon to assume responsibility for activities outside of the classroom. The professional teacher sets the example by supporting and contributing to the success of various activities and projects which are promoted by the school. He is willing to give time and talent in the interest of enhancing the position of the school in the community.

*Being Friendly and Fair.* If a teacher comes into a school wanting to become one of the members of a working team, genuinely interested in activities, and enjoying people, he will soon have congenial friends. He will find that friendship here, as everywhere, is based upon common interests, mutual understanding, and respect. In every school there are older members of the faculty who are eager to help him get his "sea legs." By accepting assistance and not claiming to have all the answers the teacher can learn the routine of the school quickly. Thus it will not be necessary to impose on the kindness of others for any appreciable length of time.

*Avoiding Hasty Judgments.* It is unwise to make up one's mind about people, school policy, or issues in a hurry. A beginning teacher or an experienced teacher in a new school might better concentrate on doing a good job of teaching, cooperate in promoting the total program, and become acquainted with the staff and school routine. If rival groups bid for control it is wise not to get involved. The teacher is not called upon to settle disputes or increase hostilities already in existence.

*Avoiding Becoming a Member of the "Gripe Clique."* Teachers have human weaknesses. It is frequently in the lounge or during the lunch hour that jealousies and dissatisfactions permeate the atmosphere and the urge to gripe makes itself felt. Some individuals gain much of their satisfaction from griping and from seeing others dissatisfied with the profession or with life in general. Such an attitude is, of course, unprofessional and disintegrating. On the whole, these teachers are in the minority, but they are often quite vocal and give the erroneous impression that everyone in the school is dissatisfied.

Working effectively with other teachers, principals, supervisors, superintendents, and parents is largely a matter of putting into practice the fourth "R": Relationships.

PROFESSIONAL ACTIVITIES

"Be it promotion policies, report cards, or the establishment of an over-all framework for a program on which a staff is working, many understandings and skills are necessary for effective involvement."[17]

*Staff Meetings.* Teachers meet usually after school to exchange ideas, discuss school problems, and plan policies. Staff meetings concern themselves with problems like the following: What can we do to improve our promotion policies? What provisions can we make in the individual classroom to provide more adequately for the gifted or other exceptional children? How can we improve our system of evaluating pupil progress and reporting to parents?

*Committee Work.* Teachers participating in committee projects

[17] Gordon Mackenzie, "Expectations That Influence Leadership," *Leadership for Improving Instruction* (Washington, D.C.: Association for Supervision and Curriculum Development, 1960), p. 73.

study, discuss, evaluate, and make recommendations for improving education in particular areas of the curriculum. The committees may be on curriculum planning, textbooks, school policies, and community relations. Teachers are frequently given time to work in such committees during school hours. In some schools they are given "professional growth credit" for this activity.

*Conferences, Conventions, and Workshops.*[18] Orientation conferences preceding the opening of school in which teachers meet with the administration personnel to become acquainted with new staff members and the philosophy, curriculum, and school policies are common. There is a chance to become familiar with classrooms and other facilities. These conferences last from two days to a week. During the school year various local and state meetings are scheduled. Teachers are encouraged, too, to participate in regional and national conventions.

Workshops are an effective way of working together for educational purposes. A group of teachers interested in the same problem or in the same curriculum area study together after school and on week ends. Such meetings are usually voluntary and are based on the expressed needs and interests of the teachers themselves.

The professional aspects of the teacher's role are bound inextricably with his relationships with the children whom he teaches, the parents with whom he communicates, and the colleagues with whom he works. These relationships cannot be minimized; the success of the teacher is dependent not alone upon the competencies and skills he exercises in the classroom but also upon his ability to work well with people.

## *The Role of the Teacher in the Community*

Professional teachers make an effort to develop friendly relations with the community. Most communities look upon teachers as use-

---

[18] Harold Spears, *Curriculum Planning Through In-Service Programs* (Englewood Cliffs, N.J.: Prentice-Hall, Inc., 1957).

ful, responsible, contributing citizens who live normal lives and participate in social and leisure-time activities. They appreciate help the teacher is willing to give with civic affairs and organizations. They appreciate the effort teachers make to become acquainted with the cultural and recreational facilities they offer. They appreciate an attitude of respect for the traditions and customs of the community, even when it appears that the usefulness of such traditions or customs is long past. Here tolerance and forebearance may be the better part of discretion. Until the teacher understands the problems and is willing to share in the hard work of community improvement, he had better withhold criticism.

*The Community's Responsibility to Teachers.*  The community should allow teachers the freedom offered a person in any other profession; it should pay a salary commensurate with the demands of the profession; it should provide living conditions which satisfy an individual of broad educational and cultural background; it should give teachers the esteem it accords to members of the medical, legal, and other professions; it should permit them the religious and political freedom that is the inherent right of any citizen in this country. Reasonable working hours, favorable working conditions, an attractive salary, and satisfying leisure-time activities do much to attract and retain highly qualified people in the teaching profession.

*The Teacher's Responsibility to the Community.*  In return, the teacher should teach effectively the children he is assigned to teach; he should continue his own education and self-improvement through advanced study, travel, and recreation; he should exemplify the ideals of democracy both in the classroom and in the community; he should preserve the cultural heritage and advance the frontiers of knowledge.

The public takes teachers at their own evaluation. They must earn the respect of the community by being competent, well-groomed, professionally minded, and active as private citizens in the affairs of the community, the state, and the nation.

*Community Participation.*  The extent to which teachers participate in community affairs is indicated by the chart below; the chart represents the findings of a nation-wide survey of classroom teachers in urban school systems with 2500 population or more. Completed questionnaires were received from 3046 of the 5000 teachers queried.

The chart reveals that although teachers presumably understand and concur with the concept of good public relations and the importance of their role in fostering them, there is a discrepancy between what they think and what they do about it. This is a result, perhaps, of the long struggle teachers have had to gain political and personal freedom and their continuing struggle to gain improved salary and working conditions.

### TEACHER PARTICIPATION IN COMMUNITY AFFAIRS

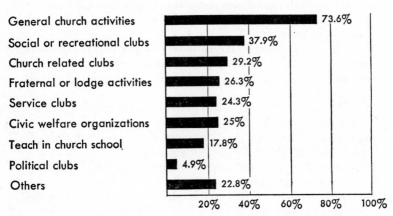

| | |
|---|---|
| General church activities | 73.6% |
| Social or recreational clubs | 37.9% |
| Church related clubs | 29.2% |
| Fraternal or lodge activities | 26.3% |
| Service clubs | 24.3% |
| Civic welfare organizations | 25% |
| Teach in church school | 17.8% |
| Political clubs | 4.9% |
| Others | 22.8% |

Source: "Better Schools Cost More," *Research Bulletin,* National Education Association, 37:40, April 1959.

To determine how far the teacher is moving in the direction of improving relations the following questionnaire is useful:

### *How Well Are You Doing in Public Relations?*[19]

Do you believe that public-relations activities should foster lay participation in the educational program?
Do you really enjoy talking and working with children?
Do you really enjoy talking and working with adults?
Are you genuinely proud to be a teacher?
Do you believe that good public relations are your responsibility?
Do you regularly visit your pupils' homes?
Do you ever send newsletters home to parents?

[19] "How Well Are You Doing in Public Relations?" *NEA Journal,* 37:14, April 1959.

Do you ever send notes to parents concerning things other than problem behavior?

Do you ever send home complimentary notes concerning your pupils who are not outstanding students?

Do you encourage your pupil's parents to visit you and the school?

Do you schedule regular conferences with parents?

Do your contacts with critical parents tend to placate them rather than increase their irritation?

Do you have a room-parent organization?

Does your school have a parent-teacher organization?

Do you regularly attend parent-teacher organization meetings?

Does your school foster parent participation in planning class work and activities?

If so, do you personally take advantage of this policy to involve parents in your classroom planning and activities?

Do you ever enlist the help of parents in the performance of routine clerical duties?

Would you recognize the parents of most of your pupils if you met them on the street?

Do you encourage your classes to invite laymen to share their experiences with the class?

Do you make an effort to bring school matters of public interest to the attention of appropriate officials or news media?

Do your classroom activities ever involve community problems and contacts with laymen?

Do you willingly accept invitations to address groups of laymen, either on school matters or on other subjects?

Do you take an active part in church, political, civic, or fraternal organizations in your community?

Do your personal actions reflect credit upon your profession?

Do your remarks in the community tend to present a constructive view of teaching and of your local school situation?

*Improving Education in the Community.* If the community wishes its children to be educated by teachers who are interested in community life, who are informed and enthusiastic, who are widely traveled and well read, it must be prepared to make it financially possible for them to live this rich, full life. "Books cost money. The . . . teacher (knowing that books are a vital tool of his profession) will think twice before purchasing one if the purchase will deny his family a necessity. The teacher who spends his summer [or his recreational hours] working in the local canning factory probably would rather be attending school for advanced work."[20]

Evidence from research as far back as 1920 shows the relationship between high-quality education and financial expenditure. The findings as summarized in a recent study suggest:

> There is a factual basis for dealing with the relationship between quality in education and its level of cost.
>
> The cost-quality relationship in education is complex and difficult to measure.
>
> The evidence now available on the effect of level of per-pupil expenditure on the quality of education is not final or complete, but it provides some valuable guidelines.
>
> A higher quality education is generally provided in school systems which spend larger amounts on their schools.
>
> . . . High quality education is seldom found in low-expenditure school systems.[21]

In pointing to the need for improving the teacher's situation Pusey warns: ". . . Nor shall we effect improvement so long as society continues to place such relatively slight value, measured in salary and prestige, on the service of teachers." That there is a brighter outlook is evidenced as he states: "Many communities are beginning to take steps to improve the standing and economic conditions of teachers. These efforts must be multiplied and accelerated."[22]

# The Role of the Teacher in Professional Organizations

Organizations are the means by which individuals with common interests, common purposes, and common problems get a hearing from other individuals and from other groups. The effect of the

[20] Robert Jewett, "Why the Able Public-School Teacher Is Dissatisfied," *Educational Research Bulletin* (Ohio State University, College of Education), 36:244, October 9, 1957.
[21] "Better Schools Cost More," *Research Bulletin*, NEA, 37:44, April 1959.
[22] Pusey, *op. cit.*, p. 200.

combined voices of individuals with a common purpose cannot be overestimated.

"In a world of special-interest groups, teachers, too, need well organized associations. In many ways, the quality of work done by the teaching profession and the security of its members are influenced by the strength of its organizations."[23]

### PURPOSES OF TEACHERS' ORGANIZATIONS

Professional organizations serve the teacher by working for the welfare of all the members, by informing the public about the problems of teachers and the needs of children, by maintaining high standards of training and performance in the profession, and by making the latest educational information available. Since the organizations are effective in improving the status and welfare of all members of the teaching profession every teacher should feel an obligation to join.

*Improving the Teachers' Economic Welfare.* Research that informs school boards and state legislatures of the salaries and working conditions of the teaching profession and makes a comparison with other professional groups requires time, funds, and skill. The united contributions of the membership make possible the funds required to carry out a research program that has their needs and interests at heart.

*Informing the Public About Needs of Children and Teachers.* A well-informed public is more likely to take steps to solve the problems currently facing the schools. The teacher functions in a twofold capacity in his role as a professional person: as an individual and as a member of professional organizations. Teachers' associations are one of the most effective ways of pooling individual efforts and alerting the public to undesirable situations.

*Maintaining Professional Standards.* The future security of child and teacher is affected by the standards maintained by members of the profession. Through associations teachers can help upgrade teaching requirements, be active in curriculum improvement, experi-

[23] Gordon E. McCloskey *et al., Introduction to Teaching in American Schools* (New York: Harcourt, Brace and Company, 1954), p. 316.

ment with new and improved methods of teaching and improved instructional aids, and encourage other teachers to be intolerant of shoddy work which discredits the profession. They can be alert to legislation that would lower certification requirements in the name of meeting the teacher shortage or any other "emergency." It has been shown that the teacher shortage is less acute in communities with high standards of professional training and qualifications. Pride in the profession is the keystone for improving the standards. Constant vigilance is the watchword of the professional teacher.

*Communicating the Results of Research and Teaching Practices.* Teachers, like other professional groups, must keep abreast of the times. New developments, new findings about the way children learn and grow must be made available to them. Research that takes place in the laboratory has no effect on the learning in the classroom unless it is used. Teachers are informed about the latest trends through journals, yearbooks, bulletins, and special studies that the associations publish. The effective teacher is not content merely to read about them. He tries them out in the classroom. Teachers' conventions, workshops, conferences, and association meetings at local, state, regional, and national levels bring teachers together to discuss problems and attack common difficulties.

## NATIONAL, STATE, LOCAL, AND INTERNATIONAL ORGANIZATIONS

With every right goes an obligation. This is especially true in professional organizations. It is not enough merely to pay dues. One must be willing to assume responsibility at every level. Representative professional organizations will be examined briefly.

*National Education Association.* Most teachers look forward to becoming members of the NEA, which they join through their state education associations. Fees are, of course, required for both the national and state organizations. Every state education association is affiliated with the national association. State and local units are closely allied with the national organization in the solution of problems that are national in scale. In purely local problems the local organization has a great deal of autonomy.

One of the best single guides for the teacher as he begins his career is the NEA Code of Ethics, which is periodically modified to meet current conditions. The following code, officially adopted by the Association's Representative Assembly in 1952, is reproduced here by permission of the National Education Association.

## Code of Ethics

We the members of the National Education Association of the United States, hold these truths to be self-evident: that the primary purpose of education in the United States is to develop citizens who will safeguard, strengthen, and improve the democracy obtained through a representative government; that the achievement of effective democracy in all aspects of American life and the maintenance of our national ideals depend upon making acceptable educational opportunities available to all; that the quality of education reflects the ideals, motives, preparation, and conduct of the members of the teaching profession; that whoever chooses teaching as a career assumes the obligation to conduct himself in accordance with the ideals of the profession.

As a guide for the teaching profession, the members of the National Education Association have adopted this code of professional ethics. Since all teachers should be members of a united profession, the basic principles herein enumerated apply to all persons engaged in the professional areas of education — elementary, secondary, and college.

FIRST PRINCIPLE: *The primary obligation of the teaching profession is to guide children, youth, and adults in the pursuit of knowledge and skills, to prepare them in the ways of democracy, and to help them to become happy, useful, self-supporting citizens. The ultimate strength of the nation lies in the social responsibility, economic competence, and moral strength of the individual American.*

In fulfilling the obligations of this first principle the teacher will:

(1) Deal justly and impartially with students regardless of their physical, mental, emotional, political, economic, social, racial, or religious characteristics.

(2) Recognize the differences among students and seek to meet their individual needs.

(3) Encourage students to formulate and work for high individual goals in the development of their physical, intellectual, creative, and spiritual endowments.

(4) Aid students to develop an understanding and appreciation not only of the opportunities and benefits of American democracy but also of their obligations to it.

(5) Respect the right of every student to have confidential information about himself withheld except when its release is to authorized agencies or is required by law.

(6) Accept no remuneration for tutoring except in accordance with the approved policies of the governing board.

SECOND PRINCIPLE: *The members of the teaching profession share with parents the task of shaping each student's purposes and acts toward socially acceptable ends. The effectiveness of many methods of teaching is dependent upon cooperative relationships with the home.*

In fulfilling the obligations of this second principle the teacher will:

(1) Respect the basic responsibility of parents for their children.

(2) Seek to establish friendly and cooperative relationships with the home.

(3) Help to increase the student's confidence in his own home and avoid disparaging remarks which might undermine that confidence.

(4) Provide parents with information that will serve the best interests of their children, and be discreet with information received from parents.

(5) Keep parents informed about the progress of their children as interpreted in terms of the purposes of the school.

THIRD PRINCIPLE: *The teaching profession occupies a position of public trust involving not only the individual teacher's personal conduct but also the interaction of the school and the community. Education is most effective when these many relationships operate in a friendly, cooperative, and constructive manner.*

In fulfilling the obligations of this third principle the teacher will:

(1) Adhere to any reasonable pattern of behavior accepted by the community for professional persons.

(2) Perform the duties of citizenship, and participate in community activities with due consideration for his obligations to his students, his family, and himself.

(3) Discuss controversial issues from an objective point of view, thereby keeping his class free from partisan opinions.

(4) Recognize that the public schools belong to the people of the community, encourage lay participation in shaping the purposes of the school, and strive to keep the public informed of the educational program which is being provided.

(5) Respect the community in which he is employed and main-

tain loyalty to the school system, the community, the state, and the nation.

(6) Work to improve education in the community and to strengthen the community's moral, spiritual, and intellectual life.

FOURTH PRINCIPLE: *The members of the teaching profession have inescapable obligations with respect to employment. These obligations are nearly always shared employer-employee responsibilities, based upon mutual respect and good faith.*

In fulfilling the obligations of this fourth principle the teacher will:

(1) Conduct professional business through the proper channels.

(2) Refrain from discussing confidential and official information with unauthorized persons.

(3) Apply for employment on the basis of competence only, and avoid asking for a specific position known to be filled by another teacher.

(4) Seek employment in a professional manner, avoiding such practices as the irresponsible distribution of applications.

(5) Refuse to accept a position when the vacancy has been created through unprofessional activity, pending controversy over professional policy, or the application of unjust personnel practices and procedures.

(6) Adhere to the conditions of a contract until service thereunder has been performed or the contract has been terminated by mutual consent or otherwise legally terminated.

(7) Give and expect due notice before a change of position is to be made.

(8) Be fair in all recommendations that are given concerning the work of other teachers.

(9) Accept no compensation from producers of instructional supplies when one's recommendations affect the local purchase or use of such teaching aids.

(10) Engage in no gainful employment outside of his contract where the employment adversely affects his professional status or impairs his standing with students, associates, and the community.

(11) Cooperate in the development of school policies and assume the professional obligations thereby incurred.

(12) Accept his obligation to the employing board to maintain a professional level of service.

FIFTH PRINCIPLE: *The teaching profession is distinguished from many other occupations by the uniqueness and quality of the professional relationships among all teachers. Community support and respect are influenced by the standards of teachers and their attitudes toward teaching and other teachers.*

In fulfilling the obligations of this fifth principle the teacher will:

(1) Deal with other members of the profession in the same manner as he himself wishes to be treated.

(2) Stand by other teachers who have acted on his behalf and at his request.

(3) Speak constructively of other teachers, but report honestly to responsible persons in matters involving the welfare of students, the school system, and the profession.

(4) Maintain active membership in professional organizations and, through participation, strive to attain the objectives that justify such organized groups.

(5) Seek to continue professional growth by such means as study, research, travel, conferences, and attendance at professional meetings.

(6) Make the teaching profession so attractive in ideals and practices that sincere and able young people will want to enter it.

Not only does the NEA collect facts and information to inform citizens, government officials, and members of the teaching profession about educational problems, conditions, and needs; it also publishes the *NEA Journal*. This is issued monthly and keeps the membership informed about current trends in economic and political activities that affect the schools and the welfare of teachers. It also provides them with recent developments in curriculum, methods, and evaluation of teaching.

Some of the thirty departments that conduct research, provide the services of consultants, hold conferences, and publish materials are as follows:

Health, Physical Education and Recreation
Higher Education
School Administrators
Supervision and Curriculum Development
Industrial Arts
Audio-Visual Instruction
Elementary School Principals
Kindergarten-Primary Education
Rural Education

Classroom Teachers
Vocational Education
Mathematics Teachers
Science Teachers
Music Education
Exceptional Children

The departments help coordinate the activities of teachers with those of principals, supervisors, and superintendents. They offer the teachers information that improves teaching at various levels and in different academic areas.

The organization of the Commission on Teacher Education and Professional Standards (TEPS) by the National Education Association in 1948 clearly indicates that the organized teachers of the nation wished to have a share in the policies that govern their professional preparation. "The leaders in the American Association of Teachers Colleges recognized a potential ally and took still another step to bring agencies into constructive relationships. Members of the Commission on Teacher Preparation were placed on all the committees of the Association in advisory or consultant relationships."[24] This action resulted in bringing classroom teachers, school superintendents, and administrative state officers into the policy-making bodies of the Association. In the initial statement of purposes the Commission declared its intent to develop an accrediting process. The alignment of forces should result in greater gains for professional preparation of the teacher than are possible with any one organization operating in isolation.

The avowed business of the Commission is to work to elevate standards for the profession to guarantee higher quality of teaching service. Among the points of general agreement reached at the Second Bowling Green Conference in regard to preparation of teachers were these:

1. That the up-grading of the preparation of teachers demands a unified approach; that this basic effort to improve the quality of education is a fundamental responsibility of the total institution.
2. That the up-grading of the preparation of teachers demands higher quality in both subject field and professional area.

[24] Donald P. Cottrell *et al., Teacher Education for a Free People* (Oneonta, N.Y.: American Association of Colleges for Teacher Education, 1956), p. 54.

3. That graduate preparation of teachers can be distinctive without being diluted; and that more and more graduate programs must be in the area of the teaching assignment.

4. That the rapid accretion of new knowledge demands new dimensions in in-service education for experienced teachers.

5. That high standards of selection and preparation are the only sure bases for guaranteeing both adequate quality of teaching and adequate quantity of teachers.

6. That the development of effective cooperative efforts to improve teacher education does not mean "total surrender" by any segment; that such development can take place only among peers; that there can be no second and third rate citizenship involved in such an enterprise.[25]

*State Education Associations.* The state association makes specific recommendations for the improvement of educational programs, teacher welfare, and teacher status. Teachers benefit from the activity of spokesmen who represent them at critical periods before the state legislatures and other organizations of the state. They cooperate with the superintendents of public instruction, school board associations, and citizens' groups to inform the general public about the purpose of state aid laws that provide for teachers' salaries and improve employment practices. The association also works with state legislatures to get laws enacted that will improve educational opportunities for children and teachers.

State associations sponsor state conventions, which all members are eligible to attend and in which problems of the profession and objectives of education are evaluated and considered. Each state association publishes a journal that emphasizes problems and educational events at the state level.

*Local Associations.* Local associations are effective rungs in the ladder leading to active participation at the state, national, and international levels. They form the seedbed for leaders and are the connecting links between teachers and organizations of other professions in the community. The success of the state and national associations depends upon the efforts and effectiveness of the organization at the local level. ". . . We must fix in mind the pattern of local organization which is best for each state and then work with all our intelli-

[25] T. M. Stinnett, "The Second Bowling Green TEPS Conference," *Phi Delta Kappan*, 40:128, 129, December 1958.

gence to achieve that pattern. Each state is different, and the pattern will vary to meet local needs."[26]

One contribution a local association can make is helping to orient the beginning teacher. School systems are making use of local teachers' associations for a number of the following tasks:

Sending information to the new teacher about the school, the community, and the local association prior to the opening of school.

Providing information about possible living quarters, churches, medical and recreational facilities in the community.

Providing information about the credit union of the local association.

Helping the new teacher get acquainted with the school system's special services.

Assigning a member of the association who is an experienced teacher as a sponsor of the beginning teacher.

Organizing workshops around the professional problems of the new teacher.

Planning social activities in advance to make the newcomer feel at home in this new situation.

Acquainting the new teacher with the various professional organizations for teachers.

The extent to which local associations are professionally oriented is mirrored in their activities. "More than one-quarter of them, for example, send a regular representative to the meetings of the local board of education. As a channel between the membership and school authorities, however, local associations as a whole are not active. Almost half presented no requests or suggestions to the school authorities during 1957–58, and about 70 per cent received no communications from such authorities. . . .

"Many local groups were active in public endeavors, work for state or federal legislation affecting education, work toward local board bond or tax levy campaigns, and efforts aimed at teacher citizenship. Teacher welfare goals were reported by a large proportion of associations, as were salary studies and recommendations and personnel policies."[27]

That there are differing opinions as to the effectiveness of the local organizations can be seen in the following quotations:

[26] Joy Elmer Morgan, "Building Foundations," *NEA Journal*, 40:249, April 1951.
[27] NEA Research Division, "Your Local Association," *Research Bulletin*, 38:43, 44, May 1960.

"The full picture of their strength, representative nature, organizational structure and complexity, and wide scope of activities would indicate clearly the strong position held and meaningful role played in the professional lives of the teachers of America by local education associations."[28]

"As for local education associations affiliated with the NEA, not even the NEA's own studies[29] venture the claim that they typically yield any real power in their communities. Occasionally an outstanding individual stimulates a local association into significant action, or conditions degenerate to the point where the local association must act or perish. . . . It is typical of local education associations to dissipate their energies in futile efforts to improve their conditions of employment. Other than this, they give teas for new teachers in the fall and retiring teachers in the spring, and perhaps listen to a few travelogues in between."[30]

*International Organizations.* Such international organizations as the Association for Childhood Education International (ACEI), World Confederation of Organizations of the Teaching Profession (WCOTP), and the *Organización Mundial Educación Preescolar* (OMEP), with which the United States National Committee for Childhood Education is affiliated, provide for a meeting of minds of different nationalities having similar concerns for educating the children of the world. Teachers who help provide the leadership and strength such organizations need are indeed ambassadors of good will. It is they who enhance the prestige of the profession and promote international understanding.

Not all teachers can be delegates to the state associations; not all are able to attend national and international meetings. However, the professional teacher recognizes that leadership must be provided at every level — local, state, national, and international. Starting at the local level he contributes ideas for vitalizing the local association with plans for interesting discussion groups, outstanding speakers, and stimulating in-service programs. He is willing to accept responsibilities as secretary, treasurer, or publicity chairman if re-

[28] *Ibid.,* p. 44.
[29] NEA Research Division, "Local Education Associations at Work," *Research Bulletin,* October, 1948.
[30] Myron Lieberman, *The Future of Public Education* (Chicago: University of Chicago Press, 1960), p. 192.

quested. Nor does he begrudge the time and effort spent in his role as a professional person. He recognizes the value of improving educational opportunities for children, colleagues, and himself.

*Improvement of Teachers' Organizations.* There is a growing belief that the teachers' organizations must become more effective in making education a profession. Lieberman[31] sets forth recommendations for strengthening them.

1. The leadership positions in teachers' organizations must be made attractive enough to compete with any other type of educational position, and with top-level positions in industry, the professions, government service, and other fields. The chief executive of such organizations as the NEA and the AAUP should be paid not less than $50,000 per year.

2. Teachers should pay at least $100 per year in dues, with perhaps $40.00 going to the national organization, $40.00 to the state organization, and $20.00 to their local organization.

3. There should be at least one full-time representative of the teachers wherever there are at least 2000 teachers in a school system or combination of systems. The national and state organizations should set minimum professional and employment standards for these representatives and be ready to assist local organizations in employing them on a permanent basis.

4. There should be a merger of the NEA and the AFT[32] on the basis of (a) an abandonment of affiliation with the labor movement and (b) adequate organizational safeguards to prevent administrator domination of the merged organization.

5. There may be a group of teachers' organizations differentiated according to their teaching fields of specialization, but there should be only one organization to represent the same kind of teachers in employer-employee affairs.

6. Organization dues should be collected by a check-off system at the source of payment.

7. Membership in the comprehensive teachers' organizations must be mandatory, though on an extralegal basis. One possible way to achieve this is for the organizations to be aggressive supporters of high administrative salaries; in return, administrative personnel must do everything they possibly can, such as instituting the check-

---

[31] *Ibid.*, pp. 273–274.

[32] American Federation of Teachers, national affiliate of the AFL–CIO. About 5 per cent of the teachers in the U.S. are enrolled in the AFT and about 60 per cent in the NEA.

off system, to strengthen the teachers' organizations. Such a *quid pro quo* would not mean administrative domination of the organizations but would be a natural alliance based upon mutual strength and respect. Every effort should be made to make membership attractive through cheap insurance, credit unions, and similar inducements.

8. The membership structure of teachers' organizations must reflect in part the certification regulations for different kinds of educational personnel; those persons with no training in common and with widely disparate levels of training should not be lumped together into one vast industrial union type organization.

9. Superintendents and other top-level managerial employees should not be allowed to join organizations which represent teachers in matters of employment.

10. Teachers' organizations should establish and enforce a code of professional ethics that would be nationwide in scope.

## The Expanding Role of Educational Television

Professor Herold C. Hunt of Harvard University has called television "our best hope for bringing today's outworn, restrictive, and unimaginative educational system out of the oxcart age and into the twentieth century." The past few years have witnessed tremendous growth in this medium of instruction; more and more commercial broadcasters are offering educational programs, and over 600 closed-circuit systems have been established. "One of the latest and most dramatic projects is sponsored by the Ford Foundation. It is known as the *Midwest Program on Airborne Television Instruction.* Beginning soon after the first of January 1961, lessons in some fifteen elementary and high school subjects will be broadcast from a plane flying at 20,000 feet at the center of an effective broadcasting range of two hundred miles radius. The broadcasts will be carried on for three hours of each school day four days a week for the rest of the school year. More than five million school children will be able to view these broadcast lessons on their school television receivers. The plane will broadcast from tapes previously prepared by a corps of master teachers who have been recruited from all parts of the country."[33]

[33] William E. Spaulding, *Look to the School* (New York: The New York Public Library, 1960), p. 24.

Another dramatic project, also sponsored by the Ford Foundation, is the closed-circuit television system in the Hagerstown, Maryland, area. Jonathan Spivak, reporting on the Hagerstown experiment in *The Wall Street Journal,* cogently cites the advantages and disadvantages of educational television:

> As educators begin to add up the balance sheet for this electronic aid to learning, they generally agree that the pluses outweigh the minuses. In its favor, they report improved pupil achievement and dollar savings on instruction; against it, some upsetting of classroom routine, scattered teacher morale problems, and a threat of mechanical standardization of the learning process.
>
> Here in Hagerstown, where televised education has gone farther than almost anywhere else, a band of 28 academic performers labors regularly from 8 A.M. to mid-afternoon to enlighten some 17,000 pupils. A closed-circuit system links 37 elementary and high schools. From six well-equipped studios in a converted recreation hall, a schedule embracing 28 subjects is transmitted each week.
>
> With only four TV teachers in foreign languages, art, and music, school officials say, the local school district can provide a wealth of courses that would otherwise require 60 teachers to offer. TV teaching has allowed the district to handle a 500-a-year increase in pupil enrollment while adding half as many teachers as would normally be needed.
>
> Even more vital, school officials claim these TV-taught students get better grades. After three years of combined TV and conventional instruction, 42% of the sixth graders scored at an eighth-grade level on achievement tests; before TV, only 15% of them hit this bracket.
>
> · · · ·
>
> During educational TV's early years, there was a good deal of teacher resentment out of fear it would cost their jobs. But this view has faded with booming school population, continued teacher shortages in many areas, and the realization that television cannot replace, but only supplements, the skilled teacher.
>
> · · · ·
>
> Television suffers most obviously from being a one-way communication process. There is no way to stop in mid-delivery and adjust to the learning pace of pupils. Unlike the skilled classroom teacher who individualizes his approach, the TV instructor must largely standardize his product for mass consumption.
>
> Certainly any attempts to rely too heavily on the magic TV box may be disastrous, educators say. "Nothing comes across with less

impact than televised mediocrity," warns *Design for ETV*, a study sponsored by the Ford Foundation.[34]

## Conclusion

A person does not become a professional teacher merely by announcing that he is one, or by joining professional organizations. He realizes that basic criteria of a profession are built upon a vast amount of scientific knowledge and require a great deal of learning on the part of its members. The professional teacher does not rely on hunch to make decisions; he makes them on the basis of a body of professional knowledge and insight.

He realizes that he must have a thorough liberal education, an understanding of the child who is to be educated and the processes involved, and the skills to impart his knowledge. He develops techniques in organizing the knowledge into learning experiences which have meaning for the child as he pursues wisdom. He respects the profession, the learners, the colleagues, and the partners in education — the parents.

He is a guide and an experimenter as he approaches problems. He helps children understand themselves, their problems, and their goals for the future. As his role becomes increasingly professional, it becomes at once more challenging and rewarding.

The reward of the teacher lies in the knowledge that through him the child's vision will be enlarged and his life enriched. ". . . We all sense, directly or indirectly, consciously or unconsciously, that to leave a vestige of oneself in the development of another is a touch of immortality. Through this we live far beyond our span of mortal years. Through this we find new and impelling reasons for being. . . ."[35]

[34] Jonathan Spivak, "Teaching by TV," *The Wall Street Journal*, December 13, 1960, pp. 1, 19.

[35] From an address by President Samuel B. Gould at an Antioch College assembly, quoted in Richard Wynn, *Careers in Education* (New York: McGraw-Hill Book Company, 1960), p. 238.

# ACTIVITIES AND QUESTIONS

1. Observe in a classroom of your choice. How many characteristics that distinguish the professional teacher did you observe?
2. How does a teacher go about becoming an accepted member of the school staff? How can the members of the staff facilitate this process?
3. Discuss the multiple role of the professional teacher. In how many of the subroles did your favorite teacher function?
4. What purposes do professional organizations serve? Interview a classroom teacher and find out to which organizations he belongs. Try to determine from your interview his attitude toward the objectives of the organizations and the extent to which he believes the organizations are achieving them.
5. What obligations and responsibilities do you expect to assume as a teacher? Discuss this question in the light of the items included in the NEA Code of Ethics.
6. Interview a principal in one of the local schools and find out what provisions are made to help teachers evaluate their effectiveness in the classroom, as members of the staff, as participants in the community, and as members of professional organizations.
7. What provisions are made locally for in-service growth of teachers?

# BIBLIOGRAPHY

American Association of Colleges for Teacher Education. *Research and Study in Teacher Education.* Oneonta, N.Y.: The Association, 1958.

Anderson, Robert H. "Time Allotment: A View on Priorities," *Educational Horizons,* 37:34–39, Winter 1958.

Association for Supervision and Curriculum Development. *Leadership for Improving Instruction.* Washington, D.C.: National Education Association, 1960.

Barr, James, Harding, Lowry W., and Jacobs, Leland. *Student Teaching in the Elementary School.* New York: Appleton-Century-Crofts, Inc., 1958.

Bridgman, Percy W. *The Way Things Are.* Cambridge: Harvard University Press, 1959.

Callahan, Raymond. *An Introduction to Education in American Society.* New York: Alfred A. Knopf, Inc., 1956.

Carman, Harry J., *et al.* "Desirable Policies for the Certification of Teachers: A Symposium," *Educational Record,* 39:253, July 1958.

Cottrell, Donald P., *et al. Teacher Education for a Free People.* Oneonta, N.Y.: American Association of Colleges for Teacher Education, 1956.

Davies, Donald. "Who Teaches the Teachers?" *Minnesota Journal of Education,* 39:17–18, September 1958.

Edmund, Neal, and Hemick, Lyle. "Ways in Which Supervisors Help Student Teachers," *Educational Research Bulletin,* 37:57–60, March 1958.

*The Education of Teachers: New Perspectives.* Report of Second Bowling Green Conference. Washington, D.C.: National Education Association, 1958.

Eichorn, John R. "Let's Consider the Teacher," *Education,* 79:22–24, September 1958.

Goodlad, John I. "Moving Forward in Teacher Education," *Educational Leadership,* 16:228–231, January 1959.

Haskew, Lawrence D. "The Profession of Teaching," in *This Is Teaching.* Chicago: Scott Foresman and Company, 1956.

Hechinger, Fred M. "Five Basic Problems in Education," *Education Digest,* 24:12–19, May 1959.

Hunt, Herold C., and Pierce, Paul R. *The Practice of School Administration.* Boston: Houghton Mifflin Company, 1959.

Jennings, Helen H. *Sociometry in Group Relations.* Washington, D.C.: American Council on Education, 1948.

Jersild, Arthur T. *When Teachers Face Themselves.* New York: Bureau of Publications, Teachers College, Columbia University, 1955.

Kearney, Nolan C. *A Teacher's Professional Guide.* Englewood Cliffs, N.J.: Prentice-Hall, Inc., 1958.

Keliher, Alice. *Talks with Teachers.* Darien, Conn.: Educational Corporation, 1958.

Lieberman, Myron. *Education as a Profession.* Englewood Cliffs, N.J.: Prentice-Hall, Inc., 1956.

Lieberman, Myron. *The Future of Public Education.* Chicago: University of Chicago Press, 1960.

Lindberg, Lucile. "The Changing Role of the Teacher," *Educational Horizons,* 33:164–165, Spring 1955.

McCloskey, Gordon E., Katterle, Zeno B., and Oviatt, Delmar T. *Introduction to Teaching in American Schools.* New York: Harcourt, Brace and Company, 1954.

Mason, S. Ward, *et al. The Beginning Teacher: A Survey of New*

*Teachers in the Public Schools, 1956–57.* Preliminary Report. Circular No. 510. Washington, D.C.: Government Printing Office, 1958.

National Commission on Teacher Education and Professional Standards. *Let's Talk About Teaching.* Washington, D.C.: National Education Association, 1959.

National Commission on Teacher Education and Professional Standards. *What Does A Teaching Certificate Mean?* Washington, D.C.: National Education Association, 1959.

National Society for the Study of Education. *Citizen Cooperation for Better Public Schools.* Fifty-Third Yearbook. Chicago: University of Chicago Press, 1954.

North, Robert D. "The Teacher Education Student," *Education Digest,* 24:44–46, May 1959.

Parrish, Louise, and Waskin, Yvonne. *Teacher-Pupil Planning for Better Classroom Learning.* New York: Harper & Brothers, 1958.

Redl, Fritz. *Teachers Study Their Children.* Washington, D.C.: American Council on Education, 1940.

Redl, Fritz. *Understanding Children's Behavior.* New York: Bureau of Publications, Teachers College, Columbia University, 1954.

Redl, Fritz, and Wartenberg, William W. *Mental Hygiene in Teaching.* New York: Harcourt, Brace and Company, 2nd ed., 1960.

Rogers, Dorothy. *Mental Hygiene in the Elementary School.* Boston: Houghton Mifflin Company, 1958.

Rubenstein, Ben O. "A Comparison Between Cultural Expectations Regarding the Rôle of the Teacher and His Actual Rôle in the Learning Process," *Educational Administration and Supervision,* 45:95–102, March 1959.

Ryans, David G. *Characteristics of Teachers.* Washington, D.C.: American Council on Education, 1960.

Stiles, Lindley J., *et al. Teacher Education in the United States.* New York: Ronald Press Company, 1960.

Strang, Ruth. *An Introduction to Child Study.* New York: The Macmillan Company, 4th ed., 1959.

"Teacher Education," *NEA Journal,* 48:14–46 (special section), April 1959.

"Teachers View Public Relations," *Research Bulletin,* National Education Association, 37:35–41, April 1959.

Wynn, Richard. *Careers in Education.* New York: McGraw-Hill Book Company, 1960.

*Yale-Fairfield Study of Elementary Teaching.* Abridged edition of the report for 1954–1955. New York: Fund for the Advancement of Education, 1956.

Yauch, Wilbur, *et al. The Beginning Teacher.* New York: Henry Holt and Company, 1955.

Young, Raymond J. "Education's Responsibility for Free Inquiry: A Challenge," *Journal of Teacher Education,* 9:291–296, September 1958.

Zimmerman, Kent A., and Lewton, Elizabeth. "Teacher Personality in School Relationships," *Education Leadership,* 8:422–428, April 1951.

# Photograph Acknowledgments

873

PICTURE ESSAY FOUR

*Page 1.* Children's Museum, Boston
*Page 2.* Duluth Public Schools, by Duluth *News Tribune*
Harvard Graduate School of Education
*Page 3.* Madison Public Schools
Harvard Graduate School of Education
*Page 4.* Columbus, Ohio, Public Schools
Duluth Public Schools, by Duluth *News Tribune*
Cincinnati Public Schools, by Marsh Photographs

PICTURE ESSAY FIVE

*Page 1.* Harvard Graduate School of Education
*Page 2.* Columbus, Ohio, Public Schools
Cincinnati Public Schools, by Marsh Photographs
New England Telephone and Telegraph Company
*Page 3.* Ken Richards, News Bureau, Florida State University
Madison Public Schools
Burbank Unified Schools
*Page 4.* Hays from Monkmeyer
Harvard Graduate School of Education

PICTURE ESSAY SIX

*Page 1.* Ken Richards, News Bureau, Florida State University
*Page 2.* Max Tharpe
Madison Public Schools
Hays from Monkmeyer
*Page 3.* San Diego City Schools
Museum of Fine Arts, Boston
*Page 4.* Ken Richards, News Bureau, Florida State University
Clemens Kalischer

PICTURE ESSAY SEVEN

*Page 1.* Stride-Rite Shoe for Children
*Page 2.* Owens-Illinois and Hedrich-Blessing

Chandoha from Foto/Find Picture Agency
National Dairy Council and Geneva, Illinois, Public
Schools

*Page 3.* Cincinnati Public Schools, by Marsh Photographs
Columbus, Ohio, Public Schools
Walter Stewart, Journalism Department, Evansville
College

*Page 4.* Harvard Graduate School of Education
Alhambra City Schools
Duluth Public Schools, by Duluth *News Tribune*

PICTURE ESSAY EIGHT

*Page 1.* Harvard Graduate School of Education
*Page 2.* Columbus, Ohio, Public Schools
Columbus, Ohio, Public Schools
*Page 3.* Harvard Graduate School of Education
Merrill-Palmer School
*Page 4.* Madison Public Schools
Columbus, Ohio, Public Schools

# Index